Uwe Engel, Lena Dahlhaus
Data Science in Social Research

Uwe Engel, Lena Dahlhaus

Data Science in Social Research

An Applied Guide to Statistical and Computational
Methods with R

DE GRUYTER

ISBN 978-3-11-068067-6
e-ISBN (PDF) 978-3-11-068068-3
e-ISBN (EPUB) 978-3-11-068077-5

Library of Congress Control Number: 2025945708

Bibliographic information published by the Deutsche Nationalbibliothek
The Deutsche Nationalbibliothek lists this publication in the Deutsche Nationalbibliografie;
detailed bibliographic data are available on the Internet at http://dnb.dnb.de.

www.degruyterbrill.com
Questions about General Product Safety Regulation:
productsafety@degruyterbrill.com

Preface

In their introduction to *data science*, Kelleher and Tierney (2018: 17) write that the term "came to prominence in the late 1990s in discussions relating to the need for statisticians to join with computer scientists to bring mathematical rigor to the computational analysis of large data sets." The history of the term and its associated concepts and methods is thus much younger than that of social science statistics, which has also relied heavily on large data sets, specifically representative surveys, since the middle of the last century. And classical statistics go back much further in history anyway.

If one looks at recent developments exclusively from the perspective of a survey researcher, one sometimes gets the impression that data science is something like a new science that is currently being discovered by social scientists. Data science will indeed seem new or different to many, but it's worth asking about the possible reasons for this.

We suspect that one reason may simply be the different technical terminology used, which refers to the same things in different ways. This, of course, obscures the commonalities between data science and social science statistics—despite all the remaining differences. And of course these differences also exist. The two fields are not identical, just as machine learning and statistical learning do not describe completely identical fields. But in both cases, there's the possibility of focusing more on the similarities or more on the differences, and we've chosen to focus more on the common core in this book, as we see it. And it's precisely the same perspective that we see in the statistical learning approach, so we've focused on it as well.

While such a perspective may make the spectrum of data science appear smaller than it actually is, this perspective is also beneficial for data science itself: It is precisely this perspective that enables not only social science statistics but also data science to derive the best of both worlds. Texts on data science often emphasize the great importance placed on accurate predictive models or on improving decision making. Diplomatically speaking, data science then focuses more on creating precise predictive models and less on models that explain the data (Kelleher and Tierney 2018: 18).

Put somewhat less diplomatically, the matter reads somewhat differently when, for example, Hofman et al. (2017: 486) in *Science* paint the accurate picture that the social sciences are often in search of causal explanations or causal mechanisms, but in doing so neglect the predictive accuracy of their models, but now the increasingly computational nature of the social sciences is reversing this traditional bias against predictions. And also, that "predictive accuracy and interpretability must be recognized as complements, not substitutes, when evaluating explanations." All of this is certainly true. But even this image only lightens one side of the story. Not only can social science data analysis practice benefit from data science, but conversely, data

https://doi.org/10.1515/9783110680683-202

science practice also benefits from the way data analysis is conducted in the social sciences.

This can be illustrated by the common method for determining predictive accuracy, as data science focuses heavily on metrics such as R^2 or the mean squared error for model evaluation. While these are excellent metrics, they still have limited power. It's not for nothing that social science statistics places so much emphasis on regression diagnostics. This is just one example. Another might be located in the area of methods that are classified as unsupervised methods in data science. The strong focus on principal component analysis is striking there, while in the social sciences, confirmatory methods in the area of latent variable analysis are also used much more extensively. What we are simply trying to exemplify is that both sides can benefit from an integrative perspective that seeks common ground rather than division.

It would be a mistake to judge data science only from the perspective of a science that works with survey data. While we can expect that survey data will remain one, perhaps even *the*, central empirical source for social research, the changing survey landscape is already accompanied by a tremendous increase in the importance of other data sources. We are convinced that the prominence of data science in social research is closely linked to the rise of *computational social science* and one of *its* underlying forces in a world of increasing digitization, namely the Internet (Engel et al. 2022a, 2022b). The central role that the Internet plays in this development is also seen in a similar way from other sides, for example when Kelleher and Tierney (2018: 19) wrote already in 2018 that "over the past 10 years there has been a tremendous growth in the amount of the data generated by online activity (online retail, social media, and online entertainment)", whose "gathering and preparing (. . .) has resulted in the need for data scientists to develop the programming and hacking skills to scrape, merge, and clean data (sometimes unstructured data) from external web sources." In the present context, we therefore also address, among other things, the collection and analysis of data from the Internet, especially text data from social media.

We have made every effort to present the contents of this textbook as accurately as possible, and hope that we have not made any errors. However, we cannot guarantee this. As is so often the case in science, we have described things as we saw them. This means that it cannot be ruled out that things could be seen and assessed differently from another perspective.

Bremen and Oldenburg, in July 2025   Uwe Engel and Lena Dahlhaus

Contents

Part I: **Description, Explanation, Prediction**

Chapter 5
R Graphics —— **144**

Part III: **Statistical Methods for Prediction, Classification, Text Analytics**

Chapter 6
Linear Models —— **175**

Chapter 7
Goodness of Fit and Predictive Power of a Linear Model —— **194**

Chapter 8
Regression Diagnostics and Corrective Measures —— **229**

Chapter 12
Statistical Learning —— 359

Chapter 13
Natural Language Processing —— 395

Chapter 1
Data Science in Social Research

1.1 Data Science

Data science[1] aims to enable data-driven decisions. Kelleher and Tierney (2018: 1) point out that the "terms *data science, machine learning*, and *data mining* are often used interchangeably" and stress as a commonality across these disciplines a focus on "improving decision making through the analysis of data". They view data science as the broadest of the three fields: While machine learning "focuses on the design and evaluation of algorithms for extracting patterns from data" and "data mining generally deals with the analysis of structured data" [. . .],

> data science also takes up other challenges, such as the capturing, cleaning, and transforming of unstructured social media and web data; the use of big-data technologies to store and process big, unstructured data sets; and questions related to data ethics and regulation (Kelleher and Tierney 2018: 1–2).

Data science is impossible without statistical algorithms because data science makes use of machine learning techniques and because algorithms represent a core element of machine learning. However, not only the implementation of algorithms requires programming, but also any digital data collection, data management, and data analysis. Additionally, methodological principles and formal rules are needed to guide design and performance of statistical analysis and the proper way of drawing inferences from it. Accordingly, data science is more comprehensive than machine learning and has at least *three* parent disciplines: statistics, computer science and research methodology.

1.2 Computational Methods in Social Research

Right from the start social research has been rooted in the behavioral sciences, survey methodology, and formal science (logic, mathematics, statistics, computer science). Computational methods in sociology have played a bearing role from the outset: The Columbia School[2] and its pioneering development work on multivariate, longitudinal, mul-

---

1 See Engel (2022: 131–133) for a review of current views of "data science", "machine learning", "big data", and "computational social science". This reference, a chapter written for the Handbook of Computational Social Science, is available in open access. https://doi.org/10.4324/9781003024583-10

2 For the history of social research, and in particular the contribution of Paul F. Lazarsfeld, the development of empirical social research in the United States, and sample-based survey research, see Schnell et al. (2018: 26–34). See also Diekmann (2007: 109–115), particularly the appreciation of Lazarsfeld's contribution (p. 113) by pointing out that after emigrating to the USA, Lazarsfeld refined and further devel-

https://doi.org/10.1515/9783110680683-001

tilevel, and latent variable analysis is certainly the best exemplification of this deep-rooted interdependency.[3] Major milestones in the history of social research are rooted in survey methodology and formal science. This includes, for instance, advancements in attribute data and multivariate analysis (Coleman 1964), survey sampling (Kish 1965; Fuller 2009; Valliant et al. 2013; Tourangeau et al. 2014), coping with survey nonresponse (Groves et al. 2002), item nonresponse and missing data treatment (Little and Rubin 2002; Enders 2010; van Buuren 2018) and uses of Paradata (Kreuter 2013). Milestones also include the psychological foundations of survey response (Tourangeau et al. 2000) and the total survey error perspective (Weisberg 2005).

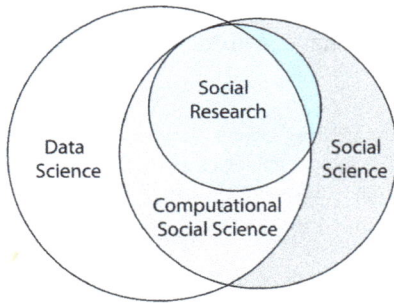

Figure 1.1: Data Science, Social Science, Computational Social Science, and Social Research.

Figure 1.1 displays an Euler diagram of the relation between data science, social science, and social research. Meanwhile much social research is directly attributable to the field of computational social science because the digitization of society has made of this field a novel, visible, highly developing area of considerably growing importance for both society and science. This development certainly helps to avoid an inadequate one-sided attribution of social research to social science, although too strict an emphasis on social media and big data analysis may produce an adverse effect as well. Not only that, it could tempt us to overlook the still paramount importance of survey data. It may also favor a view of computational social science that neglects its

---

oped the methods from his time in Vienna, "initially in the Radio Research Project at Princeton University, later within the framework of the Bureau of Applied Social Research at Columbia University in New York (Columbia School). Lazarsfeld helped shape the methodology of American social research in a variety of individual fields (communication research, content analysis, scaling, statistical methods of "third variable control," mathematical sociology, qualitative methods, etc.) and shaped modern empirical social research with his contributions" (own translation).

3 A listing reported in Engel (2022: 131–132) refers to early works on multivariate analysis (e.g., Lazarsfeld 1955; Rosenberg 1968), the mathematical study of change (Coleman 1968), methods of replication (Galtung 1969), prediction studies (e.g., Goodman 1955), the analysis of change through time by panel analysis (e.g., Lazarsfeld, Berelson, & Gaudet 1955), Lazarsfeld's latent structure analysis (McCutcheon 1987), longitudinal data analysis (Coleman 1981), and multilevel methodology (e.g., Lazarsfeld and Menzel 1969 [1961]; Coleman et al. 1966; Coleman 1990).

"social simulation modeling" area and its multilevel approach towards social complexity as detailed in Cioffi-Revilla (2017: 12–20, 205–219, 331–341, 470–484).

Computational social science cannot work without theoretical input. We usually build models that formalize the hypotheses and theories under consideration, and test the empirical validity of their implications. Common uses of mathematics in sociology have a long tradition. Already in an early work, Coleman (1964) introduced four uses of mathematics in research and theory, in his words: the "quantitative description of the various units of social science" (p. 8), the "direct measurement of observable phenomena" and the "indirect measurement of latent 'dispositional' states" (p. 25–26), the "development of quantitative empirical generalizations about behavior which relate two or more quantitative measures" (p. 9), and the provisioning of a "language for theory" (p. 9) in theory construction. Many of the highly developed measurement and scaling techniques that we currently use in social research, the highly sophisticated instruments for measuring latent variables ("disposition properties") that elude direct observation, go back to such early pioneering work. Without the use of mathematics and (e.g., propositional) logic, none of these developments would have been possible.

Computational social science covers a large but not total share in social research: Outside the overlap with data science, qualitative case studies and qualitative research in small samples may in the end be remaining attributable to social science alone, unless statistical and machine learning methods are applied to the data of such research too.

As an intersecting set of data science and social science, computational social science excludes substantial portions of both disciplines: Both parent disciplines are much broader in scope than computational social science alone. On the left of Figure 1.1, the excluded part comes about because the science of data is relevant to virtually all scientific disciplines that collect, sense, infer, and analyze data by some scientifically controlled means or other. In this spectrum of disciplines and related methods, social science covers only a small segment. On the right of Figure 1.1, although social science is an empirical science to the core, it can be pursued completely theoretically.

1.3 Web Survey Research

Surveys remain a very important tool in social research, and it would not be surprising if they were even considered a central instrument for collecting precisely those empirical data without which sociology or the social sciences could not be meaningfully pursued. However, one does not have to go that far to recognize their great importance for social research. They are undoubtedly a widely used tool. The graphs in Figure 1.2 illustrate the dimensions involved, using the example of the European context and the private market and social research institutes represented there.[4] Accordingly, the market for market and social research has, by and large, grown continuously over the past three decades.[5] At the same time, there have been significant shifts in the interview modes used: the composition of the interviews according to their survey mode has changed in three essential respects. In particular, the proportion of face-to-face interviews is declining in the long run, the proportion of telephone interviews shows a predominantly upward trend until the middle of the observation period and has been declining since then, whereas web interviews did not play a relevant role in the 1990s, but since then have predominantly shown only one direction: upwards. From a purely quantitative perspective, survey research today is primarily conducted online. Nevertheless, large academic surveys in particular still widely collect their data through face-to-face interviews, and the number of telephone interviews is anything but marginal.

1.4 Changing Survey Landscape

Lars Lyberg and Steven Heeringa (2022: 88, 97) conclude from their analysis of the changing survey landscape that they

> can echo Groves (2011) and say with confidence that 'survey research is not dying, it is changing', adding the corollary that change has always been a property of the survey landscape, and survey methodologists and practitioners have and must continue to address the challenges and take advantage of the opportunities that this change presents.

Previously, the authors had sketched one hundred years of survey research and the challenges in today's survey landscape in their article. These include declining response rates, rising survey costs, and technological effects on data collection modes. The authors also stresses the competition from alternative data sources, big data, and data science, as well as a statistical literature that over the past decade "has reflected a renewed interest in population estimation and inference from nonprobability data sources," having in mind data that "arise through automatic, voluntary or participatory processes that may be highly selective in representing populations of interest". And this, although "for almost 100 years, probability sampling or the 'representative

---

4 Data source: https://www.adm-ev.de/en/the-industry/market-research-numbers/
 We took the figures from the website of the ADM, which, as it states, is the "leading business association for German market and social research." The ADM describes itself as follows: "As a business association, the ADM represents the interests of the private market and social research institutes in Germany. The ADM member institutions achieve more than 80 percent of the industry's sales. The ADM is the only association of its kind in Germany." In the context of the tables, ESOMAR is cited as the source.
5 In the context of the cited ADM website, it is pointed out that temporal comparisons are only possible to a limited extent, "since the figures reflect changes in the market and exchange rates."

method' and design-based methods for estimation and inference have been adopted by most government, business and academic researchers as the gold standard for achieving unbiased or nearly unbiased inference in population-based research [. . .]", as well as although "even strong advocates of model-based inference acknowledged the advantage of working with data collected under probability sample designs [. . .]" (Lyberg and Heeringa 2022: 88). The authors then explain the renewed interest in population estimates and conclusions from non-probability-based data sources primarily by the fact that "most of the 'big data' that governments, businesses, and other researchers hope to utilize [. . .] are obtained from selective, convenient, volunteer or other nonrandom segments of the target population" (Lyberg and Heeringa 2022: 89). Furthermore, they rightly point to rare, highly specialized or 'hard to survey' populations that cannot be reached cost-effectively using traditional probability sampling methods.

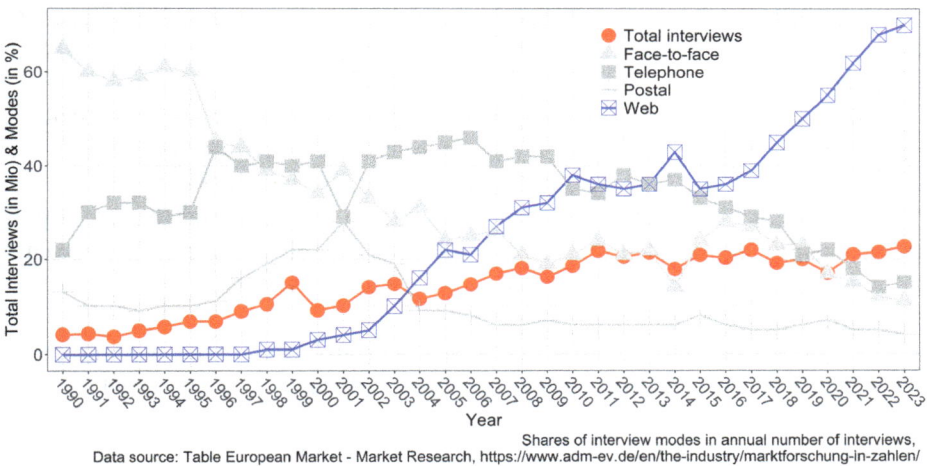

Shares of interview modes in annual number of interviews,
Data source: Table European Market - Market Research, https://www.adm-ev.de/en/the-industry/marktforschung-in-zahlen/

Figure 1.2: Trend in Survey Modes, 1990 to 2023.

1.5 Digital Trace Data

To gather empirical information for social research, we can interview people or observe their behavior. It's also conceivable to observe the traces left behind by behavior. This approach, i.e. the collection and analysis of behavioral *traces*, is particularly suitable for behavior on social media. Then it is specifically about the *digital* traces of interaction behavior and the texts that are posted. Already years ago, Quan-Haase and Sloan (2017: P. 693) wrote that the "sheer amount of digitized user-generated content is a potentially rich source of information about the social world including interactions, attitudes, opinions and virtual reactions to real-world events".

Hox (2017: 8) points out a methodological advantage of data collected from the internet or other automated sources, namely that such behavioral traces resemble what was once described as *unobtrusive measures* (Webb et al. 2000). "If subjects are aware of being research subjects, this influences their behavior, including answer behavior in surveys. Such research is reactive; subjects react to being researched." On the other hand, unobtrusive measures "collect data already generated and cannot influence that behavior." This certainly represents a methodological advantage over the survey method.

Similarly, as Keusch and Kreuter[6] (2022: 100, 103, 104) point out, the "original definition of digital trace data is limited to data that are found, that is, data created as by-product of activities not stemming from a designed research instrument." Such data are generally considered to have been collected unobtrusively, as in the case of digital trace data from social media platforms "where users post comments, share content, and interact with each other." However, the authors also show that the collection of digital trace data can be more or less obtrusive "in that the individuals who produce the data are made explicitly aware of the fact that their data are used for research purposes."

While unobtrusive measures traditionally referred to physical traces, archives, organizational and personal records, and observations, today they refer to data collected on the Internet. Hox (2017: 10) aptly points out that such data are not just "found data", but that they have been created for a purpose, "and that purpose is rarely scientific research" (Hox 2017: 10). This may be a disadvantage when it comes to potential measurement error, but it can also represent a methodological advantage.

This is because many things are expressed completely voluntarily and publicly on social media that would otherwise be rarely, or practically never, expressed in scientific surveys. For example, politically extreme or even extremist views. Social networks also reach actors who we would find extremely difficult or impossible to reach through general surveys. This makes such digital behavioral traces a valuable data source for social research on the one hand, but also sensitive in terms of data protection concerns on the other. Unlike in scientific surveys, where participation must be based on informed consent, in the case of social media data this consent is – much less centrally – anchored at best in the platform's terms of use. The rule is that content posted and shared publicly on the networks can also be read via APIs, provided the platform enables and permits this.

---

6 This reference, a chapter written by Keusch and Kreuter for the Handbook of Computational Social Science, is available in open access. https://doi.org/10.4324/9781003024583-8

1.6 Social Media Research

Social media has gained considerably in importance in recent years, both as a part of everyday life and as a field of interest for social scientists. The availability of data from social media provides researchers with unprecedented access to large-scale, and diverse data based on human communication that was previously inaccessible through traditional survey or observational methods. Social media data can capture user-generated content like posts and likes, but also more complex forms of communication between network users in form of comments or discussions. Finding out what and how people communicate online provides insights into research areas like social attitudes, cultural trends, and political mobilization, often with the possibility of including temporal and spatial information in the analysis. However, these data sources also bring significant challenges to researchers. Data acquired online requires proper computational methods of digital data collection, data management, data processing, and data analysis (Lazer et al. 2020).

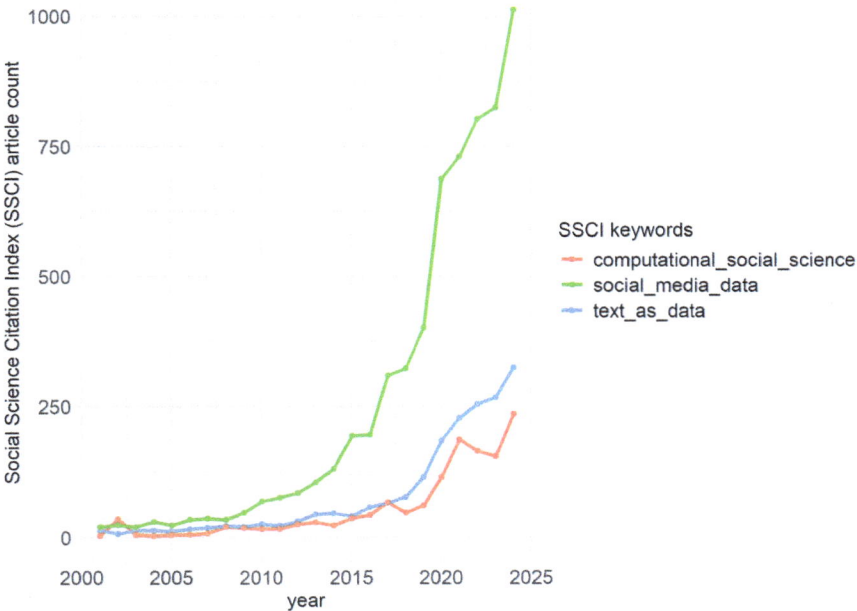

Figure 1.3: Social Media Data, Text As Data, and Computational Social Science in the Social Science Citation Index, 2000 to 2025.

In terms of data quality, social media data is often biased due to platform-specific characteristics. Different social networks are known to have differing user demographics, different approaches when it comes to algorithmic content curation, and underlying self-selection effects. Often information on such characteristics are not available to scientists. Other challenges include accessibility, privacy concerns and ethical constraints. The accessibility of social media data varies considerably between social networks. For some networks data access is possible via an Application Programming Interface (API) for free, while some platforms may give access to data only in exchange for payment or provide no legal way to access data at all. Platform policies and API restrictions may frequently change, creating instability in data availability and in turn making longitudinal studies more challenging. These circumstances also provide challenges when it comes to the development of robust, adaptive methodologies to take advantage of the full potential of social network data while navigating its complexities responsibly. Social media data differs from survey data in a crucial way. Content created by the users of a social network is not created with the possibility of it being used for research in mind and often contains sensitive information like names and pictures. Thus, careful handling is required to protect individual identities and to adhere to regulations such as the General Data Protection Regulation (GDPR).

In Figure 1.3, based on the Social Science Citation Index (SSCI), we have graphically depicted the development of articles published in scientific journals over the past 25 years for the social science disciplines (sociology, political science, and social science methods) whose full texts contain the compound keywords *computational social science*, *social media data*, and *text as data* (three separate keyword searches, with the individual terms of a keyword search linked using a logical "and"). Even though the underlying research development can only be roughly represented using such graphs, the nonlinear upward trend is clearly visible.

1.7 Big Data

Sample size plays a relevant role in survey research. In general, it is more beneficial to have a larger rather than a smaller sample size. Nevertheless, it would be wrong to claim that very large datasets are always of higher quality than large datasets simply because they are so large. Big data is undoubtedly useful for investigating rare events, examining heterogeneity, and detecting small differences (Salganik, 2018: 18–20). This also applies in principle to big *survey* datasets, not least because of the opportunities they open up for implementing convincing validation designs.

On the other hand, a very large sample size can also make data analysis more difficult. Statistical significance, for instance, loses practical relevance as a decision criterion, since even the most marginal differences can appear significant based on a huge sample size alone (Hox 2017: 10). Furthermore, sample size does not protect against hidden biases in the data. This applies even if the sample was drawn on the basis of a proper random procedure. As an example, let us consider the cumulative data set of the European Social Survey with its hundreds of thousands of units (Example Data Set 8: European Social Survey, Rounds 1 to 9). As advantageous as this large number of units is, it should not obscure the possible systematic differences that these data may contain across countries and survey rounds. In any case, the individual ESS surveys are easily interrelated due to their overall design. This is by no means a given. Pooling survey data may require prior adjustments to achieve the necessary comparability.[7]

Although random selection does not protect against selective loss of units, this loss can at least be taken into account in the modeling. With "found data" this is more difficult. In the context of his "ten common characteristics of big data", Salganik (2018: 20) writes: "While bigness does reduce the need to worry about random error, it actually *increases* the need to worry about systematic errors, the kind of errors [. . .] that arise from biases in how data are created."

1.8 Prediction and Explanation

Data science aims to make accurate predictions. *Predictive modeling* plays an important role in the machine-learning tradition (Kuhn and Johnson 2013: 1). On the other hand, observational studies in the counterfactual research tradition of social research places much weight on *causal inference*. However, since causal models often show statistically significant estimates of effect without having any substantial explanatory power (low to negligible R^2), Yarkoni and Westfall (2017: 2) quite rightly point to the tension between prediction and explanation and raise substantial doubts about the predictive power of such explanatory research. Hofman et al. (2017, 486) "argue that the increasingly computational nature of social science is beginning to reverse (the) traditional bias against prediction" and highlight the view that "predictive accuracy and interpretability must be recognized as complements, not substitutes, when evaluating explanations." James et al. (2013) show that prediction and causal inference can actually be integrated into the same approach to *statistical learning*. As stated elsewhere (Engel 2022: 134),

> balancing these two objectives in an analysis might be advantageous because prediction accuracy and generalizability cannot be maximized simultaneously. While maximizing R^2 is certainly suitable for increasing prediction accuracy, such a strategy runs the risk of overfitting and impairing the generalizability of found results. Data mining thus trusts techniques based on "replication" and "cross-validation," in which the use of training, tuning, and test samples guards

---

7 For example, Warshaw (2016: 28–31) addresses this topic in his discussion of big data in the survey context. He points to large pools of polls, taking the Roper Center for Public Opinion with its "more than 20,000 polls from hundreds of survey firms" as an example.

against overfitting (Attewell and Monaghan 2015: 14). The power of predicting unseen (out-of-sample) data can be regarded as a more relevant criterion than the size of a "theoretically privileged" regression coefficient or a model fit statistic (Yarkoni & Westfall 2017: 2).

Prediction and causal analysis can only be separated to a limited extent, since causal analysis too implies predictions that must be compared with the observed data. On the other hand, high prediction accuracy does not guarantee the conclusion of a causal relationship. Generally, however, there may well be *differences in how much emphasis is placed* on achieving predictive accuracy (e.g., by maximizing R^2) — maybe, along with determining the exact functional form of a relationship — or whether the focus is instead on finding generalizable regularities, regardless of the explanatory power of such a model in a given concrete data analysis.

For instance, Attewell and Monaghan (2015) contrast the data mining (DM) approach with what they term the "Conventional Statistical Approach" and decipher the role of predictive power as one key difference between both approaches. They point out "that the conventional statistical approach focuses on the individual coefficients for the predictors, and doesn't care much about predictive power. DM does the reverse" (Attewell and Monaghan (2015: 14). This heavy alignment of data analysis with predictive power (maximizing R^2) is likely to increase the relevance of an analysis, on the one hand. On the other hand, such an analysis runs the risk of overfitting: "Some DM applications are too effective at building a predictive model: they construct something too complicated that will not generalize to other samples (. . .) Overfitting is undesirable because it means that the complex model will not perform very well once it is applied to other data, such as the test data" (Attewell and Monaghan 2015: 32–33). The data mining approach thus trusts heavily techniques based on resampling (e.g. bootstrapping) and cross-validation as a guard against overfitting.

1.9 Outlook on the Chapters of this Textbook

This introductory chapter is followed by *Part I* with its chapters 2 and 3 on descriptive and causal inference. Part II then introduces programming in R as well as R graphics in Chapters 4 and 5, before Part III, with Chapters 6 to 13, deals with predictive modeling, statistical learning, and text analytics.

The three basic goals of a data analysis are either to describe, explain or predict reality. Against this background, chapter 2 focuses on description. The aim is usually to use sample data to draw conclusions about the prevalence of facts in precisely defined populations. For this purpose, we usually implement design-based inference. We describe how such an inference works, what prerequisites it is bound to, and what sources of error exist. Since probability samples can be severely affected by unit nonresponse, which causes theoretically unbiased statistical estimators to produce biased estimates in practice, we discuss in Chapter 2 how design-based inference can be performed using model-assisted methods to address this source of error. We also discuss how to deal with missing values in data matrices (item nonresponse) in data analysis.

Chapter 3 introduces causal inference. It introduces the counterfactual model and derives from it the relevance of implementing meaningful comparisons either experimentally or analytically by means of multivariate data analysis. We look at experimental designs and the principles of randomization and matching, and discuss causal inference in observational studies. To this end, we draw on a well-known validity typology and demonstrate how causal inference can be performed in cross-sectional and longitudinal studies. We also address the issue of unobserved heterogeneity, i.e., the case where latent variables, rather than observed ones, need to be statistically controlled.

Chapter 4 introduces data management in R. It demonstrates how to program with R and how to use RStudio for this purpose. It provides comprehensive and detailed explanations of how data can be read in and processed, and the basic structure required to perform statistical calculations. In this respect, the chapter is designed to familiarize you with some basics of exploratory statistics. Regarding R as a programming language, we describe its vector-based architecture and the advantages it offers for performing data analyses. Since R itself is constantly evolving, we'll demonstrate how this evolution is reflected in a key dimension: from the data frame to the so-called *tibble*. In effect, we're entering a newer *meta library*, the *tidyverse*, with a whole range of very useful tools for data analysis.

Chapter 5 demonstrates how to create graphs with R. Here, too, we introduce statistical concepts. We discuss graphs for exploratory, predictive, and diagnostic data analysis. As is the case throughout the textbook, the focus here is on traditional R graphs created with the *plot()* function, and otherwise on *ggplot2* graphs.

Predictive and causal modeling can be implemented technically using regression analysis. Regression analysis of observational data is also an important tool if neither *prediction* nor *causal inference* is the main focus, but rather an accurate, analytically sound *description* of a subject of investigation in question.

Chapter 6 introduces the statistical basics of linear regression and uses survey data to show how such analyses can be carried out using R. We introduce simple and multiple regression and explain the meaning of simple and partial regression coefficients. The data example used for this purpose also includes a polynomial regression to provide a first impression of how a curvilinear relation can be modelled. Chapter 6 also describes the ordinary and weighted least squares estimator and introduces and exemplifies the concept of statistical interaction.

Chapter 7 completes this introduction by showing how to assess the goodness of fit and predictive power of a linear model. We address the within-sample model fit as well as the use of the validation set, cross-validation and temporal validation design for regression analysis and structural equation modeling. Finally, in Chapter 7 we discuss the relationship between validation and replication perspectives and why both do not necessarily have to pursue the same goal.

Regardless of the objective of a regression analysis, the formal requirements of this technical tool play an important role. Despite all the differences in the modeling objectives of description, causal analysis, and prediction, it is therefore always highly recommended to use regression diagnostics to check whether and to what extent these requirements are met.

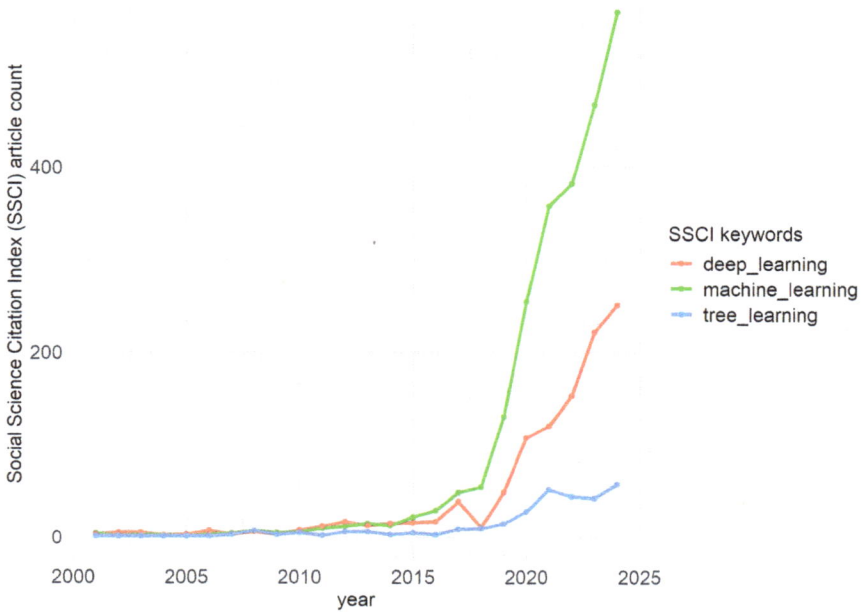

Figure 1.4: Deep Learning, Machine Learning, and Tree Learning in the Social Science Citation Index, 2000 to 2025.[8]

Chapter 8 therefore broadens the perspective on the topic of regression diagnostics and corrective actions in response to diagnostic results. For example, a diagnosis may indicate that relevant predictors are missing from the model, that a relationship under investigation is not linear but non-linear, that residuals are serially correlated or do not follow a normal curve, or that the variance of the residuals is heteroscedas-

---

8 In Figure 1.4, we graphically depict the development of articles published in scientific journals over the past 25 years for the social science disciplines (sociology, political science, and social science methods) based on the Social Science Citation Index (SSCI) whose full texts contain the compound keywords *deep learning*, *machine learning*, and *tree learning* (three separate keyword searches, with the individual terms of a keyword search linked by a logical "and"). Accordingly, machine learning in particular has experienced a dramatic increase in the past ten years. Deep learning has also experienced strong growth in recent years.

tic. In response, it may then be necessary to estimate not a linear but a linear mixed model, to switch from a linear model to a generalized linear model in order to be able to specify the random component of the model appropriately, for example by switching to the binomial distribution or the gamma distribution. We cover some of these solutions in Chapter 8, some in Chapters 9 and 10.

Chapter 9 introduces linear mixed models, in sociological contexts also known as multilevel models. We often use this modeling approach for analyzing hierarchically structured, nested data. People live in contexts and these contexts can be explicitly taken into account in modeling, for instance by considering random effects also at the context level(s) in addition to the commonly assumed random effects (residuals) at the base level.

Even if the assumption of linear variable relationships is often appropriate in sociological applications, nonlinear variable relationships should also be considered. Chapter 10 is therefore devoted to such nonlinear relationships. We consider linearizable relations, polynomial and regression splines, and generalized additive models.

A regression analysis can be used to predict conditional mean values of a metric target variable. A regression analysis can also aim to predict membership in a manifest category or latent class. Technically, this is called classification. Chapter 11 shows how a probabilistic classification can be carried out using a latent class analysis and which preparatory steps are required if this classification is to be based on weighted units of analysis. The prediction of class membership by logistic regression and WLS models for contingency tables is also covered.

Statistical learning is a prominent approach in data science. It combines the linear, generalized linear, and generalized additive models introduced in Chapters 6 to 11 with other approaches, including tree analysis, ensemble methods, and neural networks introduced in Chapter 12. Machine learning, including deep learning, represents a rapidly growing field of importance for the social sciences (Figure 1.4). We explain what machine learning means and which technical terms have evolved around a core element of data analysis, the data matrix. And we show that, despite the different terminologies, we are dealing with a field familiar from social science statistics. We will also discuss how feature engineering can be implemented using the *tidymodels* meta library.

A field of growing importance for the social sciences is social media research with its focus on data and texts as they are produced in social networks (Figure 1.3). Chapter 13 introduces the field of text data analysis, Natural Language Processing. We first introduce data collection methods (web scraping and the use of application programming interfaces (APIs)), challenges of text analysis, the required preprocessing, and the structure of textual data before introducing two prominent analysis techniques in more detail: topic modeling and sentiment analysis.

1.10 Example Data Sets Used in this Textbook

Example Data Set 1: PPSM Innovation Panel
"PPSM Innovation Panel" denotes the probability-based mixed-mode access panel, we have built for PPSM, the *Priority Programme on Survey Methodology* (2009–2013) of the German Research Foundation. During the project we realized 43,130 Interviews, 22 larger experiments on the effect of question wordings and response formats on response behavior, further mode comparisons, and five design experiments. A detailed description of the study, its survey design, samples, findings, and more is given in Engel et al. (2012) and Engel (2015). The overall survey design includes several panel surveys.

Example Data Set 2: Bremen City of Science Survey
The Bremen City of Science Survey is based on a random sample of the adult population of the city of Bremen. Following a "basic question" approach, in addition to the full version of the interview, a core version of half the length of the full interview as well as a very short version of just two basic questions were afforded. All in all, 1,183 respondents took part in the survey. The field period took three and a half weeks (April 19 to May 13, 2016). The study design is detailed in Engel and Can (2017) and Engel (2020).

Example Data Set 3: Bremen AI Delphi Survey on Human-Robot-Interaction
In late 2019, we conducted a large Delphi survey of n=297 scientists and politicians in the Bremen area (Germany) to let the respondents evaluate different scenarios. A detailed description of this web survey including selection design and questionnaire design is given in Engel and Dahlhaus (2022: 356–358).

Example Data Set 4: Web Survey on Machine Learning and Robots in Human Life
Parallel to the Delphi survey of scientists and politicians, a population survey of n=216 respondents was carried out in the Bremen area (Germany) during the 25th of November to 15th of December 2019. A detailed description of the study including sample design is given in Engel and Dahlhaus (2022: 358–360).

Example Data Set 5: "Future Perspectives of Energy Transition"
In the spring of 2022 (fieldwork: March 30 to April 3), we conducted a web survey on the dependence of the energy transition on raw materials. The questionnaire also asked for evaluations of recommendations of the committee of inquiry on "Climate Protection Strategy for the State of Bremen". The survey is representative of the adult population of Bremen and Bremerhaven (aged 18 to 70 years). We realized 330 interviews. A detailed study description is given in Engel (2022a).

Example Data Set 6: Energy Transition in the European Green Deal
The study provides insights into the acceptance of climate protection measures, which can be gained from the analysis of data from four recent Eurobarometer surveys, the

European Social Survey and the official EU statistics Eurostat. From these sources, the data set compiles a relevant set of variables at the aggregate (country) level. A detailed description of all data sources, variables and question/item wordings is given in Engel (2022b). The R data frame ("Energy.Rdata") is available at https://github.com/viewsandinsights/AI.

Example Data Set 7: Views & Insights on Climate Policy
In spring 2023 (fieldwork: April 11 to 19), we conducted N=451 interviews in the two-city state of Bremen (Germany). The web survey is representative of the adult population of Bremen aged 18 to 69. A detailed description of this study is given in Engel (2023).

Example Data Set 8: European Social Survey, Rounds 1 to 9
We prepared a cumulative data set from survey round 1 to survey round 9 of the European Social Survey (ESS) that contains a subset of variables for over 340 thousand cases from 22 European countries (N=340,215). This data set compiles two original sources downloaded from the ESS website, the European Social Survey Cumulative File, ESS 1–8 (2018)[9] and the European Social Survey Round 9 Data (2018).[10] It involves extensive coding work for a causal analysis presented in Engel (2022) and a related online appendix. All this is detailed in a freely accessible file called "R-code-to-appendix" at https://github.com/viewsandinsights/inference. The data set involves around 150 variables.

Example Data Set 9: European Social Survey, Round 10
From the official website we downloaded the dataset,[11] source questionnaire[12] and documentation[13] for Round 10 of the European Social Survey. Only data for Germany are used in this textbook. Sample size is 8,725 respondents. These data were collected in self-administered paper and web-based survey mode and took place from 05th Oct. 2021 until 04th Jan. 2022. The German sub-study of Round 10 of the European Social Survey is scientifically managed by GESIS Leibniz Institute for the Social Sciences

---

9 European Social Survey Cumulative File, ESS 1–8 (2018). Data file edition 1.0. NSD – Norwegian Centre for Research Data, Norway – Data Archive and distributor of ESS data for ESS ERIC. doi:10.21338/NSD-ESS-CUMULATIVE
10 European Social Survey Round 9 Data (2018). Data file edition 2.0. NSD – Norwegian Centre for Research Data, Norway – Data Archive and distributor of ESS data for ESS ERIC. doi:10.21338/NSD-ESS9-2018
11 European Social Survey European Research Infrastructure (ESS ERIC). (2023). ESS10 Self-completion – integrated file, edition 3.1 [Data set]. Sikt – Norwegian Agency for Shared Services in Education and Research. https://doi.org/10.21338/ess10sce03_1
12 European Social Survey (2020). *ESS Round 10 Source Questionnaire.* London: ESS ERIC Headquarters c/o City, University of London
13 European Social Survey European Research Infrastructure (ESS ERIC). (2022). ESS10 Data Documentation. Sikt – Norwegian Agency for Shared Services in Education and Research. https://doi.org/10.21338/NSD-ESS10-2020

(www.gesis.org) and implemented by infas Institute for Applied Social Sciences (www.infas.de).

Example Data Set 10: European Social Survey, Round 11
Source questionnaire (Round 11, 2023)[14] and dataset[15] (with production date: 20. Nov. 2024) were downloaded from the official website. Only data for Germany are used in this textbook. Sample size is 2,420 respondents. The data were collected in face to face survey mode, the data collection took place from 09th May 2023 until 21st Dec. 2023. The German sub-study of Round 11 of the European Social Survey is scientifically managed by GESIS Leibniz Institute for the Social Sciences (www.gesis.org) and implemented by Verian (formerly Kantar Public).

Example Data Set 11: BlueSky skeets on United Kingdom Politics
A sample of 200000 short messages from the UK Politics feed[16] on the social network BlueSky[17] published prior to the 7th of March 2025. The data were collected with the *atrrr* R package (Gruber et al. 2025).

Example Data Set 12: BlueSky skeets on Climate Change
A sample of 798 short messages from the Climate Change Science feed[18] on the social network BlueSky[19] published prior to the 7th of March 2025. The data were collected with the *atrrr* R package (Gruber et al. 2025).

Example Data Set 13: New York Times Article Information on Education
A dataset of information on 912 articles published in the New York Times in the 90 days prior to the 10th of March 2025. The data were collected using the New York Times *Article Search API*[20] and the *nytimes* (Coene 2025) R package[21]

1.11 Recommended Course Reading

The textbook is designed to impart programming skills with R and methods for the statistical analysis of survey and text data. Its focus is on statistics or data analysis courses in social science, political science, and educational science programs, but

---

14 European Social Survey (2022). *ESS Round 11 Source Questionnaire*. London: ESS ERIC Headquarters c/o City, University of London.
15 European Social Survey European Research Infrastructure (ESS ERIC)(2023). ESS11– integrated file, edition 2.0. [Data set]. Sikt – Norwegian Agency for Shared Services in Education and Research. https://doi.org/10.21338/ess11e02_0
16 https://bsky.app/profile/johnlf.bsky.social/feed/UKPolitics
17 https://bsky.app/
18 https://bsky.app/profile/kesma.bsky.social/feed/aaamxvffjaodq
19 https://bsky.app/
20 https://developer.nytimes.com/apis
21 https://github.com/news-r/nytimes

should also be relevant for economics. And, to a certain extent, for applied courses in computer science, where social science use cases should assist in imparting programming skills in R. In addition, it should be useful for professional training courses, for self-study, and as a reference source.

Table 1.1: Overview of the Thematic Focus of the Chapters.

Chapters												
1	2	3	4	5	6	7	8	9	10	11	12	13

Intro to social research, using R, stat. distributions, linear regression

Nonlinear relations, generalized models, validation, statistical learning

Descriptive and causal inference, linear mixed modeling, classification

Text analytics

Chapter 1 is a good starting point to clarify basic concepts and provide an initial orientation regarding computational methods and the main types of data in social research. It also outlines the role that data science is often assigned in the tension between the scientific goals of prediction and explanation.

For an introductory statistics or data analysis course in a bachelor's program in social sciences, political science, or education, the sequence of chapters highlighted in gray in Table 1.1 should be suitable. It introduces programming with R, the creation of R graphics, the statistical analysis of frequency distributions, and linear regression.

Following on from this, the blue-highlighted chapter sequence focuses on topics relevant to statistical learning, namely nonlinear relationships, non-additive effects, generalizations of the linear model and other statistical methods, as well as a topic that is not missing from any introduction to data science: validation designs.

While all of these statistical methods are applicable to survey data, Chapter 13, highlighted in orange, is dedicated to the analysis of text data from social media.

Therefore, if a course is already at a more advanced stage of a bachelor's or master's degree program, it would be quite possible to place less emphasis on the grayed-out topics, or even skip them, in order to go directly to the chapter route towards statistical learning and text analytics. Depending on the prerequisites the students already have in this regard.

The thematic focus and the intended objectives of a course in data analysis and statistics also determine how far the scope should be extended to include methodological questions. Particularly in social science study programs, it can be interesting to contrast the goal of data-based prediction with that of causal inference. And it may also be of interest to deal with descriptive inference, multilevel analysis and probabilistic classification. These topics are covered in the yellow-marked chapters.

Part I: **Description, Explanation, Prediction**

Chapter 2
Descriptive Inference

2.1 Descriptive and Statistical Inference

King et al. (1994: 55–57) speak of *descriptive inference* if statistical techniques are used to separate systematic from random components of phenomena of interest. Descriptive inference is essentially statistical inference[1] based on repeated measurements or observations, and replicable outcomes.[2] From the perspective of sampling and estimation, it is essentially design-based inference for "descriptive analysis of probability samples of survey populations", with the basic objective being "to describe with measurable uncertainty due to sampling a population characteristic or process as it exists in a defined finite population" (Heeringa et al. 2010: 54). The aim is usually to use sample data to draw conclusions about the prevalence of facts in precisely defined populations, for example such as the proportion of right-wing voters in Germany in a federal election. This is distinguished from analyses that go beyond descriptive analysis to analytic uses of survey data sets,[3] "—uses that estimate models to explore more universal, multivariate relationships or even to possibly understand causality in relationships among variables" (Heeringa et al. 2010: 54).

The three basic goals of a data analysis are either to describe, explain or predict reality. Against this background, this chapter focuses on description. If, for example, population parameters are to be estimated, then the aim is to describe an aspect of reality, not to explain or predict something. If we use statistical techniques for compensatory weighting of samples or imputation of missing values, then the aim is to take the necessary corrective measures to ensure data quality, but not to explain or predict a target variable. The same applies if we pursue an approach of systematic replication in order to arrive at a reliable empirical data foundation by varying the methods that en-

---

[1] For instance, the usual criteria of unbiasedness, efficiency, and consistency of sample estimators of population parameters are viewed as criteria for assessing "descriptive inferences" (King et al. 1994: 63).
[2] The importance of replicability is derivable from the point of view that systematic factors are regarded as persistent factors with consistent and predictable consequences (King et al. 1994: 62).
[3] This is where the distinction between finite populations and the so-called superpopulation model comes into play. In the words of Heeringa et al. (2010: 54): "To unify our thinking about finite population statistics versus a more universal model of processes or outcomes, sampling theoreticians have introduced the concept of a *superpopulation model*" (Heeringa et al. 2010: 54). Similarly, Fuller (2009: 341–342). Heeringa et al. (2010: 54–55) provide – using the example of a regression model – a concise description of the relationship between finite populations and a superpopulation model, and in this context also emphasize the importance of replications (of estimated regression coefficients) over finite populations when they write "Is there a replication of one's findings in surveys of other distinct finite populations? Can one make a convincing theoretical argument for a single universal model for the relationships observed in the finite populations?" (Heeringa et al. 2010: 55).

https://doi.org/10.1515/9783110680683-002

able us to create a data-based representation of empirical reality in the first place. With goals of this kind, the primary aim is not to explain or predict any target variable, but to infer a description of reality from data.

2.2 Description by Population Parameters

Given the large number of surveys conducted on behalf of media companies in Germany, Europe and worldwide to inform the public about the prevalence of political preferences or other surveyable facts among specific target groups, the importance of data-based descriptive inference cannot be overestimated. In addition, there are the surveys of institutionalized social and political reporting that have been conducted regularly for years and decades and which are at least partly geared towards descriptive inference.[4]

The aim is usually to find out what is typical for a target population and how homogeneous or heterogeneous it is in the respective respects. Percentages, mean values and measures of dispersion are often calculated for this purpose. These are easy to use, easy to communicate and, in principle, also have substantial significance. However, they must be calculated for the target population, and this can be very large. A good example is the voting population of the Federal Republic of Germany. The sheer number alone would make it practically impossible to survey all eligible voters in a short period of time or within a reasonable amount of time. Not to mention that it has been empirically proven that not every person would be reachable, able or willing to be surveyed. Trying to survey everyone would therefore be highly dysfunctional or counterproductive. The good news, however, is that this is not necessary, since statistics, with its ability to draw random samples and evaluate them using inferential statistics, provides us with excellent tools to calculate the parameters we are looking for on the basis of samples.

How should we proceed?

2.3 Selection Frame

First, the target population must be determined. This is by definition the population about which it is desired to make statements. This can be the *general population*, which is then usually restricted to a specific age range. An example is the population aged 18 and over. Occasionally the target population is expanded to include 15 + year

---

4 Although such surveys are also and especially designed in such a way that their data enable causal conclusions and predictions. The prime example of this at the European level is certainly the European Social Survey and, to some extent, the Eurobarometer studies.

olds. Sometimes other defining characteristics are added, for instance, such as the right to vote for the German Bundestag in surveys on voting behavior in Germany. It is also common to define a target population in such a way that it is limited spatially, for example regionally or locally. For example, a target population may be defined as the resident population aged 18 years and older who live in the city of Bremen on a specific date according to the register of the residents' registration office. These all are just examples.

Target Population
 > Selection frame & auxiliary data
  > Selection process & related data
   > Design & nonresponse weights
     > Missing data treatment

Figure 2.1: Target Population, Selection Frame and Related Steps.

The target can also be *specific populations*, for example, the members of an institution such as a school or university or the members of a professional group. Another example concerns social media. A target population may well be defined to target the group of users of a particular social media platform, for instance.

The researcher is generally free to determine the target population, but this determination should take into account that a practical sampling design can be developed for reaching this target. In particular, after the target population has been defined, the researcher must develop a sampling design that specifies the selection frame and related details (Figure 2.1). This selection frame should be designed in such a way that there are no significant disparities between it and the target population. Rather, it should represent the target population in its entirety, thus avoiding both under- and over-coverage.

In register samples, such as those used in *postal surveys*, the information they contain can be used to develop a selection frame. In addition, register information can help to obtain auxiliary information needed for sample weighting. If the information provided in the population register is up to date, it can provide a suitable selection frame. However, since a population register typically provides very little socio-demographic information in addition to the actual address information and this information usually only correlates weakly or not at all with the probability of participation in surveys, the register information is usually of only limited use as auxiliary information for survey weighting.

In *telephone surveys*, a suitable selection frame usually has to be created first because, at best, only a subset of landline and mobile phone numbers have been entered into the telephone register. The solution here is, in principle, to artificially generate the universe of telephone numbers that is possible in a given research context and to use this as the basis for a random selection of telephone numbers. To ensure that the process does not become too inefficient, the dialing computers check on a technical basis whether an artificially generated number leads to a real connection or not.

In *web surveys*, samples are often collected via online panels, also called access panels. Such panels represent pools of people who have agreed to be invited to participate in surveys and are often huge in terms of the number of such participants. Participants in such panels typically provide a range of socio-demographic characteristics when registering. This creates a register of personal information in the panel that can be used for sampling. In particular, the register information makes it possible to tailor the selection frame for a survey to predetermined target populations. Though the selection process itself can then be carried out on a probability basis, an online panel itself does not necessarily offer the best quality as a selection frame. This is because the selection frame itself should be randomly based and not be an opt-in volunteer panel.

Once the selection frame is defined for a specific survey, it forms the basis for drawing the required sample. This should, if possible, always be a random sample. There are a number of different ways for drawing probability-based samples. These include, for example, simple random sampling, proportional or disproportionately stratified sampling, cluster or multi-stage sampling.

We would develop a sampling design that determines which of these options to pursue in a given study. Such a design would also pay attention to the *auxiliary information* needed for the derivation of design and nonresponse weights.

2.4 Probability Sampling

Survey research uses probability samples to estimate population parameters. Sampling designs can be quite simple as in the case of simple random selection, but they can also be more complex schemes, as in the case of stratified sampling, cluster sampling or multi-stage sampling (Heeringa et al. 2010: 14–16).

The basic property of a simple random sample (srs) is that each element in the target population has the same probability of being selected.[5] A simple random sample can be selected with and without replacement. Sampling without replacement guarantees that elements cannot be selected more than once in the sample (Bethlehem 2009: 65).

Levy and Lemeshow (1999: 47–48), for instance, offer an interesting illustration when they show how rapidly the number of samples T increases that can be drawn even from a small population. To do this, they use the binomial coefficient from the

---

5 In order to technically implement random selections, statistical programs, including R, provide functions for generating random numbers and random selections.

mathematical theory of permutations and combinations to calculate the "number T of possible samples of n elements from a population of N elements" as

$$T = \binom{N}{n} = \frac{N!}{n! \cdot (N-n)!} \qquad (2.1)$$

with

$$n! = n \cdot (n-1) \cdot (n-2) \cdot \ldots \cdot (1) \quad \text{and} \quad 0! = 1 \qquad (2.2)$$

Based on this,[6] the authors introduce a *"simple random sample of n elements from a population of N elements"* as "one in which each of the $\binom{N}{n}$ possible samples of n elements has the same probability of selection, namely $1/\binom{N}{n}$", with the sampling done without replacement of elements once selected. Simple random selection certainly represents an uncomplicated and elegant way of selecting units and, if feasible in a use case, would certainly be preferable to other, more complicated ways of sampling at random.

However, in the practice of social science research, it is often unavoidable to resort to more complex methods of random sampling, for example stratified or multistage probability samples.

Stratifying a sample is quite simple. In principle, the population is first divided into subpopulations and then a random sample is drawn independently from each of these subpopulations. If the selection probability of n/N is then kept the same in each subpopulation, for example if a 10% sample is drawn each time, the result is a proportional stratified random sample. Such proportional stratification is advantageous because it retains the *self-weighting* property of a simple random selection. Simple random selection is a special type of sampling referred to by an acronym ("epsem") that refers to sampling with equal probabilities of selection. Quoting from a classic source (Kish 1965: 21):

> *Epsem* (equal probability of selection method) *sampling* describes any *sample in which the population elements have equal probabilities of selection.* (. . .) *Epsem is used widely because it usually leads to self-weighting samples*, where the simple mean of the sample cases is a good estimate of the population mean. (. . .) Epsem sampling can result either from equal probability selection throughout, or from variable probabilities that compensate each other through the several stages of multistage selection.

A stratified random sample could be considered, for example, if the student body at a university is to be surveyed. If we split the student population into subpopulations along the study programs involved, for instance, each such program represents a subpopulation from which to draw a random sample. If then the same selection probabil-

---

6 Levy and Lemeshow's description corresponds exactly to the theoretical definition of srs earlier given by Kish (1965: 39) who introduces the formula given above as (2.1) using these words: "Each possible combination of n different elements out of N has the same probability of being selected for the sample", namely $1/\binom{N}{n}$.

ity of n/N is used, the result is a proportionate stratified sample. If, however, the probability of selection varies, for example if it is set higher in low-enrollment programs, then the result is a disproportionately stratified sample. While the former selection remains self-weighting, the latter does not. This becomes relevant when a data analysis is not only about comparing students from these different programs with each other, for instance by comparing percentages in a tabular analysis, but about making statements about the student body as a whole. For this, the disproportionality would have to be balanced out by weighting.

The self-weighting property of samples is very useful in practice. We usually carry out calculations of percentages, means, measures of dispersion, correlations, regressions and the like with data from random samples in order to be able to use these calculations as estimates of the corresponding facts (parameters) in the population from which the sample was drawn. The key question is therefore whether sample statistics can easily fulfil this function?

One of the factors that plays a role in this regard is whether the sample data need to be weighted individually when calculating such percentages, averages, and the like. The key point is that such an extra-weighting would not be necessary with a self-weighting sample.[7] Then, the data of each unit (i. e., of each row in a data matrix) would simply be included in the statistical formulas with an implicit standard weight of 1.0.

This does not mean, however, that we can usually do without any case weights when using probability samples. We only use them for other reasons when necessary, namely as design or non-response weights (see below).

It is not uncommon in social research to use sampling designs for multi-stage selection, with *random selection at each stage*. For example, in a first selection step, voting districts can be selected in order to select households within selected voting districts in selection step 2 and, if necessary, household members within the selected households. To give a second example: In the European Social Survey Round 11, the sub-study for Germany was based on a two-stage probability design, in which first municipalities and then persons within these municipalities were selected from their population registers for the face-to-face interviews.[8]

When analyzing survey data, it is always important to check whether the data is based on a multi-stage sampling design. Even though such designs too can lead to self-weighting samples, they can still require design weights. In addition, multi-stage sampling (as well as cluster sampling) can come along with a so-called design effect,

---

7 Another advantage is that, apart from defining the target population and setting a suitable selection frame, the researcher does not have to determine how many units with which combinations of characteristics must be included in a sample. This too would amount to case weighting, namely a conscious weighting carried out by the researcher, as in a quota sample.

8 The sampling design also included stratification and, as is usual for the ESS, is well documented. See, for example, this web source: https://ess.sikt.no/en/study/412db4fe-c77a-4e98-8ea4-6c19007f551b

which results in larger standard errors compared to srs and thus affects the design-based inference described below.[9]

2.5 Design-based Inference

A sampling design includes two components, a "sampling plan and a method for drawing inferences from the data generated under the sampling plan" (Heeringa et al. 2010: 14). A key role is played by the combination of probability sampling as the plan with the design-based method of inference.

Probability sampling allows the calculation of sample estimates of population parameters. While e*stimator* is a technical term "to designate a rule or method of estimating a universe parameter", the particular value yielded by an estimator for a given sample is usually called an *estimate* (Som 1996:13). Popular examples of estimators are the sample mean and the sample proportion. We can imagine an estimator as a mathematical formula and ask how well it fulfills the function of estimating the parameter to be estimated. In particular, it is expected that an estimator produces unbiased, consistent and precise estimates.

A design-based approach to sampling implements a random mechanism to select sample units with a known probability of selection. The properties of estimators like bias and variance are evaluated with respect to *repeated* sampling (Valliant et al. 2013: 310). The design-based approach to sampling adopts the frequentist view that we have not only drawn the one probability sample from a population that we actually did draw in practice, but that we repeat this selection process many times, each time calculating the sample estimate that we are interested in. This creates what is called the *sampling distribution*. So, for example, if we were to take, say, 5,000 samples of the same size n from one and the same population of size N, the sampling distribution would consist of exactly these 5,000 sample estimates.[10] This sampling distribution is

---

9 We therefore often use the R library *survey()* to make appropriate design specifications for data analyses.

10 Figure 2.2 shows an example. Hypothetically, suppose that a parameter in the population is 4 (on a response scale of 1 to 11), repeatedly drawn sample estimates are normally distributed, and we conduct an experiment in which a series of random samples of equal size n are drawn from the population. Then sample estimates would be expected to be below the gray curve. However, if the population parameter were, say, 7, sample estimates would be expected to be below the orange curve. And, to take a third example, if the true value in the population is 7.5, the expected values would be below the dark red curve. Even if the true values in the population are unknown (which is usually the case, because if we knew them, sample estimates would be unnecessary), this knowledge helps us because, when testing statistical hypotheses, we can hypothesize the unknown parameters and calculate their probability based on the sample results. For the distributions in Figure 2.2, we used—purely fictitious—means of 4 and 7 and 7.5, as well as an average dispersion around the respective mean of 0.6.

now the basis for evaluating the properties of the underlying estimator, i. e. the formula or algorithm used to calculate these estimates.

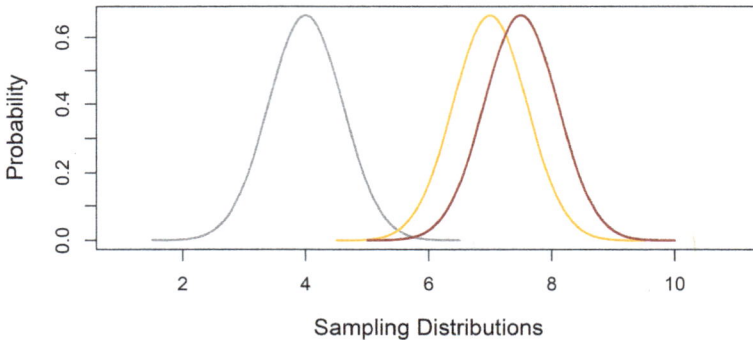

Figure 2.2: Examples of Sampling Distributions.

An estimator is considered *unbiased* if the mean of the sampling distribution coincides with the population value to be estimated. In the words of Som (1996: 14): "A sample estimator is said to be unbiased if the average value of the sample estimates for all possible samples of the same size is mathematically identical with the value of the universe parameter."

Secondly, an estimator is considered *consistent* "if it tends to the universe value with increasing sample size" (Som 1996: 15). An increasing sample size should reduce both *bias*, i. e., any difference between the mean of the sampling distribution and the population value to be estimated, and the average dispersion of the sampling distribution itself, i. e., its *variance* or *standard deviation*, with the latter then called *standard error*.

Thirdly, an estimator is considered *precise* if it has a small variance (Bethlehem and Biffignandi 2012: 69, 71–72, 98). Thus, of "two estimators, based on the same sample size, for the same universe parameter", one is more precise than the other "when its sampling variance is smaller than the other's" (Som 1996: 15–16).

In applied research, it is common practice to relate a sample estimate, such as a mean, a proportion, or a regression coefficient, to its estimated standard error. To get these estimates, there is no need to generate the underlying sampling distribution every time anew. In research practice, the resampling experiment instead functions as a pure "what if" thought experiment: What if we had drawn from the population not just the one sample on which our estimates are based, but actually many thousands, theoretically an infinite number of samples of the same size? Then we would get the sampling distribution and be able to calculate its mean, variance and standard deviation. As a rule, however, in research practice we only have the one probability sample that was actually drawn available. Once a sampling distribution is derived mathematically or via a simulation experiment, there is no need to get it confirmed again and again in research practice. There we simply use the algorithms already implemented in the statistical software to obtain sample estimates including their standard errors.

2.6 Model-Assisted, Design-Based Inference

Probability samples may suffer seriously from selective unit nonresponse. Such nonresponse can cause theoretically unbiased statistical estimators to result in biased estimates in practice. Valliant et al (2013: 310) describe this very aptly when they write that ". . . most samples that start out as probability samples do not end up that way because of nonresponse (NR) and other problems that result in the loss of some sample units." They conclude from this observation that "strictly design-based inference is usually not feasible" and describe a hybrid approach in which design-based inference is assisted by models to reflect the processes that produce a sample.[11]

Such "a hybrid approach uses both model-based and design-based thinking and is called model-assisted. A probability sample is selected, weights are calculated, and a model(s) guides the choice of the estimator. Inferences are made using the distribution generated by the probability sampling plan – not a model. [. . .] This is the approach that Särndal et al (1992) espouse" (Valliant et al. 2013: 311).

2.6.1 Use Case: Supplied Nonresponse Weights

When analyzing survey data, we usually rely on model assistance for design-based inference, particularly in the form of nonresponse or poststratification weights that are intended to compensate for systematic unit nonresponse. In practice, the standard use case is likely to include the weights provided by the data provider in data analyses to be performed. This has the great advantage that users do not have to create weighting variables themselves, but it also implies that they cannot influence the model on which the weighting is based. It is then a question of trust in the appropriateness of the weighting variables provided – a trust that appears justified in the case of large, well-conducted European social research studies such as the European Social Survey.

In the European Social Survey, for example, four weighting variables are provided:
- a design weight (called "dweight") to compensate for differential selection probabilities across participating countries. This is necessary to compensate for the fact that different sampling designs are being pursued in the participating countries.

---

11 "By contrast, a strictly model-based approach ignores the sample design and considers only the population structure (i. e., a model) in deciding on an estimator and the corresponding weights. This approach can be applied to either probability or non-probability samples" (Valliant et al. 2013: 310).

For instance, some use address-based sample, some not, so that it might become necessary to adjust for the size of the household in which the selected persons live (Kaminska 2023: 2).

– a poststratification weight (called "pspwght") that includes the design weight as well. Regarding this weight, Kaminska (2023: 2) writes: "Post-stratification weights reduce the impact of nonresponse error. Additionally, they have the advantage of correcting for coverage and sampling errors with respect to the post-stratification variables. Currently, ESS post-stratification is based on gender, age, education and geographical region."

– However, the poststratification weight does not take into account that the participating countries have different population sizes but similar sample sizes. This means that the post-stratification weight is without the population size correction. For this purpose, a population size weight called "pweight" is provided.

– Finally, an analysis weight called "anweight" is provided, which takes all the above weighting information into account. It is calculated as

$$anweight = pspwght * pweight \qquad (2.3)$$

It is recommended to always use this latter weighting variable when analyzing ESS data. Kaminska (2023: 4) writes about this:

> anweight corrects for differential selection probabilities within each country as specified by sample design, for nonresponse, for noncoverage, and for sampling error related to the four post-stratification variables, and takes into account differences in population size across countries. It is constructed by first deriving the design weight, then applying a post-stratification adjustment, and then a population size adjustment.

Since samples distorted by selective unit nonresponse can never be completely ruled out in survey research, the general recommendation is to take this possibility into account by using the weighting variables provided. As an example, let us consider an analysis using data from the Example Data Set 9 (European Social Survey Round 10, the data for Germany). In chapter 3, variation in a target variable is analyzed that is based on the answers to this survey question: "How acceptable for you would it be for Germany to have a strong leader who is above the law?" If we analyze the percentage of people who would not categorically rule out such a leader, this percentage turns out to be 35.9 percent if the sample is not weighted and this percentage turns out to be 38.8 percent if the sample is adjusted for selective unit nonresponse by using the analysis weight ("anweight") or the post-stratification weight (pspwght) both provided by the ESS team. Such 2.9 percentage points is not a small difference. The sample size is n = 8,457 respondents.

The practical implementation of weighting in R is generally straightforward, as many functions include a weighting option by default. This also applies to functions that we often use in predictive modeling, the *lm() function* for linear models and the *glm() function* for generalized linear models. For example, the structure of the *lm()* *function* looks like this:

$$lm(formula, weights, data) \tag{2.4}$$

First we specify *formula* according to the pattern "target variable ~ predictor variable(s)" and then the name of the variable that contains the case weights. Finally, *data* names the R data frame that contains the variables and cases to be analyzed. We describe all this in detail in Chapter 6 and subsequent chapters.

Since not every R function offers this weighting option, it may be advisable to take a different approach. An R library called *survey* is available for this (Lumley 2010; Lumley et al 2024). In Chapter 11, for example, we use this library to weight the frequencies in contingency tables. Since we cannot name a weighting variable in the *table()* or *ftable()* function, we use the *svytable() function* in *library(survey)* instead. To do this, the library is called, the sampling design is specified and the *svytable()* function is called based on this.

```
library(survey)
design <- survey::svydesign(id = ~1,
        weights=~weightname, data = filename)
frq <- survey::svytable(~varlist, design)
```
(2.5)

In the "survey" library, the *svydesign() function* serves the purpose of specifying complex survey designs. Options include, for instance, the specification of clusters, sampling probabilities, strata, sampling weights and a finite population correction. Of course, the data frame to be analyzed can also be named. In the present example, we only need a small part of this range of functions. Since our data example does not have a cluster structure, we indicate this with ~ *id = 1* and otherwise only specify the name of the weighting variable and the data frame. We assign these design specifications to the object named "design" in the present example, so that we can relate the subsequent *svytable() function* to this object.

2.6.2 Use Case: Models of Response Propensity

The opportunity to conduct primary research offers many design options and control over survey design, sampling, interview design and the analysis of the survey data obtained that way. This includes taking into account, right from the start, when designing the study, the possibility of compensating for systematic losses of units through selective non-response. Such systematic losses usually occur when trying to get the units selected for the sample to actually be included in the sample. General experience teaches that not all units can be reached and that of the units reached, not all are willing or can be persuaded to participate. If these losses do not occur by chance but due to systematic reasons, then selective nonresponse and thus distorted sample estimates are the result. It is then crucial to be able to recognize the systematic nature underlying such losses. This requires suitable information and a model that uses this information to predict the probability of participation in the survey, the so-called response probability or response propensity. This information can either be auxiliary information or information that can be derived from an adaptive design of the survey design itself.

According to the *random response model* (Bethlehem et al. 2011: 43–45) each individual has a specific probability of taking part in a survey once invited. However, because such response probabilities are unknown, they have to be estimated (Bethlehem et al. 2011: 330–331). Then, the amount of bias in mean estimates is quantifiable by a formula (Bethlehem 2009: 222) which relates the covariance of a target variable Y and a response probability ρ to the mean response probability. If this unknown response probability ρ is replaced with an estimated response propensity $\hat{\rho}$,

$$\hat{B}(\bar{y}_R) = \frac{Cov_{\hat{\rho}Y}}{\bar{\hat{\rho}}} \tag{2.6}$$

it becomes possible to quantify the bias in such mean estimates. (2.6) divides the covariance of the individual observed y and estimated propensity scores by the mean estimated propensity score. The resulting value is interpretable as the difference "mean value that takes the individual response propensities into account"

$$\left(\frac{\hat{\rho}_i}{\bar{\hat{\rho}}} \cdot y_i\right) \tag{2.7}$$

minus the "unweighted sample mean". Conversely to (2.8) below, here the propensity score $\hat{\rho}_i$ is used in the numerator of the fraction to weight y_i and not its inverse value.

Table 2.1 exemplifies this approach using two frequency distributions from Example Data Set 1 (PPSM Innovation Panel). It displays four quantities. First, how the score a person responds to a y variable correlates with that person's propensity to take part in the survey. Second, the bias in a mean estimate according to (2.6). Third, the sample mean, which does not take into account any response propensities, i. e. the unweighted sample mean, and fourthly, a modified version of the Horvitz-Thompson estimator, calculated as

$$\bar{y}_{HT} = \frac{1}{n} \cdot \sum_i \frac{d_i y_i}{\bar{\hat{\rho}}} \tag{2.8}$$

with d_i denoting the inverse value of the estimated individual propensity score

$$d_i = \frac{1}{\hat{\rho}_i} \tag{2.9}$$

to work as the suggested response propensity weighting estimator (Bethlehem et al. 2011: 330–331, 334–335).

In the present example, we can rely on a large sample in which the responses to the survey questions on happiness and satisfaction correlate positively, albeit only weakly, with response propensity (left column of results). The bias in the respective mean estimate is correspondingly weak (second column from the left).

Table 2.1: Bias in Sample Estimates of Mean Values of Happiness and Satisfaction with Current Life.

	$r_{\hat{\rho}Y}$	$\hat{B}(\bar{y}_R)$	$\bar{y}_R$	$\bar{y}_{HT}$
On a scale from 1 = "very unhappy" to 11 = "very happy": Where to this scale would you fit yourself in?	0.054*	0.017	7.554	7.535
How satisfied are you, all in all, with your current life? On a scale from 1 to 11 is the 1 supposed to mean that you are "very unsatisfied" and the 11 that you are "very satisfied". Using the figures in-between you can grade your assessment.	0.106*	0.033	7.896	7.862

N = 3,951 and 3,953; *sig. (p < 0.001), °p < 0.05. 11pt scales. Propensity to take part in surveys conducted within the access panel.

It is also informative to compare the unweighted sample mean (third column from the left) with the mean estimate that results when the sample is weighted by the inverse value of the response propensity as expressed in (2.8) and (2.9) (right-most column). The latter compensates for the fact that the mean, if the response propensities are taken into account, would usually be higher than the unweighted sample mean reflects (i. e., the positive bias). Based on this, the usual approach is followed to weight the data in such a way that this hidden overrepresentation is compensated for. This leads to the mean values in the right-most column.

A comparison of corresponding unweighted and weighted mean estimates now reveals the pattern that the unweighted sample mean overestimates the population mean only to a marginal degree. The differences in the respective mean values are rather small. We would therefore arrive at roughly the same conclusions here, regardless of whether we weight the data or not. This can of course look very different for other data examples.

Since the individual response probabilities required for the random response model are unknown and therefore have to be estimated as response propensities, the question arises on which basis this can be done. The answer is essentially that estimating response propensities requires auxiliary variables. Since different sets of such variables are likely to result in different estimated response propensities, the selection of proper auxiliary variables is of great importance. Though it is clear in theory which ones would be particularly effective (Bethlehem et al. 2011: 249), in survey practice one may choose only variables that are available according to circumstances

(Bethlehem and Biffignani 2012: 399). The core challenge is that information about respondents is not sufficient for corrective measures including the estimation of response propensities. This makes it difficult because non-respondents are characterized precisely by the fact that they do not participate in the survey and therefore do not contribute any data to it. So what to do?

A common option is the use of external sources of information like population registers and area data linked to the places of residence. Although this provides us with sound information for sample weighting, this weighting may be of only limited use. This is because the probability of participating in a survey may only be marginally related to demographic variables such as age and gender or the neighborhoods in which people live. In addition, survey variables and variables from population registers can be completely uncorrelated. As Lynn (2003: 239) aptly notes: "Frame data or external population data [. . .] are at best modestly correlated with the survey variables". Then any attempt at adjusting for such external sources of variation will leave potential bias in sample estimates unaffected for just those survey variables that are of interest to the researcher.

It is therefore not only sensible, but may also be the only option, to use other external sources as well. For this purpose, rich information can be obtained from "paradata" (Bethlehem et al. 2011: 454) on factors that shape the probability of gaining survey contact and cooperation. This includes efforts to design the initial contact (interview request) in such a way that it allows for flexible responses to concerns of contacted persons. Within the narrow limits set by law, this can include efforts to persuade hesitant persons to take part in an interview. Adaptive survey designs (Bethlehem et al. 2011: 395) can provide information about individuals who would normally be non-respondents also in the form of a design known as the "basic question approach" (Bethlehem 2009: 239; Bethlehem et al. 2011: 295; see also Lynn's (2003) PEDAKSI methodology). As written elsewhere (Engel 2015: 209),

> Paradata can enlarge the basis for understanding survey responses significantly. They are useful because they add relevant information to the actual survey data [. . .]. Closely related to this is an approach which pursues another aim. Instead of adding information to the body of survey data, one can try to enlarge this body itself [. . .]. A reluctant person might not be ready for a telephone interview with a length of 15 minutes, though perhaps such a person would participate in an interview of half this duration. Other people might be unwilling to participate in even such a short interview, though they would agree to answer one to three key questions of a study.

The crucial point is that such adaptive survey designs make it possible to quantify the influence of varying degrees of response propensity on the estimates of a study. Table 2.2 illustrates this by an analysis of data from Example Data Set 2 (Bremen City of Science Survey) we have presented in more detail elsewhere (Engel 2020). The table displays predicted mean interest-in-science scores for the conditions of a survey experiment on response order effects. As explained elsewhere (Engel 2020: 255–256):

Differences between entries in a row reflect differences across the two experimentally varied design features of using four vs. five response categories, and given five categories, of presenting these categories from the lowest to the highest or in reverse order. There are four such rows, one for each mode/interview condition of the adaptive survey design. In this latter regard, respondents are not allocated randomly to the four conditions.

Table 2.2: Interest in Science. Predicted y^* Latent Mean Scores (Source: author's own calculation).

			4 pt. scale	5 pt. scales		
					Scale direction	
			Low → High	All	Low → High [1]	High → Low [−1]
			A	B	C	D
x_{1g}	Mode	Interview	Predicted y^* scores			
x_{11}	CATI	Basic Questions	−0.516	−0.274	−0.427	−0.088
x_{12}	CATI	Core	−0.089	−0.286	−0.472	−0.084
x_{13}	CATI	Full	0.142	0.183	0.025	0.296
x_{14}	CAWI	Full	0.463	0.377	0.377	0.373
			N = 601	N = 570		

Note: Ordinal probit regression models. Experimental design regarding 4 pt. vs. 5 pt. scales and scale direction. *Source*: This is Table 2 in Engel (2020: 256). Reprinted with permission from Springer Nature (license agreement).

Of particular interest in the present context is column B ("All") and therein the mean comparison across the three conditions for the "CATI" telephone mode. The estimated mean values refer to the study's central target, interest in science. According to the estimates, this interest is comparatively strongest among respondents who were willing to give the full interview. The mean interest is less strong among those who did not want to give the full interview but were willing to give a core interview only that was about half as long. And interest in science turned out to be even lower among those who were willing to answer only the study's two or three "basic questions".

The result states that, as far as the CATI mode of the study is concerned, we would have overestimated the average interest in science in the population studied if we had not integrated the less willing people into the survey via the core and basic-question conditions.

2.6.3 Use Case: Quasi-Randomized Samples

Weights are used in constructing estimators. "The key goal in weight construction should, thus, be to construct good estimators" (Valliant et al. 2013: 309). However, the construction of weights is not possible without models. Valliant et al. (2013: 311) explain this using the example of volunteer surveys. "When computing weights for a volunteer survey, assumptions must be made about the mechanism that describes how likely a person is to participate. These assumptions, whether explicit or implicit, are models." If the sample is *not* probability-based, estimators can only be developed model-*based*. However, if the sample *is* probability-based, model-*assisted* estimation is possible.

Given the changing survey landscape in which probability sampling is no longer the only method used, the quasi-randomization approach described by Elliot and Valliant (2017: 255–257) appears particularly relevant as it is suitable for combining probability and non-probability sampling, for instance in the use of volunteer panels in the Internet. Elliot and Valliant (2017: 255) introduce the approach this way: "In the quasi-randomization approach, pseudo-inclusion probabilities are estimated and used to correct for selection bias. Given estimates of the pseudoprobabilities, design-based formulas are used for point estimates and variances."

Basically, a probability sample is used as a *reference sample* for the estimation of inclusion probabilities of a parallel volunteer sample:

> The statistical approach is to combine the reference sample and the sample of volunteers and fit a model to predict the probability of being in the nonprobability sample [. . .]. A key requirement of the reference survey is that it include the same covariates x_i as the volunteer survey so that a binary regression can be fitted to permit estimation of inclusion probabilities for the volunteers (Elliot and Valliant 2017: 255).

Nonresponse adjustments are required for both samples. First, to ensure that the reference sample itself is not biased by selective nonresponse, and then to adjust the volunteer sample for selection bias.[12] Beyond the connection of survey data sets, the quasi-randomization approach can also be used to connect survey data with other data via *sample matching*. This is useful when combining survey data with "found data" from social media. "The matches would be found based on covariates available in each dataset. This may be done based on individual covariate values or on propensity scores" and is "an example of predictive mean matching in which an imputation of an inclusion probability is made for each nonprobability unit" (Elliot and Valliant 2017: 256).

The availability of a suitable set of covariates is crucial. For the probability-based reference sample, in addition to the usual socio-demographics, ideally variables with a high predictive power for participation in the activity(s) that lead to the "found" data to be matched should also be included. For example, for writing and posting

---

12 Engel and Dahlhaus (2022: 358) describe how this approach was implemented in a survey.

texts of a certain type on previously determined social media platforms. Basically, this is a requirement that can be very well fulfilled as a screening task in a survey.

The set of covariates on the "found" data side, however, is much more challenging. In principle, we need the same set of covariates for statistical matching as on the reference survey side. But that is exactly what can be difficult. This is especially true when it comes to text data from online social media, and perhaps no other data other than this text data is available for matching. The challenge would then be to be able to draw conclusions about, for example, the socio-demographic characteristics of the authors of such texts from formal and stylistic elements of those texts (author profiling).

Another part of the overall task to be mastered is, however, much easier. This involves designing a suitable, even probability-based selection design for the text data from the universe of texts and postings under consideration. The application of formal models for probability-based selection is by no means limited to survey data, although this is certainly the norm in social research. Selection plans can just as easily be developed for texts and postings on social media platforms. And in principle, we also have the option of doing the selection not necessarily list-based. It can also work without a selection frame, for example in systematic random sampling.

2.7 Missing Data

2.7.1 Patterns

The applicability of methods for dealing with missing values must take into account the pattern of missing values. Citing Rubin (1976) the literature[13] usually distinguishes between three such patterns of missing values.

Data are missing *completely at random* (MCAR) when the probability of missing data on a variable of interest Y is unrelated to the values of Y and related variables in a dataset in question. Then the missing values form a simple random sample of all data values. Then missingness is completely unrelated to the data.

Data are *missing at random* (MAR) when the probability of missing data on Y is not related to the values of Y but to other measured variables. MAR is less restrictive than MCAR because it requires only that the missing values "behave like a random sample of all values within subclasses defined by observed data. In other words, MAR allows the probability that a datum is missing to depend on the datum itself, but only indirectly through quantities that are observed" (Schafer 1997: 11).

---

13 Schafer (1997: 10–11; Little and Rubin (2002: 11–12); Enders (2010: 5–12); van Buuren (2018: 8–9).

In contrast, data are called *missing not at random* (MNAR) "when the probability of missing data on a variable Y is related to the values of Y itself, even after controlling for other variables" (Enders 2010: 8).

MCAR	MAR	MNAR	
$p(R\|\Phi)$	$p(R\|Y_{obs}, \Phi)$	$p(R\|Y_{obs}, Y_{mis}, \Phi)$	(2.10)

"The key idea behind Rubin's theory is that missingness is a variable that has a probability distribution" (Enders 2010: 9). In (2.10), missingness is correspondingly represented by a missing data indicator R, which is coded 1 if a score for Y is observed and 0 if the value for Y is missing. $p()$ symbolizes a probability distribution, Y_{obs} and Y_{mis} the observed and missing parts of the data "and Φ is a parameter (or set of parameters) that describes the relationship between R and the data" (Enders 2010: 11). MCAR means that the probability of missing data on Y does not depend on the observed and missing data, MAR means that this probability depends on the observed but not the missing data, and MNAR denotes the situation that "the probability of missing data on Y can depend on other variables (i. e., Y_{obs}) as well as on the underlying values of Y itself (i. e., Y_{mis})" (Enders 2010:11).

Whereas MNAR requires specific methods,[14] the methods outlined here assume that the missing data mechanism is MAR, i. e. that the missing values are missing *at random* (Rubin 1987: 53; Enders 2010: 287).

2.7.2 Procedures

Unless a data analysis specifies otherwise, units with missing values in the relevant variables are often excluded from the analysis on a *listwise* basis by default. In this context, "listwise" refers to the set of variables to be included in a calculation, for example the target variable y and the set of predictors $x_1, \ldots, x_j$ of a linear regression. Such a listwise deletion of units with missing values results in a *complete-case analysis*.[15]

In contrast, the *pairwise* exclusion of units with missing values leads to an *available-case analysis*.[16] The option of pairwise deletion of units with missing values is,

---

14 For instance, Heckman's selection model or the pattern mixture model, e.g. for growth-curve models (Enders 2010: 291–301). We followed this route and combined a curves-of-factor latent growth curve model part with a pattern mixture model part in an analysis of data from the German PPSM Panel (Can and Engel 2015).

15 If units (cases) are excluded from a statistical analysis on a listwise or pairwise basis, this only applies to the respective statistical analysis, for example a linear regression analysis. The units themselves, i. e. the pertaining rows of the data matrix, remain in this data matrix as long as the user does not change this data matrix itself and saves these changes permanently.

16 The terms 'complete-case' and 'available-case' analysis are taken from Little and Rubin (2002: 53–54)

for example, an option in statistical analyses in which the basis of the analysis is a set of bivariate covariances or correlations. These can then be calculated either on the basis of all units with valid values *in the respective variable pairs* – regardless of whether these units simultaneously have missing values in the other variable pairs in the set or not (pairwise deletion). Or the calculation of each individual correlation can be based on the units that simultaneously have valid values *in all variables* in the set (listwise deletion).

The former option usually retains more units for an analysis than the latter, while the latter creates an identical and therefore equivalent fundament for the individual calculations. However, excluding units with missing values from statistical calculations not only reduces the sample size that remains for the calculations. Excluding units from the sample may also lead to the remaining subsample being distorted by selective item nonresponse. This happens when the missing values have *systematic* reasons. For example, when particularly high-earning people refuse to state their monthly income. Or when other questions in a survey are not answered because the answers a respondent would have to give are perceived by him or her as too sensitive or too personal to be communicated in an interview. The probability that a variable value is missing then becomes a function of this value, and the missing data pattern would no longer be random. This is much more challenging for the analysis than a reduced sample size alone.

An alternative to excluding units with missing values from a data analysis is to replace the missing values with plausible values. This replacement is called imputation.[17] Determining which values are plausible requires making substantive assumptions that can be translated into a formal model and used as the basis for the replacement process. In the simplest case, this would be the assumption that every missing value in a variable should be replaced by one and the same content value, — usually the mean of the frequency distribution. However, such a simple *mean substitution* is generally *not* recommended.

As an alternative to the general mean, *conditional* means are more suitable for replacing missing values, as these can take the particularities of each individual case into account much more closely. This can be easily achieved using a regression analysis and the set of predictors it contains with their individual feature combinations. It would then be the $\hat{y}_i$ values estimated by such a *regression imputation* for the respective feature combinations that would be used to replace the missing values. This seems sensible, as the specifics of the individual case are taken into account, but at

---

17 Imputation methods represent one class of methods in Little and Rubin's taxonomy (2002: 19–20) of missing-data methods. These are (1) procedures based on completely recorded units, (2) weighting procedures including the use of the Horvitz-Thompson estimator, (3) imputation-based procedures including hot deck imputation, mean and regression imputation, and (4) model-based procedures, including multiple imputation, "by defining a model for the observed data and basing inferences on the likelihood or posterior distribution under that model, with parameters estimated by procedures such as maximum likelihood."

the same time it is suboptimal, as an *estimated* $\hat{y}_i$ value must replace an *observed* value, and that would actually be y_i. Since $y_i = \hat{y}_i + e_i$, regression imputation realized that way therefore omits the residual or random component. This limitation is overcome in *stochastic regression imputation* by adding a random component to the estimated $\hat{y}_i$ value, which is drawn either randomly from the distribution of e_i residuals or from a probability distribution (Enders 2010: 46–48; van Buuren 2018: 13–16).

2.7.3 Multiple Imputation

Adding random noise to the prediction is an improvement but still neglects a further source of uncertainty, namely parameter uncertainty. As van Buuren (2018: 65) points out, there are two main methods for considering this uncertainty: "Bayesian methods draw the parameters directly from their posterior distributions, whereas bootstrap methods resample the observed data and re-estimate the parameters from the resampled data." These methods are called Bayesian and Bootstrap multiple imputation respectively.

Multiple imputation means that a missing value is not only replaced once by a substantial value, but – in parallel calculations – multiple times. In this way, an incomplete set of data does not result in just one completed data set but in, say $k = 5, \ldots, 10$ parallel data sets, which only differ in how the missing values are replaced with plausible substantial values. Since multiple imputation implies the performance of parallel calculations in the completed data sets, the parameter estimates obtained in this way must finally be pooled again. Multiple imputation therefore takes place in three basic steps: multiple completion of an incomplete data set (imputation phase), parallel analysis of the completed data sets (analysis phase) and then a pooling step to combine the parallel estimates into final estimates respectively (pooling phase).[18] The basis for this pooling is the rules developed by Rubin (1987: 76–77), which van Buuren (2018: 42–43) calls the "Rubin rules".[19] These rules include the formulas (2.11) to (2.15), (2.23) and (2.24) displayed below.

Sampling distributions are created by repeatedly drawing random samples from a population, each time calculating the sample estimate of interest. Based on such sampling distributions of estimates, design-based inference allows an unknown population parameter Q to be estimated by a sample estimate $\hat{Q}$ if the underlying sample estimator used possesses the required statistical properties and the applicability of the simulation model of repeated sampling is not impaired by nonresponse in a real application. Then, we could trust in $\hat{Q}$ as an estimate of Q and the associated variance-covariance, U. The

---

[18] See, e.g., Enders (2010: 188), van Buuren and Groothuis-Oudshoorn (2011: 5) or van Buuren (2018: 140).
[19] See also Enders (2010: 219, 222–226).

situation becomes more complicated when item nonresponse occurs in the sample, so that now *three analytical levels* are involved: the incomplete sample, the complete sample and the population. In the words of van Buuren (2018: 44):

> At the level of the sample, there is uncertainty about Q. This uncertainty is captured by U, the estimated variance-covariance of $\hat{Q}$ in the sample. If we have no missing data in the sample, the pair $\left(\hat{Q}, U\right)$ contains everything we know about Q. If we have incomplete data, we can distinguish three analytic levels: the population, the sample and the incomplete sample. [. . .] At the sample level we can distinguish two estimands, instead of one: $\hat{Q}$ and U. Thus, the role of the single estimand Q at the population level is taken over by the estimand pair $\left(\hat{Q}, U\right)$ at the sample level. [. . .] Note that $\hat{Q}$ is both an estimate (of Q) as well as an estimand (of $\bar{Q}$). Also, U has two roles.[20]

In this terminology, $\bar{Q}$ pertains to the incomplete sample, $\hat{Q}$ to the sample and Q to the population. $\bar{Q}$ is an estimate of $\hat{Q}$ and $\hat{Q}$ is an estimate of Q, where $\bar{Q}$ itself is obtained this way: the initially incomplete sample is completed m times, in order to get the estimate in question for each of these m imputed datasets for a calculation of their mean value across these m datasets.

$$\bar{Q} = \frac{1}{m} \cdot \sum_{l=1}^{m} \hat{Q}_l \tag{2.11}$$

Similarly, $\bar{U}$ refers to the incomplete sample and U to the sample, where $\bar{U}$ is an estimate of U. Analogous to (2.10), the calculation is carried out for the m imputed data sets with subsequent averaging. In this way we obtain the average sampling variance within the imputations

$$\bar{U} = \frac{1}{m} \cdot \sum_{l=1}^{m} \bar{U}_l \tag{2.12}$$

At the same time, we obtain the variance between the imputations as

$$B = \frac{1}{m-1} \cdot \sum_{l=1}^{m} \left(\hat{Q}_l - \bar{Q}\right)\left(\hat{Q}_l - \bar{Q}\right)' \tag{2.13}$$

and the total variance of $\bar{Q}$, "and hence of $(Q - \bar{Q})$ if $\bar{Q}$ is unbiased" (van Buuren 2018: 43), by

$$T = \bar{U} + \left(1 + \frac{1}{m}\right) \cdot B \tag{2.14}$$

---

20 Van Buuren (2018: 42) illustrates his use of the term "scientific estimand" as "a quantity of scientific interest that we can calculate" using the example of Q, i. e. a population parameter. We think the term is best translated as "quantity to be estimated".

where

$$\left(1 + \frac{1}{m}\right) \tag{2.15}$$

is a correction for finite m.

2.7.4 Predictive Mean Matching

Instead of replacing missing observed values with *estimated* values as outlined above, it is also possible to replace missing values with *observed* values from similar units. The imputation method known as *predictive mean matching* uses the predicted values from a regression analysis for assessing the similarity among the units of an analysis. It is realized in the context of multiple imputation. In the words of van Buuren (2018: 77):

> Predictive mean matching calculates the predicted value of target variable Y according to the specified imputation model. For each missing entry, the method forms a small set of candidate donors (typically with 3, 5 or 10 members) from all complete cases that have predicted values closest to the predicted value for the missing entry. One donor is randomly drawn from the candidates, and the observed value of the donor is taken to replace the missing value.

While the determination of similarity via close $\hat{y}_i$ values follows the logic of regression imputation, the random selection of observed y_i values from empirical distributions among units with close $\hat{y}_i$ resembles the logic of imputing values from nearest neighbors or similarly responding units. Since similarity is defined in terms of the $\hat{y}_i$ values whose calculation is based on a set of predictor variables, $x_{i1} \ldots x_{ij}$, the configuration of these individual x_{ij} values is also required for the units with missing y_i values.

Parameter uncertainty is taken into account by random draws from the posterior predictive distribution of the $b_j's$ calculated for the subset of complete units. Each such draw produces a new set of regression coefficients that is used for calculating the $\hat{y}_i$ values for *all* units in the analysis, including those with missing y_i values.

> Typically this would be a random draw from a multivariate normal distribution with mean b and the estimated covariance matrix of b (with an additional random draw for the residual variance). This step is necessary to produce sufficient variability in the imputed values, and is common to all "proper" methods for multiple imputation (Allison 2015).

Such random draws are accordingly repeated to create a basis for a set of differently imputed parallel data sets. In R, the whole procedure can be accomplished using the library or package "mice" developed by van Buuren and Groothuis-Oudshoorn (2011) and maintained by van Buuren. The MICE algorithm uses for multiple imputation a Fully Conditional Specification (FCS) and provides, besides predictive mean matching, a whole set of different imputation methods (van Buuren 2024).

2.7.5 Example Data

We use data from Example Data Set 4 (Web Survey on Machine Learning and Robots in Human Life) to briefly sketch the procedure using the library *mice*. There are four variables, for each of which the same six-point response scale was used in the questionnaire: (1) definitely not, (2) probably not, (3) maybe, (4) quite likely, (5) definitely, (6) don't know. Based on the auxiliary assumption that respondents expressed possible uncertainty either by answering "maybe" or "don't know", categories 3 and 6 were combined (recoded) into category 3 for the present analysis. As a result, only those values that are actually missing are considered missing in the present analysis.

The four variables considered in the present analysis have been worded as shown in Table 2.3. To better understand these questions, it should be mentioned that the survey was conducted shortly before the turn of the year from 2019 to 2020, i. e. still before the big AI hype that built up in the years that followed.

Table 2.3: Question Wordings.

Variable	Question Wording
advise	"And what if there was an app for smartphones that could advise people in important life situations: Would you consult such a personal advisor when making important decisions?"
talk	"Digital voice assistants are already being used in some private households to answer people's simple questions. Please imagine that such technical assistants would be developed so that a person could have conversations with them in the same way that people talk to each other. Could you imagine conversation situations in which a robot specialized in verbal conversation would keep you company at home?"
chores	"Research is being carried out to develop robots that will one day help people with household chores. Examples we are thinking of are: setting and clearing the table, loading and unloading the dishwasher, taking dishes out of cupboards and putting them back in, fetching and taking away objects. Please imagine for a moment that such household robots were already available today: And regardless of financial aspects: Could you imagine getting help at home in this way?"
care	"Again assuming that an assistive robot would – at some point in the future – be able to carry out its tasks competently, reliably and without errors: How about you yourself? Suppose you were to become in need of care one day. Would you agree to an assistive robot being involved in your own care?"

2.7.6 Using the Library *mice* for a Predictive Mean Matching and Multiple Imputation

At the beginning of the R script file, the data frame with the variables to be analyzed must be loaded. In this example, this is the data frame with the name "ki", which was previously saved as a file under the name "kiplus.Rdata".

Since such a data frame usually contains a large number of variables – as is the case here – we next select the variables that are to be included in the analysis. To do this, we use the *subset()* function, select the required variables and create a new R object called *kim* to temporarily store the result of this selection. Then we invoke the library *mice*. (2.16) shows us the corresponding functions in the R script.

```
load("kiplus.Rdata")
kim <- subset(ki, select = c(wgt, talk, chores,
                        care, advise))
library(mice)
```
(2.16)

Optionally, we can next examine the structure of the missing values using the *md.pattern()* function. (2.17) produces the output in (2.18).

```
md.pattern(kim, rotate.names = TRUE)
```
(2.17)

The names of the variables are at the top of the matrix. Below this, it is shown whether a variable has an existing or missing value. A "1" stands for an existing value and a "0" for a missing value. That way each *row* of the matrix indicates a pattern that is formed from a specific combination of existing and missing values in the five variables.

```
    wgt talk chores care advise
196  1   1     1    1      1   0
8    1   1     1    1      0   1
3    1   1     1    0      1   1
7    1   1     1    0      0   2
1    1   1     0    1      1   1
1    1   1     0    1      0   2
     0   0     2   10     16  28
```
(2.18)

In the first row of results, these are all ones, so no missing values are involved in this pattern. The "196" in the left-hand column for this row indicates that this particular combination of values applies to 196 units in the data set, while the "0" in the right-hand column indicates the number of zeros in the combination of this row. In the next row of the matrix we then come across "8" units that have values in *wgt, talk, chores* and *care*, but not in *advise*. The pattern in this row therefore contains one "0" that indicates the missing value for *advise*. Thus, in the leftmost column, the number of units to which the pattern of present/missing values *in the respective row* applies is counted, and on the rightmost column, the number of missing values *contained in this row pattern* is counted.

Finally, in the bottom row of the matrix, the number of units with missing values in the respective *variable* (column) is counted. While in *wgt* and *talk* no unit has missing values, meaning that these two variables were completely observed, the value for *chores* of 2 units, the value for *care* of 10 units and the value for *advise* of 16 units are missing.

Next, a call to the *mice()* function within the package *mice* generates the imputations for the variables selected by the earlier *subset()* function. $m = 5$ means that the function is specified to produce five imputed datasets, while the *seed* option guarantees reproducibility of these imputation. The result of these calculations is assigned to the R object *impu* and can be viewed in detail via *str(impu)*.

```
print(impu <- mice::mice(kim, m=5, seed=15))                    (2.19)
```

By embedding *mice()* in the *print()* function, we also get an overview of the number of imputations (here: $m = 5$), the imputation method implemented (here: *pmm*, i. e., predictive mean matching) and the predictor matrix underlying the imputations (here, all selected variables from *subset()*).

```
fit <- with(impu, glm(advise ~ talk+chores+care,
            weights = wgt, family = gaussian() ))              (2.20)
```

The next lines of the R script performs a computation of each of the now five-fold imputed data sets using *with()*. In the present case this is a regression analysis using the *glm()* function.[21] These five parallel analyses must now be merged again. To do this, we use the *pool()* function in (2.21)

```
summary (pool(fit))                                            (2.21)
```

and obtain the output displayed in (2.22). This table contains the usual result columns for a regression analysis, namely one each for the estimate of the effect, the associated standard error, the ratio of an estimate divided by its standard error as a *statistic* and the p-value to assess statistical significance.

```
   term         estimate std.error statistic      df p.value
1 (intercept)     0.888     0.227      3.92  184.07    0.00
2 talk            0.176     0.087      2.02   34.86    0.05      (2.22)
3 chores          0.026     0.071      0.36  113.30    0.72
4 care            0.278     0.072      3.86  193.03    0.00
```

In response to calling "summary(pool(fit))" in the R script. Target variable is "advise". All entries are taken from the pertaining mice output and rounded to 2 or 3 decimal places.

---

[21] The *lm()* and *glm()* functions for regression analysis are explained in detail in chapters 6 to 8.

Another column under the heading *df* gives the residual degrees of freedom for hypothesis testing. The entries are calculated according to Rubin's formulae (2.23) and (2.24)

$$v = (m-1)\left(1 + r_m^{-1}\right)^2 \tag{2.23}$$

where

$$r_m = \frac{\left(1 + m^{-1}\right)B_m}{\bar{U}_m} \tag{2.24}$$

is the relative increase in variance due to nonresponse (Rubin 1987: 77). Via (2.25)

```
print(pool(fit))
```
(2.25)

we can also display the quantities calculated from Rubin's formulae and obtain

term	ubar	b	t	riv	lambda	Fmi
1 (intercept)	0.0491	0.0002	0.0513	0.0447	0.0428	0.0531
2 talk	0.0053	0.0019	0.0076	0.4207	0.2961	0.3333
3 chores	0.0045	0.0005	0.0051	0.1327	0.1172	0.1324
4 care	0.0050	0.0001	0.0052	0.03336	0.0323	0.0422

(2.26)

A selection of table columns obtained in response to calling "print(pool(fit))" in the R script. Target variable is "advise". All entries are taken from the pertaining mice output and rounded to 4 decimal places. We get *ubar* average variance within imputations; *b* variance between imputations; *t* total variance; *riv* relative increase in variance due to nonresponse; *lambda* proportion of total variance attributable to the missing data; *fmi* fraction of missing information.

The R object *impu* generated via (2.19) contains a whole range of information about the imputations, including – in its subsection *imp* – the values imputed for the individual variables themselves. We can display this directly by (2.27).

```
impu$imp$varname
```
(2.27)

lists the data values imputed in the five datasets, where *varname* serves as a placeholder for a variable name involved in the analysis. We can also display the entire completed data set, not just the values that replace the missing values.

```
complete(impu, m)
```
(2.28)

displays such a completed dataset, with m being to be replaced by 1, 2, 3, 4 or 5 to get the corresponding imputed dataset shown. Finally,

```
fit$analyses[[m]]
```
(2.29)

provides detailed fit information for an imputed dataset, again with m taken as an placeholder for the number that indicates an involved imputed dataset.

2.8 Statistical Matching

In their discussion of new sources and data types in the survey landscape, Lyberg and Heeringa (2022: 89–90) emphasize the importance of statistical data integration and adopt the definition of the Australian Bureau of Statistics, according to which this integration consists in combining data from different administrative and/or survey sources, namely "at the unit level (i. e., for an individual person or organization) or micro level (e.g., information for a small geographic area), to produce new datasets for statistical and research purposes." A whole range of data sources are relevant here, including surveys, sensory data, geographic data, environmental data, administrative data, big data, social media or other data.

It is also particularly advantageous to link survey data with objective measurements and observer ratings. Schnell (2015b) provides a detailed discussion on the use of non-questionnaire data within surveys, including environmental data, remote sensing and street-view data, continuous behavior measurements, use of documents, and biosocial surveys.

When it comes to linking data, it is important to distinguish whether the data to be merged originates from the same or different units. For example, municipalities, cities and districts can store the data they manage on their residents or citizens in different registers. If such data were to be merged, the task would be to link data from the *same* people stored in different files. Such a task would be referred to as *record linkage*. "Record linkage seeks to identify the same objects in two different databases using a set of common identifiers or unique combinations of variables" (Schnell 2015a: 273).

Record linkage ideally requires a unique identifier that unambiguously links records, i. e., data rows, across two data sets. However, such a key is not always available, and even when it is, it can be error-prone. This means that "merging data is prone to misclassifications; in particular, we might fail to find true matches in the data (false negatives) or classify as matches observations that do not refer to the same entity (false positives)" (Enamorado 2022: 95).

Schnell (2015a: 278) discusses linkage with imperfect identifiers and an oversimplified use of string similarity measures and sees the solution to this complication in probabilistic record linkage, when it comes to decisions on potential matching records. Probabilistic record linkage is an approach that seeks a solution via a "principled framework that uses variables in common between data sets as potential identifiers," in order to "produce a probabilistic estimate for the latent matching status across pairs of records" (Enamorado 2022: 95). A set of common variables is thus used as "pseudo-identifiers" to identify the records (rows) that are likely to refer to the same entity (D'Alberto and Raggi 2024: 2136).

Table 2.4: Structure of Data in Statistical Integration of Data with Different Units but a Common Core of Variables.

Dataset A						Dataset B		
$v^A_{1\alpha}$	$\cdots$	$v^A_{1\kappa}$	$v^A_{1\lambda}$	$\cdots$	$v^A_{1\mu}$			
$\vdots$		$\vdots$	$\vdots$		$\vdots$			
$v^A_{i\alpha}$	$\cdots$	$v^A_{i\kappa}$	$v^A_{i\lambda}$	$\cdots$	$v^A_{i\mu}$	missing		
$\vdots$		$\vdots$	$\vdots$		$\vdots$			
$v^A_{n\alpha}$	$\cdots$	$v^A_{n\kappa}$	$v^A_{n\lambda}$	$\cdots$	$v^A_{n\mu}$			
			$v^B_{1\lambda}$	$\cdots$	$v^B_{1\mu}$	$v^B_{1\nu}$	$\cdots$	$v^B_{1\omega}$
			$\vdots$		$\vdots$	$\vdots$		$\vdots$
	missing		$v^B_{j\lambda}$	$\cdots$	$v^B_{j\mu}$	$v^B_{j\nu}$	$\cdots$	$v^B_{j\omega}$
			$\vdots$		$\vdots$	$\vdots$		$\vdots$
			$v^B_{m\lambda}$	$\cdots$	$v^B_{m\mu}$	$v^B_{m\nu}$	$\cdots$	$v^B_{m\omega}$

Dataset A consists of n units (i. e., rows of the data matrix) and a set of variables (i. e., columns) that is divided into two subsets. The first subset contains the variables labelled v_α to v_k which are specific to data set A, while the second subset contains the variables v_λ to v_μ which are available in *both* datasets A and B. The same applies analogously to data set B with its m units. Variables v_ν to v_ω are specific to dataset B, while variables v_λ to v_μ are available also in dataset A. In the cells of this matrix, the subscripts index *row × column*, while the superscripts index the dataset.

On the other hand, *statistical matching* or data fusion means that the data rows to be linked do not come from the same, but from *different* units. As Schnell (2015: 273) notes, "Record linkage is sometimes confused with data fusion, in which data of different units are merged to generate synthetic datasets." However, this only makes sense if only data from units that are comparable are matched. This comparability must be established. And that means that we only match units that are sufficiently similar to each other. As D' Alberto and Raggi (2024: 2137) point out, if record linkage deals with 'the same' units, statistical matching deals with units that are as much as possible similar.

This degree of similarity must, of course, be determined empirically. This requires that both data sets to be merged have some variables in common that can be used for this purpose. In the data structure shown[22] in Table 2.4, this is the subset of variables placed in the middle. More or less similar units would therefore be more or less similar *in terms of these common variables*. Second, a method is needed to measure the degree of similarity in these variables, and third, the units would have to be evaluated accordingly in order to establish suitable matches.

The data structure in Table 2.4 plays a central role in this, since statistical matching based on a common set of information can be designed as an *imputation* task and solved by, e.g., predictive mean matching of the *mice* library described above. The German Federal Statistical Office, for example, pursues this approach in a project that is located in the context of its efforts in experimental statistics.[23] Other imputation methods than predictive mean matching, which replace missing values with observed values of similar units, are also conceivable.

---

22 For a similar illustration of such a data structure, see for example D' Alberto and Raggi (2024: 2137).

23 https://www.destatis.de/DE/Service/EXSTAT/Datensaetze/erwerbsbeteiligung_schutzsuchende.html

Chapter 3
Causal Inference

3.1 Counterfactuals

"A counterfactual is a *potential* outcome, or the state of affairs that would have happened in the absence of the cause" (Guo and Fraser 2010: 24). King et al. (1994: 77–78) illustrate the difference between the factual and counterfactual condition using the example of the causal effect that can be attributed to the incumbency bonus in a political election. If an incumbent runs for election, this is the factual condition. At the same time, the counterfactual condition is that this incumbent is not the incumbent but the challenger in the same election. This condition is of course not observable, since one cannot be both the incumbent and the incumbent's challenger at the same time. The question of what percentage of the votes one and the same incumbent would have received in an election if he had not been the incumbent but the challenger in that election can therefore at best be answered *theoretically* if a causal effect is defined as the difference between the actual vote and the likely vote in the counterfactual situation.

The counterfactual model is described similarly by Morgan and Winship (2007: 5):

> The core of the counterfactual model for observational data analysis is simple. Suppose that each individual in a population of interest can be exposed to two alternative states of a cause. [. . .] In the counterfactual tradition, these alternative causal states are referred to as alternative treatments. [. . .] The key assumption of the counterfactual framework is that each individual in the population of interest has a potential outcome under each treatment state, even though each individual can be observed in only one treatment state at any point in time.

For instance, for the causal effect of feeling economically deprived vs. not deprived on self-perceived happiness, according to the counterfactual framework, deprived individuals would have a *theoretical what-if* happiness score under the condition "not deprived", and economically non-deprived individuals would have a *theoretical what-if* happiness score under the condition "deprived". "These what-if potential outcomes are counterfactual" (Morgan and Winship 2007: 5). Because it is impossible to observe *both* outcomes, "for any individual, causal effects cannot be observed or directly calculated at the individual level" (Morgan and Winship 2007: 5). Accordingly, the potential outcome in the counterfactual situation cannot be observed in real data. "Indeed, it is a missing value. Therefore, the fundamental task of any evaluation is to use known information to impute a missing value for a hypothetical and not observed outcome" (Guo and Fraser 2010: 24).

But how can we replace this missing value with a substantive value, for each unit involved in an analysis? How can we reasonably arrive at best possible proxies for the missing potential outcomes? In experimental research, in principle, by implement-

https://doi.org/10.1515/9783110680683-003

ing a structure of comparisons based on random *assignment* of units to the conditions of treatment and control; and in quasi- and nonexperimental research by *analytically* formed comparisons using techniques of multivariate data analysis and data balancing, with the units involved ideally but not necessarily coming from probability samples.

3.2 Comparing Like with Like

Meaningful comparisons ideally require that "the groups we are comparing should be the same in all relevant respects except in regard to the independent variable" (de Vaus 2001: 43), with the independent variable denoting a variable of interest whose impact on an outcome variable is to be studied. By comparing "like with like" (de Vaus 2001: 44) we should be able to isolate the effect of the independent variable on the outcome of interest.

In *experimental* designs we realize this through the principle of randomization, i. e., through the random assignment of units to the conditions of treatment and control. We can also combine the principles of randomization and matching on relevant characteristics, both in experimental and *quasi-experimental* designs, for instance, by pursuing some form of propensity score matching. Matching is also the basic principle for comparing like with like in *non-experimental* research. It is the principle through which we establish statistical controls for the impact of confounding variables. It also plays a role if, for example, response propensities are considered in the data analysis stage of observational data, e.g., directly (when included as covariates) or indirectly (when used for response weightings).

Experiments rest on the principle of *random assignment*. Units are randomly assigned to the involved conditions of treatment and control. In the simplest case, i. e., the basic experimental design, this creates one treatment and one control group, and after the intended experimental intervention has been carried out in the treatment group ($x_1 = 1$), its effects on the outcome variable y in question are determined *afterwards* by comparing, e.g., their mean y values in the two groups. Figure 3.1 shows a schematic representation of this structure, consisting of the experimental stimulus x_1 and the subsequent measurement of the outcome y, i. e., the two *posttest*-measurements $y_{g=T}^{POST}$ (for the treatment group) and $y_{g=C}^{POST}$ (for the control group).

Random assignment should produce groups with internal frequency distributions that are similar across the groups. This includes the distributions of potential confounding variables x_2, x_3, ..., x_k as well as the outcome variable y itself. On average, before any intervention takes place, the values of y should therefore not differ across the groups if the randomization was successful. In an experimental design, this can be directly taken into account. Figure 3.1 depicts the basic structure of such a design. In the randomized experiments that, for example, Shadish et al. (2002: 257–261) distinguish, this is the structure of the "Pretest-Posttest Control Group Design", with its two

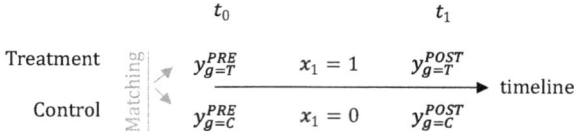

Figure 3.1: Basic Structure of an Experimental Design.

pretest-measurements $y_{g=T}^{PRE}$ (for the treatment group) and $y_{g=C}^{PRE}$ (for the control group) added to the basic design. In the case of successful randomization these two values should therefore be equal *on average*.

To ensure that this actually happens, randomization can be combined with matching. De Vaus (2001: 45–46) describes such "matched block designs", for example, as follows: first, a pretest is carried out, secondly, all participants are ranked according to their *y* pretest measurement determined in this way, and thirdly, blocks of adjacent participants are formed on the basis of this ranking. If the experiment only consists of one experimental group and one control group, i. e. of two groups in total, these blocks would each consist of two participants, one of whom is randomly assigned to the experimental group and one to the control group. You start with the two participants with the lowest *y* pretest values and work your way successively towards the higher *y* pretest values until all participants are allocated.

The matching principle also works analogously on the basis of *propensity scores*. In quasi-experimental research, for instance, such scores are used to estimate the probability of belonging to a target group of interest on the basis of auxiliary information. In a program evaluation, for example, such a group can be the target group for an educational measure to improve the chances of reintegration into the labor market. If we rank all participants according to their propensity to belong to this target group, adjacent participants in this ranking will have similar propensity scores which we can use to create twins, to randomly assign one of the two twins to the educational program and the other twin to the comparison group. However, this is only one possible approach. Propensity score matching opens up a whole range of analytical possibilities, including the choice of matching algorithms. Guo and Fraser (2010: 129) provide an overview of this.

That we can randomly assign units with the same propensity values to one or the other condition of a (quasi-)experiment, is indicated in Figure 3.1. There, this is related to the case where the (quasi-)experimental structure is made up of just two groups in total. In this case, twins are randomly assigned to one group or the other. This principle of randomly assigning units with the same propensity scores to the conditions of a (quasi-) experiment remains the same if the structure consists of more than two groups, and consequently not only pairs but also blocks consisting of three or more such units are to be randomly assigned to the groups.

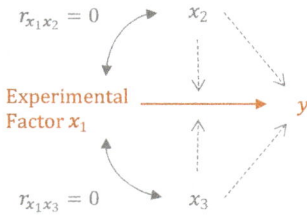

Figure 3.2: Missing Correlation of Experimental and Confounding Factors.

3.3 Limits of Randomization and Matching

Experimental designs are based on randomization. This is both their great strength and their weakness (de Vaus 2001: 71). It is a great strength because the principle of random assignment creates theoretically equivalent groups that differ from each other only by chance in their pretest measurements, and thus makes it possible to attribute any differences in the posttest measurements to the effect of the experimental factor. This feature is indeed very advantageous to identify a causal effect, at least in principle, but can the experiment be considered the gold standard of causal analysis for this reason alone? The list of methodological complications[1] of the experimental design is quite long (de Vaus 2001: 70–88) and, in addition to the usually addressed threats to internal validity (Shadish et al. 2002: 54–63; Guo and Fraser 2010: 23), also includes what de Vaus (2001: 70–72) aptly describes as "explanatory narrowness":

> Experimental research is not well suited to providing an *explanation* of the results – to identifying the mechanisms by which one variable affects another. Nor does it allow us to build a picture of the complex *set* of factors that produce a given outcome. Experiments focus on the impact of just one or two factors (de Vaus 2001: 70).

Essentially, this addresses two limitations: Experiments may be good at identifying *direct* causal effects, but not *indirect* causal effects mediated by other variables. This can lead to an underestimation of the total effect. And if an experiment has identified a direct causal effect, it is not possible to deduce from the experimental finding itself what can explain this effect.

The formal reason for this lies precisely in the purpose of randomization: the creation of equivalent within-group distributions across the groups. If this succeeds, the groups being compared no longer differ in how potential confounding variables are distributed within them, which in turn implies that randomization creates zero corre-

---

[1] A detailed account of experimental designs is outside the intended scope of this section. We refer readers who would like to delve deeper into experimental designs to two texts, namely Shadish et al (2002) and de Vaus (2001).

lations between the experimental factor and these potential confounding variables (Diekmann 2007: 339). As shown in Figure 3.2 using the example of just two such variables, we thereby lose an important link in the indirect relationships between x_1 and y, which run from x_1 via x_2 or x_3. But it is precisely this *missing link* that is needed in order to be able to assess whether x_2 or x_3 may represent *intervening* or *conditional* variables. Consequently, due to randomization, we do not know whether x_2 and x_3 represent mechanisms through which x_1 affects y. And we also do not know whether x_2 and x_3 describe relevant conditions for the effect of x_1 on y. It is conceivable, for example, that they determine whether the direct effect of x_1 on y is stronger or weaker, or whether the effect occurs at all. Such conditional effects are an expression of statistical interaction, in the present example between x_1 and x_2 or between x_1 and x_3, in their respective effect on y.

The identifiability of conditional effects is also important because they can indicate a possibly limited scope of a causal conclusion. It is conceivable, for example, that the effect of x_1 on y does not occur for certain values of x_2 or x_3. This would then limit the scope of the conclusion and thus its external validity accordingly. Conversely, it may be shown that the effect of x_1 on y occurs regardless of the values of x_2 and x_3. It would then be found that the effect of x_1 on y is generalizable across the values of x_2 and x_3. The crucial point is that this would then have been confirmed *empirically*.

A prerequisite for this, however, would be to be able to identify such interaction effects despite randomization. A randomized experiment would therefore have to be expandable to include this option. We can do this by embedding the randomized experiment in a probability survey. In this way, it was possible, for example, to calculate the effects of cognitive involvement[2] on an experimentally found response-order effect (Engel and Köster 2015: 40). It was also possible in this way to study the experimentally found impact of two methodological decisions on the frequency distribution of a target variable depending on whether the interviews were conducted on the web or by telephone as part of a full interview, a core interview or as a minimal set of three basic questions only. On the one hand, the methodological decisions concerned the number of response categories of the target variable "interest in science" (4 or 5 categories) and, on the other hand, the scale direction of its response scale (presented or read aloud from low to high or vice versa from high to low scale values). We reported on this experiment from the Bremen City of Science Survey in Chapter 2 above.

On the other hand, the matching principle too is subject to a real limitation. Matching is an operation that can only be carried out with variables that are present in a given data set. They must therefore have been measured beforehand. Randomization, on the other hand, basically refers to all conceivable confounding variables

---

2 Satisficing response behavior and perceived sensitivity of the outcome variable, a survey question about the frequency of alcohol consumption.

within the target population from which the random allocation of units to the experimental conditions takes place, regardless of whether these variables were measured in a particular study or not.

3.4 Observational Studies

An experiment can reach its limits not only through its design-related explanatory narrowness, but also through the time factor. Effects may only occur after a considerable time delay and/or be that long-lasting that it would require an unrealistically long period of time to conduct an experiment in practice, with all confounding variables effectively controlled over the entire period. Nonlinear patterns of effects may also only be able to unfold over longer periods of time. Then, nonexperimental research designs that are able to identify and isolate effects in survey data *analytically* may be superior to pure experimental settings with their limitations in practice, provided they are based on large probability samples that can be linked to suitable para- or background data.[3]

To structure the discussion, we use a well-known validity typology in experimental and quasi-experimental designs as an approximate framework (Shadish et al. 2002: 37–39), with *validity* designating "the approximate truth of an inference" (Shadish et al. 2002: 34).

3.4.1 Statistical Conclusion Validity

In this validity framework, *statistical conclusion validity* refers to the validity of conclusions drawn about the correlation (covariation) between treatment and outcome. The concept mainly addresses conditions[4] that affect statistical testing. In comparison to experimental research, the much larger sample sizes, both relatively and absolutely, that can be used in survey research offer clear advantages in this regard. On the other hand, within survey research, with regard to the frequentist approach to statistical inference, it would indeed be problematic to apply the corresponding inference rules without even having a random sample – because this approach exactly simulates the process of repeatedly drawing *random* samples. In this case, bootstrapping may be a practicable alternative, although this approach also has its limitations

---

3 As discussed in chapter 2 of this textbook.
4 Shadish et al. (2002: 45) list these nine threats to statistical conclusion validity: low statistical power, violated assumptions of statistical tests, fishing and the error rate problem, unreliability of measures, restriction of range, unreliability of treatment implementation, extraneous variance in the experimental setting, heterogeneity of units, inaccurate effect size estimation.

if the lack of random selection leads to distorted data. Because this means that only distorted data are available as a basis for the repeated random draws of this method.

3.4.2 Internal Validity

Next, the concept of *internal validity* refers to the approximate truth of an inference about whether observed covariation between treatment and outcome reflects a causal relationship. In this regard, too, Shadish et al. (2002: 55) list nine threats which can similarly play a role in non-experimental causal research.[5] First, we must be sure that the variable that represents the putative cause precedes the putative effect variable in time. In an experiment or quasi-experiment, we have the temporal sequence of pretest, experimental intervention and posttest, whereas non-experimental survey research must try in other ways to secure a causal inference. Determining a reliable temporal sequence between the variables is a particularly relevant issue in *cross-sectional* surveys, since all variables are collected at the same time (during one and the same field phase). Although a clear temporal sequence can sometimes be assumed in such studies on the basis of theoretical considerations, for example when the data of children are related to the data of the parents of these children in status attainment models, it is generally the case that an *assumed* temporal sequence might not be without alternatives. As far as the direction of causality is concerned, one can then only work with auxiliary assumptions. But having only this option available would be unsatisfactory. Therefore, already in the early days of survey research a survey design was developed that controlled the temporal sequence of measurements, namely the so-called *panel design*.

The collection and statistical analysis of panel data has been greatly refined since its beginnings and can certainly claim to be a powerful instrument for causal analysis.[6] The panel design is an elaborated *repeated-measurement* design that can effectively control both selection and measurement error. It essentially consists of a large random sample being drawn from a well-defined population and interviewed for a first round of interviews. This first round of interviews is called the first panel wave. Further panel waves follow at fixed and usually equidistant intervals, in which *the*

---

5 Ambiguous temporal precedence, selection, history, maturation, regression, attrition, testing, instrumentation, additive and interactive effects of threats to internal validity.

6 Despite the undeniable advantages that the panel design offers over the cross-sectional design for the causal analysis of observational data, it is not free of complications that were pointed out early on. For example, we are thinking of the complication that the time distance between the measurements does not correspond to the time that a causal effect needs to produce an effect (causal lag). Kessler and Greenberg (1981: 132) discussed the possibility of such disparities between temporal distance and causal lag early on. Engel (1991), for instance, developed a data-analytical solution for the special case that the causal lag is shorter than the time interval between consecutive panel waves.

same respondents are repeatedly interviewed using the same instrument (interview, questionnaire). It is precisely this repeated measurement design that makes it possible to trace constancy and change not only at the group or aggregate level, but also at the individual level. For example, we can not only determine whether *the percentage of* those who intend to vote changes or remains the same across the waves, but also whether *the individual* voting intention remains the same or changes over time. Since this measurement option is in principle available for both cause and effect variables, as well as confounding variables, the panel design offers a way of investigating even *concomitant*[7] variation of cause and effect, while controlling involved sources of error such as random and systematic measurement error.

Specific *systematic* measurement error may arise because the panel design involves repeatedly presenting the same questionnaire to respondents. This can lead to learning effects[8] and thus a response behavior that appears more consistent or predictable across the repeated measurements than it actually is. Panel data analysis is therefore designed to calculate out such undesirable method effects from the substantive relationships of a model. For example, structural equation modelling provides this option of decomposing effects into their substantial and method-related components.

Selection effects too can be statistically controlled in a panel data analysis, provided that the survey design underlying the panel was designed in such a way that the required individual propensity scores can be estimated. This applies to the initial probability sample as well as to panel attrition. Attrition means that respondents prematurely drop out of a still-running panel after perhaps having taken part in the surveys once, twice or three times. However, these losses are then not only attempted to be compensated statistically, but also by refreshing the panel with new respondents.

In addition, the multi-wave panel design can also control for confounding variables *over longer periods* of time. This applies to individual changes that occur *within*[9]

---

7 For example by suitably specified latent growth curve models or curve-of-factor models. We described this modeling technique elsewhere (Engel et al. 2007: 301–305). A growth model processes the data differently than a model that estimates stabilities and cross-lagged effects in order to take the latter as expressions of a causal relationship. As outlined elsewhere (Engel and Meyer 1996: 227–229), this earlier path-analytical cross-lagged panel model implies that *residual* variation in *y* but *not concomitant* variation of *x* and *y* is taken as an expression of a causal relationship. The causality concept of concomitant variation of cause and effect implies that the involved variables are quantities capable of changing *at the individual level*. The basic idea is that *x* can be inferred to be at least a substantial part of the cause of *y* if *changes* in *x* lead to *concurrent changes* in *y*.

8 "Testing" effects in the experimental context. "Practice, familiarity, or other forms of reactivity are the relevant mechanisms and could be mistaken for treatment effects" (Shadish et al. 2002: 60).

9 In the experimental context referred to as *maturation*. "In a study of change some of the change could be due to the passing of time rather than the experimental intervention (. . .) We need to ensure that we do not confuse the impact of an intervention for developmental or maturational changes that take place in the course of an experiment (de Vaus 2001: 73–74).

the random sample of respondents as well as to *external*[10] events, provided they can be represented as variables in the data set in question.

All in all, causal conclusions can be well secured using the panel design for observational data. The fact that it is designed to work with large samples is only an advantage. This size alone offers genuine analytical advantages over experimental settings that cannot work with thousands of randomly selected respondents. However, it is not only the sheer size of a sample that counts. The sample should and can be based on *probability* selection, directly or via quasi-randomization that uses a probability survey as reference survey (Elliot and Valliant 2017: 255).

In any case, a weighting based on individual propensity scores would be preferable to an adjustment of already aggregated (tabulated and cross-tabulated) distributions to external reference distributions, for example, of official statistics. This is because it makes it more realistic to be able to adjust the probabilities of occurrence *even of more complex value combinations* when weighting a sample, in fact including those *between suspected cause and effect variables*. In any case, effective control of selection effects requires a sampling design that enables the collection of the auxiliary information required for adequate sample weighting. This applies to cross-sectional surveys as well as to panel surveys.

3.4.3 External Validity

"External validity concerns inferences about the extent to which a causal relationship holds over variations in persons, settings, treatment, and outcomes" (Shadish et al. 2002: 83). The external validity of a data-based inference therefore concerns its generalizability, and thus replicability, over such conditions. This question naturally arises not only in experimental and quasi-experimental, but also in non-experimental designs.

In an observational study, an inference would prove *generalizable* across a set of conditions if it can be empirically shown that the underlying result is replicable across those conditions. In this case, we would expect to consistently observe similar findings. Generalizability touches on the question of whether the *intended scope* of validity of an inference can be empirically confirmed, whether it must be rejected as incorrect or whether it must be further specified. In general, this replicability can be empirically tested better and more extensively in large probability-based surveys than in experimental settings.

---

10 In the experimental context referred to as *history*. It is about external or extraneous events that occur between pretest and posttest and that may have caused changes in the posttest. De Vaus (2001: 73) states: "The problem of extraneous events is greatest in field and natural experiments in an unknown way. In such experiments we have less control over what happens to people. This lack of control is a great danger to the research as the time between pre-test and post-test increases."

3.4.4 Construct Validity

"Construct Validity involves making inferences from the sampling particulars of a study to the higher-order constructs they represent" (Shadish et al. 2002: 65). In survey research, it is quite common to measure concepts of interest using multiple indicator variables (questionnaire items). The analysis method of choice is then often a latent variable analysis, for example a confirmatory factor analysis or structural equation model. In such an analysis, the concepts are understood as latent variables that cannot be directly observed but can be measured indirectly using the manifest indicator variables. In the opening quote, these indicator variables would represent the sampling particulars and the latent variables would represent the higher-order constructs.

In such models, the relationship between manifest and latent variables is estimated using so-called *factor loadings*, which can be standardized and then used to assess *convergent validity*. In contrast, *discriminant validity* can be estimated using the *factor correlations* that exist between the latent variables, i. e. the factors of a model. Both together provide information about the *construct validity* of the measurements. While convergent validity reflects how well a latent variable is represented by the set of indicator variables used to measure it (convergent validity), factor correlations indicate how much the latent variables of a model measured in this way differ from one another (discriminant validity), in order to determine whether it is reasonable to assume that they actually represent *different* constructs.

Such models can be quite complex. The advantage, however, is that the modeling technique can still be used very well in practice, provided a large sample is used. Another advantage is that such latent variable models can also control method effects.[11] And they are of great importance for ensuring the validity of causal conclusions because they make it possible to analytically control random and systematic measurement error.

The way in which latent variable analysis is designed directs research interest primarily to the concepts to be measured, i. e., the theoretical concepts represented by the latent variables. Such concepts were also referred to early on as *global concepts* or global variables, which consist of various *components* (Rosenberg 1968). The key point is that it can be equally valuable to focus attention not only on the global concept but also on these component variables. Rosenberg (1968: 40) introduced this topic that way:

> One problem still confronting social science, as Merton notes, is the presence of propositions which are true but unspecific. Certain propositions are on such a broad level of generality that they do little to advance understanding. [. . .] Needless to say, it is of utmost importance that social science go beyond the stage of propositions so broad that they have only the vaguest empirical referents.

---

11 An example of this MTMM modeling technique from our own research can be found in Burmeister and Engel (2015).

Rosenberg was thinking of statements such as that the social environment plays an important role in the formation of attitudes, or that personality structure is an important determinant of social behavior. But he also thought about global concepts such as social class and, for example, statements that link class membership with mental health. In order to raise the question of *what exactly it is* about belonging to a social class that is responsible for the differences in mental health. Is it the prestige associated with it, the education, a more or less rewarding work, the lifestyle, or something else? If social class is considered a global concept, then such variables would be its components. In Rosenberg's words (1968: 41–42): "The general point is that many of the global concepts with which the social researcher deals are composed of a number of subconcepts which enter into it. These are *components*. Education, income, occupation, family, etc., are all part of social class." In addition to social class, variables such as age, gender, ancestry or nationality can also be understood as global concepts (Rosenberg 1968: 50). If differences are found in an analysis based on such variables, the question arises as to which of their respective components could be responsible for the result found. Let's take age as an example. If differences are found between age groups, the question arises as to what exactly it is in the real lives of people of different age groups that causes these differences. Or let's take gender as an example. Here, too, it is generally not about biological sex, but about the differences in the realities of life between men and women and other gender-related identities. An analytical perspective focused on component variables can be just as effective as, on the contrary, a perspective focused on global concepts.

3.4.5 Analytically Controlling on Third Variables

The matching principle is also a basic building block in the elaboration of relationships between variables. It is used to compare "like with like" when examining the impact of a variable x_1 on a target variable y. In German-speaking countries, this principle is also referred to in technical jargon as "keeping third variables constant". Sometimes the term "test factor" is used instead of "third variable". The matching principle of controlling on such third variables can be illustrated particularly well using a contingency table analysis. We start with a relationship between two variables x_1 and y, examine this relationship and then extend the analysis to include x_2 as a first such "third variable". We do this to see whether the original relationship between x_1 and y is changed by x_2 or whether it remains essentially the same.

If the relationship between x_1 and y holds, we can say that it has de facto generalized across the categories of x_2: we have then shown that it holds regardless of the value of x_2.

x_2 can also change the original relationship in different ways. Basically, several results are conceivable here: namely, that the relationship between x_1 and y is only maintained if x_2 also takes on a certain value or values, but not otherwise. It is also conceivable that the strength, and possibly even the sign, of the original relationship between x_1 and y depends on the values of x_2. Then we speak of statistical interaction or conditional effects, but also of the fact that the original relationship between x_1 and y is more precisely specified by x_2.

Thirdly, the inclusion of x_2 in an analysis can lead to the original relationship between x_1 and y being dissolved. How this situation is to be interpreted depends on whether the third variable is to be assessed as "intervening" or "extraneous". Since this case is particularly relevant to the question of whether an analysis allows a *causal* inference, we will discuss it in more detail in the next section. Here we would first like to exemplify the previously mentioned possible results.

A contingency table analysis with data from Example Data Set 9, i. e., the data for Germany from Round 10 of the European Social Survey, is used to illustrate the procedure. The target variable y is worded as follows: "How acceptable for you would it be for Germany to have a strong leader who is above the law?" In a first step, we compare the percentage of those who would not categorically rule out such a leader across three groups (labelled "acceptable"). These three groups represent the answers given to the following survey question: "Obedience and respect for authority are the most important values children should learn" (x_1). (3.1) shows that the percentage increases with the degree of agreement with the principle of authority as an educational goal, from 18 to 32 to 50 percent (below each percentage, the number of people on which the percentage is based is shown in gray[12]).

x_1	0	1	2	All	
Acceptable	18 %	32 %	50 %	39 %	(3.1)
n	1,666	2,101	4,438	8,205	

We now introduce x_2 as a first test factor. x_2 indicates to what extent a respondent thinks Germany should allow people from the poorer countries outside Europe to come and live here. The answers to this question again result in three groups: 0 = allow many to come and live here, 1 = allow some, 2 = allow a few/allow none. We consider this second variable, too, as a potential source of variation for the percentage in question and control this source by looking at the relationship between y and x_1 separately for the three values of x_2. In each of these separate comparisons, x_2 now represents a constant value which, as a constant, cannot influence the respective comparison any more. (3.2) shows the relationship between y and x_1 first for the case that $x_2 = 0$.

---

12 *Without* weighting – i. e., different from what the figures in the text – the frequencies from the sub-tables (3.2), (3.3) and (3.4) would add column by column to the corresponding frequencies in the overall table (3.1).

x_1	0	1	2	All	If	
Acceptable	15 %	25 %	42 %	27 %	$x_2 = 0$	(3.2)
n	672	446	627	*1,744		

As in (3.1), (3.2) also shows that the proportion of those who would not categorically rule out a strong leader above the law increases with the degree of agreement with the principle of authority as an educational goal, but this time at a somewhat lower level from 15 to 25 to 42 percent. This slightly lower level reflects the fact that we are looking at the subgroup of those who are *not* critical of the form of immigration in question ($x_2 = 0$). For this subgroup, the overall percentage of those who would not categorically rule out a strong leader who is above the law is 27 percent (column "All").

x_1	0	1	2	All	If	
Acceptable	19 %	32 %	49 %	39 %	$x_2 = 1$	(3.3)
n	753	1,142	2,169	4,064		

(3.3) now shows that in the subgroup $x_2 = 1$, the percentage increases with agreement with the principle of authority as an educational goal, namely from 19 to 32 to 49 percent. Compared with (3.2), the figures are at a slightly higher level. This also applies to the level of the subgroup as a whole, at 39 percent.

x_1	0	1	2	All	If	
Acceptable	24 %	40 %	54 %	48 %	$x_2 = 2$	(3.4)
n	263	518	1,616	2,397		

Finally, (3.4) provides information on the distribution of percentages in the subgroup $x_2 = 2$. Said percentage increases from 24 to 40 to 54 percent, and is 48 percent overall in this subgroup. Compared to (3.3), all figures are again at a slightly higher level.

(3.2), (3.3) and (3.4) can be considered as sub-tables which together form a table which can also be read *column by column*. If we do this, we can see, for example, that the percentages in the rightmost column increase from (3.2) via (3.3) to (3.4). The overall percentage of those who would not categorically rule out a strong leader above the law therefore increases in the transition from $x_2 = 0$ via $x_2 = 1$ to $x_2 = 2$, i. e. with an increasingly critical attitude towards the form of immigration in question.

We see exactly the same pattern when we compare separately for the three groups that differ in their attitude towards the principle of authority as an educational goal – that is, separately for the case where $x_1 = 0$, $x_1 = 1$ and $x_1 = 2$. Such a pattern basically signals that x_2 exerts its influence on y regardless of what value someone has in x_1 at the same time.

The analysis so far leads to the conclusion that the percentage of those who do not categorically rule out "if Germany had a strong leader who is above the law" changes with attitudes towards immigration and authority as an educational goal: the percentage in question is higher the more critical the attitude towards the form of immigration in question is or the more positively the principle of authority is viewed as an educational goal. The analysis so far also showed that these two attitudes unfold their effects independently of one another. Now, we come to the same conclusion if we also take into account another variable: the degree of satisfaction with how the democracy works.

Viewed *row by row*, Table 3.1 shows that the percentage in question is the higher the more positively the principle of authority is viewed as an educational goal (x_1), in fact regardless of the attitude towards the form of immigration in question (x_2) and the satisfaction with the way the democracy works (x_3). At the same time, a comparison of the percentage in question *in the right-hand column* for each of the three color-bordered sub-tables shows that the more critical the attitude towards the form of immigration in question is, the more likely it is that a strong leader above the law will not be categorically ruled out. Thirdly, a column-by-column comparison of *corresponding* percentages *across the three sub-tables* (again, right-hand column) shows that the percentage of people who do not categorically rule out a strong leader above the law also increases with dissatisfaction with the way the democracy works in Germany; In this regard, the main difference lies between those satisfied with it (green sub-table) and the other two groups (blue and orange bordered sub-tables).

The structure of percentages tends to suggest the same conclusions if we do not refer the column-wise comparisons to the right-hand column, but to the columns *within the sub-tables*. Analogous to the row-wise (x_1-related) comparisons of percentages, the x_2-related column-wise comparisons would take into account that x_1 and x_3 also influence the said percentage; and at the same time, the x_3-related column-wise comparisons would take into account that x_1 and x_2 also have an influence.

Table 3.1: Acceptance of a Strong Leader Above the Law, Respect for Authority, Attitude Against Immigration, and Satisfaction With the Way Democracy Works in Germany.

x_3	x_2	x_1 / y	0	1	2	
2	0	1	11 %	22 %	33 %	22 %
		n	278	198	270	746
2	1	1	12 %	22 %	39 %	28 %
		n	302	403	684	*1,388
2	2	1	14 %	25 %	46 %	36 %
		n	74	115	322	*510

Table 3.1 (continued)

x_3	x_2	x_1 / y	0	1	2	
1	0	1	19 %	24 %	49 %	31 %
		n	272	180	238	690
1	1	1	21 %	38 %	52 %	42 %
		n	305	531	926	1,762
1	2	1	28 %	43 %	59 %	52 %
		n	81	199	590	870
0	0	1	14 %	29 %	46 %	29 %
		n	115	70	113	298
0	1	1	28 %	34 %	56 %	46 %
		n	148	202	519	869
0	2	1	28 %	43 %	55 %	49 %
		n	108	201	693	1,002

Source (dataset): European Social Survey, Round 10, dataset for Germany
y indicates: "How acceptable for you would it be for Germany to have a strong leader who is above the law?" In each case, the percentage of people who would not categorically rule out such a leader is shown.
x_1 indicates: "To what extent do you agree or disagree that obedience and respect for authority are the most important values children should learn?" 5pt scale recoded to 3 categories: 0 = disagree (strongly); 1 = neither agree nor disagree; 2 = agree (strongly). x_2 indicates: ". . ., to what extent do you think Germany should allow people from the poorer countries outside Europe to come and live here?" 4 pt scale recoded to 3 categories: 0 = allow many to come and live here, 1 = allow some, 2 = allow a few /allow none. x_3 indicates: ". . . on the whole, how satisfied are you with the way democracy works in Germany?" The 11pt scale ranges from 0 = extremely dissatisfied", over 1, 2, 3, . . ., to 10 = "extremely satisfied". Here, this scale is recoded to 3 categories: (0, 1, 2, 3, 4 = 0)(5, 6, 7 = 1)(8, 9, 10 = 2). "anweight" – weighted frequency distribution. In each cell, the number of respondents to whom a percentage refers is indicated in grey (percentage basis). All figures rounded to 0 decimal places. *Includes a small rounding inaccuracy.

However, the more percentages to be compared, the more difficult it becomes to recognize the inherent structure of a multivariate frequency distribution with the naked eye, i. e. just by looking at it visually. In the present example, 27 percentages are already involved in the table, plus the 9 percentages in the right-hand column. Simply including one further x_k variable would greatly increase the number of value combinations and thus the complexity of the distribution. And even then, it must be said that the example takes into account only relatively few variables.

This is to indicate that contingency table analysis has its limits. On the one hand, it is advantageous when complexity is low (few variables, perhaps each with few categories only) because of the clarity of the results obtained that way. In the present thematic context, it is also advantageous that this method can be used to demonstrate the principle of matching on third variables, in order to compare like with like. As complexity increases, however, the results become more difficult to interpret, even when the structure of observed percentages actually appears to be quite clear. As is actually the case in the present example. But even then, the need arises to check whether this structure actually indicates what it seems to indicate: namely, that the three x_k variables exert their influence on y *independently of each other*.

To ensure that we can draw such a conclusion from the structure of observed percentages, it is best to change the method of analysis and perform a regression analysis instead of a contingency table analysis. For this we "translate" the present contingency table analysis into a regression model that reflects the assumption that the effects of x_1, x_2 and x_3 on y are independent of each other. In regression analysis, such a model is called a *main effects model*. In addition, we "translate" the present analysis into a second regression model for comparison purposes. Specifically, a model that takes into account statistical interaction between them in addition to the independent effects of x_1, x_2 and x_3 on y.

Table 3.2: Logistic Regression Estimates of Main Effects & Statistical Interactions.

	Main effects		plus Interactions	
	b_k	z_k	b_k	z_k
x_1	0.69	18.7	0.69	8.1
x_2	0.21	5.4	0.24	2.5
x_3	-0.28	-8.1	-0.42	-4.6
$x_1 \cdot x_2$			-0.05	-0.9
$x_1 \cdot x_3$			0.05	1.1
$x_2 \cdot x_3$			0.05	1.0
Const.	-1.38	-17.0	-1.31	-9.3

N = 8,135 respondents. "anweight"-weighted estimates. All b's are rounded to two decimal places, each $z_k = b_k/s.e_{b_k}$ value is rounded to one decimal place. Pseudo R^2 = 0.068 (main effects only) and 0.069 (main effects & statistical interaction terms). The target variable y is a binary variable coded 0 and 1. To ensure comparability with the contingency table analysis, the three x_k variables remain recoded into the three categories 0, 1, and 2.

Since y is a 0/1 coded binary variable, we calculated a *logistic* regression. We present this method in more detail in chapters 8.7 and 11.1. Table 3.2 reports the result of the calculations for the variables of the present contingency table analysis. In each case, the estimate of the effect of an x_k variable, b_k, is shown, as well as this estimate divided by its standard error $b_k/s.e_{b_k}$, the respective z_k entry in Table 3.2.

Such an estimate of effect achieves statistical significance when its strength attains at least approximately twice its (also estimated) standard error. This clearly applies to all main effects, but clearly not to the three interactions. We conclude that the main effect model describes the data better than a model that also assumes interactions between x_1, x_2 and x_3. It is important to consider that the explanatory power of the three x_k variables is only around 6.8 percent. A significant part of the variation in y cannot therefore be explained by the three x_k variables and must therefore be attributed to other variables.

$$Pr(y=1|x_k) = \frac{1}{1+e^{-\left(b_0+b_1\cdot x_1+b_2\cdot x_2+b_3\cdot x_3\right)}} \tag{3.5}$$

If we replace the $b_k's$ in (3.5) by their estimates from Table 3.2, we can estimate for each combination of values of the three x_k variables the probability of having the value 1 ("acceptable") in the target variable, i. e., the probability of not categorically excluding a strong leader above the law.

Table 3.3: Are the Effects Found Generalizable Across the Group of Men and Women and the Age Spectrum?

| | Main effects | |
	b_k	z_k
x_1	0.60	14.1
x_2	0.48	5.1
x_3	−0.07	−6.4
$x_1 \cdot x_4$	−0.16	−2.8
$x_2 \cdot x_5$	−0.01	−2.9
x_4	0.60	3.8
x_5	−0.04	−5.9
x_6	0.0004	5.7
Const.	−0.99	−4.5

Again, logistic regression estimates are displayed. N = 7,659 respondents. "anweight"-weighted estimates. All b's are rounded to two decimal places, each $z_k = b_k/s.e_{b_k}$ value is rounded to one decimal place. Pseudo $R^2 = 0.076$. The target variable y is a binary variable coded 0 (strong leader above the law is categorically ruled out, i. e. not accepted) and 1 (is basically accepted). x_1 "authority": original 5pt scale recoded to reverse scale direction, now coded as follows: 0 = disagree strongly, 1 = disagree, 2 = neither agree nor disagree, 3 = agree, 4 = agree strongly. x_2 "against immigration". The original 4pt scale is retained, except for starting the sequence of codes with 0, not 1. These codes are used: 0 = allow many immigrants from the poorer countries outside Europe to come and live here, 1 = allow some, 2 = allow a few, 3 = allow none. x_3 "satisfaction with the way democracy works". Original 11pt scale used, ranging from 0 = "extremely dissatisfied" to 10 = "extremely satisfied"; x_4 = gender: 0 = male; 1 = female; x_5 age (in years); x_6 is age-squared (technical term added to the equation, in order to estimate a curvilinear age effect by x_5 and x_6 taken together.

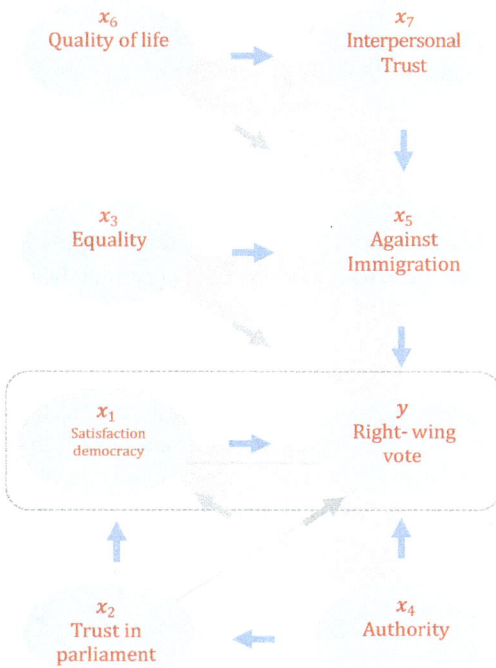

Figure 3.3: Right-Wing Vote as a Function of Value Orientations, Trust in Men and Institutions, and Satisfaction with the Way Democracy Works in Germany.

From the analysis so far, we now know that the two attitudes towards the principle of authority as an educational goal and towards the form of immigration in question, as well as satisfaction with how democracy functions in the country, have their effect here independently of each other. By extending the regression model to include variables such as gender and age, for instance, we can now try to *determine the scope* of such a statement empirically. To do this, we stick with our modeling technique and extend the model with terms that can indicate whether there are interactions between the above variables on the one hand and variables such as gender and age on the other. Table 3.3 illustrates such an analysis.

x_1, x_2 and x_3 denote, as before, the three initial variables (x_1 = in favor of the principle of authority, x_2 = against immigration, x_3 = satisfaction with the functioning of democracy). x_4 denotes gender (0 = male, 1 = female), x_5 stands for age in years and x_6 for age-squared. The coding scheme is explained in the notes below Table 3.3.

The model in Table 3.3 is based on an intermediate step. First, a model was calculated that contained both interaction terms for each of the three initial variables x_1, x_2 and x_3, i. e. one such multiplicative term for x_4 (gender) and one such term for x_5 (age). Of these, only those terms that turned out to be statistically significant in this purely data-driven procedure are taken into account in the model shown in Table 3.3. That is the multiplicative term $x_1 \cdot x_4$ and the multiplicative term $x_2 \cdot x_5$.

The result is quite interesting. The conclusion that the probability of not categorically ruling out a strong leader who is above the law does not change per se: The probability increases the more positive the attitude towards the principle of authority and the more critical the attitude towards immigration, whereas the probability decreases with people's satisfaction with the way democracy works.

However, only the latter effect (due to x_3) turns out to be independent of gender and age. In contrast, the effect of x_1 (attitude towards authority) on y is systematically weaker among women ($x_4 = 1$) than among men, and the strong effect of x_2 (immigration) on y is slightly weakened with increasing age (x_5). The scope of the two, x_1 and x_2-related statements is therefore limited and thus to be specified accordingly.

Finally, it should be noted that the probability of not categorically excluding a strong leader above the law is systematically higher among women than among men (main effect of x_4), and that this probability is comparatively higher among younger and older people than among middle-aged people. This is indicated by the curvilinear age effect, whose linear component is represented by x_5 and whose quadratic component is represented by x_6.

3.4.6 Causal Inference

We locate the most uncertain form of causal inference in cross-sectional data and there in the practice of interpreting slope coefficients of a regression analysis in the sense of a hypothetical experiment:[13] If x_k changes by one scale unit, then the expected change in y is $b_k \cdot y$ scale units. This is exactly what b_k would lead us to expect, and this expectation may indeed turn out to be correct.

But cross-sectional data offer no guarantee of this. Strictly speaking, a slope coefficient in cross-sectional data does *not* reflect the expected *change* in y for a unit change in x_k, but rather the expected mean *difference* in y when comparing units that differ by one x_k scale unit from each other. What is analytically separated here is only a *systematic* from the *random* part of the variation of a target variable y in question. As such, regression analysis can provide most valuable insights, but not every systematic difference identified in this way reflects a causal relationship.

Causal relationships are rather linked to prerequisites: In particular, it must be reasonable to assume that a systematic $x_k \rightarrow y$ relationship is indeed a causal rela-

---

[13] The slope of a regression line is usually interpreted to indicate "the magnitude of the change in Y for a unit change in X" (Blalock 1981: 385).

tionship.[14] Four criteria for inferring causal relationships have been formulated for this purpose (e.g., de Vaus 2001: 34–39).

1. The covariation between two initial variables, say, x and y, proves to be *not spurious*. This would be the case if the (x, y) covariation tends to zero (i. e., disappears) when a third variable (test factor) z is included that must reasonably be assumed to be temporally or causally prior to the two initial variables x and y. In an early book on the subject (Rosenberg 1968: 27), the term "extraneous variable" was chosen for such a test factor.[15] In Rosenberg's (1968: 28) words at that time:

   > Strictly speaking, there is no such thing as a spurious relationship; there are only spurious interpretations. It is customary to use the term "spurious relationship," however, to refer to a case in which there is no meaningful or inherent link between the two variables; the relationship is due solely to the fact that each of the variables happens accidentally to be associated with some other variables.

2. Since an effect cannot precede its cause, *time order* matters. It is therefore extremely important to be able to replace the lack of temporal order in cross-sectional data (and thus their lack of verifiability) with convincing auxiliary assumptions when causal conclusions are to be drawn from cross-sectional data.

3. The target (i. e., dependent) variable must be *capable of change*. Accordingly, it would be nonsensical to attempt to use a causal model to explain variation in characteristics that do not change at all on an individual level, i. e. that are constant over time for each individual. This criterion is weaker than one that requires that a *causal variable too* must be capable of change. The latter would be the case with a concept of causality that expects that *changes* in x lead to corresponding *changes* in y.

4. It must be *theoretically* plausible to assume a cause-effect relationship. An empirical causal analysis is actually unthinkable without an adequate theory about the subject area in question. And it is precisely this substantive theory that needs to be translated into a suitable formal model in order to then be able to conclude to what extent systematic differences reflect cause-effect relationships. This implies that *theoretical* plausibility can only be verified in conjunction with *methodological* criteria, such as those from *covariance structure analysis*.

---

14 This is not always the case. A slope may, but does not necessarily, have a causal interpretation. Agresti and Finlay (1986: 259) illustrate this latter case with an example in which they relate two statistical rates in a linear regression.

15 The examples of the somewhat misleading term "spurious correlation" that are occasionally used in statistical literature have also been around for a long time (Rosenberg 1968: 28). The classic example is certainly the relationship between the number of storks in an area and the number of children born in that area (assumed test factor: rural-urban location) or the relationship between the number of firefighters at a fire and the amount of damage caused (assumed test factor: size of the fire). However, real data examples are not always so clearly recognizable as being so absurd as these "classics" here.

Cross-sectional data in particular force us to make auxiliary assumptions about causal relationships, namely with regard to both assumed causal directions and the structure of direct and indirect causal paths. The more complex this structure is, i. e., the more precise the prediction of a covariance structure is, the more certain the conclusion is about causal relationships based on the observation of observed systematic differences. To do this, we can compose the overall structure of a causal model *using elementary variable triangles*. This will be illustrated by the example in Figure 3.3, in conjunction with the corresponding results from Tables 3.4 and 3.5. In order to demonstrate this development from simple to complex, we have broken down the model into individual equations.[16]

$$\frac{Pr(y=1|x_1)}{1-Pr(y=1|x_1)} = e^{b_0} \cdot e^{b_1 x_1} \tag{3.6}$$

Our starting point is (3.6). Accordingly,[17] the odds of voting for a politically far-right party (y) decrease by a factor of $e^{-0.5} = 0.6$ for each unit increase in satisfaction with the functioning of democracy in Germany (x_1). The strength of the logistic regression estimate is about 12.1 times its standard error and thus much larger than the rule of thumb of twice its standard error would have to indicate for a statistically significant estimate. The effect is strong and statistically significant and goes in the theoretically expected direction. The figures are taken from equation 1 in Table 3.4.

The fact that dissatisfaction with the way democracy works in Germany strengthens parties on the right pole of the political spectrum is not surprising per se, but it does clearly confirm a connection that is widely discussed in public. A first question might now be whether there is an inherent link between satisfaction with democracy and right-wing voting or whether the relationship is instead spurious, i. e. an accidental relationship that goes back to a common cause. We assumed that the attitude towards the principle of authority might be a candidate for such a common cause, namely based on the assumption that such basic attitudes are generally established earlier rather than later in a person's life. In Figure 3.3 we are now in the shaded variable triangle of the model region at the bottom right. The expectation is accordingly that the attitude towards the principle of authority (x_4) is an extraneous test factor that might account for the observed $x_1 \rightarrow y$ relation. So this original relationship between satisfaction with democracy and vote for the far-right should dissolve, i. e., tend to zero, if the equation is enlarged by this "third variable" (3.7).

$$\frac{Pr(y=1|x_1)}{1-Pr(y=1|x_1)} = e^{b_0} \cdot e^{b_1 x_1} \cdot e^{b_4 x_4} \tag{3.7}$$

---

16 Alternatively, we could have chosen to relate the variance/covariance structure implied by the model *as a whole* to the observed structure using a statistical goodness-of-fit test.
17 See the notes below Table 3.4.

The estimates are reported as equation 2 in Table 3.4. If we compare the corresponding estimates of effect of x_1 (satisfaction with democracy) on y (right-wing vote) in columns 1 and 2, we see that the effect of x_1 on y has remained essentially unchanged, and the attitude towards the principle of authority (x_4) has an additional independent effect on y. Both variables are systematically linked to the odds of voting right-wing.

At the same time, the estimate in eq. 10 in Table 3.5 shows that a positive attitude towards the principle of authority (x_4) is systematically associated with lower satisfaction with democracy (x_1). This association too is strong and statistically significant. Thus, as to the shaded variable triangle at the bottom right of the diagram, despite a stable and accordingly *not*-spurious relationship between x_1 and y two strong effects of x_4 were identified, one upon x_1 and another one upon y.

We can next turn to an imaginary variable triangle at the bottom left of the diagram. There we can start from the relationship between trust in parliament and right-wing voting. This estimate of effect of x_2 on y is reported as eq. 4 in Table 3.4 and signals that higher trust in the parliament (x_2) is systematically associated with lower odds of voting right-wing (y). We are here inclined to say that x_2 has thus a strong and statistically significant effect on y in the expected direction.

We now ask if x_1 might explain *why* x_2 is associated with y. Since x_1 is associated with x_2 (eq. 11, Table 3.5), x_1 may provide an option for this. We thus enlarge the picture accordingly, in order to check how the estimate of x_2 on y changes if x_1 is added to the equation. Equations 4 and 5 provide the required comparison.

The main result is that the effect of x_2 on y weakens slightly, but remains at a strong and statistically significant level. The same applies analogously to the effect of x_1. This becomes evident in Table 3.4 by comparing the corresponding values from Eq. 1 and 5. Thus, when controlling for each other, *both* variables x_1 and x_2 retain strong effects of their own on y. We cannot therefore conclude that x_1 is an intervening variable in the relationship between x_2 and y. For this to happen, the effect of x_2 would have to approach zero. But that is exactly what did not happen.

Table 3.4: Logistic Regression Estimates of Effect on Right-Wing Vote.

Target					y				
Eq.	1	2	3	4	5	6	7	8	9
b_0	−0.57	−1.69	−4.45	−0.91	−0.30	−1.42	−3.90	−4.82	−0.82
	−3.8	−4.1	−12.9	−8.5	−2.4	−4.7	−9.1	−17.5	−1.6
x_1	−0.50	−0.48			−0.29				−0.26
	−12.1	−11.7			−7.2				−6.3
x_2				−0.53	−0.36				−0.37
				−14.0	−8.0				−7.9

Table 3.4 (continued)

Target						y			
Eq.	1	2	3	4	5	6	7	8	9
x_3						−0.30	−0.23		−0.22
						−4.0	−3.0		−2.9
x_4		0.33	0.60						0.13
		3.0	5.9						1.3
x_5							0.88	0.89	0.36
							8.9	9.3	3.5
R^2_{McF}	0.199	0.209	0.037	0.203	0.245	0.013	0.082	0.072	0.283

Source (dataset): European Social Survey, Round 11, dataset for Germany. Source (questionnaire): Codebook ESS11 – integrated file, edition 2.0; doi:10.21338/ess11e02_0. All computations are based on the "anweight" – weighted frequency distributions. Each column reports the outcome of a separate logistic regression equation. R^2_{McF} McFadden's Pseudo-R^2. N = 2,420 (sample size) minus respondents with missing values in the variables of a given equation: Average valid N (median) over the 14 equations is 2,387 respondents; the middle 50 percent of valid Ns are between the 1st quartile = 2,362 and the 3rd quartile = 2,398. Min/Max valid N's are 2,278/2,412. The y and x_k variable names correspond to those in Figure 3.3.

- y is an index that combines two responses: if a respondent did vote in Germany's last national election & he/she voted for the Alternative for Germany (AFD), and/or if the respondent affirmed that there is a particular political party he/she feels closer to than all the other parties & this party is the Alternative for Germany (AFD).
- x_1 indicates: ". . . on the whole, how satisfied are you with the way democracy works in Germany?" The 11pt scale ranges from 0 = "extremely dissatisfied", over 1, 2, 3, . . ., to 10 = "extremely satisfied".
- x_2 indicates: ". . ., please tell me on a score of 0–10 how much you personally trust each of the institutions I read out. 0 means you do not trust an institution at all, and 10 means you have complete trust. Firstly . . . . . . Germany's parliament?"
- x_3 indicates: "Now I will briefly describe some people. Please listen to each description and tell me how much each person is or is not like you. . . . She/he thinks it is important that every person in the world should be treated equally." (Scale direction reversed, to let the assigned codes reflect *ascending* likeness): 5 = Very much like me, 4 = Like me, 3 = Somewhat like me, 2 = A little like me, 1 = not like me, 0 = not like me at all.
- x_4 indicates: "To what extent do you agree or disagree that obedience and respect for authority are the most important values children should learn?" Scale direction reversed to let the codes reflect ascending agreement: 0 = disagree strongly; 1 = disagree, 2 = neither agree nor disagree; 3 = agree, 4 = agree strongly
- x_5 indicates: ". . ., to what extent do you think Germany should allow people from the poorer countries outside Europe to come and live here?" 0 = allow many to come and live here, 1 = allow some, 2 = allow a few 3 = allow none.
- x_6 indicates: "Taking all things together, how happy would you say you are?" 11pt scale, ranging from 0 = "extremely unhappy" to 10 = "extremely happy"
- x_7 indicates: ". . ., generally speaking, would you say that most people can be trusted, or that you can't be too careful in dealing with people? Please tell me on a score of 0 to 10, where 0 means you can't be too careful and 10 means that most people can be trusted."

Table 3.5: Linear Regression Estimates of Effect on Trust in the German Parliament, Prejudice Formation and Satisfaction With Democracy.

Target	x_1			x_2	x_5
Eq.	10	11	12	13	14
b_0	6.79	2.79	2.42	6.26	3.51
	45.6	18.9	29.8	41.1	33.0
x_2		0.64	0.65		
		42.2	43.8		
x_3					−0.14
					−7.5
x_4	−0.45	−0.12		−0.55	
	−9.1	−3.0		−10.8	
x_6					−0.05
					−5.3
x_7					−0.07
					−10.2
R^2	0.034	0.449	0.446	0.047	0.082

See the explanations to Table 3.4

Using the same logic, we can now examine other triangular relationships: for example, in the bottom left of the diagram in Figure 3.3, the putative role of x_2 as an intervening variable for the relationship between x_4 and x_1. Since x_4 is associated with x_2 (Eq.13), this would be possible. We ask whether the $x_4 \rightarrow x_1$ relationship (eq. 10) dissolves when x_2 is added to the equation (eq. 11), and observe that the effect weakens substantially, but also retains statistical significance. Since x_2 is also associated with x_1 (eq. 12), the only conclusion that can be drawn is that x_4 (authority) is associated with x_1 both directly and indirectly via x_2. Usually, one then speaks of a direct and an indirect effect.

We can now proceed in a completely analogous manner with the triangular relationships in the upper part of diagram 3.3 and ask, for example, why are quality of life (x_6) and an anti-immigration attitude (x_5) negatively associated? Eq. 14 shows that this is the case, but Eq. 14 also shows that this systematic relationship exists despite variables that could mediate this effect (x_3, x_7). Here, too, we primarily observe three independent, i. e. "direct" effects on the target variable of an equation (here, anti-immigration attitude, x_5).

Finally, we can look at the diagram in Figure 3.3 starting from the effect of x_4 (authority) on y (eq. 3). The effect is strong, statistically significant and shows the expected sign. And we already know that the effect remains substantial when x_1 (satisfaction) is also taken into account (eq. 2). An interesting specification can then be derived from an intermediate step towards eq. 9 in Table 3.4. This equation takes into account the impact of all five x_k variables, which are expected to have a direct effect on y, since we have essentially found a main effects structure so far. This specification consists in the fact that x_4 (authority) loses its direct effect precisely when x_1 (satisfaction) and/or x_2 (trust in parliament) are included in the equation, *but only under the condition* that x_3 (equality) and x_5 (against immigration) are also included in the equation. Only then do x_1 (satisfaction with democracy) and x_2 (trust in parliament) act as intervening variables through which x_4 (authority) affects y (odds of right-wing voting). Or only then does x_4 act as an antecedent variable in this causal chain.

This analysis of data from Round 11 of the European Social Survey illustrates one aspect particularly well, namely that not every systematic factor must also be causal. We identified a number of relevant factors in the odds of voting right-wing. These factors proved to be strong, statistically significant and with the expected sign. And in light of a McFadden's $R^2_{McF} = 0.283$ (eq. 9), they proved to be quite explanatory. Thus, based on this analysis, we would be in a fairly good position to *predict* the conditional odds of voting right-wing. Nevertheless, exactly the same analysis suggests that these factors may have only limited causal relevance. Why is this? Because we were essentially only able to identify *direct* systematic effects. In contrast, we had to largely abandon our ideas for a structure that also includes *indirect* effects and *conditional covariances equal to zero*. Of course, this does not necessarily have to be a problem in itself; in fact, it may be considered completely irrelevant how indirectly one variable affects another variable. However, with the degree of complexity of an assumed causal structure, the options for its empirical testing increase. If a model does not exclude any possible effect, it cannot be tested in principle, as it can only reproduce the observed variance/covariance matrix. However, the more detailed and complex an assumed causal structure is, the more testing options it offers to assess whether observed systematic differences may also indicate causal effects.

But even then, caution is still required. In terms of propositional logic, we remain in a weak position as long as we can only confirm that the implications of a model are compatible with corresponding data.[18] If it turns out that model and data are compatible[19] indeed, however, we have not proven the model in this way. To do so, we would have to be able to rule out all model alternatives that have the same implications as the model we are currently testing. What is usually not possible.

We cannot therefore achieve ultimate certainty on the basis of this test logic. Nevertheless, it makes sense to strive to specify a suspected causal structure as precisely as possible. Why? This does not only provide testing opportunities. The more precise the predictions of a model are, the more potential consequences it excludes from the

---

18 For example, if a model-implied and observed variance/covariance matrix coincide.
19 This topic is occasionally addressed in sociological methodology. The formal basis is the implication relationship. See, for example, Stinchcombe (1987: 17–20). Galtung (1969: 454–455) too provides an insightful discussion in his chapter on "Theories".

outset, the higher its information content and falsifiability and thus its practical relevance.

Longitudinal data are superior to cross-sectional data in that they can help fix the temporal sequence between variables. Since an effect cannot occur before its cause, it is important for causal analyses to be able to determine this sequence. Covariance structure analysis is therefore by no means limited to cross-sectional data, but is also a standard instrument in the analysis of panel data. While *covariance* is a basic building block for the analysis of metric scales, categorical variable analysis involves statistical measures other than this covariance, for example, *transition probabilities* and *transition rates* in the case of panel data. This does not change the principle, but only the statistical measure suitable for a given analysis. We would therefore like to conclude this section on causal inference with the example of a *categorical data analysis* in order to illustrate an advantage that arises when causal analysis can be based on panel data.

Table 3.6: Frequencies of Four Conditional Turnover Tables.

		If LS = 1			If LS = 2			If LS = 3			If LS = 4	
	t_2	happy			happy			happy			happy	
t_1		0	1		0	1		0	1		0	1
0		99	101	0	61	76	0	21	44	0	10	31
1		52	279	1	68	722	1	19	524	1	17	520

N = 2,644 persons with their responses at two panel waves from Example Data Set 1 (PPSM Innovation Panel). Question wordings: "Please imagine the picture of a ladder with 11 steps. The top step is supposed to stand for the best possible living standard, such as you would want it for you. And the lowermost step 1 is supposed to stand for the living standard that would be the worst for you. If you think of your current living standard: On which step would you settle it?" Here, the 11 steps were recoded to LS to come as close as possible to four approximately equally sized groups. This was only possible to a limited extent: LS = 1 (22.3%), LS = 2 (35.5%), LS = 3 (21.9%), LS = 4 (20.4%) using the following recoding scheme: (1, 2, 3, 4, 5 = 1)(6, 7 = 2)(8 = 3)(9, 10, 11 = 4). Happiness: "If you think of how matters develop for you currently: What would you say? Are you currently more happy or more unhappy?" Coded 1 if more happy, 0 if more unhappy.

Transition probabilities are easy to calculate on the basis of turnover tables. Table 3.6 describes the simple example where we know for each participant in a panel survey whether he or she was happy or unhappy at time t_1 and whether he or she was happy or unhappy at a later time t_2. Cross-tabulation results in the frequencies with which the four possible combinations occurred over the two points in time: unhappy at both points in time (0, 0), happy at both points in time (1, 1), unhappy at the first point in time but happy at the second (0, 1), and conversely happy at the first point in time but unhappy at the second (1, 0).

Table 3.6 shows these four frequencies separately for four subsamples of the panel, which were formed according to the values of a presumed cause of happiness, i. e., the standard of living. The structure of this example is simple in that only the presumed effect variable enters the model as a time-varying quantity, but the presumed cause only via its values at t_1. This means that these data cannot be used to map causality in the sense of concomitant variation of cause and effect. If we wanted to pursue such a dynamic concept of causality, the present data structure would be unsuitable. It is only possible to determine to what extent the t_1 condition represents a prerequisite for becoming happy rather than unhappy over time, or for remaining happy. This is done in order to be able to trace time-related transitions or stabilities in a presumed *effect* back to a prerequisite that may be considered as a *causal* condition of such courses.

Using[20] (3.8), transition probabilities are easily calculated for the four fourfold tables in Table 3.6.

$$p_{01} = \frac{f_{01}}{f_{0+}} \qquad\qquad p_{10} = \frac{f_{10}}{f_{1+}} \qquad\qquad (3.8)$$

They refer to t_1 and t_2 and are therefore dependent on this time interval. This is then referred to as a discrete-time model. If desired, this can be converted into a continuous-time model by mathematically allowing the time distance between t_1 and t_2 to tend towards zero (3.9).

$$q_{ij} = lim_{\Delta t \to 0} p_{ij(t,t+\Delta t)} \qquad\qquad (3.9)$$

This converts a transition probability p_{ij} into a transition rate q_{ij}. As Coleman (1981: 9) explains, "this rate has a lower bound of zero if there is no direct transition from i to j and is unbounded above." The transition rate represents the central parameter of the mathematical model of the discrete-state, continuous-time stochastic process on which Coleman (1964; 1981) based his modeling approach. This approach allows a flexible linear and exponential decomposition of transition rates into analytical components with potentially causal relevance.

---

20 In the usual way, the double subscript in (3.8) first marks row i, then column j of the table, with the + sign replacing the missing column in the marginal frequency of a row. The calculation is done row by row by dividing a relevant cell frequency by the marginal frequency of its row. This marginal frequency is not displayed in the respective table, but simply results as the sum of the two cell frequencies of a row.

Table 3.7: Transition Rates Towards Happiness and in the Opposite Direction, Depending on the Standard of Living.

LS = 1	LS = 2	LS = 3	LS = 4
$q_{01.1} = 0.83$	$q_{01.2} = 0.89$	$q_{01.3} = 1.18$	$q_{01.4} = 1.49$

$q_{10.1} = 0.26$	$q_{10.2} = 0.14$	$q_{10.3} = 0.06$	$q_{10.4} = 0.06$

Even though the present data example is very simple, it can already illustrate the basic idea: the separation of random and systematic sources of variation of transition rates and thereby the identification of their relevant causes. Such causes can be such that they have an effect in both directions with the same but opposite effect strength. However, transition rates that unfold freely in both directions can also be modeled. This would then be a situation in which different causes are responsible for one or the other direction of transition. In the present example,[21] we can see with the naked eye that as the standard of living increases, two things happen:[22] the transition rate towards happiness is strengthened and at the same time the transition rate in the opposite direction is weakened. A corresponding formal model could therefore operate with such an effect assumption. However, we do not want to go into the modelling task itself here. Instead, we are only interested in outlining the considerations on the basis of which we might possibly conclude from a time-varying quantity to a causal variable, which itself can only be included in the model as a time-constant quantity.

3.4.7 Unobserved Heterogeneity

Alipourfard et al. (2022: 269–270) provide a vivid example of Simpson's paradox hat the sign of a statistical relationship between two variables can be reversed in groups

---

21 For the sake of simplicity, a formula by Coleman (1964: 137) was used to calculate the observed qij's from the transition probabilities (see also Plewis 1985: 152–153): $q_{01} = p_{01} \cdot W$, $q_{10} = p_{10} \cdot W$, $W = \frac{-\ln(1 - p_{10} - p_{01})}{t(p_{10} + p_{01})}$

22 Moreover, not only do the transition rates vary as a function of the standard of living, but also the stability of being happy at both points in time (f_{11}/f_{++}). In particular, the probability of being happy at both points in time increases from 0.525 to 0.779 and 0.862 to 0.900 when we go from LS = 1 to LS = 4. This type of evidence, too, contributes to strengthen the inference that the standard of living has a causal impact on a person's happiness.

within a study population.[23] Since this possibility exists, it is important to take such group memberships into account. It is conceivable that such a group membership can be represented in the model using an *observed* variable, i. e., a usual categorical variable, but it is also conceivable that such a membership cannot be directly queried in an interview, but can only be inferred indirectly.[24] This would then be about membership in a so-called *latent* group and a proper analysis method would be the probabilistic classification method usually referred to in sociology as "latent class analysis". We can use this classification method to disaggregate the data and identify possible confounding effects of latent group membership. If they are ignored, this may lead to an observed frequency distribution actually manifesting a *mixture of* frequency distributions that then remain undetected. If data analysis ignores such hidden memberships, these memberships may well function as potential "latent confounders" of observed variable relationships; with the result that *unobserved* heterogeneity is not taken into account and can thus lead to distorted results. An illustrating example is given below.

As part of a survey on views & insights on climate policy we collected data on the heating transition for the building sector (y_1), intergenerational justice (y_2) and climate rationality (y_3). The data collection took place in the spring of 2023 at a time when a controversial legislative proposal was being lively debated in Germany. At its core, it was about a "heating law" that required homeowners to switch to climate-friendly heating. On the one hand, the climate protection it aimed at was welcomed, but on the other hand, it was seen as too extensive a state intervention in private life. Our survey question should be seen against the background of this polarizing public debate:

Table 3.8: Wordings of Scale Poles, Assigned Response Codes and Percentages.

Code	−3	−2	−1	0	1	2	3
			Is the heating transition for the building sector justified ?				
y_1	"Yes, we need every possible saving in CO_2 to protect the climate."			neutral	"No, the heating transition demands far too much from citizens."		
	14.0%	15.5%	15.8%	22.1%	9.7%	9.9%	13.1%

---

23 In the words of Pearl et al. (2016: 1): "Named after Edward Simpson (born 1922), the statistician who first popularized it, the paradox refers to the existence of data in which a statistical association that holds for an entire population is reversed in every subpopulation."
24 In section 3.4.5, the technique of analytical controlling on third variables was introduced. These were *observed* variables. Here, the focus is now on controlling on *latent* rather than observed confounding variables.

Table 3.8 (continued)

Code	−3	−2	−1	0	1	2	3
			Intergenerational justice in the financial burden of climate change				
y_2	"Climate protection justifies any taking on debts"			neutral	"This debt puts far too much of a burden on future generations."		
	13.1%	10.9%	13.8%	15.4%	15.1%	13.6%	18.0%
			Climate rationality				
y_3	"Germany should not impose strict climate protection targets as long as other countries continue to put much greater strain on the earth's climate than Germany."			neutral	"Even though Germany has recently contributed only just under two percent to global CO_2 emissions, it should definitely take the lead with strict climate protection measures."		
	16.1%	10.3%	10.5%	20.1%	13.2%	13.4%	16.5%

y_1 was placed in the middle part of the questionnaire, y_2 was the second question in the survey and y_3 was the last question in the survey. The three survey questions were therefore asked far apart from each other. This is advantageous for the present analysis because this placement minimizes the likelihood of answering a later question too consistently just because an answer to a previous question is still too fresh in memory. Instead of the sequence of assigned response code −3, −2, −1, 0, 1, 2, 3 shown here, the sequence of symbols ⋘, ≪, <, 0, >, ≫, ⋙ was used in the questionnaire to avoid the impression of an implicit evaluation of the response alternatives. This bipolar scale was placed exactly *between* the statements on the left and right in order to highlight through the question design which statement corresponds to which *pole* of the scale. The percentage bases are (from top to bottom) n = 444, 449 and 448.

"In 2022, greenhouse gas emissions in Germany amounted to 761 million tons. For 2024, it is now expected that the switch to renewable energies for heating will lead to a saving of around 1.4 percent of emissions in the building sector. Do these figures justify the heating transition for the building sector that the federal government is aiming for?" Table 3.8 shows in the upper segment how the question was continued.

A second survey question related to the aspect of intergenerational equity in the financing of climate protection measures. It is important to know that the two-city state of Bremen is heavily indebted and, despite this very strained budget situation, wanted and wants to invest considerable resources in climate protection measures. The public debate was correspondingly lively. We wanted to know how accepted measures against climate change are if they have to be financed through loans. On the one hand, such borrowing may enable the necessary measures to counteract climate change, but on the other hand, debts also have to be repaid. The more debt is taken on today, the more it will limit the financial scope that remains for future government investments and services. This was our survey question:

"The Bremen Parliament recently approved a credit line of 2.5 billion euros for climate protection projects in its first reading. Which of these two views is closest to your personal assessment?" Table 3.8 shows in the middle segment how the question was continued.

Table 3.9: Conditional Item Response Probabilities and Predicted Class Memberships.

		Conditional item response probabilities						
		-3	**-2**	**-1**	**0**	**1**	**2**	**3**
		Is the heating transition for the building sector justified?						
y_1	Class 1	0.004	0.143	0.266	0.372	0.120	0.095	0.000
	Class 2	0.024	0.000	0.000	0.059	0.139	0.192	0.586
	Class 3	0.594	0.349	0.057	0.000	0.000	0.000	0.000
		Intergenerational justice in the financial burden of climate change						
y_2	Class 1	0.011	0.120	0.226	0.227	0.257	0.101	0.060
	Class 2	0.000	0.010	0.031	0.076	0.017	0.282	0.585
	Class 3	0.551	0.200	0.035	0.029	0.032	0.079	0.076
		Climate rationality						
y_3	Class 1	0.018	0.074	0.139	0.325	0.226	0.151	0.067
	Class 2	0.580	0.167	0.085	0.076	0.034	0.058	0.000
	Class 3	0.097	0.123	0.027	0.000	0.000	0.183	0.570
N = 446		Predicted class memberships						
		Class 1 = 0.567		Class 2 = 0.227		Class 3 = 0.206		

N = 446; Chi^2 goodness of fit = 460.4, df = 286, p = 1.0

Finally we addressed the question of what is a rational response to climate change in view of the fact that single cities, regions or even countries can contribute only rather limited CO_2 savings. One would restrict oneself or incur costs without directly benefiting from this. However, it would be a contribution to *global* CO_2 savings and therefore a relevant contribution to the fight against global warming, ergo a rational behavioral response to climate change. On the other hand, it could be argued that the CO_2 saving potential is far too low to protect coastal cities like Bremen or Bremerhaven or a country like Germany from the consequences of climate change, as long as other countries continue to pollute the climate as before. A person might then ask herself why she should limit herself if other CO_2 emitters do not, especially since the consequences of climate change for the person would be pretty much the same, regardless of whether she practices individual renunciation or not. At the end of the online interview, our respondents were therefore confronted with two corresponding opposing statements shown in the lower segment of Table 3.8, combined with this question:

"Which of these two opinions would you agree with more?"

What is striking about the three frequency distributions reported in Table 3.8 is that they do not have the form of distribution that one might expect, namely one in which the frequencies clearly fall towards the poles of the scale. Rather, it looks as if the frequencies are distributed much more evenly across the entire response spectrum. We recognize the pattern that the frequencies first fall from the neutral center of the bipolar scale towards the sides before rising again towards the poles. We therefore assume that each of these observed frequency distributions actually reflects *three* distributions attributable to different latent population groups. A latent class analysis is therefore used to test the assumption that the y distributions are confounded in this sense.

A solution assuming 3 latent classes proved acceptable. Table 3.9 displays the conditional response probabilities given estimated class membership. Each of the probability distributions should be read row-wise. For class 1, we see the pattern that the probability values decrease towards both poles of the response scale. This applies equally to all three y variables. Respondents here obviously tended towards the middle rather than the poles of the scale. The situation is completely different for the other two classes. For both classes 2 and 3, there is a strong tendency to respond towards one of the two poles. A strong contrast is created by the fact that the two classes tend towards the *opposite* pole of the scale in their response behavior, which strongly indicates a pronounced polarization effect in the climate of opinion. While 56.7 percent of the population tends to a neutral stance (class 1), 22.7 percent were opposed to too much climate protection (class 2) and 20.6 percent expressed a positive attitude towards climate protection (class 3).

3.5 Replication

In principle, any analysis of observational data can be subject to potential sources of error, regardless of its modeling objective. It therefore makes sense to take these sources into account and to check whether and to what extent they (could) be relevant when conducting a data analysis. In this context, the influence of the analytical decisions of the researcher or data analyst on the result of the data analysis is particularly important.

Any analysis of data from nonexperimental social research implies unavoidable decisions with regard to how the analysis should be designed, how the modeling should be carried out and how the validity of the conclusions drawn from it should be evaluated. Since theoretically any analytical decision made in this regard can influence the final result and the conclusions drawn from it, we consider the conceptualization, modeling, and validation of a data analysis itself as possible sources of outcome variation.

The key question is therefore how much a result remains invariant to changes in the method used to obtain this result. This key question was asked early on in the context of the Columbia School of Social Research and is linked there to an approach of systematic replication (Galtung 1969: 437–450). We can now embed this approach in a broader classification of replications in the quantitative social sciences. This classification distinguishes four possible replication goals (Freese and Peterson 2017: 152): *verifiability* to check if the results of an original study are reproducible if the same analysis is performed on the same data, *robustness* to check how far target findings are "merely the result of analytic decisions" if a "reanalysis on the original data" uses "alternative specifications", *repeatability* to determine whether key results of a study can be replicated by applying the original procedures to new data, and *generalization* to check "if similar findings may be observed consistently across different methods or settings".

It Is clear that such replication goals only make sense if they are pursued transparently. Systematic replications should therefore be viewed as the instrument of an *open science,* in this case specifically of an open *computational social science* (Voelkel and Freese 2022).

Concept.	Modeling		Validation		
Measurement	Estimation	Within-	Out-of-sample		
			RANDOMLY		PURPOSELY
		Cross-	Independent		
			Concurrent		Prognostic

Figure 3.4: Conceptualization, Modeling, and Validation as Sources of Variation in Nonexperimental Research.

Each data analysis is concretized by decisions on how certain tasks should be practically implemented. Figure 3.4 therefore relates the conceptualization, modeling and validation of a data analysis *in an interleaved structure* to the concretely involved tasks of measurement, estimation, and validation.

3.5.1 Conceptualization > Measurement

A first source of outcome variation concerns the theoretical constructs of an analysis in relation to their supposed indicator variables. We have to ask what indicator variable(s) best suit the theoretical concept(s). Achieving content validity can be quite challenging, as it should be reasonable to view the indicator variables included as a representative selection from the universe of indicators that could theoretically have been selected. The fact that this is an assumption that is difficult to test in practice only underlines the importance of trying to replicate an analysis with alternative sets of indicator variables.

Conceptualizing a study also means determining who should be included in a empirical study and in what way. This requires determining how the selection of units should be operationally realized. A fundamental choice here is between probability and non-probability sampling. A related choice concerns the collection of auxiliary information for handling unit nonresponse.

3.5.2 Measurement > Modeling

Next, given a theoretical concept, we have to decide which method or measurement model we want to use to link the theoretical construct(s) with their indicator variable (s). Possible models link a hypothetical construct in question with only a single indicator variable or simultaneously with more than one such indicator. The link can be established by using principal component or confirmatory factor analysis[25] or some other method of index formation. A latent variable model that explicitly takes into account different scale levels of the observed and latent variables involved, such as a structural equation or latent class model, represent another option.

In the *triangle of conceptualization > measurement > modeling* it is thus a leading question which conceptual quantity do I want to measure with which indicator variables in which specific way. This implies the construction of a questionnaire or interview and that in turn implies taking into account expected mode and response effects.

For instance, research in survey methodology has shown that the results of a survey can be influenced by the underlying survey mode. Especially for survey questions whose answers touch on norms of social desirability, it matters whether survey interviews are mediated by an interviewer or conducted online. Response effects are also important. These are effects that arise from question wordings or response formats. Such effects are numerous and occasionally they are stronger, for example in the case of scales that ask about *the frequency of* a behavior (Engel et al. 2012: chapter 13). The cognitive involvement in answering survey questions and how sensitive a question is perceived also plays an important role (Engel and Köster 2015) and should therefore be taken into account by implementing corresponding para- and meta-questions when constructing a questionnaire or interview.

The scope that a question allows for its answer is another source of response variation. Implicit framing effects can arise when a survey question does not provide any framework, so it is entirely up to the respondent how he/she wants to understand a question. On the contrary, framing effects can arise intentionally when a framework for answering the question is provided explicitly from the outset and then ideally integrated into a systematic comparison, as is done with the quasi-experimental question format respectively the factorial survey design (Engel and Köster 2015a).

---

25 For example, the factor-score scales in chapter 7.2, are derived from confirmatory factor analysis.

In general, experiments or quasi-experiments are suitable means to control the effects of question wordings and question/response formats when built into a survey questionnaire. It can also be helpful to design a survey interview from the outset in such a way that statistical methods specifically designed to control measurement error can be used in the later data analysis phase. Structural equation modeling is a case in point. In this approach to data analysis, latent variables play a key role in controlling random and systematic measurement error in both cross-sectional and repeated measurement designs.[26] So-called MTMM models can be estimated to take into account, for example, different survey modes, question wordings and response formats. "MTMM" is the usual acronym for the "MultiTrait-MultiMethod" approach to survey measurements (Burmeister and Engel 2015). Although an application of this approach to data analysis requires considerable effort, in theory and in practice such models can be estimated routinely.

3.5.3 Modeling > Estimation

There are various estimation methods that can be used routinely, so a choice must be made here (explicitly or implicitly by adopting default settings).

Especially in predictive modeling, a decision must also be made about the functional form, which is assumed to be the way in which the variables included in a data analysis are linked to one another.

A relationship between two variables can be linear or nonlinear, but it can also contain various random effects in addition to such systematic effects. This applies, for example, to models for hierarchical data structures, in which random effects are taken into account at aggregate levels in addition to the base level.

Another point to consider is the scale level of the variables included in an analysis, especially its target variable. Depending on whether it is a metric or categorical variable, we may be dealing with a classification task.

Also of crucial importance is the random distribution of the target variable or the residuals that a model has to take into account, i. e., for instance, whether we have to estimate a linear model or a generalized linear model.

Finally, samples can only provide correct estimation results on the basis of a reliable data quality. This applies, for example, to quality impairments caused by unit and item nonresponse or random and systematic measurement errors.[27]

All respective modeling/ estimation options require decisions on how to proceed and, theoretically, any of these decisions can affect the final score.

---

26 If designed properly, latent variable modeling enables different formalizations of causality, for instance via time-lagged effects or concomitant variation of putative cause and effect, and they enable the control of random and systematic measurement errors (Engel and Meyer 1996; Engel et al. 2007). Examples of the structural equation modeling approach are given in Engel (2013: 92–99).

27 This topic is covered in Chapter 2.

3.5.4 Estimation > Validation

Model fit is assessable in different ways. Validation thus requires fixing relevant evaluation metrics. If fit criteria suggest contrary decisions as to the acceptability of a model, the situation is comparable to the so-called *p*-hacking strategy. Yarkoni and Westfal (2017: 4–5), for instance, describe *p*-hacking as a practice of procedural overfitting, "of flexibly selecting analytical procedures based in part on the quality of the results they produce". Similarly, Freese and Peterson (2017: 155) trace the "abiding concern [. . .] that published findings represent a best-case scenario among all the arbitrary and debatable decisions made over the course of analyzing data" back to "p-hacking, in which a researcher runs different analyses until they find support for their preferred hypothesis".

In addition to the evaluation metric, the validation design itself also represents a potential cause of outcome variation. "Within-sample" design means avoiding randomly splitting the sample into a training and test or holdout sample. It is then quite possible to work with a very sophisticated set of evaluation metrics (as in structural equation modeling, for example), but to apply these metrics to the same data that were used to develop the model itself.

In contrast, data science places great emphasis on *not* using the same data that was used to develop the model to test it. Instead, the validation standard is to separate the data into training and test or holdout (sub-)samples, and this on a random basis. While a cross-validation design represents a compromise between within- and out-of-sample validation by randomly splitting the sample into subsamples and using each of them once as a test sample in an iterative process, the validation set design pursues pure out-of-sample validation. This is done by randomly splitting the sample into a training and test or holdout sample in order to test the model on data that remains completely unseen during the training phase. To train and test a model, independent subsamples are drawn from a random sample. Such subsamples are independent but concurrent because they come from the same parent sample and its immanent data-collection period. The time axis is therefore only involved insofar as it concerns this data collection period (i. e., the field phase in a survey). Otherwise, not. In social research, however, large surveys conducted using a trend design offer the additional opportunity to use *future* data to validate models and thus evaluate their *prognostic* validity.

Even this rough sketch of choices and related sources of outcome variation shows great scope in the conception and implementation of data analyses. How exactly this is scope to be handled depends on the replication goal and the methods involved. Robustness is such a replication goal (Freese and Peterson 2017: 152). A target finding would be considered *robust* if *alternative specifications* of an analysis, applied to the same data, leads to the same finding, so that it can be concluded that the result is invariant or insensitive to the analytical decisions made. When pursuing this sensitivity question, it would be good to be able to show that a target result remains stable against changes in the method used to achieve the result.

However, this does not apply to all use cases. For example, methods can differ in their ability to deliver precise and error-controlled results. *Sampling* is a good example of this. Probability sampling allows for a much better control of the selection process of units than non-probability sampling. A sampling design that combines probability sampling with the collection of auxiliary information for propensity weighting offers more analytical options for handling unit nonresponse than probability sampling alone could do. Analogously, questionnaire designs can differ in their ability to control measurement error that comes along with specific survey modes, question wordings and response formats. Methods of data analysis too can offer different levels of capability in precision and error control. Therefore, if it turns out that results are not invariant to the methods used.to obtain them, then it makes sense to also take such quality aspects into account.

Testing the extent to which results are *generalizable* is another replication goal where it cannot be expected that results are always replicable across the tested conditions. Because non-replicability across a tested condition would only mean that the empirical result needs to be further specified.

Part II: **Using R**

Chapter 4
Data Management in R

4.1 R and R-Studio

The R Project for Statistical Computing writes on its website[1]: "R is a free software environment for statistical computing and graphics". R is also characterized as a language for object-oriented and functional programming[2] and as a "scripting language for statistical data manipulation and analysis" (Matloff 2011: xix). R benefits greatly from the contributions of a huge community of software developers and thus offers its users from a wide range of scientific disciplines the best conditions for conducting statistical analysis and data science. The R Project for Statistical Computing is a network of researchers who support free science and its progress in extremely useful ways by extending the core[3] of R with packages[4], or libraries. You can download the software free of charge from a CRAN Mirror for your country[5], with CRAN denoting "The Comprehensive R Archive Network".

RStudio simplifies the use of R a lot. RStudio is an open-source IDE (integrated development environment) that often serves as a graphical user interface for working with R. RStudio Desktop is available in a free edition[6].

Figures 4.1 and 4.2 are screenshots of the RStudio user interface with its four windows. The R console with its R prompt > in the lower left window is used for *interactive* use of R. Commands are entered after the >, and the results are displayed directly below.

The upper left window is used for using R in *batch* mode. R scripts are written into this window or loaded from an existing R script file into this window—and from there they are executed in whole or in part. Such scripts consist of sequences of R instructions (commands) that are then available for repeated use, modification, additions, etc. Figure 4.1 shows an example of such an R script *before* it is executed, and Figure 4.2 shows the screen *after* it has been executed: Initially, the R console in the lower left window and the Global Environment in the upper right window are empty, then filled with the results of this execution. We describe what the entries mean below. Finally, in the lower right window, we see the current directory of files. This

---

1 https://www.r-project.org/ (last access: March 08, 2025)
2 See section 4.5.2 below.
3 The development and further development of this core as well as the R infrastructure is in the hands of the *R Core Team*. Who is a member of this team can be found here: https://www.r-project.org/contributors.html (last access: March 08, 2025)
4 Access to all packages is available via https://cran.r-project.org/web/packages/ (last access: March 08, 2025)
5 https://cran.r-project.org/mirrors.html (last access: March 08, 2025)
6 https://posit.co/downloads/ (last access April 11, 2025)

https://doi.org/10.1515/9783110680683-004

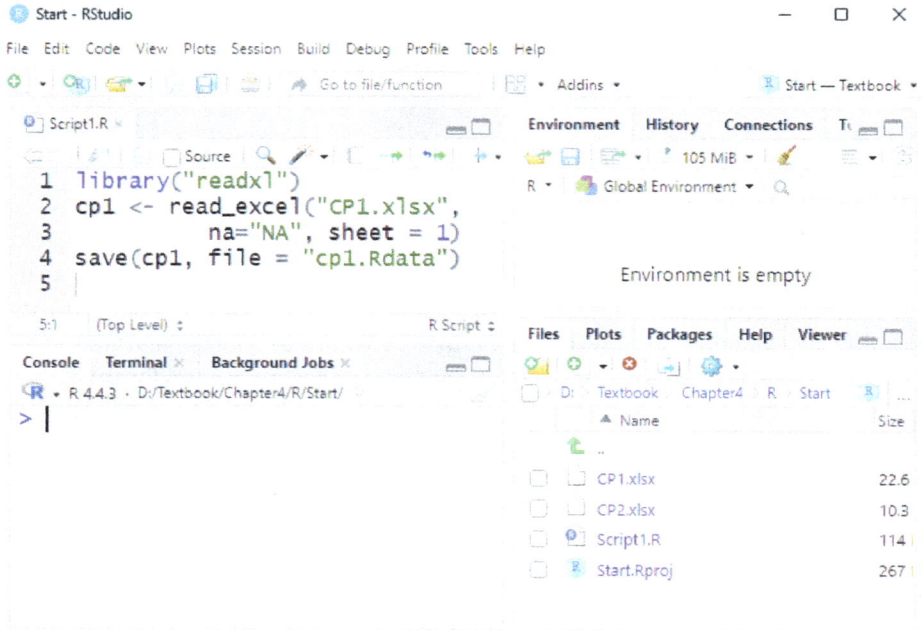

Figure 4.1: RStudio Interface before Having Executed an R Script.

"Files" window can also be switched to another window, for example, one that displays any generated "Plots."

The approach followed in this textbook for the many R applications is generally to work in batch mode, i. e. with R scripts.

4.2 Importing Data From Excel and Stata

We use a small selection of variables from the much larger Example Data Set 7 on Views & Insights on Climate Policy to illustrate a possible way of importing survey data into an R frame[7]. This way consists in importing the data from an Excel file which had previously been exported from a survey tool such as lime survey. For this we ran the sequence of instructions in (4.1).

```
library("readxl")
cp1 <- read_excel("CP1.xlsx", na="NA", sheet = 1)                    (4.1)
save(cp1, file = "cp1.Rdata")
```

---

7 Using our survey platform on https://limesurvey.viewsandinsights.com/

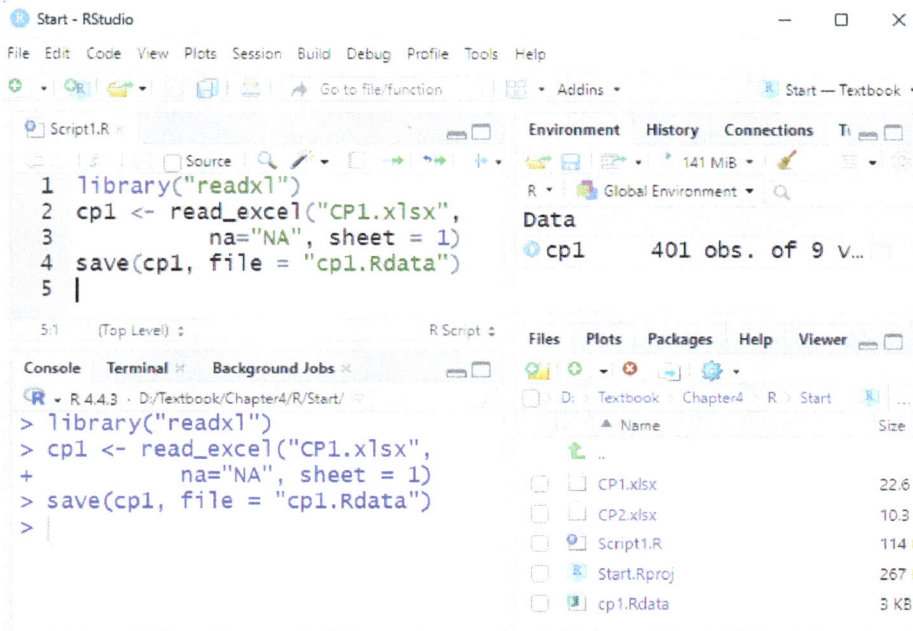

Figure 4.2: RStudio Interface after Having Executed an R Script.

First, the library *readxl* is called, which contains the required function *read_excel()*. This function, in turn, requires the name of the Excel file to be read (*CP1.xlsx*) and a specification of how to handle missing values, i. e., blank cells in the relevant columns of the Excel file. Here, the instruction says to assign the corresponding standard code in R, namely *NA*, to such cells of the data matrix. Finally, *sheet = 1* specifies the sheet to read from the file *CP1.xlsx*, here the first (only) sheet in this file.

The instruction in this line of the R script also causes the imported data to be assigned to the R object with the freely chosen name *cp1*, whereby this object is automatically created as a data frame. In other words, the data frame is stored under the object name *cp1* and as such is temporarily available for the duration of the R session.

The following line of instructions then only serves to permanently save this data frame so that it remains stored even after the R session has ended. Before we execute these lines of instructions, RStudio looks like shown in Figure 4.1, after they are executed, it looks like shown in Figure 4.2.

Figure 4.3 provides the screenshot of a view on the first ten units in the data frame *cp1*. We obtained this view via (4.2).

```
View(cp1)
```
(4.2)

The variable names listed in the header of the data frame were imported from the Excel file during the data import. When exporting the data from the survey tool, we had previously selected the technical option to import these names from the survey tool into the first row of the Excel file. Thus, the variable names originally come from the survey tool and could be chosen quite freely *there*.

We mention this path not only to show the steps how the raw data gets into the data frame, but also for another reason. When exporting data from the survey tool, it may be necessary to rename the variable names for survey questions that require or allow multiple responses before they can be imported into R. In this example, this concerns the variables DQ11_1, DQ11_2 and DQ11_3. These variables belong to survey question DQ11 and were written out by the survey tool itself as DQ11[1], DQ11[2] and DQ11[3] in the first row of the Excel file. In R, however, the square bracket [] is reserved for addressing elements in vectors and matrices and is therefore not permitted as part of variable names. Therefore, we manually replaced the square brackets in these variable names with the underscores shown in Figure 4.3 between export from the survey tool and import into R.

	DQ03	DQ06	DQ11_1	DQ11_2	DQ11_3	VQ01	VQ02	P01	P02
1	4	1	4	2	1	7	1	1	26
2	3	1	5	3	2	8	2	2	23
3	3	1	4	7	9	6	1	2	22
4	3	2	2	1	7	8	1	1	20
5	2	3	1	7	3	7	2	1	26
6	2	2	5	NA	NA	7	2	1	64
7	1	1	1	3	2	8	1	1	54
8	NA	1	2	6	1	NA	2	1	50
9	2	1	2	8	3	5	0	2	40
10	3	1	1	2	7	8	2	1	52

Showing 1 to 10 of 401 entries, 9 total columns

Figure 4.3: A View on the first 10 Units in the Data Frame "cp1".

With the data frame *cp1* saved in *cp1.Rdata*, the import of the survey data is complete — and normally, this would be the point at which to begin the statistical analysis of the data from the, here, 401 respondents. In the present case, however, the data collection marked only an intermediate step in an ongoing process, with the data of another 50 respondents to be added — using exactly the same questionnaire. These additional survey data were also exported from the survey tool to an Excel file (*CP2.xlsx*) and from there imported into an R data frame *cp2*, which in turn was saved in *cp2.Rdata*. As shown in (4.3), the two structurally identical data frames were then loaded into a new R session, and their rows were concatenated using the *rbind()* function. In other words, the 50 rows of the second data frame were appended to the 401 rows of the first data frame, so that the resulting data frame, stored under the object name *cp* in *cp.Rdata*, now contains 451 data rows, i. e., the survey data from 451 units or respondents.

```
load("cp1.Rdata")
load("cp2.Rdata")
cp <- rbind(cp1, cp2)
save(cp, file = "cp.Rdata")
```
(4.3)

Data can be available as an Excel file, but also in another format. Datasets are often offered for download as SPSS or STATA files, i. e., in the format of one of the software products for statistical analysis that have been established for decades. This applies, for example, to the data files of the Eurobarometer studies or the European Social Survey. Such surveys provide extremely important datasets for empirical research in political science, sociology, and psychology. It is therefore very advantageous that R provides a convenient and uncomplicated option for reading such data formats into R.

```
library(haven)
ESS11_DE <- read_dta("ESS11-DE.dta")
save(ESS11_DE, file = "ess11.Rdata")
```
(4.4)

The *haven* library can be used for this purpose. Specifically (4.4) is used to import a Stata file. In this example, data for Germany from Round 11 of the European Social Survey are imported. We had previously downloaded this Round 11 data from the official website of the European Social Survey. The sequence of instructions in (4.4) comes from the R script we created for this purpose. However, we could also have used the R Studio menu. Selecting *File > Import Dataset > From Stata . . .* opens a window with the *Browse . . .* option, allowing you to specify the file to be imported and import it using the *Import* button.

4.3 The Elements of a Data Frame

A data frame organizes data in the basic form required for many analyses. Each column represents a variable, each row a unit (here, a respondent). Each cell of the matrix therefore contains information about the value a unit (i. e., a respondent) has in a variable. As shown in Figure 4.3, this value is usually represented by a number, i. e., a numeric code. The meaning of this code for each variable is derived from a coding rule that assigns numbers to the values of that variable. The researcher usually determines such an assignment during questionnaire development by assigning numbers to the clickable answer fields for variables with a closed response format. These are then precisely the numbers that are transferred into the data matrix. How these numbers can be used for data analysis depends largely on the *scale level* of the respective variable. This level depends on the nature of the variable or how the property to be measured is operationally defined.

A *thought experiment* can help outline this point. Imagine randomly selecting two units from the data frame and comparing the numbers these two units have in a variable of interest. The key question is then: What exactly does this numerical relation indicate?

At the *nominal* scale level, the *numerical relation* can only reflect an *empirical relation* of this kind: the two randomly selected units belong to the same or to different response categories. If the two numbers are equal, the two units belong to the same response category, if the numbers are unequal, to different categories. A meaningful comparison is therefore restricted to the equal/unequal ($=, \neq$) relation.

The gender of a respondent is an example. In the present data frame, this is variable P01, with its response categories "male" (assigned number = 1), "female" (assigned number = 2), and "diverse" (assigned number = 3). With a variable of this type, the assigned numbers serve solely to indicate membership in a category, nothing more. Accordingly, the researcher has complete freedom to determine which number is assigned to which category. The numbers themselves are completely meaningless for data analysis as long as the coding rule is always applied in exactly the same way to all included units.

In an *ordinal* scale, the relation between two numbers can be interpreted in terms of "less than", "equal to" or "greater than" ($<, =, >$). This means: If the numbers that two randomly selected units have in a variable differ from each other, the smaller of the two numbers can be taken to mean that this unit has less of the property in question than the unit with the larger number. For example, one is happier than the other, is less satisfied with their life than the other, rates the public infrastructure for charging the batteries of electric cars better than the other, has a higher standard of living than the other, etc. The requirement for an ordinal scale is that the sequence of gradations between the ordered response categories (e.g., from "not at all satisfied" to "very satisfied") must be appropriately mirrored by the sequence of assigned numbers. It must always remain a monotonically increasing or monotonically decreasing sequence of numbers. This somewhat reduces the researcher's scope in assigning numbers to the response categories.

As an example, let us consider variable VQ02 in the data frame of Figure 4.3. The question was "What can you as an individual contribute to climate protection?" and there were four possible answers to choose from:

3	very much
2	a lot
1	not so much
0	practically nothing

Respondents could grade their answers accordingly, from "practically nothing" to "very much", as follows: very much > a lot > not so much > practically nothing. The empirical relations expressed therein must always be preserved by the accompanying numerical relations. Here, we have chosen the simplest case and assigned this sequence of numbers: 3 > 2 > 1 > 0. However, it would have been equally legitimate to assign this monotone sequence of numbers: 4 > 3 > 2 > 1, but not this semi-monotone sequence of 4 > 2 < 3 > 1. The only reason for starting the sequence with zero here was that "zero" should provide the respondent with a suitable equivalent to the practically empty set, i. e., "practically nothing." However, this is a survey-related, not a data-analytical, reason. When assigning numbers to response categories of variables, one should always ensure that these can also make intuitive sense to the respondents. An incongruent impression could be created in this regard by reversing the assigned number sequence, for example, an assignment like this: 0 = very much, 1 = a lot, 2 = not so much, 3 = practically nothing. This assignment would be acceptable from a scale level perspective, but possibly unfavorable from a survey psychology perspective.

The next higher scale level is achieved with an *interval* scale of measurement. With such a scale, the intervals between individual values can also be interpreted. Kühnel and Krebs[8] (2006: 31) illustrate this using the example of a person's year of birth: "If three people were born in 1960, 1961, and 1963, then the birth interval between the first and second person is only half as large as the interval between the second and third person." However, "if the age in years is calculated from the year of birth, a ratio scale results, since birth () establishes an absolute reference point (zero point)."[9] The essential difference between an interval scale and a ratio scale is that a *ratio* scale has a uniform ("absolute") zero point, whereas an interval scale does not. To stay with the example: The calendar underlying the three birth years is based on a zero point that is not shared by other calendars. In contrast, the birth of a person essentially establishes a unique zero point. The general argument is then simply that it only makes sense to directly relate two measurements to each other if they were measured on a scale with such a unique zero point. Applied to the age variable, it would therefore be a meaningful statement that a forty-years-old person is twice as old as a twenty-years-old person, or that a 45-years-old is three times as old as a 15-years-old, etc.

Whereas in statistics textbooks, the classic "counterexample" is temperature measured on an interval scale. This can be measured in degrees Celsius, Fahrenheit, or Kelvin. And since each scale has a different zero point, the argument here would be

---

8 Kühnel and Krebs (2006: 28–36) provide an instructive introduction to the topics of "scale level" and "permissible transformations" of scales in their German-language statistics textbook. The topic of scale level is essentially a classic topic in statistics textbooks. See, for example, Blalock (1981: 15–19) or Agresti and Finlay (2009: 11–14).

9 Own translation

that it doesn't make sense to say that 30° Celsius is twice as warm as 15° Celsius, since this relationship would be numerically quite different if the two temperatures were read on one of the other two scales.

Interval and ratio scales are considered *metric* scales and are considered a prerequisite for the meaningful applicability of statistical procedures *that calculate with the scale values themselves*. Only if these numbers are sufficiently empirically determined can the mathematical operations performed with them lead to a meaningfully interpretable result. If a researcher is free to choose which numbers to assign to the response categories of a variable, it makes little sense to calculate, for example, the arithmetic mean or the variance from these assigned numbers, simply because the result would be different if other numbers had been assigned beforehand. Accordingly, interest in metric scales is strong, especially since the information content increases with the scale level. However, we encounter ordinal scales much more frequently than metric scales in empirical social research. Ordinal scales are therefore often treated as if they were metric scales. For variables that have only a few ordered response categories, say, three to five, this is certainly a problematic practice. For scales with, say, seven to eleven response categories, however, it might be more reasonable to argue that such a scale would already behave like a metric scale, so that it can be treated as a quasi-metric scale.

However, the achievable scale level also depends on the *operational definition* of the characteristic to be measured. For example, it is possible to measure the degree of agreement with a topic on a Likert scale, thus achieving an ordinal scale level. It is also possible to measure agreement with a topic using multiple statements that can be answered with "yes" or "no," and use the number of "yes" statements for measurement. This would then be a ratio scale level measurement, since the scale rests on counting and contains the empty set as zero if none of the items is answered with "yes." Furthermore, social science statistics has highly developed analytical methods at its disposal that allow the integration of ordinal scales into analyses that imply *latent* metric scales. For instance, ordinal regression can be specified that way (Long 1997: 116–122). Structural equation modeling too allows for ordinal scales or mixtures of ordinal and metric scales (Beaujean 2014). Thus, based on suitable measurement models, a metric scale level can also be achieved for ordinal variables.

4.4 Univariate Frequency Distributions

Looking at a single *column* of the data matrix, we can see which values have occurred for that variable among all units, and we can determine the univariate frequency distribution of that variable by simply counting the frequency of each of these values. In Figure 4.3, for example, we find the variable P01 in the second column from the right and the numbers 1 and 2 below it. This is the variable "gender," for which the questionnaire provided three response categories: "male" (coded with 1), "female" (coded with 2), and "diverse" (coded with 3). Now, if we start a new R session and let the software count how often these three numbers occurred — for that variable (i. e., column) among the 451 respondents (i. e., rows) in the data frame, using the sequence of instructions in (4.5),

```
load("cp.Rdata")
addmargins(table(cp$P01))
```
(4.5)

R Studio reports the output shown in (4.6) in its lower left window (R console):

```
  1    2    3   Sum
213  236   2   451
```
(4.6)

The *table()* function performs the counting. It finds 213 times the number one, 236 times the number two, and 2 times the number three for variable *P01* in data frame *cp* (*cp$P01*). Thus, the data frame contains 213 males, 236 females, and 2 respondents who consider themselves to be in the "diverse" category. The *table()* function alone would only provide us with the three cell frequencies (213, 236 and 2), but not the marginal frequency or their sum (451). We obtain the latter by embedding *table()* within the *addmargins()* function.

Let us look at another variable in the data frame, namely DQ06. It shares one property with P01, namely the *scale level*. Both variables have nominal response scales. DQ06 is a variable that was posed in the survey as follows: "A thought experiment: Imagine that politicians had to choose between a secure and a climate-neutral energy supply for the country, and—completely fictitiously—both couldn't be achieved simultaneously. What would be your recommendation: Which of these two goals should politicians choose?" There were three response categories offered:

"For a secure energy supply" (coded 1), "For a climate-neutral energy supply" (coded 2) and "I don't know, I can't say" (coded 3). First, we count the frequencies using (4.7)

```
addmargins(table(cp$DQ06))
```
(4.7)

and get the frequencies presented in (4.8)

```
  1    2    3   Sum
284  120   41  445
```
(4.8)

These numbers now represent the absolute frequencies of the univariate frequency distribution of the variable DQ06. The attribute *absolute* is chosen to distinguish them from the corresponding relative frequencies, which result when the absolute numbers are converted into proportions which add up to 1.0 or to percentages which add up to 100.

```
round(100 * prop.table(table(cp$DQ06)), digits=1)                    (4.9)
```

To do this, we embed the *table()* function within the *prop.table()* function to get the relative frequencies calculated as shares of 1.0. We then multiply these frequencies by 100 to express them as percentages. Finally, we embed the expression within the *round()* function to round the percentages to one decimal place. The result is shown in (4.10).

```
   1     2    3
63.8  27.0  9.2                                                      (4.10)
```

Two points are still worth noting: First, the sum of the frequencies in (4.8) is 445 and not 451. Six respondents were therefore automatically excluded from the tabulation due to missing values, i. e., NAs, in the variable.

Second, category 3 of this variable deserves special attention. In survey research, it can be useful to explicitly give respondents the opportunity to express themselves if they feel overwhelmed or have no opinion on a question. The reason for including an explicit "don't know" category here was that we were asking for answers to a *fictitious* situation. However, with a *nominal* scale – as in this case – this hardly complicates the analysis of the data, since each category has to be considered separately anyway.

However, the situation is somewhat different if the scale level is ordinal or metric, i. e. higher than the nominal scale level. If the analysis then aims to exploit this ordinality or metric, then this cannot be easily done for the "don't-know" category. It is not uncommon for the "don't know" units to be excluded from such an analysis and consequently treated as if they were NAs, i. e., units with missing values in the variable in question. As an example, consider the following survey question DQ03, which requested answers on an *ordinal* scale. We asked: "The construction of wind turbines is a good example of how renewable energy also requires local acceptance. However, it's often the case that wind turbines are only acceptable as an energy source as long as they're not located in my neighborhood. Should climate policy respect this attitude?" Respondents could choose their answer from five categories, which were presented to all respondents in the same fixed order:

1	Yes, should accept without exception
2	Yes, should generally accept (exceptions allowed)
3	No, should generally not accept (exceptions allowed)
4	No, should not accept without exception
5	Don't know, can't say

The crucial point is that only the first four categories reflect ordinally graded responses, but not the fifth category. We ran the two instructions in (4.11) and obtained the frequency distribution in (4.12).

```
addmargins(table(cp$DQ03))
round(100 * prop.table(table(cp$DQ03)), digits=1)
```
(4.11)

Renewable energies in general, and wind power in particular, are actually very popular among the population. Nevertheless, the well-known "NIMBY" ("Not In My Backyard") phenomenon also exists in Germany. And as the frequencies of the two yes answers show, the NIMBY attitude is held by slightly less than half of Bremen's adult population (48%).

```
   1    2    3    4    5  Sum
  62  154  127   50   57  450


   1    2    3    4    5
13.8  34.2 28.2 11.1 12.7
```
(4.12)

This is the result if we exclude no unit with valid values from the analysis. As it should be. However, if the percentages were calculated without the "don't know" units, the proportion of both "yes" answers combined would be 55 percent, thus exceeding the 50 percent mark. Of course, there would be no need for such an approach in a tabular analysis such as the one presented here. However, this does not apply so completely to other methods of data analysis. For example, in a regression analysis, we could not simply include this scale as a single 5-point scale (1, 2, . . ., 5) due to the break between the ordered categories 1 to 4 on the one hand and category 5 on the other. And if we were to simply exclude the units with the value 5, we would also change the result, but in a much more hidden way than with a table analysis like this one. Here, we essentially encounter the same issue as with missing values, or NAs. If the percentage is high, this poses a high potential for bias in an analysis that simply excludes such units from the analysis—especially since "don't know" responses too, like NAs, can go back to *systematic* reasons.

It may then be reasonable to consider the possibility of alternatives to excluding units. Elsewhere (Engel and Dahlhaus 2022: 356) we described an ordinal scale to rate the degree of belief in the validity of statements that ranges from "not at all", "probably not", "possibly", and "quite probable", to "quite certain". In addition, each respondent had the option of "don't know." Since this option was used only by a few (1.3% on average), we considered it reasonable to recode these "don't know" responses to the mid category "possibly", acting on the auxiliary assumption that both categories equivalently express maximal uncertainty. However, whether a scale allows for such recoding must always be examined on a case-by-case basis.

Returning to Figure 4.3, the fourth column from the right contains the variable VQ01. The underlying survey question was formulated as follows: "How much do you feel personally responsible for contributing to reducing climate change?" Followed by an eleven-point scale from 0 to 10, where only the poles are labeled: 0 = "not at all" and 10 = "very much".

```
addmargins(table(cp$VQ01))
round(100 * prop.table(table(cp$VQ01)), digits=1)
plot(round(100 * prop.table(table(cp$VQ01)), digits=1))
```
(4.13)

We use the instructions in (4.13) and obtain the absolute and relative frequencies in (4.14) in the lower left window and the graph shown in Figure 4.4 in the lower right window of the R Studio interface:

```
 0   1   2    3    4    5    6    7    8    9   10   Sum
32   9   9   25   19   78   70   83   51   28   43   447

 0      1     2     3     4      5      6      7      8     9    10
7.2    2.0   2.0   5.6   4.3   17.4   15.7   18.6   11.4   6.3   9.6
```
(4.14)

While a graphic can be exported directly from the interface's plot window using one of the common graphic formats, this may not be of sufficient image quality in terms of resolution. The height and width of the graphic also depend on the variably adjustable size of the lower right window. This can lead to suboptimal ratios of width and height and thus distorted appearing graphs. It may therefore be more advantageous to specify the key parameters (format, height, width, resolution) explicitly.

```
 tiff("VQ01-600.tiff", units="in", width=9,
     height = 4, res=600 )
plot(round(100 * prop.table(table(cp$VQ01)), digits=1))
dev.off()
```
(4.15)

For that purpose R provides graphics devices for common formats such as *jpeg()*, *png()* and *tiff()*. Here, we use the **.tiff* function and specify the output file, the width and height of the graphics and the units in which height and width are given. Here, this is inches, while the resolution is specified in ppi (pixels per inch) or dpi (dots per inch). *dev.off()* returns the number and name of the active device and is required to finalize the process.

An advantage is that a distribution of frequencies, as shown in (4.14), can also be easily represented graphically. To do this, we use the *plot(table)* function[10] in R, which can be applied to both absolute and relative frequencies. Here, we have applied it to the relative frequencies by simply embedding their calculation in the plot() function (last line in (4.13)).

The graph gives an immediate impression that this distribution doesn't even come close to following a normal distribution. The distribution has multiple peaks, not just one, making it multimodal. And even if we were to assume that the frequencies attributable to scale values 5, 6, and 7 form something like a plateau (ignoring the slightly lower frequency for scale value 6), we still couldn't claim that the frequencies decline to either side from there. The values only fall initially, but then rise again towards the poles. We have already observed a similar distribution pattern for three other variables in this study and attributed it to the polarized public opinion climate at the time of data collection. We mention this here only to illustrate with an example that the choice of mean values and measures of dispersion should take into account not only the scale level but also the shape of a frequency distribution.

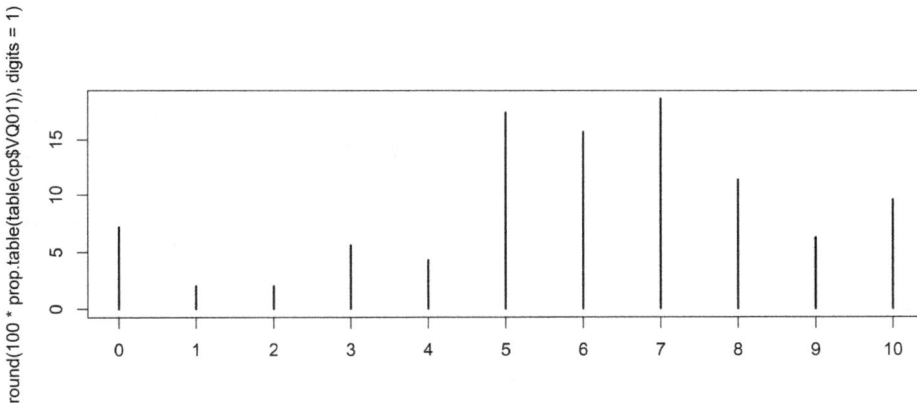

Figure 4.4: The *plot(table)* Function Applied to the Relative Frequencies of Variable VQ01.

Mean values serve to indicate what typical values are for a population or sample. Assuming a metric scale, the arithmetic mean can be calculated.

---

10 Murrell (2011: 25–33) provides an excellent introduction to the graphics capabilities of R, including, as one of many options, the plot(table) function (p. 33).

$$\bar{x} = \frac{\sum_{i=1}^{n} x_i}{n} \tag{4.16}$$

For variable *VQ1* from data frame *cp*, (4.17) performs the calculation. As always in R, the link between data frame and variable name is established by the dollar sign.

```
mean(cp$VQ01, na.rm = TRUE)                                              (4.17)
```

The result is 5.95 on a scale from 0 to 10, so 6.0 if we round to one decimal place. Thus, typically, the perceived responsibility for contributing to reducing climate change is at 6.0, i. e., slightly above the nominal midpoint of the scale, which is at 5.0.

However, this description is still incomplete. We still need further information about how well or poorly the mean value can fulfill the function of characterizing a typical value for the population or sample. In statistics, a measure of dispersion is usually used for this purpose; in the case of the arithmetic mean, this is the standard deviation.

$$s_x = \sqrt{\frac{\sum_{i=1}^{n} (x_i - \bar{x})^2}{n-1}} \tag{4.18}$$

This measure indicates the average dispersion of the individual values around their arithmetic mean. To get this measure, we take the sum of the squared deviations of the individual x_i values from their mean $\bar{x}$ and divide this sum by $n-1$ (with n indicating the number of x_i values that go into the calculation; for the sake of simplicity often referred to as sample size[11]). This yields the variance, of which we take the square root to obtain the standard deviation. In R, the standard deviation is easily obtained by the *sd()* function, here applied to variable *VQ01* from the data frame *cp* (4.19). As in (4.17), we activate the option to remove NAs. As a result of this calculation we get the value 2.65, so 2.7, if we round to one decimal place again.

```
sd(cp$VQ01, na.rm = TRUE)                                               (4.19)
```

It is then usual to consider the range $\bar{x} \pm 1s$, i. e. the range of the arithmetic mean plus/minus 1 standard deviation. For variable VQ01 this would be the range from 3.3 to 8.6. If the frequency distribution were normally distributed, —which it is not here—, approximately 68% of all units[12] would fall into this range. This would then be the information used to assess how homogeneous or heterogeneous the sample appears with respect to the variable under investigation. This is also the range used to assess how

---

11 A formulation that, strictly speaking, ignores the number of excluded cases with missing values in the variable in question.
12 Agresti and Finlay (2009: 79), for example, use an informative graphic to explain the normal distribution specifically in this respect.

well the arithmetic mean can fulfill its function of characterizing the value typical for the population or sample. This function can be fulfilled better the more closely the individual values are scattered around their mean, i. e., the more homogeneous the sample is in this respect.

Strictly speaking, the calculation of the arithmetic mean and standard deviation requires a metric scale. If this scale level is not achieved, the mean value of the frequency distribution should be determined using a measure suitable for ordinal scales, namely the median. At the same time, the spread should be determined not using the standard deviation, but rather the interquartile range. These measures are suitable for ordinal scales. They are also recommendable in the case of metric scales whose frequency distributions are skewed, i. e. deviate from a symmetric, typically bell-shaped distribution.

We demonstrate the calculation of the median and the interquartile range using variable VQ01. To do this, we consider its empirical distribution function, i. e. the distribution of the cumulative relative frequencies. A quick way is to embed one script line in (4.13) into the *cumsum()* function, to get (4.20)

```
cumsum(round(100 * prop.table(table(cp$VQ01)), digits=1))        (4.20)
```

This instruction produces the sequence of percentages shown in (4.21).

$$
\begin{array}{ccccccccccc}
0 & 1 & 2 & 3 & 4 & 5 & 6 & 7 & 8 & 9 & 10 \\
7.2 & 9.2 & 11.2 & 16.8 & 21.1 & 38.5 & 54.2 & 72.8 & 84.2 & 90.5 & 100.1
\end{array}
\tag{4.21}
$$

Because we've rounded to one decimal place for better readability, a small rounding inaccuracy arises, which is evident in the fact that the percentages add up to 100.1 instead of 100.0. To avoid this, we would simply change "digits = 1" to "digits = 2" in (4.20) to round the numbers to two decimal places.

A disadvantage of the standard outputs of the absolute, relative and cumulative relative frequencies in (4.14) and (4.21) is certainly that the information is provided in a fragmented, not very compact, form. However, we can easily change this with a little trick. It consists in defining the table itself as a data frame. This changes the display format while retaining the ability to calculate the required values. (4.22) shows the required sequence of instructions.

```
addmargins(frq <- table(cp$VQ01))
tb <- as.data.frame(frq)
tb$Perc <- round(100 * (tb$Freq/sum(tb$Freq)), 1)        (4.22)
tb$CumPerc <- cumsum(tb$Perc)
print(tb)
```

This yields an output consisting of two parts. First, the absolute frequencies are displayed as already known from (4.14), followed by the table in (4.23).

	Var1	Freq	Perc	CumPerc
1	0	32	7.2	7.2
2	1	9	2.0	9.2
3	2	9	2.0	11.2
4	3	25	5.6	16.8
5	4	19	4.3	21.1
6	5	78	17.4	38.5
7	6	70	15.7	54.2
8	7	83	18.6	72.8
9	8	51	11.4	84.2
10	9	28	6.3	90.5
11	10	43	9.6	100.1

(4.23)

This table now has the typical format for frequency tables, with three columns for absolute frequencies (Freq), relative frequencies expressed as percentages (Perc), and the cumulative percentages in the rightmost column. The values of the variable itself are located in the column headed "Var1". This label is automatically generated and should actually be "VQ01" in this example. The left column is also automatically generated. It simply numbers the rows and can —and should— be ignored here.

To understand the median and interquartile range, the rightmost column in (4.23) is relevant. It represents the empirical distribution function and, as such, displays quantiles. Quantile is the generic term for, for example, quartiles, quintiles, or deciles, which can be used to divide a distribution into quarters, fifths, tenths, etc., as needed. The division into quarters is probably the most common variant, especially because the median represents nothing other than the second quartile.

To understand such measures, we need to imagine the values of the scale as an ordered series. First come the units with the smallest values on the scale, then those with the next largest values, up to the units with the largest values. For variable VQ01, this would first be the 32 respondents with the value 0, then the 9 respondents with the value 1, up to the 43 respondents with the value 10. The median is then the value of the middle person, i. e., the value of the respondent that halves such a series of values. For example, the person who stands, so to speak, in the middle of the ordered series, with theoretically equal numbers of persons to their right and left. And the first quartile would represent the value of the person who separates the first quarter of the distribution from the remaining three quarters. Similarly, the third quartile would be the value of the person who separates the first three quarters from the remaining quarter of people. Consequently, the middle 50 percent of the units with their values in the variable under consideration lie between the 1st and 3rd quartile. Where the difference 3rd quartile minus 1st quartile indicates the interquartile range.

The closer the two quartiles are to each other, the more homogeneous the sample is in the variable under investigation. We can either read the required values in (4.23) from the rightmost column or simply calculate them using the summary() function:

summary(cp$VQ01)   (4.24)

The *summary()* function returns the smallest and largest values, the first, second, and third quartiles, and the arithmetic mean of the frequency distribution. It also returns the number of NAs, i. e., units with missing values in the variable. (4.25) contains all these numbers.

```
Min. 1st Qu.  Median   Mean 3rd Qu.    Max.  NA's
0.000   5.000   6.000  5.949   8.000  10.000     4
```
                                                                                     (4.25)

We see that the arithmetic mean and median differ little from each other. One would therefore come to the same conclusion: that respondents typically rate their sense of responsibility to contribute to reducing climate change at six on a scale of 0 to 10. It also becomes clear that the middle 50 percent of responses range between five and eight on this scale, meaning that respondents typically gave an answer within this spectrum.

Characterizing a frequency distribution by its quartiles offers the advantage of being useful for ordinal scales and skewed distributions. However, a disadvantage may arise from the fact that they are too coarse for subtle comparisons. This can tempt one to calculate the arithmetic mean instead of the median, for example, when it comes to comparing mean values across groups. Then, in principle, it can be considered to include the quartiles in interpolated form. Figure 4.5 illustrates this scheme using the median for the frequency distribution of the variable VQ01. It only shows a partial representation of this distribution; the complete distribution can be seen in (4.23).

To calculate the interpolated mean, we first check which category it will fall into. Theoretically, the median is the scale value at which 50.0% would be found in the empirical distribution function in the far right column of (4.23). However, we see there —as in Figure 4.5— that this value itself doesn't appear at all. Instead, we see that 38.5 percent of respondents have an observed scale value less than or equal to 5, and 54.2 percent have an observed scale value less than or equal to 6. This implies that the median must be sought in the context of category 6.

Two auxiliary assumptions come into play here. First, that a scale point represents the midpoint of a surrounding interval and, secondly, that the responses are evenly distributed within each such interval. Here, the class width is one, but could be larger for grouped data. The interpolation then takes as a reference point the lower bound of the interval under consideration, which for the median is 5.5, in order to add to this lower bound exactly the share of the class width that is required to reach the sought (here, 2nd) quartile.

VQ01 $k =$	5		6		7	8
lb_k	4.5		5.5		6.5	7.5
cp_k		38.5 %		54.2 %		72.8 %
		$cp_{k-1} \longrightarrow$	$\dfrac{q_k - cp_{k-1}}{p_k}$			
			15.7 %			

lb_k lower bound of category or class k; cp_k cumulative percent up to and including k

Figure 4.5: Interpolated Median for the Frequencies of Variable VQ01.

(4.26) provides the formula for this computation. Q_k denotes the sought interpolated quartile, lb_k the lower bound of the category or class k in question, and q_k the quantile sought in that k. This value is 25 for the 1s quartile, 50 for the second and 75 for the 3rd quartile.

$$Q_k = lb_k + \left(\frac{q_k - cp_{k-1}}{p_k}\right) \times width \qquad (4.26)$$

Applied to the relevant percentages in (4.23), (4.26) yields the outcome shown in (4.27).

$$1st\ Quartile = 4.5 + \left(\frac{25 - 21.1}{17.4}\right) \times 1 = 4.7$$

$$Median = 5.5 + \left(\frac{50 - 38.5}{15.7}\right) \times 1 = 6.2 \qquad (4.27)$$

$$3rd\ Quartile = 7.5 + \left(\frac{75 - 72.8}{11.4}\right) \times 1 = 7.7$$

However, we can get the same result much more easily if we use the function in *library(psych)* that performs these calculations:

```
library(psych)
round(psych::interp.quartiles(cp$VQ01, w=1,
                na.rm = TRUE), digits = 1)
```
(4.28)

This produces the output shown in (4.29):

```
library(psych)
    Q1  Median  Q3
   4.7    6.2   7.7
```
(4.29)

In the case of nominal scales, the options are more limited. As a measure of a typical value, the most frequently occurring value of a distribution, i. e., the mode, may be considered. However, this would only make sense if the distribution is single-peaked, i. e. has only one such value.

It is even more difficult to define a meaningful measure for the dispersion of a nominally scaled variable. Jann (2002: 50–52) suggests the *entropy* as a possible measure:

$$H = -1 \cdot \sum_{cat=1}^{C} (p_{cat} \cdot ln(p_{cat})) \tag{4.30}$$

As an example, let us consider the variable DQ06, for which we have shown the relative frequencies of its three categories in (4.10). Category 1 expressed a preference for a secure energy supply, category 2 for a climate-neutral energy supply and category 3 for expressing a "don't know" answer. If we express the three percentages in (4.10) as proportions, we can use (4.31) to calculate the entropy H and the relative entropy rH for this distribution of relative frequencies[13].

```
p <- c(0.638, 0.270, 0.092)
H <- -1 * sum(p * log(p))                                          (4.31)
print(rH <- H/log(length(p)))
```

The entropy measure can be used to determine the degree of predictability inherent in the distribution of units over the categories of a discrete variable. The entropy is maximal when units are evenly distributed across the categories of such a variable; then predictability is lowest and the uncertainty associated with a prediction is accordingly highest. Conversely, the uncertainty of a prediction is lowest and predictability is highest, when all units are concentrated in one category of the variable. Then the entropy is zero. The maximum value of H is $ln(C)$, with C indicating the number of categories of the variable. Dividing H by H_{max} results in the *relative entropy* with its maximum value of 1.

For variable DQ06 we get an H of 0.86. The maximum entropy is equal to the logarithm of 3, since three categories or proportions are involved, and the relative entropy is 0.783. But how can this number support the interpretation of the result, considering that the three observed frequencies in (4.21) deviate significantly from a uniform distribution, but 0.783 is numerically quite close to the number of 1.0 achieved with a uniform distribution? Probably only when comparing frequency distributions of nominally scaled variables.

In (4.31), we first define a vector consisting of the three elements and assign it the object name *p*, so that the calculation of the entropy H in the following line can be

---

13 See Chapter 11.4.9 for entropy as a measure of classification quality.

related to this *p*. Finally, we divide *H* by the maximum value that *H* can have by relating *H* to the logarithm of the length of the vector, i. e., to the logarithm of the number of elements it contains. We assign the result of this calculation to the object name *rH* (for relative entropy) and embed the calculation including this assignment in the *print()* function to get the numerical result printed.

4.5 Vectors

4.5.1 Vector, Matrix, List, Data Frame

In R, data is organized into vectors. Matloff (2011: 10) calls them the "R workhorse", because it is "hard to imagine R code, or even an interactive R session, that doesn't involve vectors". A *vector* consists of one or more than one elements of the same *mode, or data type*. We have *numeric* vectors (all entries are numbers), *character* vectors (all entries are text) and *logical* vectors with their possible entries TRUE and FALSE.

Vectors can form matrices. "An R matrix corresponds to the mathematical concept of the same name: a rectangular array of numbers. Technically, a matrix is a vector, but with two additional attributes: the number of rows and the number of columns" (Matloff 2011: 11–12).

In contrast, *lists* can consist of elements of *different* modes. "Like an R vector, an R list is a container for values, but its contents can be items of different data types" (Matloff 2011: 12). As Buttrey and Whitacker (2018: 8, 62) put it: "A *list* is an R object that can hold other R objects" (. . .) "a list might include a numeric matrix, a character vector, a function, another list, or any other R object." The R objects we get in return to function calls are often organized as lists.

Since in data science we often deal with both numbers and text—i. e., different data types—we need a format that overcomes the restriction of a *matrix*, which can only consist of a single data type. In R, this is the *data frame*. "A data frame in R is a list, with each component of the list being a vector corresponding to a column in our "matrix" of data" (Matloff 2011: 14).

4.5.2 Objects and Functions

R "incorporates features found in object-oriented and functional programming languages". Matloff (2011: xx-xxi) exemplifies *object-oriented programming* by means of a statistical regression analysis. When using "the lm() regression function in R, the function returns an *object* containing all the results—the estimated coefficients, their standard errors, residuals, and so on. You then pick and choose, programmatically, which parts of that object to extract."

As Buttrey and Whitaker (2018: 8–9) express[14] it, "An *object* is a general word for anything in R. Usually we will use this to refer to data objects such as vectors, matrices, lists, or data frames, but we might use "object" to refer to a function, a file handle, or anything else with a name in R", to continue a bit later that a *"function* is a kind of R object that can take an action". Such actions are made comparatively easy for the user: "As is typical in functional programming languages, a common theme in R programming is avoidance of explicit iteration. Instead of coding loops, you exploit R's functional features, which let you express iterative behavior implicitly" (Matloff 2011: xxi)[15].

4.5.3 Using the c() and cbind() Functions

(4.32) is an example of a *numeric* vector consisting of eight elements.

```
c(5, 2, 1, 7, 4, 3, 6, 9)                    (4.32)
```

When we execute this expression, we get the following output in the lower left window, i. e., in the R Console, of the R Studio Interface:

```
[1] 5 2 1 7 4 3 6 9                           (4.33)
```

The same output is produced if we assign the vector to a name with the left-arrow followed by typing this name in the next line of the R script:

```
X <- c(5, 2, 1, 7, 4, 3, 6, 9)
X                                             (4.34)
```

In R we often assign functions or calculations, i. e. R objects, to object names.

Logical vectors are most often constructed by R in response to an operation on other vectors (Buttrey and Whitaker 2018: 23). Table 4.1 lists common R operators, including those that perform comparisons[16].

---

14 Adler (2010: 50–51) describes it in the same sense.

15 Similarly, Kuhn and Silge (2022: 21) stress the aspect of functional programming: „R has excellent tools for creating, changing, and operating on functions, making it a great language for functional programming. This approach can replace iterative loops in many situations [. . .]."

16 A complete list, including operator precedence, can be found in Adler (2010: 64–66). Wickham and Grolemund (2017: 56) also briefly describe arithmetic operators(+, -, *, /, ^) and modular arithmetic, i. e., %/% (integer division) and %% (remainder). Some further examples. When we raise a number to the power of 0.5 (i. e., if we calculate x^0.5), this means we take the square root, which we also obtain via sqrt(x). exp() and log() refer to the exponential and logarithmic functions, respectively. For calcu-

Table 4.1: Some R Operators.

<	less than	+ -	Add, subtract
< =	less than or equal	* /	Multiply, divide
>	greater than	^	Exponentiation (right to left)
> =	greater than or equal	&	And
==	is equal to	|	Or
! =	is not equal to	%any%	Special operators

For example, if we let R perform a comparison on (4.32) to learn to which of its elements a specific condition applies (here, being greater than or equal to 5),

```
c(5, 2, 1, 7, 4, 3, 6, 9) >= 5
```
(4.35)

this creates vector (4.36):

```
[1] TRUE FALSE FALSE TRUE FALSE FALSE TRUE TRUE
```
(4.36)

Now we build a second numeric vector using (4.37)

```
y <- c(8, 4, 3, 5, 6, 1, 8, 5)
y
```
(4.37)

and get the following returned:

```
[1] 8 4 3 5 6 1 8 5
```
(4.38)

Now we have two numerical vectors of equal *length*, i. e. each with the same number of elements, which we can combine to form a matrix. To do this, we use the *cbind()* function to bind the two vectors together to create two *columns*. As before, the names, —here *x, y* and *m*—, are freely chosen.

```
m <- cbind(x,y)
m
```
(4.39)

We now have a matrix with two columns and eight rows, as well as subscripts in the square brackets on the left, which indicate the row number before the comma. Such

---

lating with matrices (matrix algebra): The function t() transposes a matrix, %*% is the operator for matrix multiplication and solve() is the function for matrix inversion (Hatzinger et al. 2014: 175–176).

numerical subscripts can be used to address or extract elements of vectors or matrices.

```
      x  y
[1,]  5  8
[2,]  2  4
[3,]  1  3
[4,]  7  5                                                    (4.40)
[5,]  4  6
[6,]  3  1
[7,]  6  8
[8,]  9  5
```

In (4.40), the element in row 6 and column 1 would be returned via

```
m[6,1]                                                        (4.41)
```

as

```
x
3                                                            (4.42)
```

and following the same logic, *m[4, 2]* would return the value 5 (for *y*). In a matrix, an element can be addressed via the intersection of [row, column], i. e., via a double subscript. In a vector, a single subscript suffices. In (4.34), for example, the expression *x [4]* would return the value of the fourth element, i. e. the 7.

(4.40) is an example of a data matrix in the format of a *matrix()*. Such a matrix is essentially a vector, arrayed in a two-dimensional rectangle (Buttrey and Whitaker 2018: 53). That is, we get the same matrix as (4.40) if we use, for example, (4.43).

```
ma <- matrix(c(5, 2, 1, 7, 4, 3, 6, 9,
               8, 4, 3, 5, 6, 1, 8, 5), nrow=8, ncol=2)     (4.43)
ma
```

namely (4.44)

```
      [,1] [,2]
[1,]    5    8
[2,]    2    4
[3,]    1    3
[4,]    7    5                                                (4.44)
[5,]    4    6
```

```
[6,]    3    1
[7,]    6    8
[8,]    9    5
```

Instead of a numerical subscript, a *logical subscript* can also be specified— in the case of a *matrix* for example to form a subset of *rows* that satisfies a certain criterion. In (4.45) this criterion is that *x* is greater than or equal to 7. This applies to the entries in row 4 and row 8, i. e., to the numbers 7 and 9.

```
z <- m[x >= 7]
z
```
(4.45)

The R script lines in (4.45) select these two numbers along with the numbers for *y* of that rows, and assigns this subset to the object name *z*.

```
[1] 7 9 5 5
```
(4.46)

According to the same logic, the subscript *m[x <= 3]* would yield the outcome in (4.47). The condition applies to the row numbers 2, 3 and 6. (4.47) shows the three numbers for *x* first, followed by the corresponding numbers for *y*.

```
[1] 2 1 3 4 3 1
```
(4.47)

This structure is unfavorable because it destroys the original structure of the matrix (4.40). (4.48) corrects this,

```
matrix(c(2, 1, 3, 4, 3, 1), nrow=3, ncol=2)
```
(4.48)

by producing the subset of (4.40) shown in (4.49).

```
       [,1]  [,2]
[1,]    2    4
[2,]    1    3
[3,]    3    1
```
(4.49)

A characteristic of the *matrix()* format is that it can only contain one data type—in this case, numeric data. However, if we want to combine numeric vectors and character vectors in a matrix, we need another format, namely a *data frame*. One way to achieve this is shown in (4.50). Here again, the assigned object name is freely chosen.

```
f <- as.data.frame(m)
```
(4.50)

We create a *character vector* consisting of eight elements. For the sake of simplicity, we use the alphabet, but we could also have put other alphanumeric characters in the quotation marks.

```
t <- c("a", "b", "c", "d", "e", "f", "g", "h")
t
```
(4.51)

The two R script lines return the output shown in (4.52).

```
[1] "a" "b" "c" "d" "e" "f" "g" "h"
```
(4.52)

We now integrate this vector consisting of alphanumeric characters into the data frame using *cbind()*, with *df* being a freely chosen name.

```
df <- cbind(f, t)
df
```
(4.53)

This adds the vector *t* to the data frame and returns the output shown in (4.54).

```
   x  y  t
1  5  8  a
2  2  4  b
3  1  3  c
4  7  5  d
5  4  6  e
6  3  1  f
7  6  8  g
8  9  5  h
```
(4.54)

To verify the data format for each column, we can inspect the structure of the object—here, of the data frame with the object name *df.* For this we use the *str()* function.

```
str(df)
```
(4.55)

This function provides useful, specific information in the context of many analyses in R. Here, it provides this specific information:

```
'data.frame': 8 obs. of 3 variables:
 $ x: num  5 2 1 7 4 3 6 9
 $ y: num  8 4 3 5 6 1 8 5
 $ t: chr  "a" "b" "c" "d" ...
```
(4.56)

Logical subscripts can also be formulated in the context of a data frame. (4.57) is an example. To do this, we apply the general rule of linking the name of the data frame and the variable to be called within it using the dollar sign.

```
df$y[y>=6]
```
(4.57)

Whereby we now produce a result that is limited to the extraction of the relevant values for the variable formulated in the condition in square brackets.

```
[1]  8  6  8
```
(4.58)

However, we will see below that in the context of data frames we can work easily and flexibly with the *subset()* function.

4.5.4 Vector Operations

In R, arithmetic operations on vectors produce vectors (Buttrey and Whitaker 2018: 24). For example, in *matrix m* (4.40) we can add the values of vectors x and y or take their product, square the values of a vector, take their square root, take their logarithm, all as needed. Starting again with the vectors x and y, such (and further) mathematical operations are easily performed,

```
x  <-  c(5, 2, 1, 7, 4, 3, 6, 9)
y  <-  c(8, 4, 3, 5, 6, 1, 8, 5)
p  <-  x+y
q  <-  x*y
r  <-  x^2
u  <-  sqrt(y)
v  <-  log(x)
m  <-  cbind(x,y,p,q,r,u,v)
m
```
(4.59)

and produce the output shown in (4.60).

```
       x   y   p    q    r        u          v
[1,]   5   8   13   40   25   2.828427   1.6094379
[2,]   2   4   6    8    4    2.000000   0.6931472
[3,]   1   3   4    3    1    1.732051   0.0000000
[4,]   7   5   12   35   49   2.236068   1.9459101
[5,]   4   6   10   24   16   2.449490   1.3862944
```
(4.60)

```
[6,]  3  1   4   3   9  1.000000  1.0986123
[7,]  6  8  14  48  36  2.828427  1.7917595
[8,]  9  5  14  45  81  2.236068  2.1972246
```

Following on from (4.53), the script lines in (4.61) would perform the same mathematical operations if the data are organized in a *data frame*.

```
df$p <- df$x+df$y
df$q <- df$x*df$y
df$r <- df$x^2                                                    (4.61)
df$u <- sqrt(df$y)
df$v <- log(df$x)
df
```

This extends (4.54) into the data frame shown in (4.62)

```
    x  y  t  p   q   r        u          v
1   5  8  a  13  40  25  2.828427  1.6094379
2   2  4  b   6   8   4  2.000000  0.6931472
3   1  3  c   4   3   1  1.732051  0.0000000
4   7  5  d  12  35  49  2.236068  1.9459101       (4.62)
5   4  6  e  10  24  16  2.449490  1.3862944
6   3  1  f   4   3   9  1.000000  1.0986123
7   6  8  g  14  48  36  2.828427  1.7917595
8   9  5  h  14  45  81  2.236068  2.1972246
```

So it makes no difference whether the calculations are performed in the context of the format of a *matrix()* or a *data.frame()*. The main purpose of this example, however, is to demonstrate how the calculations for the two vectors x and y are performed simultaneously *for each of their elements*. This becomes clear when you go through the calculations *line by line*.

Although calculations —unlike in the present example— do not always result in a vector of the same length as the vector(s) to which a calculation refers, Buttrey and Whitaker (2018: 25) aptly put it, "one of the sources of R's power is the ability to perform computations on every element of a vector at once."

4.5.5 Statistical Results as Numerical Vectors

Especially in statistical analyses, we often apply mathematical operations to the elements of vectors *that only result in a single number* (i. e., producing a numerical vector of length 1). Examples include common statistical formulae and functions used to compute them in R, such as the arithmetic mean and *mean()*, the variance and *var()*, the standard deviation and *sd()*, the Pearson correlation and *cor()*, etc. The same applies to functions like *sum()*, which adds the values of a vector *vertically*, i. e., *within* a column, or *length()*, which counts the number of elements a vector consists of. Here, too, their application results in a single number, i. e., a vector of length 1. In contrast, the *summary()* function creates a numeric vector consisting of a small set of numbers, namely the smallest and largest scale value, the 1st, 2nd and 3rd quartile, and the mean. Just to name a few examples of statistical functions.

The fact that such statistical results are immediately available as numerical vectors in R is an advantage because they can then be easily included in *user-defined* calculations. For example, returning to data frame (4.62), the script line

```
summary(df$x)
```
(4.63)

produces the output shown in (4.64)

```
Min.  1st Qu.  Median   Mean  3rd Qu.   Max.
1.000   2.750   4.500  4.625   6.250  9.000
```
(4.64)

while (4.66) is produced if we embed *summary()* in the *str() function* to understand the structure of the object created by R in response to *summary()*. Thus, (4.65)

```
str(summary(df$x))
```
(4.65)

yields an output that shows how (4.64) is internally organized as an R object, including the numerical vector with its six entries and their labels:

```
'summaryDefault' Named num [1:6] 1 2.75 4.5 4.62 6.25 ...
- attr(*, 'names')= chr [1:6] "Min." "1st Qu." "Median" "Mean" ..
```
(4.66)

Now suppose we want to extract the arithmetic mean from this summary vector. To do this, we would have to address the fourth element from the left. We achieve this by means of a corresponding subscript, i. e., by

```
df$mean <- summary(df$x)[4]
df$mean
```
(4.67)

The object name *df$mean* is freely chosen after the dollar sign; even though we wanted to extract the mean here, we could have chosen a completely different name. The *df* before the dollar sign, however, is fixed, since we want to refer to this specific data frame. (4.67) produces the following output:

```
[1] 4.625 4.625 4.625 4.625 4.625 4.625 4.625 4.625
```
(4.68)

We see that the correct value was extracted, but we also see that we get this value eight times. This is because the data frame consists of eight rows of data, and R automatically replicated the value accordingly. In R, this is called *recycling* (Buttrey and Whitaker 2018: 26) —here, recycling a vector of length 1, i. e., the previously extracted mean value. The vector can therefore easily be incorporated into calculations with the other variables of the data frame. For example, by calculating the difference between each individual x value and the arithmetic mean in the variable x and squaring this difference.

```
df$sqd <- (df$x-df$mean)^2
```
(4.69)

If we were to type *df$sqd* (again a freely chosen name, here for squared difference), the eight individual values of this variable would again be displayed as a vector. However, since our data frame is very small—and we want to see how our calculations affect it—we'll just type *df* to see the entire data frame.

```
df
```
(4.70)

This produces the output shown in (4.71).

	x	y	t	p	q	r	u	v	mean	sqd
1	5	8	a	13	40	25	2.828427	1.6094379	4.625	0.140625
2	2	4	b	6	8	4	2.000000	0.6931472	4.625	6.890625
3	1	3	c	4	3	1	1.732051	0.0000000	4.625	13.140625
4	7	5	d	12	35	49	2.236068	1.9459101	4.625	5.640625
5	4	6	e	10	24	16	2.449490	1.3862944	4.625	0.390625
6	3	1	f	4	3	9	1.000000	1.0986123	4.625	2.640625
7	6	8	g	14	48	36	2.828427	1.7917595	4.625	1.890625
8	9	5	h	14	45	81	2.236068	2.1972246	4.625	19.140625

(4.71)

We see the recycled vector with the mean value again, and to the right of it, the result of the calculation of (4.69), i. e., the squared difference of each individual x value from the arithmetic mean of its frequency distribution. Following on from formula (4.18) for the standard deviation, we could now calculate the sum of these squared deviations, divide this sum by n-1, i. e., in this case, by 8 minus 1, and take the square root of the resulting expression.

```
sqrt(sum(df$sqd)/(8-1))
```
(4.72)

If we've chosen the subjunctive here to express that we *could have* proceeded this way, it's for good reason. Standard deviation is one of the statistical functions for which R has a standard implementation, namely *sd()*. (4.72) and (4.73) therefore give the same result.

```
sd(df$x)
```
(4.73)

So, if we were only interested in calculating this measure, we wouldn't have had to generate either *mean* or *sqd*, but would have simply called (4.73). *R then does the rest automatically*[17]. And even if we had wanted to program the standard deviation formula ourselves, we wouldn't have had to write the intermediate steps, i. e., *mean* and *sqd*, into the data frame. We essentially only did that here to illustrate recycling. We could have used the script line (4.74) instead (to be resolved from the inside out).

```
sqrt((sum((df$x-(summary(df$x)[4]))^2))/(8-1))
```
(4.74)

Each calculation method produces the same result for the 8 values of the variable *x* in data frame *df*, namely a standard deviation of 2.67.

When calculating a statistical formula, such as the standard deviation in this case, we would generally use the function that is already implemented for precisely this purpose—in this example, the *sd()* function—and save ourselves the trouble of doing the calculations ourselves.

However, In the present context, in addition to recycling, we also wanted to illustrate the advantage that *the results* of statistical calculations *are themselves vectors* in R—and thus addressable or extractable. And that is exactly what we occasionally take advantage of, especially in more complex data analyses.

In the example above, we used the *summary()* function to illustrate this. First, the mean was extracted from the vector of summary values, then this *external* value was returned back into the data frame for further calculations. However, the *summary()* function produces a relatively small object (as exemplified in (4.66)), other statistical methods can produce much more complex objects. How exactly such an R object is structured, what information it contains in its various sections and how exactly these sections can be addressed during programming can be seen from the *str()* function when it is applied to the object in question. We occasionally demonstrate this possibility for a variety of purposes in Chapters[18] 6 to 11 and would like to illustrate this option only very briefly here.

---

[17] Wickham and Grolemund (2017: 56) describe this for arithmetic operators (+, -, *, /, ^) in such a way that "these are all vectorized, using the so-called "recycling rules." If one parameter is shorter than the other, it will automatically extended to be the same length."

[18] Especially in In section 6.4 (Table 6.1), section 6.5 (Table 6.3), section 6.6 (Table 6.4), section 7.1 (Table 7.3), section 7.2 (Table 7.5), section 8.1 (Table 8.1), section 9.4, (Table 9.3), section 10.2

For example, linear regression involves predicting values for a target variable. We explain this in more detail in Chapter 6. These predicted values are stored in an R object and are thus available for subsequent calculations. For example, using data from Example Dataset 6 on the energy transition in the European Green Deal, (4.75) performs a linear regression with country data to predict for each country the percentage of people who support political regulation of AI interventions[19], using the country's purchasing power standard for this purpose (with an explained variance of 27.7 percent $\left(R^2 = 0.277\right)$ and a substantial positive effect of a country's purchasing power involved).

```
ai <- lm(eudata$public ~ eudata$KKS)
boxplot(ai$fitted.values,
 xlab= "If only the purchasing power of a country were relevant:      (4.75)
\nEstimated shares for AI requires political intervention",
         ylab="Percentages")
```

To do this, we use the *lm()* function ("lm" stands for linear model), name the target variable to the left of the tilde ~, and the variable used for prediction to the right. The result of these calculations is assigned to the freely chosen object name *ai*. Using *str(ai)*, we can inspect this object and see that it consists of a *list* of 12 elements, including numeric vectors that can be used for further calculations. One of these vectors contains the predicted values and can be addressed or extracted via *modelname$fitted.values*. We do this here only for a small example, which consists of creating a so-called boxplot for these predicted values (Figure 4.6). For this boxplot, *xlab* and *ylab* is optional, but is used here for labeling. The embedded character string "\n" serves as a line break.

A boxplot is a commonly used diagram to visualize the range of the middle 50 percent of responses in a frequency distribution. This range is indicated by the upper and lower boundaries of the box. The horizontal line within the box represents the median. The point at the very top of the image represents an outlier, i. e., an atypical value.

(Table 10.11), section 10.3 (Table 10.13), section 11.1 (Table 11.2), section 11.4.6 (Table 11.9), section 11.4.9 (Table 11.11)

19 The question wording for the variable "public" was as follows: "To ensure that applications of artificial intelligence are developed in an ethical manner, political intervention is required."

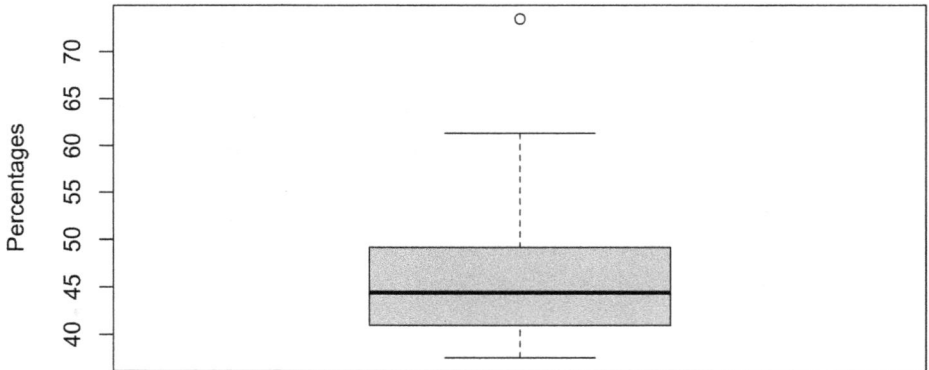

If only the purchasing power of a country were relevant:
Estimated shares for AI requires political intervention

Figure 4.6: Boxplot of the Predicted Values From a Preceding Regression Analysis.

4.6 Recoding the Values of Variables with recode() and ifelse()

Let's return to the data frame in Figure 4.3. In the far right column is variable P02, age in years. Using *summary(cp$P02)*, we obtain some descriptive statistics for the frequency distribution of this variable.

$$
\begin{array}{llllll}
\text{Min.} & \text{1st Qu.} & \text{Median} & \text{Mean} & \text{3rd Qu.} & \text{Max.} \\
18.00 & 31.00 & 39.00 & 41.69 & 54.00 & 69.00
\end{array}
\tag{4.76}
$$

We see that the range is between 18 and 69 years, that the mean age is 39 if we use the median, and 41.7 if we use the arithmetic mean. And we see that the middle 50 percent of respondents are between 31 and 54 years old. What we are particularly interested in in this section, however, is the *number of* ages given. While *table(cp$P02)* provides us with the frequency distribution of the age variable itself (so that we could determine the number of ages mentioned simply by counting), *str(table(cp$P02))* provides us with the information we are looking for in a more compact form (4.77): A total of 52 different ages were given by the respondents.

```
'table' int [1:52(1d)] 4 6 4 7 5 10 7 16 11 12 ...
- attr(*, "dimnames")=List of 1
  ..$ : chr [1:52] "18" "19" "20" "21" ...
```
(4.77)

A large number of different values for a metric variable is actually advantageous, as is the case in the present example of the age variable, and does not necessarily provide a reason to group the values into classes. However, the researcher may want to present the results in a compact form, or conduct an analysis with *grouped* variable values for one reason or another. In this case, the original *codes* of the variable are said to be *recoded*.

We can accomplish this task quite easily using the recoding function from a package that acts as a *Companion to Applied Regression* and is called via 'car'.

```
library(car)                                                    (4.78)
```

We then perform the recoding as described in (4.79). In this example, we used the general rule of linking the function to the package it originates from using a double colon.

```
cp$agegroup <- car::recode(cp$P02,
                    recodes ='18:24=1;
                             25:29=2;
                             30:39=3;                            (4.79)
                             40:49=4;
                             50:59=5;
                             60:70=6')
```

Alternatively, we could have used a function from base R, for which we do not need the package (i. e., the library) 'car' at all, but is a little more complex to program: the *ifelse()* function.

The *ifelse()* function assigns a value to a target variable if one condition is met, and another otherwise. Example: If a certain condition is met, the target receives a 1; otherwise ("else"), a 0. If only a single condition needs to be formulated, a single *ifelse()* statement is sufficient. For multiple related conditions, the value that would specify the "else" component is replaced by another *ifelse()* statement. This applies to all conditions except the last one, since then a remaining set can actually be addressed. This creates a nested structure of *ifelse()* statements, as can be seen for our age example in (4.80). To specify conditions, we use operators that perform comparisons. We have briefly discussed such operators in the context of Table 4.1 and "logical vectors".

In (4.80), the target variable is named *cp$agroup*. Since we want to group the individual values into six age groups, we need five *ifelse()* statements. In each row in (4.80), the inner brackets specify the condition (with the two sub-conditions linked together by the logical "and"), and after the comma, the value to be assigned to the target variable. Only the last row is assigned *two* values: 5 if the condition of this row is true, and 6 otherwise. The 6 is thus assigned to all age values that are not covered by any of the five explicit assignments—in our example, this creates the oldest group.

```
cp$agroup <-
  ifelse( (cp$P02 <= 24), 1,
    ifelse( (cp$P02 >= 25 & cp$P02 <= 29), 2,
      ifelse( (cp$P02 >= 30 & cp$P02 <= 39), 3,
        ifelse( (cp$P02 >= 40 & cp$P02 <= 49), 4,
          ifelse( (cp$P02 >= 50 & cp$P02 <= 59), 5, 6)))))
```
(4.80)

(4.79) and (4.80) produce an identical output (4.81).

```
> addmargins(table(cp$agegroup))
   1    2    3    4    5    6  Sum
  43   57  126   78   88   59  451

> addmargins(table(cp$agroup))
   1    2    3    4    5    6  Sum
  43   57  126   78   88   59  451
```
(4.81)

A characteristic of the recoding of the frequency distribution in (4.79) is that the resulting groups represent intervals of varying lengths. The first age group consists of 18– to 24–year-olds (each including) and thus covers 7 years; the second age group covers five years, the third 10 years, and so on. Another approach could have been to create age intervals of equal length. R includes the *cut()* function for this type of task. To illustrate this with an example, we create variable *cp$ag*.

```
cp$ag <- cut(cp$P02, 6)
```
(4.82)

R automatically created a factor consisting of six levels, i. e. the six age classes. In R, a *factor* is a data type for categorical variables (not a factor in the statistical sense of factor analysis). In response to *str(cp$ag)* we get the following information:

```
Factor w/ 6 levels "(17.9,26.5]",..: 1 1 1 1 1 6 5 4 3 4 . . .
```
(4.83)

We calculate the frequency table of this factor by (4.84),

```
table(cp$ag)
```
(4.84)

and obtain in response to this output (4.85)

$$
\begin{array}{cccccc}
\texttt{(17.9,26.5]} & \texttt{(26.5,35]} & \texttt{(35,43.5]} & \texttt{(43.5,52]} & \texttt{(52,60.5]} & \texttt{(60.5,69.1]} \\
70 & 111 & 77 & 70 & 73 & 50
\end{array}
\tag{4.85}
$$

The sequence (] as opening and closing brackets means, described here using the example of the first age group: older than 17.9 up to and including 26.5 years. We obtain age intervals of 8.5 years each, in the youngest and oldest groups it is 8.6 years.

In the *ifelse()* statements of (4.80), we have linked the two sub-conditions within the inner parentheses with a logical "and" using the & symbol. How a link with a logical "or" works using the | symbol is illustrated in (4.86) for another data example. For this purpose, we draw on the variable DQ03 outlined above, which dealt with the "NIMBY" (Not in My Backyard) phenomenon in the case of wind turbines. The response format provided for four graded answer options, two of which were semantically introduced with "yes, . . ." and two with "no, . . ."

```
cp$nimby <-
  ifelse( (cp$DQ03 == 1 | cp$DQ03 == 2), 1,                    (4.86)
    ifelse ( (cp$DQ03 == 3 | cp$DQ03 == 4), -1, 0))
```

We might now consider combining the two yes and two no answer options. In (4.86), we do this and assign the values 1 (for "accept") and -1 (for "not accept") to the outcome variable. This leaves the fifth category, "don't know., can't say". Regarding this category, we could make the auxiliary assumption that it expresses something like ambivalence or uncertainty, in contrast to the definitive response tendencies toward yes or no. If—and only if—this assumption were considered tenable, we could consider this category as a middle category between 1 and -1, and assign it the value 0. The assignment of 1, 0, and -1 in (4.86) would remain syntactically correct even if we were to reject this auxiliary assumption; however, the assigned numerical sequence of 1, 0, and -1 would then not be able to be attributed the meaning just outlined. There would then simply be three response categories, whose meaning would have to be determined differently by the researcher.

```
> addmargins(table(cp$DQ03))
 1    2    3   4   5  Sum
62  154  127  50  57  450
> addmargins(table(cp$nimby))                                  (4.87)

 -1    0    1  Sum
177   57  216  450
```

(4.87) then allows the comparison of the frequency distributions of the initial variable and the outcome variable (where we already know the distribution of DQ03 from (4.12)). Another point deserves special attention. A look at the sums in (4.87) shows that (4.86) with its two ifelse() statements refers to 450 units. However, the data frame contains a total of 451 units. This means that we have one respondent having an NA in the variable that is automatically excluded from the variable transformation. Stated otherwise, *ifelse()* doesn't collect such NAs in the final residual category (i. e., the 0 in the present example).

This is different from the case where we want to explicitly declare values of a variable as missing in order to exclude them from calculations—for example, temporarily for a single statistical analysis. In the present example, we might consider excluding the "don't know" cases from a possible calculation. Although this would be strongly discouraged in the present example (because this alone would exclude around 12.7% of the units), it could technically be easily implemented using an *ifelse()* statement such as (4.88).

```
cp$nimby2 <-
  ifelse( (cp$DQ03 == 1 | cp$DQ03 == 2), 1,                        (4.88)
    ifelse ( (cp$DQ03 == 3 | cp$DQ03 == 4), -1, NA))
```

4.7 Creating Subsets with subset() and sample()

We load the data frame *cp* and make a systematic selection of units, i. e., a selection of rows from the data frame. In (4.89), for example, this is the condition that the variable *P01* must have the value *1*, i. e., that the respondent must be male.

```
load("cp.Rdata")
sset <- subset(cp, P01 == 1)                                        (4.89)
```

While after loading *cp* into the global environment, we can see in the upper right window of our R Studio interface that *cp* consists of "451 obs. of 9 variables," we now see in the line below that *sset* consists of "213 obs. of 9 variables." These are the 213 males in the dataset (compare, for example, the frequency distribution in 4.6). *sset* is a freely chosen object name for the creation of this subset of *cp*. It should also be noted that the condition *P01 = = 1* is just a simple example of such a condition. The *subset()* function is just another function for which we have a variety of operators available to perform logical comparisons. We discussed the topic of operators and logical vectors above in the context of Table 4.1. We can also combine different sub-conditions using the logical "and" or "or" clauses, thus defining quite complex conditions.

The *subset()* function is used not only to select from the *rows* of the data frame, but also from its *columns*, i. e., from the variables available in the data frame. The *select* option is used for this purpose. For example, we could have extended the *subset()* line in (4.89) with such a *select* instruction.

```
sset <- subset(cp, P01 == 1, select=c(DQ11_1, DQ11_2, DQ11_3))          (4.90)
```

And would then read in the "Global Environment", i. e. the upper right window in the R Studio Interface, that *sset* contains of "213 obs. of 3 variables". The option to create subsets of variables using *subset()* can be advantageous in data analysis for two reasons. First, some statistical functions in R expect the set of variables to be processed in a function to be fixed *before*. Secondly, by limiting the set of variables to exactly the subset of variables that is actually needed in a subsequent statistical calculation, the subset of units that have NAs (missing values) in the variables in question can be easily excluded. While statistical functions themselves also offer the function of handling NAs, their prior control may nevertheless be necessary, for example, in calculations that have to bridge subsets, for example a training and test data set.

```
sset <- subset(cp, select=c(VQ01, P02))
sset <- na.omit(sset)
```
(4.91)

First, we exemplify how NAs can be handled: The first instruction in (4.91) limits the variables to the two we want to include in a subsequent regression analysis. Next, we apply the *na.omit()* function to this subset. In this example, this excludes four units with missing values in the variables involved. *sset* now consists of "447 obs. of 2 variables", as we learn from the corresponding entry in the Global Environment of the R Studio Interface.

```
set.seed(123)
tr <- sample(447, 313, replace=FALSE)
```
(4.92)

The exclusion of cases with missing values can only be a suboptimal solution, but seems justified[20] if, as in this case, only very few units are lost. For a random split between training and test data, we next realize a simple random selection of about 70% of the 447 respondents, without replacement of a unit once drawn, using the *sample()* function. This *sample()* function is preceded with the *set.seed()* function in order to set a seed for the random number generator. This makes it possible to reproduce the result of an analysis when it is repeated. "seed" is a freely chosen single value, interpreted as an integer.

```
summary(trainmodel <- glm(VQ01 ~ P02,
family=gaussian(),data=sset, subset=tr))
mean((sset$VQ01-predict(trainmodel, sset))[-tr]^2)
```
(4.93)

---

[20] Otherwise, other techniques for handling missing data must be used. We discussed this topic in Chapter 2.

The training data consists of 313 units and is assigned to the object named *tr* in (4.92). We then access the remaining set, i. e., the test data, simply by prefixing it with a minus sign, i. e., *-tr*. We can derive practical benefits from this, for example, in the context of regression analyses. For example, by relating the values of a target variable *as predicted in the training data set* to the values *observed* for the variable *in the test data set*. This can be used to calculate, for example, the mean squared error or the explained variance. (4.93) illustrates this with respect to the MSE. (4.93) is an example of the *glm()* function with its options to specify both *data* and *subset*. (4.93) also takes advantage of the *predict()* function. We explain the details of proceeding this way in the context of an analysis in section 7.2.

4.8 Statistical Calculations with Weighted Units

From Chapter 2, we know that estimates from random samples can be biased by non-response, so it may be necessary to compensate for these biases by weighting the units of analysis. It may also be the case that the survey design itself requires a weighting of units. This topic thus encompasses both design and nonresponse weights. Calculating with "weighted units" then practically only means that these units, for example, respondents with their data, are not included in the calculation of statistical formulas with the standard weight of 1, but rather with a weight that differs from this for each individual.

Working with weighted frequency distributions in R isn't a major hurdle, because many of the functions we use for statistical calculations include a weighting option. We can also rely on a *survey* package that greatly simplifies weighting. However, this requires that a suitable weighting variable has been developed beforehand for the dataset being analyzed. While such weighting variables are included in the datasets of large social science studies such as the European Social Survey or the Eurobarometer studies, a researcher must develop the weighting variables themselves if they want to conduct their own study using their own data. However, describing *how to construct* such a weighting variable would go well beyond the intended scope of this section. Instead, we will limit ourselves to a simple application, which consists in showing how we can work with weighted units *using an existing weighting* variable.

For this purpose, we again use Example Data Set 7 on Views & Insights on Climate Policy and refer to three of the variables shown in Figure 4.3 above, DQ11_1 to DQ11_3. First, we load the data frame[21] and the *survey* package. This library contains a variety

---

21 Above, we created and used a small selection of variables from this dataset, as shown in Figure 4.3. Since the resulting data frame *cp* does not contain the weight variable we now need, we will use Example Dataset 7 itself for the data analysis in this section.

of relevant functions, of which we will only use the weighting function here. The process is two-step: first, we specify the sampling design via *svydesign()* to reference it in subsequent calculations.

```
load("klimapolitik1.Rdata")
library(survey)
design <- survey::svydesign(ids = ~1, weights=~kpo$wg,
                           data = kpo)
addmargins(frq <- survey::svytable(~kpo$DQ11_1, design,
                                   round=TRUE))
```
(4.94)

We see the relevant part of the R script in (4.94). First, the *svydesign()* function is used. This function allows you to specify the sampling design more comprehensively than we do here. For example, you can specify strata, cluster sampling probabilities, a correction for finite populations, or, as in this example, sampling weights. In (4.94), *ids = ~1* means that we have no clusters here, names the weighting variable and the data frame. The resulting object is assigned the freely chosen name *design* for later reference.

The *survey* library provides a whole range of statistical functions for this purpose, of which we will use the *svytable()* function here. It's linked to the *survey* library via the double colon and is used here to calculate the weighted frequency distribution for variable *DQ11_1*. *design* establishes the connection to *svydesign()* and *round* indicates that we want to round the frequencies to whole numbers. Otherwise, the frequencies can also be fractional numbers due to weighting. The result is assigned to the object name *frq* so that it can be addressed in a subsequent calculation. Finally, we embed the expression in *addmargins()* to get also the marginal frequencies displayed. The result, the weighted frequency distribution of DQ11_1, is then shown in (4.95) .

```
kpo$DQ11_1
  1    2    3   4   5   6   7   8   9   Sum
140  115  53  49  12  35  23   6  10   443
```
(4.95)

As shown above, we can obtain a compact representation of a frequency distribution using a small sequence of instructions, as is the case here.

```
tb <- as.data.frame(frq)
tb$perc <- round(100 * (tb$Freq/sum(tb$Freq)), 1)
tb$cumperc <- cumsum(tb$perc)
tb
```
(4.96)

Thus, (4.96) produces the output in (4.97), where the meaning of the codes becomes clear from (4.98).

kpo.DQ11_1		Freq	perc	cumperc
1	1	140	31.6	31.6
2	2	115	26.0	57.6
3	3	53	12.0	69.6
4	4	49	11.1	80.7
5	5	12	2.7	83.4
6	6	35	7.9	91.3
7	7	23	5.2	96.5
8	8	6	1.4	97.9
9	9	10	2.3	100.2

$$(4.97)$$

Weighting frequency distributions is not limited to univariate distributions; we can also apply it to any bivariate and multivariate frequency distributions.

4.9 Multiple Responses and Rankings

Survey questions can be designed to allow multiple responses. In this case, each possible answer becomes a separate variable in the data matrix, which is then binary coded to indicate whether a respondent chose it or not.

A similar data structure arises when respondents are asked to rank their preferences. Only that the answers to be given are no longer independent of each other. The question underlying Q11 is an example of this. The question was formulated as follows: "Which sources should Germany use to meet its energy needs in the future? Please list your three to five favorites in the desired order." Accordingly, we have a survey question here that not only allows multiple answers, but actually implies them. This is because the question only makes sense if respondents name their favorites, which they would like to rank *first, second, and third*, etc. These favorites had to be selected from the following set of options (in the dataset with the assigned numeric codes as shown in (4.98).

1 Wind power
2 Solar power
3 Hydropower
4 Nuclear power
5 Coal $\qquad$ (4.98)
6 Natural gas
7 Biomass
8 Crude oil
9 Wood

If a survey question allows or implies multiple answers, each such answer becomes a separate variable. If, as in this example, we want to consider which energy source was ranked first, second and third by a respondent, we need a variable for the first rank, a variable for the second place and a variable for the third place. A total of three columns are therefore required in the data frame. Here, these are *DQ11_1* (1st rank), *DQ11_2* (2nd place) and *DQ11_3* (3rd place). Consequently, we can look at *three* univariate frequency distributions (reported in (4.97) and (4.99), the latter produced as part of (4.100)).

```
> addmargins(survey::svytable(~kpo$DQ11_2, design,
+                             round=TRUE))
kpo$DQ11_2
  1   2   3  4  5  6  7  8  9 Sum
112 128  72 13 13 37 33 19 10 437
> addmargins(survey::svytable(~kpo$DQ11_3, design,
+                             round=TRUE))
kpo$DQ11_3
 1  2   3  4  5  6  7  8  9 Sum
64 85 141 23 13 26 47 16 18 433
```

(4.99)

However, these would then be three *uni*variate distributions, each showing how the preference for various energy sources is distributed in the sample when distinguishing between first, second, and third choices. However, the first, second, and third choices cannot be made independently of each other, since the selection is made without replacement of an element once drawn: If an energy source is placed on rank 1, it is no longer available for places 2 and 3, and so on. Consequently, it makes more sense to look at the *individual combinations* of these preferences for ranks 1, 2, and 3.

```
load("klimapolitik1.Rdata")
library(survey)
design <- survey::svydesign(ids = ~1, weights=~kpo$wg,
                            data = kpo)
addmargins(survey::svytable(~kpo$DQ11_2, design,
                   round=TRUE))
addmargins(survey::svytable(~kpo$DQ11_3, design,
                   round=TRUE))
addmargins(top123 <- survey::svytable(~kpo$DQ11_1
                       +kpo$DQ11_2
                       +kpo$DQ11_3,
                       design,
                       addNA=TRUE,
                       round=TRUE))
```

(4.100)

(4.100) yields the configurations in the typical form of cross tabulating the 1st and 2nd variable separately for the values of the 3rd variable. Since each of these variables has nine answer options plus an NA category (the latter considered by the *addNA* option in *svytable()*), this creates ten single tables, each with $10 \cdot 10 = 100$ cells for the frequencies of the value combinations. Using (4.101), we therefore transform these 10 individual tables into a more compact form by transforming the table object *top123* into a data frame. This data frame has the structure partially outlined in Table 4.2. Each row represents one of the possible value combinations of DQ11_1, DQ11_2, and DQ11_3 (including NAs) and shows the weighted frequencies as absolute frequencies (*Freq*), relative frequencies (*perc*), and cumulative relative frequencies (*cumperc*) for each of these combinations. The column with the cumulative frequencies is of only marginal importance and is only included here because it gives an intuitive impression that once 100% has been reached, all configurations are included. In total, this data frame consists of 1,000 rows, many of which, however, have a frequency of zero.

```
tb <- as.data.frame(top123)
tbs <- subset(tb, Freq > 0)
tbs$perc <- round(100 * (tbs$Freq/sum(tbs$Freq)), 2)                    (4.101)
tbs$cumperc <- cumsum(tbs$perc)
tbs
```

We therefore limit this frame to all combinations that have empirically occurred *at least once* using the *subset()* function in (4.101). This reduces the table to 144 rows, the first and last of which are shown[22] in Table 4.2. Since a small number of respondents indicated only two, one, or no preferences, a few *NAs* are included at the bottom of the table.

Table 4.2: Individual Value Combinations and Their Frequencies.

Line		R Output					
		kpo.DQ11_1	kpo.DQ11_2	kpo.DQ11_3	Freq	perc	cumperc
1							
2	13	3	2	1	13	2.84	2.84
3	14	4	2	1	7	1.53	4.37
4	16	6	2	1	4	0.88	5.25
5	17	7	2	1	4	0.88	6.13
6	22	2	3	1	12	2.63	8.76
7							
8	.	.	.	.	.	.	.

---

[22] Just as a side note, the row numbers on the far left were taken over from the parent data frame, and therefore the numbers of those rows that were excluded by the subset() statement are now missing.

Table 4.2 (continued)

Line				R Output				
9	•	•	•	•	•	•		•
10	•	•	•	•	•	•		•
11								
12	864	4	7	9	1	0.22		95.61
13	871	1	8	9	1	0.22		95.83
14	876	6	8	9	2	0.44		96.27
15	911	1	2	< NA >	1	0.22		96.49
16	927	7	3	< NA >	2	0.44		96.93
17	993	3	< NA >	< NA >	1	0.22		97.15
18	995	5	< NA >	< NA >	2	0.44		97.59
19	998	8	< NA >	< NA >	2	0.44		98.03
20	999	9	< NA >	< NA >	2	0.44		98.47
21	1000	< NA >	< NA >	< NA >	8	1.75		100.22

We can now examine this table to determine how frequently each specific combination of energy sources was chosen. To make this task a little easier, we sort the table in descending order of this frequency using the *arrange()* function from the *tidyverse* metapackage (4.102). Our attention is focused on the columns *Freq* and *perc*. At the same time, the column with the cumulative frequencies (*cumperc*) has lost its function *with the sorting* and should be completely ignored here.

```
library(tidyverse)
as_tibble(tbs)                                                        (4.102)
arrange(tbs, desc(Freq))
```

The first ten rows of this rearranged table are shown in Table 4.3. We see that the most common combination is that energy source 2 (solar energy) is ranked first, energy source 1 (wind energy) is ranked second, and energy source 3 (hydropower) is ranked third. This combination is chosen 56 times, or in 12.25 percent of all combinations. The combinations listed below that first row also refer to these three sources—in different orders—and underscore their popularity. Another energy source, namely biomass (code 7), only appears in seventh and eighth place in the combinations sorted by frequency.

Table 4.3: Rearranged Frequency Table.

Line		R Output					
1		kpo.DQ11_1	kpo.DQ11_2	kpo.DQ11_3	Freq	perc	cumperc
2	1	2	1	3	56	12.25	45.13
3	2	1	2	3	53	11.60	58.27
4	3	1	3	2	29	6.35	25.64
5	4	3	1	2	14	3.06	16.88

Table 4.3 (continued)

Line					R Output		
6	5	3	2	1	13	2.84	2.84
7	6	2	3	1	12	2.63	8.76
8	7	1	2	7	11	2.41	82.86
9	8	2	1	7	8	1.75	79.79
10	9	< NA >	< NA >	< NA >	8	1.75	100.22
11	10	4	2	1	7	1.53	4.37

This outlines a possible path we can take to determine the frequency or probability with which such preference orders occur *empirically*. Although the following step is not required, it can be useful for benchmarking these empirical values with theoretical values. Combinatorics provides a possible reference for this.

To do this, we determine the number of ways for forming subsets of 3 from a set of 9, taking the selection order into account. We can calculate this by the number of permutations that can be formed by selecting r objects from a set of n objects, with n and r being positive integers and $r \leq n$ (Hagle 1995: 19; Kühnel and Krebs 2006: 140–141). In factorial notation, the formula may be written as

$$V = \frac{n!}{(n-r)!} \tag{4.103}$$

The formula calculates the number of ways to select r from n elements without replacement, taking selection order into account, with each of these ways having the same probability of $1/V$. In this example, these are

$$\frac{9!}{(9-3)!} = 504 \tag{4.104}$$

ways, each with a probability of $1/504 = 0.002$. If we use this *a priori* probability as a benchmark, it becomes clear that the empirical probabilities found above are significantly higher than this point of reference.

4.10 Data Frame and Tibble

In Section 4.5.2, we discussed the difference between the formats of a matrix and a data frame. Here, we'll show how a data frame can be transformed into a "tibble." To do this, we'll first create a data frame, but this time not by importing data from Excel or Stata (as shown above in Section 4.2), but using the *c()* and *cbind()* functions already familiar from Section 4.5.3. But this is just to demonstrate this method of creating a data frame. Regardless of which of these methods a data frame was created by, it can be transformed into a tibble.

Table 4.4: R Script to Build a Data Frame and Tibble.

Line	R Script
1	`KKS <- c(128, 118,  51,  91, 92, 123, 129,`
2	`        82,  91, 111, 104, 66,  64,  71,`
3	`       190,  97,  81, 261, 69, 100, 130,`
4	`        71,  78,  65, 120, 87,  71)`
5	`EPclimate <- c(12.9, 18.6,  2.1,  2.6,  7.2, 17.0,`
6	`              25.6, 11.5,  5.6, 15.2, 12.4,  3.4,`
7	`               4.5,  5.4, 19.5,  3.1,  7.4, 20.0,`
8	`               3.5, 13.8, 25.0,  5.2, 11.5,  3.6,`
9	`              25.5,  8.9,  8.0)`
10	`public <- c(39.6, 49.3, 33.8, 56.1, 33.4, 62.4, 62.9,`
11	`            39.8, 49.8, 59.8, 56.5, 51.3, 32.6, 29.7,`
12	`            50.0, 51.0, 40.0, 57.8, 33.4, 33.7, 77.5,`
13	`            31.3, 45.6, 19.0, 71.7, 47.7, 31.4)`
14	`df <- data.frame(cbind(KKS, EPclimate, public))`
15	`cntry <- c("AT", "BE", "BG", "CY", "CZ",`
16	`           "DE", "DK", "EE", "ES", "FI",`
17	`           "FR", "GR", "HR", "HU", "IE",`
18	`           "IT", "LT", "LU", "LV", "MT",`
19	`           "NL", "PL", "PT", "RO", "SE",`
20	`           "SI", "SK")`
21	`eudata <- cbind(df, cntry)`
22	`library(tidyverse)`
23	`eu <- as_tibble(eudata)`
24	`eudata`
25	`eu`
26	`save(eudata, file = "eudata.Rdata")`
27	`save(eu, file = "eu.Rdata")`

Lines are explained in the accompanying text

To illustrate this with an example, we use a small selection of variables from Example Data Set 6 on Energy Transition in the European Green Deal. This selection involves three of its variables: a country's purchasing power standard (KKS), the percentage of people who support political regulation of AI interventions (public), and the percentage that would like to see action against climate change prioritized by the European Parliament (EPclimate).

The R script used for this purpose can be seen in Table 4.4. First, three numeric vectors are created for the variables *KKS*, *EPclimate*, and *public* and bound to the data frame *df* using *cbind()* within *data.frame()*. We then create a character vector for the variable with the identifiers of the 27 participating countries. We add this vector to the data frame *df* and assign the name *eudata* to this extended data frame. (4.105) shows the structure of this data frame for the first ten of these 27 units.

```
> eudata
   KKS EPclimate public cntry
1  128       12.9    39.6    AT
2  118       18.6    49.3    BE
3   51        2.1    33.8    BG
4   91        2.6    56.1    CY
5   92        7.2    33.4    CZ
6  123       17.0    62.4    DE
7  129       25.6    62.9    DK
8   82       11.5    39.8    EE
9   91        5.6    49.8    ES
10 111       15.2    59.8    FI
```

(4.105)

To transform this data frame into a tibble, we call the *tidyverse* library. tidyverse isn't actually an R package, but rather a kind of R *metapackage* consisting of a number of libraries that can also be called individually. We consider Wickham and Grolemund (2017) as a primary reference for information about the structure, libraries, and functions of the tidyverse. Following this source[23], "Tibbles are data frames, but slightly tweaked to work better in the tidyverse" and "There are two main differences in the usage of a tibble versus a classic data.frame: printing and subsetting"

(Wickham and Grolemund 2017: 44, 121). We immediately see one of these two differences when we convert the data frame into a tibble using the *as_tibble()* function (Table 4.4). The same data frame, now defined as a tibble, then appears in the printout as in (4.106).

```
> eu
# A tibble: 27 × 4
    KKS EPclimate public cntry
   <dbl>     <dbl>  <dbl> <chr>
1   128      12.9    39.6 AT
2   118      18.6    49.3 BE
3    51       2.1    33.8 BG
4    91       2.6    56.1 CY
5    92       7.2    33.4 CZ
6   123      17      62.4 DE
7   129      25.6    62.9 DK
8    82      11.5    39.8 EE
```

(4.106)

---

23 To quote another relevant source: "A *tibble* is a modern class of data frame within R, available in the dplyr and tibble packages, that has a convenient print method, will not convert strings to factors, and does not use row names" (Silge and Robinson 2017: 3).

```
9     91      5.6   49.8 ES
10    111     15.2  59.8 FI
# i 17 more rows
# i Use `print(n = . . .)` to see more rows
```

The entries are, of course, the same, but the headers are different. We now directly obtain information about the format of the vectors involved, —information we would otherwise obtain via *str()*. Wickham and Grolemund (2017: 44–45) explain the possible abbreviations, just to mention three of them: *int* stands for integers, *dbl* stands for doubles, or real numbers, and *chr* stands for character vectors, or strings.

Defining a data frame as a tibble opens up the possibility of using alternatives to functions from base R, for example the *subset()* function[24]. We're thinking of the functions *filter()* and *select()*. Furthermore, a tibble can be sorted using *arrange()*. And *mutate()* can be used to create new variables as functions of existing variables, just as we might otherwise do with *ifelse()*.

We would like to outline these options only very briefly here. To illustrate the filter function, we can, for example, take a country's purchasing power standard, the variable *KKS*. This way, we could perhaps be interested in EU countries with particularly high purchasing power standards and subsume all countries whose purchasing power lies above the third quartile of the frequency distribution for KKS. Therefore, we first let R calculate this value using *summary(eu$KKS)*,

```
> summary(eu$KKS)
  Min. 1st Qu.  Median   Mean 3rd Qu.   Max.                    (4.107)
  51.0    71.0    91.0  101.5   119.0  261.0
```

to be able to fix the required numeric value for the *filter()* function

```
(euw <- filter(eu, KKS > 119))                                   (4.108)
```

filter() selects those *rows* of the tibble for which the condition *PKS > 119* applies. These are the seven rows in (4.109). Because we placed the instruction (4.108) in the outer parentheses, the result is displayed immediately in the R console (the lower left window in the R Studio interface), without having to call the object name, in this case *euw*, again in a following line within the R script. This is a general option in R (i. e., not restricted to the tidyverse).

---

[24] These functions belong to the "dplyr Basics" as described by Wickham and Grolemund (2017: 45) in the context of Chapter 3 of their work, where "dplyr" refers to one of the packages from the tidyverse metapackage.

```
# A tibble: 7 × 4
    KKS EPclimate public cntry
  <dbl>     <dbl>  <dbl> <chr>
1   128      12.9   39.6 AT
2   123      17     62.4 DE
3   129      25.6   62.9 DK
4   190      19.5   50   IE
5   261      20     57.8 LU
6   130      25     77.5 NL
7   120      25.5   71.7 SE
```

(4.109)

Just as we can select rows of a tibble, we can also select *columns*, i. e., variables. The *select()* function is provided for this purpose. (4.110) is an example of this.

```
euc <- select(eu, public, cntry)
print(euc, n=3)
```

(4.110)

To get only the first three rows of the tibble instead of the first ten by default, we use the *print()* option shown here. The result is reported in (4.111).

```
# A tibble: 27 × 2
  public cntry
   <dbl> <chr>
1   39.6 AT
2   49.3 BE
3   33.8 BG
# i 24 more rows
# i Use `print(n = . . .)` to see more rows
```

(4.111)

Finally, we would like to demonstrate the *mutate()* function with an example, although here only with a simple calculation.

```
eum <- mutate(eu,
       dev = KKS - mean(KKS))
print(eum, n=3)
```

(4.112)

We see that *mutate()* generates a new variable, here freely named *dev*, and adds it to the tibble as a new column on the far right.

```
# A tibble: 27 × 5
    KKS EPclimate public cntry    dev
  <dbl>     <dbl>   <dbl> <chr> <dbl>
1   128      12.9    39.6 AT     26.5
2   118      18.6    49.3 BE     16.5
3    51       2.1    33.8 BG    -50.5
# i 24 more rows
# i Use `print(n = . . .)` to see more rows
```

(4.113)

This newly generated variable consists of the difference values that result when the arithmetic mean of the frequency distribution of the *KKS* values is subtracted from the individual *KKS* values of a country.

4.11 Convert a Tibble From Wide to Long Format

Options for *modifying* a basic data structure are contained in the *tidyr* library of the tidyverse metapackage. We'll illustrate the *gather()* function from this library. This can be used, for example, to convert a dataset from a wide to a long data format. Such a conversion is relevant, for example, when converting panel data into a form suitable for modeling growth curves, to name just one prominent application scenario[25].

The panel design is characterized by the repeated survey of a random sample of individuals at fixed time intervals. Typically, this design involves a very large initial sample and a questionnaire in which standardized survey variables are repeatedly asked in an unchanged form. This creates a data structure in which the dataset contains the variables from the first wave of the survey first, then the same variables from the second wave, then the same variables from the third wave, and so on. In the following fictitious example, we consider only a single variable and, for simplicity, refer to this variable as *t1*, *t2*, and *t3*, depending on whether the responses to it were collected at the first (t1), second (t2), or third time point (t3).

In order to be able to keep track of the change in the data structure, our example contains only four respondents, to whom we simply assign a consecutive number 1, 2, 3, 4 as an ID. We also replaced the answers, *which actually vary individually*, with fixed values to keep track of whether an answer came from t1, t2, or t3. Thus, in the fictitious tibble, *11* represents an answer from t1, *22* represents an answer from t2, and *33* represents an answer from t3.

---

[25] The conversion of a tibble from wide to long format using *gather()* is also exemplified in section 8.5 and Table 8.7.

```
library(tidyverse)
t1 <- c(11,11,11,11)
t2 <- c(22,22,22,22)
t3 <- c(33,33,33,33)
id <- c(1,2,3,4)
(as_tibble(w <- data.frame(cbind(t1, t2, t3, id))))
```

(4.114)

This way we generate the tibble shown in (4.115) via (4.114). This structure is sometimes referred to as a *wide* format. It is essentially nothing more than the basic form of a data matrix, in which columns represent variables and rows represent units.

```
# A tibble: 4 × 4
      t1     t2     t3     id
   <dbl>  <dbl>  <dbl>  <dbl>
1     11     22     33      1
2     11     22     33      2
3     11     22     33      3
4     11     22     33      4
```

(4.115)

We can now transform this structure into a *long* data format using the *gather()* function. We create this format using (4.116) and see the result in (4.117).

```
ml <- w %>%gather(t1,t2,t3,
                  key = "year", value="obs")
ml
```

(4.116)

The following happened: the t1, t2 and t3 values of a unit, which are next to each other in a row in the wide format, are now arranged one below the other.

```
   id year obs
1   1   t1  11
2   2   t1  11
3   3   t1  11
4   4   t1  11
5   1   t2  22
6   2   t2  22
7   3   t2  22
8   4   t2  22
9   1   t3  33
10  2   t3  33
11  3   t3  33
12  4   t3  33
```

(4.117)

The resulting structure may become even clearer if we reorder the rows of (4.117) using the *arrange()* function in (4.118).

```
arrange(ml, id, year)
```
(4.118)

(4.119) then shows the typical hierarchical data structure as we use it for statistical multilevel analyses, namely here for time-related repeated measurements "within" each unit (person).

```
   id year obs
1   1   t1   11
2   1   t2   22
3   1   t3   33
4   2   t1   11
5   2   t2   22
6   2   t3   33
7   3   t1   11
8   3   t2   22
9   3   t3   33
10  4   t1   11
11  4   t2   22
12  4   t3   33
```
(4.119)

4.12 The Pipe Operator

When programming with R, there can be multiple ways to achieve the same result. Sometimes it's simply a matter of programming style as to which option is preferred, but sometimes a programming option can make the work much easier. The use of the *pipe operator* is certainly an example of both motives. It comes in two versions: as a native pipe (Kuhn and Silge 2022: 21) and within the tidyverse as part of the *magrittr* package (Wickham and Grolemund 2017: 261–266). As an example, we use the selection of variables from Example Data Set 7 on Views & Insights on Climate Policy, with which we started this chapter.

```
load("cp.Rdata")
(sset1 <- na.omit(subset(cp, P01 == 1,
              select=c(VQ01, P02)))))
```
(4.120)

After data frame *cp* is loaded, (4.120) should accomplish two things: First, select a set of rows (*P01 == 1*) and simultaneously a set of columns (*VQ01, P02*) from this data frame. To do this, the *subset()* function is used. Second, the *na.omit()* function is applied to this subset to exclude units with missing values in the two selected variables. To do this, *subset()* is embedded within *na.omit()* —and the expression is resolved from the inside out: first *subset*, then *na.omit*. Assigned to *sset1*, the data frame now consists of "210 obs. of 2 variables"[26], as indicated in the Global Environment, i. e., the upper right window of the R Studio Interface. And by putting the whole expression in the outer brackets, we immediately get an (abbreviated) printout of the resulting date frame in the R console, i. e. in the lower left window of the R Studio interface.

Instead of embedding *subset()* in *na.omit()* and resolving the expression from the inside out, we can also use the native pipe operator | > and append *na.omit()* to *subset()*.

```
(sset2 <- subset(cp, P01 == 1,
            select=c(VQ01, P02))|>na.omit())
```
(4.121)

As Kuhn and Silge (2022: 21) explain, the "pipe operator substitutes the value of the left-hand side of the operator as the first argument to the right-hand side". Alternatively, we could have called the *tidyverse* library and used the pipe operator % >% instead of | > .

```
load("cp.Rdata")
m <- lm(VQ01 ~ P02, data = cp)
f <- m$fitted.values
s <- summary(f)
s
```
(4.122)

Another example: Suppose we want to calculate and print the descriptive statistics of the *predicted values* of a linear regression. We can do this via a cascade of intermediate objects (as shown in (4.122)) or by directly nesting the functions within each other[27] (as shown in 4.123)).

```
summary(fitted.values(lm(VQ01 ~ P02, data = cp)))
```
(4.123)

The result would be the same (4.124).

---

26 Subset() itself reduces the data frame to 213 units ("observations"), of which three respondents have missing values in the two variables.
27 Instead of *fitted.values* we could also have used the *predict()* function, for example: *mean(predict (lm(VQ01 ~ P02, data = cp)))* may also be obtained via *library(magrittr); lm(VQ01 ~ P02, data = cp)% >% predict()% >%mean()*

```
Min. 1st Qu. Median Mean 3rd Qu.  Max.
5.839  5.897  5.936  5.949   6.006  6.076
```
(4.124)

We could extend the nesting even further, for example, to round the entries in *summary()* to 2 decimal places.

```
round(summary(fitted.values(lm(VQ01 ~ P02,
                  data = cp))), 2)
```
(4.125)

The result would then look like (4.126).

```
Min.  1st Qu.  Median  Mean  3rd Qu.  Max.
5.84    5.90    5.94  5.95    6.01  6.08
```
(4.126)

While the piped version of the nested structure of functions would look like

```
lm(VQ01 ~ P02, data = cp)|>
   fitted.values()|>summary()|>round(2)
```
(4.127)

Here too we could use the % >% pipe operator instead of the native | > pipe operator, but we would have to call either the *magrittr* library or the *tidyverse* metapackage.

```
library(magrittr)
lm(VQ01 ~ P02, data = cp)%>%
   fitted.values()%>%summary()%>%round(2)
```
(4.128)

4.13 Tidy Text Format

Following Hadley Wickham, Silge and Robinson (2017: 1) characterize tidy data as follows: "tidy data has a specific structure: each variable is a column, each observation is a row, each type of observational unit is a table. We thus define the tidy text format as being *a table with one token per row*." The two authors developed the *tidytext* package for such a data structure. The *tidy text format* is just one possible data structure for analyzing textual data. Another common format is the document-term matrix, which we introduce in Chapter 13. There, we also introduce some basics and options for collecting and analyzing textual data. Here we limit ourselves to a brief sketch of how to create a tibble with text in the tidy text format, following Silge and Robinson (2017: 2 – 4).

A fictitious survey asked about future scenarios. The researchers wanted to know how artificial intelligence (AI) will change the world. They posed an open-ended question and received, among other things, the following three answers:

```
text <- c("AI will be more creative than human intelligence",
          "Robots will replace nurses in care",                        (4.129)
          "People will trust AI more than their own abilities")
```

(4.129) is a character vector, which we will next convert into a data frame. We will stay in the *tidyverse* and use the *dplyr* library.

```
library(dplyr)
wide <- tibble(line=1:3, text=text)                                    (4.130)
wide
```

The result is a tibble with three rows, one for each respondent, and two columns. While the first column simply numbers the rows from 1 to 3, thus easily providing a participant ID, the second column contains the sentences with which the three respondents answered the survey question (4.131).

```
# A tibble: 3 × 2
   line text
  <int> <chr>
1     1 AI will be more creative than human intelligence               (4.131)
2     2 Robots will replace nurses in care
3     3 People will trust AI more than their own abilities
```

We now have a tibble in the basic form of the "wide" data format. We will now convert this into the "long" format, as we know it from multilevel analysis and demonstrated in Section 4.11 using the "panel data" example and *gather()*. Here, we use the *unnest_tokens()* function from the *tidytext* package for it.

```
library(tidytext)
long <- wide%>%
   unnest_tokens(word, text)                                           (4.132)
print(long,n=15)
```

The result is a tibble that now consists of 23 rows, because the three answers together consist of 23 words (4.133).

```
# A tibble: 23 × 2
    line word
    <int> <chr>
1       1 ai
2       1 will
3       1 be
4       1 more
5       1 creative
6       1 than
7       1 human
8       1 intelligence                                          (4.133)
9       2 robots
10      2 will
11      2 replace
12      2 nurses
13      2 in
14      2 care
15      3 people
# i 8 more rows
# i Use `print(n = . . .)` to see more rows
```

These 23 words are now arranged one below the other in a column and are all lower-case to facilitate analysis. Which word belongs to which answer, i. e., to which respondent, is simultaneously preserved by the information in the other column. Translated into the terminology of multilevel statistical analysis, the assigned values 1, 2, and 3 would now function as Level 2 IDs.

The example demonstrates the default setting for *tokenization* in *unnest_tokens()* in that each original row is split so that each row contains only one word (Silge and Robinson 2017: 4). This structure could now be used, for example, to count word frequencies. Though in conjunction with additional functions, more complex analyses, such as sentiment analysis, are also possible. Furthermore, there is the option to convert the tidy text format to other data formats and back. In this textbook, we have devoted Chapter 13 to methods for collecting and analyzing textual data.

Chapter 5
R Graphics

5.1 R's Plot() Function

Murrell (2011: 26) describes the *plot()* function as an important high-level function, which in many cases represents the simplest way to generate a complete plot in R. It also includes a wide variety of graphic design options.

plot() is a generic function. This means that when applied to the same data, it can easily create different types of graphs. This also means that different data types can generate different types of graphs (Murrell 2011: 27). For example, for visualizing characteristics of univariate, bivariate, and multivariate frequency distributions. Another data type concerns predictive modeling, which involves generating diagnostic plots for such models.

We will make extensive use of the possibilities offered by R's graphics library in the chapters of this textbook. Since these chapters focus on *statistical* topics—rather than on how a graph is created with R—we will focus here on R's graphics library itself. Given the wide variety of options offered by this library,[1] it is inevitable that we will only be able to present a selection of these options here. To this end, we focus on plots for exploratory, predictive, and diagnostic data analysis.

When using R via the R Studio interface, the instructions required to create a graph can be entered in an R script (upper left window) or via the R console prompt (lower left window), while the resulting graph is displayed in the lower right window of this interface. While it is possible to save the graph in this *Plots* window to a file, the options are quite limited. Furthermore, the appearance of the graph depends heavily on the variable size of this Plots window, which impairs the exact reproducibility of a graph. Therefore, more precise control over the appearance of the graph seems advisable. This is possible by controlling the graphics device.

In the words of Murrell (2011: 306), "In R's terminology, graphical output is directed to a particular *graphics device*." [. . .] "Graphics formats that R supports and the functions that open an appropriate graphics device" include *vector* formats, such as "PDF, PostScript, and SVG", while examples of *raster* formats "are PNG, JPEG, TIFF, and all screen devices" (Murrell 2011: 308–309). In the present textbook usually the file-based *tiff()* format is used, with *dev.off()* to close the device.

---

1 Murrell (2011: 25–115) is an excellent reference to *R*'s Traditional Graphics Model, including its simple usage as well as its customizing.

https://doi.org/10.1515/9783110680683-005

5.2 Exploratory Graphs

5.2.1 Distributional Shape, Mean Values and Dispersion

We start with data from Example Data Set 1 (PPSM Innovation Panel). Among other things, we asked respondents to rate their standard of living on a scale whose poles they could determine themselves. One pole represented the best possible standard of living and the other the worst possible standard of living, as the respondents themselves imagined it. The question wording was as follows: "I would now like you to imagine a ladder with 11 rungs. The top rung, 11, represents the best possible standard of living, as you would wish for it. And the bottom rung, 1, represents the standard of living that would be the worst for you. When you think about your current standard of living, which rung would you place it on?" This scale followed:

On ladder rung	11
	10
	9
	8
	7
	6
	5
	4
	3
	2
On ladder rung	1

We determine the absolute and relative frequencies of this distribution in the same way as shown in Chapter 4, using the *table()* and *prop.table()* functions (5.1), and obtain the results shown in (5.2).[2] The two graphics in Figure 5.1 then serve to visualize the shape, mean values and dispersion of the distribution.

```
load("ls.Rdata")
addmargins(table(ls$LS11))                                          (5.1)
round(100 * prop.table(table(ls$LS11)), digits=1)
```

This produces this output (absolute and relative frequencies):

1	2	3	4	5	6	7	8	9	10	11	Sum
38	38	124	222	482	705	731	885	550	183	93	4051

(5.2)

1	2	3	4	5	6	7	8	9	10	11
0.9	0.9	3.1	5.5	11.9	17.4	18.0	21.8	13.6	4.5	2.3

---

2 This subsection supplements Section 4.4 on univariate frequency distributions.

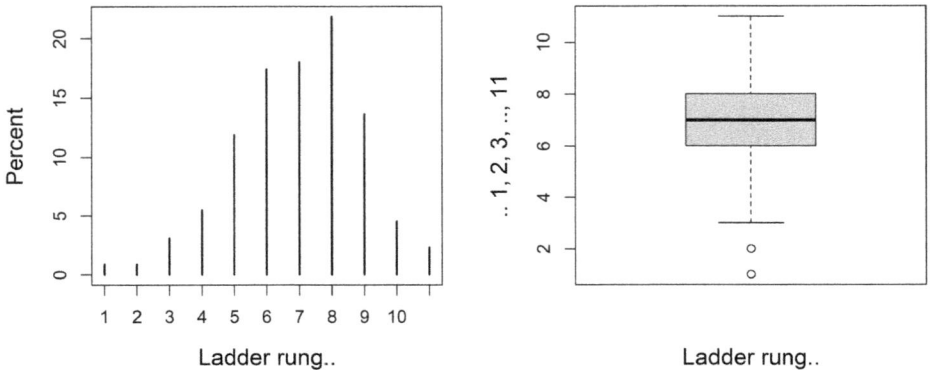

Figure 5.1: Two Plots of a Univariate Distribution.

Table 5.1: Script to Figure 5.1 Two Plots of a Univariate Distribution.

Line	R Script
1	`load("ls.Rdata")`
2	`tiff("fig51.tiff", units = "in", width = 9,`
3	`    height = 4.5, res = 600 )`
4	`par(mfrow = c(1,2))`
5	`plot(round(100 * prop.table(table(ls$LS11)),`
6	`        digits = 1), cex.lab = 1.3,`
7	`    xlab = "Ladder rung..",`
8	`    ylab = "Percent")`
9	`boxplot(ls$LS11, xlab = "Ladder rung..",`
10	`        ylab =".. 1, 2, 3, .., 11",`
11	`        cex.lab = 1.3)`
12	`dev.off()`

Lines explained

Line 1 loads the data frame. Lines 2 and 3 control the graphics device, here using the *.tiff format. The file name, width, height, and nominal resolution (in pixels per inch (ppi)) of the two following graphics are specified within the parentheses. The instructions in lines 2 and 3 refer not only to the following graphic, but to the *two* following graphics, because these two graphics are integrated into a common structure via *par()* in line 4. *par()* can set diverse graphical parameters, here it is used along with *mfrow = c(nr, nc)* to array the two graphics in 1 row and 2 columns. Lines 5 and 6 specify a nested structure of functions, with the *table()* function at the very inside, the *plot()* function at the very outside, and *prop.table()* and *round()* in-between. In lines 7 and 8, *xlab* and *ylab* serve as axis labels whose font size is specified by *cex.lab* in line 6. They can be included, but are not required. Lines 9 to 11 generate the boxplot for the variable *LS11* from data frame *ls*. Here, too, the same options are used for axis labeling. Finally, line 12 shuts down the active graphics device.

We use (5.3) to obtain the usual measures of mean and dispersion values, here for the variable *LS11* from the data frame *ls*, including the option to remove *NA* values from the calculation.

```
mean(ls$LS11, na.rm = TRUE)
sd(ls$LS11, na.rm = TRUE)                                                    (5.3)
summary(ls$LS11, na.rm = TRUE)
```

The *mean()* function computes the arithmetic mean and the *sd() function* the standard deviation. Applied to the distribution of current living standards, we obtain the arithmetic mean value of 6.9 on the scale of 1 to 11 and the standard deviation value of 1.9. As outlined in chapter 4.4., it is then usual to consider the range $\bar{x} \pm 1s$, i. e. the range of the arithmetic mean plus/minus 1 standard deviation. If the frequency distribution were normally distributed, approximately 68% of the living standard assessments would fall into this range, that is in the range from 5.0 to 8.8. From the left graphic in Figure 5.1, we see that the normal distribution assumption probably does not hold. The distribution deviates too significantly from symmetry —especially with regard to the frequency with which rung 8 was chosen— and is instead slightly skewed to the left.[3]

Third, using *summary()*, we obtain the first, second, and third quartiles of the frequency distribution, in addition to the arithmetic mean. These three quartiles are the values that are visualized in the boxplot via the upper and lower edges of the box, as well as the median line displayed within it. This boxplot is shown in the right graphic in Figure 5.1, while (5.4) shows the corresponding output to summary(). There, we also see that the median is slightly above the arithmetic mean (7.0 vs. 6.9). Such a mean < median relationship is typical for distributions skewed to the left, whereas the opposite mean > median relationship can indicate a distribution skewed to the right. However, since the shape of frequency distributions can vary greatly —they can, for example, be single- or multi-peaked, they can be U-shaped instead of bell-shaped, they can be a mixture of both—, it is always safer to look at a plot to get a visual impression of the distributional shape.

```
  Min. 1st Qu.  Median    Mean 3rd Qu.    Max.
 1.000   6.000   7.000   6.915   8.000  11.000                               (5.4)
```

A boxplot provides us with an often preferred alternative to considering mean and standard deviation, even when the scale level is metric and we could therefore calculate both measures. However, distributions can typically be skewed, for example, the

---

3 For example, Agresti and Finlay (2009: 38, 43–45) provide a vivid comparison between bell-shaped and skewed distributions in their chapter on descriptive statistics, and also compare the properties of mean and median.

distribution of monthly income, with significantly more low- and middle-income earn-ers than high-income earners. Then the median, i. e., the 2nd quartile, is often pre-ferred as an indication of the typical value of a distribution, while the range of the middle 50 percent of the values are favored to indicate their typical spread, i. e. de-gree of homogeneity or heterogeneity. In this example, the middle 50 percent of stan-dard-of-living assessments fall in the scale range from 6 to 8.

5.2.2 Scatterplots

We stick with our data example and add as a second variable the answers to a ques-tion that was asked in the interview immediately after the question about the current standard of living: "And when you think about what standard of living you think you would fairly be entitled to, what level would that be?" Followed by the same eleven-point ladder scale as for the current standard of living. We can now examine where respondents see their *current* standard of living and the standard of living they would consider *fair*. A *scatterplot* of the joint (bivariate) frequency distribution of these two variables can be considered as a graphical aid. The result is shown in the left graph in Figure 5.2.

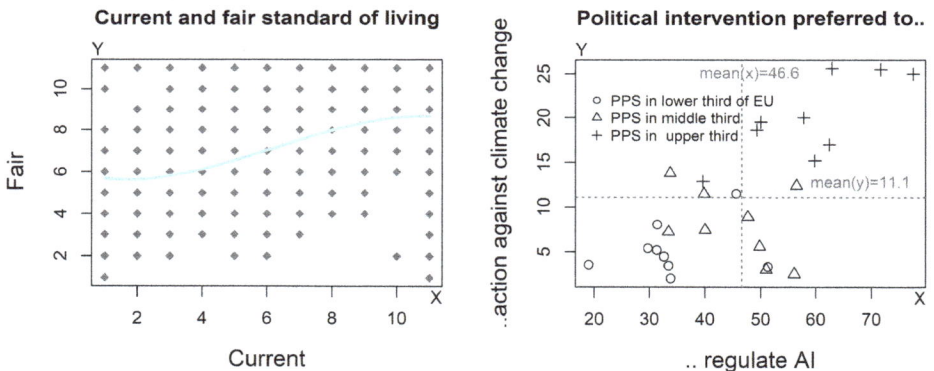

Figure 5.2: Scatterplots With Two and Three Variables.

The image is created as a space made up of $11 \cdot 11 = 121$ possible value combinations. So far, so good. What is remarkable, however, is that this cloud of (x, y) value combi-nations fills almost the entire area, making it difficult to recognize a pattern.

With this, we want to point out that a scattergram is not always helpful, but can even be misleading. In the present example, this is because the cloud of (x, y) value combinations gives the impression at first glance that the two variables are weakly correlated at best, although both variables are in fact quite strongly correlated with each other with r = 0.58. To illustrate this, we calculated a prediction curve and placed it over the cloud. The crucial point is: Without this prediction curve, which here is based on a third-degree polynomial, the plot would only hint at said positive correlation if one is ready to interpret the diagonally running blank areas in the top left and bottom right of the image in this way.

The right scatterplot in Figure 5.2 uses data from Example Data Set 6 on Energy Transition in the European Green Deal. We created this dataset by compiling variables from different sources[4] to characterize the 27 countries of the European Union through aggregate data analysis. Working with such aggregate data has the advantage of being able to easily link the records of data from different sources, but it also has the disadvantage of omitting substantial variation below the country level. This limits the significance of the analysis accordingly.

The scatter plot visualizes the relationship between two population shares of a country: the percentage of those who regard action against climate change as a first priority of the European Parliament[5] and the percentage of those who think that "political intervention" is required to ensure "that artificial intelligence applications are developed ethically"[6]

The cloud of (x, y) combinations in these percentage values runs from the bottom left to the top right in the image and thus suggests a positive relationship between the two population values: the higher one value, the higher the other. We have also included the two reference lines in the diagram to indicate the arithmetic means of the two frequency distributions. The resulting four quadrants can be used to clarify the statement in the following way: Above-average values in one variable tend to be associated with above-average values in the other variable, and vice versa. The bivariate frequency distribution extends accordingly particularly over the two quadrants from bottom left to top right. This is precisely the expression of a *positive* covariance in the sense of the covariance formula (5.5).[7] Whereas a *negative* covariance would indicate a relationship of the following type: Above-average values in one variable tend to be associated with below-average values in the other variable, and vice versa. The bivariate frequency distribution would then extend mainly over the two quadrants from top left to bottom right.

$$cov_{xy} = \frac{\sum_{i=1}^{n}(x_i - \bar{x}) \cdot (y_i - \bar{y})}{n} \tag{5.5}$$

---

4 The data sources and question wordings involved in the sections of this chapter are given below in this and the following section 5.3.

5 Source: Eurobarometer 95.1

6 Source: Eurobarometer 92.3

7 For each unit i, its values in x and y are expressed as the difference from the respective arithmetic mean of the frequency distribution, the two differences are multiplied together, and the sum of these products across all units is divided by the number of these units.

And zero covariance would indicate that neither of these two structures is present. The sign of the covariance reveals the *direction* of the bivariate relationship. If the covariance is converted into a *correlation*, its *strength* can also be easily interpreted, since the correlation coefficient r indicates this strength in a standardized form on a scale from -1 via 0 to $+1$.

$$r = \frac{cov_{xy}}{s_x \cdot s_y} \tag{5.6}$$

One of the various ways to calculate the Pearson correlation is shown in (5.6). It simply consists of dividing the covariance by the product of the standard deviations of the two variables.[8] Typically, r is calculated directly using the function *cor()*, which is applied here to relate the two variables *EPclimate* and *public*, both from the data frame *eu* (5.7).

```
cor(eu$EPclimate, eu$public,
    use = "complete.obs")
```
(5.7)

Alternatively, the covariance and the two standard deviations could have been calculated explicitly and incorporated into the formula for r. In (5.8), we chose the variant of dividing the covariance by the square root of the product of the two variances involved (5.8).

```
cov(eu$EPclimate, eu$public,
    use = "complete.obs")/
    sqrt(var(eu$public, na.rm = TRUE) *
    var(eu$EPclimate, na.rm = TRUE))
```
(5.8)

The individual elements, i. e. the covariance and the two standard deviations, are summarized in (5.9).

$$cov_{xy} = 74.521 \qquad s_x = 14.118 \qquad s_y = 7.483 \qquad b = 0.374 \tag{5.9}$$

The calculations according to (5.7) and (5.8) result in a quite strong correlation of r_{xy}=0.71.

Alternatively, r can be calculated by multiplying the slope b of a simple linear regression (as explained in Chapter 6.1) by the ratio of the standard deviations of the two variables.

---

8 Blalock (1981: 398). In the context of linear regression, for example, r is also given as the correlation between the predicted and observed y values or as the square root of the multiple R^2.

$$r = \left(\frac{s_x}{s_y}\right) \cdot b \qquad (5.10)$$

In this way, the standardized regression coefficient β is actually created, so that a correlation may also be interpreted "as the value the slope would equal if the variables were equally spread out" (Agresti and Finlay 2009: 270). For this, we can use (5.11) to get the required b slope. Here, this b slope came out as indicated in (5.9).

```
lm(eu$EPclimate ~ eu$public)                              (5.11)
```

We now want to extend the analysis to include a third variable, namely the purchasing power standard of a country (named *KKS*), and ask how this variable correlates with the other two variables.

```
eu <- na.omit(subset(energy,
      select=c(EPclimate, public, KKS)))                  (5.12)
round(cor(eu),2)
```

This could also be achieved in various ways; here, we have chosen the approach shown in (5.12). This involves selecting only those variables from the data frame that are to be correlated with each other and excluding all units with missing values from this subset. Accordingly, *subset()* is embedded in *na.omit()*. To be able to refer to this matrix in the subsequent instruction, it is assigned an object name, and the correlation function is referenced to it. Embedding it in the rounding function only serves to keep the resulting correlation matrix (5.13) readable.

```
          EPclimate public  KKS
EPclimate      1.00   0.71 0.69
public         0.71   1.00 0.53                           (5.13)
KKS            0.69   0.53 1.00
```

As printed, this matrix is redundant because it shows each correlation twice, once below the main diagonal and once above it. It is therefore sufficient to consider only the sub diagonal part of the matrix. There we see again the already known correlation between the two initial variables of r = 0.71. We also see that both variables also correlate positively with the third variable, namely 0.69 and 0.53. This means that the two population shares expressing a preference for political intervention (on the one hand, with regard to AI, on the other hand, with regard to climate change) not only correlate positively *with each other*, but *also with the purchasing power* of a country. In other words: the higher the purchasing power of a country, the higher the two shares tend to be. Political interventions to regulate AI and combat climate change are therefore an issue that appears to concern the population in wealthy countries more than in less wealthy countries. This is certainly not surprising: those who must primarily strive for economic security will certainly set their priorities elsewhere than AI and climate change.

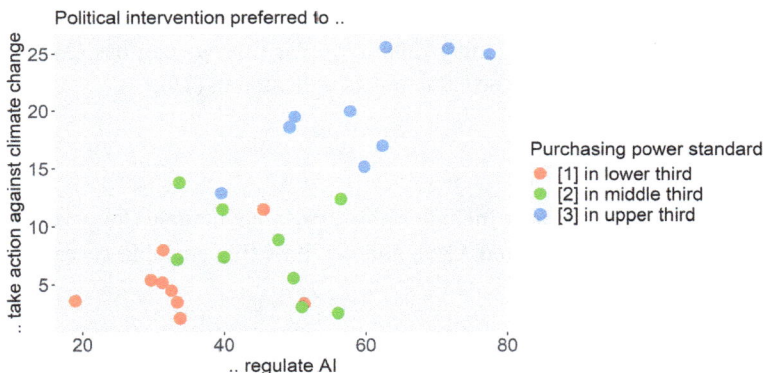

Figure 5.3: A ggplot2 Scatterplot for 3 variables.

A scatterplot can visualize a correlation pattern consisting of three variables if the values of the third variable are suitably marked. In this case, this applies to the purchasing power variable. For example, the right-hand diagram in Figure 5.2 results from differentiating the purchasing power standard values with respect to the terciles of the underlying frequency distribution.

To create such a diagram, a long list of R plotting symbols are available. Wickham and Grolemund (2017: 11–12) provide this list in full and Murrell (2011: 64) provides excerpts. The easiest way, however, is to access the required information via the R documentation itself. To get access to the list of available symbols, you may proceed as follows: First, from the prompt in the R Console or from your current R script, run the line instruction

?par   (5.14)

to get —via the *Set or Query Graphical Parameters* help window— the list of graphical parameters. Scroll down this long list to *pch* and its explanatory text and follow the link to *points* for getting the *Add Points to a Plot* help window, with its explanation of the *pch* values and the list of 26 R plotting symbols and their assigned *pch* integer values.

As an alternative to *traditional R graphics*, we can also use the *ggplot2* graphics package in R (Wickham 2016) to create a plot of the relationships we are currently discussing. The result is shown in Figure 5.3. Regarding the cloud of (*x, y*) value combinations, the right-hand graph in Figure 5.2 and the graph in Figure 5.3 convey the same information, except that instead of different plotting symbols, different colors are used. However, the graph in Figure 5.3 certainly appears more elegant in its presentation than the standard graph in Figure 5.2, so the desire for a presentation graphic may be the deciding factor in favor of the plot in Figure 5.3.

We'll stick with this graphics library to conclude this section with a scatter plot using data from Example Data Set 4 on Machine Learning and Robots in Human Life.

In this study, we asked: "We would like to ask you two questions below: first, in which areas should robots be used primarily, and second, in which areas should robots not be used at all, if possible?" For each of these two questions, the following instruction followed: "Please select up to five areas from the list (. . .). First, assign rank 1, then rank 2, then rank 3, etc." The 15 areas indicated in the legend to Figure 5.4 were available for selection.

Using these data, we calculated the respective probability that a region is part of the TOP 5 ranking set. To visualize the result in a graph, we have compiled these probabilities in a data frame (5.15):

```
> robotareas
# A tibble: 15 × 3
      yes    no area
    <dbl> <dbl> <fct>
 1 0.755 0.009 industry
 2 0.389 0.023 manufacturing
 3 0.097 0.241 service
 4 0.069 0.495 privatelives
 5 0.431 0.107 healthcare
 6 0.074 0.62  care
 7 0.046 0.486 education                                    (5.15)
 8 0.514 0.046 rescue
 9 0.745 0.005 space
10 0.685 0     deepsea
11 0.037 0.37  leisure
12 0.352 0.065 transport
13 0.199 0.107 agriculture
14 0.153 0.384 military
15 0.019 0.088 noarea
```

We originally created this graphic for an open-access chapter on robotic assistance (Beetz et al. 2023: 6–8). We present this original graph here again to highlight a particular aspect that can be addressed with a scatter plot: Namely, a scatterplot does not necessarily have to be about determining the covariance or correlation between two variables or a prediction curve between them, although these are certainly its main applications. It can also be about identifying any polarities that may be present in the data.

Here, these would be the areas where preferences are clearly distributed among the population: many are *in favor of*, and only a few are *against*, the use of robots in a particular area. Similarly, few are *in favor of*, and many are *against*, the use of robots in a particular area. In the plot, these would be areas that tend toward the top left corner or the bottom right corner. And just to visually support this contrast, we've drawn a diagonal line in the diagram.

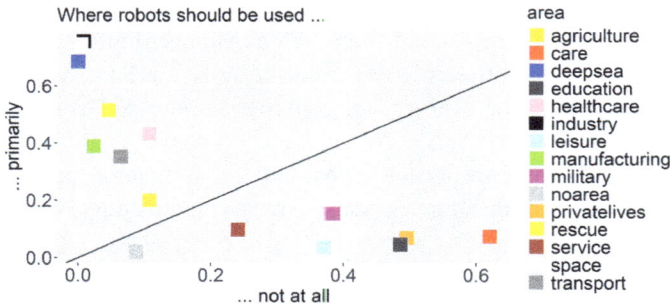

Figure 5.4: Preferred and Rejected Areas of Robots: In Search of Polarity Instead of Covariance. Source: This is Figure 1.1 in a chapter on "Trustworthiness and Well-Being: The Ethical, Legal, and Social Challenge of Robotic Assistance" (Beetz et al. 2023: 8) published — in Open Access — by Springer in the SpringerBriefs in Sociology series.[9]

A *ggplot2* plot consists of three basic components (Murrell 2011: 148–149):
1. the data to be plotted, as defined by creating an empty plot object with ggplot().
2. the graphics or geometric shapes, or *geoms*, (e.g., data symbols or lines) to be added to the empty plot via functions such as geom_point() or geom_line().
3. the features, or *aesthetics*, of such geometric shapes to be used to represent the data values, via the aes() function.

Using a scatter plot as an example: A scatter plot represents each combination of values of *x* and *y* as a *point* in the coordinate system of these two variables. Each such point has a feature such as its size, color and shape. "These attributes are called **aesthetics**, and are the properties that can be perceived on the graphic" (Wickham 2016: 78).

As Murrell (2011: 148) summarizes it, "a plot is created by mapping data values via aesthetics to the features of geometric shapes."

After *library(ggplot2)* has been called, we usually start the relevant part of the R script with a first line of instruction to determine the data to be plotted. In the R script in Table 5.4, for example, this line is

```
ggplot(data = robotareas) +
```
(5.16)

---

9 https://doi.org/10.1007/978-3-031-11447-2

with *robotareas* being the name of the data frame prepared for this graphic (5.15). The line is terminated with the + operator to link it to the subsequent lines of the R script. In the words of Murrell (2011: 148), a *ggplot2* plot is built up "by creating plot components, or *layers*, and combining them using the + operator." In our example, the first of these layers looks like this:

$$
\begin{aligned}
&\texttt{geom\_point(mapping = aes(x=no, y=yes, color = area),} \\
&\qquad\texttt{size = 6, shape = 15) +}
\end{aligned}
\qquad (5.17)
$$

As the geometric shape, the *point* is used as the data symbol, with its features *size*, *shape* and *color* mapped to the variables *yes*, *no* and *area* (as displayed in (5.15)), using the *aes()* function. The assignment of 15 to *shape* refers to the list of *pch* values that we explained above in the context of (5.14). As documented in the R script in Table 5.4, further layers connected with the + operator follow, in particular for labeling, manual assignment of colors and setting font sizes.

Table 5.2: Script to Figure 5.2 Scatterplots With Two and Three Variables.

Line	R Script
1	`load("ls.Rdata")`
2	`load("eudata.Rdata")`
3	`eudata$KKS3 <- ifelse(eudata$KKS <= 78, 1,`
4	`                     ifelse(eudata$KKS <= 104, 2, 3))`
5	`tiff("fig52.tiff", units="in", width=9,`
6	`       height = 4, res = 600 )`
7	`par(mfrow = c(1,2))`
8	`plot(ls$LS11, ls$LS12, pch=18,`
9	`       cex=1.1, col="grey50", cex.lab = 1.3,`
10	`       main="Current and fair standard of living",`
11	`       xlab="Current",`
12	`       ylab = "Fair")`
13	`mtext("X", adj = 1, side = 1)`
14	`mtext("Y", adj = 0, side = 3)`
15	`x <- seq(from = 1.0, to = 11.0, by = 0.1)`
16	`y <- c(6.01 - 0.44*x + 0.15*x^2 - 0.008*x^3)`
17	`lines (x, y, lwd=3.0, lty = 1, col = "lightblue")`
18	`plot(eudata$public, eudata$EPclimate,`
19	`       pch = as.numeric(eudata$KKS3), cex = 1.1, cex.lab = 1.3,`
20	`       xlab=".. regulate AI",`
21	`       ylab = "..action against climate change",`
22	`       main = "Political intervention preferred to..")`
23	`mtext("X", adj=1, side=1)`
24	`mtext("Y", adj=0, side=3)`
25	`legend(18.0,24.0, c("PPS in lower third of EU",`

Table 5.2 (continued)

Line	R Script
26	"PFS in middle third",
27	"PFS in upper third"),
28	cex=0.85, pch=1:3, bty="n")
29	abline(h=11.1, col="grey50", lty="dotted", lwd=1.5)
30	text(68, 12.7, "mean(y)=11.1", col="grey50", cex=0.9)
31	abline(v=46.6, col="grey50", lty="dotted", lwd=1.5)
32	text(48, 25, "mean(x)=46.6", col="grey50", cex=0.9)
33	dev.off()

Lines explained

Lines 1 and 2 load the required data frames. Lines 3 and 4 recodes the values of variable *KKS* into 3 groups. Lines 5 and 6 control the graphics device in terms of format, file name, width, height and resolution in pixels per inch (ppi) for the two graphics, which are integrated into a common structure via *par()* in line 7, and line 33 switches this graphics device off again. *par()* can set diverse graphical parameters, here it is used along with *mfrow* = *c(nr, nc)* to array the two graphics in 1 row and 2 columns.

The script then contains the instructions for the two plots, in lines 8 to 17 for the left graph and in lines 18 to 32 for the right graph in Figure 5.2. For both graphics, the setup is basically structured the same: first comes the *plot()* function itself, followed by additional graphics functions, in this case to add *lines* and *text* as well as a *legend* to the graphic for annotation.

The arguments to *plot()* involve the variables to be plotted, the data symbol (*pch*), the factor by which plotting text and symbols should be magnified relative to the default (*cex*), the color (*col*), and the labeling of the headline (*main*) as well as the labeling of the x-axis (*xlab*) and y-axis (*ylab*) and their relative font size (*cex.lab*). *mtext()* writes *X* and *Y* on the bottom and top margins of the figure region, aligned bottom/right and top/left (lines 13 and 14 as well as 23 and 24).

Lines 15 and 16 are required for the prediction curve to be drawn by *lines()* in line 17. Line 15 defines the x-scale as a sequence of values from 1 to 11, spaced 0.1 times. Line 16 then specifies the functional form of the (x, y) relationship. It defines *y* as a function of *x* and uses the result of a previously performed third-degree polynomial regression. The arguments to *lines()* involve the line width (*lwd*), line type (*lty*) and line color (*col*).

Lines 25 to 28 add a legend to the plot. Arguments to the legend() function involve the *x* and *y* coordinates to be used to position the legend, its text in *c()*, the relative size of this text (*cex*), and the plotting symbols to be used (*pch*). The specification *pch* = *1:3* means that the first three symbols from the list of R plotting symbols are taken (We have outlined access to this list in the context of (5.14)). *bty* = *"n"* suppresses the box otherwise drawn about the legend.

Lines 29 and 31 call to *abline()* to add straight lines through the plot. *h* specifies the *y* value for a horizontal line, and *v* the *x* value for a vertical line. In addition, color (*col*), line type (*lty*) and line width (*lwd*) are specified.

Lines 30 and 32 call to *text()* to add the quoted text at the specified (x, y) coordinates. In addition, color (*col*) and relative size (*cex*) of the text is fixed.

Table 5.3: R Script to Figure 5.3 Preference for Political Intervention.

Line	R Script
1	`load("Energy2.Rdata")`
2	`energy$KKS3 <- ifelse(energy$KKS <= 78,`
3	`"[1] in lower third",`
4	`ifelse(energy$KKS <= 104,`
5	`"[2] in middle third",`
6	`"[3] in upper third"))`
7	`eu <- na.omit(subset(energy,`
8	`select = c(KKS3, public, EPclimate)))`
9	`library(ggplot2)`
10	`tiff("fig 53.tiff", units = "in", width = 9,`
11	`height = 4.5, res = 600 )`
12	`ggplot (data = eu) +`
13	`geom_point(mapping = aes(x = public,`
14	`y = EPclimate, color = KKS3), size = 4.5) +`
15	`ylab(".. take action against climate change") +`
16	`xlab(".. regulate AI") +`
17	`labs(color = "Purchasing power standard",`
18	`title = "Political intervention preferred to ..") +`
19	`theme(legend.title = element_text(size= 16)) +`
20	`theme(axis.text.x = element_text(size = 16)) +`
21	`theme(axis.text.y = element_text(size = 16)) +`
22	`theme(legend.text = element_text(size = 16)) +`
23	`theme(axis.title = element_text(size = 16)) +`
24	`theme(plot.title = element_text(size = 16))`
25	`dev.off()`

Lines explained

Line 1 loads the required data frame. Lines 2 to 6 recode the values of variable KKS to three groups using *ifelse()*. For this purpose, *ifelse()* is used again, this time in such a way that the outcome variable is not assigned numerical values, but the character strings enclosed in quotes. This has the advantage that these character strings are automatically transferred to the subsequent graphic. Lines 7 and 8 reduce the data frame to the three variables to be plotted and omits possible units with missing values in these variables. Line 9 invokes the *ggplot2* library. Lines 10, 11, and 25 control the graphics device as described in the context of the previous plots of this chapter. The only difference is that the instructions only refer to the one subsequent plot.

Lines 12 to 24 contain the instructions for creating the plot. Since we also need instructions of this type in the following R script (Table 5.4), we explain their meaning there – as well as in the text in the context of Figure 5.4.

Table 5.4: R Script to Figure 5.4 Preferred and Rejected Areas of Robots: In Search of Polarity Instead of Covariance.

Line	R Script
1	`load("areas.Rdata")`
2	`library(ggplot2)`
3	`tiff("fig54.tiff", units = "in", width = 9,`
4	`    height = 4.2, res =600 )`
5	`ggplot(data = robotareas) +`
6	`  geom_point(mapping = aes(x = no, y = yes, color = area),`
7	`               size = 6, shape = 15 ) +`
8	`  ylab("... primarily") +`
9	`  xlab("... not at all") +`
10	`  labs(title = "Where robots should be used ...") +`
11	`  geom_abline(intercept = 0, slope = 1) +`
12	`  scale_color_manual(`
13	`    values = c(industry = "black",`
14	`                manufacturing = "green",`
15	`                service = "brown",`
16	`                privatelives = "orange",`
17	`                healthcare = "pink",`
18	`                care = "red",`
19	`                education = "grey35",`
20	`                rescue = "yellow",`
21	`                space = "white",`
22	`                deepsea = "blue",`
23	`                leisure = "lightblue",`
24	`                transport = "grey60",`
25	`                agriculture = "gold",`
26	`                military = "magenta",`
27	`                noarea = "grey80"`
28	`                )) +`
29	`  theme(legend.title = element_text(size = 18)) +`
30	`  theme(axis.text.x = element_text(size = 18))  +`
31	`  theme(axis.text.y = element_text(size = 18))  +`
32	`  theme(legend.text = element_text(size = 18))  +`
33	`  theme(axis.title = element_text(size = 18))  +`
34	`  theme(plot.title = element_text(size = 18))`
35	`dev.off()`

Lines explained

Line 1 loads the data frame created specifically as input for this graph (5.15). Line 2 calls the required graphics library, *ggplot2*. Lines 3, 4, and 35 again control the graphics device, in the same way as explained for previous graphs in this chapter. The actual plot instructions follow in lines 5 to 34. Lines 5 to 7 are explained in the context of (5.16) and (5.17). Lines 8 to 10 are used for labeling. Line 11 is used to draw the diagonal line in the graph. Lines 12 to 28 individually assign the colors to the values of the (third) variable *area* that are to be used in the graph. Finally, the respective font sizes are set via lines 29 to 34.

5.3 Predictive Graphs

A prediction curve expresses the functional form of the (x, y) relationship, and we consider it important to attempt to determine this functional form, even if the cloud of (x, y) value points itself reveals some structure. Even then, by determining the functional form of a relationship, we can significantly increase the information content of a predictive or inferential analysis. This is because such an analysis excludes more alternatives the more precisely the functional relationship is specified.

The four scatterplots in Figure 5.5 again use data from Example Data Set 6 on Energy Transition in the European Green Deal.

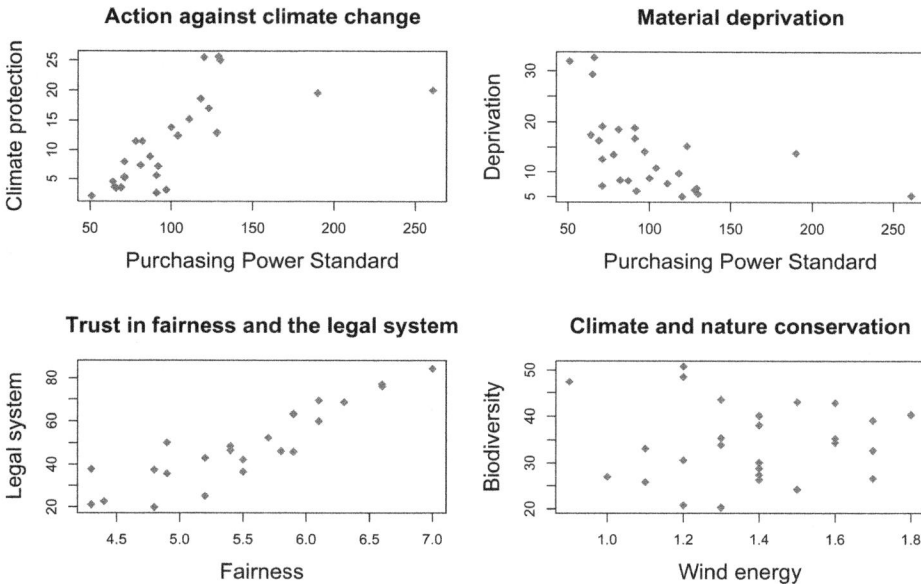

Figure 5.5: Four Scatterplots.

The two upper diagrams refer to the purchasing power standard of a country.[10] In the top left graph, this measure is related to the proportion of a country's population that

---

10 The measure comes from Eurostat and is described on the European Union website as follows: "In calculating the standard of living, the price of certain goods and services in each country is measured relative to the income in that country. A common national currency, the purchasing power standard (PPS), is used. A comparison of gross domestic product (GDP) per capita in PPS provides an overview of the standard of living in the EU." https://european-union.europa.eu/principles-countries-history/key-facts-and-figures/life-eu_de

wants the European Parliament to prioritize action against climate change.[11] We see that this proportion of the population is higher the higher the purchasing power standard of a country is. However, we also see that this relationship may be non-linear.

The situation is similar in the diagram above right, except that the relationship depicted there suggests a negative covariance: The higher a country's purchasing power index, the smaller the proportion of the population characterized by material deprivation.[12] Here, too, the relationship appears nonlinear rather than linear.

These are the two diagrams that we use in Chapter 6 and more extensively in Chapter 10 to introduce nonlinear variable relationships.

While the two upper diagrams suggest a relationship between the respective variables, the diagram in the lower right is a scatter plot, which rather suggests that there is probably no relationship between the two variables. For this example, we have selected one variable that is relevant for nature conservation and a second variable that is relevant for climate protection: namely, how positive or negative the impacts of wind energy[13] and the protection of biodiversity[14] are assessed (r = 0.0).

In contrast to the diagram at the bottom right, the diagram at the bottom left indicates a close and apparently linear relationship between the two variables shown there (r = 0.9). Both variables are intended to measure the degree of trust, in one's fellow human beings on the one hand, and in the legal system on the other. These two

---

11 The variable was collected as part of Eurobarometer 95.1 (ZA7781). The question was worded as follows: "Which of the following issues would you like to see addressed by the European Parliament as a priority? First, . . ." "Action against climate change" Source: European Commission and European Parliament, Brussels: Eurobarometer 95.1, March-April 2021. Kantar Public, Brussels [Producer]; GESIS, Cologne [Publisher]: ZA7781, dataset version 1.0.0, doi:10.4232/1.13791

12 The measure comes from Eurostat. It is the material deprivation rate (according to the EU-SILC survey) for 2020. "The indicator is defined as the percentage of the population that does not have access to at least three of the nine material deprivation items in the dimension 'Economic strain and durables'." https://ec.europa.eu/eurostat/databrowser/view/tessi080/default/table

13 The item about *wind energy* comes from Eurobarometer 95.2 (ZA7782). Question wording: "The following list shows areas in which new technologies are currently being developed. For each area, please indicate whether you think this will have a positive, negative, or no impact on how we live in the next 20 years". The response options for each technology were: "very positive impact (+2)," "somewhat positive impact (+1)," "somewhat negative impact (−1)," "very negative impact (−2)," "no impact (0)." The numbers in brackets were not part of the question, but were subsequently assigned to the answer options for the calculation of country means. European Commission, Brussels: Eurobarometer 95.2, April-May 2021. Kantar Public, Brussels [Producer]; GESIS, Cologne [Publisher]: ZA7782, dataset version 1.0.0, doi:10.4232/1.13884

14 The biodiversity item comes from Eurobarometer 95.3 (ZA7783). Question wording: "Which of the following objectives do you think should be the top priority of a European Green Deal—that is, a set of measures to protect the environment and combat climate change?" . . . "Protection of biodiversity" European Commission, Brussels: Eurobarometer 95.3, June-July 2021. Kantar Public, Brussels [Producer]; GESIS, Cologne [Publisher]: ZA7783, dataset version 1.0.0, doi:10.4232/1.13826

variables also come from different data sources.[15] But although the relationship between both variables appears to be linear, and would then be best characterized by a straight prediction line, we will see that another functional form of the relationship can also be considered.

To create Figure 5.5, we use —as in some graphs above— the option to arrange several plots, in this case in a 2×2 array.

```
par(mfrow = c(2,2))                                                      (5.18)
```

The R script then contains four plotting instructions, each with identically specified graphic parameters, but related to four different pairs of variables and correspondingly adjusted labels for the heading and *x*- and *y*-axes. For example, the first of these four *plot()* functions looks like this:

```
plot(energy$KKS, energy$EPclimate, type="p",
     pch=18, cex=1.3, col="grey50",
     cex.main=1.5, cex.lab = 1.5,                                        (5.19)
     xlab="Purchasing Power Standard",
     ylab= "Climate protection",
     main = "Action against climate change")
```

The arguments to this *plot()* function involves the pair of variables (*KKS* and *EPclimate* from data frame *energy*), the *type* of plot (*p* for points), the plotting symbol (*pch* = 18 for a diamond), its *color* (grey in medium intensity) and relative size (*cex*), as well as the labeling of headline (*main*), x- axis (*xlab*) and y-axis (*ylab*) and their relative font sizes (*cex.main, cex.lab*).

Although the relationship between trust in one's fellow human beings and the legal system appears to be linear, another functional form of the relationship can also be considered. To illustrate this, we calculated a linear and third-order polynomial regression and superimposed both prediction graphs over the scatter plot. This is shown in Figure 5.6.

---

15 The trust-in-fairness variable comes from European Social Survey Round 9. On a 11pt scale, respondents were asked to indicate whether they think most people would try to take advantage of them if given the chance (score: 0) or whether they would try to be fair? (score: 10). Source: https://www.europeansocialsurvey.org/data/ Based on this data, we computed country means.

The second variable comes from Eurobarometer 92.3 (ZA7601, dataset version 1.0.0, doi:10.4232/1.13564). Question wording: "I would now like to know how much trust you have in certain media and institutions. Please tell me for the following media and institutions whether you tend to trust them or tend to distrust them. What about . . .?" . . . "justice, legal system". Each country is characterized by the percentage of those who trust the respective institution in their own country (vs. 'do not trust' or 'don't know').

Trust in fairness and the legal system

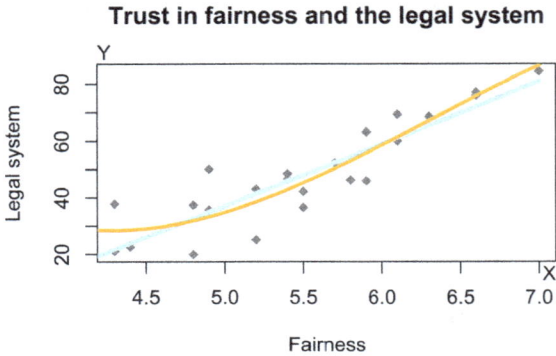

Figure 5.6: Trust in Fairness and the Legal System: Two Prediction Graphs Compared.

To overlay the two graphs on the cloud of (x, y) value combinations in Figure 5.6, we proceeded as described for another data example in the R script in Table 5.2.

```
x <- seq(from = 4.0, to = 7.0, by = 0.1)
y1 <- c(-72.59 + 21.95*x )
lines (x, y1, lwd=4.0, lty=1, col = "lightblue")          (5.20)
y3 <- c(481.92 - 255.71*x + 45.25*x^2 - 2.398*x^3)
lines (x, y3, lwd=3.0, lty=1, col = "orange")
```

First, we define an *x*-scale as a sequence of values from 4 to 7 spaced 0.1 apart. Next, we define two functional forms of the (*x, y*) relationship, one for the light blue prediction line (*y1*) and one for the orange prediction curve (*y3*). Both define the respective target variable (*y1* or *y3*) as a function of *x*, using the results of previously performed regression analyses. The arguments of the two *lines()* statements concern the line width (*lwd*), the line type (*lty*), and the line color (*col*).

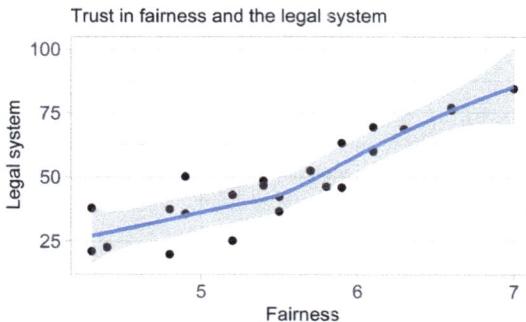

Figure 5.7: Use of Local Polynomial Regression Fitting in the Trust in Fairness and the Legal System Example.

Alternatively, a method called "Local Polynomial Regression Fitting" was used. As explained in the R Documentation, *loess()* fits a locally polynomial surface determined by one or more numerical predictors, using local fitting and (weighted) least squares.

In principle, this works in such a way that to determine the slope of the prediction graph at a point x, only points that fall within a narrow interval around x are used. The slope is thus determined only by the points in the immediate vicinity of x, in fact weighted by their distance from x. In this sense, the slope is determined *locally*. To achieve this for all x values, the method implies to shift this interval on the x axis from the small to the larger x values, in order to obtain locally determined predictions for the whole spectrum of x values.

To prepare this analysis, we first reduced the *energy* data frame to the two required variables *pplfair* and *justice*, and excluded countries from the calculation that have missing values in these variables.

```
eu <- na.omit(subset(energy,
      select=c(pplfair,justice)))
```
(5.21)

Then, the required *loess()* smoothing function can conveniently be called from the *ggplot2* graphics library, namely by adding this function as a layer to *ggplot()* using the geometric shape *geom_smooth()*. The corresponding passage in the R script looks like this:

```
library(ggplot2)
ggplot(eu, aes(x=pplfair, y=justice)) +
  geom_point()+
  geom_smooth() +
```
(5.22)

The *ggplot2* graphics library includes a *theme* system, "which allows you to exercise fine control over the non-data elements of your plot" (Wickham 2016: 169). The system allows you to set entire themes or modify individual theme components. This creates a variety of options for customizing the appearance of a plot.

```
  theme_light() +
  labs(title="Trust in fairness and the legal system") +
  xlab("Fairness") + ylab("Legal system") +
  theme(plot.title = element_text(size= 10)) +
  theme(axis.text.x = element_text(size = 10)) +
  theme(axis.text.y = element_text(size = 10)) +
  theme(axis.title = element_text(size=10))
```
(5.23)

In addition to labeling via *labs()*, *xlab()* and *ylab()* we used both basic options: on the one hand by setting the *theme_light()* theme and on the other hand by using individual *theme()* statements to control the font size of various text elements.

The result is shown in Figure 5.7. Here, too, we see that the prediction graph, instead of a straight line, tends toward a very weak curve.

5.4 Diagnostic Graphs

To begin with the topic of diagnostic plots, we'll refer to the two regression models in Figure 5.6. There, we saw that even if the scatter plot strongly suggests a linear relationship, and a very close one at that, a curvilinear relationship can also be considered. This raises the question of which of these two models should ultimately be favored. First, we can consider the explained variance. In this regard, the two R^2 differ only minimal $\left(R^2_{Lin} = 0.80; \ R^2_{Poly} = 0.83 \right)$. This is at best a slight advantage for the polynomial regression. However, it is always advisable to carry out regression diagnostics in addition to R^2 in order to check to what extent the requirements of a regression analysis are met. We have done this below for both model variants (Figure 5.8).

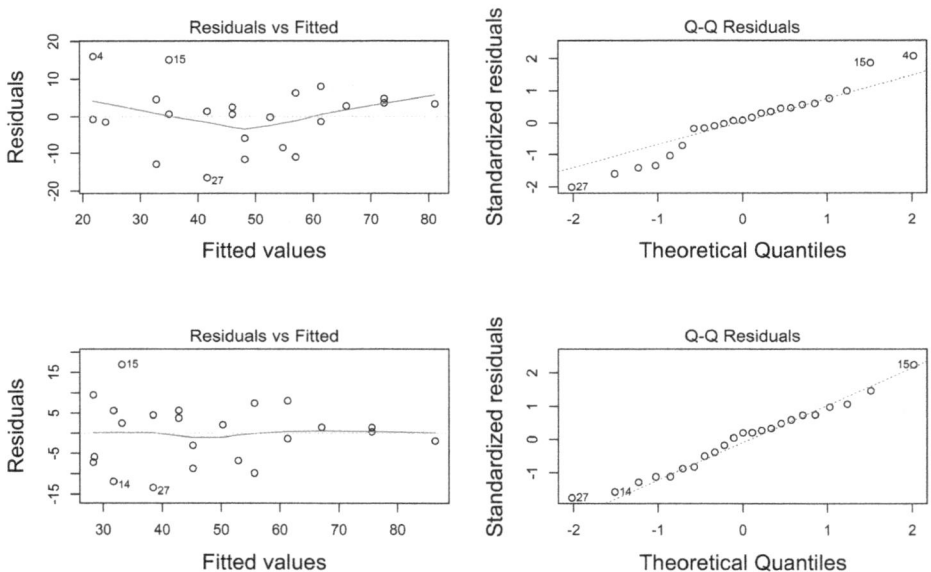

Figure 5.8: Four diagnostic plots for the models in Figure 5.6.

Four graphs plot residuals or standardized residuals against fitted values or theoretical quantiles

Following *na.omit(subset())* in (5.21) to handle missing data, *tiff()* to control the graphics device and *par(mfrow = c(2,2))* to arrange the four plots shown in Figure 5.8 in a 2 × 2 array, the four *plot()* functions described in (5.24) followed in the R script.

```
plot(lm(justice ~ pplfair,
          data=eu),which=c(1),
    cex.main=1.5, cex.lab = 1.5)
plot(lm(justice ~ pplfair,
          data=eu),which=c(2),
    cex.main=1.5, cex.lab = 1.5)
plot(lm(justice ~ poly(pplfair, 3,
          raw=TRUE), data=eu),
          which=c(1),
    cex.main=1.5, cex.lab = 1.5)
plot(lm(justice ~ poly(pplfair, 3,
          raw=TRUE), data=eu),
          which=c(2),
    cex.main=1.5, cex.lab = 1.5)
```

$$(5.24)$$

To create these four diagnostic plots, we use the option to embed the *lm()* function in the *plot()* function. Since *plot()* is a generic function, the nested function structure automatically provides us with four diagnostic plots that can be accessed *interactively* via the R console, including the two types of diagnostic plots accessed here, namely the Residuals vs. Fitted Plot and the Q-Q Plot. In order to retrieve these two plots specifically in *batch* mode, we use the *which()* function, as shown, to select the first and second diagnostic plots, i.e. the RvF and Q-Q plots, from the series of four interactively offered plots via *c(1)* and *c(2)*.

The first two plot functions in (5.24) serve to generate these two diagnostic plots for the *linear* regression of the model, which is the *light blue prediction line* in Figure 5.6. These two diagnostic plots form the top row in Figure 5.8.

In contrast, the third and fourth plot functions in (5.24) produce these diagnostic plots for the model's *polynomial* regression, which is the *orange prediction curve* in Figure 5.6. These two diagnostic plots form the bottom row in Figure 5.8.

We discuss these two types of diagnostic plots and how they can be interpreted in great detail in Chapter 8. Given the background outlined there, it would be reasonable to conclude that polynomial regression better meets the requirements: the residuals lie, on average, almost perfectly on both reference lines: the horizontal zero line in the lower left diagram and the expected line of the theoretical quantiles in the lower right diagram. In the present example, this clearly speaks in favor of the polynomial regression.

For the final data example of this chapter,[16] we proceed as described earlier for the two models in Figures 5.6 and 5.8 (Figure 5.9). We start again—in the plot at the

---

16 We add one variable from the European Social Survey Round 9 for 2018. The underlying survey question reflects the respondent's assessment of household income with regard to possible feelings of

top left—with a scattergram between two variables and inquire about the functional form that might connect these two variables. A linear regression (the light blue prediction line in the plot at the top left) serves as the reference and starting point. A polynomial regression (the orange prediction curve) is also calculated. Based on the coefficients of these two regression analyses, we overlaid these two graphs on the cloud of *(x, y)* value combinations using the following script lines:

```
x <- seq(from = 0.0, to = 80.0, by = 1.0)
y1 <- c(6.5 - 0.043*x )
lines (x, y1, lwd=3.0, lty=1, col = "lightblue")              (5.25)
y2 <- c(7.21 - 0.098*x + 0.00081*x^2)
lines (x, y2, lwd=3.0, lty=1, col = "orange")
```

This time, from the outset, the visual impression is that the relationship between the two variables is nonlinear rather than linear. This impression is further reinforced by the fact that the (nonlinear) orange prediction — measured by the R^2 — achieves a higher prediction accuracy than the (linear) light blue prediction (0.63 vs. 0.53).

The regression diagnostics also demonstrate that the assumption of a nonlinear relationship is indeed more appropriate here. In the *Residual vs. Fitted* plot at the top right, we see that the linear prediction is accompanied by a clearly irregular pattern. In contrast, the *Residual vs. Fitted* plot at the bottom left for the polynomial regression shows a pattern that comes the theoretical expectation of a mean residual of zero much closer. Furthermore, the *Q-Q* plot also shows a quite acceptable pattern.

To create the 2×2 arrangement of the four plots, we proceeded as described in detail above for other examples. Therefore, we only want to show the passage from the R script for the two lower plots here, and only to draw attention to the specification of *which()*, which requests both diagnostic plots in a single statement via the vector *c(1, 2)*.

```
plot(m2 <- lm(pplfair ~ poly(hincfel34, 2,
          raw=TRUE), data=eu), which=c(1,2),              (5.26)
     cex.main=1.5, cex.lab = 1.5)
```

One topic we explore in more detail in Chapter 10 concerns influential cases. There, as here, we calculate a common measure to determine this influence, namely Cook's Distance. We also address the topic of "outliers" in Chapter 10.

---

deprivation (ESS Round 9 Source Questionnaire, p. 60, survey question F42). Respondents were asked which of the four descriptions "comes closest to how you feel about your household's income today? Living comfortably with current income (1), managing with current income (2), struggling with current income (3), and finding it very difficult with current income (4)." We combined (3) and (4) into one category and calculated the corresponding percentage for each country.

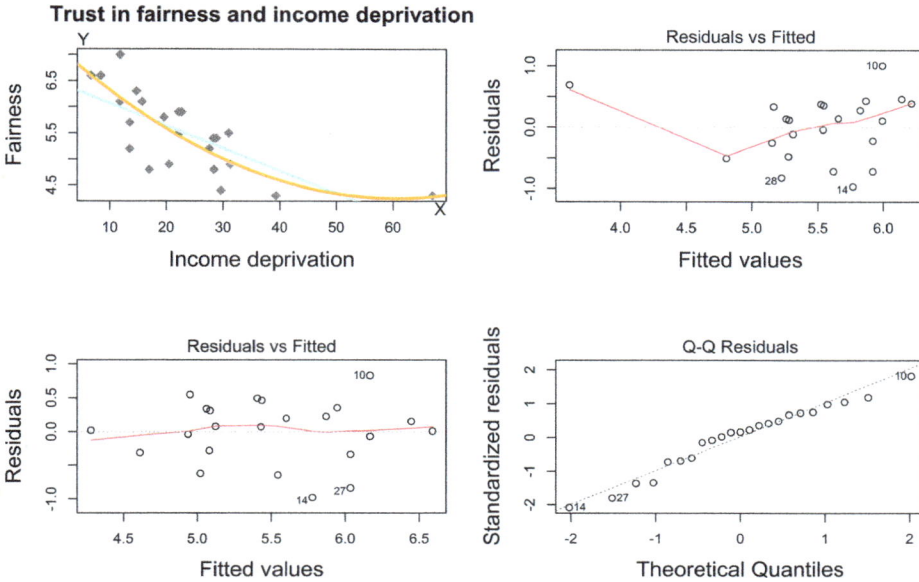

Figure 5.9: Linear and Polynomial Model and Related Diagnostic Plots.

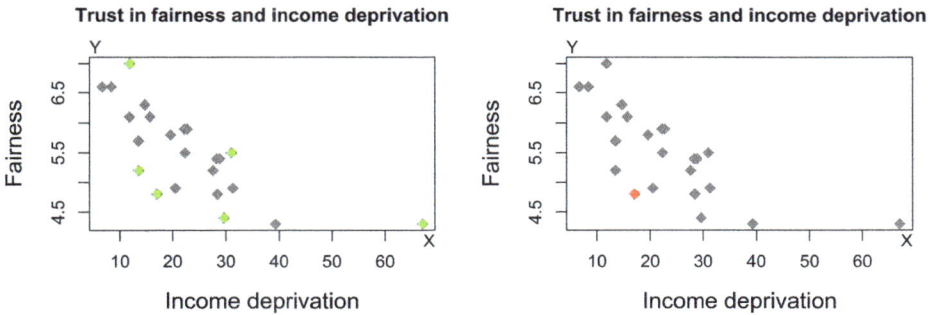

Figure 5.10: Cook's D and Outliers Visualized for the Polynomial Model.

The data example may then allow these influential cases and outliers to be visualized in the scatter plot by highlighting them in color. This is illustrated in Figure 5.10. Regarding the substantive discussion of Cook's D and outliers, we refer to Chapter 10 and focus here on showing how such plots can be created. (5.27) quotes the first of three passages from the underlying R script in Table 5.5. It serves to use the polynomial regression, which will be referred to later—via the object name *m2*—to perform two calculations.

```
m2 <- lm(pplfair ~ poly(hincfel34, 2,
                    raw=TRUE), data=eu)
```
(5.27)

The first of these two calculations refers to Cook's D (5.28) and the second to the out-liers (5.29). Cook's D itself can be easily calculated using the *cooks.distance()* function. The next line of the script defines an object that should specify the threshold value that must be exceeded to be considered an influential case. As is often the case, differ-ent threshold values are conceivable here. To ensure that the selection of such a value is at least well-founded, we calculated a summary of the distribution of Cook's D val-ues and set the 3rd quartile as the threshold.

```
cd <- cooks.distance(m2)
thrs <- 0.043 # 3rd Quartile
cd_obs <- which(cd > thrs)                          (5.28)
points(eu$hincfel34[cd_obs], eu$pplfair[cd_obs],
       col="green", pch=19)
```

Once this threshold is set, the next task is to identify those units whose value is greater than the threshold. To do this, we use the *which()* function, both for the left plot (5.28, for Cook's D) and the right plot (5.29, for outliers).

```
outl <- which(abs(resid(m2)) > 2.0 * sd(resid(m2)))
points(eu$hincfel34[outl], eu$pplfair[outl],           (5.29)
       col="red", pch=19)
```

The selection function *which()* works by converting the logical vector that is automati-cally generated[17] when a condition is set into a numeric one. "It returns the indices (i. e., position numbers) of the elements that are TRUE" (Buttrey and Whitaker 2018: 33–34). This means that we get the positions within a vector at which the specified condition occurs (Matloff 2011: 47).

We want to illustrate this using the example of (5.28) that Cook's D > 0.043. To keep the vectors in question clear, we round the entries to three decimal places.

```
> round(cd <- cooks.distance(m2),3)
    1     2     3     4     5     6     8
0.014 0.003 0.579 0.029 0.014 0.001 0.019
    9    10    11    12    14    15    16
0.000 0.131 0.022 0.015 0.083 0.000 0.005         (5.30)
   17    18    20    22    23    24    26
0.011 0.001 0.053 0.010 0.033 0.017 0.000
   27    28
0.096 0.061
```

---

17 See also Chapter 4, section 4.5.3 on vectors, including logical vectors

First, we display the vector with Cook's D entries for the 23 included countries in
(5.30). Since these data were extracted via subset() from a larger data frame originally
composed of 28 units, the numbering of the positions runs from 1, . . ., 28, skipping the
positions of the omitted units.

```
> thrs <- 0.043 # 3rd Quartile
> (lv <- cd > thrs)
    1     2     3     4     5     6     8
FALSE FALSE  TRUE FALSE FALSE FALSE FALSE
    9    10    11    12    14    15    16
FALSE  TRUE FALSE FALSE  TRUE FALSE FALSE
   17    18    20    22    23    24    26
FALSE FALSE  TRUE FALSE FALSE FALSE FALSE
   27    28
 TRUE  TRUE
```
(5.31)

Next, we formulate the condition in (5.31) that *cd > thrs*. This is the condition we used
as an argument to *which()*. The assignment of this condition to an object name, in this
case *lv*, would not be necessary. We do this only to be able to view the automatically
generated *logical* vector. The outer brackets serve only to ensure that this vector is
readily displayed. The sequence of numbers from 1, . . ., 28 again identifies the positions of the 23 units. TRUE indicates that the condition *cd > thrs* is true for this unit,
and FALSE indicates that this condition is false.

```
> (cd_obs <- which(cd > thrs))
 3 10 14 20 27 28
 3  9 12 17 22 23
```
(5.32)

Normally, we wouldn't even need to look at the logical vector itself. Instead, we can display the TRUE positions directly using *which()*. This actually gives us two sequences of
position numbers: one relative to the original data frame (top row in (5.32)) and one relative to the data frame reduced by *subset()* (bottom row in 5.32). While we can easily relate
the upper row to (5.31) (position numbers for TRUE), we can easily relate the lower row
to (5.33) and (5.34) (*x* and *y* values of the TRUE cases when addressing these units via []).

```
> eu$hincfel34
 [1] 14.7 19.6 67.0 39.3 28.3 11.8 22.2 22.3
 [9] 11.8 22.7 13.5 17.0 31.3 15.7 28.4 27.6
[17] 31.0  8.4 20.5 28.8  6.7 13.5 29.6
> eu$hincfel34[cd_obs]
[1] 67.0 11.8 17.0 31.0 13.5 29.
```
(5.33)

To illustrate this, we first consider the vector with the 23 values, and then the vector of the six units for which the condition $cd > thrs$ applies. These are the values of the third, ninth, twelfth, seventeenth, twenty-second and twenty-third units.

```
> eu$pplfair
 [1] 6.3 5.8 4.3 4.3 5.4 6.1 5.9 5.5 7.0 5.9
[11] 5.7 4.8 4.9 6.1 4.8 5.2 5.5 6.6 4.9 5.4
[21] 6.6 5.2 4.4
> eu$pplfair[cd_obs]
[1] 4.3 7.0 4.8 5.5 5.2 4.4
```

$$(5.34)$$

Analogously, we can now reconstruct (5.34) in the same way.

Table 5.5: R Script to Figure 5.10 Cook's D and Outliers Visualized for the Polynomial Model.

Line	R Script
1	load("Energy2.Rdata")
2	eu <- na.omit(subset(energy,
3	select = c(pplfair,hincfel34)))
4	m2 <- lm(pplfair ~ poly(hincfel34, 2,
5	raw = TRUE), data = eu)
6	tiff("fig510.tiff", units = "in", width = 9,
7	height = 3.5, res =1200)
8	par(mfrow = c(1,2))
9	plot(eu$hincfel34, eu$pplfair, type = "p", cex =1.5,
10	pch=18,col="grey50", cex.main=1.1,
11	cex.lab = 1.3,
12	xlab="Income deprivation",
13	ylab= "Fairness",
14	main = "Trust in fairness and income deprivation")
15	mtext("X", adj=1, side=1)
16	mtext("Y", adj=0, side=3)
17	cd <- cooks.distance(m2)
18	summary(cd) # 3rd quartile 0.043
19	thrs <- 0.043 # 3rd Quartile
20	cd_obs <- which(cd > thrs)
21	points(eu$hincfel34[cd_obs], eu$pplfair[cd_obs],
22	col="green", pch=19)
23	plot(eu$hincfel34, eu$pplfair, type="p", cex=1.5,
24	pch=18, col="grey50",
25	cex.main=1.1, cex.lab = 1.3,
26	xlab="Income deprivation",
27	ylab= "Fairness",

Table 5.5 (continued)

Line	R Script
28	main = "Trust in fairness and income deprivation")
29	mtext("X", adj=1, side=1)
30	mtext("Y", adj=0, side=3)
31	outl <- which(abs(resid(m2))>2.0 * sd(resid(m2)))
32	points(eu$hincfel34[outl], eu$pplfair[outl],
33	col="red", pch=19)
34	dev.off()

Lines explained

We attach this R script primarily to demonstrate the overall structure of an R script for creating a plot using Figure 5.10 as an example. We have already presented and explained the individual instructions in the context of the preceding diagrams and in the accompanying text.

Line 1 loads the data frame. Lines 2 and 3 use the nested *na.omit(subset))* structure for variable selection and missing data control. Lines 4 and 5 calculate the polynomial regression, which the subsequent diagnostic plots refer to. Lines 6, 7, and 34 control the graphics device. Line 8 arranges the two plots in a 1 x 2 structure. Lines 9 to 22 then refer to the left plot and lines 23 to 33 to the right plot. For both *plot()* functions, the parameters are used that we have already described in detail in the context of the previous plots in this chapter. Regarding the coloring of the points in the cloud of (x, y) value combinations, we described the logic of the procedure – via *which()* – in the accompanying text to this graphic (lines 17 to 20 and line 31). We now use this selection function for the two *points()* functions, and therein via the [] specification (lines 21 and 22, 32 and 33). While the selection criterion for COOK's D was that this index value is > 3rd quartile of all index values (line 19), we assumed as a possible criterion for defining an outlier that an absolute residual of the polynomial regression exceeds twice the standard deviation of all residual values (line 31).

Part III: **Statistical Methods for Prediction, Classification, Text Analytics**

Chapter 6
Linear Models

6.1 Simple Regression

$$y_i = a + b \cdot x_i + e_i \qquad i = 1, \ldots, n \tag{6.1}$$

In this equation y_i and x_i represent observed values and a and b stands for the un-known parameters to be estimated. The subscript i refers to the units of analysis, often called "cases". The index runs from the first to the last, i. e., n^{th} case in the data matrix, of which each such case constitutes a row.

In this most simple use-case of a linear regression, estimates of intercept and slope, a and b, may be obtained by dividing the covariance of x and y by the variance of x

$$b = \frac{cov_{xy}}{s_x^2} \tag{6.2}$$

and by subtracting the man values of x and y as shown in (6.3):

$$a = \bar{y} - b \cdot \bar{x} \tag{6.3}$$

In general, instead, standard estimation algorithms are used to obtain the estimates of effect of regression models. In linear regression this are usually *least-squares* esti-mates of the unknown parameters. The standard algorithm is called Ordinary Least Squares, its acronym OLS is often used to denote this computational approach.

$$Q = \sum_{i=1}^{n} e_i^2 = \sum_{i=1}^{n} (y_i - \hat{y}_i)^2 \tag{6.4}$$

OLS estimates are obtained by minimizing the expression displayed in (6.4). In partic-ular, we obtain OLS estimates by minimizing the sum of squared differences between the pairs of y values observed and estimated for a unit i. Applied to equation (6.1), for instance, the result is an equation that predicts a value of y given x for each case i.

$$\hat{y}_i = a + b \cdot x_i \tag{6.5}$$

Illustrating Example

Example Data Set 6 on Energy Transition in the European Green Deal is used for an illustration of a simple regression. This data sets describes the EU countries in terms of variables from several data sources. This includes a characterization of each country by the percentage of its population that would like to see action against climate change pri-oritized by the European Parliament. In the present example this is the target variable y (labeled *EUclimate* in the data set). Another variable indicates a country's living stan-dard by its official purchasing power standard (*PPS*). PPS measures the price of certain goods and services relative to income in a country. In the present example this is variable *x* (labelled *KKS* in the data set). The number of cases is N = 27, namely the 27 EU countries. In the R script we named the data set *energy*.

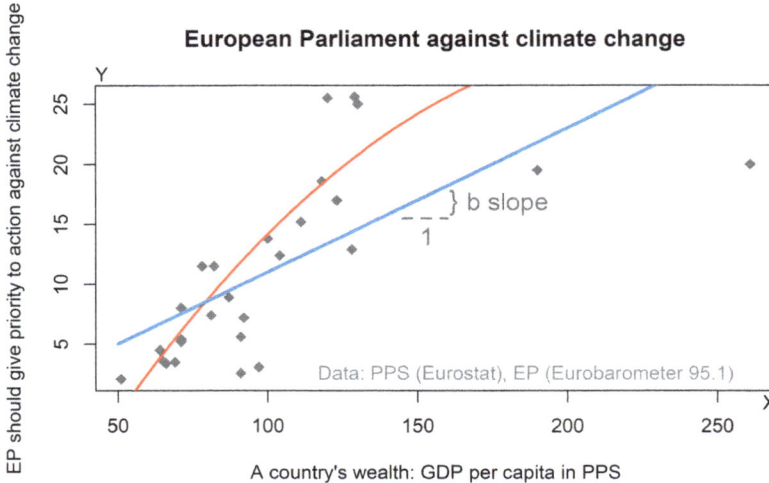

Figure 6.1: Linear and Polynomial Regression.

To estimate the said population share of a country, we use the *lm()* function:

$$lm(formula, weights, data) \tag{6.6}$$

lm stands for *linear model*. First we specify *formula* according to the pattern: target variable ~ predictor variable. Since case weighting is not needed in this example, we ignore the *weights* option here. This implies that each case (=country) is included in the calculation with the standard weight of 1. Finally, *data* names the R data frame that contains the variables and cases to be analyzed. Then, the *lm()* function looks like this:

$$lm(EPclimate \sim KKS, \ data = energy) \tag{6.7}$$

That would be the most economical way. However, it is often a good idea to save the calculations under an explicit object name — for example for subsequent calculations or model comparisons. Such object names can be freely chosen, here we use *sr* to indicate simple regression. If the script line embeds *lm()* in the *summary()* function at the same time, we immediately get the standard output.

$$summary(sr < -lm(EPclimate \sim KKS, \ data = energy)) \tag{6.8}$$

This standard output includes information about the residuals, the estimated coefficients, and the model fit. In this introductory example, we take from this overall set only three pieces of information, namely the intercept (*a* = − 0.97), the slope (*b* = 0.12), and the multiple R-squared ($R^2 = 0.474$). In Figure 6.1, these values for intercept and slope result in the light-blue regression line.

The *b* slope is often interpreted in terms of a hypothetical experiment to indicate the expected change in y_i for a unit change in x_i. An increase in a country's purchasing power index by one index point would therefore result in an expected increase in the respective population share by 0.12 (where the *y* scale expresses this share in percentages).

The intercept *a* estimates the *y* value in the case that the predictor variable *x* is equal to zero. This becomes apparent if x_i is set to zero in (6.5). Then $b \cdot x_i$ also becomes zero and in this way reduces (6.5) to $\hat{y}_i = a$. However, it should be noted that this way we get an artificial reference value when $x_i = 0$ falls outside the range of the *x* scale.

A simple regression assumes a linear relationship between *y* and *x*. Such a relationship is characterized by a straight line, as exemplified by the light-blue graph in Figure 6.1. Linearity means to assume a linear *effect* of *x* on *y*. Such an effect implies the same expected change in *y* for a unit change in *x* across the whole scale range of *x*: the *b* slope is then assumed the same regardless of whether a smaller or larger *x* value is assumed to change. Polynomial regression allows us to relax this assumption by estimating the possible *nonlinear* effect *x* might exercise on *y*.

6.2 Polynomial Regression

A polynomial regression may be computed by nesting the *poly()* function in *lm()*. In the illustrating example, this would change the R script line from (6.8) to (6.9), where again the object name is freely chosen (here *pr* to indicate polynomial regression).

$$summary(pr < -lm(EPclimate \sim poly(KKS, 2, raw = TRUE), data = energy)) \qquad (6.9)$$

This R script line calls for a *2nd -degree* polynomial. Such a polynomial raises *x* to the 2nd power as shown in (6.10), where b_0 replaces *a* as the symbol for the intercept:

$$y_i = b_0 + b_1 \cdot x_i + b_2 \cdot x_i^2 + e_i \qquad (6.10)$$

to arrive at the involved estimates

$$\hat{y}_i = b_0 + b_1 \cdot x_i + b_2 \cdot x_i^2 \qquad (6.11)$$

for b_0, b_1, b_2 as shown in (6.11). Instead of using *poly()*, we could have expanded the set of predictor variables with an *artificially created* variable, x^2 (the square of *x*). This results in estimates for the intercept ($b_0 = -20.82$), a linear ($b_1 = 0.45$) and quadratic ($b_2 = -0.001$) effect component of *x* on *y*, and a multiple R-squared ($R^2 = 0.685$). In Figure 6.1, these intercept and slope estimates result in the red regression curve.

This raises the question of which of the two graphs better approximates the underlying scatterplot. For this we have to assess the model fit. A measure for this is the multiple R-squared. R^2 is usually interpreted in terms of explained variance. In the illustrating example R^2 is 0.474 if we assume a linear effect, and R^2 is 0.685 if we assume a non-linear effect of x on y. The latter explains much more variance than the former, namely 68.5 percent vs. 47.4 percent of the variance of the target variable y.

6.3 Multiple Regression

While simple regression uses just one x variable for a prediction equation, multiple regression uses more than one. Adding additional x variables is straightforward. For example, a second variable would expand (6.1) like this:

$$y_i = b_0 + b_1 \cdot x_{1i} + b_2 \cdot x_{2i} + e_i \tag{6.12}$$

While in general k variables may be added to the prediction equation:

$$y_i = b_0 + b_1 \cdot x_{1i} + b_2 \cdot x_{2i} + \ldots + b_k \cdot x_{ki} + e_i \tag{6.13}$$

Let x_1 denote as before a country's official purchasing power standard, and x_2 the percentage of a country's population at risk of poverty or social exclusion (labeled *Povertyrisk* in the data set). Then, (6.8) changes to

$$summary\left(mr < -lm\left(\begin{array}{c} EPclimate \sim KKS + Povertyrisk, \\ data = energy \end{array}\right)\right) \tag{6.14}$$

where mr is a freely chosen object name (here, to indicate multiple regression). A corresponding function call computes the least-squares estimates $b_0 = 11.43$, $b_1 = 0.10$ and $b_2 = -0.49$ as well as a predicted y value for each case i if these estimates were inserted in the prediction equation (6.15)

$$\hat{y}_i = 11.43 + 0.10 \cdot x_{1i} - 0.49 \cdot x_{2i} \tag{6.15}$$

The model explains 57.8 percent of the y variance ($R^2 = 0.578$). The additional inclusion of a second predictor variable has thus raised the explained variance from $R^2 = 0.474$ to 0.578.

6.4 Ordinary Least Squares

In practice, OLS estimates are easily achieved by a function call to *lm()*. All necessary calculations are then carried out automatically. This involves minimizing Q in (6.4). Just to give an idea of the involved calculations, we rewrite each multiplication of $b_k \cdot x_{ki}$ in (6.12) by its equivalent $x_{ki} \cdot b_k$ and add a term x_{0i} which is 1 for all cases i. This constant term is necessary for computing the intercept. We obtain this way the equation (6.12) in a form

$$y_i = x_{0i} \cdot b_0 + x_{1i} \cdot b_1 + x_{2i} \cdot b_2 + e_i \qquad x_{0i} = 1 \text{ for all } i \tag{6.16}$$

that may be expressed in matrix notation as

$$Y = Xb + e \qquad (6.17)$$

In the illustrating example, with its $i = 1, \ldots, 27$ cases and their observed values in y, x_1, and x_2, the overall structure of Y, X, b, and e is shown in (6.18).

$$
\begin{matrix} Y_{[27 \cdot 1]} & X_{[27 \cdot 3]} & b_{[3 \cdot 1]} & e_{[27 \cdot 1]} \end{matrix}
$$

$$
\begin{bmatrix} 12.9 \\ 18.6 \\ 2.1 \\ 2.6 \\ 7.2 \\ 17.0 \\ 25.6 \\ 11.5 \\ 5.6 \\ 15.2 \\ 12.4 \\ 3.4 \\ 4.5 \\ 5.4 \\ 19.5 \\ 3.1 \\ 7.4 \\ 20.0 \\ 3.5 \\ 13.8 \\ 25.0 \\ 5.2 \\ 11.5 \\ 3.6 \\ 25.5 \\ 8.9 \\ 8.0 \end{bmatrix}
=
\begin{bmatrix} 1 & 128 & 16.9 \\ 1 & 118 & 19.5 \\ 1 & 51 & 32.8 \\ 1 & 91 & 22.3 \\ 1 & 92 & 12.5 \\ 1 & 123 & 17.4 \\ 1 & 129 & 16.3 \\ 1 & 82 & 24.3 \\ 1 & 91 & 25.3 \\ 1 & 111 & 15.6 \\ 1 & 104 & 17.9 \\ 1 & 66 & 30.0 \\ 1 & 64 & 23.3 \\ 1 & 71 & 18.9 \\ 1 & 190 & 20.6 \\ 1 & 97 & 25.6 \\ 1 & 81 & 26.3 \\ 1 & 261 & 20.6 \\ 1 & 69 & 27.3 \\ 1 & 100 & 20.1 \\ 1 & 130 & 16.5 \\ 1 & 71 & 18.2 \\ 1 & 78 & 21.6 \\ 1 & 65 & 31.2 \\ 1 & 120 & 18.8 \\ 1 & 87 & 14.4 \\ 1 & 71 & 16.4 \end{bmatrix}
\cdot
\begin{bmatrix} b_0 \\ b_1 \\ b_2 \end{bmatrix}
+
\begin{bmatrix} e_1 \\ e_2 \\ e_3 \\ e_4 \\ e_5 \\ e_6 \\ e_7 \\ e_8 \\ e_9 \\ e_{10} \\ e_{11} \\ e_{12} \\ e_{13} \\ e_{14} \\ e_{15} \\ e_{16} \\ e_{17} \\ e_{18} \\ e_{19} \\ e_{20} \\ e_{21} \\ e_{22} \\ e_{23} \\ e_{24} \\ e_{25} \\ e_{26} \\ e_{27} \end{bmatrix}
\qquad (6.18)
$$

Corresponding to (6.16), equation (6.19) yields the *predicted* y_i value for each case i.

$$\hat{y}_i = x_{0i} \cdot b_0 + x_{1i} \cdot b_1 + x_{2i} \cdot b_2 \qquad x_{0i} = 1 \text{ for all } i \tag{6.19}$$

This enables us to replace $\hat{y}_i$ in (6.4) with the right-hand side of (6.19), to obtain

$$Q = \sum_{i=1}^{n} e_i^2 = \sum_{i=1}^{n} \left(y_i - (x_{0i} \cdot b_0 + x_{1i} \cdot b_1 + x_{2i} \cdot b_2) \right)^2 \tag{6.20}$$

and (6.21), after the inner brackets have been eliminated.

$$Q = \sum_{i=1}^{n} e_i^2 = \sum_{i=1}^{n} \left(y_i - x_{0i} \cdot b_0 - x_{1i} \cdot b_1 - x_{2i} \cdot b_2 \right)^2 \tag{6.21}$$

OLS estimates are obtained if we write out equation (6.16) for each case i, set the first partial derivatives of Q with respect to b_0, b_1 and b_2 equal to zero and solve the resulting system of equations. Using matrix algebra, this is usually done via the least-squares *normal equations*

$$(X'X)b = X'Y \tag{6.22}$$

where X' denotes the transpose of X. The normal equations are solved by pre-multiplying (6.22) by $(X'X)^{-1}$. The result is an expression $(X'X)^{-1}(X'X)b = (X'X)^{-1}X'Y$ that reduces to the estimator

$$b = (X'X)^{-1}X'Y \tag{6.23}$$

because $(X'X)^{-1}(X'X) = I$ is an identity matrix. Thus, in the example, using (6.23) we get exactly the OLS estimates b_0, b_1 and b_2 we are looking for. The required R script lines are part of the script shown in Table 6.1.

Table 6.1: OLS Estimates of Effect.

Line	R Script
1	`load("Energy2.Rdata")`
2	`# Simple regression`
3	`summary(sr <- lm(EPclimate ~ KKS, data = energy))`
4	`# Multiple regression`
5	`summary(mr <- lm(EPclimate ~ KKS + Povertyrisk, data = energy))`
6	`#input y and x`
7	`y <- mr$model$'EPclimate'`
8	`x0 <- rep(1, length(mr$model$'EPclimate'))`
9	`x1 <- mr$model$'KKS'`
10	`x2 <- mr$model$'Povertyrisk'`
11	`x <- cbind(x0, x1, x2)`
12	`xtx <- (t(x)%*%x)`

Table 6.1 (continued)

Line	R Script
13	invxtx <- solve(xtx)
14	b <- invxtx%*%t(x)%*%y
15	round(b, 5)

Lines explained

Line 1 loads the data frame. Line 2: Optional comment. Line 3: *lm()* nested in the *summary()* function. *lm()* specifies the formula in terms of target $y \sim$ predictor x, names the involved data frame, and assigns all of the involved model specifications and computations to the object named *sr*. Line 4: Optional comment. Line 5: *lm()* nested in the *summary()* function. Here, *lm()* specifies the formula in terms of target $\bar{y}$ predictor variables $x_1 + x_2$, names the involved data frame, and assigns all of the involved model specifications and computations to the object named *mr*. Line 6: Optional comment. Lines 7 to 10 build the vectors for y, x_0, x_1 and x_2. The corresponding empirical values are displayed in (6.18). We use the option to import the required observed values directly from the previously created object *mr*, where script line 8 is used to create a vector of 1s, with the number of 1s fixed via the length (=number of rows) of the y vector. Line 11 combines the three x vectors to a matrix denoted using the column-bind function. Lines 12 to 14 realize the computations for (6.23). Line 12 pre-multiplies X with its transpose, line 13 inverts this $X'X$ matrix, to get $(X'X)^{-1}$. Line 14 multiplies this matrix with $X'Y$, to obtain b. Line 15 optionally rounds the b values to 5 decimal places in order to be able to compare the values directly with the corresponding values produced by the *lm()* function.

As expected, the *lm()* function and the direct calculation produce identical b estimates: $b_0 = 11.42954$, $b_1 = 0.09827$, $b_2 = -0.48887$. An increase in a country's purchasing power standard (x_{1i}) by one index point would accordingly result in an expected increase in y_i, the percentage of its population that would like to see action against climate change prioritized by the European Parliament, by 0.098 y scale units, "holding constant" the second predictor variable (x_{2i}) at the same time. While an increase in this second predictor x_{2i}, the percentage of a country's population at risk of poverty or social exclusion, by one scale unit (percentage) would let us expect a decrease in the percentage of its population that would like to see action against climate change prioritized by the European Parliament, by -0.489. b_1 and b_2 are now *partial* regression coefficients whose meaning is detailed in the next section.

6.5 Partial Regression Coefficients

We speak of *simple* regression when only one x variable is used to predict the target variable y and we speak of *multiple* regression when more than one x variable is used for this purpose. Secondly, the technical term usually implies that both y and the x

variables are measured on metric scales, and, thirdly, that the distributional assumptions associated with the linear regression model hold. Fourth, it is common practice to calculate the b's based on data from random samples, in order to use them as sample estimates of population parameters.

In this section we would first like to show how the b's of a simple regression differ from the b's of a multiple regression. Figure 6.2 displays the structure of the example used to illustrate the difference.

Simple Regression   Multiple Regression

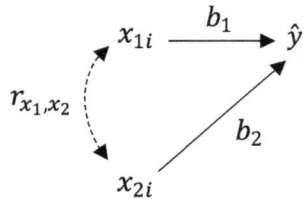

Figure 6.2: Simple and Multiple Regression Structure.

We use three eleven-point scales from Example Data Set 4, Web Survey on Machine Learning and Robots in Human Life. The target variable y is happiness, using this question wording: "On a scale of 1 = "very unhappy" to 11 = "very happy", where would you place yourself on this scale?" In the data frame ki this variable is referred to as *happy*.

x_1 measures a respondent's standard of living using this question wording: "We ask you to imagine the image of a ladder with 11 rungs. The top rung 11 should represent the best possible standard of living, just as you would want it. And the bottom rung 1 should represent the standard of living that would be the worst for you. Two questions about this: 1.) If you think about your current standard of living. Which rung of the ladder would you place him on? 2.) Which rung of the ladder do you see your standard of living on in five years?" Here we use the first of these two scales, i. e., the scale on the *current* standard of living. In the data frame ki this variable is referred to as *livstand*.

x_2 measures how confident a respondent is about his or her personal future. We asked: "How do you assess your personal future? Are you more confident or skeptical about it?" A response was requested on two consecutive scales, first on a categorical scale ("confident", "skeptical", "neither/nor", "don't know"), then on the eleven-point scale used here: "On a scale of 1 = "not at all confident" to 11 = "very confident", where would you place yourself on this scale?" In the data frame ki this variable is referred to as *confidence*.

To illustrate the difference between simple and partial regression coefficients, we run three corresponding models:

$$summary\left(hl < -lm\left(\begin{array}{l} happy \sim livstand, \\ weights = cwt, \quad data = ki \end{array}\right)\right) \qquad (6.24)$$

$$summary\left(hc < -lm\left(\begin{array}{l} happy \sim confidence, \\ weights = cwt, \quad data = ki \end{array}\right)\right) \qquad (6.25)$$

$$summary\left(hlc < -lm\left(\begin{array}{l} happy \sim livstand + confidence, \\ weights = cwt, \quad data = ki \end{array}\right)\right) \qquad (6.26)$$

Where again *hl*, *hc* and *hlc* are freely chosen object names, *happy*, *livstand* and *confidence* name y, x_1 and x_2, *cwt* names the case weight, and *ki* the data frame in which these four variables are stored. The first and second model are simple regression models and the third is a multiple regression model that brings together the two previously separate predictors into one equation. A comparison of corresponding estimates of effect yields the result shown in Table 6.2.

Table 6.2: Corresponding Simple and Partial Regression Coefficients.

b coefficient	livstand	confidence
Simple	0.5715	0.5611
Partial	0.4329	0.3963

It becomes evident that both simple estimates exceed their partial counterpart. This is due to the fact that persons in good standard of living tend to be confident as well. The two ratings are correlated $\left(r_{x_1 x_2} = 0.43\right)$ and indicate this particular relationship: Persons with higher *livstand*-scores tend also to higher *confidence*- scores, and vice versa. The two partial regression coefficients consider this correlation, the simple regression coefficients do not. If then, as here, both predictors are also correlated with the target variable y, the effect of x_1 on y will implicitly reflect part of the effect of x_2 on y, and the effect of x_2 on y will also partially reflect the effect of x_1 on y. We are then talking of *confounded effects*. Exactly this mixing of effects from different variables is ruled out by computing partial coefficients. In case of regression analysis such partial coefficients remove specifically the influence of correlating predictors from the estimate of effect a given predictor variable exercises on a target variable y. Partial coefficients have the same meaning as simple coefficients when interpreted as hypothetical experiment: The *b*'s from a multiple regression too indicate expected change in a target variable y for a unit change in a predictor variable x_k, however now while "holding constant" all other predictors in a given equation. Thus the hypothetical experiment is carried out under an explicit set of statistical controls.

In practice, calling the *lm()* function evokes all required computations automatically, nothing more is required to get partial regression coefficients. When we decompose a multiple regression into a series of simple regressions in the present context, so only to illustrate what it means to say that we free an estimate of effect from the influence of a confounding factor. An early description of this technique is given in Draper and Smith (1981: 196–204). Here, we use (6.26) to regress *happy* on *livstand* and *confidence*. Excluding cases with missing values in *y*, x_1 and x_2 on a listwise base, the remaining valid *n* is 209 cases. Where the two subjective ratings of living standard and confidence explain 51.4 percent of the target variable *y*, i. e., the subjective rating of happiness $\left(adj.R^2 = 0.514\right)$. The associated regression equation may be written as (6.27):

$$y_i = x_{0i} \cdot b_0 + x_{1i} \cdot b_1 + x_{2i} \cdot b_2 + e_i \qquad x_{0i} = 1 \text{ for all } i \qquad (6.27)$$

Since the function call uses the *weights* option, *weighted* least squares estimates are computed. We obtain as intercept $b_0 = 1.536$ and as *b* slopes the two partial regression coefficients $b_1 = 0.4329$ and $b_2 = 0.3963$. If we take the *partial* b_1 coefficient as an example, we could also have calculated this coefficient via the *simple* regression (6.28)

$$(y_i - \hat{y}_i) = b_1(x_{1i} - \hat{x}_{1i}) + e_i \qquad (6.28)$$

Where in this equation the differences in the brackets, $(y_i - \hat{y}_i)$ and $(x_{1i} - \hat{x}_{1i})$, represent the *residuals* that occur when x_2 is used to predict x_1 and *y* in two separate simple regressions. For each case *i* those residual values indicate the target variation x_2 can*not* predict. If then residual-*y* is regressed on residual-x_1, this simple regression yields an intercept of zero and the same b_1 as the multiple regression yields. Schematically this is shown in Figure 6.3. The same partial b_1 also results if, instead of residual-*y*, *y* itself is regressed on residual-x_1, but then the intercept is unequal to zero. Partial b_2 can be calculated using the same technique, except that the influence of x_1 must now be partialed out. Table 6.3 shows the associated R script.

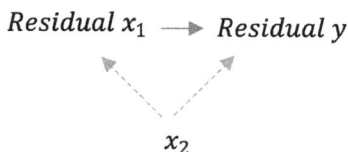

Figure 6.3: Multiple Regression Decomposed to Obtain Partial b_1.

Table 6.3: R Script to Auxiliary Effect Decomposition.

Line	R Script
1	`load("ki.Rdata")`
2	`# Simple regression`
3	`summary(hl <- lm(happy ~ livstand, weights = cwt, data = ki))`
4	`summary(hc <- lm(happy ~ confidence, weights = cwt, data = ki))`
5	`# Multiple regression`
6	`summary(hlc <- lm(happy ~ livstand + confidence,`
7	`            weights = cwt, data = ki))`
8	`# Correlated predictor variables`
9	`cor(hlc$model$livstand, hlc$model$confidence,`
10	`            method = c("pearson"))`
11	`# Auxiliary effect decomposition`
12	`aux1 <- lm(hlc$model$happy ~ hlc$model$confidence,`
13	`            weights = hlc$weights)`
14	`aux2 <- lm(hlc$model$livstand ~ hlc$model$confidence,`
15	`            weights = hlc$weights)`
16	`summary(aux3 <- lm(aux1$residuals ~ aux2$residuals,`
17	`            weights = aux1$weights))`

Lines explained

Line 1 loads the data frame. Line 2: Optional comment. Lines 3 and 4: *lm()* nested in the *summary()* function. *lm ()* specifies the formula in terms of target $y \sim$ predictor x, names the involved weight and data frame, and assigns all specifications and computations to the objects named *hl* and *hc* respectively. Line 5: Optional comment. Lines 6 and 7: *lm()* nested in the *summary()* function. Same setup as described above. Line 8: Optional comment. Lines 9 and 10 compute the Pearson correlation between x_1 and x_2. For this the required observed values are directly imported from the previously created object *hlc*. Line 11: Optional comment. Lines 12 to 17 specify the three functions required for the auxiliary effect decomposition resulting in (6.28). Here again the required values are imported from previously created objects: the *observed* values are taken from *hlc* and the residuals are taken from *aux1* and *aux2*.

6.6 Weighting the Units of Analysis

The weighted least squares estimator can be used to consider individually varying weights. In practice, this is realized by creating a variable to be addressed in the *weights* option of the *lm()* function. In the present example this is the variable named *cwt* in the data frame.

In survey research weighting is usually done to adjust observed survey data for requirements of the survey design and/or for unit nonresponse that occur in realizing probability samples. Accordingly we then talk of design weights and nonresponse weights. If both adjustment requirements arise, then we would always have to create a single weighting variable that combines both requirements. Such variables are usually developed in an early phase of a study, for example immediately after the completion of a survey's field phase (data collection). It is common practice in social research that survey data providers supply these weighting variables as part of delivered data sets. Thus such variables are usually available ahead of statistical analysis. They do not have to be created again and again. In practice they are simply called in the lm() function.

In WLS analysis the weights are in general the elements of the inverse of the estimated variance-covariance matrix of Y. This gives more weight to elements that have smaller sampling variances, "that is, to the elements in which we have more confidence" (Forthofer and Lehnen 1981:26). We expand (6.23) accordingly by V_Y^{-1} to obtain the weighted least squares estimator (6.29):

$$b = \left(X'V_Y^{-1}X\right)^{-1}X'V_Y^{-1}Y \tag{6.29}$$

Here we use this WLS estimator specifically in conjunction with the units' weights. The associated R script is explained in Table 6.4.

Table 6.4: WLS Estimates of Effect.

Line	R Script
1	load("ki.Rdata")
2	summary(hlc <- lm(happy ~ livstand + confidence,
3	weights = cwt, data = ki))
4	# input Y, weights, X
5	y <- c(hlc$model$happy)
6	w <- c(hlc$weights)
7	x0 <- rep(1, length(hlc$model$happy))
8	x1 <- hlc$model$livstand
9	x2 <- hlc$model$confidence
10	x <- cbind(x0,x1,x2)
11	# Computing b
12	v <- diag(u <- (1/w))
13	invv <- solve(v)
14	b <- (solve(t(x)%*%invv%*%x))%*%t(x)%*%invv%*%y
15	round(b, 5)

Lines explained

Line 1 loads the data frame. Lines 2 and 3: *lm()* nested in the *summary()* function. *lm()* specifies the formula in terms of target y ~ predictors $x_1 + x_2$, names the involved weight variable and data frame, and assigns all specifications and computations to the object named *hlc*. Line 4: Optional comment. Lines 5 to 9 import the empirical input: target y, weight w, x_1 and x_2. Line 7 specifically provides x_0, i. e., the vector of 1s required for the intercept, where the required number of 1s is specified by the embedded *length()* function. Line 10 binds together the vectors x_0, x_1 and x_2 to the matrix x. Line 11: Optional comment. Lines 12 to 14 specify the required computations to get b according to the WLS estimator (6.29). Line 12 calculates the inverse values of the weights and embeds them in the diagonal matrix v. Line 13 inverts this matrix. Line 14 computes b according to (6.29). Line 15 rounds the output of b to five significant decimal places.

6.7 Statistical Interaction in the Standard Use Case

The standard multiple regression model estimates linear and additive effects. This phrase specifically refers to the main effects of predictors. However, the linearity as well as the additivity assumption may be relaxed. For instance, while a polynomial and spline regression model respectively is apt to estimate non-*linear* effects, non-*additive* effects may be covered by models that consider *statistical interaction* between some or all predictors of an equation in addition to the single main effects of such x_k variables.

Statistical interaction represents the very part of an overall effect of a set of predictor variables that exceeds the sum of their main effects. Statistical interaction indicates an *emergent effect* that — across a set of x_k variables — arise out of specific value configurations of those variables. The presence of statistical interaction represents certainly a practical instance of what is meant by the famous sentence that the whole thing is more than the sum of its parts.

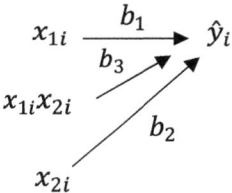

Figure 6.4: Synthetic Interaction Term Added.

Main effects are calculated in such a way that they do not overlap. They break down the overall influence of a set of correlated predictors into single independent effects. Where the main effect of a variable is independent in the sense that it excludes possible interactions with other predictors. Therefore, in case of *linear* effects: *one x, one b slope*. Interactions weaken this principle because they make the strength and even direction of a b slope dependent on the context of other predictors in the equation (Jaccard 2001: 14). To illustrate this, let's go back to our multiple regression example above, here rewritten as (6.30).

$$\hat{y}_i = b_0 + b \cdot x_{1i} + b_2 x_{2i} \tag{6.30}$$

(6.30) considers the main effects of x_{1i} and x_{2i} only, labeled b and b_2 . Next we formulate the idea that the effect of x_{1i} on $\hat{y}_i$, b, is a linear function of x_{2i}. This means that it depends on the value a person i has on x_{2i} if the effect of x_{1i} on $\hat{y}_i$ becomes weaker or stronger.

$$b = b_1 + b_3 x_{2i} \tag{6.31}$$

According to (6.31), for a unit change of x_{2i}, the effect of x_{1i} on $\hat{y}_i$, b, changes by b_3.

Replacing b in (6.30) with the right-hand side of (6.31), yields

$$\hat{y}_i = b_0 + (b_1 + b_3 x_{2i}) x_{1i} + b_2 x_{2i} \qquad (6.32)$$

Multiplying out the brackets and rearranging terms, yields

$$\hat{y}_i = b_0 + b_1 x_{1i} + b_2 x_{2i} + b_3 x_{1i} x_{2i} \qquad (6.33)$$

Where b_1 and b_2 represent main effects and b_3 represents an interaction effect. Special attention deserves the expression following this b_3, namely $x_{1i} x_{2i}$. This is the product of x_{1i} and x_{2i} and exemplifies the standard technique of implementing statistical interaction in regression analysis: by creating a synthetic variable defined as the product of two (or more) parent variables. In practice, this variable is created first and then taken up in the *lm()* function call as an additional predictor (Figure 6.4). Alternatively, the operators ":" and "*" may be used to create the product of x_{1i} and x_{2i}. The associated R script lines are shown in Table 6.5.

Table 6.5: Specifications of Statistical Interaction.

Line	R Script
1	`load("ki.Rdata")`
2	`ki$lico <- ki$livstand * ki$confidence`
3	`summary(hlcl <-lm(happy ~ livstand + confidence +`
4	`lico, weights = cwt, data = ki))`
5	`# Alternative to lines 3 and 4,`
6	`# given that script line 2 is omitted`
7	`summary(hlcint <- lm(happy ~ livstand + confidence +`
8	`livstand:confidence,`
9	`weights = cwt, data = ki))`
10	`summary(hlcint2 <- lm(happy ~ livstand * confidence,`
11	`weights = cwt, data = ki))`

Lines explained
Line 1 loads the data frame. Line 2 creates the synthetic variable named *lico* as product of x_1 and x_2. Lines 3 and 4: *lm()* nested in the *summary()* function. *lm()* specifies the formula in terms of target $y \sim$ predictors $x_1 + x_2 + x_3$, names the involved weight variable and data frame, and assigns all specifications and computations to the object named *hlcl*. Lines 5 and 6: Optional comment. Lines 7 to 9 call a model formulation that uses the ":" operator to add only the product of x_1 and x_2 to x_1 and x_2. Lines 10 and 11 formulate a second alternative procedure. It uses the "*" operator to specify x_1 and x_2 as well as its product at once.

While the main effects of living standard and confidence explain 51.4 percent of happiness, the two predictors explain 58.6 percent if additionally their interaction is considered $(adj.R^2 = 0.586)$. (6.34) inserts the numerical estimates in the equation.

$$\hat{y}_i = -4.7498 + 1.2515 \cdot x_{1i} + 1.2995 \cdot x_{2i} - 0.1147 \cdot x_{1i}x_{2i} \qquad (6.34)$$

Both main effects are positive ($b_1 = 1.2515$ and $b_2 = 1.2995$) and thus indicate an expected increase in happiness in case of rising living standard and confidence respectively. At the same time the interaction is negative ($b_3 = -0.1147$). For a given individual standard-of-living score, say $x_{1i} = 6$, its positive main effect on happiness, $1.2515 \cdot 6$, is weakened the more, the higher the individual x_{2i} confidence score at the same time, and vice versa. Analogously this also applies to a given confidence score, depending on whether the standard of living score is larger or smaller. This means that without taking the interaction into account, the overall effect of the two predictors would have been overestimated.

An interaction model consisting of *two metric scales* x_{1i} and x_{2i} and their mathematical product $x_{1i}x_{2i}$ as a third variable exemplifies the standard implementation of statistical interaction in multiple regression. This nucleus of x_{1i}, x_{2i} and $x_{1i}x_{2i}$ is easily extendable to models with more than two x variables and then also to additional interactions and even higher-order interactions between three and more x variables at a time. All this by multiplying the x variables as wanted and implementing their products as synthetic variables in the prediction model.

6.8 Statistical Interaction in the Mixed-Scales Use Case

Interaction may also occur between variables of different scale levels, for instance between a *metric* and *categorical* variable. Due to the completely arbitrary nature of assignment of scores to the single categories of categorical variables, it would be senseless to multiply such scores by scores of, for instance, metric variables. The solution of this complicating factor is to transform these categories into a set of synthetic variables, known as dummy variables, before doing any further calculations. Such dummy variables are binary variables coded 1 if a condition applies, and zero otherwise. Here, "condition" stands for membership in a given response category, or if necessary also in a collapsed category of two or more individual categories.

To illustrate the dummy-coding technique in the present mixed-scales use context of statistical interaction analysis, we stay with the eleven-point happiness and standard-of-living scales but switch to a categorial measure of confidence. As outlined above, we asked the respondents how they assess their personal future in a two-step response format. First we asked if they were more confident or skeptical about it, followed by the response categories "confident", "skeptical", "neither/nor", "don't know". Then the eleven-step ladder scale was used (without any filtering in this sequence of survey questions) that we have used in the previous illustrative example. Applied to the four categories of the assessment of one's personal future, the dummy-coding technique may be exemplified as shown in Table 6.6.

Table 6.6: Dummy Coding Scheme Exemplified.

	x_{2i}	x_{4i}
Confident	1	0
Skeptical	0	0
Other (neither/nor & don't know)	0	1

As before the metric scale is x_{1i}, the standard of living. x_{2i}, x_{3i} and x_{4i} are the three 0/1 coded dummy variables that map the categories of the parent variable "future":

This is being *confident* and *skeptical* respectively as well as *other*. This last condition merges two original categories: *neither/nor* and a very few *don't know*. We omit one of these dummy variables, in fact x_{3i}=skeptical, to make this the implicit reference category for the effect of the remaining two dummy variables, x_{2i} and x_{4i}. In Table 6.6 this is the condition coded zero throughout.

Alternatively, we could have chosen one of the other two categories as the implicit reference category as well. However, since we primarily want to contrast the conditions confident vs. skeptical, *skeptical* was chosen as the reference category. The second dummy variable then provides the contrast *other* vs. *skeptical*. This second variable is included primarily to keep the reference category *skeptical* unconfounded, i. e. not merged with cases from the categories *neither/nor* and *don't know*. Thus the contrast *other* vs. *skeptical* primarily serves as a statistical control.

As a general recommendation, choose the reference category so that the explicitly estimated effects can be interpreted in the best possible way. Therefore, a residual category should never be chosen as a reference category. Additionally, the reference category itself should comprise a substantial number of cases.

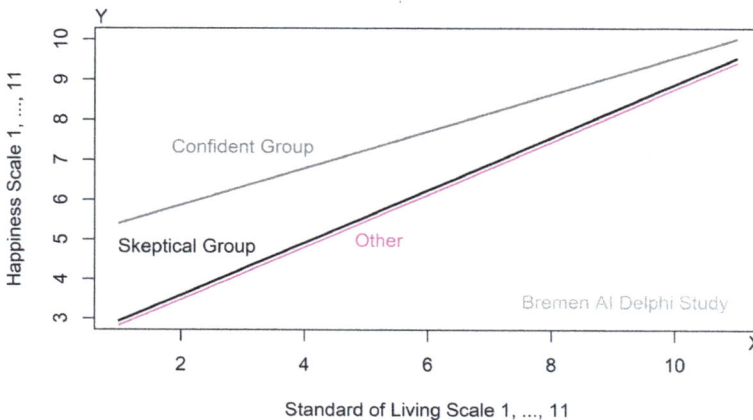

Figure 6.5: Interaction in the Mixed-Scales Use Case.

The prediction model comprises the metric scale x_{1i} (standard of living), x_{2i} (confident) and x_{4i} (other) as well as the product $x_{1i}x_{2i}$ to cover the interaction of x_{1i} and x_{2i}. To predict happiness by these variables, we specify (6.35) in conjunction with (6.36), replace b in (6.35) with the right-hand side of (6.36), and get in this way an equation (6.37) that indicates how the slope of the metric scale of x_{1i}, b_1, is modified by the 0/1 coded dummy variable x_{2i} (being 1 = confident vs. 0 = skeptical). Multiplying out the brackets and rearranging terms, yields (6.38). This equation estimates an intercept b_0, the main effect of living standard, b_1, the main effect of being confident (vs. skeptical), b_2, the main effect of other (vs. skeptical), b_4, and the interaction effect of living standard and being confident, b_5.

$$\hat{y}_i = b_0 + b \cdot x_{1i} + b_2 x_{2i} + b_4 x_{4i} \tag{6.35}$$

$$b = b_1 + b_5 x_{2i} \tag{6.36}$$

$$\hat{y}_i = b_0 + (b_1 + b_5 x_{2i}) x_{1i} + b_2 x_{2i} + b_4 x_{4i} \tag{6.37}$$

$$\hat{y}_i = b_0 + b_1 x_{1i} + b_2 x_{2i} + b_4 x_{4i} + b_5 x_{1i} x_{2i} \tag{6.38}$$

Table 6.7 displays the R script lines used for dummy coding, the synthetic interaction variable, and the *lm()* function call. Replacing the b's in (6.38) with their estimated values, yields (6.39).

$$\hat{y}_i = 2.28 + 0.66 \cdot x_{1i} + 2.67 \cdot x_{2i} - 0.11 \cdot x_{4i} - 0.20 \cdot x_{1i} x_{2i} \tag{6.39}$$

As expected the main effect of living standard is positive ($b_1 = 0.66$). We observe also a positive effect due to being confident (vs. skeptical) about the personal future ($b_2 = 2.67$). In this case of $x_{2i} = 1$, the interaction effect ($b_5 = -0.20$) becomes effective too, since this condition implies $-0.20 \cdot x_{1i} \cdot 1$. For the group of confident people the effect of living standard on happiness, i. e. its slope, thus amounts to 0.66–0.20 = 0.46 for a unit change of x_{1i}.

Table 6.7: R Script for Implementing Dummy Coding in the Use Case "Interaction between Metric and Categorical Scales".

Line	R Script
1	load("ki.Rdata")
2	addmargins(table(ki$future))
3	ki$confident <- ifelse(ki$future == 1, 1, 0)
4	ki$skeptical <- ifelse(ki$future == 2, 1, 0)
5	ki$other <- ifelse((ki$future == 3	
6	ki$future == 4), 1, 0)

Table 6.7 (continued)

Line	R Script
7	ki$int <- ki$livstand * ki$confident
8	summary(hlci <-lm(happy ~ livstand + confident +
9	other + int, weights = cwt, data = ki))

Lines explained

Line 1 loads the data frame. Line 2 embeds *table()* in the *addmargins()* function to get the frequency distribution of the variable named *future*. Lines 3 to 6 realize dummy coding of the parent variable *future* using *ifelse()* logic. These 0/1 coded dummy variables are named *confident, skeptical* and *other*. Line 7 creates a synthetic interaction variable by multiplying the metric scale *livstand* with the previously created dummy variable *confident*. Lines 8 and 9: *lm()* nested in the *summary()* function. *lm()* specifies the formula in terms of target y ~ predictors $x_1 + x_2 + x_3 + x_4$, names the involved weight variable and data frame, and assigns all specifications and computations to the object named *hlci*.

On the other hand, if someone is not confident, i. e. skeptical, x_{2i} becomes zero. This results in $-0.20 \cdot x_{1i} \cdot 0$ and thus in zero on the whole (since multiplication with zero makes the whole expression and thus the interaction vanish). For the group of skeptical people the effect of living standard on happiness thus amounts to 0.66 for a unit change of this metric x_{1i} variable. x_{2i} acts accordingly as a group-forming variable that moderates the effect of the metrically scaled living standard x_{1i}.

The last configuration refers to $x_{4i} = 1$, i. e. the "other" group (of persons who responded *neither/nor* or *don't know* to said survey question). Compared to the skeptical group, membership in this group results in a marginally lower expected happiness value. Figure 6.5 picture the overall finding. Parallel regression lines indicate the absence of interaction, non-parallel lines indicate its presence. The associated R script lines are shown in Table 6.8.

Coleman's approach to longitudinal multivariate analysis is focused on qualitative attribute data. Such data is essentially transformable to 0/1 coded binary data. Related to this kind of data, Coleman (1964: 224–235) introduced different kinds of interaction effect, including the popular intensifying effect. In addition, Coleman (1981: 32–33) developed a formula to estimate interaction also in terms of sameness or difference in the values of attribute data. For the case of two such attributes k and j, this formula may be written as (6.40).

$$x_{kj} = x_k \cdot x_j + (1 - x_k)(1 - x_j) \tag{6.40}$$

Table 6.8: Syntax to Build Figure 6.5.

Line	R Script
1	x <- seq(from = 1, to = 11, by = 1)
2	y1 <- c(2.28 + 0.66*x) # skeptical
3	y2 <- c(2.28 + (0.66-0.20)*x + 2.67) # confident
4	y3 <- c(2.28 + 0.66*x - 0.11) # other
5	tiff("fig65.tiff", units = "in", width = 7, height = 4.5, res = 600)
6	plot(x, y1, type = "l", lwd = 2, cex = 1.0, col = "black", ylim = c(3, 10),
7	xlab = "Standard of Living Scale 1, ..., 11",
8	ylab = "Happiness Scale 1, ..., 11")
9	lines (x, y2, lwd = 2, cex = 1, col = "grey50")
10	lines (x, y3, lwd = 1.5, cex = 1, col = "magenta")
11	text(3, 7.3, "Confident Group", cex = 1.0, col = "grey50")
12	text(2.1, 4.8, "Skeptical Group", cex = 1.0, col = "black")
13	text(5.2, 5, "Other", cex = 1.0, col = "magenta")
14	mtext("X", adj = 1, side = 1)
15	mtext("Y", adj = 0, side = 3)
16	text(9.2, 3.4, "Bremen AI Delphi Study", cex = 1.0, col = "grey65")
17	dev.off()

Lines explained

Line 1 defines the x axis. Lines 2 to 4 specify the respective functions in terms of $y = f(x)$ for the skeptical, confident and other group. Line 5 defines the graphic in terms of format, name, unit, width and height in inch, and resolution. Lines 6 to 8 specify details of the *plot()* function in terms of the x axis and function to be plotted (*y1*), the *line* as symbol used to plot the function (*type*), line width (*lwd*), font size relative to standard size (*cex*, character expansion factor), line color (*col*), scale range of the y axis (*ylim*), labeling of x and y axis (*xlab, ylab*). Lines 9 to 16 specify related instructions. Lines 9 and 10 add the two remaining graphs in terms of *x, y*, line width, font size and color. Lines 11 to 13 as well as line 16 add the respective quoted text at the respective x-y coordinates, and defines font size and color. Lines 14 and 15 write the quoted text in the margins of the figure. *adj = 1* in conjunction with *side = 1* provide right alignment at bottom, and *adj = 0* in conjunction with *side = 3* left alignment at top. Line 17 shuts down the graphic device activated by *tiff()* in line 5.

Chapter 7
Goodness of Fit and Predictive Power of a Linear Model

7.1 Within-Sample Model Fit: How Well Does a Linear Model Fit the Data?

Table 7.1 contains the output to the interaction model in the standard use case of section 6.7 above. It refers specifically to equation (6.34) of this earlier example. The output consists of several blocks of information. First the function call issued from the associated R script is reprinted. The output then informs about the summary statistics (min/max value, 1st quartile, median, 3rd quartile) for the residual variable. Next we see the "Coefficients" block of the estimated regression coefficients together with their associated standard errors, t values and statistical significance. Finally the output reports the block of information required to assess how well the model fits the data. We have two measures at our disposal: the residual standard error, RSE, and the coefficient of determination, R^2. Third, an F-statistic is reported to assess the statistical significance of R^2.

Table 7.1: Output from the Interaction Model in the Standard Use Case (refers to eq. 6.34).

Line	R Output
1	Call:
2	lm(formula = happy ~ livstand + confidence + lico, data = ki,
3	weights = cwt)
4	
5	Weighted Residuals:
6	Min 1Q Median 3Q Max
7	-5.4063 -0.5870 0.0119 0.5820 4.7745
8	
9	Coefficients:
10	Estimate Std. Error t value Pr(>|t|)
11	(Intercept) -4.74976 1.10926 -4.282 2.85e-05 ***
12	livstand 1.25147 0.14185 8.822 4.93e-16 ***
13	confidence 1.29947 0.15556 8.353 9.91e-15 ***
14	lico -0.11472 0.01886 -6.081 5.75e-09 ***
15	---
16	Signif. codes: 0 '***' 0.001 '**' 0.01 '*' 0.05 '.' 0.1 ' ' 1
17	
18	Residual standard error: 1.258 on 205 degrees of freedom

https://doi.org/10.1515/9783110680683-007

Table 7.1 (continued)

Line	R Output
19	(7 observations deleted due to missingness)
20	Multiple R-squared: 0.5919, Adjusted R-squared: 0.5859
21	F-statistic: 99.12 on 3 and 205 DF, p-value: < 2.2e-16

Lines explained

Lines 1 to 3 reprint the function call issued from the R script. Lines 5 to 7 provide the summary statistics (min/max value, 1st quartile, median, 3rd quartile) for the residual variable. Lines 9 to 16 report the "Coefficients" block of the estimated regression coefficients together with their associated standard errors, t values and statistical significance. Lines 18 to 21 report the block of information about the model fit. The number of units i is n=209.

The left outcome column of the table of "Coefficients" reports the least squares estimates for the intercept and the slopes of equation (6.34) that was introduced in section 6.7 above. To the right of this the associated standard error estimates are printed.

In the frequentist model, the standard error is the average spread, i.e. the standard deviation, of the sampling distribution of the sample estimates of a population parameter. Related to this is the idea that random samples are taken from the population not just once, but repeatedly, each time the relevant sample estimate is calculated and noted, and the standard deviation is calculated from this distribution of sample estimates. In research practice, this is a purely theoretical model, as *only one* random sample is actually drawn (and thus just one sample estimate, for instance, of a slope parameter is available). However, the theoretical model can be derived mathematically and also proved experimentally.

If an estimate is divided by its standard error, the resulting ratio is given in the third column as *t value*. The reference to *t* designates the relevant probability distribution. Finally, the probability value associated with the respective t value is shown in the fourth column. For instance, the probability of obtaining a t value greater than the absolute value of −6.081, i.e. of $|-6.081|$, is $5.75 \times 10^{-9} = 0.00000000575$, that is zero. In line 16 of the output this is indicated by the associated significance code.

Conceptually a linear regression model decomposes the deviation of an individual y_i value from the mean value, $\bar{y}$, of its frequency distribution into two segments (Figure 7.1).

Computationally this is realized by decomposing the overall sum of squares into two parts, in fact a residual sum of squares and an explained sum of squares.

Table 7.2: Analysis of Variance Table for Output in Table 7.1.

Line	R Output
1	Analysis of Variance Table
2	
3	Response: happy
4	Df Sum Sq Mean Sq F value Pr(>F)
5	livstand 1 295.77 295.767 187.024 < 2.2e-16 ***
6	confidence 1 116.00 115.996 73.349 2.593e-15 ***
7	lico 1 58.48 58.483 36.981 5.750e-09 ***
8	Residuals 205 324.19 1.581
9	---
10	Signif. codes: 0 '***' 0.001 '**' 0.01 '*' 0.05 '.' 0.1 ' ' 1

Lines explained

Line 1 indicates the type of table and line 3 the target variable. In lines 5 to 8 the table itself reports the consumed and remaining degrees of freedom, the respective sums of squares, mean squares, F values and associated probability values. The number of units i is n=209. This implies that we have available n-1 = 208 degrees of freedom, of which we "consume" one per predictor variable to estimate their effects. Given k=3 predictors, as in the present analysis, this results in n-k-1 = 209 – 3 – 1 = 205 residual degrees of freedom. The left outcome column indicates these df. The column to the right reports the sums of squares. Next, these sums of squares are divided (row-wise) by their degrees of freedom and reported as mean squares. The F value results if the mean squares of a predictor is divided by the residual mean square. In lines 5 and 7, for instance, by computing 295.767 ÷ 1.581434 = 187.025 and 58.483÷1.581434 = 36.98 respectively (using more decimal places than printed above to minimize rounding error; cf. line 14 in Table 7.3). If we compute the sum of the sum of squares over the three predictors and divide this sum by the sum of involved degrees of freedom, (295.767 + 115.996 + 58.483)/3, we obtain the *model's* mean square and df. Now if we divide this mean square by the residual mean square, we obtain the F value reported in the bottom line of the standard output in Table 7.1 along with the associated numerator and denominator degrees of freedom (99.12 on 3 and 205 df). The associated p-value of 2.2e-16, i.e. of 2.2×10^{-16}, indicates a highly significant value when testing the null hypothesis that the effects of all three predictors are zero, in fact against the alternative hypothesis that at least one of these effects deviate from zero. Since this null hypothesis implies an $R^2 = 0$, the F test is used to test the statistical significance of R^2 as well.

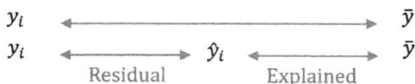

Figure 7.1: Individual Variation Decomposed.

$$\underset{i=1}{\overset{n}{\sum}} (y_i - \bar{y})^2 = \underset{i=1}{\overset{n}{\sum}} (y_i - \hat{y}_i)^2 + \underset{i=1}{\overset{n}{\sum}} (\hat{y}_i - \bar{y})^2 \tag{7.1}$$

$$\text{Overall} \qquad\quad \text{Residual} \qquad\;\; \text{Explained}$$

Least squares estimates of intercept and slope(s) are obtained by minimizing the *residual* sum of squared differences between the pairs of y values observed and estimated for a unit i. If units are individually weighted, then the sum of these *weighted* squared differences is minimized.

$$\sum_{i=1}^{n} w_i (y_i - \hat{y}_i)^2 \tag{7.2}$$

Such analyses thus require always a variable that provides the weight for each unit. For instance, in the present analysis this information is stored in the variable named *cwt*.

If the residual sum of squares is divided by the associated (i.e., the residual) degrees of freedom, the square root of this quantity is known as the *Residual Standard Error* (RSE). In this formula n indicates the number of units i and k the number of predictor variables (not counting the intercept).

$$RSE = \sqrt{\frac{1}{n-k-1} \sum_{i=1}^{n} w_i (y_i - \hat{y}_i)^2} \tag{7.3}$$

The RSE is an estimate of the standard deviation of the residuals in the population from which the sample data underlying the RSE calculation was randomly drawn. Along with another measure, the R^2, it is considered a measure for assessing model accuracy (James et al. 2013: 68 – 71). Table 7.3 refers to the model whose estimates and model fit information are reprinted in Tables 7.1, 7.2 and 7.4.

Since for *each* unit i both values, the observed y_i and the estimated $\hat{y}_i$, are available, across all units the correlation known as *multiple R* can be computed. If we square this coefficient, we obtain R^2, the coefficient of determination.

$$R^2 = r_{\hat{y},y}^2 \tag{7.4}$$

R^2 can take values between 0 and 1 and is usually interpreted as the proportion of *explained variance* of target variable y. It is also common to interpret this measure in terms of the *proportional reduction of prediction error*

$$R^2 = \frac{s_y^2 - s_e^2}{s_y^2} \tag{7.5}$$

Formula (7.5) relates two estimates of the prediction error to each other: the prediction is based only on the frequency distribution of the target variable itself and the prediction is based on the joint frequency distribution of that target variable with one

Table 7.3: Residual Standard Error & Sum of Squares.

Line	R Script
1	load("ki.Rdata")
2	summary(hlcl <-lm(happy ~ livstand + confidence +
3	lico, weights=cwt, data=ki))
4	n <- length(hlcl$residuals) # 209
5	k <- (hlcl$rank - 1) # 3
6	y <- hlcl$model$happy
7	w <- hlcl$weights
8	r <- hlcl$residuals
9	f <- hlcl$fitted
10	summary(wr <- r * sqrt(w))
11	anova(hlcl)
12	rss <- sum(w*(y - f)^2) # 324.1941
13	rse <- sqrt(rss/(n-k-1)) # 1.257551
14	rv <- rss / (n-k-1) # 1.581434
15	summary(hlcl2 <-glm(happy ~ livstand + confidence +
16	lico, family = gaussian(),
17	weights=cwt, data=ki))

Lines explained

Line 1 loads the data frame. Lines 2 and 3 specify the function call as explained earlier (Table 6.5). Already this call produces the output reprinted in Table 7.1 (no further script lines required). The rest of this script provides additional information to help understand the calculation of individual quantities of this output in Table 7.1 (weighted residuals, residual sum of squares, residual standard error, residual variance). In addition, the associated variance analysis table is called, also a comparative calculation using the *glm()* function. Lines 4 to 9 directly access information obtained from the function call above. This information is stored in object *hlcl*. Line 4 uses the *length()* function to fix *n*, the number of units that went into the analysis (here, 209 units). Line 5 determines *k*, the number of predictor variables (excluding the intercept). Line 6 accesses the target variable (*y*), line 7 the weights (*w*), line 8 the residuals (*r*), and line 9 the fitted values (*f*) (the respective new variable names in brackets). Line 10 multiplies each residual by the square root of its weight, assigns this product to object *wr*, and calculates the summary statistics for this variable. In Table 7.1, this summary statistics is displayed under the heading *Weighted Residuals*. Line 11 calls the associated analysis of variance table (as reprinted in Table 7.2). Lines 12 to 14 refer to the residual sum of squares (*rss*). First this quantity is computed according to (7.2). Next it is divided by the associated degrees of freedom. While line 14 assigns this division to object *rv* (indicating residual variance), line 13 takes the square root of this division to get *rse*, the Residual Standard Error. Lines 15 to 17 specify the function call for the present model if the *glm()* function is used for it. This function call generates the output shown in the main part of Table 7.4.

or more predictor variables. In the former case, the mean value is the best choice for an educated guess of the y value of a randomly drawn unit i while the overall y variance quantifies the prediction error. In the latter case the *conditional* y mean given x, i.e. the estimated y value, is the best choice while the *residual* variance quantifies the prediction error. Formula (7.5) subtracts the residual variance from the overall variance and expresses this difference as share in the overall variance.

$$R_{adj}^2 = R^2 - \frac{k \cdot (1 - R^2)}{n - k - 1}$$ (7.6)

The *adjusted* R^2 considers additionally the number of predictor variables, k. Formula (7.6) reduces a given R^2 the more the more predictor variables were needed to achieve its value. Sparse models in terms of k are thus advantaged. This attenuation effect due to k is more effective the smaller the number of units n that went into the calculation of R^2.

R^2 is widely used to assess linear regression models. Attewell and Monaghan (2015: 13 – 15) regard it a measure of "predictive power" and James et al. (2013: 68 – 71) a measure of "model accuracy". In contrast, Kuhn and Johnson (2013: 95–97) do not consider R^2 as an accuracy measure in their treatise of quantitative measures of performance in regression models. Rather, they emphasize that R^2 is a correlation measure, not an accuracy measure. This may be seen as such if accuracy is to be defined in absolute terms — like an agreement coefficient such as κ (kappa) — and not in relative terms. Longitudinal panel research addressed a similar topic early on, namely the difference between absolute and relative change. At that time, Kessler and Greenberg (1981: 8) drew attention to the point that a perfect correlation between corresponding measures at t_1 and t_2 can indicate quite different facts: namely that all respondents remained in their respective states over time (high absolute stability) or that all respondents changed their respective states in the same way (high relative but low absolute stability).

Table 7.4: Output from the Interaction Model Using the glm() Function.

Line	R Output
1	Call:
2	glm(formula = happy ~ livstand + confidence + lico,
3	family = gaussian(), data = ki, weights = cwt)
4	
5	Coefficients:
6	Estimate Std. Error t value Pr(>|t|)
7	(Intercept) -4.74976 1.10926 -4.282 2.85e-05 ***
8	livstand 1.25147 0.14185 8.822 4.93e-16 ***
9	confidence 1.29947 0.15556 8.353 9.91e-15 ***
10	lico -0.11472 0.01886 -6.081 5.75e-09 ***
11	– – –
12	Signif. codes: 0 '***' 0.001 '**' 0.01 '*' 0.05 '.' 0.1 ' ' 1

Table 7.4 (continued)

Line	R Output
13	
14	(Dispersion parameter for gaussian family taken to be 1.581434)
15	
16	Null deviance: 794.44 on 208 degrees of freedom
17	Residual deviance: 324.19 on 205 degrees of freedom
18	(7 observations deleted due to missingness)
19	AIC: 761.86
20	
21	Number of Fisher Scoring iterations: 2

Lines explained

Lines 1 to 3 reprint the function call issued from the R script. Lines 5 to 12 report the "Coefficients" block of estimates, standard errors, t values and significance information. We realize that *glm()* and *lm()* produce identical results. Lines 14 to 19 inform about the model-fit block of information. Across *lm()*, *anova()* and *glm()* three pairs of quantities correspond to each other:

Table 7.1		Table 7.2		Table 7.3		Table 7.4	
lm()		anova()		script		glm()	
Line	Value	Line	Value	Line	Value	Line	Value
The square of the residual standard error, i.e. the residual variance, corresponds to the dispersion parameter for gaussian family.							
18	1.258^2	8	1.581	14	1.581434	14	1.581434
				13	1.257551		
The residual sum of squares corresponds to the residual deviance.							
		8	324.19	12	324.1941	17	324.19
The overall sum of squares corresponds to the null deviance.							
		5 to 8	794.44*			16	794.44

*Sum of sums of squares (295.77+116+58.48 +324.19 = 794.44)

7.2 Linear Regression in the Validation Set Design

In the words of Kelleher and Tierney (2018: 145), a paradigm of data science can be described with the sentence: "The golden rule for evaluating models is that models should never be tested on the same data they were trained on." Consequently, one solution is to randomly split an original data set (Figure 7.2), in the simplest case into a training and a test set, which is then sometimes referred to as a holdout or validation set (James et al. 2013: 176–177; Ghani and Schierholz 2017: 174). This "hold-out sampling" is probably the simplest and most appropriate form of sampling in this context "when we have very large datasets from which we can take samples" (Kelleher et al. 2020: 541).

In addition, the data science literature also suggests a design that randomly splits the dataset into *three* parts: a training set, a validation set and a test set (Kelleher and Tierney 2018: 147; Kuhn and Silge 2022: 134–135). First, an initial set of models is trained in the training set in order to compare their performance in a second step using the unseen data of the validation set. "The validation set is used when data outside the training set is required in order to tune particular aspects of a model" (Kelleher et al. 2020: 541).

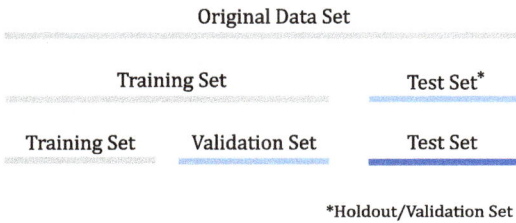

Figure 7.2: Validation Set Design.

Such tuning is not always necessary. In a simple linear regression, for instance, there is almost no scope for modeling the relationship. In this case, a random split into a training and test set will usually be completely sufficient. This may be different for more complex models. In this regard, we are thinking of different kinds of models. For instance models that involve nonlinear effects of unknown shape or statistical interactions in addition to main effects or latent variables. Additional complexity arises out of the different ways categorical variables and metric scales may go into formal models. In such cases, it may indeed be helpful to identify a best model via an intermediate tuning phase.

Once such a best model has been selected, the training and validation set can be merged back together into a larger training set, in order to relate this larger training set to the final test set. In doing this, it is crucial that the test set was completely left out of the preceding training and validation step, i.e. has actually remained unseen by the trained model (Kelleher et al. 2020: 536), and that the test set is not used for a final adaptation to the data (model tuning). Then the test set can be used to estimate the generalization performance of the best model from the previous step, "that is, how well the model is likely to do on unseen data" (Kelleher and Tierney 2018: 145, 147).

We first stick with the data example from Section 7.1 and the output for the regression equation (6.34) shown in Table 7.1. The R script shown in Table 7.5 performs four basic tasks for this analysis: handling item nonresponse, holdout sampling, running the regression for the training set, and calculating the residual standard error and R^2 with respect to the test set.

Table 7.5: Script to Interaction Model (6.34) in the Validation Set Design.

Line	R Script
1	`load("ki.Rdata")`
2	`sset <- subset(ki, select = c(happy, livstand,`
3	`                        confidence, lico, cwt))`
4	`sset <- na.omit(sset) # 209`
5	`set.seed(123)`
6	`tr <- sample(209, 146, replace = FALSE)`
7	`summary(trainmodel <- lm(happy ~ livstand + confidence + lico,`
8	`        weights=cwt, subset = tr, data=sset))`
9	`n <- length(sset$cwt) - length(trainmodel$weights) # 63`
10	`k <- trainmodel$rank - 1 # 3`
11	`print(rss <- sum((sset$happy-predict(trainmodel, sset))[-tr]^2))`
12	`print(rse <- sqrt(rss/(n-k-1)))`
13	`print(rv <- rss/(n-k-1))`
14	`obs.happy <- sset$happy[-tr]`
15	`prd.happy <- predict(trainmodel, sset)[-tr]`
16	`print(R2 <- cor(obs.happy, prd.happy, use="everything",`
17	`        method = "pearson")^2) # 0.5474`
18	`print(test.mse <- mean((sset$happy-predict(trainmodel,`
19	`                        sset))[-tr]^2))`
20	`print(train.mse <- mean(trainmodel$residuals^2))`

Lines explained

Line 1 loads the data frame. Lines 2 and 3 select the required variables using the *select* argument of the *subset()* function and assigns the result to the new data frame named *sset*. Line 4 applies the *na.omit()* function to this new data frame for a listwise exclusion of units with missing values in the selected variables. Line 5 sets a seed for the random number generator to ensure reproducible results when carrying out the random sampling of row numbers in the subsequent line 6. This random sampling is realized without replacement of a unit once drawn. The result of this sampling is assigned to object *tr* in order to be addressable in subsequent steps of analysis. Lines 7 and 8 invoke the *lm()* function with the usually required specifications, this time including the *subset=tr* argument The result is assigned to *trainmodel* and all this embedded in the *summary()* function. Lines 9 and 10 are auxiliary computations to get the values for *n* and *k* in lines 12 and 13. Since the *length()* function requires a variable name for which the length is to be determined, the weight variables just serve as such a variable. Line 10 provides the number of predictor variables excluding the intercept. Line 11 calculates the residual sum of squares for the test or holdout sample. Note the reference to *[-tr]*, while at the same time the *predict()* function relates to *trainmodel*, i.e., the training set. The result of the computation is assigned to object *rss* and embedded in the *print()* function to get it printed. Line 12 divides the residual sum of squares by *n-k-1* and takes the square root of this, in order to get the residual standard error *rse*. Similarly, line 13 calculates the residual variance by omitting the square root. Lines 14 to 17 are written to calculate R^2. Line 14 assigns the observed y values of the holdout set to *obs.happy*, while line 15 assigns the predicted values from the training set to *prd.happy*. Lines 16 and 17 then serve the purpose of computing the correlation between these two vectors, square this correlation, and assign the result to *R2*. Embedded in *print()*, we get the value of R2 printed. Lines 18 and 19 calculate the mean squared error with respect to the test set and line 20 calculates the MSE for the training set.

Table 7.6: Output from the Interaction Model (6.34) When Applied to the Training Set.

Line	R Output
1	Call:
2	lm(formula = happy ~ livstand + confidence + lico, data = sset,
3	subset = tr, weights = cwt)
4	
5	Weighted Residuals:
6	Min 1Q Median 3Q Max
7	-5.6728 -0.7008 -0.0784 0.5832 4.3829
8	
9	Coefficients:
10	Estimate Std. Error t value Pr(>|t|)
11	(Intercept) -4.29695 1.34096 -3.204 0.00167 **
12	livstand 1.26684 0.16642 7.612 3.42e-12 ***
13	confidence 1.26536 0.18731 6.756 3.39e-10 ***
14	lico -0.11768 0.02249 -5.233 5.87e-07 ***
15	– – –
16	Signif. codes: 0 '***' 0.001 '**' 0.01 '*' 0.05 '.' 0.1 ' ' 1
17	
18	Residual standard error: 1.294 on 142 degrees of freedom
19	Multiple R-squared: 0.5468, Adjusted R-squared: 0.5373
20	F-statistic: 57.12 on 3 and 142 DF, p-value: < 2.2e-16

Lines explained in Table 7.1

First, the data frame *ki* is loaded and the *subset()* function is used to select the required variables including the sample weight *cwt*. The resulting new data frame is named *sset* and contains only these five variables. Then, the *na.omit()* function serves the purpose of reducing this latter data frame listwise to the units with valid values in these variables. This listwise exclusion leads to a slightly reduced sample size of 209 units (respondents).

Next we draw a random sample of 70 percent of these 209 units without replacement of a unit once drawn. For this purpose, we precede the *sample()* function with the *set.seed()* function in order to first set a seed for the random number generator. This makes it possible to reproduce the result of an analysis when it is repeated. James et al. (2013: 191) write in this context:

> It is generally a good idea to set a random seed when performing an analysis such as cross-validation that contains an element of randomness, so that the results obtained can be reproduced precisely at a later time.

The *sample()* function essentially generates a random selection of row numbers that subsequent calculations can refer to. To make this possible, we assign the result of this random selection to the (freely chosen) object name *tr*. This *tr* now represents the training set and can be addressed, for example, within both the *lm()* and *glm()* functions via their respective *subset* option. This option only complements the usual model specification as described earlier in this textbook. Via *summary(model name)* we obtain the standard output for the training set as displayed in Table 7.6. It corresponds to the output from Table 7.1, except that this time the analysis refers to the training set.

The model is calculated on the training set *tr* with its 146 units (respondents). Next we calculate the residual standard error *RSE* and R^2 with respect to the test set. Regarding this calculation we can in principle proceed as described in Table 7.3. However, in the *validation set design* we have to relate the predicted values from the *training* set to the observed values from the *test* set. At the operational level, we achieve this through the possibility to address all units of the dataset who are *not* part of the training set by placing a minus sign in front of *tr* when calculating the residual sum of squares, *rss*.

Embedded in this script line is the *predict()* function with its built-in capacity to transfer predicted values from *tr* to where they are missing but needed, namely to -*tr*. They are needed there in particular to relate them to the observed values of the test set when calculating the residual sum of squares, which in turn is needed to get the *RSE* and R^2. This built-in capacity is essentially the ability to perform a procedure known as *regression imputation* (van Buuren 2018: 13). This procedure is one of several methods for dealing with missing values in data sets.[1]

First, the regression model is estimated for the subset without missing values. In the present context, this is the training set. As a result, we obtain the regression coefficients as reported in Table 7.6. If inserted into the regression equation (7.7), i.e. equation (6.34) with the *b* estimates of the training model replacing the initial estimates,

$$\hat{y}_i = -4.2970 + 1.2668 \cdot x_{1i} + 1.2654 \cdot x_{2i} - 0.1177 \cdot x_{1i}x_{2i} \tag{7.7}$$

these coefficients provide us with the predicted values in the target variable *y*, namely for each unit with his/her specific combination of values in the predictor variables. Exactly these predicted values are now missing in the test set.

There we only have the observed values for *y* and the *x* variables available. However, we can assign a predicted *y* value to each unit of the test data set by inserting his/her combination of *x* values into the regression equation with its *b* estimates from the training set. In this way, for each unit of the test data set, we obtain exactly the pair of information (*y* estimated and *y* observed) that we need to calculate the R^2, the residual standard error *RSE*, the residual variance *RV* and the mean squared error *MSE*. The *RV* and *MSE* metrics differ only in whether the residual sum of squares is

---

[1] An overview of such "traditional methods" for dealing with missing data is given, for example, by Enders (2010: 37–55), including the method called regression imputation (pp. 44–46).

divided by *n* or by *n-k-1*. In the relevant literature, the MSE is a prominent measure in this context (e.g., James et al. 2013: 191).

It is important to note that the user does not have to perform these steps himself, as they are executed automatically via the *predict()* function together with the *-tr* specification in the [] brackets. It is thus a straightforward way of bridging the two subsets *tr* (training set) and *-tr* (test set) by this built-in form of regression imputation.

Table 7.7: Evaluation Metrics for Interaction Model (6.34) Compared.

	all	tr	-tr
R^2	0.592	0.547	0.547
RSE	1.258	1.294	1.355
RV	1.583	1.674	1.835
MSE	1.567	1.580	1.718
n	209	146	63

Table 7.7 reports the values of the three evaluation metrics for the full sample (acc. to Table 7.1), the training set (acc. to Table 7.6) and the test set when using for the calculation the predicted values from the training set. The column headed with *-tr* would be the relevant column if we follow the data-science recommendation to evaluate the model via the validation set design. The columns to the left of this are just for comparing how this procedure would affect the evaluation result in the example at hand. It is important to stress that the usual way is to *first* carry out holdout sampling and *only then* start with the regression analysis on the training set. Here we only wanted to use a data example that has already been introduced.

A relevant topic is sample size. In the present example the n=209 units already represent a relatively small sample. Kelleher et al. (2020: 541) write that there were no fixed recommendations "for how large the different datasets should be when hold-out sampling is used, although training:validation:test splits of 50:20:30 or 40:20:40 are common." Similarly, Ghani and Schierholz (2017: 174) note in relation to the split between training set and test set that "typically the splits range from 50–50 to 80–20, depending on the size of the data set". In the present analysis we performed a 70:30 split and this led us to just 63 units in the holdout set which is already a very small sample.

We will stick with the validation set design to illustrate with another example that this form of validation can be used not only for linear regression models. Via the *glm()* function with its various distributional arguments, other regression models, such as logit or probit models, can also be implemented into this validation scheme. We use data from Example Data Set 8 from the European Social Survey, Rounds 1 to 9, to exemplify this point by a type of regression whose foundations are explained in chapter 8, section 8.7.2, namely a probit regression. This data example is part of the research tradition on the authoritarian personality and asks to what extent right-wing extremism can be explained by the tendency toward authoritarianism. In Figure 7.3 this is the

$$x_1 \rightarrow y \tag{7.8}$$

relationship (equation 1). y measures the affinity to the political far right via the closeness to or the election of parties on the *far right* of the political spectrum. If this affinity is given, y is coded 1 and 0 otherwise. Since y is thus a binary variable, we have to choose a probit (or alternatively, a logit) regression here.

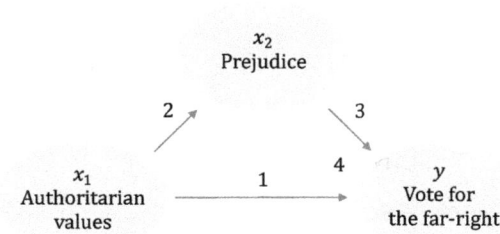

Figure 7.3: Vote for the Far-Right as a Function of Prejudice Formation and Authoritarian Value Orientation.

While the predictor variable x_1 is a scale of *factor-scores*. Such scales are derived from confirmatory factor analysis and represent the scores of underlying latent variables.[2] In the present example, also x_2 is such a scale of factor scores.

We can now proceed exactly as outlined for the above validation-set example. First, we load the data frame and select the required variables.

```
load("ess19.Rdata")
sset <- subset(ess19, select = c(authoritarian,          (7.9)
                        prejudice, rw2, wt))
```

We then exclude units with missing values in these variables on a listwise base. This reduces the number of units from 340,215 by 40,239 to 299,976 units.[3]

---

2 Details of the measurement model are documented in Engel (2022c) and a related R script.

3 This form of missing data treatment implies a loss of units for data analysis. We specifically lose 11.8 percent of the initial sample size due to item nonresponse. In large samples this is unproblematic as long as the missing values are missing at random. Only a more detailed missing data analysis

```
sset <- na.omit(sset)
```
(7.10)

Next we do the holdout sampling. (7.11) realizes this sampling by a 70:30 random split for the training : holdout sample. Again a seed for the random generator is set for reproducible results.

```
set.seed(123)
tr <- sample(299976, 209984)
```
(7.11)

Then the next script lines refer to the regression model itself. The only difference to the earlier example is that we relate the procedure here to the *glm()* function and thereby to a probability distribution other than the normal distribution.

```
summary(eq1 <- glm(rw2 ~ authoritarian, weights = wt,
    family=quasibinomial(probit), subset = tr, data=sset))
```
(7.12)

In a concluding step the mean squared error is computed with respect to the hold-out set.

```
mean((sset$rw2-predict(m1, sset))[-tr]^2)
```
(7.13)

The script lines (7.12) and (7.13) refer to *equation 1* in Figure 7.3. As with a linear regression, with a probit regression we obtain estimates of the regression coefficients involved, in this case estimates for the intercept and the effect of x_1 (authoritarian values) on y (vote for the far-right). Table 7.8 reports these two estimates together with the test or holdout *MSE* in its first row of findings.

Table 7.8: Estimates of Effect for the Model in Figure 7.3.

Eq.	Target	Form	Intercept	x_1	x_2	MSE
			b_0	b_1	b_2	
1	y	Probit	−2.189	0.106 (9.1)		4.889
2	x_2	Linear	0.014	0.213 (82.0)		0.565
3	y	Probit	−2.283		0.387 (38.5)	5.271
4	y	Probit	−2.284	0.041 (3.5)	0.383 (37.7)	5.278

In brackets: $b_v/s.e_v$ (estimate divided by its standard error)

would show whether there are also systematic reasons involved. Since we address the topic of item nonresponse elsewhere in this textbook, we skip this further analysis here.

We proceed in a similar way for the other target variables and thus obtain the values shown in Table 7.8. A characteristic of this procedure is that we calculate the four regression equations separately from one another, i.e. in four separate models. The effects shown are all significant in a statistical sense.

We do this here especially for a specific comparison: Does the effect of x_1 on y disappear when equation 1 is supplemented by x_2? This is done via equation 4. If we now compare the corresponding values in column b_1 of Table 7.8 with each other (0.106 vs. 0.041), we see that b_1 does not disappear completely: It does not become zero, but remains with a substantially reduced effect strength. This means that x_2 only partially acts as an intervening[4] variable, so the effect of x_1 on y can only partially be explained by the "mechanism" x_2. But even if a direct $x_1 \rightarrow y$ effect remains, an authoritarian value orientation also leads to the aforementioned voting behavior because this value orientation strengthens the formation of prejudice and this prejudice formation in turn favors the voting behavior.

7.3 Validation Set and Temporal Validation Design in Structural Equation Modeling

Instead of calculating the equations separately, we can also integrate them into a structural equation model. Structural equation modeling is an analytical tool that is both highly advanced and routinely applicable.

A structural equation model consists of two basic parts: a measurement part that relates observed indicator variables to latent variables by factor loadings and the structural equations that relate such latent concepts to each other. Both the measurement equations and the structural equations can be specified as, e.g., linear, logit, probit or Poisson regression equations, depending on the type and scale level of the respective target variables. The R library *lavaan* provides us with a tool that enables the flexible estimation of SEMs and provides a wide range of metrics for model evaluation. Beaujean (2014: 153–166) and Byrne (2012: 66–77), for example, provide a good overview of these fit measures.

A systematic introduction to these fit measures would be far outside the scope of this section. The same applies to an introduction to structural equation modeling.[5] Here, we would like to limit ourselves to one of the common fit measures, the SRMR, using the data example from Figure 7.3. The main focus will be on incorporating this

---

4 For an early introduction to "intervening variables", refer, e.g., to Rosenberg (1968: 57–58).
5 A number of textbooks are available for this purpose, including, for example, Bollen (1989), Byrne (2012), and the excellent German-language introduction by Reinecke (2014).

Table 7.9: Measurement of Authoritarian Value Orientation.

Item*		Loadings
x_1	Important to live in secure and safe surroundings	0.62
x_2	Important that government is strong and ensures safety	0.60
x_3	Important to behave properly	0.61
x_4	Important to do what is told and follow rules	0.54
x_5	Important to follow traditions and customs	0.52

*Selection of items from the Human Values Scale of the European Social Survey. *ESS* item names and more details are reported in Engel (2022c). Standardized factor loadings (n= 209,984 units (training set)). 6 pt. scales, original scale direction reversed. In the model treated as metric scales. If the scales are alternatively treated as ordinal scales, the factor loadings are nearly the same: 0.66 (x_1); 0.66 (x_2); 0.65 (x_3); 0.56 (x_4); 0.55 (x_5).

measure into a random-based and a time-based validation design.[6] Regarding the training set, Tables 7.9 and 7.10 report the measurement part[7] of the structural equation model and Table 7.11 its structural part.[8] According to this structural part, an authoritarian value orientation strengthens the affinity to the political right by forming prejudices against immigrants. This affinity to the political far right is again measured via the closeness to or the election of parties on the far right of the political spectrum. If this affinity is given, the variable is coded 1 and 0 otherwise. This variable enters

---

6 In structural equation modeling one evaluation metric is called the "expected value of the cross-validation index" (ECVI). It has been developed to avoid splitting the available data to form two samples, namely what Browne and Cudeck (1993: 147) termed the "calibration sample", i.e. the training set in the present context, and the "validation sample". Analogous to the scheme described in the present section, the model "is fitted to the calibration sample covariance matrix [. . .], yielding a fitted covariance matrix" [. . .], the cross-validation index (CVI) is "the discrepancy between the validation sample covariance matrix [. . .] and the fitted model [. . .] obtained from the calibration sample" (Browne and Cudeck 1993: 147). Given this, the *expected value of* the cross-validation index (ECVI) is a single-sample approximation of the CVI that avoids the split in calibration and validation sample (Browne and Cudeck 1993: 148). As the authors point out, "the ECVI is not helpful for choosing a parsimonious model when *n* is very large" (Browne and Cudeck 1993: 157). This means that it is not suitable for the example we discuss in this section. However we can compute this measure via *fitmeasures(rw.fit, fit. measures = c("ecvi"))* and get an ECVI=0.005. Beaujean (2014: 160–161) provides the formula for the ECVI and point out that the ECVI was designed "to be a single-sample approximation to the cross-validation coefficient obtained from a validation sample [. . .] Smaller values indicate better fit."
7 According to the factor loadings, only a mediocre measurement quality is achieved for the authoritarian value orientation, while prejudice formation appears to be measured very well by its three related items.
8 The common within-sample measures for assessing approximate fit all indicate an acceptable model (Comparative Fit Index CFI=1.0; Tucker-Lewis Index TLI=0.999; Root Mean Square Error of Approximation RMSEA=0.013; Standardized Root Mean Square Residual SRMR=0.023. Training set n=209,984 units.

the model as an observed binary variable. The data come again from Example Data Set 8 from the European Social Survey, Rounds 1 to 9.

Table 7.10: Measurement of Prejudice Formation.

Item*		Loadings
x_6	Country should allow people of the same race or ethnic group as most [country] people to come and live here	0.86
x_7	How about people of a different race or ethnic group from most [country] people?	0.98
x_8	How about people from the poorer countries outside Europe?	0.88

*Items come from the European Social Survey. *ESS* item names and further details are reported in Engel (2022c). Standardized factor loadings (n= 209,984 units (training set)). 4pt. scales: 1=allow many to come, 2=allow some, 3=allow a few, 4=allow none. In the model treated as ordinal scales.

The R programming starts analogously to (7.10) and (7.11), except that the selection of variables now focuses on the original variables and not the factor value scales derived from them. As before the resulting sample size is 299,976 units.

```
load("ess19.Rdata")
sset <- subset(ess19, select = c( x1, x2, x3, x4,
                    x5, x6, x7, x8, rw2, wt))
sset <- na.omit(sset)
```
(7.14)

Next we do the holdout sampling. (7.15) realizes this sampling again by a 70:30 random split for the training:holdout sample using the same seed for the random generator. This time we add two script lines to assign [tr,] and [-tr,] to different object names.

```
set.seed(123)
tr <- sample(299976, 209984)
traindata <- sset[ tr,]
testdata  <- sset[-tr,]
```
(7.15)

Next, *library(lavaan)* is invoked and the two model parts are specified according to the syntax rules of this library. This specification basically follows the usual way of specifying regression equations. If an equation specifically concerns factor loadings, the =~ symbol is used, otherwise the ~ symbol, with the respective target variable being placed left of the symbol.[9] (7.16) shows the script lines and its assignment to a model name.

---

9 Beaujean (2014) provides a good introduction to the syntax rules.

```
library(lavaan)
rw.model <- '
author =~ x1 + x2 + x3 + x4 + x5
prej =~ x6 + x7 + x8
rw2 ~ author + prej
prej ~ author
'
```
(7.16)

Once the model is specified, the next step is to estimate its parameters. To do this, we use the *sem()* function with its arguments. These include the reference to the model name, the data frame and the sample weights. We also determine the scale level if not assumed metric. In the present example this concerns the items on prejudice formation and the voting behavior. The *ordered* option collects these variables and implicitly controls in this way that we specify probit equations for these variables (otherwise linear regression equations are assumed by default). Finally, we assign the result of this model estimation to the object *rw.fit* in order to be able to address it in the subsequent *summary()* function. (7.17) shows how the *sem()* function was specified in detail.

```
rw.fit <- sem(rw.model, data=traindata,
              sampling.weights="wt",
              ordered=c("x6", "x7", "x8", "rw2"))
```
(7.17)

We use the *summary()* function to control the information to be included in the output. In the present example we used the sequence of script lines displayed in (7.18) and got a large amount of information, of which only a little part is reported in Tables 7.9 to 7.11.

```
summary(rw.fit, fit.measures = TRUE, estimates = TRUE,
standardized = TRUE, rsquare=TRUE)
```
(7.18)

Table 7.11: Estimates of Effect for the Model in Figure 7.3.

Target	Predictor	b_v	$b_v/s.e_v$	β_v	R^2
Right-wing					0.085
	Authoritarian	0.021	1.25	0.016	
	Prejudice	0.335	24.97	0.287	
Prejudice					0.049
	Authoritarian	0.251	48.96	0.222	

*b_v unstandardized regression effect; $b_v/s.e_v$ divides b_v by its standard error; β_v standardized regression effect

If the analysis would be based on the entire sample, we could have ended it at this point with the output and the numerous information it contained. However, we have based the analysis on the training set and now need to complete one more step: validating the model fit, specifically the SRMR measure.

To do this, the model-implied variance/covariance matrix of the model that we have just calculated for the *training* set must be related to the corresponding observed variance/covariance matrix for the *test* or *holdout* set. Both matrices are accessible using *str(rw.fit)*. This function shows all the information contained in the object *rw.fit* and how it can be accessed within this object. This allows us to easily incorporate them into subsequent calculations.

However, both matrices are designed as *full* matrices, which means that each individual covariance is contained twice: once below and once above the main diagonal. However, for computing the test SRMR, we only need each (observed and model-implied) covariance element once and not twice. We do this by setting the redundant entries above the main diagonal to zero. Only this calculation step requires a little more effort, since the *auxiliary matrix* required for it must be adapted to the size of the variance/covariance matrix. Since the present model consists of $v = 9$ observed variables, their variance/covariance matrix consists of 9 rows and 9 columns. To eliminate their redundant entries above the main diagonal, we multiply them by zero, while all required entries are multiplied by 1. We only need the auxiliary matrix for this multiplication. Like the variance/covariance matrix itself, it is a 9 x 9 matrix whose internal structure of ones and zeros will produce the desired structure. (7.19) reports the script lines used to create this auxiliary matrix. First, we define 9 vectors representing the rows, then the *rbind()* function combines these 9 rows into a matrix. This matrix can be referenced in subsequent calculations under the object name *m*.

```
r1 <- c(1, 0, 0, 0, 0, 0, 0, 0, 0)
r2 <- c(1, 1, 0, 0, 0, 0, 0, 0, 0)
r3 <- c(1, 1, 1, 0, 0, 0, 0, 0, 0)
r4 <- c(1, 1, 1, 1, 0, 0, 0, 0, 0)
r5 <- c(1, 1, 1, 1, 1, 0, 0, 0, 0)
r6 <- c(1, 1, 1, 1, 1, 1, 0, 0, 0)
r7 <- c(1, 1, 1, 1, 1, 1, 1, 0, 0)
r8 <- c(1, 1, 1, 1, 1, 1, 1, 1, 0)
r9 <- c(1, 1, 1, 1, 1, 1, 1, 1, 1)
m  <- rbind(r1, r2, r3, r4, r5, r6, r7, r8, r9)
```

$$(7.19)$$

In such a matrix the number of ones follows the general formula

$$\frac{v \cdot (v+1)}{2}$$

$$(7.20)$$

The present model consists of $v = 9$ observed variables. In the subsequent calculations, we therefore have to take into account a total of

$$\frac{9 \cdot 10}{2} = 45 \tag{7.21}$$

elements of the variance/covariance matrix on and below the main diagonal. It is these 45 elements to which the SRMR measure refers.

```
x <- unlist(rw.fit@SampleStats@cov)
obs <- x * m                                                    (7.22)
observed <- cov2cor(obs)
```

Having built this auxiliary matrix, we export the observed variance/covariance matrix from object *rw.fit.* and assign it to the object named *x* (7.22). The *unlist()* function is used to be able to involve the subsequent multiplication with the just-calculated auxiliary matrix *m*. The *cov2cor()* function is then used to convert the variance/covariance matrix into a correlation matrix named *observed*.

Next we do the same for model-implied variance/covariance matrix (7.23) named *implied*.

```
y <- unlist(rw.fit@implied$cov)
impl <- y * m                                                   (7.23)
implied <- cov2cor(impl)
```

For the planned holdout validation, it would actually have been sufficient to calculate only *implied*, since we want to relate exactly this matrix to the observed variance/covariance matrix of the *test* set. But since we now have both, *observed* and *implied*, we can also compute the training SRMR.[10]

Byrne (2012: 76) aptly describes the Standardized Root Mean Squared Residual (SRMR) in these words: "The SRMR represents the average value across all standardized residuals, and ranges from zero to 1.00; in a well-fitting model, this value will be small (say,.05 or less)."

The SRMR may be expressed as follows:[11]

---

10 Since the *summary(rw.fit, ...)* function above also returns this evaluation metric, normally it would not need to be calculated separately.

11 The SRMR formula is also presented in the literature in a version in which the correlation between variables i and j is not represented directly via the r_{ij} correlation symbol as here; instead, r_{ij} is then replaced by the equivalent expression in terms of the covariance and variance elements involved. See, e.g., Bollen (1989: 258) or Reinecke (2014: 119). Beaujean (2014: 164) describes the calculation in text form.

$$SRMR = \left[\frac{\sum_{i=1}^{v} \sum_{j=1}^{i} \left(r_{ij} - \hat{r}_{ij} \right)^2}{\frac{v \cdot (v+1)}{2}} \right]^{\frac{1}{2}} \tag{7.24}$$

In (7.24), r_{ij} indicates an element of the observed correlation matrix and $\hat{r}_{ij}$ the corresponding element of the model-implied correlation matrix. For each such pair of entries we compute the squared difference between the observed and model-implied correlation, sum these quantities over all elements,[12] and divide this sum by the number of elements in order to arrive at its mean value. Finally, the square root is taken from this average squared difference. Since we use as the basic element the correlation instead of the covariance, the SRMR yields this average residual in standardized form.

(7.25) shows the script lines used to calculate the training SRMR in the present example.

```
TrainSRMR <- sqrt(sum((observed - implied)^2)/45)
TrainSRMR
```
(7.25)

The calculation results in a value of 0.023 and can, in Byrne's (2012: 76) words, be interpreted as follows: "Given that the SRMR represents the average discrepancy between the observed sample and hypothesized correlation matrices, we can interpret this value as meaning that the model explains the correlations to within an average error of . . ." here,.023. The holdout validation will now show how this value changes if we relate the model-implied correlation matrix of the *training* set to the observed correlation matrix of the *test* set. Since we have already calculated the model-implied matrix, all we are missing is the matrix of the observed correlations. The easiest way to obtain this matrix is to calculate the above *sem()* function again, but this time applying it to the test set.

```
rwt.fit <- sem(rw.model, data=testdata, sampling.weights="wt",
          ordered=c("x6", "x7", "x8", "rw2"))
```
(7.26)

We do not need to continue with the *summary()* function here, as we do not want to produce any output. Instead, we continue the calculations analogously to (7.22)

```
xt <- unlist(rwt.fit@SampleStats@cov)
obst <- xt * m
observedt <- cov2cor(obst)
```
(7.27)

---

[12] In (7.24) *i* represents the row index, *j* the column index, and *v* the number of observed variables involved. If the formula were applied exactly as shown, then the elements within each row *i* would first be added up across the columns *j* before the row sums themselves are added up to a total value.

in order to export the observed variance/covariance matrix from object *rwt.fit*, eliminate the elements above its main diagonal, and convert the covariances to correlations. Analogous to (7.25) we finally calculate the test SRMR as

```
TestSRMR <- sqrt(sum((observedt - implied)^2)/45)
TestSRMR
```
(7.28)

and obtain as the result a value of 0.026.

Period		Training Set		Test Set
A				
B				
C				
D				

Figure 7.4: Temporal Validation Scheme.

The validation set design is based on *randomly* splitting the training set and test set. However, based on the idea of *predictive* validity, it can be just as convincing to split the data *along the time axis*. For example, using data and calculations from one year to make a forecast for the following year. In other words, trying to predict the future under scientifically controlled conditions and then test the following year to what extent the forecast was accurate. Since we have an infrastructure of time-related survey data available in social research, we can actually put this idea into practice. In the present context, for example, we again use the data from the first nine survey rounds of the European Social Survey (Table 7.12).

As to validation along the time axis, Ghani and Schierholz (2017: 175–176), for example, speak of *temporal validation* and Kelleher et al. (2020: 546–547) of *out-of-time sampling*. In this context, both groups of authors discuss the topic of possible time dependencies in data. Ghani and Schierholz (2017: 175), for example, point out that in practice an assumption of the cross-validation and holdout set approach is "almost always" violated, namely the assumption "that the data have no time dependencies and that the distribution is stationary over time." Kelleher et al. (2020: 547) regard out-of-time sampling essentially as "a form of hold-out sampling in which sampling is done in a targeted rather than random fashion". In this context, they illustrate with an example that "we should be careful to ensure that the times from which the training and test sets are taken do not introduce a bias into the evaluation process, because the two different time samples are not really representative." This leads the authors to conclude that "the time spans are large enough to take into account any cyclical behavioral patterns or that other approaches are used to account for these" (Kelleher et al. 2020: 547).

Table 7.12: The Training and Test Sets Mapped to ESS Survey Rounds.

Round	1	2	3	4	5	6	7	8	9
Year	2002	2004	2006	2008	2010	2012	2014	2016	2018
Period									
A									
B									
C									
D									

In the data example presented here, this is ensured insofar as the time spans for training and test set are based on the given structure of the ESS survey rounds that take place every two years (Table 7.12). Each of these periods is therefore the same length, namely 2 years, and also long enough to avoid any distortions caused by too short or incomparable time intervals. The nine survey rounds contained in the dataset were divided in such a way that the test set always covers such a 2-year interval. As far as the time spans for the training sets are concerned, we could have extended them cumulatively from period to period if we started with round 1 each time. In principle, this would have been in line with the scheme used by Ghani and Schierholz (2017: 175) to describe their "temporal validation" concept. However, this would level out any existing differences along the time axis, including possible trends. To avoid this, the training data sets also follow a temporal gradation that ensures that no survey round serves as a training data set more than once. Figure 7.4 and Table 7.12 show the characteristics created in this way.

As far as implementation is concerned, we proceed in the same way as described above, except that we now carry out holdout sampling not randomly but systematically according to survey rounds. Accordingly, the variable selection in (7.14) must be extended by the variable *essround* (survey round). (7.14) is here correspondingly converted to (7.29)

```
load("ess19.Rdata")
sset <- subset(ess19, select = c( essround, x1, x2, x3, x4,
                         x5, x6, x7, x8, rw2, wt))
sset <- na.omit(sset)
```
(7.29)

As before, this results in 299,976 units with valid values in all selected variables. Next, the random selection in (7.15) is replaced by a systematic selection as exemplified in (7.30) for *Period A*. Regarding (7.15), the random selection by the *sample()* function is replaced by two additional *subset()* functions that refer to *sset* and thus to the preceding *subset()* function.

```
traindata <-subset(sset, essround <= 3)
testdata  <-subset(sset, essround == 4)
```
(7.30)

Period A uses the data from survey rounds 1 to 3 as the training set and the data from survey round 4 as the test or holdout set. This results in the following number of units: Training set (n=93,356) and test set (n=32,474).

Everything else is then carried out completely analogously to the procedure described above. This means that the script lines (7.16) to (7.28) are adopted unchanged in order to estimate exactly the model described above in the manner described and to validate it using the SRMR evaluation metric. This results in a training SRMR of 0.025 and a test SRMR of 0.033 for this first period.

For periods B, C and D we now proceed completely analogously to period A by modifying the two subset() functions in (7.30) accordingly. We do this successively in separate runs. For *Period B* this leads to (7.31).

```
traindata <-subset(sset, (essround == 4 | essround == 5))
testdata  <-subset(sset, essround == 6)
```
(7.31)

Period B uses the data from survey rounds 4 and 5 as the training set (n=66,359) and the data from survey round 6 as the test or holdout set (37,045). This results in a training SRMR of 0.027 and a test SRMR of 0.037 for this second period. Next, (7.32) does the selection for *Period C*.

```
traindata <-subset(sset, (essround == 6 | essround == 7))
testdata  <-subset(sset, essround == 8)
```
(7.32)

This split leads to a training n of 70,847 units and a test n of 35,004 units. The training SRMR is 0.023 and the test SRMR=0.034. Finally, *Period D* is accessed via (7.33)

```
traindata <-subset(sset, essround == 8)
testdata  <-subset(sset, essround == 9)
```
(7.33)

This final split leads to a training n of 35,004 units and a test n of 34,410 units. The training SRMR is 0.028 and the test SRMR=0.040.

In an assessment of these SRMR values, two aspects can be highlighted: All values are smaller than 0.05 and thus indicate an acceptable model fit in light of this evaluation metric. This would mean saying that the model explains the correlations between the indicator variables with a still acceptable average error. And the second conclusion is that the test value is always slightly higher than the training value.

Table 7.13: Summary Table of SRMR and R^2 for Periods A to D.

Period	SRMR		R^2_{Train}	
	Training	Test	Right-wing	prejudice
A	0.025	0.033	0.067	0.043
B	0.027	0.037	0.053	0.047
C	0.023	0.034	0.122	0.057
D	0.028	0.040	0.122	0.084

In the overview of Table 7.13 we also see that the explanatory power of the model for the target variable *prejudice formation* increases over the four periods. While the explanatory power for the target variable *right-wing vote* is such that it initially decreases slightly from period A to B, before moving to a significantly increased level in periods C and D.

7.4 Cross-Validation

An alternative to the validation set design is *cross-validation*. Figure 7.5 illustrates the data splitting scheme. First, the dataset is randomly split into a training and a test set. The training dataset is then resampled k times. This means it is randomly split into k *partitions* or *folds* and each of these partitions is iteratively used once as an assessment set, while the remaining k-1 partitions serve as an analysis set. The desired calculations are therefore carried out k times and then summarized via averaging.

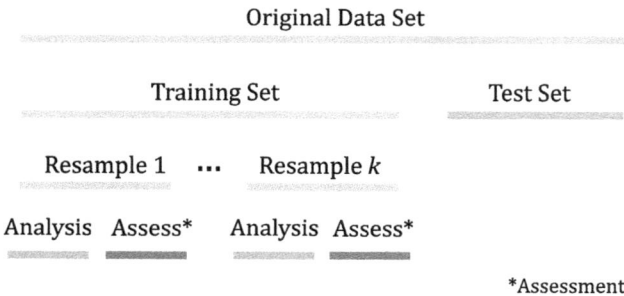

Figure 7.5: Data Splitting Scheme Involving Resampling.

To illustrate the scheme and procedure, we again use the EU data frame with its 27 units (countries).[13] First, we load this data frame and exclude possible units with missing data in the relevant variables. In this example, none of the 27 EU countries need to be excluded from the calculations. Next step is to invoke the *tidymodels* library (Kuhn and Silge 2022: 39). This is actually a *metapackage* that loads a number of individual packages itself. This includes, for instance, the *rsample* package for data splitting and resampling.

```
load("Energy2.Rdata")
eu <- na.omit(subset(energy,
      select=c(cntry, KKS,Povertyrisk))) # 27 EU countries          (7.34)
library(tidymodels)
eu <- as_tibble(eu)
```

The next script line in (7.34) is optional. It converts the data frame into a tibble. Next, we set a seed for the random number stream to be able to reproduce the result. Using *vfold_cv(eu, v=3)* we randomly split the data frame *eu* into 3 partitions (7.35).

```
set.seed(15)
(sfolds <- vfold_cv(eu, v=3))                                       (7.35)
```

The outer bracket only serves to obtain the corresponding output without having to call the created object *sfolds* again. (7.35) produces the following output in the R console.

```
#   3-fold cross-validation
# A tibble: 3 × 2
  splits         id
  <list>         <chr>
1 <split [18/9]> Fold1                                              (7.36)
2 <split [18/9]> Fold2
3 <split [18/9]> Fold3
```

The three generated partitions are displayed. Furthermore, for each of these folds, it is shown that 18 of the 27 units were assigned to the *analysis set* and 9 of the 27 units

---

13 Example Data Set 6 on Energy Transition in the European Green Deal. The KKS (purchasing power standard) variable was introduced in chapter 5. The "Poverty Risk" variable also comes from Eurostat. It is the percentage of a country's population at risk of poverty or social exclusion in 2020.

were assigned to the *assessment set*. If we now want to know which countries were assigned to which set,[14] we can use the instructions in (7.37).

```
sfolds$splits[[1]] %>% analysis()
sfolds$splits[[1]] %>% assessment()
sfolds$splits[[2]] %>% analysis()
sfolds$splits[[2]] %>% assessment()
sfolds$splits[[3]] %>% analysis()
sfolds$splits[[3]] %>% assessment()
```
(7.37)

This will identify the respective data frames or tibbles. And since each of these data frames contains, among other things, the country code as a variable, we can use this to reconstruct the respective random selection. We have summarized the results for this country code in Table 7.14.

The key principle is that the *assessment* sets are mutually exclusive across the three resampling runs or folds (i.e., the splits 1, 2, and 3) and together represent the entirety of the 27 units. In Table 7.14, these are the grayed-out fields.

Also, *within* a random split, analysis and assessment sets are mutually exclusive. For each such split, "one fold is held out for assessment statistics and the remaining folds are substrate for the model" (Kuhn and Silge 2022: 130).

While *across* the random splits, units from the analysis sets are used twice (i.e., k-1 times).

If we then want to calculate a linear regression, for example, we can do so in the context of the *tidymodel* framework using the sequence of instructions shown in (7.38).

```
model <-
  linear_reg() %>%
    set_engine("lm")
(fit <-
  model %>%
  fit(Povertyrisk ~ KKS, data=eu)%>%
  extract_fit_engine() %>% summary())
```
(7.38)

---

14 A very clear illustration of the principle of cross-validation can be found, for example, in Kuhn and Silge (2022: 129–131).

Table 7.14: Cross-Validation Scheme for 3 Folds and 27 Units (EU Countries).

cntry	Split 1 analysis	Split 1 assess	Split 2 analysis	Split 2 assess	Split 3 analysis	Split 3 assess
AT	○			+	○	
BE	○		○			+
BG		+	○		○	
CY	○			+	○	
CZ	○		○			+
DE	○			+	○	
DK	○		○			+
EE	○			+	○	
ES	○		○			+
FI	○			+	○	
FR	○			+	○	
GR		+	○		○	
HR		+	○		○	
HU	○		○			+
IE	○			+	○	
IT		+	○		○	
LT	○		○			+
LU	○		○			+
LV		+	○		○	
MT		+	○		○	
NL	○		○			+
PL	○			+	○	
PT	○		○			+
RO		+	○		○	
SE		+	○		○	
SI	○			+	○	
SK		+	○		○	
27	18	9	18	9	18	9

This does exactly the same thing as a standard call to the function *lm()*, as shown in (7.39), and we also get the standard output[15] of this function (as already presented above).

```
stats::lm(formula = Povertyrisk ~ KKS, data = data)
```
(7.39)

---

15 Since our purpose here is to illustrate the cross-validation principle, we only briefly mention the coefficients of the linear regression: Intercept $b_0 = 25.4$; Slope $b_1 = -0.042$; $R^2 = 0.119$; RMSE=4.84. Countries with higher purchasing power standards would accordingly be predicted to have a lower risk of poverty.

However, within the *tidymodel* package, we can also easily perform cross-validation using the *fit_resamples()* and *collect_metrics()* functions. The latter provides us, in particular, the root mean squared error (RMSE) and R^2, the coefficient of determination.

The *mean squared error* (MSE) measures model accuracy (James et al. 2013: 29; Kuhn and Silge 2022: 109). The smaller the MSE, the greater the prediction accuracy, and thus the better the model. However, the MSE determines the mean *squared* difference between predicted and observed values of a regression model, which can complicate its interpretability. Ghani and Schierholz (2017: 176) point this out, emphasizing that the RMSE is more intuitive "as it is a measure of mean differences on the original scale of the response variable" (Ghani and Schierholz 2017: 176).

```
(cv <-
    model %>%
    fit_resamples(resamples=sfolds,                          (7.40)
                  Povertyrisk ~ KKS))
collect_metrics(cv)
```

(7.40) yields the two statistics RMSE and R^2. For v=3, three estimates of these statistics result. While *collect_metrics()* returns their averages, the individual estimates themselves are returned if the option *summarize=FALSE* is used for this function.

```
collect_metrics(cv, summarize = FALSE)                       (7.41)
```

A look at these values can help to see how much they fluctuate across folds and thus possibly indicate a low stability in these estimates. In the words of Kuhn and Silge (2022: 132): "Depending on data size or other characteristics, the resampling estimate produced by *V*-fold cross-validation may be excessively noisy"; the authors continue: "As with many statistical problems, one way to reduce noise is to gather more data. For cross-validation, this means averaging more than *V* statistics." This consideration leads the authors to *Repeated Cross-Validation*: "To create *R* repeats of *V*-fold cross-validation, the same fold generation process is done *R* times to generate *R* collections of *V* partitions. Now instead of averaging *V* statistics, $V \times R$ statistics produce the final resampling estimate" (Kuhn and Silge (2022: 132).

This approach may indeed be helpful, but it does not solve the problem of samples being too small. As in this case, with only 27 units (a number that would in principle be even smaller if we had initially performed the recommended random split into training and test data sets). Repeating the fold generation process only increases the number of replicates that can be included in the averaging, but not the number of available units itself.

In practice, however, the implementation of repeated cross-validation is straightforward. We simply add the required specification to (7.35), here for instance to repeat the fold generation process 3 times.

```
(sfolds <- vfold_cv(eu, v=3, repeats = 3))                              (7.42)
```

Then, the split structure is as shown in (7.43).

```
#   3-fold cross-validation repeated 3 times
# A tibble: 9 × 3
  splits          id      id2
  <list>          <chr>   <chr>
1 <split [18/9]> Repeat1 Fold1
2 <split [18/9]> Repeat1 Fold2
3 <split [18/9]> Repeat1 Fold3                                          (7.43)
4 <split [18/9]> Repeat2 Fold1
5 <split [18/9]> Repeat2 Fold2
6 <split [18/9]> Repeat2 Fold3
7 <split [18/9]> Repeat3 Fold1
8 <split [18/9]> Repeat3 Fold2
9 <split [18/9]> Repeat3 Fold3
```

Kuhn and Silge (2022: 130) describe it aptly: "Using V=3 is a good choice to illustrate cross-validation, but it is a poor choice in practice because it is too low to generate reliable estimates". They continue in reporting that "In practice, values of V are most often 5 or 10" and that they "generally prefer 10-fold cross-validation as a default because it is large enough for good results in most situations." Ghani and Schierholz (2017: 174) report about cross-validation that "Typically, k is set to 5 or 10." James et al. (2013: 181–182) discuss k-fold cross-validation and the use of k=5 or k=10 instead of k=n.

For an illustration, a medium-sized dataset should be more suitable than a large dataset, since the simpler validation set design should generally suffice for the latter. For this purpose, we use Example Data Set 1 (PPSM Panel).

Analogous to (7.34), we load the dataset and the *tidymodels* library, perform simple missing data management, and optionally convert the data frame to a tibble. We then implement a random 70:30 split into a training and a test dataset.

```
set.seed(123)
(sset_split <- initial_split(sset, prop = 0.70))
train <- training(sset_split)                                          (7.44)
test <- testing(sset_split)
```

Based on the *initial_split()* function, we get the following random split:

```
<Training/Testing/Total>
<1923/825/2748>                                                        (7.45)
```

Next, we formulate a model statement analogous to the upper part of (7.38)

```
model <-
  linear_reg() %>%                                                          (7.46)
  set_engine("lm")
```

and then add — analogously to (7.35) — the necessary statements for the intended cross-validation structure, i.e., the *vfold_cv()* function in conjunction with control statements for keeping the predicted values.

```
set.seed(350)
(sfolds <- vfold_cv(train, v=10, repeats = 5))                             (7.47)
pred <- control_resamples(save_pred = TRUE)
```

The *sfold* statement creates the structure shown in (7.48). We see there for the first of 5 repeats that the 1923 units of the *training* dataset are distributed over the 10 folds (3·193 units and 7·192 units), in this way forming the 10 assessment sets. For each split, we also see the number of units in the analysis set (1730 and 1731 respectively), where the analysis and assessment sets in each split add up to the 1923 units of the training data set.

```
#   10-fold cross-validation repeated 5 times
# A tibble: 50 × 3
    splits              id      id2
    <list>              <chr>   <chr>
 1 <split [1730/193]> Repeat1 Fold01
 2 <split [1730/193]> Repeat1 Fold02
 3 <split [1730/193]> Repeat1 Fold03
 4 <split [1731/192]> Repeat1 Fold04
 5 <split [1731/192]> Repeat1 Fold05                                        (7.48)
 6 <split [1731/192]> Repeat1 Fold06
 7 <split [1731/192]> Repeat1 Fold07
 8 <split [1731/192]> Repeat1 Fold08
 9 <split [1731/192]> Repeat1 Fold09
10 <split [1731/192]> Repeat1 Fold10
# i 40 more rows
# i Use `print(n = . . .)` to see more rows
```

Next, we apply the *fit_resamples()* function to this data structure, whose arguments include the reference to the data structure and the regression equation.

```
fit <-
    model %>%
    fit_resamples(resamples=sfolds, KL7 ~ LS11+EDUC6+just10,
                  control = pred)
```
(7.49)

Finally, via (7.50) we obtain the average values of the two standard fit measures, the root mean squared error (RMSE) and R^2 in conjunction with their standard error estimates.

```
collect_metrics(fit)
```
(7.50)

In this case we obtain an RMSE of 1.53 and an R^2 of 0.041. It is important to note that these values refer exclusively to the training dataset and not to the initially created test dataset. The cross-validation procedure described here primarily serves the goal of developing the most optimal model *for this training dataset* by performing something like model tuning or model fitting.

In order to gain any insight or benefit from this approach, a procedure that — as here— only includes a single model specification (i.e., the regression equation in (7.49)) would be of little help. Instead, meaningful model comparisons should be made in order to be able to identify something like a best model by comparing the respective model fits. Even within the limited framework offered by our small data example, this would still be possible in principle: we could test whether a model that allows for interactions in addition to the main effects would fit the data better. We could also test whether – contrary to what is assumed here – nonlinear effects are also involved, and if so, which functional form would best approximate the data. However, we will forego such a comparative analysis here.

Second, it should be noted that the assessment of model fit should not be based solely on measures such as MSE, RMSE, or R^2, but should also include more in-depth diagnostics.

And third, care should be taken not to overfit the models, as this could severely impair their generalizability. That's why the last step is so important: applying the best model to test data that was not used in the model development. Although this final step can also be carried out in the context of the *tidymodels* library, we will stick to the procedure already introduced above.

```
set.seed(123)
tr <- sample(2748, 1923)
m <- lm(KL7 ~ LS11+EDUC6+just10, data=sset,
                subset=tr)
(mse <- mean((sset$KL7-predict(m, sset))[-tr]^2))
(rmse <- sqrt(mse))
```
(7.51)

Using (7.51),[16] we get a test MSE of 2.10 and a test RMSE of 1.45.

7.5 Generalizing Across Samples, Methods, and Settings

In a broader sense, generalization implies replicability of findings not only across datasets but also across different ways of conceptualization, measurement, data collection, and data analysis. It thus makes sense to check through an approach to *systematic replication* the extent to which empirical findings depend on the specific method used to obtain them[17] (Galtung 1969). As a first example, let us consider the case in which an alternative model specification is applied to the same data. In the structural equation model above, an analytical decision refers to the assumed scale level. In the specification of model (7.16) above, the 6pt. scales for the measurement of an authoritarian value orientation were defined as metric scales, while the 4pt. scales for measuring prejudice formation were treated as ordinal scales (7.17). We have pointed this out in the context of Tables 7.9 and 7.10. Alternatively, we could have assumed an ordinal scale level also for the 6pt. scales. We do this here by extending the list of variables defined as *ordered* in the *sem()* function in (7.17) accordingly, in order to check how stable the result remains despite this analytic decision.

---

16 The model itself is of only marginal interest here, but will be briefly outlined for the sake of completeness. As a target variable, we use an indicator of a value-rational attitude: willingness to accept a personal disadvantage for the sake of a collective good. The target variable *KL7* measures the willingness to accept higher costs for climate protection (7-point scale from 1 = completely disagree to 7 = completely,agree). The predictor *LS11* assesses the living standards on an 11-point scale ranging from 1 to 11. The question wording was as follows: "I would now like you to imagine a ladder with 11 rungs. The top rung, 11, represents the best possible standard of living, as you would wish for it. And the bottom rung, 1, represents the standard of living that would be the worst for you. When you think about your current standard of living, which rung would you place it on?" The variable *EDUC6* measures the educational status on a 6-point scale. Variable *just10* asks if it is fair to pass on wealth to children so that they have better opportunities (7-point scale from 1 = completely disagree to 7 = completely agree). We use this variable here as an indicator of a purposive-rational attitude that prioritizes individual or particular self-interest. When this model is applied to the *test* data, the following coefficients are obtained (standard errors in brackets): $b_0 = 3.64$; $b_{1(LS11)} = 0.135$ (4.91); $b_{2(EDUC6)} = 0.106$ (3.37); $b_{3(just10)} = -0.064$ (−2.05); Residual standard error 1.45 on 821 degrees of freedom. The residual vs. fitted and Q-Q plots show acceptable, though slightly suboptimal patterns.

17 In Galtung's (1969: 437) own words: "Under the present heading of 'replication' we shall discuss efforts to *increase* the degree of confirmation by *decreasing* the tenability of the argument that the findings are artefacts of the method. The obvious way of doing this is to show that they are invariant of variations in the method, at least within a reasonable range." Galtung's approach is directed at the four sources of variation when acquiring survey data, namely the *units*, the *variables*, their *values*, and the *data-collection*. The approach is detailed in Galtung (1969: 437–450).

```
rw.fit <- sem(rw.model, data=traindata,
          sampling.weights="wt",
          ordered=c("x1", "x2", "x3", "x4", "x5",
                    "x6", "x7", "x8", "rw2"))
```
(7.52)

Table 7.15 reports the findings. These show that, with one exception, we obtain nearly the same estimates when we compare them with the values in Table 7.11. This exception refers to the strength of the effect of the authoritarian value orientation on the right-wing target variable. This effect now appears stronger and almost reaches statistical significance (1.90 is only slightly below the critical value of 1.96 that we would have to achieve in a two-tailed test). Strictly speaking, we would therefore be led to the same conclusion as above, namely that an authoritarian value orientation strengthens the affinity to the political right *by forming prejudices* against immigrants. But it was close and we would have had to conclude that prejudice formation can *only partially* explain the effect of authoritarian value orientation on right wing votes (we discussed this topic in the context of Table 7.8).

Table 7.15: Estimates of Effect for the Model in Figure 7.3 (all scales as ordinal scales).

Target	Predictor	b_v	$b_v/s.e_v$	β_v	R^2
Right-wing					0.085
	Authoritarian	0.035	1.90	0.023	
	Prejudice	0.333	25.09	0.286	
Prejudice					0.047
	Authoritarian	0.279	50.29	0.216	

b_v unstandardized regression effect; $b_v/s.e_v$ divides b_v by its standard error; β_v standardized regression effect; all scales treated as ordinal scales. Training SRMR=0.024; Test SRMR=0.027. Factor loadings as described in Tables 7.9 and 7.10.

Another example is equation 2 in Table 7.8. We used this equation above in the training set to predict prejudice formation based on an authoritarian value orientation. Based on this equation the estimate of effect turned out to be 0.213 and proved to be strong when related to its standard error ($b_1/s.e_1 = 82.0$). A similar numerical estimate is obtained in chapter 9, section 9.2, equation (9.15), when the model is based on the *full* data set $b_1 = 0.216$ $\left(b_1/s.e_{b_1} = 101.0\right)$. However, it is also shown there how this estimate changes when the model allows the intercept and slope coefficient to (co-)vary randomly across the 22 countries involved. Such a random-intercept-and-slope model leads to the estimates shown there in (9.17): $b_1 = 0.173$ $\left(b_1/s.e_{b_1} = 9.97\right)$. We find that the analytical decision to allow random variation at the country level slightly reduces the effect in light of the slope and strongly in light of the slope/standard error ratio.

A third example concerns the *operational definition* of the right-wing target variable. In the analysis above, we measured the affinity to the political far right via the closeness to or the election of parties on the *far right* of the political spectrum. As an alternative to an indicator that reflects self-reported *behavior*, we could also have chosen an indicator that relates to self-classification on the left-right spectrum. In the European Social Survey, this classification is assessed using an eleven-point scale. Elsewhere (Engel 2022c), we were therefore also able to show what the result would have been if, instead of the above behavioral indicator, we had used as the target group those who chose the rightmost scale value 10 on this scale when surveyed.

Such robustness checks therefore touch on one specific aspect of the broader replication goal of determining whether/how well results are generalizable across different methods or settings.

It is crucial to recognize that this replication-oriented perspective does not necessarily pursue the same goal as a validation set design, which divides the dataset into a training, validation and test set in order to first find the best-fitting model via validation before determining its generalizability by reference to the test set. Systematic replication also involves understanding the conditions under which a result is replicable or not. The implementation of a validation set design should therefore not lead the analyst to neglect or mask this central task.

Chapter 8
Regression Diagnostics and Corrective Measures

8.1 Regression Diagnostics – Going Beyond R^2

How well does a linear regression model fit the data? This question is often answered with its predictive or explanatory power, i. e. by referring to the strength and significance of R^2. This answer is not wrong, but it is incomplete. A regression model relies on a number of assumptions that must also be met. These assumptions refer to the least squares estimates.

First, the regression equation must be *identifiable*. In survey research, this condition is usually met because the number n of units (observations) is usually significantly larger than the number k of parameters to be estimated in a regression model. However, if a regression model is calculated for *aggregated* data, it may happen that k has to be kept smaller than wanted in order to fulfill this condition. At the beginning of Chapter 6 we had an example of aggregate-level data with the EU countries, and thus with only 27 units of analysis. However, this topic concerns also *aggregated individual*-level data in categorical data analysis when regression models for contingency tables are to be estimated. Then it is quite realistic to ask if a model is under-identified ($n < k$), just identified (saturated, $n = k$) or over-identified ($n > k$). Besides, the x matrix of predictors must not contain linear dependencies. This is usually not an issue either. Though it would be one if, for example, we tried to model statistical interactions via differences between x variables and not via products of such variables.

Second, the *systematic* part of the regression model must be correctly specified. For instance in terms of possible non-additive and nonlinear effects respectively. When estimating nonlinear effects using linear models, it is important to note that this is only possible with functions that can be linearized. For that the relationship between y and x must be linear *in the coefficients* (James et al. 2013: 266; Daniel and Wood 1999: 19; Fox 1991: 59; Berry and Feldman 1985: 57). This condition is fulfilled in two cases. First, if the relationship *itself* is linear and thus displayable as straight line. Secondly, if a nonlinear relationship is linearizable for parameter estimation purposes and in fact linearized and estimated using a linear equation. A prime example of this latter case is polynomial regression. The correct specification of the systematic part of the regression model, especially concerning nonlinear relations, is the subject of chapter 10.

Third, the *random* part of the regression model must also be correctly specified. In particular, ordinary least squares estimation requires that a couple of assumptions about the residuals of a linear regression be met. In particular, the residuals should have an expected value of zero and constant variance, they should follow a normal distribution and be independent of each other (Blalock 1981: 387; Draper and Smith 1981: 141).

Otherwise we would be faced with the following impairments:

https://doi.org/10.1515/9783110680683-008

Biased least squares estimates result especially when the expected value of the residuals is nonzero or when a curvilinear relationship is incorrectly specified as linear relationship.

Though still unbiased least squares estimates result when the residual variance is not constant (Draper and Smith 1981: 110), the "standard errors, confidence intervals, and hypothesis tests associated with the linear model rely upon" the assumption "that the error terms have a constant variance" (James et al. 2013: 95). Similarly, Fox (1991: 49) remarks that although "the least-squares estimator is unbiased and consistent even when the error variance is not constant, its efficiency is impaired and the usual formulas for coefficient standard errors are inaccurate."

In addition, the assumption that the residuals are normally distributed is also required for making tests, namely for tests "which depend on the assumption of normality, such as t- or F-tests, or for obtaining confidence intervals based on the t- and F-distributions" (Draper and Smith 1981: 87). Whereby however the F-statistic at least *approximately* follows a F-distribution if the residuals are *not* normally-distributed but the sample size n is large (James et al. 2013: 76). Similarly, Fox (1991: 40) states that "the central-limit theorem assures that under very broad conditions inference based on the least-squares estimators is approximately valid in all but small samples."

The usual assumption of normally-distributed residuals having an expected value of zero and constant variance, $N(0, \sigma^2)$, implies that these residuals are independent of each other, that is that they are pairwise uncorrelated (Draper and Smith 1981: 162–163; Kmenta 1986: 298). Chatterjee and Price (1977: 123–124) discuss reasons for autocorrelation and point out that the presence of autocorrelation leads to inefficient ("in the sense that they no longer have minimum variance") but unbiased least squares estimates. The authors add that the "estimate of σ^2 and the standard errors of the regression coefficients may be seriously understated [. . .] giving a spurious impression of accuracy." In addition, "confidence intervals and the various tests of significance commonly employed would no longer be strictly valid." In order to secure the conclusions that can be drawn from a linear regression model, it is therefore necessary to test this assumption of serially uncorrelated observations as well.

When calculating linear regression models, it is thus important to use appropriate diagnostics to ensure that all associated assumptions are fulfilled indeed. The standard instruments in this regard include diagnostic plots and metrics, which we present in this chapter. We focus in particular on two basic diagnostic plots and two metrics:
- The first plot is the Residual-vs.-Fitted Plot to check three possibilities:
    - Does the model possibly suffer from omitted but relevant predictor variables?
    - Is the relation between target and predictor variable possibly nonlinear instead of linear?
    - Is the residual variance possibly heteroskedastic instead of constant?
- The second plot is the Q-Q plot to check if the residuals follow a normal curve.
- The first metric is the Durbin-Watson test to check if the residuals might be serially (pairwise) correlated.

– The second metric is Cook's D to identify influential units of analysis.

In addition, we raise the question of what can be done if diagnostic plots or metrics suggest that
– relevant predictors are missing from the model (section 8.2)
– a relationship under study is nonlinear (chapter 10)
– residuals are serially correlated (section 8.3 and chapter 9)
– residuals do not follow a normal curve (section 8.4),
– the residual variance is heteroscedastic (sections 8.6 and 8.7),
– a few influential units of analysis unduly influence a regression analysis (chapter 10).

8.2 Residual-vs.-Fitted Plot as Diagnostic Instrument

In a linear regression model, two types of influencing variables can be distinguished: on the one hand, the x variables whose effects are estimated and, on the other hand, all other variables that might have an impact on the target y as well. Typically, a regression model is incomplete in the sense that its estimated b_k slopes will only represent a subset of all effects on a target variable. So how can these b_k effects be estimated without bias?

This is only possible if it can be reasonably assumed that the impact of these other variables is zero. A common assumption is accordingly that these other variables are numerous, neutralize each other in their overall effect on the target y, and this way produce a residual expected value of zero (Blalock1981: 397). Consequently, this assumption ensures that the variables not taken into account cannot distort the estimates of the b_k effects. In essence, this assumption of an expected residual value of zero, $E(e_i) = 0$, formally closes an actually incomplete model. It must therefore be checked whether this assumption can be made with justification.

This check is made possible by a graphic that plots the residuals against the predicted values. This residual-vs.-fitted plot is a standard instrument in regression diagnostics. An application of this diagnostic instrument to a linear regression model can result in scatterplots like the ones shown schematically in Figure 8.1.

In a properly specified linear regression model, the residuals should scatter randomly around the zero line, where the mean residual values lie exactly on this line. Whether this is empirically true can be tested by computing an auxiliary regression that estimates the residuals as a function of the predicted values. As with any other regression, *conditional* mean values are estimated – here, conditional mean *residual* values.

Using the interaction model (6.34) as an example, we demonstrate this approach in the R script in Table 8.1 and the result of this computation in Figure 8.3. To do this, we deliberately do not estimate a straight line equation, but rather a third degree polynomial regression in order to give the model enough scope for different curve shapes. Figure 8.3 shows that *despite this scope*, the estimated conditional mean residual values are almost all perfectly on the zero line. Consequently, in this example we can assume that the expected value of the residuals is zero.

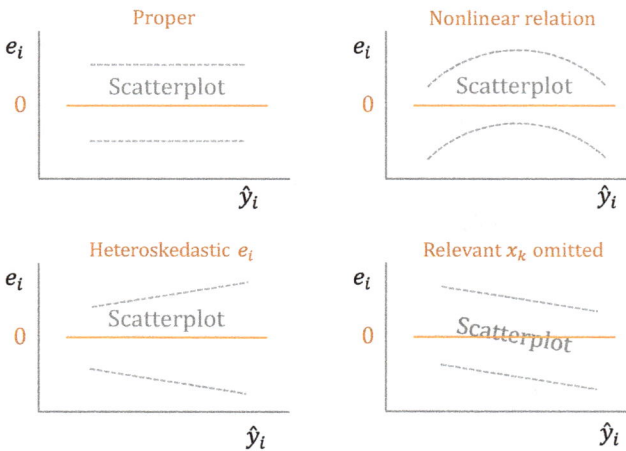

Figure 8.1: Scheme of Possible Outcomes from a Residual-vs.-Fitted Plot.

But what if this assumption were not true? As already suggested, this would lead to the conclusion that the model has neglected one or more than one relevant predictor. For instance, if model (8.1) is estimated

$$y_i = b_0 + b_1 x_{1i} + e_i \qquad (8.1)$$

while model (8.2) is true,

$$y_i = b_0 + b_1 x_{1i} + b_2 x_{2i} + e_i \qquad (8.2)$$

then the expected residual value of model (8.1) cannot be zero but would deviate from this by $b_2 x_{2i}$. Just what does it mean for the estimated b_k coefficients themselves if a model has omitted relevant x_k? What does it imply when a residuals-vs-fitted plot indicates a pattern like that shown schematically in Figure 8.2?

The pattern becomes understandable if the formal definition of a residual is taken as a starting point. According to this definition,

$$e_i = y_i - \hat{y}_i \qquad (8.3)$$

the estimated y value is subtracted from the observed y value. A positive residual thus indicates that the observed value is greater than the estimated value, that the observed value is therefore *under*estimated. On the other hand, a negative residual indicates that an observed value is *over*estimated.

The question then is whether positive and negative residuals, i. e. the underestimation and overestimation of observed values, concentrate on certain regions of the $\hat{y}_i$ scale, so that one can speak of a systematic connection in this regard.

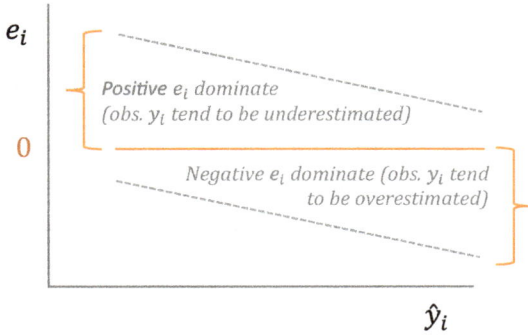

Figure 8.2: Detection of Biased Slope Estimates Using the Residual vs. Fitted Plot.

Figure 8.2 actually shows such a relationship: observed values tend to be underestimated when the estimated values themselves are smaller, and observed values tend to be overestimated when the estimated values themselves are larger. This means that smaller estimates tend to be too small and larger estimates tend to be too large to adequately reflect the observed values. And this in turn indicates that the b_k slope underlying these $\hat{y}_i$ estimates *over*estimates its true effect size. In contrast, a scatterplot *rising* from left to right in Figure 8.2 would have indicated a b_k slope that *under*estimates its true effect size.

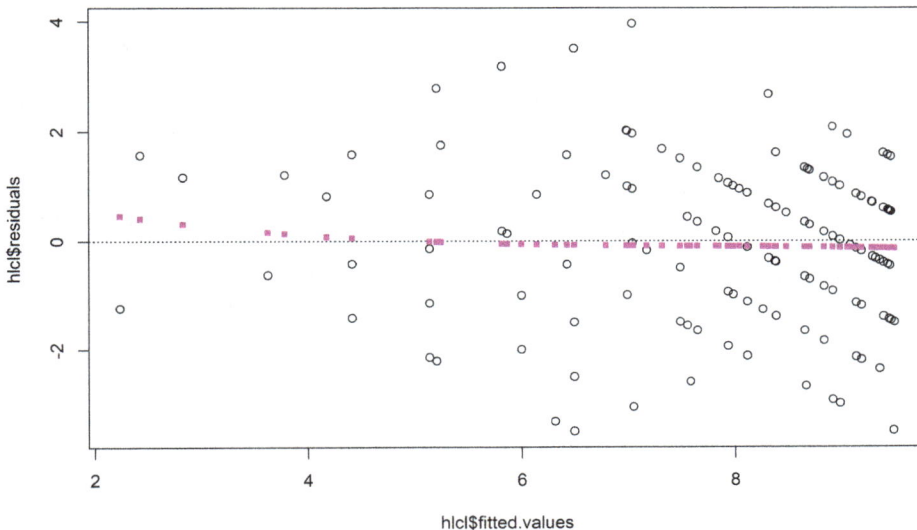

Figure 8.3: Residual-vs.-Fitted Plot to Interaction Model (6.34).

If a residual-vs.-fitted plot suggests an omitted x_k variable, a useful addition is a graphic that plots the residuals against the values of such potentially omitted x_k "candidates". It can also be useful to trace the residuals – as a target variable – back to potentially omitted predictors in a further regression.

Table 8.1: Script to Residual-vs.-Fitted Plot to Interaction Model (6.34).

Line	R Script
1	`load("ki.Rdata")`
2	`ki$lico <- ki$livstand * ki$confidence # interaction`
3	`summary(hlcl <-lm(happy ~ livstand + confidence +`
4	`            lico, weights=cwt, data=ki))`
5	`summary(z <- lm(hlcl$residuals ~ poly(hlcl$fitted.values, 3,`
6	`                  raw=TRUE), weights = hlcl$cwt))`
7	`tiff("fig83.tiff", units="in", width=9,`
8	`                  height = 6, res=600 )`
9	`x <- hlcl$fitted.value`
10	`y <- 1.373 - 0.544*x + 0.069*x^2 - 0.003*x^3`
11	`plot(hlcl$fitted.values, hlcl$residuals)`
12	`abline(h=0.0, lty="dotted")`
13	`points (x, y, pch=22, cex=0.7, col = "magenta", bg="magenta")`
14	`dev.off()`

Lines explained

Line 1 loads the data frame. Line 2 creates the synthetic variable named *lico* as product of x_1 and x_2. Lines 3 and 4: *lm()* nested in the *summary()* function. *lm()* specifies the formula in terms of target $y\sim$ predictors $x_1 + x_2 + x_3$, names the involved weight variable and data frame, and assigns all specifications and computations to the object named *hlcl*. Lines 5 and 6: *poly()* nested in *lm()* which in turn is nested in the *summary()* function. *lm()* specifies a 3rd degree polynomial, to prepare an element of the fitted-vs.-residual plot below. Target is the residual variable from the multiple regression computed in lines 3 and 4 and the predictor variable is given by the fitted values from this same regression. Both scales are imported from object *hlcl*. Lines 7 and 8 define the graphic in terms of format (*tiff*), name (fig 83.tiff), units (*inch*), width and *height* in inch, *resolution* (600dpi). Line 9 creates a variable named *x* as a copy of the fitted-values variable from the earlier multiple regression, just to simplify the specification in lines 10 and 13. Line 10 writes down the outcome of the polynomial regression called in lines 5 and 6. Line 11 calls the *plot()* function for the fitted-vs.-residual plot. Lines 12 and 13 are lines associated with the *plot()* function above. Line 12 draws a horizontal dotted line at 0.0 of the vertical (residual) scale. Line 13 draws the predicted y values of the polynomial regression, i. e. the expected conditional means of *y* given *x*. In a perfect model, these sequence of conditional y values should coincide with the dotted zero line created in line 12. The specifications for *points* in line 13 involve the symbol used (*pch = 22* defines squares), its font size relative to standard (*cex*), as well as the color for their shape (*col*) and filling (*bg*). Line 14 shuts down the graphic device activated by *tiff()* in line 7.

A residual-vs.-fitted plot is a useful graphical device. However, it has limitations as a diagnostic tool if the sample size is very large. Then it seems advantageous to randomly draw a subset of points from the scatterplot in order to include this subset in the diagnostic plot. Technically, this can be achieved by subsampling rows of a data frame (Buttrey and Whitaker 2018: 79–80). Using data from Example Data Set 8 (European Social Survey, Rounds 1 to 9), the procedure is explained in the R script in Table 8.2 (esp. lines 4 to 7) while the resulting residuals-vs.-fitted plot is displayed in Figure 8.4.

Table 8.2: Script to the Residual-vs.-Fitted Plot in the Large-N Use Case.

Line	R Script
1	`load("ess19.Rdata")`
2	`summary(sr <- lm(prejudice ~ authoritarian, weights = wt,`
3	`     ess19))`
4	`df <- data.frame(sr$residuals, sr$fitted.values, sr$weights)`
5	`set.seed(15)`
6	`ss <- sample(nrow(df), 450) # 0.0015 of 307901`
7	`selection <- df[ss,]`
8	`summary(pr <- lm(selection$sr.residuals ~`
9	`             poly(selection$sr.fitted.values, 3,`
10	`             raw=TRUE), weights = selection$sr.weights))`
11	`tiff("fig84.tiff", units="in", width=9,`
12	`     height = 6, res=600 )`
13	`x <- selection$sr.fitted.values`
14	`y <- -0.084 + 0.950*x + 1.491*x^2 - 15.947*x^3`
15	`plot(selection$sr.fitted.values, selection$sr.residuals)`
16	`abline(h=0.0, lty="dotted")`
17	`points (x, y, pch=22, cex=0.7, col = "lightblue",`
18	`         bg="lightblue")`
19	`dev.off()`

Lines explained
Line 1 loads the data frame. Lines 2 and 3: *lm()* nested in the *summary()* function. Line 4 creates a data frame consisting of the residuals, fitted values and weights from the *sr* regression above and assigns the object name *df* to it. Line 5 sets a random seed to ensure reproducible sampling below. Line 6 samples at random, without replacement, 450 row numbers from the 307,901 rows of data frame *df* and assigns this vector of row indices to object name *ss*. Line 7 does the sampling, i. e. this script line reduces data frame *df* to the rows whose numbers were selected in line 6 and stores this subset of data frame *df* in a new object named *selection*. Lines 8 to 10 compute a 3rd degree polynomial to get for line 14 the required conditional *y* mean estimates given *x*. Lines 11 to 19 contain the instructions for the residual-vs-fitted plot for the random subset of *df* drawn earlier. These instructions follow the same logic as in the corresponding residual-vs-fitted plot above, and are explained there.

8.3 Reducing Autocorrelation in Residuals by Linear Mixed Models

Chatterjee and Price (1977: 123) rightly noticed early on that "adjacent residuals tend to be similar in both temporal *and* spatial dimensions (emphasis added)". "Autocorrelation" of residuals is accordingly a relevant topic not only for its main field of econometric time series analysis, but also for any sociological analysis that has to deal with data with an inherent spatial structure. If then regression diagnostics point to autocorrelated residuals of a linear regression model, this autocorrelation may prove reducible if this same model is recalculated as a linear mixed model. The example of a big, spatially structured data set (persons within countries) presented in chapter 9 is used to illustrate the case.

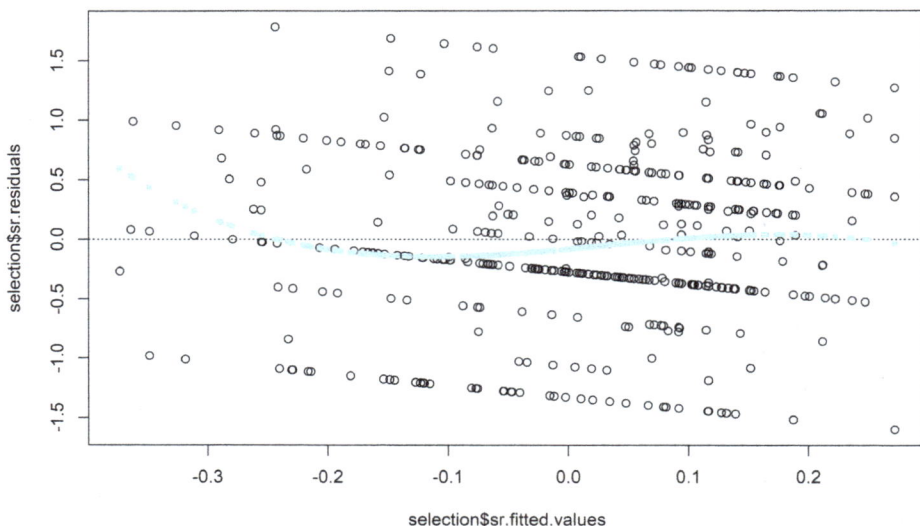

Figure 8.4: Residual-vs.-Fitted Plot in the Large-N Use Case.

This is the proposed procedure: We start with the *lm()* function, carry out a Durbin-Watson test for autocorrelation, recalculate the model using the *lmer()* or *lme()* function, and calculate the autocorrelation again to see whether a model that respects the spatial data structure leads to a reduction in autocorrelation.

Chatterjee and Price (1977: 125) point out that the Durbin-Watson test is based on the assumption that the errors constitute a first-order autoregressive series, here written as (8.4),

$$\varepsilon_i = \rho \cdot \varepsilon_{i-1} + z_i \qquad |\rho| < 1 \qquad (8.4)$$

where $z_i \sim N(0, \sigma^2)$ is assumed to be normally independently distributed with zero mean and constant variance. Draper and Smith (1981: 163) explicate the full set of test assumptions and demonstrate that these imply the usually made assumption of normally distributed residuals with zero mean and constant variance if the null hypothesis of uncorrelated errors, H_0: $\rho = 0$, is valid. Similarly, if we replace ρ with zero in (8.4), this reduces the error ε_i to the random component z_i and its above-cited distributional assumptions.

The null hypothesis of the Durbin-Watson statistic assumes that the residuals are uncorrelated ($\rho = 0$). We compute a statistic d that compares pairs of successive residuals. It starts with the first such pair by subtracting the first residual from the second, and squares this difference. This way the algorithm runs successively through the pairs of residuals by subtracting the second from the third, the third from the fourth, and so on until the last residual value is reached. It takes the sum of these n-1 squared difference values and divides this sum by the sum of the n squared residuals, to obtain the required test statistic (8.5).

$$d = \frac{\sum_{i=2}^{n} (e_i - e_{i-1})^2}{\sum_{i=1}^{n} e_i^2} \tag{8.5}$$

We then determine on the basis of the value of d whether or not to reject the null hypothesis H_0 of *no* autocorrelation against an H_1 that states one of three possible alternatives to H_0: that the correlation is unequal to zero (two-sided test) or that the correlation is either positive or negative (one-sided tests).

Draper and Smith (1981: 163–167) describe the complete testing procedure and decision rules of the classical Durbin-Watson Test. These rules refer to the *two* critical values, the test implies for each combination of significance level, number of predictive variables and number of observations, namely d_L (lower limit) and d_U (upper limit).

- One-sided test against H_1: $\rho > 0$: Reject H_0, at level α, if $d < d_L$. Do not reject H_0 if $d > d_U$.
- One-sided test against H_1: $\rho < 0$: Reject H_0, at level α, if $4 - d < d_L$. Do not reject H_0 if $4 - d > d_U$.
- Two sided equal-tailed test against H_1:$\rho \neq 0$. Reject H_0, at level 2α, if $d < d_L$ or $4 - d < d_L$. Do not reject H_0 at level 2α if $d > d_U$ and $4 - d > d_U$.
- Otherwise the test is regarded as inconclusive.

Based on the approximately holding relationship $d \approx 2 \cdot (1 - r)$, where ρ is estimated by r, it becomes clear that d is close to 2 when $r = 0$ and near to zero when $r = 1$. "Therefore values of d close to 2 will lead to the acceptance of the null hypothesis, whereas those close to zero (or close to 4) will lead to its rejection" (Kmenta 1986: 329). Similarly, "the closer the sample value of d to 2, the firmer the evidence that there is no autocorrelation present in the error. Evidence of autocorrelation is indicated by the deviation of d from the numerical value of 2" (Chatterjee and Price 1977: 127).

Since the critical values d_L and d_U are required for manual testing, these values were included *in tabulated form* in relevant textbooks. The tables in Chatterjee and Price (1977: 223–224), Draper and Smith (1981: 164–166) and Kmenta (1986: 763–768) are examples of this practice. Nowadays, of course, the test would be carried out computer-assisted. When using the R environment for this, the testing procedure simplifies to a script line that invokes the test as part of the "Companion to Applied Regression" ("car") library. Therein a function called *durbinWatsonTest()* computes residual autocorrelations and generalized Durbin-Watson statistics and their bootstrapped p-values. How to carry out this test is explained in the lower parts of the R scripts in Table 9.1 and Table 9.3 while their associated outputs in Table 9.2 and Table 9.4 document the results.

A Durbin-Watson test related to the linear model in section 9.2 reveals an autocorrelation of 0.117 along with a value of $d = 1.767$. The reported p value of 0 belongs to a two-sided test where H_0 ($\rho = 0$, residuals are uncorrelated) is tested against an H_1 that states that the residuals are correlated indeed ($\rho \neq 0$). The same holds true if we test H_0 against an H_1 that states that the residuals are *positively* correlated ($\rho > 0$).

A p value of zero let us reject the null hypothesis and accordingly conclude that the residuals are correlated. Since p = 0 indicates the probability of obtaining a d-value of 1.767 in the sample, assuming at the same time that ρ is zero in the population, H_0 is rejected as too unlikely.

If we now calculate the corresponding multilevel model and its d-value, this value is d = 1.926 and thus much closer to the reference value of 2 than the 1.767 of the previous *lm()* model. This suggests that the autocorrelation of the residuals (and thus an important source of model mis-specification) was reduced by estimating the linear model again as a *mixed-effects* model. That is, as a model that allows the intercept and slope of a linear model to (co-)vary across the 22 countries.

The example illustrates that autocorrelated residuals may be a source of mis-specified regression models. However that doesn't mean that autocorrelation impairs any model. The interaction model (6.34) introduced in chapter 6 for the standard use case, for instance, does not suffer from serially correlated residuals. A Durbin-Watson test related to this interaction model reveals an autocorrelation of -0.045 along with a value of $d = 2.087$. The test yields a p value of 0.48. It belongs to a two-sided test where H_0 ($\rho = 0$, residuals are uncorrelated) is tested against an H_1 that states that the residuals are correlated ($\rho \neq 0$). From this we have to conclude that we cannot reject the null hypothesis that the residuals are uncorrelated. The null hypothesis cannot be rejected because the probability p of the sample finding would be too high for it (p > 0.05). p indicates the probability of the sample finding under the assumption that $\rho = 0$ in the population.

8.4 Normally Distributed Residuals

A Quantile-Quantile Plot (Q-Q Plot) is the commonly used instrument to check if the standardized residuals of a linear regression model are normally distributed. This plot compares specifically the empirical quantile values with their theoretical counterparts and plots these pairs of values against each other.

Using again interaction model (6.34) as an example, Figure 8.5 displays the associated Q-Q Plot, while Table 8.3 explains the underlying R script. According to this plot, the empirical residuals follow a normal curve only in its middle scale range, below and above this middle range they tend to more extreme values than the normal curve would let us expect. Since they *tend to their respective poles*, this makes the empirical distribution more heterogeneous than would be expected with a normal distribution.

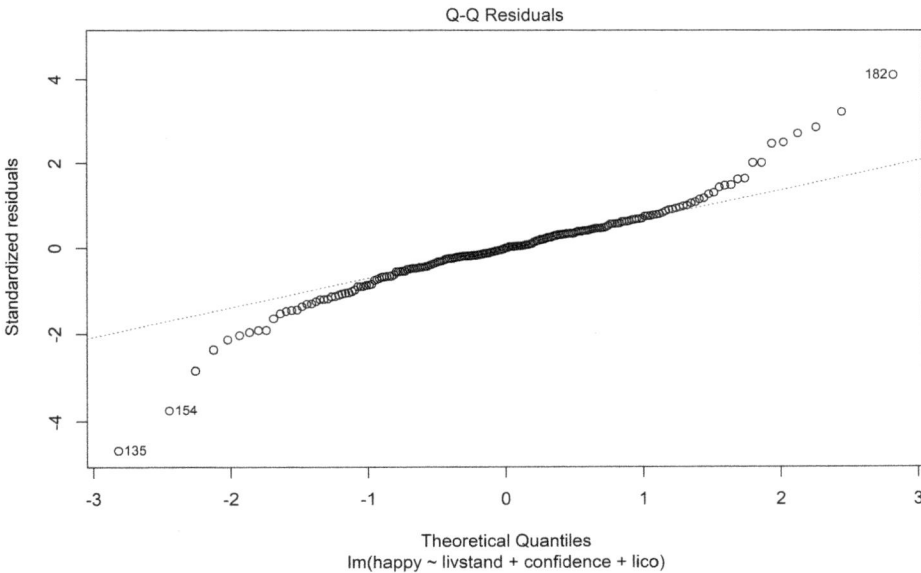

Figure 8.5: Q-Q Plot to Interaction Model (6.34).

Quantiles can be computed for both empirical frequency and theoretical probability distributions, in order to determine which scale values (quantile *values*) correspond to which quantile *shares*. The frequently used quartiles are possibly better known than the generic term *quantile*. Quartiles represent nothing else than special quantiles.

One way to determine such quartiles of a frequency distribution, for instance, is to sort the observed scale values in ascending order and to use the associated cumulative percentage shares to determine three particular scale values: In fact those scale values for which 25% (1st quartile), 50% (2nd quartile, median) and 75% (3rd quartile) respectively have the respective or smaller scale value. Instead of quartering distributions, we

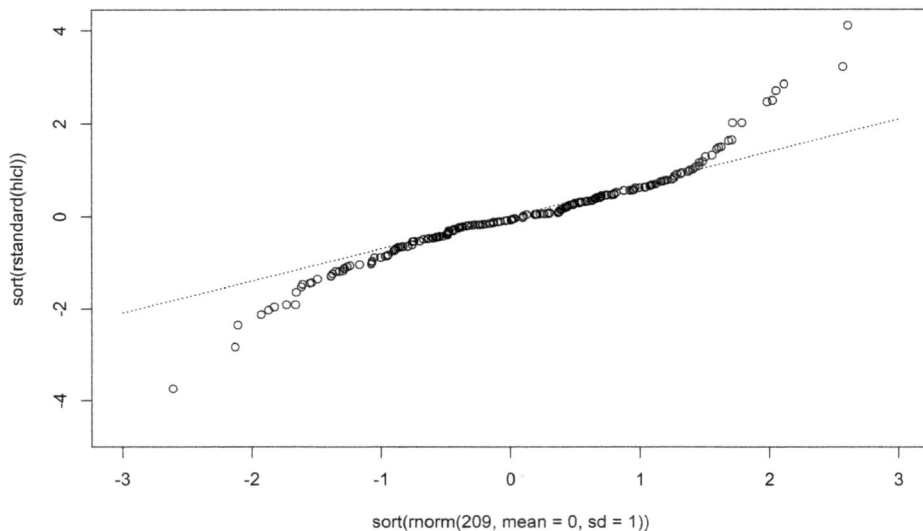

Figure 8.6: Alternative Q-Q Plot to Interaction Model (6.34).

Table 8.3: Script to the Q-Q Plot to the Interaction Model.

Line	R Script
1	load("ki.Rdata") # Q-Q Plot to interaction model
2	ki$lico <- ki$livstand * ki$confidence # interaction
3	summary(hlcl <-lm(happy ~ livstand + confidence +
4	lico, weights=cwt, data=ki))
5	tiff("fig85.tiff", units="in", width=9,
6	height = 6, res=600)
7	plot(hlcl, which = c(2))
8	dev.off()
9	# The Q-Q Plot detailed.
10	summary (sort(rstandard(hlcl)))
11	set.seed(15)
12	summary(sort(rnorm(209, mean=0, sd=1)))
13	x <- seq(from= -3, to= +3, by = 0.01)
14	y <- 0.697*x
15	tiff("fig86.tiff", units="in", width=9,
16	height = 6, res=600)

Table 8.3 (continued)

Line	R Script
17	plot(sort(rnorm(209, mean=0, sd=1)), sort(rstandard(hlcl)),
18	xlim=c(-3, 3))
19	lines(x, y, lty="dotted")
20	dev.off()

Lines explained

Lines 1 to 4 are the same as the lines in the R script in Table 6.5. They are used to calculate interaction model (6.34). Details are given there. Here we only need it as a reference for the Q-Q plot. Lines 5 and 6 define the graphic in terms of format (*tiff*), name (*fig 85.tiff*), units (*inch*), *width* and *height* in inch, *resolution* (600dpi). Line 7 relates the *plot ()* function to object *hlcl* and selects one out of a couple of standard plots by the *which* option. Following the equal sign is the specification of a vector *c()* and the reference number *2* for the Q-Q plot. Line 8 shuts down the graphic device activated by *tiff()* in line 5. Line 9: Comment. Lines 10 to 20 present an alternative to the *which* option to construct the essential components of a Q-Q plot. Lines 10 to 12 are required only to obtain the slope in the equation in line14. First, line 10 represents a nested structure of functions in that it embeds *rstandard()* within *sort()* within *summary()*. Importing the information from object *hlcl* line 10 calculates standardized residuals, sorts these residuals in ascending order, and calculates the summary statistics of this distribution, specifically to get its 1st and 3rd quartile. Line 11 sets a random seed for assuring reproducible results from line 12. Line 12 generates 209 normally distributed random variates with zero mean and a standard deviation of one, sorts these variates in ascending order and calculates the summary statistics of this distribution. Here again we are interested in the 1st and 3rd quartile of this distribution. Namely to subtract the 1st quartile from the 3rd for the empirical distribution, to do the same for the theoretical distribution, in order to take the ratio of the two differences of quartiles as slope of the expected line in the figure (because in a Q-Q plot the slope is defined to depend on the quartiles of the theoretical distribution). Line 13 produces a sequence of *x* values from -3 to + 3 in 0.01 steps, line 14 defines the slope by the just-explained ratio of differences, and line 19 draws the resulting line. Lines 15 and 16 specify the usual details of a graph, while lines 17 and 18 call and specify the function that plots the empirical and theoretical distribution, with their respective values sorted in ascending order, against each other. Line 20 shuts down the graphic device activated by *tiff()* in line 15.

can just as easily, for example, divide distributions into fifths or tenths and calculate quintiles or deciles accordingly. Or we can simply calculate the corresponding quantile shares for all of the observed scale values. Be that as it may, in any case it is necessary to sort the observed measurements in ascending order.

And this is exactly what we are doing in the present context, on the one hand with the standardized residuals of the empirical frequency distribution and, on the other hand, with the generated random variates that follow a standard normal distribution. The procedure is explained in the lower part of the R script in Table 8.3, while the result of this programming is shown in Figure 8.6.

8.5 Specifying the Random Component by a Generalized Linear Model

A linear model can be viewed as a special case of a generalized linear model (Nelder and Wedderburn 1972). *Generalized Linear Models* (GLMs) represent a prominent class of statistical models for distributions in the exponential family. A GLM consists of three parts (McCullagh and Nelder 1989: 26 – 32, 43):

1. A random part that specifies the distribution of a variable Y, with mean $E(Y_i) = \mu_i$
2. A systematic part that specifies effects of covariates on a quantity called linear predictor η_i
3. A link function $g(\cdot)$ that relates, for each unit $i = 1, \ldots, n$, η_i to μ_i in the link function $\eta_i = g(\mu_i)$.

The *glm()* function implemented in R expects input in terms of these three components. It also expects the designation of a data frame, and possibly the name of a variable used for weighting the observations (units of analysis).

$$glm(formula, \ family, \ weights, \ data) \tag{8.6}$$

In a classical linear model the components of Y have independent Normal distributions with $E(Y) = \mu$ and constant variance σ^2. In terms of a GLM, the random and systematic part is linked by the identity $\mu = \eta$. Then we can also use the *lm()* function.

$$lm(formula, \ weights, \ data) \tag{8.7}$$

First, *formula* specifies the systematic part of a GLM in the form target ~ covariate(s). Instead of *covariate* we could also have used terms such as *predictor, explanatory variable* and *feature*. The terms are used interchangeably. It is this systematic part in which the model is specified in terms of linear and nonlinear as well as additive and non-additive effects. In addition, the random part of the model must be specified in terms of distribution and link function.

In social research, random samples are often drawn from populations of interest in order to use this sample data for analysis. To draw a random sample, each of its units must be selected independently at random. Such a repeated drawing of units creates random variation in the units' variables, which must be taken into account in statistical models. This also applies to GLMs. In particular, the probability distribution of the target variable Y and a link function must be determined. In (8.6) this is done by specifying *family*.

$$family = distribution(link = function) \tag{8.8}$$

Commonly used distributions are the Gaussian distribution (normal curve), the binomial distribution (if Y is a binary variable), the Poisson distribution (if Y is a count variable), and the Gamma distribution (if variability in Y increases as its mean increases (Agresti and Finlay 2009: 460–461). If *binomial* is replaced by *quasibinomial*, possible overdispersion is considered.

A link function is associated with each distribution in the following way: Gaussian (*link = identity*), binomial (*link = logit*) and binomial (*link = probit*) respectively, Poisson (*link = log*), Gamma(*link = inverse*).

8.6 When the Variance of a Distribution Increases with its Mean: Assessing the Occurrence of Future Events Using the Gamma Distribution

The OLS criterion of constant variance cannot be met if the variability of a target variable increases as its mean increases. But that is exactly the expectation when it comes to forecasts. Subjective predictions are always subject to uncertainty. However, this uncertainty becomes the more pronounced the more distant the future for which an event is predicted. Then, when specifying the random part of a GLM, a gamma rather than normal distribution should be considered, so that the model assumes data with constant *coefficient of variation* instead of constant variance (McCullagh and Nelder 1989: 285–292).

Shape parameters let the gamma distribution have variable shapes. Selections of such shapes along with their underlying parameters are given in Johnson et al. (1994: 342) and Evans et al. (2000: 100). The density functions given there convey a good visual impression that, depending on these shape parameters, gamma distributions do have the ability "to mimic closely a normal distribution" (Johnson et al. 1994: 344).

To illustrate the use of the gamma distribution in the context of generalized linear modeling, we can use Example Data Set 3, the Bremen AI Delphi Survey on Human-Robot-Interaction. In this survey the following survey question was asked:

"The technical development of AI involves solving highly complex tasks. By when do you think AI will have the following capabilities?"

Table 8.4: Thirteen Items on AI, their Means, Standard Deviations, and Coefficients of Variation.

	M	SD	CV
Robots can navigate autonomously through the rooms of an apartment.	1.8	1.3	0.7
For example, robots can move towards people in the room of an apartment (quickly, carefully, . . .) or move away from them in the same way that people do with each other.	3.0	1.9	0.7
Drones can deliver mail and packages reliably and safely to any recipient address in cities.	3.3	2.1	0.6
Robots can autonomously carry out activities in the care of people in need of care. Example 1: Give bedridden people something to eat and drink (feed them, let them drink from a glass), raise the bed to eat and then lower it again.	3.6	2.1	0.6
Autonomous driving is possible safely and reliably in cities.	4.1	1.9	0.5
Assistant robots can take on household tasks such as preparing food, setting and clearing the table, operating the dishwasher and washing machine, and loading and unloading.	4.2	2.0	0.5
Robots can autonomously carry out activities in the care of people in need of care. Example 2: Being able to have personal conversations with people in need of care in a personalized communication style (tailored to the person and learned from interaction with them).	4.6	2.6	0.6
Robots can infer underlying behavioral intentions by observing verbal and extraverbal human behavior.	4.6	2.5	0.6
Robots program themselves.	4.9	3.0	0.6
Robots can autonomously carry out activities in the care of people in need of care. Example 3: Being able to have personal, content-related conversations with people in need of care (being able to build on previous conversation content).	5.1	2.5	0.5
Like humans, robots can transfer solution ideas from one problem area to another.	5.5	2.6	0.5
The reference data sets available for training robots are as extensive as the biographical experiences that humans typically learn.	5.6	2.9	0.5
If you don't have the experience to solve a problem, "common sense" may be able to offer a second-best solution. Robots are now also able to develop an understanding of problems in a context-related manner.	5.9	2.5	0.4

CV Coefficient of variation = SD/Mean. Means and standard deviations correlate r = 0.85 across the thirteen items.

Respondents were asked to assess a list of thirteen such capabilities. These thirteen items are displayed in Table 8.4. For each of these items we asked for an evaluation by means of the following nine-point time scale:

1	Already possible
2	By 2025
3	By 2030
4	By 2035
5	By 2040
6	By 2045
7	By 2050
8	Later
9	Not at all

Table 8.4 reorders the initial sequence of these items to report three corresponding quantities in ascending order of the items' mean values: the respective mean value and its associated standard deviation and coefficient of variation. For an item k this coefficient expresses the size of the standard deviation relative to that of the mean (Blalock 1981: 84).

$$CV_k = \frac{s_k}{\bar{x}_k} \tag{8.9}$$

Table 8.4 reveals the expected tendency that an item's spread increases with its mean: Means and standard deviations correlate r = 0.85 across the thirteen items. Accordingly, most (i. e., 10 in 13) $CV_k's$ are very similar to each other, they narrowly range between 0.5 and 0.6. This is certainly not a perfect though nevertheless pretty apt relationship, given one expects identical $CV_k's$.

This describes a situation for which the gamma distribution can be taken into account when specifying the random component of a GLM. Before we get to specifying and estimating a model for our data example, we have to take an intermediate step that is due to the special structure of this example. This intermediate step consists of converting the dataset's underlying *wide format* to a *long format*. In this way, we realize a task that we can similarly encounter in other contexts of social science data analysis, for example when modeling growth curves in the analysis of longitudinal data.

Table 8.5: Wide Format of a Data Frame.

row	y_1	...	y_7	...	y_{13}	x_1	id
1	5		5		6	1	1
2	2		4		4	1	2
3	2		2		7	1	3
.	.		.		.	.	.
113	.		.		.		113

The wide data format is the usual standard: Each row of the data frame represents one unit of analysis. In survey research this is typically a responding person with her answers to the survey questions. Table 8.5 illustrates this structure regarding the present example. Since we have 113 respondents, the data frame consists of 113 rows. y_1 to y_{13} represent the thirteen survey items listed in Table 8.4 and x_1 represents one of the predictor variables used in this example. Then, id is simply a running number from 1 to 113 that will serve as an abstract numerical key in the rearranged data structure of the long format. We thus see that each row represents a respondent, while all variables with the values of this respondent are arranged next to each other.

Table 8.6: Long Format of a Data Frame.

row	x_1	id	y	obs
1	1	1	y_1	5
2	1	2	y_1	2
3	1	3	y_1	2
.	.	.	.	.
679	1	1	y_7	5
680	1	2	y_7	4
681	1	3	y_7	2
.	.	.	.	.
1357	1	1	y_{13}	6
1358	1	2	y_{13}	4
1359	1	3	y_{13}	7
.	.	.	.	.
1469	.	113	y_{13}	.

The *gather()* function from the *tidyverse* library is used to rearrange the data frame. The script in Table 8.7 shows the required instructions and Table 8.6 outlines the resulting structure in long format for selected values of the first three respondents.

The most striking difference between wide and long format is that for each unit i the values of $y_1. \ldots, y_{13}$ are next to each other in wide format and one below the other in long format, thus forming the y column. The 113 units (respondents) with their 13 y_k variables per unit result that way in a data frame with a total of $113 \cdot 19 = 1,469$ rows: the *first* 113 rows reproduce the observed y_1 values along with the associated x_1 values, the *next* 113 rows reproduce the observed y_2 values along with the associated x_1 values, then the next 113 rows do the same for y_3, and so on until y_{13} and the 113th unit is reached in row 1,469.

Two further features are worth noting. The first refers to the units' x variables. In Table 8.6 this is x_1 only, with one observed value per respondent. Since these 113 values do not vary when converting the 113 rows in the $113 \cdot 19 = 1,469$ rows, the x_1 values are the same in all of the nineteen blocks of 113 rows each. When converting the wide into long format, the matrix of x variables is simply repeated (copied) from the 1st block of rows.

The second feature concerns the *id* variable. In the present context this is simply the running number from 1 to 113. When converting the data frame from wide to long format, this running number is required to keep traceable which y and x values belong to which respondent.

In another context, namely growth curve modeling, this key would represent the *level-2 id* in an analytical 2-level data structure, with the x values located at level 2 and the y values at level 1. In such a modeling framework all variables that enter a model as variables *not* assumed changing over time would be settled at level 2, while the time- varying variables would be located at level 1. Such a data structure is hierarchical in the sense that level-1 data are nested within level-2 data. Growth curve modeling is an approach that applies the multilevel framework to longitudinal data. There too the long data format is used when analyzing panel and trend data. It is also a useful instrument when it comes to the analysis of multivariate data structures as in the present context.

In the next step we specify a GLM for the data in long format. Both topics, data format and specification of a GLM, generally represent two completely distinct topics, but are needed specifically for this data example in conjunction with each other. Because of the 2-level data structure, we specifically estimate a generalized linear mixed model using the *glmer()* function from the R library *lme4*. The R script is explained in Table 8.7, the associated output is printed in Table 8.8 and the related null model in Table 8.9. Since a detailed introduction to linear mixed modeling is the subject of chapter 9, the present context focuses more on explaining the implications of using the *inverse* link of the gamma distribution and less on *mixed* modeling and its inherent multilevel aspect.

First of all, the null model reveals an interesting result. We use this model for variance decomposition. Its random-effects block shows specifically that 1 percent of variance is located at level 2 and 99 percent is located at level 1. Despite the usual labeling as *Groups* level in the *Random effects* block of the output, in the special data arrangement of this example level 2 represents the respondents themselves and not groups of them. The 1: 99 percent split indicates specifically that almost all variance in y emerges from a respondent's ratings of the thirteen survey items, while just 1 percent represents differences between those respondents. The observed variation therefore reflects almost exclusively differences in the statements being evaluated and only marginally possible differences in the people evaluating. For example, in evaluation research, different response styles could be a source of interpersonal variation that doesn't reflect variation across the objects to be evaluated.

In the present data example, we are interested in the respondents' AI self-rated expertise (x_1) and institutional context (x_2) and how these two features affect the respondents' ratings on the thirteen survey items. We distinguish three groups of respondents, namely actors in politics, scientists in engineering & natural sciences and scientists in the social sciences. Since x_2 represents a categorical variable, dummy coding is used to convert its three categories into 0/1 binary terms.

We explained this coding technique in section 6.8. In general k-1 dummy terms are used to estimate their effects in terms of expected differences to the omitted kth category. In the present analysis we specifically compare the groups of politicians (x_{2POL}) and social scientists (x_{2SOC}) respectively with the implicit reference group of engineers and natural scientists (x_{2ESC}).

In the present example the features x_1 and x_2 will not be able to explain much. If only 1 percent of the variance is at level 2, then only 1 percent of the variance can be explained at this level. We can of course ask how much of this explainable part is actually explained by the level-2 variables x_1, x_{2POL} and x_{2SOC}. To do this, we need to calculate how much an inclusion of these variables helps to reduce the prediction error. The calculation follows the same logic as in section 7.1 and section 9.3: we relate the residual variance of the model that contains these predictors to the corresponding variance of the null model, here specifically in relation to the level-2 variance.

$$R^2 = \left(\frac{\tau_{0|null}^2 - \tau_{0|model}^2}{\tau_{0|null}^2} \right) \tag{8.10}$$

With the two corresponding figures for the *Intercept*-Variance from Tables 8.8 and 8.9 inserted in (8.10), the level-2 variables reduce the prediction error by marginal 0.33 percent only. When responding to the thirteen survey items, it therefore plays almost no role at all whether "knowledge of AI" . . . "represents the core of [the respondent's] professional activity", is "indispensable" or "important" (taken together coded 1), or whether knowledge of AI is "not that important" (coded 0; question wordings in quotation marks). Furthermore, the professional background turns out to be virtually meaningless when it comes to assessing the thirteen AI scenarios.

It fits into this picture that no estimate of effect reaches any significant strength. As in section 9.2 explained, in measuring the strength of such an estimate here too we take the ratio to its standard error without wanting to draw a conclusion about its significance in the statistical sense from the associated t value. In the present context, because the analysis is not based on a random sample.

The random part of a GLM is specified by the *family* option. In the script in Table 8.7 this is the *family* = "Gamma"(*link* = "inverse") instruction. The link function deserves special attention in this specification. Gamma implies the *inverse* link (McCullagh and Nelder 1989: 30, 32) and thus predicts the reciprocal value μ^{-1} instead of μ. Applied to the present example, the linear predictor in the equation

$$\eta_{ki} = b_0 + b_1 x_{1i} + b_2 x_{2i} + b_3 x_{3i} + u_{0i} + e_{ki} \tag{8.11}$$

thus is

$$\eta_{ki} = \frac{1}{\mu_{ki}} \tag{8.12}$$

In this equation x_1 represents the respondents' AI self-rated expertise, x_2 the first dummy term x_{2POL} and x_3 the second dummy term x_{2SOC}. Subscripts indicate the respondents i ($i = 1, \ldots, 113$) and survey items k ($k = 1, \ldots, 13$), with the respondents located at level 2 and the items located at level 1 of the long format of the data frame (Table 8.6). u_{0i} and e_{ki} designate the random effects (i. e., the residuals) at level 2 and level 1 whose variances τ_0^2 and σ_e^2 are printed in the *random-effects* block of the output in Table 8.8. Transforming (8.11) and (8.12) to (8.13)

$$\mu_{ki} = \frac{1}{b_0 + b_1 x_{1i} + b_2 x_{2i} + b_3 x_{3i} + u_{0i} + e_{ki}} \tag{8.13}$$

yields the wanted predicted values via equation (8.14).

$$\hat{\mu}_{ki} = \frac{1}{b_0 + b_1 x_{1i} + b_2 x_{2i} + b_3 x_{3i}} \tag{8.14}$$

This transformation should be taken into account when interpreting the sign of a b_k, because predicting μ instead of μ^{-1} reverses its sign: a *plus* becomes *minus* and vice versa.

Based on the nine-point time scale described at the beginning of this section, we are analyzing the responses to the survey question about by when AI will have thirteen capabilities under consideration. The response scale increases in 5-years periods and ranges from 1 (already possible) until 9 (not at all). This means: the higher the response score, the later AI is expected to have acquired a skill in question. So a positive b effect would actually mean *later* and a negative effect would mean *earlier*. However, since equation (8.11) is not predicting μ, but rather μ^{-1}, the situation is exactly the opposite. Thus, when using the gamma specification, we should consider that the reversed sign of a fixed effect indicates if this is a positive or negative effect on μ.

Table 8.10 shows the result if the present model uses the normal curve instead of gamma. Then implicitly *link* = "*identity*" is used instead of *link* = "*inverse*". Both models produce equivalent predictions: If we compare the predicted μ's of both models with each other, the two vectors prove to be almost perfectly correlated (r = 0.996), with the deviance value for the gamma-specification of the model's random part indicating a comparatively better model fit.

Table 8.7: Script to *gather()*, *glmer()* Using the Gamma Distribution, and *lmer()*.

Line	R Script
1	`load("forecast.Rdata")`
2	`data$x2POL <- ifelse(data$x2 == "POL", 1, 0)`
3	`data$x2SOC <- ifelse(data$x2 == "GW", 1, 0)`
4	`data$x2ESC <- ifelse(data$x2 == "TNW", 1, 0)`
5	`data$id <- seq_len(113) # respondent id`
6	`data <- subset(data,`
7	`              select = c(y1, y2, y3, y4, y5, y6, y7,`
8	`                         y8, y9, y10, y11, y12, y13,`
9	`                         x1, x2POL, x2SOC, x2ESC, id))`
10	`library(DataEditR)`
11	`data_edit(data)`
12	`library(tidyverse)`
13	`as_tibble(data)`
14	`ml <- data %>%`
15	`gather('y1', 'y2', 'y3', 'y4', 'y5', 'y6', 'y7', 'y8',`
16	`       'y9', 'y10', 'y11', 'y12', 'y13', key = "y",`
17	`     value = "obs")`
18	`data_edit(ml)`
19	`library(lme4)`
20	`summary(glmer(obs ~ (1|id) + x1+x2POL+x2SOC, data = ml,`
21	`             family = "Gamma"(link= "inverse")))`
22	`summary(glmer(obs ~ (1|id), data = ml,`
23	`             family = "Gamma"(link= "inverse")))`
24	`summary(lmer(obs ~ (1|id) + x1+x2POL+x2SOC,`
25	`             REML = FALSE, data = ml))`

Lines explained

Line 1 loads the data frame. Lines 2 to 4 create the dummy terms using *ifelse()* logic. Line 5 creates a running number to be used as level-2 respondent id. Lines 6 to 9 selects the relevant subset of *y* and *x* variables and the respondent *id*. The *subset()* function excludes specifically from the data frame named *data* all variables that are not involved in the subsequent data transformation from wide to long format. Line 10 calls the library required for the data editor and line 11 loads the data into this editor. Line 12 calls the *tidyverse* library to get access to the *as_tibble()* and *gather()* and the programming features around these functions. In the Tidyverse, *tibble* is the coinage for an advanced data frame. Tibbles evolve from data frames, so line 13 defines the present data frame as a tibble. Line 14 to 17 use the *gather()* function to transform this tibble from wide to long format. For it we have to name the 13 *y* variables along with a key and a name for the column to write the observed *y* values in. Line 14 assigns the transformed data to object *ml*. Line 18 loads this data in the editor, just to check its structure. Then a concluding set of script lines call the functions required for the estimation of generalized linear mixed models and linear mixed models, both from library *lme4* (line 19). The specification of both functions, *glmer()* and *lmer()*, follow the same rules. We specify *target ~ covariates* for the fixed effects, and the random effects in brackets. *(1|id)* specifies the intercept as varying across the *id* units (respondents). In addition we have to name the data frame, family/link, and the estimator (here, ML). See also chapter 9 for linear mixed models.

Table 8.8: Output to *glmer()* Using the Gamma distribution.

Line	R Output
1	Generalized linear mixed model fit by maximum likelihood
2	(Laplace Approximation) ['glmerMod']
3	Family: Gamma (inverse)
4	Formula: obs ~ (1 | id) + x1 + x2POL + x2SOC
5	Data: ml
6	
7	AIC BIC logLik deviance df.resid
8	6469.9 6501.7 -3228.9 6457.9 1463
9	
10	Scaled residuals:
11	Min 1Q Median 3Q Max
12	-1.4992 -0.7572 -0.1139 0.5793 3.2247
13	
14	Random effects:
15	Groups Name Variance Std.Dev.
16	id (Intercept) 0.003009 0.05486
17	Residual 0.304794 0.55208
18	Number of obs: 1469, groups: id, 113
19	
20	Fixed effects:
21	Estimate Std. Error t value Pr(>|z|)
22	(Intercept) 0.256497 0.019151 13.393 <2e-16 ***
23	x1 -0.009465 0.018341 -0.516 0.606
24	x2POL 0.028632 0.026361 1.086 0.277
25	x2SOC 0.007638 0.019368 0.394 0.693
26	---
27	Signif. codes: 0 '***' 0.001 '**' 0.01 '*' 0.05 '.' 0.1 ' ' 1
28	
29	Correlation of Fixed Effects:
30	(Intr) x1 x2POL
31	x1 -0.670
32	x2POL -0.563 0.264
33	x2SOC -0.611 0.114 0.421

Lines explained

Lines 1 to 5 specify details of the function call. Lines 7 and 8 report the metrics for comparative model evaluation: The information-theoretic criteria AIC (Akaike's information criterion), BIC (Bayesian information criterion), loglikelihood, deviance, and residual degrees of freedom. Lines 10 to 12: Summary statistics for the residuals. Lines 14 to 17: *Random effects* block of information. Line 16 names the level-2 id along with the variance and standard deviation of the intercept at this level. Line 17 reports the residual variance and standard deviation at level 1. Line 18 prints the number of observations as 1,469 grouped within 113 units. Lines 20 to 27 report the *fixed effects* block in the usual way as estimate and its associated standard error and t ratio.

Table 8.9: Output to the Null Model Using *glmer()* and the Gamma distribution.

Line	R Output
1	Generalized linear mixed model fit by maximum likelihood
2	(Laplace Approximation) ['glmerMod']
3	Family: Gamma (inverse)
4	Formula: obs ~ (1 | id)
5	Data: ml
6	
7	AIC BIC logLik deviance df.resid
8	6465.8 6481.7 -3229.9 6459.8 1466
9	
10	Scaled residuals:
11	Min 1Q Median 3Q Max
12	-1.4947 -0.7501 -0.1078 0.6093 3.2588
13	
14	Random effects:
15	Groups Name Variance Std.Dev.
16	id (Intercept) 0.003019 0.05495
17	Residual 0.304937 0.55221
18	Number of obs: 1469, groups: id, 113
19	
20	Fixed effects:
21	Estimate Std. Error t value Pr(>|z|)
22	(Intercept) 0.25935 0.00905 28.66 <2e-16 ***
23	---
24	Signif. codes: 0 '***' 0.001 '**' 0.01 '*' 0.05 '.' 0.1 ' ' 1

Lines explained
Analogous to Table 8.8 the corresponding null model is printed.

Table 8.10: Output to *lmer()* Using the Normal Distribution.

Line	R Output
1	Linear mixed model fit by maximum likelihood ['lmerMod']
2	Formula: obs ~ (1 | id) + x1 + x2POL + x2SOC
3	Data: ml
4	
5	AIC BIC logLik deviance df.resid
6	6782.7 6814.5 -3385.4 6770.7 1463
7	
8	Scaled residuals:
9	Min 1Q Median 3Q Max
10	-2.1702 -0.7050 -0.1359 0.5603 2.4568
11	
12	Random effects:

Table 8.10 (continued)

Line	R Output
13	Groups Name Variance Std.Dev.
14	id (Intercept) 1.451 1.205
15	Residual 5.226 2.286
16	Number of obs: 1469, groups: id, 113
17	
18	Fixed effects:
19	Estimate Std. Error t value
20	(Intercept) 4.38117 0.28027 15.632
21	x1 0.05109 0.26986 0.189
22	x2POL -0.11573 0.38378 -0.302
23	x2SOC -0.16773 0.28492 -0.589
24	
25	Correlation of Fixed Effects:
26	(Intr) x1 x2POL
27	x1 -0.672
28	x2POL -0.589 0.280
29	x2SOC -0.615 0.111 0.425

Lines explained

The table provides the corresponding information for a linear mixed model that uses the normal curve instead of the gamma distribution. A detailed description of the output of such a model is provided in chapter 9.

8.7 When the Variance of a Distribution is a Function of its Mean: Using the Binomial Distribution

How does the frequency distribution of a binary variable looks like? Such a variable consists of two states usually coded 1 if an attribute of interest is present, and 0 otherwise. Imagine you have 10 observations, seven 1s and three 0s, then their arithmetic mean $\bar{y} = 0.7$ is simply the share p of 1s in the n = 10 observations.

And the average spread of a binary 0/1 variable? If the mean of the distribution is denoted p, then its standard deviation is $\sqrt{p \cdot (1-p)}$. This expression may look strange but it simply emerges from the well-known standard-deviation formula (here expressed for a variable y and a sample of n observations)

$$s_y = \sqrt{\frac{\sum_{i=1}^{n} (y_i - \bar{y})^2}{n}} \tag{8.15}$$

if applied to a binary variable consisting of values 1 and 0. Because then the mean value is p and only two types of quantities represent the squared deviations from it: $(1-p)^2$ and $(0-p)^2$, with $n \cdot p$ ones and $n \cdot (1-p)$ zeros in the sum of squares. Defining $q = 1 - p$, Blalock (1981: 196–197) demonstrates the few required algebraic steps to arrive at $\sqrt{p \cdot q}$.

More important than presenting these computational steps again, however, is to recognize that in case of binary variables the average spread of a frequency distribution is a function of its mean value. This is an important fact because a linear regression analysis always estimates (conditional) mean values. Then, the more these mean values differ from each other, the more the spread differs too. Which in turn means: Although linear regression offers a meaningful interpretation even in the case of a binary target variable, it is usually *not* recommended to use it because of the violated criterion of constant variance (homoscedasticity). It *does* offer a meaningful interpretation because it always estimates the conditional probability of being in state $y = 1$ of a 0/1 coded target variable, with the conditions emerging from the configuration of the x_k variables involved in a prediction. However, the implied heteroscedasticity violates a requirement for the ordinary least squares estimator. This is the first standard objection to the linear probability model. Then, a second standard objection commonly raised is that irregular $\hat{y}$ estimates may occur. This refers to estimated values outside the range of zero and one, as these then exclude a probability interpretation (Agresti 1990: 84–85; Long 1997: 38–39).

Accordingly, for a binary target variable, it is unanimously recommended to run a logistic or probit regression instead of a linear regression. We would like to illustrate this with the following data example.

8.7.1 Example Data

In Example Data Set 1, the PPSM Innovation Panel, we asked the respondents this question: "Just think about how things are going for you right now. What would you say? Are you currently happy or unhappy?" Of n = 3,949 respondents, 18.3 percent perceived themselves as "rather unhappy" and 81.7 percent as "rather happy". In Table 8.11 this is variable y. Coding the variable $y = 1$ for happy and $y = 0$ for unhappy, the share of 1's in the n observations, $Pr(y = 1) = 0.817$, is just the arithmetic mean of its frequency distribution.

Variable x measures the respondents' current standard of living on an eleven-point scale. They were asked to imagine the image of a ladder with 11 rungs, with rung 11 representing the best possible standard of living and rung 1 representing the worst one. Table 8.11 shows in column n the absolute frequencies, with which respondents placed their standard of living on the respective ladder rung. The mean rung is $\bar{x} = 6.9$, with mean dispersion of $s_x = 1.9$ around it. The frequency distribution of ladder rungs is skewed, with a median of 7 and the middle 50 percent of ratings in the range of 6 (1st quartile) and 8 (3rd quartile).

In addition, Table 8.11 displays the bivariate frequency distribution of x and y, standard of living and perceived happiness, with the proportion of happy respondents given a certain standard of living reported in the far right column. With this information, Table 8.11 describes the basic structure of the present data example. In the analysis below the variables are named y (happiness) and x (standard of living) and the data frame is named *happy*.

Table 8.11: Structure of Data Example.

	y			$Pr(y = 1\|x)$
x	0	1	n	
1	28	9	37	0.243
2	19	19	38	0.500
3	64	52	116	0.448
4	78	129	207	0.623
5	150	320	470	0.681
6	134	549	683	0.804
7	100	610	710	0.859
8	92	781	873	0.895
9	38	504	542	0.930
10	11	169	180	0.939
11	9	84	93	0.903
All	723	3,226	3,949	0.817

8.7.2 Linear Probability, Logistic, and Probit Model

We outlined in section 8.5 that a Generalized Linear Model (GLM) uses link functions $\eta_i = g(\mu_i)$ to relate, for each observation $i = 1, \ldots, n$, the linear predictor η_i to μ_i. In the classical linear model with its assumption of *normally* distributed residuals and constant residual variance, this is the *identity* link

$$\eta_i = \mu_i \tag{8.16}$$

For the *binomial* distribution, with $0 < \mu < 1$, a link function should satisfy the condition that it maps the interval (0, 1) on to the whole real line (McCullagh and Nelder 1989: 31). Customary link functions for it involve the *probit* and *logit* link.

A class of models for *binary* responses has specifically the form

$$\pi(x) = F(\alpha + \beta x) \tag{8.17}$$

where $\pi(x)$ indicates the probability of being in state 1 of variable y given x, $Pr(y = 1|x)$, and F is a standard continuous *cdf* (cumulative distribution function)[1]. "When F is strictly increasing over the entire real line", (8.17) "is a GLM with link function equal to the inverse of F"

---

1 The acronym *cdf* denotes the "cumulative distribution function" $F(v)$ of a random variable V. $F(v)$ gives the probability that V takes a value less than or equal to v, $F(v) = Pr(V \le v)$, where instead of

$$F^{-1}[\pi(x)] = a + \beta x \tag{8.18}$$

that maps "the (0,1) range of probabilities onto $(-\infty, \infty)$, the range of linear predictors such as $a + \beta x$" (Agresti 1990: 90). Model (8.17) is the *probit* model, with link

$$\eta_i = \Phi^{-1}(\mu_i) \tag{8.19}$$

(McCullagh and Nelder 1989: 31, 108, 110), when F is the *standard normal* cdf $\Phi(\cdot)$, and it is the *logistic* model, with link function (8.20)

$$\eta_i = \ln\left(\frac{\mu_i}{1 - \mu_i}\right) \tag{8.20}$$

when F is the standardized *logistic* cdf, i. e., (8.21)

$$F(x) = \frac{e^{\left[\frac{(x-\mu)}{\tau}\right]}}{1 + e^{\left[\frac{(x-\mu)}{\tau}\right]}} = \frac{1}{1 + e^{\left[\frac{-(x-\mu)}{\tau}\right]}} \qquad -\infty < x < \infty \tag{8.21}$$

(Agresti 1990: 90; Evans et al. 2000: 124, 126) with location parameter $\mu = 0$ and scale parameter $\tau = 1$, resulting in the simplified expression

$$F(x) = \frac{e^x}{1 + e^x} = \frac{1}{1 + e^{-x}} \tag{8.22}$$

While in a linear regression model the error variance is *estimated*, in the binary response model this variance is *assumed*. For the Probit model, the error is assumed to be distributed normally with mean 0 and $Var(\epsilon) = 1$, while for the logit model the errors are assumed to have a *standard* logistic distribution with mean 0 and variance $Var(\epsilon) = \pi^2/3$ (Long 1997: 42, 47; Long and Freese 2006: 133–134)[2], here with π indicating the mathematical constant $Pi = 3.1416$. Due to these assumptions, the estimates of corresponding logit and probit effects differ approximately by the ratio of the two built-in normalization factors $\sqrt{\pi^2/3}$ and $\sqrt{1}$, i. e., by a ratio of about 1.8 (Aldrich and Nelson 1984: 41, 44; Long 1997: 47–48). However, as will be exemplified below, their empirical predictions are nearly the same. Figure 8.7. gives an impression of the sigmoid (S-shaped) shape of the normal and logistic distribution functions.

With *happiness* denoted by y, *standard of living* by x, and with the data frame named *happy*, (8.23) specifies *the glm()* function for the *linear probability model* for the example data.

"cumulative distribution function" often the simpler term "distribution function" is used (Daly et al. 1995: 69; Kühnel and Krebs 2006: 150).

2 If the logistic distribution is rescaled to have unit variance, the result is the *standardized* logistic distribution, then with nearly identical logistic and normal *cdf*'s (Long 1997: 43).

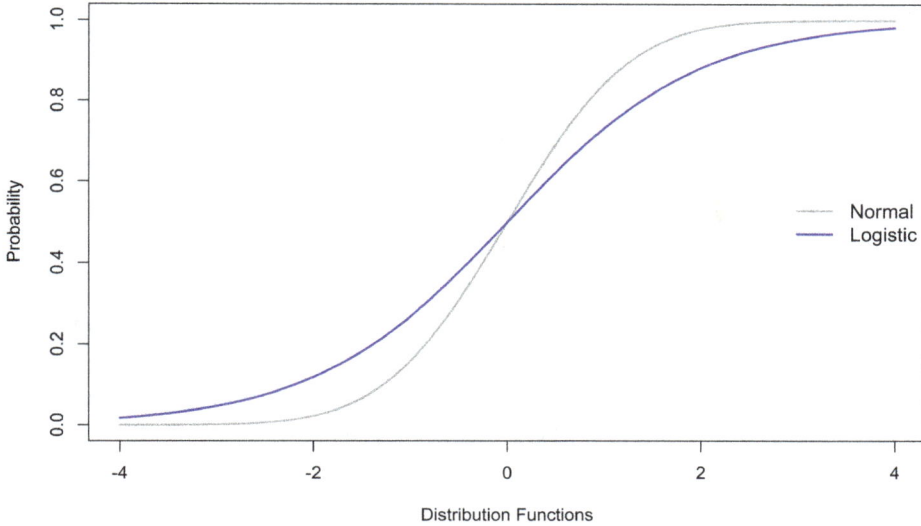

Figure 8.7: Normal and Logistic Distribution Functions.

$$summary\left(LP< - glm\left(\begin{array}{l}y\sim x,\\ family=gaussian(link="identity"),\\ data=happy\end{array}\right)\right)\qquad(8.23)$$

This function call produces the same estimates of effect when $glm()$ is replaced with the corresponding $lm()$ because of the same underlying distributional assumptions. In addition, both function calls produce equivalent model-fit information, for instance as exemplified in section 7.1. The model estimates the probability of being rather happy as a function of the respondents' standard of living

$$Pr(y=1|x)=b_0+b_1x\qquad(8.24)$$

The OLS estimates of intercept and slope are displayed in Table 8.12. The blue regression line in Figure 8.8 results if we insert these estimates into (8.24). Accordingly, we can expect that the probability of rating oneself as happy increases by 0.0615 when standard of living increases by one rung. A plausible result: the higher the personal standard of living, the more likely personal happiness is.

However, special attention deserves the upper pole of the x scale, particularly the rungs 9, 10, and 11. Inserted into (8.24), the resulting $Pr(y=1|x)$ estimates are

$$0.9437 \ for \ x=9$$

$$1.0052 \ for \ x=10$$

$$1.0667 \ for \ x=11$$

Table 8.12: Data Example: Linear Probability Model.

Linear Probability Model (LP)			
	b_k	$s.e(b_k)$	$b_k/s.e(b_k)$
Intercept	0.3902	0.0219	17.85
x	0.0615	0.0030	20.25

McFadden's $R^2 = 0.094$

While respondents on rung 9 have an estimated probability of 0.94 of being happy, the corresponding estimates for rungs 10 and 11, namely 1.01 and 1.07, exceed the upper bound 1.0 of a probability. This exemplifies one of the two standard objections to the linear probability model. There is also the second standard objection: heteroscedasticity.

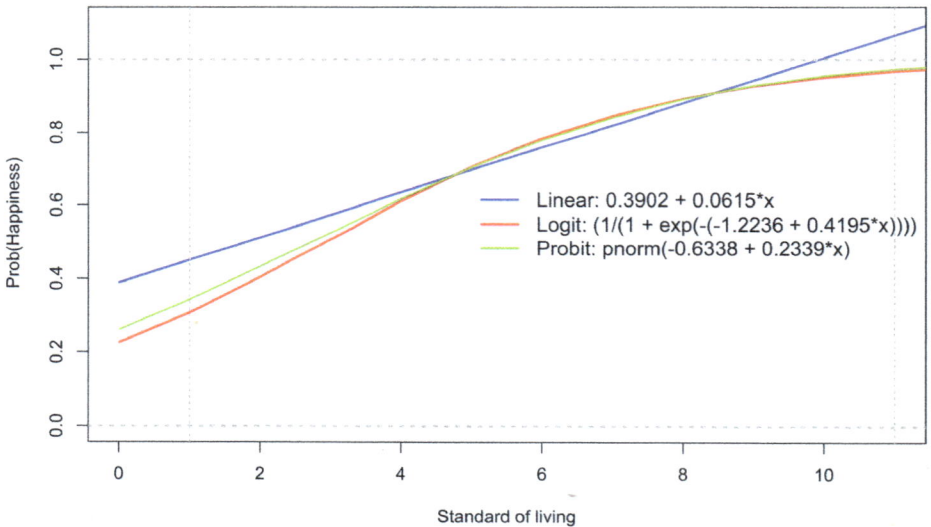

Figure 8.8: Predictions of Linear, Logit and Probit Model Compared.

Already the range of the *observed Pr* values in Table 8.11, in fact 0.243 to 0.903, suggests that the *estimated Pr* values too will differ substantially from one another across the eleven respondent groups $x = 1, \ldots, 11$. Consequently, the variances $Pr \cdot (1 - Pr)$ must also differ.

Again with *happiness* denoted by *y*, *standard of living* by *x*, and with the data frame named *happy*, (8.25) specifies the *glm()* function for the *probit model* for the example data.

$$summary\left(PT<-\ glm\left(\begin{array}{c}y\sim x,\\ family=binomial(link="probit"),\\ data=happy\end{array}\right)\right) \tag{8.25}$$

The *glm()* function uses as estimator iteratively reweighted least squares. The estimates of intercept and slope are displayed in Table 8.13. The green regression curve in Figure 8.8 results if we insert these estimates into (8.26).

Table 8.13: Data Example: Probit Model.

	Probit Model (PT)		
	b_k	$s.e(b_k)$	$b_k/s.e(b_k)$
Intercept	−0.6338	0.0861	−7.362
x	0.2339	0.0129	18.085

McFadden's $R^2 = 0.096$

$$Pr(y=1|x) = \Phi(b_0 + b_1 x) \tag{8.26}$$

$\Phi(b_0 + b_1 x)$ returns the probability that a standard normal variate takes a value less than or equal to $b_0 + b_1 x$. The probit model predicts quantile values z_a and takes the associated probabilities a of the distribution function as estimates of $Pr(y=1|x)$. The *glm()* function returns for each respondent the estimated quantile value z_a as *linear predictor* and a as *fitted value*.

With the link function altered to *logit*, the function call (8.27)

$$summary\left(LC<-\ glm\left(\begin{array}{c}y\sim x,\\ family=binomial(link="logit"),\\ data=happy\end{array}\right)\right) \tag{8.27}$$

provides the estimates of effect of the logistic model for the example data. These estimates are reported in Table 8.14. If inserted into (8.28), the red curve in Figure 8.8 results.

$$Pr(y=1|x) = \frac{e^{(b_0 + b_1 x)}}{1 + e^{(b_0 + b_1 x)}} = \frac{1}{1 + e^{-(b_0 + b_1 x)}} \tag{8.28}$$

Here, the *glm()* function returns for each respondent the estimated logit (8.29) as *linear predictor* and (8.28), the estimated $Pr(y=1|x)$, as *fitted value*. It is this transformation that contributes much to the practical significance of the logistic model. On the one hand, it enables a useful interpretation in terms of the probability of being in a state of interest, in the present data, for instance, this state is being a happy person.

$$ln\left(\frac{Pr(y=1|x)}{1-Pr(y=1|x)}\right) = b_0 + b_1 x \tag{8.29}$$

On the other hand, we have the quantity called *logit* that helps to map the (0,1) range of probabilities onto the full range of a linear predictor. Aldrich and Nelson (1984: 31–32) made this point: Transformation of Pr to the ratio $Pr/(1-Pr)$ eliminates the upper bound, $Pr=1$, because as Pr approaches one, $Pr/(1-Pr)$ goes to infinity. While taking the logarithm of this ratio eliminates the lower bound of zero, "the result of which can be any real number from negative to positive infinity."

Table 8.14: Data Example: Logistic Model.

| | **Logistic Model (LC)** | | |
	b_k	$s.e(b_k)$	$b_k/s.e(b_k)$
Intercept	−1.2236	0.1484	−8.245
x	0.4195	0.0233	18.045

McFadden's $R^2 = 0.098$

Models for binary responses may thus use both the standard normal and logistic *cdf* for a mapping that excludes Pr estimates outside the (0,1) range of probabilities. The green and red curve in Figure 8.8 show this advantage specifically for the upper limit of the (0, 1) range, since this upper bound is only asymptotically approximated but not reached.

However, the said use of the *cdf*'s implies that the strength of the effect of x on $Pr(y=1|x)$ varies depending on the value of x. Then it might be reasonable to compute the *marginal* effect for a selected x value. In the present example this is the median value $x=7$. A marginal effect is conceived of as an instantaneous rate of change at the selected point (Hilbe 2009: 605–609). In the present example it results as the product of the b_1- slope 0.4195 and the derivative of (8.28),

$$e^{(b_0+b_1\cdot 7)} \cdot \left(\left(1+e^{(b_0+b_1\cdot 7)}\right)^{-2}\right) \tag{8.30}$$

to express with it the limiting value $\lim_{\Delta x \to 0}(\Delta Pr(y=1)/\Delta x)$ of the ratio of the difference in $Pr(y=1)$ to the difference in x when this latter difference approaches zero[3]. In Figure 8.9, this is the slope of the tangent line at $x=7$ and amounts to 0.0543.

Despite different parameterization, the probit and logit models originate approximately the same predictions of $Pr(y=1|x)$. Both vectors of fitted values are nearly perfectly correlated and the average distance between them is vanishingly small.

---

3 Fox (2009: 59–66) provides a detailed introduction to the derivative of a function.

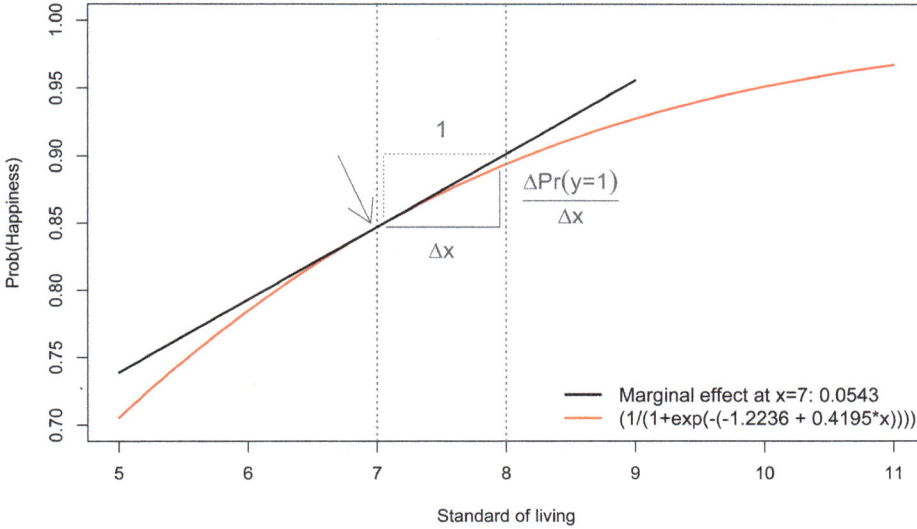

Figure 8.9: Marginal Effect at x = 7.

Table 8.15 reports the figures, with r indicating the Pearson correlation and d a distance metric (8.31)

$$d = \frac{1}{n} \cdot \sum_i \left| Pr_{(i)LC} - Pr_{(i)PT} \right| \tag{8.31}$$

that simply takes the average, over the i respondents, of the absolute differences between the corresponding model predictions. At the same time, the estimate of the effect of standard of living on the probability of happiness in the logit model turns out to be 1.79 times the corresponding estimate in the probit model, thus nearly approaching the expected ratio of 1.8 as outlined above.

Table 8.15: Correlation and Average Distance Between Model Predictions.

Models	r	d
LP — LC	0.962	0.025
LP — PT	0.973	0.021
LC — PT	0.999	0.005

Furthermore, the calculations in Table 8.15 indicate comparatively larger differences in the predictions of the probit and logit model on the one hand and the linear probability model on the other. Whereby the average distance between the linear probability (LP) and logit model (LC) appears slightly greater than the average distance between the linear probability (LP) and probit model (PT).

8.7.3 Logistic Link Function

The link function (8.20) respectively (8.29) provides an alternative to the analysis of $Pr(y = 1)$. Instead of analyzing the *probability* of being in state 1 of a binary variable of interest, we can also analyze the *odds* of being in this state. A simple transformation of the logit, i. e., the log of the odds, yields the odds

$$\frac{Pr(y = 1|x)}{1 - Pr(y = 1|x)} = e^{b_0 + b_1 x} = e^{b_0} \cdot e^{b_1 x} \tag{8.32}$$

With the estimates of intercept and slope from Table 8.14, we get

$$\frac{Pr(y = 1|x)}{1 - Pr(y = 1|x)} = e^{-1.2236} \cdot e^{0.4195 \cdot x} \tag{8.33}$$

With the data structured as in Table 8.11, we have eleven odds, one for each x value respectively row. An estimated intercept of $e^{-1.2236} = 0.29$ indicates that, given $x = 0$, we expect to observe for every happy person $0.29^{-1} = 3.5$ unhappy persons. Since $x = 0$ cannot occur empirically in the present example ($x = 1, \ldots, 11$), this is only a theoretical reference value. Then, the estimated slope e^{b_1} indicates the *odds ratio* between consecutive odds. In this regard, the odds of being happy are expected to increase by a factor of e^{b_1} for each higher rung of the ladder-scale.

8.7.4 Weighting the $Pr(y = 1|x)$

Replacing the linear probability model with the probit or logit model is the standard way to handle binary response variables. The *glm()* function uses iteratively reweighted least squares instead of ordinary least squares, and copes that way with the heteroscedasticity involved in the prediction of $Pr(= 1)$: the more the estimated Pr values differ from one another across the eleven respondent groups $x = 1, \ldots, 11$, their variances $Pr \cdot (1 - Pr)$ must also differ.

   An alternative route to dealing with this heteroscedasticity is to estimate the probability directly from the *aggregated data* of Table 8.11. We would then simply use an approach designed for categorical data analysis. If there is access to the original data set (of, in the present example, the n = 3,949 respondents), this alternative route would be unnecessary. However, if there is access to the aggregated data only, perhaps as published contingency table, then this alternative route might be useful. This approach goes back to Coleman (1964), an elaboration of the WLS approach for aggregated data can also be found in Forthofer and Lehnen (1981). Coleman's approach con-

Table 8.16: Data Example: Linear Probability Model.

Linear Probability Model for Aggregated Data			
	b_k	$s.e(b_k)$	$b_k/s.e(b_k)$
Intercept	0.4526	0.0666	6.80
X	0.0530	0.0085	6.27

$R^2 = 0.814$

sists of weighting each *estimated* $Pr(y=1)$ with the inverse value (8.34) of its sampling variance,

$$((Pr \cdot (1-Pr))/n)^{-1} \tag{8.34}$$

Using R, this calculation can be easily carried out. We use the *lm()* function for this and the weighting option in it, to get WLS estimates of intercept and slope for the now *eleven* appropriately weighted units of analysis. Table 8.17 reports the R script, while Table 8.16 informs about the resulting WLS estimates of effect. Please note that the R^2 of 0.814 reported below this table for the *aggregated* data is not comparable to the R^2 of 0.094 when using the *individual-level* survey data of the previous section.

8.7.5 Inference With the Binomial Distribution

The binomial distribution is the probability distribution of the *frequency* with which a *binary* element occurs in a simple random selection in which each drawn element is put back before the next element is drawn (i. e., sampling with replacement). The probability of observing x successes and $n-x$ failures is given by the binomial distribution

$$Pr(X=x) = \binom{n}{x} p^x (1-p)^{n-x} \tag{8.35}$$

Table 8.17: R Script to WLS Estimates for the Aggregated Data Example.

Line	R Script
1	load("Happy.Rdata")
2	happy <- subset(happy, select = c(x, y))
3	happy <- (na.omit(happy))
4	ftm <- as.matrix(ftable(happy$x, happy$y))
5	n <- c(ftm [, 1] + ftm [, 2])

Table 8.17 (continued)

Line	R Script
6	Pr <- c(ftm [,2])/n
7	x <- seq_len(11)
8	obs <- round(cbind(ftm, x, n, Pr),3)
9	vPr <- c((Pr*(1-Pr))/n)
10	w <- c(1/vPr)
11	summary(lm(Pr ~ x, weights = w))
12	# WLS
13	y <- Pr
14	x0 <- c(1,1,1,1,1,1,1,1,1,1,1)
15	x1 <- c(1,2,3,4,5,6,7,8,9,10,11)
16	x <- cbind(x0,x1)
17	v <- diag(vPr)
18	invv <- solve(v)
19	round(b <- ((solve(t(x)%*%invv%*%x))%*%t(x)%*%invv%*%y),4)

Lines explained

Line 1 loads the data frame. Lines 2 and 3 reduce this frame to the target and predictor variable and the observations with valid values in both variables. Lines 4 to 8 create the aggregated input as displayed as Table 8.11. First, the contingency table is defined as matrix (line 4) to sum the frequencies row-wise (line 5) and calculate Pr (line 6). Then line 7 creates a sequence of numbers from 1 to 11 to represent the empirical values of *x*. Finally, line 8 binds the initial matrix together with these calculations and assigns the result to the object named *obs* (for the empirical observations). Lines 9 and 10 then create the weight variable that is used in the *lm()* function call in line 11. Line 12: Comment. Alternatively, lines 13 to 19 show how the WLS estimates of intercept and slope can be calculated directly. We addressed this topic in section 6.6.

where x is any integer between 0 and n, inclusive. $p^x (1-p)^{n-x}$ expresses the probability of observing x successes and $n-x$ failures in a *particular* sequence, while the binomial coefficient

$$\binom{n}{x} = \frac{n!}{(n-x)! \cdot x!} \tag{8.36}$$

gives the *number* of different sequences of x successes and $n-x$ failures (Fox 2009: 99; Evans et al. 2000: 44; Kühnel and Krebs 2006: 168). Daly et al. (1995: 78) describe the binomial probability model as "probability model for the total number of successes in a sequence of n independent Bernoulli trials, in which the probability of success in a single trial is p."

A random sample of size n results if we realize n independent random draws from a population of interest, in order to select n of its N elements. Each of the single draws represents a random experiment that originates a chance outcome. We are then specifically talking about a *Bernoulli trial* when a single draw can produce one of two outcomes, success or failure, with probability of success being p. A Bernoulli variate is the special case, for $n = 1$, of the general binomial variate involving n trials. A Bernoulli distribution has a mean of p and a variance of $p \cdot (1-p)$ (Evans et al. 2000: 31).

Imagine the selection of items from an urn, with a finite population N of which $N \cdot p$ are successes and $N \cdot (1-p)$ are not. Then a "Bernoulli variate corresponds to selecting one item ($n = 1$) with probability p of success in choosing the desired type" (Evans et al. 2000: 33), while the binomial variate is the *number x of successes* in n independent selections, with a drawn element put back before the next draw ("with replacement"). As Evans et al. (2000: 43) phrase it: The "binomial variate **B:** n, p is the number of successes in n-independent Bernoulli trials, where the probability of success at each trial is p and the probability of failure is $q = 1 - p$." The mean of the binomial variate is accordingly $n \cdot p$ and the variance is $n \cdot p \cdot (1-p)$ (Evans et al. 2000: 44). These formulae relate to the *absolute* frequencies, while the corresponding formulae for *relative* frequencies (i. e., proportions) are p and $p \cdot (1-p)/n$ (Kühnel and Krebs 2006: 171–172).

Table 8.18: 1,500 Random Draws of Samples of Size $n = 4$.

x	p	Freq.	%
0	0.00	32	1.07
1	0.25	217	7.23
2	0.50	803	26.77
3	0.75	1,222	40.73
4	1.00	726	24.20
		3,000	100

For instance, when drawing samples of size $n = 4$, with respect to x the five outcomes shown in Table 8.18 are possible. If we convert x into p, the corresponding shares of successes x in sample units n, p, are 0.0, 0.25, 0.5, 0.75 and 1.0. This describes the outcome space for which we carried out 3,000 random draws using the function[4]

$$rbinom(n, size, prob) \tag{8.37}$$

with $n = 3000$, *size* = 4 and $p = 0.7$. In this way we simulate the draws of 3,000 random samples of size 4 from a population with true value of $p = 0.7$. Doing this results in the compositions as displayed in Table 8.18: 1.07 percent of the 3,000 samples contained none success. In 7.23 percent of the 3,000 samples $x = 1$ success in $n = 4$ elements was observed, while 26.77 percent of the samples showed two, 40.73 percent three, and

---

[4] Adler (2010: 338–341) presents a useful overview of functions to let R generate probability distributions.

24.20 percent four successes in four elements. With a sample size of $n = 4$, only the five *p*-values of the outcome space can occur empirically, but not the true population value of 0.7. However, the frequency distribution already shows very clearly that most samples are concentrated around the nearest value of 0.75.

Table 8.19: Increasing Sample Size.

Sample n	4	8	16	32	64
Mean(p)	0.69942	0.69692	0.69351	0.70126	0.69780
s.e.(p)	0.22926	0.16249	0.11526	0.08091	0.05740

We repeated this sampling experiment with sample sizes $n = 8$, $n = 16$, $n = 32$ and $n = 64$ to give an idea of the impact of increasing the sample size. Table 8.19 reports the results. First, each of the experiments confirm that the mean of the sampling distribution tends to the true population value. This illustrates that the sample proportion can be viewed as an unbiased estimator of the population proportion. Secondly, it becomes clear that an increase of the sample size by a factor of four halves the standard error. As the sample size increases, their estimates become more accurate because they are spread more closely around the true value from the start (Agresti and Finlay 2009: 114). Figure 8.10 illustrates this with respect to the five sampling experiments. Where the fact that the five graphs also differ in the percentage values in which their *p* values (i. e., proportions of successes *x* in sample units *n*) occur, is due to the fact that *the number of such* p values increases as the sample size increases, so that each individual *p* value occurs comparably less frequently. This explains why the five graphs in Figure 8.10 appear so arranged one on top of the other.

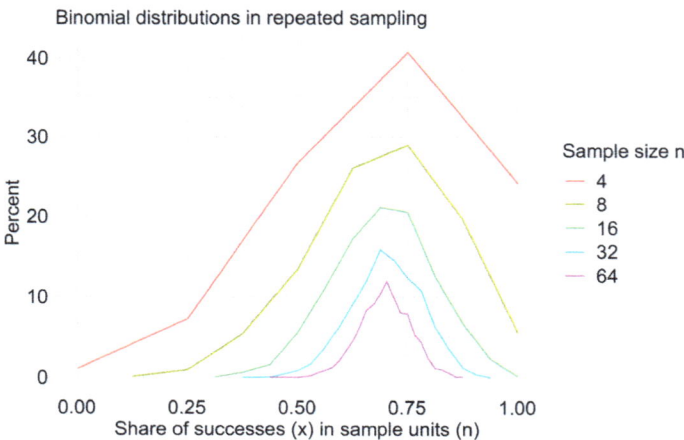

Figure 8.10: Binomial Distributions in Repeated Sampling.

The shapes of the graphs in Figure 8.10 also show that they become more symmetrical as n increases. The population variance σ_y^2 of a variable and the sample size n are the most important factors that affect the standard error of an estimate. In the case of a proportion the variance is $\pi \cdot (1 - \pi)$, with the population parameter π estimated by its sample estimate p.

$$s.e_p = \sqrt{\frac{\pi \cdot (1 - \pi)}{n}} \tag{8.38}$$

The sample size is also the decisive factor in the transition of finite-sample toward asymptotic sampling distributions. The sampling distribution of a proportion, for instance, is the normal curve instead of the binomial distribution if

$$n \cdot \frac{\pi}{1 - \pi} > 9 \text{ and } n \cdot \frac{1 - \pi}{\pi} > 9 \tag{8.39}$$

As Kühnel and Krebs (2006: 204–207) outline, this applies, for instance, if n is about 25 to 30 and $0.25 \leq \pi \leq 0.75$. If we have to estimate π by p, then the sample size should additionally be $n > 60$. Similar to (8.37), Blalock (1981: 172) reported earlier as criterion $n \cdot \pi > 5$.

Given sampling is *without* replacement from a relatively small population, the sampling distribution is the *hypergeometric* distribution (Blalock 1981: 171; Kühnel and Krebs 2006: 163–164)

$$Pr(X = x) = \frac{\binom{N_1}{x} \cdot \binom{N - N_1}{n - x}}{\binom{N}{n}} \tag{8.40}$$

where N denotes population size, n sample size, N_1 the frequency of successes in the population and x the number of successes in the sample.

The hypergeometric distribution approaches the binomial distribution asymptotically and the approximation is said to be sufficiently precise if $N/n > 20$ (Kühnel and Krebs 2006: 176). In practical terms, this means that we can ignore whether sampling is done with or without replacement if the population is larger than the sample by a factor of more than 20. Then we can refer to the binomial distribution regardless of whether the sample was drawn with or without replacement. If the conditions for the sample size outlined above do also apply, statistical inference can be based on the normal distribution.

Chapter 9
Linear Mixed Models

9.1 Fixed and Random Effects

Spatial proximity often creates social similarity in ways of thinking and behaving. When people repeatedly meet in contexts such as families, school classes, neighborhoods, peer groups, etc., they influence each other simply through the unavoidable social interaction in such contexts. When people come together to form groups, it is thus not uncommon for social similarity within such structures to be more pronounced than across such structures. It has therefore long been part of the standard repertoire of sociological data analysis to explicitly take spatial data structures into account. This is essentially done by models for nested data structures that include aggregate levels of analysis as spatial and social contexts respectively. Examples are persons within households, households within neighborhoods, neighborhoods within urban municipalities and counties. Other sequences of nested levels of analysis are conceivable too, for instance persons within households within electoral districts or pupils within school classes. Their choice ultimately depends only on the research interest and the availability of data sets with a desired nested data structure.

In statistical terms such a multilevel data analysis relaxes the standard assumption that intercept and slope(s) of a regression model are fixed quantities that do not (co-)vary across aggregate units. Equation (9.1) exemplifies this standard assumption for a simple regression with an intercept b_0 and just one slope b_1. The subscript $i = 1, \ldots, n$ runs from the first to the nth observation (unit of analysis).

$$y_i = b_0 + b_1 x_{1i} + e_i \qquad \qquad Var(e_i) = \sigma_e^2 \qquad\qquad (9.1)$$

Instead, in a multilevel model both intercept and slope(s) are allowed to (co-)vary across group-level units $g = 1, \ldots, G$. The fixed quantities b_0 and b_1 from Equation (9.1) thus become the *variable* quantities b_{0g} and b_{1g} in a level-1 equation (9.2), while the associated level-2 equations (9.3) and (9.4) specify their variability across aggregate units $g = 1, \ldots, G$.

$$y_{ig} = b_{0g} + b_{1g} x_{1ig} + e_{ig} \qquad \qquad Var(e_{ig}) = \sigma_e^2 \qquad\qquad (9.2)$$

Equation (9.3) specifies specifically the *intercept* for aggregate unit g, b_{0g}, as function of a mean value b_0 plus element u_{0g} that expresses the random deviation of b_{0g} from b_0 .

$$b_{0g} = b_0 + u_{0g} \qquad \qquad Var(u_{0g}) = \tau_0^2 \qquad\qquad (9.3)$$

https://doi.org/10.1515/9783110680683-009

Analogously, equation (9.4) specifies specifically the *slope* for aggregate unit g, b_{1g}, as function of a mean value b_1 plus element u_{1g} that expresses the random deviation of b_{1g} from b_1.

$$b_{1g} = b_1 + u_{1g} \qquad\qquad Var(u_{1g}) = \tau_1^2 \qquad\qquad (9.4)$$

We can conceive of u_{0g} and u_{1g} as random effects or simply as residuals at level 2 that add to the common level-1 residuals e_{ig}. If we let the right-hand sides of the level-2 equations (9.3) and (9.4) replace b_{0g} and b_{1g} in the level-1 equation (9.2), the resulting equation (9.5)

$$y_{ig} = (b_0 + u_{0g}) + (b_1 + u_{1g})x_{1ig} + e_{ig} \qquad\qquad (9.5)$$

may be transformed into (9.6) by eliminating the brackets and rearranging terms,

$$y_{ig} = b_0 + b_1 x_{1ig} + u_{0g} + u_{1g}x_{1ig} + e_{ig} \qquad\qquad (9.6)$$

to reveal the fixed-part

$$b_0 + b_1 x_{1ig} \qquad\qquad (9.7)$$

and random-part

$$u_{0g} + u_{1g}x_{1ig} + e_{ig} \qquad\qquad (9.8)$$

of the model. Since a multilevel model estimates two kinds of effects, namely fixed and random effects, this type of modeling is also known as linear *mixed* and linear *mixed-effects* modeling respectively.

When we estimate such a model, a primary interest is usually in the b coefficients of the fixed part, here b_0 and b_1, and the *variance components* of the coefficients of the random part. For the present model these components are shown next to equation (9.2), (9.3) and (9.4), and may be used, for instance, to assess average spread around b_0

$$b_0 \pm \sqrt{\tau_0^2} \qquad\qquad (9.9)$$

and b_1

$$b_1 \pm \sqrt{\tau_1^2} \qquad\qquad (9.10)$$

Usually the *intercept-slope covariance* is also of substantial research interest.

$$Cov(u_{0g}, u_{1g}) = \tau_{01} \qquad\qquad (9.11)$$

One would at least let the intercept of a regression model vary randomly. We then speak of a random-intercept model. Such a model leads to parallel regression lines across the aggregate units (Figure 9.1, upper-right graph). On the other hand, we are talking about a random-intercept-and-slope model if it allows also the slopes of a regression model to vary and covary randomly across the aggregate units of an analysis. The lower left and lower right graphs in Figure 9.1 depict schematically the two opposing cases of positive and negative intercept-slope covariance.

The upper left diagram in Figure 9.1 too shows a possible result that can occur when testing a multilevel regression model: If, for example, a random-intercept-and-slope model is being estimated, it may turn out that intercept and slope do *not* differ across the aggregate units. Such a result would then reduce the model to the standard use case of a regression with residual variance only at level 1.

We can go beyond linear mixed models that consider at the aggregate level *random* effects only. In addition to random effects such models can also estimate the *systematic* effects of group-level variables simply by expanding the level-2 equations accordingly. For instance, the addition of one such group-level variable would expand equation (9.3) to (9.12)

$$b_{0g} = b_0 + b_2 x_{2g} + u_{0g} \tag{9.12}$$

and equation (9.4) to (9.13).

$$b_{1g} = b_1 + b_2 x_{2g} + u_{1g} \tag{9.13}$$

Sociological methodology developed a typology of such collective properties (Lazarsfeld and Menzel 1969) early on. If we follow Coleman (1990), the multilevel approach would even be a core element of sociological explanations.

9.2 Linear and Linear Mixed Model Compared

We use again data from Example Data Set 8 (European Social Survey, Rounds 1 to 9). In section 8.2 we estimated a linear model to demonstrate the procedure with a Residual-vs.-Fitted Plot in big surveys. Here we use this same model again to compare it with the corresponding random-intercept-and-slope model. To do this, we start with the *lm()* function. Table 9.1 prints the R script and Table 9.2 the associated output. The analysis is based on $n = 307,901$ respondents with valid values in both *prejudice* and *authoritarian*. We obtain the usual blocks of information for the *lm()* function, as detailed in section 7.1. In the present context it is sufficient to point to two findings.

First, the $adj.R^2 = 0.032$ indicates a reduction in prediction error by 3.2 percent when prejudice formation is predicted by authoritarianism.

Secondly, the effect of such an attitude on prejudice formation appears to be very strong when measured by the t value.

In measuring the strength of an estimate of effect as a ratio to its standard error, we adopt a data analysis practice such as that pursued throughout Coleman (1981).

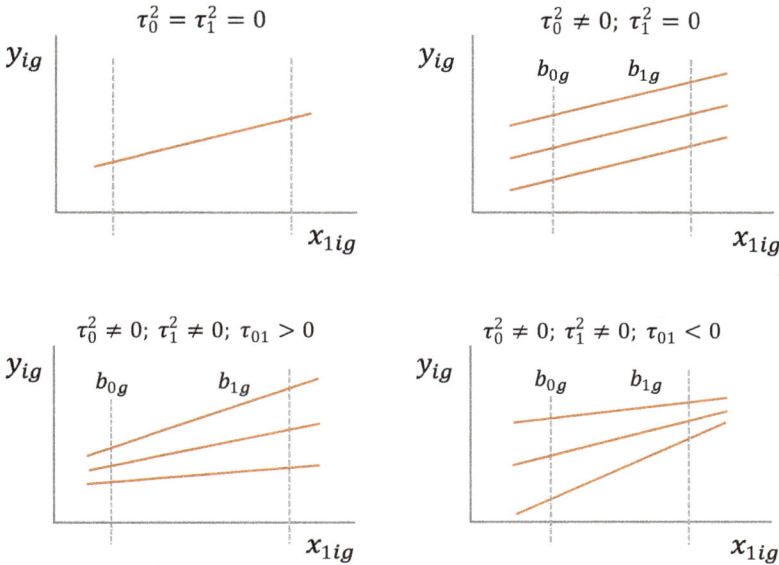

Figure 9.1: Group-Level Regression Lines With Varying Intercept-Slope Patterns.

Since in this practice the standard error only acts as a uniform benchmark without wanting to draw conclusions about statistical significance from the associated t value, this technique is suitable, for example, in big samples, because even the most minimal effects quickly reach significance in such samples simply due to the sheer sample size.

With reference to Table 9.2, we have to report the following b estimates along with their associated standard errors and t values:

$$b_0 = 0.017 \ \left(s.e_{b_0} = 0.001; \ t = b_0/s.e_{b_0} = 12.61\right) \tag{9.14}$$

and

$$b_1 = 0.216 \ \left(s.e_{b_1} = 0.002; \ t = b_1/s.e_{b_1} = 101.0\right) \tag{9.15}$$

However, as already remarked in section 8.3, when a model is impaired by correlated residuals, this is a condition that is generally expected to lead to underestimated standard errors of the least-squares estimates and thus to overestimated t values. This expectation also applies in the present example. It is suggested by the comparison of (9.14) with (9.16) as well as by the comparison of (9.15) with (9.17), if additionally is taken into account that the autocorrelation of the residuals proves to be stronger in the linear model than in the linear mixed model.

Next we estimate the model as random-intercept-and-slope model. To do this, we use two functions available in R for parallel calculations: on the one hand, the *lmer()* function (Bates et al. 2015), and on the other hand, the *lme()* function. Although both calculations produce identical results, they differ in the way in which the weighting variable is to be specified. Details are explained in the R script in Table 9.3, while Table 9.4 reports the output when using the *lmer()* function.

As before the analysis is based on $i = 1, \ldots, 307,901$ respondents, however now additionally considering that these persons come out of $g = 1, \ldots, 22$ countries.

Analogous to a linear model, a linear mixed model too estimates fixed effects. For the present model we obtain two estimates along with their associated standard errors and t values, namely

$$b_0 = 0.061 \ \left(s.e_{b_0} = 0.045; \ t = b_0/s.e_{b_0} = 1.349\right) \tag{9.16}$$

and

$$b_1 = 0.173 \ \left(s.e_{b_1} = 0.017; \ t = b_1/s.e_{b_1} = 9.971\right) \tag{9.17}$$

The fixed effects b_0 and b_1 may be conceived of as mean values of their country-specific values. According to (9.9) and (9.10), the average country-level spread around the respective mean value is captured by the standard deviation

$$\sqrt{\tau_0^2} \text{ for } b_0 \text{ and } \sqrt{\tau_1^2} \text{ for } b_1 \tag{9.18}$$

Both the respective variance and standard deviation is given in the *Random effects* block of information in Table 9.4. Inserting these estimates in (9.9) and (9.10) yields

$$0.061 \pm \sqrt{0.045} = 0.061 \pm 0.212 \tag{9.19}$$

for the intercept and

$$0.173 \pm \sqrt{0.006} = 0.173 \pm 0.079 \tag{9.20}$$

for the slope. It can be seen that the average spread around the mean intercept is particularly pronounced.

In addition the output reports the residual (i. e., within-country) variation in terms of variance and standard deviation.

Finally, the intercept-slope covariance (9.11) is reported as correlation and amounts to $r_{01} = -0.33$. Taken together, this results in the overall picture shown in Figure 9.2. The figure depicts the 22 country-specific regression lines along with their mean regression line.

While the mean regression (red line) is based on the fixed-effects estimates $b_0 = 0.061$ and $b_1 = 0.173$ only, the 22 country-specific lines result when we consider additionally the random effects. To do this, we replace in equation (9.5) the random ef-

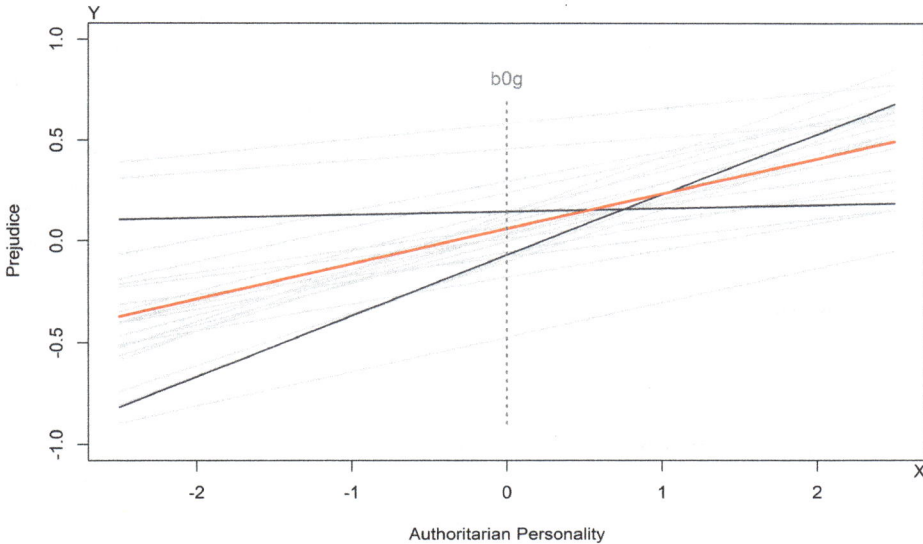

Figure 9.2: Regression Lines of Intercept-and-Slope Model: Mean (red line) and Country-specific.

fects u_{0g} and u_{1g} with their respective numerical estimates. These random effects or level-2 residuals are displayed in Table 9.5, while the last two script lines in Table 9.3 show how to get access to these values.

The two regression lines highlighted in black belong to the two countries with the weakest and strongest effect of an authoritarian attitude on prejudice formation, i. e. the regression lines with the flattest and steepest slope. They are only highlighted to make it easier to recognize the structure of the all in all 22 country-specific regression lines displayed in the graph, namely with particular attention to the relationship between b_{0g} and b_{1g}. This relationship may be phrased as follows: the lower b_{0g}, the higher b_{1g}, and vice versa. It is exactly the direction and strength of this relationship that is captured by the intercept-slope covariance or correlation.

To understand this relationship, it may help to first understand the meaning of an intercept. For example, the present model is based on equation (9.6) with its fixed part (9.7). This fixed part reduces to b_0 if the predictor variable x_{1ig} is zero, because multiplication of b_1 with zero let the second term of (9.7), $b_1 \cdot x_{1ig}$, vanish. And this in turn reduces the fixed-part prediction to $\hat{y}_{ig} = b_0$. An intercept thus estimates the target value given the x variable(s) is/are zero. In the present context this meaning of an intercept is applicable to b_0 of the red regression line as well as to b_{0g} of any of the country-specific lines.

But now the follow-up question arises as to whether an x variable can actually take on the value zero or not, since the meaning of an intercept that has just been derived can only be used sensibly for interpretation if $x = 0$ can actually occur.

In the present example, the question can be answered in the affirmative because variable x represents factor scores, and such factor-score scales have a mean value of zero. b_0 and b_{0g} thus estimate the mean prejudice level given a mean intensity of authoritarian attitude, namely global or country-specific. The regularity "the lower b_{0g}, the higher b_{1g}" then simply implies that the strength of the effect of an authoritarian attitude on prejudice formation varies that way: the effect, i. e., the expected increase in mean prejudice level for an increase of attitude intensity by one scale unit (i. e., the slope), is stronger in countries where a *mean* intensity of this attitude is associated with a comparably lower mean prejudice level. While at the same time the effect is weaker in countries where a *mean* intensity of this attitude is already associated with a comparably higher mean prejudice level.

9.3 Comparative Model Evaluation

The present model is a "random-intercept-and-slope" model. A defining characteristic of such a model is that its random part is largely unrestricted: It allows for random variation of both intercept and slope as well as for covariation between these two components to unfold. Now, for a comparative model evaluation, various restrictions can be imposed on this model. A common approach is to compare it with a random-intercept model. The way we do this is that we impose two restrictions on it: that the slope has no random variation and therefore there can also be no intercept-slope covariance. In such a pairwise comparison, the random-intercept-and-slope model would act as a so-called full model, while the random-intercept model would act as the corresponding restricted model, since two freely-to-estimate coefficients of the first model are fixed to zero in the second model. When using Maximum Likelihood as estimator, it is common practice to use the models' *deviance* values for such comparative evaluations. A deviance value is defined as $-2 \times -logLik$. For the random-intercept-and-slope model Table 9.4 reports both values in its upper part, while the corresponding information is provided in Table 9.7 for the random-intercept model. In addition, Table 9.6 reports the R script used to get the series of required information.

The deviance value of the random-intercept-and-slope model amounts to 892,077.1, while the deviance value of the random-intercept model amounts to 892,968.3, with the smaller value indicating the comparably better goodness of fit. The difference of these two deviance values is $\chi^2_{df=2} = 891.2$ and follows a Chi^2 distribution with degrees of freedom equal to the difference in the number of freely estimated parameters. Here this difference is 2, since we get one degree of freedom for each coefficient *not* being estimated in the random-intercept model: one for the variance of b_1 and another one for the intercept-slope covariation. Given two degrees of freedom, a chi^2 value of 891.2 is highly significant in the statistical sense. This let us conclude that the random-intercept-and-slope model (with its smaller deviance value) attains a significant better goodness of fit than the random-intercept model (with its larger deviance value).

We can benchmark the random-intercept-and-slope model and the random-intercept model respectively against the corresponding *null model*. Such a model consists only of the intercept and its random variation at levels 1 and 2. Table 9.6 and Table 9.7 provide the details. For this reference model we notice a deviance value of 902,495.1. Since it omits one parameter estimated in the random-intercept model (i. e., b_1), the difference to this model is $\chi^2_{df=1} = 9,526.8$. This simply means that the inclusion of the b_1 effect considerably improves the model fit. The same is true if we form the difference between the random-intercept-and-slope model and the null model ($\chi^2_{df=3} = 10,418$).

It is useful to assess a model also by the amount it helps to reduce the prediction error. The basic idea was already introduced in section 7.1. A detailed description is also given in Hox (2010: 69–73). Here it is applicable to the random-intercept model, while using the null model as baseline.

$$R^2 = \left(\frac{s^2_{res|null} - s^2_{res|model}}{s^2_{res|null}} \right) \tag{9.21}$$

We proceed by adding the level 1 and level 2 variance for both models, $s^2_{res} = \tau^2_0 + s^2_e$, and inserting their sums in (9.21). For the present example we find these values in the two *Random effects* blocks in Table 9.7. The figures are 0.04268 + 0.51305 = 0.5557 for the random-intercept model, and 0.04864 + 0.52916 = 0.5778 for the null model. Since this yields an R^2 of 0.0382, we conclude that the prediction error is reduced by 3.8 percent.

9.4 Variance Decomposition

In addition, the two variance components τ^2_0 and s^2_e can be used to decompose the overall variance into the shares allocable to level 1 and level 2. In the null model, for instance, this share is 0.04864/0.5778 = 0.084 (deviance value = 902,495.1). Accordingly, 8.4 percent of the overall variance in prejudice formation is variance *between* the 22 European countries, while 91.6 percent represents variance *within* these countries.

We can refine this picture by adding a second group-level variable, namely the survey round. Table 9.8 prints the R script and Table 9.9 the associated output for the above null model and two further variance decompositions. These two models differ primarily in how they decompose the group-level variance, taking into account that the respondents have two group memberships at the same time: as a member of a country and a member of a survey round.

One of them decomposes the variance into the *nested* (i. e., hierarchical) data structure of respondents within survey rounds and survey rounds within countries.

Variance . . .	Component	
. . . between the 22 countries	0.04585	8.0 %
. . . between the all in all 178 survey rounds within the countries	0.01989	3.5 %
. . . between the all in all 307,901 respondents within the survey rounds	0.50852	88.6 %
Sum:	0.57426	100 %

Deviance value: 890,798.0

Accordingly, the variance in prejudice formation represent 8.0 percent variance between the countries, 3.5 percent variance between survey rounds *within* the countries, and 88.6 percent variance between respondents within the survey rounds.

Then a final model handles country and survey round as non-nested grouping factors by fully crossing the two factors. Under this assumption, the variance decomposition results in the following values:

Variance . . .	Component	
. . . between the 22 countries	0.04985	8.6 %
. . . between the 9 survey rounds	0.00584	1.0 %
. . . between the 307,901 respondents within the countries & survey rounds	0.52430	90.4 %
Sum:	0.57999	100 %

Deviance value: 899,700.5

Accordingly, the variance in prejudice formation represent 8.6 percent variance between the countries, 1.0 percent variance between the survey rounds, and 90.4 percent variance between respondents within the countries and survey rounds.

The three models decompose the variance in prejudice formation in different ways. It is therefore not surprising that different model assumptions lead to different results. Despite these differences, however, it can be clearly stated that the largest shares in variance indicate variability between respondents within the countries and time points, not between them: Depending on the model, the proportions of variance at level 1 range between 88.6 and 91.6 percent. On the other hand, the models see 8.0 to 8.6 percent of variability as variance between countries, and only 1.0 to 3.5 percent as time-related variance of prejudice formation.

9.5 Tables to the Models on Prejudice Formation and Authoritarian Personality

Table 9.1: Script to *lm()* and the related Durbin-Watson Statistic.

Line	R Script
1	load("ess19.Rdata")
2	sset <- subset(ess19, select= c(prejudice, authoritarian,
3	cntry, wt))
4	sset <- na.omit(sset)
5	library(car)
6	summary(sr <- lm(prejudice ~ authoritarian, weights = wt,
7	data = sset))
8	durbinWatsonTest(sr, max.lag=1, alternative=c("two.sided"),
9	simulate=TRUE, reps = 1000)

Lines explained

Line 1 loads the data frame. Lines 2 and 3 use the *subset ()* function to select the target variable *prejudice*, the predictor variable *authoritarian*, a group-level variable *cntry* (denoting *country*; here, this variable is actually not required but it is used in the corresponding linear mixed model below), and the sample weight *wt*. This reduces the data frame *ess19* (column-wise) to these variables and stores it as a new data frame named *sset*. Line 4 reduces this data frame to the units (rows of the data frame) with valid values in all selected variables. Line 5 invokes the library "Companion to Applied Regression" (*car*) because it is required for the Durbin-Watson test. Lines 6 and 7 issue the *lm()* function call embedded in the *summary ()* function. The target variable is *prejudice*, the predictor variable is *authoritarian*. Related to this regression object *sr*, lines 8 and 9 address the Durbin-Watson test. Here, a two-sided test is specified. Alternatively, one-sided tests would result by replacing *two.sided* by *positive* or *negative*. The maximum lag is set to 1 (adjacent residuals only), while the *simulate* option invokes bootstrapping, with 1000 replications, to obtain a p-value.

Table 9.2: Output to *lm()* and the related Durbin-Watson Statistic.

Line	R Output
1	Call:
2	lm(formula = prejudice ~ authoritarian, data = sset, weights = wt)
3	
4	Weighted Residuals:
5	Min 1Q Median 3Q Max
6	−6.7690 −0.2864 −0.0050 0.3610 6.2003
7	
8	Coefficients:
9	Estimate Std. Error t value Pr(>|t|)
10	(Intercept) 0.017059 0.001353 12.61 <2e-16 ***
11	authoritarian 0.215922 0.002138 101.01 <2e-16 ***

Table 9.2 (continued)

Line	R Output
12	---
13	Signif. codes: 0 '***' 0.001 '**' 0.01 '*' 0.05 '.' 0.1 ' ' 1
14	
15	Residual standard error: 0.7331 on 307899 degrees of freedom
16	Multiple R-squared: 0.03208, Adjusted R-squared: 0.03207
17	F-statistic: 1.02e+04 on 1 and 307899 DF, p-value: < 2.2e-16
18	
19	> durbinWatsonTest(sr, max.lag=1, alternative=c("two.sided"),
20	+ simulate=TRUE, reps = 1000)
21	lag Autocorrelation D-W Statistic p-value
22	1 0.1166183 1.766748 0
23	Alternative hypothesis: rho != 0

Lines explained

Lines 1 and 2 reprint the function call. Lines 4 to 17 represent the standard output to the *lm()* function, for instance as detailed in section 7.1 and Table 7.1, especially the weighted residuals, the *Coefficients* block of information, and the block of information about the model fit. Lines 19 and 20 reprint the call to the Durbin-Watson Test and lines 21 to 23 print the associated numerical results.

Table 9.3: Script to the Random-Intercept-and-Slope Model.

Line	R Script
1	load("ess19.Rdata")
2	sset <- subset(ess19, select= c(prejudice, authoritarian,
3	cntry, wt))
4	sset <- na.omit(sset)
5	library(lme4)
6	# Random-intercept-and-slope model using lmer()
7	# and weight "wt"
8	summary(rism <- lme4::lmer(prejudice ~ authoritarian +
9	(authoritarian | cntry),
10	weights = wt, REML=FALSE, sset))
11	library(car)
12	resid <- c(rism@resp$y - predict(rism))
13	durbinWatsonTest(resid) # 1.926404
14	# Same model using lme() and inverse weight
15	library(nlme)
16	summary(rism2 <- lme(fixed=prejudice ~ authoritarian,
17	data=sset, method="ML",
18	random = ~authoritarian	cntry,
19	weights = ~(wt)^-1))
20	resid2 <- c(rism2$data$prejudice - predict(rism2))

Table 9.3 (continued)

Line	R Script
21	durbinWatsonTest(resid2) # 1.926404
22	round(rism2$coefficients$fixed, 3)
23	round(rism2$coefficients$random$cntry, 3)

Lines explained

As in the R script in Table 9.1, line 1 loads the data frame. Lines 2 and 3 use the *subset ()* function to select the target variable *prejudice*, the predictor variable *authoritarian*, the group-level variable *cntry*, and the sample weight *wt*. This reduces the data frame *ess19* (column-wise) to these variables and stores it as a new data frame named *sset*. Line 4 reduces this data frame to the units (rows of the data frame) with valid values in all selected variables. Line 5 invokes the library *lme4* for *Linear Mixed-Effects Models*. Lines 6 and 7: Comments. Lines 8 to 10 specify the call to function *lmer()*, assigns the result of this function call to the object named *rism* (a freely-to-choose object name, here representing the acronym for *random-intercept-slope model*), and embed all this in *summary()*. The model is defined in terms of *target ~ predictor* (fixed effects) plus the random effects at the group level *cntry* in brackets. It also addresses the weight *wt*, the estimator *ML* (log-likelihood) and the data frame. Line 11 invokes the library *Companion to Applied Regression* (*car*) for calculating the Durbin Watson Test. Line 12 calculates the residuals for model object *rism*, i. e. the above random-intercept-and-slope model, by creating a vector *c()* of difference values that result from subtracting the predicted from the observed values of the target variable, and assigns this vector to the object named *resid*. Line 13 addresses this object when calling the Durbin-Watson test. Line 14: Comment. Line 15 invokes the library *nlme* for *Linear and Nonlinear Mixed Effects Models* required for function *lme()*. Lines 16 to 19 specify the corresponding model for the above random-intercept-and-slope model, this time using the *lme()* function. The result of this function call is assigned to object *rism2*, while the call itself is embedded in *summary()*. Line 16 defines the model for the fixed effects according to *target ~ predictor*. Line 17 names the data frame and specifies the estimator (Maximum Likelihood). Line 18 specifies the random effects using *cntry* (country) as group-level variable. Then, line 19 specifies the variable for weighting the units of analysis. Note that the *lme()* function requires this information as the inverse value of the actual weight. Line 20 calculates the vector of residuals, as above by subtracting the predicted values from the observed values, and assigns the result of this calculation to the object named *resid2*. Line 21 calculates the Durbin Watson test for this vector of residuals. Line 22 extracts from model *rism2* the two estimated fixed effects and rounds their printing to three decimal places, while line 23 does the same with the level-2 residuals for the 22 countries. The output to lines 22 and 23 is displayed in Table 9.5.

Table 9.4: Output Using Function *lmer()*.

Line	R Output
1	Linear mixed model fit by maximum likelihood ['lmerMod']
2	Formula: prejudice ~ authoritarian + (authoritarian | cntry)
3	Data: sset
4	Weights: wt
5	
6	AIC BIC logLik deviance df.resid
7	892089.1 892152.9 -446038.5 892077.1 307895

Table 9.4 (continued)

Line	R Output
8	
9	Scaled residuals:
10	Min 1Q Median 3Q Max
11	-10.2121 -0.4280 -0.0043 0.4454 8.2812
12	
13	Random effects:
14	Groups Name Variance Std.Dev. Corr
15	cntry (Intercept) 0.04494 0.21199
16	authoritarian 0.00626 0.07912 -0.33
17	Residual 0.51144 0.71515
18	Number of obs: 307901, groups: cntry, 22
19	
20	Fixed effects:
21	Estimate Std. Error t value
22	(Intercept) 0.06108 0.04527 1.349
23	authoritarian 0.17320 0.01737 9.971
24	
25	Correlation of Fixed Effects:
26	(Intr)
27	authoritarn -0.319
28	
29	[1] 1.926404

Lines explained

Line 1: Heading. Lines 2 to 4: Details of the Function Call. Lines 6 and 7 report the metrics for comparative model evaluation: The information-theoretic criteria AIC (Akaike's information criterion), BIC (Bayesian information criterion), loglikelihood, deviance, and residual degrees of freedom. Line 9 to 11: Summary statistics for the residuals (min/max, 1st, 2nd and 3rd quartile). Lines 13 to 18: *Random effects* block of information. Line 15 names the group-level variable *cntry* and the variance and standard deviation of the intercept at this group level. Line 16 reports the corresponding information about the effect of *authoritarian* on the target *prejudice*. The line also reports the intercept-slope correlation at the group level. Line 17 informs about the residual, i. e. the within-group variance of target variable *prejudice*. Line 18 prints the number of observations at the individual and group level. Lines 20 to 27 provide information about the *fixed effects*. Lines 22 prints the estimate and associated standard error of the intercept. The *t* value results as ratio of estimate to standard error (est./se). Line 23 reports the corresponding values for the effect of *authoritarian* on *prejudice*. In this type of model the estimates of intercept and slope represent mean values whose group-level dispersion and covariance is considered via the dispersion/covariance of the estimated random effects. Line 29 reports the associated Durbin Watson value.

Table 9.5: Fixed and Random Effects Using Function *lme()*.

Line	R Output (in extracts)
1	> round(rism2$coefficients$fixed, 3)
2	(Intercept) authoritarian
3	0.061 0.173
4	> round(rism2$coefficients$random$cntry, 3)
5	(Intercept) authoritarian
6	AT 0.070 0.114
7	BE -0.020 0.069
8	CH -0.144 0.116
9	CZ 0.395 -0.115
10	DE -0.163 0.082
11	DK -0.028 0.027
12	EE 0.178 -0.002
13	ES -0.130 0.126
14	FI 0.087 0.026
15	FR 0.052 0.082
16	GB 0.029 0.021
17	HU 0.521 -0.096
18	IE -0.117 -0.033
19	IT 0.009 -0.060
20	LT -0.049 -0.077
21	NL -0.031 -0.001
22	NO -0.239 -0.041
23	PL -0.140 -0.080
24	PT 0.235 -0.028
25	SE -0.534 -0.004
26	SI -0.064 0.032
27	SK 0.084 -0.157

Lines explained

Line 1 reprints the script line that imports from regression object *rism2* the fixed effects, and rounds their printing to three decimal places. Lines 2 and 3 display the corresponding results. Line 4 reprints the script line that imports from regression object *rism2* the random effects or level-2 residuals, and rounds their printing to three decimal places. Lines 5 to 27 display the corresponding results for the 22 involved European countries.

Table 9.6: Script to Comparative Model Evaluation.

Line	R Script (in extracts)
1	library(lme4)
2	# Random-intercept-and-slope model using lmer()
3	summary(rism <- lme4::lmer(prejudice ~ authoritarian +
4	(authoritarian | cntry),
5	weights = wt, REML=FALSE, sset))

Table 9.6 (continued)

Line	R Script (in extracts)
6	# Random-intercept model
7	summary(rim <- lmer(rism@frame$prejudice ~
8	(1 | rism@frame$cntry) +
9	rism@frame$authoritarian,
10	weights = rism@resp$weights,
11	REML=FALSE,sset))
12	# Random-intercept null model
13	summary(nmodel <- lmer(rism@frame$prejudice ~
14	(1 | rism@frame$cntry),
15	weights = rism@resp$weights,
16	REML=FALSE,sset))

Lines explained

Line 1 invokes the library required for the *lmer()* function. The following lines are the corresponding function calls for the three model specifications compared in the present context: Lines 3 to 5 for the random-intercept-and-slope model *rism* (as explained in Table 9.3), lines 7 to 11 for the random-intercept model *rim*, and lines 13 to 16 for the random-intercept null model. One aspect should be highlighted here: the syntax represents a series in that the specification of the second and third model imports the required information from the first object (*rism*). This strategy helps to assure an identical sample of valid observations for the estimation of each the three models. However, such a strategy is only necessary if the listwise exclusion of observations with missing values in prejudice and/or authoritarian is not already carried out by the *na.omit()* function (as, for example realized in Table 9.3, script line 4). When using this *na.omit ()* function, we can then address the empirical variables also directly. This is shown, for instance, in Table 9.8.

Table 9.7: Output to Comparative Model Evaluation.

Line	R Output (in extracts)
1	# Random-intercept model
2	AIC BIC logLik deviance df.resid
3	892976.3 893018.9 -446484.2 892968.3 307897
4	
5	Random effects:
6	Groups Name Variance Std.Dev.
7	rism@frame$cntry (Intercept) 0.04268 0.2066
8	Residual 0.51305 0.7163
9	Number of obs: 307901, groups: rism@frame$cntry, 22
10	
11	Fixed effects:
12	Estimate Std. Error t value
13	(Intercept) 0.056090 0.044114 1.271
14	rism@frame$authoritarian 0.213558 0.002171 98.365

Table 9.7 (continued)

Line	R Output (in extracts)
15	
16	# Random-intercept null model
17	AIC BIC logLik deviance df.resid
18	902501.1 902533.0 -451247.5 902495.1 307898
19	
20	Random effects:
21	Groups Name Variance Std.Dev.
22	rism@frame$cntry (Intercept) 0.04864 0.2206
23	Residual 0.52916 0.7274
24	Number of obs: 307901, groups: rism@frame$cntry, 22
25	
26	Fixed effects:
27	Estimate Std.Error t value
28	(Intercept) 0.05851 0.04709 1.242

Lines explained
Lines 1 to 15 report in extracts the output to the random-intercept model and lines 16 to 28 to the random-intercept null model. For each of the two models the comparative model-fit block, the random-effects block and the fixed-effects block is printed.

Table 9.8: Script to Alternative Variance Decompositions.

Line	R Script (in extracts)
1	load("ess19.Rdata")
2	sset <- subset(ess19, select= c(prejudice, authoritarian,
3	cntry, essround, wt))
4	sset <- na.omit(sset)
5	library(lme4)
6	
7	# Random-intercept null model
8	summary(nm1 <- lmer(prejudice ~
9	(1 | cntry),
10	weights = wt, REML=FALSE,sset))
11	
12	# Intercept varies among g1 (cntry) and g2 (essround) within g1
13	summary(nm2 <- lmer(prejudice ~
14	(1 | cntry/essround),
15	weights = wt, REML=FALSE,sset))
16	

Table 9.8 (continued)

Line	R Script (in extracts)
17	# Intercept varies among cntry and essround
18	summary(nm3 <- lmer(prejudice ~
19	(1 | cntry)
20	+ (1 | essround),
21	weights = wt, REML=FALSE,sset))

Lines explained

Line 1 loads the data frame. Lines 2 and 3 select the five required variables (target, predictor, country, survey round, weight) and stores this subset as a new data frame named *sset*. Note that we added the survey round to this subset. Line 4 reduces this subset to the observations (individual units of analysis) with valid values in all selected variables. Then, lines 7 to 21 provide the script lines for three models that differ in the specification of the random effects only. This concerns line 9, line 14, and lines 19 and 20. Line 9 specifies at level 2 a random intercept across the countries. Line 14 does the same across the countries and the survey rounds within each of the countries. Finally, lines 19 and 20 specifies random variation across country and survey round without establishing a nested structure for it.

Table 9.9: Output to Alternative Variance Decompositions.

Line	R Output (in extracts)
1	> # Random-intercept null model
2	AIC BIC logLik deviance df.resid
3	902501.1 902533.0 -451247.5 902495.1 307898
4	
5	Random effects:
6	Groups Name Variance Std.Dev.
7	cntry (Intercept) 0.04864 0.2206
8	Residual 0.52916 0.7274
9	Number of obs: 307901, groups: cntry, 22
10	
11	Fixed effects:
12	Estimate Std. Error t value
13	(Intercept) 0.05851 0.04709 1.242
14	
15	> # Intercept varies among g1 (cntry)
16	# and g2 (essround) within g1
17	AIC BIC logLik deviance df.resid
18	890806.0 890848.6 -445399.0 890798.0 307897
19	
20	Random effects:
21	Groups Name Variance Std.Dev.
22	essround:cntry (Intercept) 0.01989 0.1410
23	cntry (Intercept) 0.04585 0.2141
24	Residual 0.50852 0.7131

Table 9.9 (continued)

Line	R Output (in extracts)
25	Number of obs: 307901, groups: essround:cntry, 178; cntry, 22
26	
27	Fixed effects:
28	Estimate Std. Error t value
29	(Intercept) 0.05970 0.04701 1.27
30	
31	> # Intercept varies among cntry and essround
32	AIC BIC logLik deviance df.resid
33	899708.5 899751.0 -449850.2 899700.5 307897
34	Random effects:
35	Groups Name Variance Std.Dev.
36	cntry (Intercept) 0.04985 0.22327
37	essround (Intercept) 0.00584 0.07642
38	Residual 0.52430 0.72409
39	Number of obs: 307901, groups: cntry, 22; essround, 9
40	
41	Fixed effects:
42	Estimate Std. Error t value
43	(Intercept) 0.06678 0.05405 1.236

Lines explained

Lines 1 to 43 report in extracts the output to three alternative variance decompositions. For each of the models three blocks of information are printed: the comparative model-fit block, the random-effects block and the fixed-effects block. The decomposed variance components at level 2 and level 1 are displayed in the random-effects block of each model and explained in section 9.4.

Chapter 10
Nonlinear Relations

10.1 Linearizable Relations

While a linear relationship can be represented as a straight line, nonlinear relationships can lead to very different curves. A practically important question is then whether a nonlinear relationship can be linearized to facilitate the estimation of its parameters. One such form of linearizable functions are polynomials, an example of which was introduced in section 6.1. This was a second degree polynomial:

$$y_i = b_0 + b_1 \cdot x_i + b_2 \cdot x_i^2 \tag{10.1}$$

This is the gray graph on the left in Figure 10.1 (where this graph reproduces the red graph in Figure 6.1). We have two x variables and thus two b coefficients. In the polynomial case, however, these two coefficients cannot vary freely because it is not possible to vary x while keeping x^2 constant at the same time. Thus, the general interpretation of partial slope coefficients given in section 6.5 doesn't apply in case of polynomials (Berry and Feldman 1985: 58). However, if we take the derivative[1] of

$$b_1 x + b_2 x^2 \tag{10.2}$$

with respect to x, the resulting expression shows how

$$b_1 + 2 \cdot b_2 x \tag{10.3}$$

the overall effect of x is decomposed into a constant component and another one whose strength depends on the value of x. This provides good guidance for interpretation. Furthermore we can use *the implications of* a polynomial regression for interpretation, namely in terms of the estimated *curve shape*.

This also applies to higher degree polynomial regressions[2]. Polynomials are generally suitable for models in which the slope is expected to change sign one or more times as the value of x increases, i. e., in nonmonotonic nonlinear relationships (Fox 1991: 59). There are also nonlinear model specifications that assume the slope maintains the same sign but either decreases or increases in magnitude as x increases (Berry and Feldman 1985: 57), i. e., monotonic nonlinear relationships.

Linearizable functions are such that nonlinear relations between original variables are converted into linear relationships between suitably transformed variables.

---

[1] We converted x^m to $m \cdot x^{(m-1)}$

[2] We continue the route using polynomial regression, regression splines, and generalized additive models in Section 10.2 and 10.3 below.

https://doi.org/10.1515/9783110680683-010

Such transformations may combine each of the three functions of y, namely $y, 1/y$ and $\ln y$, with each of the corresponding functions of x (Daniel and Wood 1999: 19–22).

We stick with the data example from Section 6.1. There we used aggregate data that describe the EU countries (Example Data Set 6 on Energy Transition in the European Green Deal). This includes a characterization of each country by the percentage of its population that would like to see that the European Parliament prioritizes action against climate change. Here again this is the target variable y. And as there, we also use a country's living standard as measured by its official purchasing power standard (PPS) as the predictor variable x.

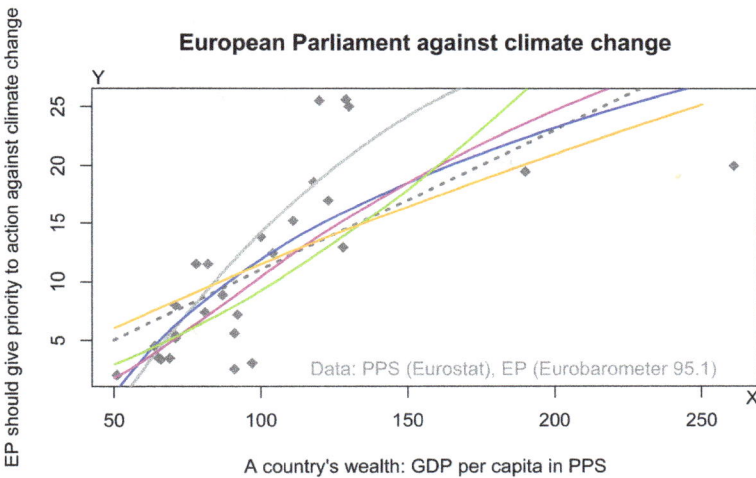

Figure 10.1: Curve Shapes of Five Nonlinear Functions.

Based on this data example and inspired by the shape of the associated polynomial regression curve from Section 6.1, a small selection from the list of possible variable transformations should illustrate the procedure.

A first option relates the logarithm of x_i to the original y_i, to get the equation

$$y_i = a + b \cdot (\ln x_i) \tag{10.4}$$

(Daniel and Wood 1999: 21). The function call is easily accomplished by the instruction

$$lm(y \sim \log(x), data = energy) \tag{10.5}$$

where *energy* is the name of the data frame. The function call yields an intercept of $a = -63.39$ and a slope of $b = 16.35$. In Figure 10.1 the blue curve results if we insert these estimates in (10.4). Compared to the gray polynomial curve, the blue curve takes the two data points (i. e., countries) on the far right of the diagram much more into account.

A second option leads to the magenta curve in Figure 10.1. It starts from equation

$$y_i = a \cdot e^{\frac{b}{x_i}} \tag{10.6}$$

to arrive at its linear form

$$\ln y_i = \ln a + \frac{b}{x_i} \tag{10.7}$$

(Daniel and Wood 1999: 22). Since b/x_i is equal to $b \cdot 1/x_i$, (10.7) can be rewritten as

$$\ln y_i = \ln a + b \cdot \frac{1}{x_i} \tag{10.8}$$

to realize the combination of required variable transformations, in fact the logarithm of y along with the inverse value of x. We also see that a linear regression with y and x values transformed in this way estimates two coefficients, namely the logarithm of a as well as b. To obtain these estimates we create a synthetic variable that is defined as the inverse value of x, name this variable ix (a freely chosen name), and use this variable as predictor in the function call

$$lm(log(y) \sim ix, \, data = energy) \tag{10.9}$$

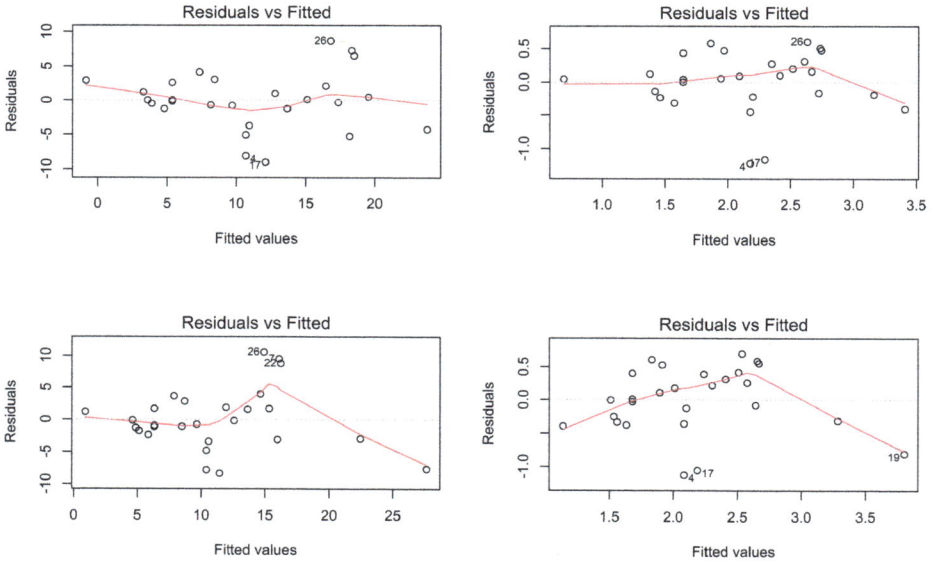

Figure 10.2: Residual-vs-Fitted Plots.

This function call produces an output[3] that reports two estimates in its *Coefficients* table: 4.0664 in the row labeled *(Intercept)* and below a −172.0016 in the row labeled *ix*. Since 4.0664 represents ln a, a itself is obtained as $e^{4.0664} = 58.35$. In contrast, b can be read directly from the output, namely as −172.0. Thus the magenta curve in Figure 10.1 results if 58.35 and −172.0 replaces a and b in (10.6)

$$y_i = 58.35 \cdot e^{\frac{-172.0}{x_i}} \tag{10.10}$$

Another option is an exponential model,

$$y_i = a \cdot x_i^b \tag{10.11}$$

whose linear form is obtained by taking the logarithm of both sides of the equation.

$$ln(y_i) = \ln a + b \cdot (\ln x_i) \tag{10.12}$$

(Berry and Feldman 1985: 60). In a linear model b indicates the expected change in y for a *unit* change in x. We obtain a constant slope, in the present data example for instance as the dotted line[4] in Figure 10.1. In contrast, the b from the present exponential model indicates the *elasticity* of y with respect to x, that is, "the approximate percentage of change in y corresponding to a 1% change in x_j" (Fox 1991: 61; Berry and Feldman 1985: 60). The function call

$$lm(\log(y) \sim \log(x), data = energy) \tag{10.13}$$

produces an output that reports two estimates in its *Coefficients* table: −5.2753 in the row labeled *(Intercept)* and below a 1.6313 in the row labeled *log(x)*. Since −5.2753 represents ln a, a itself is obtained as $e^{-5.2753} = 0.0051$. In contrast, b can be read directly from the output, namely as 1.6313. If we insert these numerical estimates in (10.11), the result is the green curve in Figure 10.1.

All four functions are linearizable and were thus estimated using ordinary least squares. For it we used functions of x and y, i.e. the variable transformations shown above, and calls to the *lm()* function. Given a nonlinear function is not linearizable, its parameters may instead be estimable by nonlinear least squares using the *nls()* function. Just to exemplify its use, we adopt a formula originally known from another scientific field (enzyme kinetics). However, in the present context we use this formula only figuratively to estimate y_i as a function of x_i using two parameters, where a denotes the maximum value of the response and b the x value at which half the maximum response is attained.

$$y_i = \frac{a \cdot x_i}{b + x_i} \tag{10.14}$$

---

3 The R outputs of this section are documented in Tables 10.1 to 10.3.
4 This line reproduces the corresponding line in Figure 6.1.

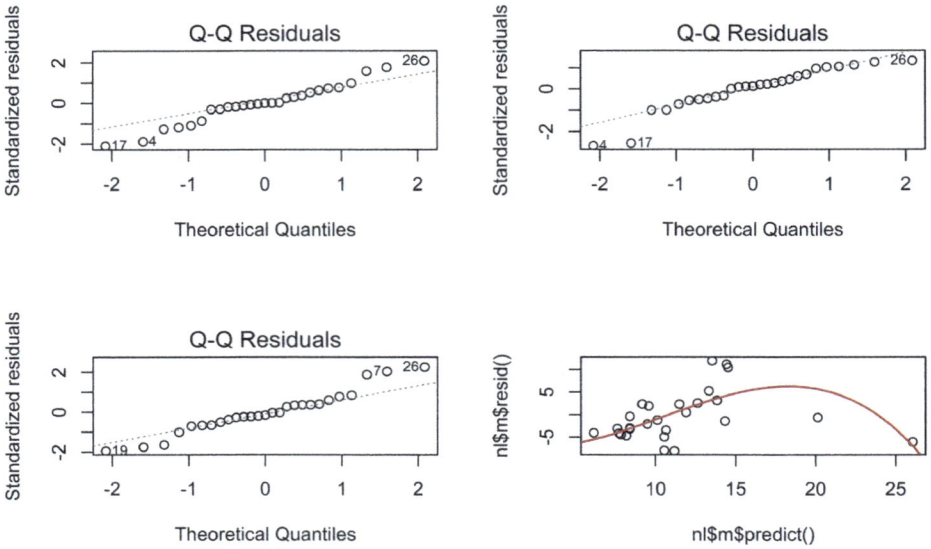

Figure 10.3: Q-Q Plots.

The associated *nls()* function call is

$$nls\left(\begin{array}{c} y \sim (a \cdot x)/(b + x), \\ start = list(a = 25, b = 90), data = energy \end{array}\right) \tag{10.15}$$

and contains the formula in the first row and the starting values for a and b in the row below. The function call produces $a = 122.5$ and $b = 966.4$ that rescaled correspond to 12.25 and 96.64 in Figure 10.1. If a and b are inserted into (10.14), we get the orange curve in Figure 10.1. The associated output is reprinted in Table 10.3.

Now, Figure 10.1 shows a series of similar curves for our data example. Through it the current example nicely illustrates that there can be more than one functional form to describe the same data. This naturally raises the question of which of these curves should ultimately be selected. If the aim is to empirically test a theory and this theory is formulated so precisely that a certain functional form can be derived from it, then the decision would be clear. However, this is not the norm. Instead, the rule is that there is scope for how theoretical considerations may be formalized and confronted with data. In addition, specifically data science is characterized by the ability to gain valuable insights directly from the data.

Be that as it may, care must always be taken to ensure that the functional form can be interpreted in terms of content, as this is the only way to derive meaningful insights from such an analysis. At the same time, it must be ensured that the model describes the data precisely enough. In this regard we have five models applied to the same data and thus a comparative evaluation may help to select the best fitting of these models. In

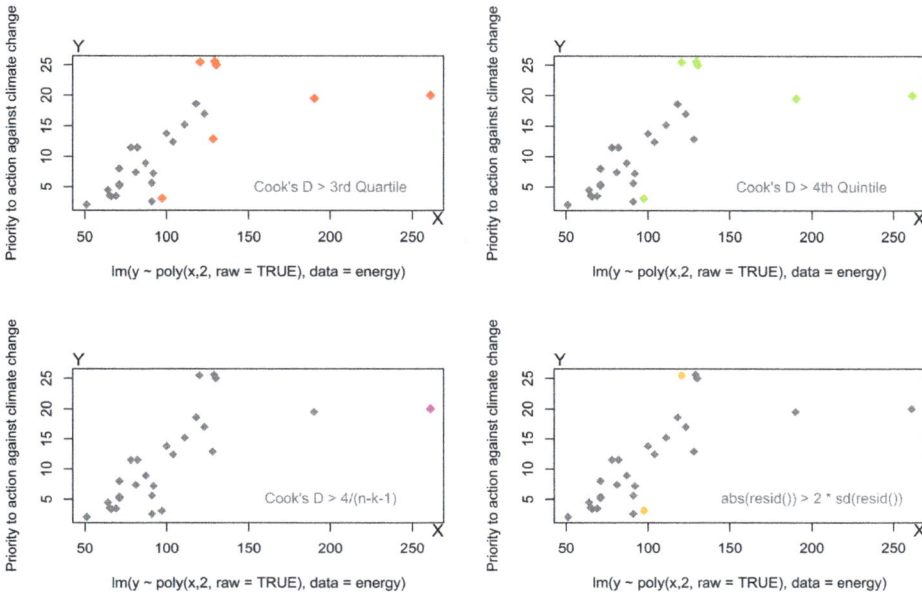

Figure 10.4: Influential Units in the Polynomial Regression Example.

terms of multiple R^2, the gray (polynomial) curve attains the best value $\left(R^2 = 0.685\right)$, followed by the magenta curve $\left(R^2 = 0.640\right)$, the blue curve $\left(R^2 = 0.599\right)$, the green curve $\left(R^2 = 0.579\right)$ and the orange curve $\left(McFadden\ R^2 = 0.485\right)$.

As outlined in chapter 8, however, additional diagnostics should also be performed to evaluate model fit. For it we can use the instruments explained there, particularly the Residuals-vs.-Fitted Plot and the Q-Q Plot. In this regard especially the gray and magenta curves tend to exhibit just about acceptable albeit clearly suboptimal results (upper left and right diagrams in Figures 10.2 and 10.3), while the green and blue curves do more poorly in both regards.

In Figures 10.2 and 10.3, the upper left plots pertain to the polynomial regression (gray curve in Figure 10.1). Concerning the Residuals-vs.-Fitted Plot in Figure 10.2, the mean values oscillate only slightly around the horizontal reference line, while the corresponding Q-Q Plot in Figure 10.3 indicates a pattern that appears widely compatible with the theoretical expectation.

The diagnosis for the magenta curve in Figure 10.1 (i. e., the curve that relates ln y to the inverse of x) produces a roughly similar, at best only marginally worse, picture (upper right diagrams in Figures 10.2 and 10.3).

In contrast, the other curves show greater deviations from the ideal image of a Residuals-vs.-Fitted Plot. For the blue curve in Figure 10.1 (i. e. the curve that relates y to ln x), the associated diagnosis plots are the lower left diagrams in Figures 10.2 and

10.3. While the lower right diagram in Figure 10.2 expresses the comparably poor pattern for the green curve in Figure 10.1 (i. e., for the curve that relates ln y to ln x).

The same applies in principle to the orange curve in Figure 10.1, i. e. the nonlinear function estimated via *nls()*. The corresponding Residuals-vs.-Fitted Plot is the lower right diagram in Figure 10.3. We built it using the method explained in section 8.2. Underlying the dark-red line is a 3rd degree polynomial that relates the residuals to the predicted values of the orange curve.

This suggests that we should only consider the polynomial model (gray curve) and the exponential model (magenta curve) as we proceed. Regarding these two models, Figures 10.4 and 10.5 illustrate another tool of regression diagnostics, namely the identification of influential units (observations) and outliers. Here, *influential* means influential on the coefficients to be estimated, i. e. intercept and slope. This is definitely one of the bigger points in regression diagnostics. On the one hand, there are several diagnostic options (of which we would only like to present Cook's D here). On the other hand, it is important to answer the question of what can actually be done if units prove to be too or unduly influential, as is sometimes said. This question touches on two discussions of more general importance.

First, when is something *too* influential? Where exactly is this transition point or cutoff value? For Cook's D, 4/n-k-1 was suggested (Fox 1991: 34). Even if this should be a sensible recommendation, it remains arbitrary. It therefore makes sense to consider alternative criteria for setting a cutoff value as well. To do this, we based ourselves on the frequency distribution of D values and used also the 3rd quartile and 4th quintile as cutoffs. The values greater than these cutoffs would then be considered *too* influential, i. e. the 25% or 20% largest values of the distribution of D values. In the two upper diagrams and the lower left diagram of Figure 10.4 and 10.5 all data points exceeding the respective cutoff are marked in color. Meanwhile, the colored data points in the bottom right diagram show which data points should be considered outliers.

Secondly, the recommendation to exclude outliers from the analysis must be viewed as critical (Fox 1991: 39). It is true that outliers, i. e. observations with an atypical x-y configuration, can strongly influence the estimation of intercept and slope. But exclude such a data point from the analysis because of that? The present data example shows that exactly this can be unacceptable and should in any case be assessed very critically. Why? Because we are operating here with just 27 units and eliminating one unit would mean excluding an entire EU country from the analysis simply because it may differ too much from the other countries in a certain respect.

Against the background of both points mentioned, it appears to be much more productive to be able to use an approach of systematic replication to assess and quantify the influence that decisions made in the context of a statistical analysis have on the result. This implies precise documentation of all methodological decisions and analysis steps as well as an examination of how invariant (robust) the result of a data analysis remains in relation to variations in the design and implementation of this analysis.

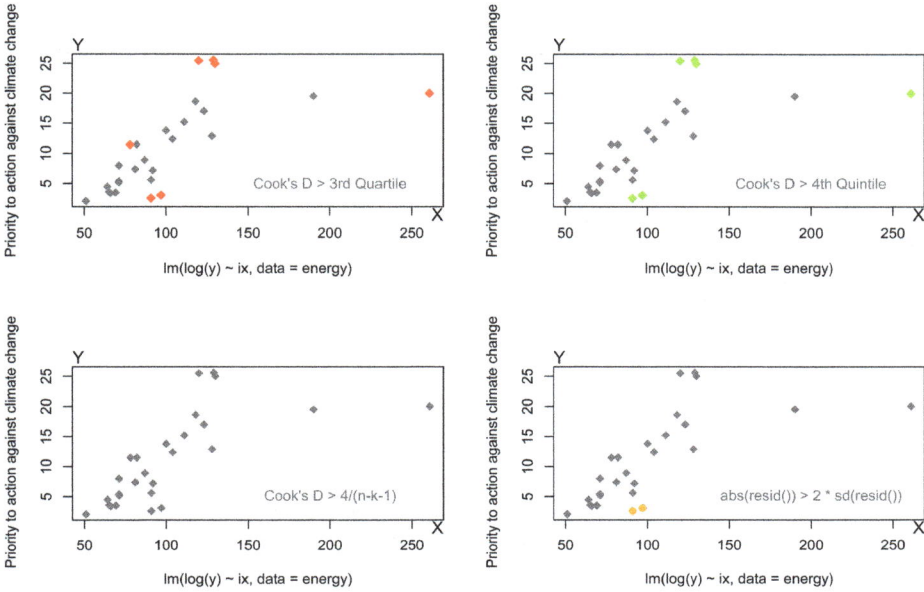

Figure 10.5: Influential Units in the log(y)/inverse(x) Transformation Example.

Table 10.1: Output to $y = poly(x, 2)$ and $y = log(x)$.

Line	R Output
1	Call:
2	lm(formula = y ~ poly(x, 2, raw = TRUE), data = energy)
3	
4	Residuals:
5	Min 1Q Median 3Q Max
6	-9.0032 -1.2676 0.0143 2.4016 8.7006
7	
8	Coefficients:
9	Estimate Std. Error t value Pr(>|t|)
10	(Intercept) -2.082e+01 5.402e+00 -3.855 0.000760 ***
11	poly(x, 2, raw = TRUE)1 4.488e-01 8.457e-02 5.306 1.92e-05 ***
12	poly(x, 2, raw = TRUE)2 -1.127e-03 2.808e-04 -4.014 0.000509 ***
13	---
14	Signif. codes: 0 '***' 0.001 '**' 0.01 '*' 0.05 '.' 0.1 ' ' 1
15	
16	Residual standard error: 4.37 on 24 degrees of freedom
17	Multiple R-squared: 0.6853, Adjusted R-squared: 0.659
18	F-statistic: 26.13 on 2 and 24 DF, p-value: 9.445e-07
19	
20	Call:

Table 10.1 (continued)

Line	R Output
21	lm(formula = y ~ log(x), data = energy)
22	
23	Residuals:
24	Min 1Q Median 3Q Max
25	-8.3241 -2.6364 -0.7448 1.7851 10.5962
26	
27	Coefficients:
28	Estimate Std. Error t value Pr(>|t|)
29	(Intercept) -63.387 12.220 -5.187 2.30e-05 ***
30	log(x) 16.353 2.676 6.111 2.18e-06 ***
31	---
32	Signif. codes: 0 '***' 0.001 '**' 0.01 '*' 0.05 '.' 0.1 ' ' 1
33	
34	Residual standard error: 4.833 on 25 degrees of freedom
35	Multiple R-squared: 0.599, Adjusted R-squared: 0.583
36	F-statistic: 37.34 on 1 and 25 DF, p-value: 2.183e-06

Lines explained:

Lines 1 to 18 refer to a first *lm()* function call and lines 20 to 36 to a second one. Each of them contains the same blocks of information. First, the function call is reprinted. This is followed by a summary statistics of the residuals (smallest/largest value, first, second and third quartiles). The coefficient block provides information about intercept an slope estimates and their associated standard errors, t-ratios and significance information. The overall model can be evaluated via the model-fit block, i. e., through R^2, *adj.* R^2 and the associated *F*-test.

Table 10.2: Output to $log(y) \sim inverse(x)$ and $log(y) \sim log(x)$.

Line	R Output
1	Call:
2	lm(formula = log(y) ~ ix, data = energy)
3	
4	Residuals:
5	Min 1Q Median 3Q Max
6	-1.22080 -0.20677 0.05851 0.29630 0.60558
7	
8	Coefficients:
9	Estimate Std. Error t value Pr(>|t|)
10	(Intercept) 4.0664 0.3009 13.516 5.39e-13 ***
11	ix -172.0016 25.8161 -6.663 5.56e-07 ***
12	---
13	Signif. codes: 0 '***' 0.001 '**' 0.01 '*' 0.05 '.' 0.1 ' ' 1
14	

Table 10.2 (continued)

Line	R Output
15	Residual standard error: 0.4648 on 25 degrees of freedom
16	Multiple R-squared: 0.6397, Adjusted R-squared: 0.6253
17	F-statistic: 44.39 on 1 and 25 DF, p-value: 5.559e-07
18	
19	Call:
20	lm(formula = log(y) ~ log(x), data = energy)
21	
22	Residuals:
23	Min 1Q Median 3Q Max
24	-1.1278 -0.3246 0.0080 0.3943 0.7042
25	
26	Coefficients:
27	Estimate Std. Error t value Pr(>|t|)
28	(Intercept) -5.2753 1.2704 -4.153 0.000335 ***
29	log(x) 1.6313 0.2782 5.864 4.07e-06 ***
30	---
31	Signif. codes: 0 '***' 0.001 '**' 0.01 '*' 0.05 '.' 0.1 ' ' 1
32	
33	Residual standard error: 0.5024 on 25 degrees of freedom
34	Multiple R-squared: 0.579, Adjusted R-squared: 0.5622
35	F-statistic: 34.39 on 1 and 25 DF, p-value: 4.069e-06

Lines explained:

Lines 1 to 17 refer to a first *lm()* function call and lines 19 to 35 to a second one. Each of them contains the same blocks of information and is structured as described in the previous table. The calculations refer to the transformed variables.

The influence on a coefficient depends on the two factors called *leverage* and *discrepancy*. Specifically the "combination of high leverage with an outlier produces substantial influence on the regression coefficients" (Fox 1991: 21), where an outlier is an observation whose dependent variable is unusual *given the value of the independent variable*. Cook's D_i statistic is defined as

$$D_i = \frac{e'^2_i}{k+1} \cdot \frac{h_i}{1-h_i} \tag{10.16}$$

(Fox 1991: 30). The first term on the right-hand side of (10.16) is a measure of *discrepancy*: For each observation the squared standardized residual is divided by $k+1$, with k denoting the number of b's in the equation, excluding the intercept (here, $k = 1$). The standardized residual itself results if each observed residual e_i is transformed to

$$\acute{e}_i = \frac{e_i}{s \cdot \sqrt{1 - h_{ii}}} \tag{10.17}$$

with s calculated as

$$s = \sqrt{\frac{\sum e_i^2}{n - k - 1}} \tag{10.18}$$

(Fox 1991: 25). Then, the second term on the right-hand side of (10.16) is a measure of *leverage*. It refers, for each observation, to a so-called *hat-value* h_i that expresses the fitted values in terms of the observed values. In simple-regression analysis such hat-values measure distance from the mean of x (Fox 1991: 25).

$$h_i = \frac{1}{n} + \frac{(x_i - \bar{x})^2}{\sum\limits_{j=1}^{n} (x_j - \bar{x})^2} \tag{10.19}$$

Table 10.3: Output to $y \sim (a \cdot x)/(b + x)$.

Line	R Output
1	Formula: y ~ (a * x)/(b + x)
2	
3	Parameters:
4	Estimate Std. Error t value Pr(>|t|)
5	a 122.5 191.4 0.640 0.528
6	b 966.4 1716.5 0.563 0.578
7	
8	Residual standard error: 5.477 on 25 degrees of freedom
9	
10	Number of iterations to convergence: 12
11	Achieved convergence tolerance: 7.925e-06

Lines explained:
This output refers to the use of nonlinear least squares via *nls()* function call. The model is outlined around (10.14) and (10.15). Line 1 reprints the formula of this function call. The *Parameters* block of information provides, in the usual way, the estimates and their associated standard errors, t ratios, and significance information.

For a another analysis we stick with the same Example Data Set 6 on Energy Transition in the European Green Deal but switch to another target variable. This variable too comes from Eurostat and is defined as the percentage of the population that does not have access to at least three of nine items of material deprivation in the dimension 'Economic burden and durable goods'. This *rate of deprivation* is the target variable y. And as before we use a country's living standard as measured by its official purchasing power standard (PPS) as the predictor variable x.

Figure 10.6 shows the scatterplot. We see that the bulk of the data points consists of 22 countries (oriented diagonally towards the bottom left corner in the diagram), of which three countries are separated towards the top left and two countries are separated towards the bottom right. As with the previous example, it would not be acceptable to simply exclude these countries from the analysis due to their more or less atypical position in the diagram. Instead, here too it is important to find a function that can approximate the data points *in their entirety*.

To do this, we use three of the functions that we already described for the previous example. In Figure 10.6, the blue, magenta and orange curves each indicate the same functional form as in the previous example. That the curves look completely different, it is only because of the opposite signs of the relations analyzed here and above.

Material Deprivation and Wealth

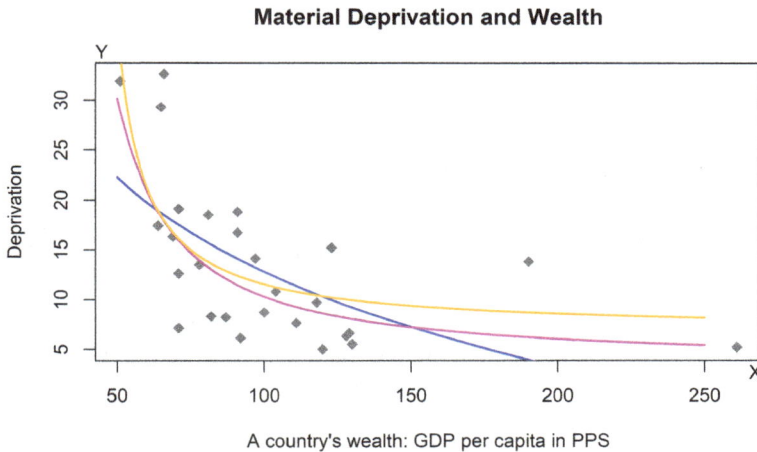

Figure 10.6: Three Nonlinear Curve Shapes in the Deprivation Example.

A comparative model evaluation reveals that the orange curve approximates the data best, with a McFadden's $R^2 = 0.52$ and an acceptable Residual-vs-Fitted Plot[5] (lower left diagram in Figure 10.7). The second best fit attains the magenta curve with $R^2 = 0.467$ and acceptable Residual-vs.-Fitted and Q-Q Plots (upper right and lower right diagrams in Figure 10.7). Then, the blue curve attains only an $R^2 = 0.381$ and clearly the less acceptable Residual-vs.-Fitted Plot (upper left diagram in Figure 10.7).

───────────

5 Again the method described in section 8.2 was used. Initially a 3rd degree polynomial was employed to regress the residuals on the predicted values. Because all three effect components turned out to be completely insignificant, we simplified it to a simple regression (the straight line displayed in the lower left diagram in Figure 10.7).

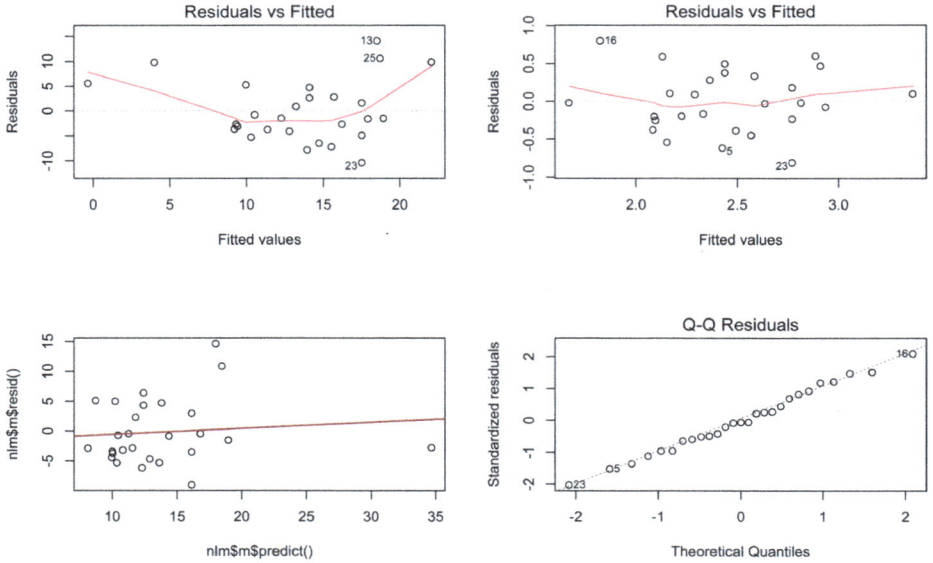

Figure 10.7: Diagnostic Plots for the Deprivation Example.

10.2 Polynomial Regression and Regression Splines

As outlined in section 8.5, a Generalized Linear Model (GLM) consists of three parts:
1. A random part that specifies the distribution of a variable Y, with mean $E(Y_i) = \mu_i$
2. A systematic part that specifies effects of covariates on a quantity called linear predictor η_i
3. A link function $g(\cdot)$ that relates, for each unit $i = 1, \ldots, n$, η_i to μ_i in the link function $\eta_i = g(\mu_i)$.

The *glm()* function

$$glm(formula, family, weights, data) \tag{10.20}$$

accordingly expects input in each of these respects: *formula* specifies the systematic part in the form *target variable ~ covariate(s)*, while *family*, along with *link*,

$$family = distribution(link = function) \tag{10.21}$$

specifies the random part. While sections 8.5 to 8.7 address primarily topics concerning the random part of a GLM (specifically the gamma and binomial *distribution* and the probit and logit *link*), the present section pays particular attention to the systematic part of a GLM. Because as far as this systematic part is concerned, it also opens up choices such that the assumed effects are linear or nonlinear in one functional form or another. This is realized via an approach that relates η_i not to x itself,

$$\eta_i = \beta_0 + \beta_1 b_1(x_i) + \beta_2 b_2(x_i) + \beta_3 b_3(x_i) + \ldots + \beta_K b_K(x_i) \qquad (10.22)$$

but to a *basis function of* x, namely $b_j(x_i)$ (James et al. 2013: 270). In this equation the β_j represent the regression slopes and the $b_j(x_i)$ the functions of x, that is, the predictors. For polynomial regression, for instance, these functions were $b_j(x_i) = x_i^j$. The approach accordingly includes functions on both sides of the equation that connects η to x: namely the link function on one side and a function of x on the other side. We would like to illustrate this for polynomial regression, regression splines and generalized additive models (GAMs) using an example that applies four corresponding models to the same data (Table 10.4).

Table 10.4: Examples for *formula* in *glm()* or *gam()*.

formula = y ~ x	GLM, Linear Effect
formula = y ~ poly(x, 3)	3rd-degree polynomial GLM
formula = y ~ bs(x, knots = c(k₁, k₂, k₃), degree = 3)	3rd-degree spline GLM
formula = y ~ s(x, 3)	3rd-degree GAM

The data come from Example Data Set 7 on Views & Insights on Climate Policy. The target variable y is based on this question wording: "Bremen as a federal state wants to be climate neutral by 2038, Germany by 2045 and the European Union by 2050. Do you think it is right or wrong that Bremen wants climate neutrality achieving faster than Germany and the EU?" Possible responses are "Bremen's schedule is right" (coded 1) vs. "too ambitious" (coded 0). 56.3 percent voted for "schedule is right" and 43.7 percent for "schedule is too ambitious" (n = 375). The predictor variable x is age measured in years.

First, we start with a probit model that assumes a *linear* effect of x. The systematic part of the model therefore only consists of the intercept and one slope coefficient. The estimates are $\beta_0 = 0.952$ and $\beta_1 = -0.018$, and McFadden's[6] $R^2 = 0.032$. The resulting regression line is displayed in the upper left diagram of Figure 10.8 and the associated output is reprinted in Table 10.5.

Next, we estimate a 3rd degree *polynomial* regression. This is a cubic regression model *over the entire range of* x. The equation is

$$\eta_i = \beta_0 + \beta_1 x_i + \beta_2 x_i^2 + \beta_3 x_i^3 \qquad (10.23)$$

---

6 This is a Pseudo-R^2 measure that compares a model with just the intercept to a model with all parameters (Long and Freese 2006: 109). Here, we use the deviance values reported in Table 10.5 for its computation: $1 - (Res.dev/Null.dev)$.

The estimates are reprinted in Table 10.6. If inserted into (10.23), the result is the upper right graph in Figure 10.8. McFadden's $R^2 = 0.045$.

We then continue with the idea of not fitting a polynomial regression over the entire range of x, but instead fitting separate polynomials *over different regions of x*. Such *piecewise* polynomials would therefore estimate a complete set of b coefficients for each of these regions. For instance, for a cubic regression model such as (10.23) *all* β coefficients would be obtained for *each* region, with the x scale points that separate these regions called *knots*. If there were only two such regions the single knot c would allocate the x values according to $x_i < c$ and $x_i \geq c$.

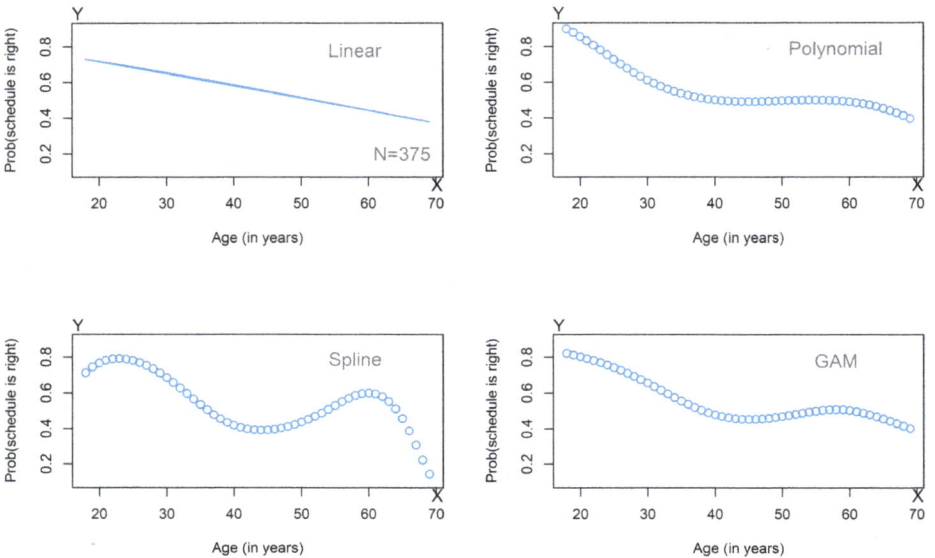

Figure 10.8: Linear Effect and Nonlinear Curve Shapes when Applying Four Models to the Same Data.

On the one hand, such a piecewise polynomial regression allows for finer curve shapes because different sets of b estimates may result for the different regions. On the other hand, further model restrictions are required to allow the curves of adjacent regions on the x scale to directly flow into one another. Then a *regression spline* results if we fit a piecewise degree-d polynomial regression under the constraint that the fitted curve is continuous and has continuous first and second derivatives (James et al. 2013: 271–272). We adopt basis model (10.22) to represent a cubic spline with 3 knots. For it we follow James et al. (2013: 273) and start off "with a basis for a cubic polynomial—namely, x, x^2, x^3—and then add one *truncated power basis* function per knot." Such a function is defined as

$$h(x, \xi) = (x - \xi)^3_+ = \begin{cases} (x - \xi)^3 & \text{if } x > \xi \\ 0 & \text{otherwise} \end{cases} \tag{10.24}$$

with ξ denoting a knot (James et al. 2013: 273). We take the first, second and third quartile of the distribution of x values as the three knots, to implement a formula[7]

$$formula = y \sim bs(x, \; knots = c(30, 39, 54), \; degree = 3) \tag{10.25}$$

that relates to

$$\eta_i = \beta_0 + \beta_1 b_1(x_i) + \beta_2 b_2(x_i) + \beta_3 b_3(x_i)$$
$$+ \beta_4 b_4(x_i) + \beta_5 b_5(x_i) + \beta_6 b_6(x_i) \tag{10.26}$$

It produces the output reprinted in Table 10.8[8], while the associated *plot()* function yields the lower left graph in Figure 10.8. McFadden's $R^2 = 0.068$.

Table 10.5: Output to *glm(y ~ x)*.

Line	R Output
1	Call:
2	glm(formula = kpo$y ~ kpo$x, family = quasibinomial(link = probit),
3	weights = kpo$wg)
4	
5	Coefficients:
6	Estimate Std. Error t value Pr(>|t|)
7	(Intercept) 0.951497 0.204632 4.650 4.62e-06 ***
8	kpo$x -0.018169 0.004518 -4.021 7.01e-05 ***
9	---
10	Signif. codes: 0 '***' 0.001 '**' 0.01 '*' 0.05 '.' 0.1 ' ' 1
11	
12	(Dispersion parameter for quasibinomial family taken to
13	be 1.00869)
14	
15	Null deviance: 515.55 on 374 degrees of freedom
16	Residual deviance: 499.10 on 373 degrees of freedom

---

7 The results of the calculations are shown in Table 10.8, along with the function call in the header of this table. The *splines* library required for the calculation can be accessed via *library(gam)*, which was developed for Generalized Additive Models and also imports *splines* for this purpose. From a user perspective, working with *library(gam)* is certainly the most straightforward approach. However, Table 10.11 also shows how the calculation of a spline model can be realized using the *tidymodels* interface.

8 If such an output is produced via *library(tidymodels)*, in principle we obtain the same output except for a marginally different labeling of the *bs* coefficients.

Table 10.5 (continued)

Line	R Output
17	AIC: NA
18	Number of Fisher Scoring iterations: 3

Lines explained

Lines 1 to 3 reprint the function call. Lines 5 to 10 report the *Coefficients* block of information. It includes the estimates (in this section labelled β_j), each with its standard error, t ratio (β/s.e) and significance information. Lines 12 and 13: Dispersion. The specification *quasibinomial* allows for overdispersion (i. e., for deviating from an otherwise fixed 1.0). Lines 15 to 16: Model fit information in terms of deviance values.

Table 10.6: Output to $glm(y \sim poly(x, 3))$.

Line	R Output
1	Call:
2	glm(formula = kpo$y ~ poly(kpo$x, 3, raw = TRUE),
3	family = quasibinomial(link = probit), weights = kpo$wg)
4	
5	Coefficients:
6	Estimate Std. Error t value Pr(>|t|)
7	(Intercept) 4.905e+00 2.074e+00 2.365 0.0185 *
8	poly(kpo$x, 3,raw = TRUE)1 -2.958e-01 1.578e-01 -1.875 0.0616 .
9	poly(kpo$x, 3,raw = TRUE)2 5.906e-03 3.767e-03 1.568 0.1178
10	poly(kpo$x, 3,raw = TRUE)3 -3.913e-05 2.852e-05 -1.372 0.1709
11	---
12	Signif. codes: 0 '***' 0.001 '**' 0.01 '*' 0.05 '.' 0.1 ' ' 1
13	
14	(Dispersion parameter for quasibinomial family taken
15	to be 1.030515)
16	
17	Null deviance: 515.55 on 374 degrees of freedom
18	Residual deviance: 492.52 on 371 degrees of freedom
19	AIC: NA
20	
21	Number of Fisher Scoring iterations: 5

Lines explained

Lines 1 to 3 reprint the function call. It specifies the model in terms of $y \sim x$, allows for overdispersion, chooses the probit link and names the variable that weights each unit. Lines 5 to 12: Here the *Coefficients* block of information reports the linear, quadratic and cubic component of the effect of x along with the usual information that accompanies the estimates: standard error, t ratio, significance information.

Exactly the same curve is also obtained if we run the *glm()* function with variable x and five functions of x, namely: x, x^2, x^3, $(x-30)^3$, $(x-39)^3$, $(x-54)^3$, with the latter three terms, one for each knot, constructed according to (10.24), with the condition "*if* $x > \xi$, 0 *otherwise*" realized by *ifelse()* logic (Table 10.7). However, in this way we do not get the same estimates as in Table 10.8, since the solution there is based on a parameterization that differentiates between the $b's$ and $\beta's$. But the models' *implications* including their fit measures are identical. We would see this equivalence very clearly if we superimposed the left and right curves in Figure 10.9. The red graph belongs to the spline regression in Table 10.8 and the blue graph belongs to the cubic polynomial model with a truncated power basis function added per knot. Accordingly we also get identical fit values in terms of null deviance (515.55 on 374 df), residual deviance (480.33 on 368 df), and dispersion parameter for quasibinomial family (1.020971).

Table 10.7: Cubic Polynomial Plus Truncated Power Basis Function Per Knot.

Line	R Script
1	`load("klimapolitik1.Rdata")`
2	`kpo <- subset(kpo, select=c(y,x,wg))`
3	`kpo <- kpo[complete.cases(kpo$y, kpo$x, kpo$wg),]`
4	`kpo$x2 <- kpo$x * kpo$x`
5	`kpo$x3 <- kpo$x * kpo$x * kpo$x`
6	`kpo$xk1 <- ifelse(kpo$x > 30, (kpo$x-30)^3, 0)`
7	`kpo$xk2 <- ifelse(kpo$x > 39, (kpo$x-39)^3, 0)`
8	`kpo$xk3 <- ifelse(kpo$x > 54, (kpo$x-54)^3, 0)`
9	`summary(m3a <- glm(formula=kpo$y ~ kpo$x + kpo$x2 +`
10	`kpo$x3 + kpo$xk1 + kpo$xk2 + kpo$xk3,`
11	`family=quasibinomial(link=probit),`
12	`weights=kpo$wg))`

Lines explained
Line 1 loads the data frame. Line 2 selects the variables to be used in the analysis, including the sample weight. Line 3 refers to the data frame subset in the line above it to reduce this frame to the units with valid information in all of its involved variables, using within the square brackets the *complete.cases()* function. Lines 4 to 8 create the synthetic variables to be addressed in the *glm()* function call in lines 9 to 12.

Returning to (10.26), the related Table 10.8 reports in its *Coefficients* block the intercept β_0 and the six β_j slope estimates. In contrast, we only get the $b_j's$ by accessing the R object that is created in the course of calculating the regression. A variety of information is stored in this object, including these b_j coefficients. Since these have been calculated for each individual unit i and since we have 375 units and six such coefficients per unit, the values are stored in a 375×6 matrix. Via script line *str(object)*, one gets access to the structure of any R object previously calculated in a running session and the information stored therein, where *object* is to be replaced with the assigned object name in the R script. In the present example this object name is *m3* (denoting the 3ʳᵈ of the four corre-

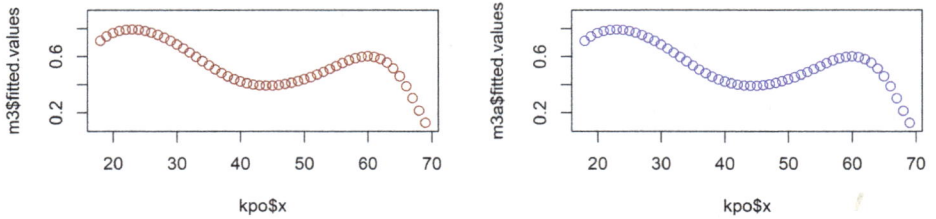

Figure 10.9: Identical Curve Shapes of the Spline Regression (Red Graph) and the Cubic Polynomial With a Truncated Power Basis Function Added Per Knot (Blue Graph).

sponding models as indicated in Table 10.4). Inspection of this *m3* object reveals how the required information is stored therein. (10.27) mirrors exactly this internal object structure when performing the calculations via the *tidymodels* route (Table 10.11)[9]. Although not required, rounding may help increase the readability of the requested information.

$$\text{round}(\texttt{m3\$fit\$fit\$fit\$data}, 4) \tag{10.27}$$

This way we get access to the $b_j's$ (Table 10.9)[10], for instance to reconstruct how these predictors get involved in (10.26) to obtain for each unit i the predicted η_i value, i.e., the linear predictor of the *glm()*. We illustrate this for the three of the 375 units which correspond to rows 1, 6, and 9 of the matrix in Table 10.9. With the β_j estimates from Table 10.8 and the b_j of the selected rows in Table 10.9, (10.26) predicts $\eta_1 = 0.7426$, $\eta_6 = -0.0716$ and $\eta_9 = -0.2823$ using the script lines (10.28) to (10.30).

Unit 1

$$\begin{aligned} eta1 < \ & -0.5602 + 0.4549 \cdot 0.4671 + 0.0646 \cdot 0.4394 - 1.0360 \cdot 0.0546 \\ & - 0.6524 \cdot 0.0 + 0.1261 \cdot 0.0 - 1.6825 \cdot 0.0 \end{aligned} \tag{10.28}$$

Unit 6

$$\begin{aligned} eta6 < \ & -0.5602 + 0.4549 \cdot 0.0 + 0.0646 \cdot 0.0006 - 1.0360 \cdot 0.2778 \\ & - 0.6524 \cdot 0.5588 + 0.1261 \cdot 0.1627 - 1.6825 \cdot 0.0 \end{aligned} \tag{10.29}$$

---

9 Alternatively, if the same model is calculated via *splines* and *library(gam)*, we would obtain this matrix via *round(m3$model$`bs(kpo$x, knots = c(30, 39, 54), degree = 3)`,4)*. However, no matter which library is used: after an R *object* has been calculated, it is easy to check via *str(object)* how it is internally structured – and in which of the internal sections the desired information is stored in order to export this information appropriately.

10 When using the *library (tidymodels)* this matrix is output as a *tibble*, with a seventh column added for *y*.

Unit 9

$$eta9 < -0.5602 + 0.4549 \cdot 0.0 + 0.0646 \cdot 0.0 - 1.0360 \cdot 0.0015$$
$$- 0.6524 \cdot 0.0525 + 0.1261 \cdot 0.4340 - 1.6825 \cdot 0.5120 \tag{10.30}$$

The three linear predictors can also be extracted directly from the R object. For the first 10 units (10.31)

$$\text{round(m3\$fit\$fit\$fit\$linear.predictors[1:10],4)} \tag{10.31}$$

provides this information (here split into two outcome lines) as follows:

```
     1       2       3       4       5
 0.7426  0.8189  0.8112  0.7339  -0.1554
```
$$\tag{10.32}$$
```
     6       7       8       9      10
-0.0716  0.0215  -0.0452  -0.2823  -0.2651
```

The probit model predicts quantile values z_α and takes the associated probabilities α of the distribution function as estimates of $Pr(y = 1|x)$. Since we are calculating such a probit regression here, we can address both the z values, i. e. the linear predictors, and the associated probability values. One way to get these probabilities is by embedding the above expression *m3\$fit\$fit\$fit\$linear.predictors[1:10]* in the *pnorm()* function before rounding:

$$\text{round(pnorm(m3\$fit\$fit\$fit\$linear.predictors[1:10]),4)} \tag{10.33}$$

It results an outcome (again split into two outcome lines)

```
     1       2       3       4       5
 0.7711  0.7936  0.7914  0.7685  0.4383
```
$$\tag{10.34}$$
```
     6       7       8       9      10
 0.4715  0.5086  0.4820  0.3889  0.3955
```

that can also be extracted from the R object by directly addressing its *fitted values* via

$$\text{round(m3\$fit\$fit\$fit\$fitted.values[1:10],4)} \tag{10.35}$$

Usually it is these fitted values that we are interested in as target in a probit regression.

Table 10.8: Output to $glm(y \sim bs(x, knots = c(30, 39, 54), degree = 3))$.

Line	R Output
1	Call:
2	glm(formula = kpo$y ~ bs(kpo$x, knots = c(30, 39, 54),
3	degree = 3), family = quasibinomial(link = probit),
4	weights = kpo$wg)
5	
6	Coefficients:
7	Estimate Std. Error t value Pr(>|t|)
8	(Intercept) 0.56023 0.44852 1.249 0.2124
9	bs(kpo$x, ..)1 0.45489 0.80444 0.565 0.5721
10	bs(kpo$x, ..)2 0.06461 0.53057 0.122 0.9031
11	bs(kpo$x, ..)3 -1.03600 0.63634 -1.628 0.1044
12	bs(kpo$x, ..)4 -0.65239 0.63882 -1.021 0.3078
13	bs(kpo$x, ..)5 0.12605 0.67206 0.188 0.8513
14	bs(kpo$x, ..)6 -1.68245 0.65033 -2.587 0.0101 *
15	---
16	Signif. codes: 0 '***' 0.001 '**' 0.01 '*' 0.05 '.'
17	0.1 ' ' 1
18	
19	(Dispersion parameter for quasibinomial family
20	taken to be 1.020971)
21	
22	Null deviance: 515.55 on 374 degrees of freedom
23	Residual deviance: 480.33 on 368 degrees of freedom
24	AIC: NA
25	
26	Number of Fisher Scoring iterations: 4

Lines explained
Lines 6 to 17: The *Coefficients* block reports the β estimates along with associated information (standard error, t-ratio, significance information).

A fourth model follows the statistical approach outlined in the next section. It is a generalized additive model (GAM). We include it in this section for two purposes: First, to complete the picture that emerges when we apply four relevant models to the same data. Then the main question is whether these models lead us to the same or different conclusions. Secondly, to illustrate that the *gam()* function provides access to stored results beyond the standard output that is similar to the regression-spline case just dealt with. Third, to give a first impression that we determine the flexibility of smoothing splines via degrees of freedom. The statistical approach itself will then be presented in more detail in the next section using a more extensive model example.

Table 10.9: Output to the b_j's: first 10 rows of the 375×6 matrix.

Line	R Output
1	1 2 3 4 5 6
2	[1,] 0.4671 0.4394 0.0564 0.0000 0.0000 0.0000
3	[2,] 0.5688 0.2189 0.0138 0.0000 0.0000 0.0000
4	[3,] 0.5465 0.1502 0.0071 0.0000 0.0000 0.0000
5	[4,] 0.3778 0.0426 0.0009 0.0000 0.0000 0.0000
6	[5,] 0.0000 0.0049 0.3740 0.5224 0.0986 0.0000
7	[6,] 0.0000 0.0006 0.2778 0.5588 0.1627 0.0000
8	[7,] 0.0068 0.4337 0.5339 0.0256 0.0000 0.0000
9	[8,] 0.0020 0.3743 0.5830 0.0407 0.0000 0.0000
10	[9,] 0.0000 0.0000 0.0015 0.0525 0.4340 0.5120
11	[10,] 0.0000 0.1027 0.6523 0.2403 0.0047 0.0000

We invoke *library(gam)* and specify the function call as follows:

$$gam \left(\begin{array}{l} formula = kpo\$y \sim s(kpo\$x, 3), \\ family = quasibinomial(link = probit),\ weights = kpo\$wg \end{array} \right) \tag{10.36}$$

This function call relates to an equation that may be written as

$$\eta_i = \beta_0 + \gamma_1 \cdot x_i + s_i \tag{10.37}$$

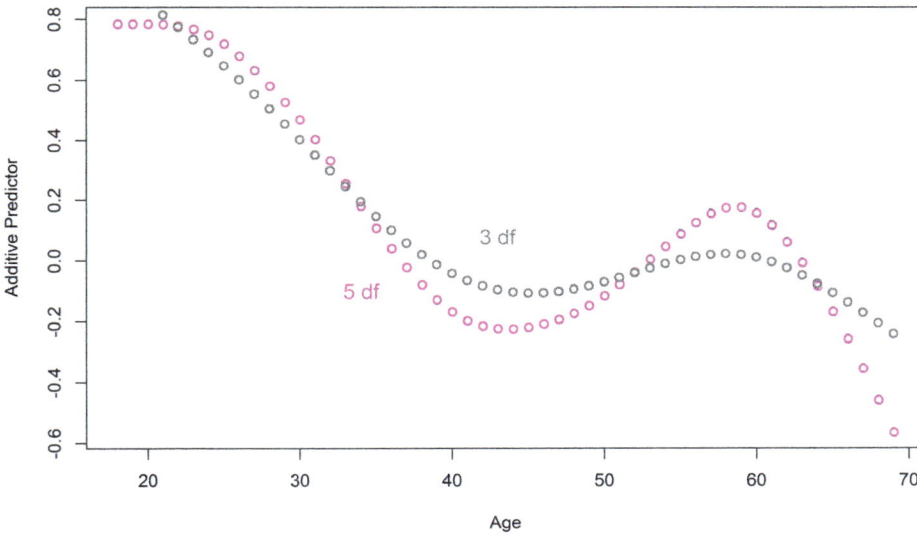

Figure 10.10: Curve Shapes of Two Smoothing Splines with 3 and 5 degrees of Freedom Applied to the Same Data.

It produces the output reprinted in Table 10.10, while the associated *plot()* function yields the lower right graph in Figure 10.8. McFadden's $R^2 = 0.055$. Equation (10.37) predicts for each unit the additive predictor. If this additive predictor, as it is called, is plotted against the values of the x variable, the result is a curve as shown in Figure 10.10. The number of degrees of freedom determines the permitted flexibility of the estimated curve. Figure 10.10 was created on the basis of (10.37), whereby the gray curve with $df = 3$ comes from the function call (10.36). In contrast, the magenta curve estimates the same model with 5 df, as will also be done in the following section 10.3.

To see how this prediction is accomplished, we extract the required information from the R object. Since we named this object *m4* (denoting the 4th of the four corresponding models discussed in this section), the linear model part is extracted first:

$$m4\$coefficients \tag{10.38}$$

For the intercept we obtain as estimate $\beta_0 = 0.942892$ and for the linear effect component $\gamma_1 = -0.017998$. The remaining information required is specific to each unit. For the 1st unit in the data frame, for instance, this information is accessible by

$$m4\$smooth[1] \tag{10.39}$$

and

$$m4\$smooth.frame\$`s(kpo\$x, 3)`[1] \tag{10.40}$$

That way we obtain $s_1 = 0.127570$ and $x_1 = 26$, i. e. the unit in the first row of the data frame is 26 years old. If we insert these values in (10.37),

$$\eta_1 = 0.942892 - 0.017998 \cdot 26 + 0.127570 \tag{10.41}$$

we get as result a predicted $\eta_1 = 0.602514$. This is the additive predictor for this first unit. This value is also obtainable via

$$m4\$additive.predictors[1] \tag{10.42}$$

and corresponds to

$$pnorm(m4\$additive.predictors[1]) \tag{10.43}$$

and

$$m4\$fitted.values[1]) \tag{10.44}$$

For this first unit this probability value is 0.7266. For getting access to the predictions for other units one has simply to change the number in the square brackets. For instance, for the unit in row 6 of the involved data frame the prediction is

$$\eta_6 = 0.942892 - 0.017998 \cdot 52 - 0.046951 \tag{10.45}$$

and results in the additive predictor $\eta_6 = -0.03996$ and the corresponding probability $pnorm(-0.039956) = 0.48406$.

Table 10.10: Output to $gam(y \sim s(x, 3))$.

Line	R Output
1	Call: gam(formula = kpo$y ~ s(kpo$x, 3),
2	family = quasibinomial(link = probit), weights = kpo$wg)
3	Deviance Residuals:
4	Min 1Q Median 3Q Max
5	-2.6665 -1.1042 0.6699 1.0909 1.8497
6	
7	(Dispersion Parameter for quasibinomial family taken to be 1.0017)
8	
9	Null Deviance: 515.5495 on 374 degrees of freedom
10	Residual Deviance: 487.171 on 371 degrees of freedom
11	AIC: NA
12	
13	Number of Local Scoring Iterations: NA
14	
15	Anova for Parametric Effects
16	Df Sum Sq Mean Sq F value Pr(>F)
17	s(kpo$x, 3) 1 15.53 15.5312 15.504 9.831e-05 ***
18	Residuals 371 371.64 1.0017
19	---
20	Signif. codes: 0 '***' 0.001 '**' 0.01 '*' 0.05 '.' 0.1 ' ' 1
21	
22	Anova for Nonparametric Effects
23	Npar Df Npar F Pr(F)
24	(Intercept)
25	s(kpo$x, 3) 2 5.917 0.002954 **
26	---
27	Signif. codes: 0 '***' 0.001 '**' 0.01 '*' 0.05 '.' 0.1 ' ' 1

Lines explained
Lines 1 and 2 reprint the function call. Lines 3 to 5: Summary statistics of deviance residuals. Line 7 to 10: Model fit block of information: dispersion parameter and deviance values. Lines 15 to 27 report the details of two analyses of variance. The first ANOVA refers to the linear effect component and the second ANOVA to the nonlinear effect component. Regarding the former parametric effect of x, line 17 reports five pieces of information: degrees of freedom, sum of squares, mean square, F value and its associated probability. Line 25: Similarly, degrees of freedom, F value and its associated probability are reported for the second ANOVA. Both F tests indicate statistically significant effect components.

Table 10.11: R Instructions Corresponding to the Four Different Formulae in Table 10.4.

Line	R Script
1	`load("klimapolitik1.Rdata")`
2	`kpo <- subset(kpo, select=c(y,x,wg))`
3	`kpo <- kpo[complete.cases(kpo$y, kpo$x, kpo$wg),]`
4	`summary(m1 <-glm(formula = kpo$y ~ kpo$x,`
5	`family=quasibinomial(link=probit),`
6	`weights = kpo$wg))`
7	`summary(m2 <- glm(formula=kpo$y ~ poly(kpo$x,3,`
8	`raw = TRUE),`
9	`family=quasibinomial(link=probit),`
10	`weights = kpo$wg))`
11	`library(tidymodels)`
12	`kpo <- as_tibble(kpo)`
13	`model <-`
14	`linear_reg() %>%`
15	`set_engine("glm",`
16	`family = stats::quasibinomial(link="probit"))%>%`
17	`translate()`
18	`rec <- recipe(y ~ x, data=kpo)%>%`
19	`step_bs(x, degree = 3,`
20	`options = list(knots=c(30,39,54)))`
21	`lmwflow <-`
22	`workflow() %>%`
23	`add_model(model)%>%`
24	`add_recipe(rec)`
25	`m3 <-`
26	`fit(lmwflow,kpo)`
27	`get_model <-`
28	`function(x) {`
29	`extract_fit_parsnip(x) %>% tidy()`
30	`}`
31	`get_model(m3)`
32	`m3 %>% extract_fit_engine() %>% summary()`
33	`round(m3$fit$fit$fit$data,4)`
34	`library(gam)`
35	`summary(m4 <- gam(formula=kpo$y ~ s(kpo$x, 3),`

Table 10.11 (continued)

Line	R Script
36	`family=quasibinomial(link=probit),`
37	`weights=kpo$wg))`

Lines explained

Line 1 loads the data frame. Line 2 uses the *select* option of the *subset()* function to confine the data frame to the variables to be used in the analysis. Line 3 reduces the data frame to the units with valid values in all analysis variables by use of the *complete.cases()* function in the square brackets. Lines 4 to 6: *glm()* function for the 1ˢᵗ model (linear-effect model). Lines 7 to 10: *glm()* function for the 2ⁿᵈ model (polynomial regression). Line 11 to 33: Instructions for the 3ʳᵈ model (regression spline, without case weights). Line 11 invokes *library(tidymodels)*. Line 12 defines the data frame as *tibble*. Then, four major components are implemented: a *model* statement that specifies a function along with its specifications (lines 13 to 17), a *recipe* for the required feature engineering (lines 18 to 20), a *workflow* to combine model and recipe (lines 21 to 24), and the *fit* function in lines 25 and 26, in fact along with instructions to get the fit results extracted in the parsnip way and the way, the addressed function — here the *glm()* function— reports the results (lines 27 to 32). Line 33 accesses the matrix of *b*'s, the first ten rows of which are listed in Table 10.9. Line 34 invokes the library *gam*, followed by the *gam()* function used for model *m4* in lines 35 to 37.

10.3 Generalized Additive Models

A generalized additive model is a "generalized linear model with a linear predictor involving a sum of smooth functions of covariates" (Wood 2017: 161). The difference between the two approaches is accordingly not on the side of the link function, i. e. to the left of the equal sign of the predicting equation, but to the right of it on the side of the covariates. The smooth function f_j makes the difference.

Yee (2015: 49–50) distinguishes four broad categories of smoothing methods: Regression or series smoothers (e.g., polynomial regression, regression splines), smoothing splines (with roughness penalties, e.g. cubic smoothing splines), local regression (e.g., loess), and nearest-neighbor smoothers (running means, running lines, running medians).

As to regression splines, there are two common bases for cubic splines: truncated power series and B-splines, with *bs()* and *ns()* as two implementations of such "Basic" or "Basis"-splines (Yee 2015: 53).

If a generalized additive model uses *natural splines* for the f_j, least squares can be used to fit the model "because natural splines can be constructed using an appropriately chosen set of basis functions" (James et al. 2013: 284). However, if the f_j are *smoothing splines*, least squares is to be replaced with another algorithm (James et al. 2013: 283–285). Then, instead of using predefined basis function to achieve nonlinearities, the generalized additive model uses, more flexibly, unspecified smooth functions f_j for it (Hastie et al. 2009: 296).

$$\eta_i = \beta_0 + f_1(x_1) + f_2(x_2) + \ldots + f_p(x_p) \tag{10.46}$$

Such a prediction equation can be generally specified for p covariates. In our data example there will be four such predictor variables. For fitting such equations, Hastie et al. (2009: 297–298) use a so-called "Backfitting Algorithm" whose building block is a "scatterplot smoother for fitting nonlinear effects in a flexible way", for instance the cubic smoothing spline (James et al. 2013: 284–285, 294). "It is called an *additive* model because we calculate a separate f_j for each X_j, and then add together all of their contributions" (James et al. 2013: 283).

When estimating the f_j smooth functions, they are decomposed into a linear and a nonlinear component. "The linear component is a weighted least squares linear fit of the fitted curve on the predictor, while the nonlinear part is the residual" (Hastie et al. 2009: 301).

The following data example may exemplify the procedure. We first introduce the variables involved. The data come again from Example Data Set 7 on Views & Insights on Climate Policy. We also stick with the target variable y that has been worded as follows: "Bremen as a federal state wants to be climate neutral by 2038, Germany by 2045 and the European Union by 2050. Do you think it is right or wrong that Bremen wants climate neutrality achieving faster than Germany and the EU?" Possible responses are "Bremen's schedule is right" (coded 1) vs. "too ambitious" (coded 0).

As in the previous section a first predictor is *age* measured in years. We expect a negative sign of its linear effect component, since younger people are likely to recognize that they will be exposed to the consequences of climate change for longer biographical time periods than older people, and that these consequences could be even more serious than they are today. It follows that younger people should actually have a greater interest than older people in ensuring that measures against climate change are implemented as quickly as possible.

A second predictor is *climate responsibility*. A core element of responsibility is taking into account the consequences that one's own actions, one's own decisions and one's own behavioral habits have on others. Taking responsibility accordingly means taking responsibility for these consequences. It is therefore very important whether/ to what extent this responsibility is felt as a personal responsibility. We used this survey question for it: "How much do you feel personally responsible for making a contribution to reducing climate change?" Responses were requested on an eleven-point scale ranging from 0 = "not at all" to 10 = "very strong". Using this coding, we expect a positive sign of the linear effect component of this felt responsibility on the probability of accepting Bremen's time schedule as right.

A third predictor is *climate rationality*. However, what is rational behavior in the face of climate change? What might a rational behavioral response to climate change look like *from the perspective of an individual actor*?

On the one hand, this person could argue that the achievable CO_2 savings potential of only two percent may not be able to protect coastal cities like Bremen and Bremerhaven or a country like Germany as a whole from the consequences of climate change. For the savings potential would be too small for it. But it would be a contribution to *global CO_2* savings and therefore a relevant contribution to the fight against global warming, ergo a rational behavioral response to climate change.

On the other hand, it could be argued that the CO_2 saving potential is far too low to protect cities like Bremen or Bremerhaven or a country like Germany from the consequences of climate change, as long as other countries continue to pollute the climate as before. A person might then ask herself why she should limit herself if other CO_2 emitters do not, especially since the consequences of climate change for the person would be pretty much the same, regardless of whether she practices individual renunciation or not.

Thus, basically, each person has the choice of which rationality to adopt. In our Views & Insights on Climate Policy Survey, we accordingly contrasted both views by use of a *bipolar* scale. We constructed this scale so that respondents could intuitively recognize their bipolar character without favoring either viewpoint. In particular, it was necessary to avoid a *response effect* that could have arisen from respondents seeing a plus sign as a plus in the evaluative sense and a minus sign as a minus in the evaluative sense. We therefore did not use a sequence of numbers such as -3, -2, -1, 0, +1, +2, +3 and instead worked with intuitively understandable symbols:

Which of these two opinions would you agree with more?							
Left text	⋘	≪	<	0	>	≫	⋙	*Right text*

Where the two opposing views were worded as quoted below:

Left text is replaced by "Germany should not impose strict climate protection targets as long as other countries continue to put much greater strain on the earth's climate than Germany."

Right text is replaced by "Even though Germany recently contributed just under two percent to global CO_2 emissions, it should definitely move forward with strict climate protection measures." In the present analysis the response scale is coded 1, 2, . . ., 7 from left to right. Using this coding, we expect a positive sign of the linear effect component of this type of rationality on the probability of accepting Bremen's time schedule as right.

The response distribution indicates a polarized opinion climate on this topic:

Which of these two opinions would you agree with more?							
Left text	16%	10%	11%	20%	13%	13%	17%	*Right text*

Finally, a fourth predictor is *intergenerational justice* when it comes to the financial burden of climate change. The topic is certainly more complex than the aspect we were able to cover in the survey. But it is nonetheless an important aspect. We wanted to know how accepted measures against climate change are if they have to be financed through loans. On the one hand, such borrowing may enable the necessary measures to counteract climate change, but on the other hand, debts also have to be repaid. The more debt is taken on today, the more it will limit the financial scope that remains for future government investments and services. We asked the respondents this survey question: "The Bremen parliament recently approved a credit line of 2.5 billion euros for climate protection projects in the first reading. Which of these two views comes closest to your personal assessment?" Just as described for the predictor "rationality," we also worked here with a bipolar scale that contrasts two opposing statements. *Left text* is replaced by "Climate protection justifies any taking on debts" and *right text* is replaced by "This debt puts far too much of a burden on future generations." In the present analysis the response scale is coded 1, 2, . . ., 7 from left to right. Using this coding, we expect a negative sign of the linear effect component of intergenerational justice on the probability of accepting Bremen's time schedule as right[11].

Since we have four predictors, the equation for the additive predictor (10.46) becomes

$$\eta_i = \beta_0 + f_1(x_1) + f_2(x_2) + f_3(x_3) + f_4(x_4) \tag{10.47}$$

respectively

$$\eta_i = \beta_0 + f_1(age) + f_2(responsibility) + f_3(rationality) + f_4(justice) \tag{10.48}$$

if the abstract x_j notation is replaced with the four predictor names. We invoke *library(gam)* and issue the function call

---

11 We replenished the two bipolar scales for climate rationality and intergenerational justice with a third bipolar scale to run the probabilistic classification (latent class analysis) detailed in section 11.4. This third scale follows the same construction logic as the two presented above. This survey question related to an extremely lively public discussion in 2023 about a controversial heating law. The following wording was used to introduce the question: "In 2022, greenhouse gas emissions in Germany were 761 million tons. For 2024, it is now expected that the switch to renewable energies for heating will lead to savings of around 1.4 percent of emissions in the building sector. Do these figures justify the heating transition for the building sector that the federal government is aiming for?" *Left text*: "Yes, we need every possible saving in CO_2 to protect the climate." Right text: "No, the heating transition demands far too much from citizens." A solution assuming 3 latent classes proved fully acceptable (n = 443; likelihood ratio = 6.72; Chi^2 = 6.36 (df = 6)). The estimated class population shares were as follows: 36.4% were opposed to too much climate protection. 40.6% expressed a positive attitude towards climate protection. 23.0% expressed a neutral stance.

$$m5 < - gam(formula = y \sim s(age, 5) + s(responsibility, 3)$$
$$+ s(rationality, 2) + s(justice, 3),$$
$$family = quasibinomial(link = probit),$$
$$weights = wg, data = kpo)$$

(10.49)

to fit the model to the data. The $s()$ function is used to specify a *smoothing* spline with associated degrees of freedom (James et al. 2013: 294) that control the flexibility of the smoother (Yee 2015: 59–60). As exemplified in (10.48) the individual $s()$ functions may have different degrees of freedom.

As outlined above, the statistical approach involves a decomposition of a f_j into a linear and nonlinear component. This means that the prediction equation for each individual unit must take into account both effect components per predictor. The prediction equation (10.47) can therefore also be written as

$$\eta_i = \beta_0 + \gamma_1 x_{1i} + s_{1i} + \gamma_2 x_{2i} + s_{2i}$$
$$+ \gamma_3 x_{3i} + s_{3i} + \gamma_4 x_{4i} + s_{4i}$$

(10.50)

with γ_j denoting the (parametric) linear effect component of f_j and with s_{ji} denoting the respective individual (nonparametric) nonlinear effect component of f_j.

A closer look at the standard output of a *gam()* function call reveals that it essentially contains information about the quality of model fit and the statistical significance of the effect components, but not these effect components themselves (Table 10.12). So it may be good to know how to get access to them. For it we extract this information from the R object to which the results of the *gam()* function call were assigned. In the present case this is the object named *m5*, a freely chosen name. Via *str(m5)* you can see beforehand how the object is structured and how desired information is stored in it. In this way we would see that the intercept β_0 and the γ_j coefficients of the parametric model part can be obtained by

```
m5$coefficients
```
(10.51)

Running this script line produces output (10.52):

```
(Intercept)  s(age, 5)    s(responsibility, 3)
0.19126760 -0.02163211              0.15062687
```

(10.52)

```
s(rationality, 2)      s(justice, 3)
      0.18266282        -0.18044893
```

Similarly, access to the s_{ji} is possible by running a script line such as

$$\text{m5\$smooth[1,]} \tag{10.53}$$

to get the information for selected units, here for instance for the unit in the first row of the 371×4 smooth matrix (371 units and 4 entries per unit). Running script line (10.53) produces output (10.54):

```
s(age, 5)    s(responsibility, 3)    s(rationality, 2)
0.22807566              0.05188225           0.07894895
```

$$\tag{10.54}$$

```
s(justice, 3)
-0.21095274
```

In a similar way, we can now extract the empirical information from the R object that we would need to complete the prediction regarding this first respondent.

$$\text{m5\$model\$`s(age, 5)`[1]} \tag{10.55}$$

$$\text{m5\$model\$`s(responsibility, 3)`[1]} \tag{10.56}$$

$$\text{m5\$model\$`s(rationality, 2)`[1]} \tag{10.57}$$

$$\text{m5\$model\$`s(justice, 3)`[1]} \tag{10.58}$$

These script lines reveal that the respondent in the first row of the involved data frame has an age of 26, a responsibility score of 7, a rationality score of 4, and a justice score of 4. Together with these four observed x values, we now have all the information for the prediction equation.

	β_0	$\gamma_j x_{ji} + s_{ji}$	**Predictor**
$\eta_1 =$	0.1913	$-0.0216 \cdot 26 + 0.2281$	Age
		$+0.1506 \cdot 7 + 0.0519$	Responsibility
		$+0.1827 \cdot 4 + 0.0790$	Rationality
		$-0.1805 \cdot 4 - 0.2110$	Justice

$$\tag{10.59}$$

Rounded to 2 decimal places, the equation predicts $\eta_1 = 0.84$. Exactly the same result (identical to 6 decimal places) can be extracted from object *m5* via script line

$$\text{m5\$additive.predictors[1]} \tag{10.60}$$

Since we are carrying out a probit regression, this predicted value represents a quantile value z_α of the standard normal distribution function whose probability α is the associated quantile probability $\Phi(z_a) = Pr(Z \leq z_a) = \alpha$. Since the usual interest is in this probability, we can use the *pnorm()* function

$$pnorm(m5\$additive.predictors[1]) \tag{10.61}$$

respectively

$$m5\$fitted.values[1] \tag{10.62}$$

to get access to the predicted probability of being in state $y = 1$, given the individual configuration of predictor variables. For the respondent in row 1 of the involved data frame, this probability is $Pr(0.84) = 0.7996$.

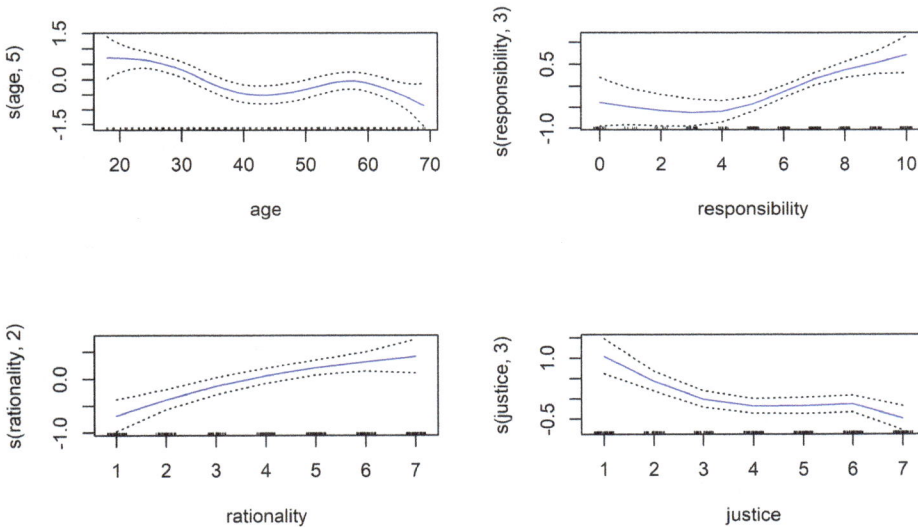

Figure 10.11: Curve Shapes of the Nonlinear Effects of Age, Responsibility, Rationality and Justice on the Additive Predictor.

In (10.49) we used as *family* specification *quasibinomial()* instead of *binomial()*. The difference is that the dispersion parameter is now not fixed to one. This is done to adjust the nominal binomial variance[12] for possible overdispersion that arise, for instance, from clustered data (McCullagh and Nelder 1989: 124–125). More generally, this is done

---

12 Another reason for using quasibinomial() instead of binomial() may be the use of the *weights* option in a *glm()* or *gam()* function call, since this weighting might lead to non-integer "successes". Then we obtain a warning message below the standard output. A comparison of the quasibinomial and binomial version of the model reveals identical results, except for the ANOVA for the nonparametric effects and

by equating the nominal variance "with some constant multiple of the formula given by the sampling model" (Agresti 1990: 42). For binary data, this means multiplying the nominal variance by a factor σ^2 (McCullagh and Nelder 1989: 125). This factor is estimated and as dispersion parameter reported in the output. However, as can be seen from Table 10.12, in the present example we are dealing with a case of *under*-dispersion.

An annotated version of the R script to this analysis is documented in Table 10.13.

What insights can be gained from such an analysis? If desired, predictions could even be unit-oriented. However, when analyzing survey data, as is the case here, the usual focus is more likely to be on determining the contributions of the individual predictors on the target. In the present example, this target is the probability that Bremen's schedule to achieve climate neutrality faster than Germany and the EU is considered right. Of interest are then the effects of the predictors on this probability. To assess these effects, four aspects deserve special attention:

- the general tendency of the effect as indicated by the sign of the linear effect component in (10.52)
- the statistical significance of this linear component as indicated by the ANOVA for Parametric Effects in Table 10.12
- the specific form of nonlinearity (curve shape) that becomes visible when the prediction target, i. e., the additive predictor η_i, is plotted against an involved predictor (Figure 10.11)
- the statistical significance of the nonlinear effect component as indicated by the ANOVA for Nonparametric Effects in Table 10.12

Also of interest is the overall model fit, as can be read off from the deviance values in Table 10.12, for instance by deriving McFadden's-R^2 from them. Here, this $R^2 = 0.344$. Compared to the goodness of fit of model (10.37) that involves only age as predictor (McFadden's $R^2 = 0.055$), the additional inclusion of responsibility, rationality and justice raises the predictive power of the model considerably, where each of these concepts is operationally defined as described above.

First, the linear effect component of age has a negative sign. This is shown in (10.52). Related to this effect component, the ANOVA for Parametric Effects in Table 10.12 indicates that this effect component is statistically significant. This is suggested by the F value and its probability given the null hypothesis that this effect component is zero. At the same time, the ANOVA for Nonparametric Effects indicate that the nonlinear effect component is statistically significant too.

A simple and convenient way to identify the specific form of nonlinearity of an effect is possible through a diagram that plots the additive predictor η_i against the predicting x_{ji} variable(s) used for the prediction. Because the present example uses four such x_{ji}

----

specifically the Chi^2 values calculated therein. All other results are identical including $coefficients, $smooth, $additive.predictors, $fitted.values, and the deviance values.

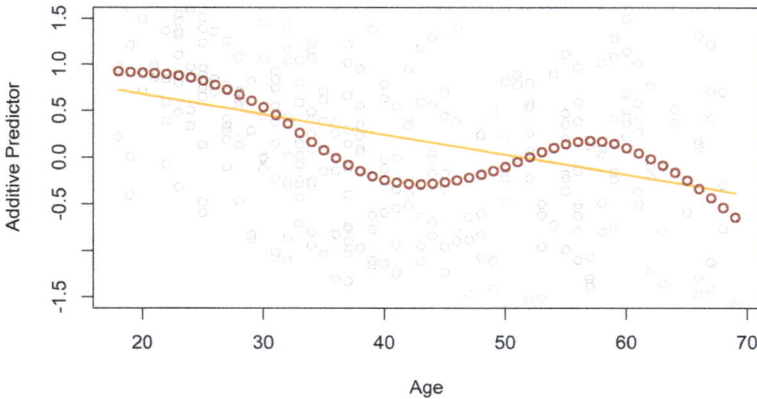

Figure 10.12: Nonlinear Shape of the Age Effect and Its Linear Component.

variables, we require one such plot for each of them. When using the *gam()* library, we get these four plots automatically by calling the *plot()* function subsequently to the *gam()* function. The link between *gam()* and *plot()* is done via the name of the object to which the *gam()* calculations were assigned, in this example *m5* according to (10.49). The diagrams reported in Figure 10.11 are obtained if we let the following two script lines follow the *gam()* function call (10.49) above.

$$\text{par(mfrow = c(2,2))} \tag{10.63}$$

$$\text{plot(m5, se=TRUE, col="blue")} \tag{10.64}$$

First, (10.63) defines the 2×2 structure of rows and columns required for the all in all four diagrams. Then (10.64) calls the plot function and specifies it in such a way that the confidence intervals are also displayed and the curves themselves are colored blue.

Returning to the effect of age, the upper left diagram in Figure 10.11 confirms the slightly *falling* trend captured by the negative sign of the linear effect component. It indicates a falling trend if the whole spectrum of age values is taken into account. Adding this linear trend line to the diagram makes the falling trend over the age spectrum more visible. In Figure 10.12 this is the orange line, while the dark-red line repeats the curve from the upper left diagram of Figure 10.11. The two graphs in Figure 10.12 are based on equation (10.50), once with s_{1i} included and once without this nonlinear effect component. At the same time the individual values for responsibility $(x_{2i} + s_{2i})$, rationality $(x_{3i} + s_{3i})$ and justice $(x_{4i} + s_{4i})$ are replaced with their respective mean values to hold them constant. We conclude from the evidence shown in Figure 10.12 that age has generally a negative effect on the target, however with varying slopes within different regions of the age spectrum. This target is the additive predictor and thus *implicitly* also the probability of considering Bremen's schedule to be right (as was shown above by

(10.60), (10.61) and (10.62) for a selected unit). In general, this probability is therefore higher among younger people than among older people, as the orange line shows. At the same time the dark-red curve describes the variation around this *general* trend. The curve starts with 18-year-olds. First we see an increasing *decline* in the target probability before this *nonlinear* trend is reversed in people in their early 40s. From then on, the probability increases again until the late 50s, after which it decreases again.

Age is the prototype of a predictor variable where nonlinear effects must always be taken into account. As a rule, their values cover a wide spectrum in finely graded manner, such as the spectrum of 18 to 70 year olds in 1-years-steps here. This variable therefore stands in some contrast to other scales commonly used in social research, such as those with 5, 7 or 11 scale points. Even if such scales are generally well-founded, they do not necessarily provide the space that would be required for non-linear effects to unfold. On the one hand, because they contain too few scale points or gradations, and on the other hand, because the range of answers asked for is too narrow.

But even if the age variable is almost predestined to reveal nonlinearities, it is not necessarily trivial to recognize their substantive significance. This also applies to the present data example, since here, as in general, the reasons behind the age effect curve can be quite varied. This is due to the fact that age can be seen as a variable that implicitly reflects the influence of many other variables (Rosenberg 1968). Thus, without further information, we can only speculate as to what might explain the specific curve shape from a sociological perspective. But it is at least likely that there is a typical biographical pattern involved behind this: first, an occupational career must be built in order to achieve the prosperity and social security that one desires for oneself and possibly one's family. Many will have achieved these goals by their early 40s and will thus have gained the material basis to personally focus on higher goals, for example in the context of climate protection.

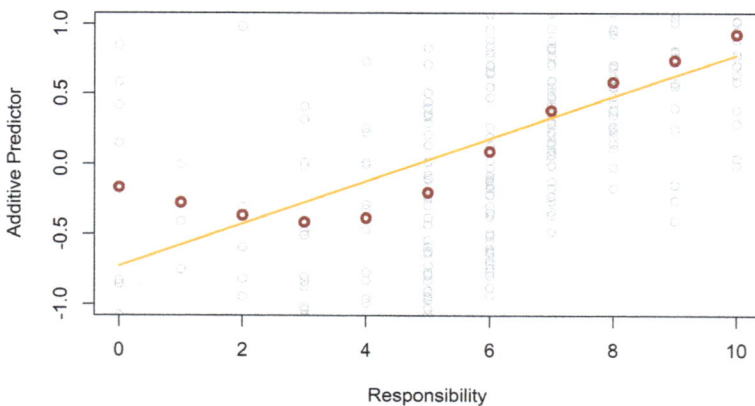

Figure 10.13: Nonlinear Shape of the Responsibility Effect and Its Linear Component.

Contrary to age, felt climate responsibility goes hand in hand with a slightly *rising* trend captured by the positive sign of the linear effect component. We briefly illustrate this case too. The two graphs in Figure 10.13 are based on equation (10.50) too, once with s_{2i} included and once without this nonlinear effect component. At the same time the individual values for age ($x_{1i} + s_{1i}$), rationality ($x_{3i} + s_{3i}$) and justice ($x_{4i} + s_{4i}$) are replaced with their respective mean values to hold them constant. We therefore proceed analogously to what we just described for the predictor *age*, keeping the other predictors constant.

We conclude from Figure 10.13 an effect pattern of felt climate responsibility that confirms the expected "the stronger this responsibility, the more likely Bremen's schedule is considered right" only for responsibility scores greater than 3. In contrast, this situation is reversed in the scale range from 0 to 3 below. From the two ANOVAs in Table 10.12 it can be seen that both effect components are statistically significant.

In a similar way, the influence of the two predictors *rationality* and *intergenerational justice* can now be examined. Figure 10.11 shows a positive trend for rationality and a negative trend for justice, provided that the two concepts are operationally defined as described above in the text. It should perhaps be emphasized that only the nonlinear component of the rationality effect turns out to be statistically insignificant.

Table 10.12: Output to the GAM Model.

Line	R Output
1	Call: gam(formula = y ~ s(age, 5) + s(responsibility, 3) +
2	s(rationality, 2) + s(justice, 3),
3	family = quasibinomial(link = probit),
4	data = kpo, weights = wg)
5	Deviance Residuals:
6	Min 1Q Median 3Q Max
7	-2.6017 -0.6777 0.2173 0.7387 2.2084
8	
9	(Dispersion Parameter for quasibinomial family taken to be 0.8377)
10	
11	Null Deviance: 511.2982 on 370 degrees of freedom
12	Residual Deviance: 335.1894 on 356.9999 degrees of freedom
13	AIC: NA
14	
15	Number of Local Scoring Iterations: NA
16	
17	Anova for Parametric Effects
18	Df Sum Sq Mean Sq F value Pr(>F)
19	s(age, 5) 1 9.196 9.196 10.978 0.001016 **
20	s(responsibility, 3) 1 41.330 41.330 49.337 1.096e-11 ***
21	s(rationality, 2) 1 21.170 21.170 25.271 7.898e-07 ***
22	s(justice, 3) 1 17.434 17.434 20.811 6.979e-06 ***

Table 10.12 (continued)

Line	R Output
23	Residuals 357 299.066 0.838
24	---
25	Signif. codes: 0 '***' 0.001 '**' 0.01 '*' 0.05 '.' 0.1 ' ' 1
26	
27	Anova for Nonparametric Effects
28	Npar Df Npar F Pr(F)
29	(Intercept)
30	s(age, 5) 4 5.0495 0.0005716 ***
31	s(responsibility, 3) 2 5.7545 0.0034698 **
32	s(rationality, 2) 1 2.3206 0.1285563
33	s(justice, 3) 2 8.1122 0.0003587 ***
34	---
35	Signif. codes: 0 '***' 0.001 '**' 0.01 '*' 0.05 '.' 0.1 ' ' 1

Lines explained

Lines 1 to 4 reprint the function call. Lines 5 to 7: Summary statistics of deviance residuals. Line 9 to 12: Model fit information: dispersion parameter and deviance values. Lines 17 to 25 report the details of a first analysis of variance. It refers to the linear effect components and reports five pieces of information: degrees of freedom, sum of squares, mean square, F value and associated probability. Lines 27 to 35 report the outcome of a second analysis of variance, in fact regarding the nonlinear effect component. Similarly, degrees of freedom, F value and associated probability are reported. The F tests may be used to assess the statistical significance of the various effect components.

Table 10.13: R Script to the Generalized Additive Model Example.

Line	R Script
1	load("klimapolitik1.Rdata")
2	kpo <- subset(kpo, select=c(y,age, responsibility,
3	rationality, justice, wg))
4	kpo <- kpo[complete.cases(kpoy, kpoage,
5	kpo$responsibility, kpo$rationality,
6	kpo$justice, kpo$wg),]
7	library(gam)
8	summary(m5 <- gam(formula = y ~ s(age, 5) +
9	s(responsibility, 3) +
10	s(rationality, 2) + s(justice, 3),
11	family=quasibinomial(link=probit),
12	weights=wg, data = kpo))
13	tiff("fig1011.tiff", units="in", width=7,
14	height = 4.5, res=600)
15	par(mfrow = c(2,2))
16	plot(m5, se=TRUE, col="blue")

Table 10.13 (continued)

Line	R Script
17	dev.off()
18	m5$coefficients
19	m5$smooth[1,]
20	m5$model$`s(age, 5)`[1]
21	m5$model$`s(responsibility, 3)`[1]
22	m5$model$`s(rationality, 2)`[1]
23	m5$model$`s(justice, 3)`[1]
24	eta1 <- 0.19126760 -
25	0.02163211*26 + 0.22807566 + # age
26	0.15062687*7 + 0.05188225 + # responsibility
27	0.18266282*4 + 0.07894895 - # rationality
28	0.18044893*4 - 0.21095274 # justice # 0.8400305
29	m5$additive.predictors[1] # 0.8400304
30	pnorm(m5$additive.predictors[1]) # 0.7995543
31	m5$fitted.values[1] # 0.7995543

Lines explained

Line 1 loads the data frame. Lines 2 and 3 use the *select* option of the *subset()* function to confine the data frame to the variables to be used in the analysis. Lines 4 to 6 reduce the data frame to the units with valid values in all analysis variables by use of the *complete.cases()* function in the square brackets. Line 7 invokes the library *gam*. Lines 8 to 12 specify the *gam()* function call, assign its output to object *m5* and embed all this in the *summary ()* function. Lines 13 to 17 refer to the associated outcome plot as shown in Figure 10.11. The specification includes the format (*tiff*), name (*fig1011.tiff*), unit (*inch*), size in terms of *width* and *height*, and the *resolution*. Line 15 defines the 2×2 structure for the four diagrams in Figure 10.11. Line 16 invokes the *plot ()* function that generates these four diagrams, one for each predictor. Line 17 shuts down the graphics device previously opened with the *tiff()* line. Line 18 provides the outcome for the parametric model part, i. e., the linear effect components. Then, lines 19 to 23 and 29 to 31 refer to entries that vary from unit to unit. Here the unit in the first row of the involved data frame is used as an example, as indicated by the number in the square brackets. This information is required, for instance, to see how the additive predictor for this first unit is obtained. This is shown in lines 24 to 28, again for the 1st unit. R interprets text that follows the # symbol as a comment.

Chapter 11
Classification

11.1 Predicting Class Membership by Logistic Regression

Section 8.7.1 introduced logistic and probit regression and exemplified their use for predicting the probability of being in state 1 of a binary, 0/1 coded response variable. This prediction can be used as the final result, but it can also be used in a further step to predict class membership. Here we would like to illustrate this additional step using the example of the logistic model introduced in section 8.7.1.

Using data from Example Data Set 1, the PPSM Innovation Panel, we asked the respondents this question: "Just think about how things are going for you right now. What would you say? Are you currently happy or unhappy?" We coded this variable $y = 1$ for happy and $y = 0$ for unhappy and used as predictor variable x the respondents' current standard of living on an eleven-point scale. The analysis is based on data from n = 3,949 respondents. As detailed in section 8.7.1, function call (8.27) was used to estimate the probability of being happy as a function of one's standard of living

$$Pr(y = 1|x) = \frac{1}{1 + e^{-(b_0 + b_1 x)}} \tag{11.1}$$

We obtained the estimates $b_0 = -1.2236$ and $b_1 = 0.4195$ (Table 8.14) and graphed the outcome in Figure 8.8. We will continue this example to show how this regression can be used for classification. We distinguish between two classes and try to predict, based on the standard of living, whether a respondent belongs to the class of happy or unhappy people. Such a step implies a quite relevant methodological intervention: namely, the determination of the value that divides the scale of predicted probability values into the two classes. Even if a decomposition into $p \leq 0.5$ (unhappy class, coded 0) and $p > 0.5$ (happy class, coded 1) seems reasonable for this specific purpose, the setting of such cuts remains in general an intervention that must be carefully considered, as it can affect the result of an analysis. Using this decomposition, we obtain a cross-tabulation of predicted versus observed frequencies, commonly referred to as a confusion matrix. The R script in Table 11.2 shows the steps required to get this table, here referenced as (11.2).

```
        predicted
observed   0     1    Sum
     0    47   676    723
     1    28  3198   3226
   Sum    75  3874   3949
```
(11.2)

When proceeding in this way, it may be advantageous to be able to determine the classification quality using such a so-called confusion matrix and related statistical

https://doi.org/10.1515/9783110680683-011

concepts. Table 11.1 displays the general structure of this table and introduces the notation used to identify the cell frequencies in the related formulae. These formulae define different evaluation metrics, including among others accuracy, precision and recall (Ghani and Schierholz 2017: 177–178; Lantz 2019: 320 – 331).

Accuracy indicates the ratio of correct predictions to all predictions. Accordingly, the sum of the cell frequencies in the main diagonal of the confusion matrix is divided by the sum of all cell frequencies.

$$Accuracy = \frac{TP + TN}{TP + TN + FP + FN} \tag{11.3}$$

In the present example, this yields an accuracy of 0.8217. Accordingly, 82.2 percent of the predictions are correct. We can refine this accuracy metric by relating this observed accuracy to the accuracy expected by chance. This may be done using Cohen's κ coefficient of agreement. Kappa

$$\kappa = \frac{p_o - p_e}{1 - p_e} \tag{11.4}$$

is the probability of observed matches, p_o, minus the probability of matches expected by chance, p_e, divided by one minus the probability of expected matches. κ is built such that it expresses the excess of observed over expected agreement as share of the maximal possible excess. This scope for excess is $1 - p_e$, since p_o becomes 1 with perfect observed agreement[1].

Table 11.1: Structure of Confusion Matrix.

		Predicted Class	
		0	1
True Class	0	TN True Negatives	FP False Positives
	1	FN False Negatives	TP True Positives

Typically, you will use functions from relevant R libraries to calculate κ, for example *cohen.kappa()* from *library(psych)*. Then it would not be necessary to calculate the expected frequencies yourself. However, if you still want to do this, the *CrossTable()* function from library(gmodels) provides a simple solution. Alternatively, you can of course carry out the calculations yourself. The probability of expected matches may

---

1 Then all units lie on the main diagonal of the confusion matrix. In the case of perfect observed agreement κ also becomes 1, because (11.4) is then $\kappa = (1 - p_e)/(1 - p_e)$.

then be computed by multiplying for each cell on the main diagonal of the confusion matrix the observed row and column probabilities at whose intersection the cell lies, and then summing up these figures. With the observed marginal frequences from (11.2) taken as calculation basis, we obtain

$$p_e = \left(\frac{723}{3949} \cdot \frac{75}{3949}\right) + \left(\frac{3226}{3949} \cdot \frac{3874}{3949}\right) = 0.8049 \tag{11.5}$$

Accordingly,

$$\kappa = \frac{0.8217 - 0.8049}{1 - 0.8049} = 0.0861 \tag{11.6}$$

This value indicates that the observed agreement of observed and predicted class membership exceeds the expected agreement by 8.6% of the maximum possible excess.

Two further metrics refer to the true *positives* only. One of these two metrics is called *precision*. It relates the number of correct positive predictions to all positive predictions

$$Precision = \frac{TP}{TP + FP} \tag{11.7}$$

and thus answers the question: If the prediction is positive, how often is it correct? Precision is also called positive predictive value. In the present example, the precision is 0.8255 which means that 82.6 percent of the positive predictions are correct.

Table 11.2: Script to the Confusion Matrix Example.

Line	R Script
1	`load("Happy.RData")`
2	`summary(LC <- glm(q15r ~ LS11,`
3	`                family=binomial(link = "logit"),`
4	`                data = happy))`
5	`observed <- LC$model$q15r`
6	`predicted <- rep(0, 3949)`
7	`predicted[LC$fitted.values > .5] = 1`
8	`addmargins(table(observed, predicted ))`
9	`cm <- as.matrix(table(observed, predicted ))`
10	`print(accuracy <- (cm[2,2] + cm[1,1])/(cm[2,2]`
11	`                + cm[1,1] + cm[1,2] + cm[2,1]))`
12	`print(precision <- cm[2,2]/(cm[2,2] + cm[1,2]))`
13	`print(recall <- cm[2,2]/(cm[2,2] + cm[2,1]))`
14	`print(pe <-`
15	`    (((((cm[1,1] + cm[1,2]) * (cm[1,1] + cm[2,1])) +`

Table 11.2 (continued)

Line	R Script
16	`((cm[2,2] + cm[2,1]) * (cm[2,2] + cm[1,2]))) /`
17	`(cm[1,1] + cm[1,2] + cm[2,1] + cm[2,2]))/`
18	`(cm[1,1] + cm[1,2] + cm[2,1] + cm[2,2]))`
19	`library(gmodels)`
20	`CrossTable(cm, expected = TRUE)`
21	`library(psych)`
22	`cohen.kappa(cm)`

Lines explained

Line 1 loads the data frame. Lines 2 to 4 call the *glm()* function to specify the logistic model already explained in section 8.7.1. Line 5 assigns the observed values of the target variable to the object named *observed*. We also extract this empirical information from object *LC* to ensure that we only include those units for which we also have predicted values available (control of missing values). These predicted values too are extracted from object *LC*. To do this, line 6 generates a vector of 3949 zeros to change these zeros – via line 7 – to ones, provided the condition in square brackets is met, i. e. the predicted values are greater than 0.5. Line 8 embeds *table()* in the *addmargins()* function to get the crosstabulation of observed and predicted values. Line 9 defines this table as matrix and assigns it to the object named *cm*. This is done to be able to address the cells of this matrix in the subsequent script lines 10 to 18. This is done by adding the relevant [row, column] index in square brackets. The calculations are assigned to object names that indicate the respective metric. We embed these calculations in *print()* to get the result printed. Lines 19 and 20 provide an alternative way to the expected frequencies *pe* in lines 14 to 18, in fact by the cross-table function from *library(gmodels)*. Finally, lines 21 and 22 provide an easy way to get Cohen's kappa through a function from *library(psych)*.

The second of the two metrics is called *recall*. It relates the number of correct positive predictions not to all positive predictions but to all positive units in the data

$$Recall = \frac{TP}{TP + FN} \tag{11.8}$$

This metric is also called sensitivity or true positive rate and indicates the ability of the classifier to find positive cases. Here, recall is 0.9913 which means that the classification detects 99.1 percent of the positive units, i. e., happy persons, in the data.

11.2 Contingency Tables of Weighted Units of Analysis

A classification that is based on logistic regression contains a probabilistic component, namely that it is based on the conditional probability of being in the target state of interest, given a configuration of predictor variables, $Pr(y = 1|x)$. In this sense, this is a *probabilistic* classification.

The same applies if the predictors too are categorical variables, so that the conditional probability is calculated on the basis of an appropriately built contingency table. In R, for example, the *ftable()* function would provide this structure.

However, such classifications also contain a *non*-probabilistic element in that membership in the target class are based purely on self-assignment by the respondents. In the example of the previous section, this concerned the decision of respondents for counting themselves to the categories of happy or unhappy persons. This can also be described as self-assignment to a formal class with a probability of one or zero, depending on which underlying response category of the *y* variable was chosen.

However, we arrive at a more comprehensive probabilistic classification if class membership itself is understood as an *unobserved* membership that can be inferred from *manifest* responses to appropriate survey items. This is then referred to as *latent* class membership.

We will introduce the method for estimating such memberships, the so-called Latent Class Analysis (LCA), in section 11.4 below. Beforehand we will describe a technique of creating the *ftable()* structure as well as a technique of creating the empirical input for an LCA, with each method *based on weighted units*.

11.2.1 Example Data

For this purpose we will rely on data from Example Data Set 5 on Future Perspectives of Energy Transition. The variables are taken from a larger list of survey items. This item list was introduced as follows:

> Transportation transition means: away from coal, natural gas and oil – towards renewable "green" energy. In addition to climate protection, the dependence on Russian natural gas is currently a major topic of discussion. However, electric motors, batteries, solar modules and wind turbines also require raw materials, the mining and processing of which is concentrated in only a few countries and is often accompanied by significant environmental impacts, impairments to the quality of life and human rights violations of the local population. How should Germany's energy transition take this into account? Multiple answers possible.

This opening text was followed by ten statements from which respondents could select their answers. The three statements taken into account in this analysis come from this list. The target variable *y* is based on this item wording: "Mine/process required raw materials only in Europe as quickly as possible". This variable is named *raw materials* in the data frame. Here it is coded 1 if a respondent ticked this box and 0 otherwise.

Two further items are taken as predictor variables:

First, an item named *nature conservation* in the data frame. It is worded as follows: "Pay attention to nature conservation *in your own country too*" (coded 1 if a respondent ticked this box, 0 otherwise).

Second, an item named *save energy* in the data frame: "Significantly reduce Germany's energy needs" (coded 1 if a respondent ticked this box, 0 otherwise).

In addition *gender* is considered coded 1 if female and 0 if male.

11.2.2 Weighting the Units of Analysis for *ftable()* Structures and LCA Input

First[2], the *svydesign()* function from *library(survey)* is used for being able to include individual weights in the subsequent statistical calculations. Such survey weights are calculated once after the field phase of a survey and stored as a variable in the data frame. In the present data frame this variable is named *wg*.

```
library(survey)
design <- survey::svydesign(id = ~1,                                 (11.9)
          weights=~wg, data = ksr)
```

Next, the contingency table is built by the *svytable()* function. This function builds a table with weighted frequencies in the same structure as *table()* does with unweighted frequencies. In the present example, this means that for each value of the third variable specified in the *svytable()* call, a table is calculated for the first two of these three variables. In the present example, we therefore get two tables with the bivariate frequency distribution of raw materials against nature conservation, in fact one for males (female = 0) and another one for females (female = 1). The difference between *table()* and *svytable()* is therefore only that the cells of the contingency tables contain unweighted frequencies on the one hand and weighted frequencies on the other.

```
frq <- survey::svytable(~rawmaterials+
          natureconservation+female, design)                        (11.10)
```

Such a table structure is not very compact and can quickly become confusing if the cross-tabulation is made up of more than three variables or if variables have more than two values rather than just two. It then makes sense to make the crosstabulation more compact by defining it as a data frame. Since weighted frequencies generally have decimal places, it also seems sensible to round them to zero decimal places for further analysis steps.

---

2 The successive script lines described in this subsection and the beginning of section 11.3 form together the corresponding R script in the order presented. In parallel, the largely identical R script for a larger data example, not split up, can be found further down in Table 11.6.

```
tabinput <- as.data.frame(frq)
tabinput$Freq <- round(tabinput$Freq, 0)
```
(11.11)

In the present example this new data frame is named *tabinput,* a freely chosen name. The definition as data frame generates a structure that combines the design matrix of all involved value configurations with a variable denoted as *Freq* (11.12). This variable indicates how often each configuration occurs. In the present example, we have $2 \cdot 2 \cdot 2 = 8$ such configurations, of which, for example, the first has occurred 95 times, the second 12 times, and so on. By the script line *print(tabinput)* we obtain the following output in the R console.

	rawmaterials	natureconservation	female	Freq
1	0	0	0	95
2	1	0	0	12
3	0	1	0	46
4	1	1	0	15
5	0	0	1	68
6	1	0	1	16
7	0	1	1	45
8	1	1	1	33

(11.12)

We make use of this structure for the next step by creating another new data frame in which each occurring configuration gets an own row. For example, the first row in (11.12) is copied so often that the new data frame contains 95 rows with this specific value configuration. Following the same logic, the subsequent rows are replicated, each with the value of *Freq* serving as a multiplier. With this step, we are simply converting an *aggregated* data set back into an *individual-level* data set, in which each row represents one respondent. This time, however, in a composition according to the *weighted* frequency of each configuration.

```
library(hutils)
weightedinput <- weight2rows(tabinput, "Freq")
```
(11.13)

This is done via the *weight2rows()* function from *library(hutils)*. The result is a data table respectively data frame that consists of the same four columns (variables) as (11.12) but now with 330 rows, each representing one unit of analysis (respondent). We assign this data to the freely chosen object name *weightedinput*. By the script line *print(weightedinput)* we get an extract from this data table printed in the R console. In particular, the first and last five cases are shown, here reprinted as (11.14).

	rawmaterials	natureconservation	female	Freq
1:	0	0	0	1
2:	0	0	0	1
3:	0	0	0	1
4:	0	0	0	1
5:	0	0	0	1

326:	1	1	1	1
327:	1	1	1	1
328:	1	1	1	1
329:	1	1	1	1
330:	1	1	1	1

$$(11.14)$$

We describe this specific data management for two completely unrelated purposes: on the one hand to demonstrate how to prepare an *ftable()* structure for weighted units of analysis. On the other hand, the same data management can be used to prepare the empirical input for a *latent* classification (as exemplified in section 11.4.)

In the remainder of this sub-section the *ftable()* function is used to continue the present data example. The procedure is basically the same as in the standard case: we call this function and specify therein the variables to be tabulated. The only difference is that when specifying these variables we refer to the data frame that has been created in the last step (i. e., the frame named *weightedinput*) and not to the initial, unweighted one.

```
print(CT <- ftable(weightedinput$female,
            weightedinput$natureconservation,
            weightedinput$rawmaterials, ⌐            (11.15)
            dnn=c("female", "nature.conservation",
                "raw.materials")))
```

This is realizable through the usual $ sign used in R to connect a variable with the data frame in which it resides. We assign the table built in this way to the object named *CT* (a freely chosen name for indicating contingency table) and embed all this in *print()* to get the result. This produces the output referenced as (11.16).

		raw.materials	0	1
female	nature.conservation			
0	0		95	12
	1		46	15
1	0		68	16
	1		45	33

$$(11.16)$$

The structure becomes clear if this table is compared to the structure of (11.12). The *frequencies* of two consecutive table rows are arranged next to each other. This is a useful rearrangement when the resulting column variable (with its values 0 and 1) is to be treated as a target variable whose variation as a function of the remaining variables is to be studied. In this example, there are two such variables with two values each, resulting in four value combinations. Consequently, the rearranged table has four rows.

When reorganizing the table, it is important to note the order in which the variables are to be addressed in the function call[3]. While (11.12) is based on the order in (11.10), (11.16) is based on the *reverse* order in (11.15). The *dnn = c()* option generates the labeling of the table by including the variable names and not just their values in the table.

11.3 Predicting Class Membership by WLS Models for Contingency Tables

An *ftable()* structure can be used to estimate how the belonging to, for example, sociological categories affect the probability of being in state 1 or 0 of a categorical target variable. To do this, we can restrict ourselves to one of these two states and, for example, calculate the proportion of respondents who are in state 1 of the dichotomous target variable.

For the present data example, the three script lines in (11.17) would make this possible. In the first line *CT* is defined as a matrix to preserve the labeling of the configurations. In the second line row marginals are created by summing the entries in column 1 *[, 1]* and column 2 *[, 2]* of *CT* row-wise, then these sums are assigned to *n*. In the third line the entries in column 2 are divided by *n*, the resulting proportion *prop* is rounded, here to four decimal places, and then assigned to *Pr1*.

```
CT <- as.matrix(CT)
n <- CT [, 1] + CT [, 2]                                    (11.17)
Pr1 <- round(prop <- (CT [,2])/n, 4)
```

Depending on your choice, these calculations can then complement the underlying table (11.16) or be treated separately. This simply depends on which columns are combined when using the *cbind()* function.

```
print(comtable <- cbind(CT, Pr1, n))                        (11.18)
```

---

3 Controlling the table structure via the order in which the variables are named is certainly the easiest way. However, *ftable()* also includes the options *row.vars* and *col.vars* to steer this structure.

When using (11.18), *Pr1* and *n* are added to the table, resulting in (11.19)

```
      0    1     Pr1      n
0_0  95   12   0.1121   107
0_1  46   15   0.2459    61
1_0  68   16   0.1905    84
1_1  45   33   0.4231    78
```

(11.19)

When using (11.20), for instance,

```
print(septable <- cbind(Pr1, n))
```

(11.20)

we only get (11.21) for a study of how *Pr1* varies across the four configurations.

```
      Pr1     n
0_0  0.1121  107
0_1  0.2459   61
1_0  0.1905   84
1_1  0.4231   78
```

(11.21)

In small tables such as (11.21) this variation can be described well without further calculations. But even here it is already advantageous to apply the principle of controlling for third variables in contingency table analysis. If we denote nature conservation by x_1, female by x_2, *Pr1* as p_g, and the row marginals as n_g, a notation taken from Coleman's (1964) attribute data analysis may be used to exemplify this principle (Table 11.3).

Table 11.3: Data Structure and Design Matrix for the Initial $2 \cdot 2 \cdot 2$ Contingency Table.

Group	x_2	x_1	x_0	p_g	n_g
$g = 1$	0	0	1	$p.$	$n.$
$g = 2$	0	1	1	p_1	n_1
$g = 3$	1	0	1	p_2	n_2
$g = 4$	1	1	1	p_{12}	n_{12}

x_0 Intercept term; x_1 Nature conservation;
x_2 Female

First we calculate the effect of x_1 on p_g *for equal values of* x_2,

$$a_1 = \frac{1}{2} \left(p_{12} - p_2 + p_1 - p. \right)$$

(11.22)

then we calculate the effect of x_2 on p_g *for equal values of* x_1

$$a_2 = \frac{1}{2} \ (p_{12} - p_1 + p_2 - p_.)$$ (11.23)

where such an *effect* is algebraically derivable as the mean difference between the proportions related to each other in this way. We proceed according to exactly the same logic in larger tables. For example, if we extend the analysis to additionally include the variable *save energy* (R script below in Table 11.6), we obtain the frequency distribution and the *Pr1* values in (11.24)

```
        0    1    Pr1      n
0_0_0  73    9  0.1098   82
0_0_1  24    4  0.1429   28
0_1_0  22    3  0.1200   25
0_1_1  22   11  0.3333   33
1_0_0  55   14  0.2029   69
1_0_1  26   20  0.4348   46
1_1_0  13    2  0.1333   15
1_1_1  19   14  0.4242   33
```
(11.24)

Now *three* dichotomous predictors are involved to predict the target *raw materials*, resulting in $2 \cdot 2 \cdot 2 = 8$ configurations (table rows). Using the notation in Table 11.4, the first of the three main effects involved is derivable as the *mean difference*

$$a_1 = \frac{1}{4} (p_{123} - p_{23} + p_{12} - p_2 + p_{13} - p_3 + p_1 - p_.)$$ (11.25)

in p_g between the two groups $x_1 = 1$ (respondent is member of this group) and $x_1 = 0$ (respondent is not member of this group) *for equal configurations of* x_2 and x_3. These are the four $x_2 \cdot x_3$ configurations 1 1, 1 0, 0 1 and 0 0. We therefore systematically vary the possible source of variation x_1, while at the same time holding the other two possible sources of variation x_2 and x_3 constant. Following the same logic, the main effect of x_2 is the mean difference

$$a_2 = \frac{1}{4} (p_{123} - p_{13} + p_{12} - p_1 + p_{23} - p_3 + p_2 - p_.)$$ (11.26)

in p_g between the two groups $x_2 = 1$ (respondent is member of this group) and $x_2 = 0$ (respondent is not member of this group) *for equal configurations of* x_1 and x_3. These are the four $x_1 \cdot x_3$ configurations 1 1, 1 0, 0 1 and 0 0. And finally the main effect of x_3 can be derived as mean difference

$$a_3 = \frac{1}{4}(p_{123} - p_{12} + p_{13} - p_1 + p_{23} - p_2 + p_3 - p.) \tag{11.27}$$

in p_g between the two groups $x_3 = 1$ (respondent is member of this group) and $x_3 = 0$ (respondent is not member of this group) *for equal configurations of* x_1 and x_2. These are the four $x_1 \cdot x_2$ configurations 1 1, 1 0, 0 1 and 0 0.

Table 11.4: Data Structure and Design Matrix for the Initial $2 \cdot 2 \cdot 2 \cdot 2$ Contingency Table.

Group	x_3	x_2	x_1	x_0	p_g	n_g
g = 1	0	0	0	1	$p.$	$n.$
g = 2	0	0	1	1	p_1	n_1
g = 3	0	1	0	1	p_2	n_2
g = 4	0	1	1	1	p_{12}	n_{12}
g = 5	1	0	0	1	p_3	n_3
g = 6	1	0	1	1	p_{13}	n_{13}
g = 7	1	1	0	1	p_{23}	n_{23}
g = 8	1	1	1	1	p_{123}	n_{123}

x_0 Intercept term; x_1 Nature conservation;
x_2 Save energy; x_3 Female

The principle of systematically varying only one condition at a time while keeping the other conditions constant also applies when the number of predictors is increased to *four* or more than four. Only the number of conditions respectively predictor configurations that have to be kept constant increases accordingly. For example, in the above case with three predictors we had to keep the two-digit configurations 11 10 01 00 constant, with four predictors these would be the eight three-digit configurations 1 1 1, 0 1 1, 1 0 1, 0 0 1, 1 1 0, 0 1 0, 1 0 0, 0 0 0, and so on.

This approach follows a common idea in contingency table analysis. If only two proportions were to be related to each other, it would not be unusual to calculate the *difference between them* in order to interpret this difference as an expression of an effect of the dichotomous variable for whose values the proportions were calculated. This idea is generalized here by calculating such differences *for comparable pairs of proportions,* in order to take their *mean* difference as an effect measure.

However, the mean difference in proportions can also be derived algebraically as an effect measure. For this we need a data structure and design matrix such as the ones exemplified in Tables 11.3 and 11.4 as well as an algorithm to reduce over-identification when there are fewer unknowns to be estimated in a system of equations than there are pieces of empirical information available. For the model in Table 11.3, for example, this would be three unknowns (a_0, a_1, a_2) in four observed n_g from the equations that result if the model is written out for each of the aggregated cases ($g = 1, 2, 3, 4$), while the Least Squares estimator may be used as algorithm. In its basic form this is Ordinary Least Squares (OLS),

$$Q = \sum_{g=1}^{4} (p_g - \hat{p}_g)^2 = min \tag{11.28}$$

here applied to minimize the sum of squared differences between observed and estimated proportions. If we replace, in (11.28), each estimated $\hat{p}_g$ by its right-hand side of the equation that replaces each "one" in the design matrix, i. e., each condition for an effect, by this very effect,

$$
\begin{aligned}
\hat{p}_. &= a_0 \\
\hat{p}_1 &= a_0 + a_1 \\
\hat{p}_2 &= a_0 \qquad\quad + a_2 \\
\hat{p}_{12} &= a_0 + a_1 + a_2
\end{aligned}
\tag{11.29}
$$

then Q becomes

$$Q = (p_. - a_0)^2 + (p_1 - a_0 - a_1)^2 + (p_2 - a_0 - a_2)^2 + (p_{12} - a_0 - a_1 - a_2)^2 \tag{11.30}$$

In the present example, the four brackets in (11.30) would have to be squared, the first partial derivatives of the resulting algebraic expression of Q with respect to a_0, a_1 and a_2 would have to be set equal to zero and the resulting system of equations would have to be solved. The result of this calculation would then be exactly the a_1 and a_2 expressions shown in (11.22) and (11.23) along with an expression for the intercept a_0

$$a_0 = \frac{1}{4} (-p_{12} + p_2 + p_1 + 3p_.) \tag{11.31}$$

With the observed *Pr1* values from (11.21), we get the three estimates of effect $a_0 = 0.0874$, $a_1 = 0.1832$ and $a_2 = 0.1278$ as functions of the *observed p_g* values.

However, we obtain exactly the same estimates of effect if we avoid the detour via the algebraic calculations and instead calculate an OLS regression directly with the observed *Pr1* values from (11.21) and the design matrix from Table 11.3 (R script below Table 11.5). In practice, data analysis will therefore usually be carried out directly by a regression analysis of this kind. Nevertheless the mathematical equivalence offers us a second route of *interpreting* such estimates of effect. Commonly a regression slope is interpreted as *expected change* in *y* for a unit change in *x* (as detailed in chapter 6). This interpretation is also applicable here. However, a slope can also be interpreted as *mean difference* in observed proportions, percentages or mean values. This opens up another option for interpreting *ordinary* least squares estimates of effect.

The mathematical equivalence can also be achieved with *weighted* least squares estimates if for each effect component (difference in two proportions) the sampling variance is additionally taken into account. For each x_k variable such a WLS estimate of effect may be calculated as

$$a'_k = \frac{1}{\sum_j w_j} \times \sum_j w_j \cdot d_j \qquad (11.32)$$

where the summation runs over the effect components j of the underlying OLS effect. In (11.22), for instance, j runs from 1 to 2, since this effect consists of two components, namely the differences $d_1 = (p_{12} - p_2)$ and $d_2 = (p_1 - p_.)$. We weight (i.e., multiply) each difference by the inverse of its estimated sampling variance,
   for instance d_1 by w_1,

$$w_1 = \frac{1}{\hat{\sigma}^2(p_{12}) + \hat{\sigma}^2(p_2)} \qquad (11.33)$$

do the same for d_2,

$$w_2 = \frac{1}{\hat{\sigma}^2(p_1) + \hat{\sigma}^2(p_.)} \qquad (11.34)$$

take the sum of both products and divide this sum by the sum of the two weights. We would then proceed analogously with the second effect (11.23). Since the sampling variance of a proportion is

$$\hat{\sigma}^2_{p_g} = p_g \times (1 - p_g)/n_g \qquad (11.35)$$

this approach also takes into account that the p_g are based on different group sizes n_g. The four aggregated units in the present example are therefore not included in the calculation with a standard weight (factor) of 1, but rather with a weight that is largely determined by group size. Consequently, the larger the group for which a proportion is calculated, the greater the weight it receives in the calculations. This allows the interpretation of a regression slope to be refined as an average difference in accordingly weighted proportions.

Here too, we obtain exactly the same estimates of effect if we avoid the detour via the algebraic calculations and instead calculate a WLS regression directly with the observed *Pr1* values from (11.21) and the design matrix from Table 11.3 (R script below Table 11.5). The model contains an x_0 (intercept) and the two variables x_1 (nature conservation) and x_2 (female). With the observed *Pr1* values from (11.21), the associated WLS estimates of effect are $a'_0 = 0.1018$, $a'_1 = 0.1777$ and $a'_2 = 0.1090$.

The larger of the two models of this section contains one more x_k variable. There we have an x_0 (intercept), x_1 (nature conservation), x_2 (save energy) and x_3 (female) along with their associated WLS estimates of effect $a'_0 = 0.0914$, $a'_1 = 0.1595$, $a'_2 = 0.0253$ and $a'_3 = 0.1185$.

Table 11.5: Script to the OLS and WLS Estimates of Effect.

Line	R Script
1	y <- c(0.1121, 0.2459, 0.1905, 0.4231); matrix(y,nrow=4, ncol=1)
2	x0 <- c(1,1,1,1)
3	x1 <- c(0,1,0,1)
4	x2 <- c(0,0,1,1)
5	x <- cbind(x2,x1,x0)
6	xtx <- (t(x)%*%x)
7	ix <- solve(xtx)
8	print(b <- ix%*%t(x)%*%y)
9	m <- c(107, 61, 84, 78); matrix(m,nrow=4, ncol=1)
10	v <- diag(u <- (y*(1-y)/m))
11	iv <- solve(v)
12	ivx <- solve(t(x)%*%iv%*%x)
13	print(bw <- ivx%*%t(x)%*%iv%*%y)
14	# Second data example
15	y <- c(0.1098, 0.1429, 0.1200, 0.3333,
16	0.2029,0.4348,0.1333, 0.4242); matrix(y,nrow=8, ncol=1)
17	x0 <- c(1,1,1,1,1,1,1,1)
18	x1 <- c(0,1,0,1,0,1,0,1)
19	x2 <- c(0,0,1,1,0,0,1,1)
20	x3 <- c(0,0,0,0,1,1,1,1)
21	x <- cbind(x3,x2,x1,x0)
22	xtx <- (t(x)%*%x)
23	ix <- solve(xtx)
24	print(b <- ix%*%t(x)%*%y)
25	m <- c(82,28,25,33,69,46,15,33); matrix(m,nrow=8, ncol=1)
26	v <- diag(u <- (y*(1-y)/m))
27	iv <- solve(v)
28	ivx <- solve(t(x)%*%iv%*%x)
29	print(bw <- ivx%*%t(x)%*%iv%*%y)

Lines explained

Lines 1 to 13 refer to the smaller data example, lines 15 to 29 to the larger. For each data example, first the observed proportions are provided as y (line 1 resp. lines 15 and 16), then the design matrix x is specified (lines 2 to 5 resp. 17 to 21). Lines 6 to 8 resp. 22 to 24 realize the OLS computations. Line 6 resp. 22 pre-multiplies X with its transpose, line 7 resp. 23 inverts this $X'X$ matrix, to get $(X'X)^{-1}$. Line 8 resp. 24 multiplies this matrix with $X'Y$, to obtain b. We proceeded in a similar way for the OLS calculations in Chapter 6 (there (6.23) and Table 6.1).

For obtaining the WLS estimates additional empirical input is required, namely the row frequencies resp. group sizes m, and provided in line 9 resp. 25. Lines 10 to 13 resp. 26 to 29 specify the required computations to get b according to the WLS estimator, for instance as expressed in chapter 6 in (6.29) and Table 6.4. Line 10 resp. 26 calculates the inverse values of the weights and embeds them in the diagonal matrix v. Line 11 resp. 27 inverts this matrix to embed this in lines 12 and 13 resp. 28 and 29 for the matrix multiplications required according to the WLS estimator. We proceeded in a similar way for the WLS calculations in Chapter 6 (there (6.29) and Table 6.4).

For this larger model too the target is the proportion of respondents who agree that raw materials needed for the energy transition should be mined/processed only in Europe as quickly as possible. Expressed as *percentage*, this figure is 9.1 percent among males ($x_3 = 0$) who did *not* tick both that one should pay attention to nature conservation in one's own country too ($x_1 = 0$) and that one should significantly reduce Germany's energy needs ($x_2 = 0$). The effects of these two attitudes change the initial reference value. If we express each of these effects as a properly weighted average percentage *difference*, again rounded to one decimal place a difference of plus 16 percent is traced back to attitude x_1 (nature conservation) and a plus of 2.5 percent to attitude x_2 (save energy). In addition a plus of 11.9 percent is attributable to the respondents' belonging to the group of females ($x_3 = 1$).

Table 11.6: Script to the *ftable()* Structure and *Pr1* Values of (11.24).

Line	R Script
1	library(survey)
2	design <- survey::svydesign(id = ~1,
3	weights=~wg, data = ksr)
4	frq <- survey::svytable(~rawmaterials+natureconservation
5	+saveenergy+female, design)
6	tabinput <- as.data.frame(frq)
7	tabinput$Freq <- round(tabinput$Freq, 0)
8	library(hutils)
9	weightedinput <- weight2rows(tabinput, "Freq")
10	CT <- ftable(weightedinput$female, weightedinput$saveenergy,
11	weightedinput$natureconservation,
12	weightedinput$rawmaterials)
13	CT <- as.matrix(CT)
14	n <- c(CT [, 1] + CT [, 2])
15	Pr1 <- round(prop <- (c(CT [,2]))/n, 4)
16	CT <- as.matrix(CT)
17	n <- CT [, 1] + CT [, 2]
18	Pr1 <- round(prop <- (CT [,2])/n, 4)
19	print(contingencytable <- cbind(CT, Pr1, n))

Lines explained
This is the largely identical R script referred to at the beginning of subsection 11.2.2 where the script lines are explained in the text.

11.4 Probabilistic Classification by Latent Class Analysis

11.4.1 Latent Structure Analysis

Latent Variable Analysis is used to identify hidden structures in data. It contains two types of variables: manifest and latent variables. Instead of manifest variables, we also speak of observed or measured variables. They contain the responses to the questions asked in a questionnaire or interview. In contrast, latent variables are understood as variables whose values cannot be directly queried in a survey, but whose values can be inferred from the responses given therein. Typically, sets of variables or items are used for this purpose to infer the values of a latent variable.

Latent variable analysis is a generic term for different forms of analysis. Originally, the term Latent Structure Analysis was also used, for example in a typology that goes back to Paul F. Lazarsfeld. This typology relates the assumed scale level of the latent variable(s) to the scale level of the observed variables. It distinguishes whether the respective scale level is metric (continuous) or non-metric (discrete) and thus arrives at four combinations or forms of analysis. A factor analysis, for example, combines metric scales on both levels. On the other hand, we speak of a Latent Class Analysis as a "qualitative data analog to factor analysis which enables researchers to empirically identify discrete latent variables from two or more discrete observed variables" (McCutcheon 1987: 7).

11.4.2 Basic Model

The empirical input of a latent class analysis is generally a multivariate contingency table of indicator variables. In our data example, this table will consist of three such variables, each with three categories. So this will be a $3 \cdot 3 \cdot 3$ table with its 27 possible response combinations. Below, this multivariate frequency distribution is shown in (11.48) along with the observed and expected frequencies. It is the column of *observed* frequencies shown there that represents the empirical input in absolute figures. We transform the 27 absolute frequencies $f_{y_1 y_2 y_3}$ to relative frequencies $p_{y_1 y_2 y_3}$ to arrive at the distribution of figures to be estimated by the latent class model. If we do exactly this, we will obtain an expected frequency for each observed frequency. It is these model-implied frequencies $\hat{p}_{y_1 y_2 y_3}$ that are then analytically broken down into components.

First, the model assumes that the units are not only distributed across the 27 response combinations, but that they are also distributed across the latent classes *within each configuration*. Of the units in a $y_1 y_2 y_3$ configuration, some belong to class $k = 1$, some to class $k = 2$, and some to class $k = 3$. How many "some" are exactly is the result of the model's estimation. Regardless of how they are distributed, they add up to the total number of units within a configuration. Equation (11.36) expresses this for our data example with *three* assumed latent classes.

$$\hat{p}_{y_1 y_2 y_3} = \sum_{k=1}^{3} \hat{p}_{k y_1 y_2 y_3} \qquad (11.36)$$

with

$$\hat{p}_{ky_1y_2y_3} = \hat{p}_k \cdot \hat{p}_{y_1y_2y_3|k} = \hat{p}_k \cdot \hat{p}_{y_1|k} \cdot \hat{p}_{y_2|k} \cdot \hat{p}_{y_3|k} \tag{11.37}$$

The expression $\hat{p}_{ky_1y_2y_3}$ accordingly gives the expected relative frequency of units in class k within response configuration $y_1y_2y_3$. It is exactly this relative frequency that is analytically broken down into components, namely the probability of class membership $\hat{p}_k$ and, given this membership, into conditional response probabilities $\hat{p}_{y_j|k}$. This is expressed by equation (11.37), which multiplicatively relates these probabilities.

11.4.3 Example Data

The data come again from Example Data Set 7 on Views & Insights on Climate Policy. The three bipolar scales detailed in section 10.3 serve as a basis. These three scales were placed far apart from each other in the questionnaire, namely at the beginning, in the middle and at the end. They are heating transition for the building sector (y_1), intergenerational justice (y_2) and climate rationality (y_3), with each scale mapping the response spectrum onto seven categories ($\lll$, $\ll$, $<$, 0, $>$, $\gg$, $\ggg$).

Now it would be ideal to be able to stick with these seven response categories in the present data example too. For this, however, we would need a larger sample to ensure that ideally each, realistically as many of them as possible, of the 343 cells of the underlying $7 \cdot 7 \cdot 7$ contingency table contains a sufficient number of units (ideally, 5+ for valid Chi^2 testing). In addition, sticking with the seven response categories would complicate the exemplification of some basic elements of the method. Therefore, in this data example we will collapse each scale to three categories, one for each direction with a neutral middle category in-between ($<$, 0, $>$). These three categories are coded 1 for $<$, 2 for 0 and 3 for $>$ in the present analysis.

The scale recoding simplifies the empirical input to a $3 \cdot 3 \cdot 3$ table, and thus only consists of 27 theoretical response combinations.

We use the R library *poLCA* to calculate the model. As standard output we get sections on the conditional response probabilities, class sizes and model fit. A printout of these sections is reproduced as (11.38), (11.39) and (11.40). The R script is documented in Table 11.7. Further calculations follow below in the Tables 11.9 to 11.12.

11.4.4 Conditional Response Probabilities

How likely is it to choose response category 1, 2 or 3 for an indicator variable given the class membership? (11.38) shows this for the three indicator variables y_1, y_2 and y_3.

The figures add up to 1.0 in each row.

```
Conditional item response (column) probabilities,
 by outcome variable, for each class (row)
```

```
$kpo.y1
                1       2       3
class 1:    0.1014  0.0873  0.8113
class 2:    0.9283  0.0671  0.0046
class 3:    0.1629  0.6965  0.1406
```

```
$kpo.y2
                1       2       3
class 1:    0.0933  0.0803  0.8265
class 2:    0.7506  0.0603  0.1891
class 3:    0.1756  0.4445  0.3800
```

(11.38)

```
$kpo.y3
                1       2       3
class 1:    0.6888  0.0616  0.2496
class 2:    0.2511  0.0427  0.7062
class 3:    0.0657  0.7019  0.2324
```

Conditional response probabilities make it possible to infer two basic aspects of a latent class analysis: the measurement quality of the model and the meaning of the latent classes involved. What is crucial is the pattern of these probabilities.

Table 11.7: Script to Preparatory Weighting and Main Specification of the Latent Class Analysis (LCA).

Line	R Script
1	`load("klimapolitik1.Rdata")`
2	`library(survey)`
3	`kpdesign <- survey::svydesign(id = ~1,`
4	`            weights=~kpo$wg, data = kpo)`
5	`frq <- survey::svytable(~kpo$y1`
6	`                +kpo$y2`
7	`                +kpo$y3,`
8	`                kpdesign)`
9	`lcinput <- as.data.frame(frq)`
10	`lcinput$Freq <- round(lcinput$Freq, 0)`

Table 11.7 (continued)

Line	R Script
11	library(hutils)
12	weightedinput <- weight2rows(lcinput, "Freq")
13	library(poLCA)
14	f <- cbind(kpo.y1,
15	kpo.y2,
16	kpo.y3)~1
17	m <- poLCA(f, weightedinput, nclass = 3)

Lines explained

Lines 1 loads the data frame *kpo*. Except for the variables and the data frame, lines 2 to 12 are basically identical to the script lines explained at the beginning of subsection 11.2.2 in the context of (11.9) to (11.13). Line 13 invokes library *poLCA*. Lines 14 to 16 use the column-bind function to restrict the input to the required variables, adds ~ *1* to specify that no covariates are involved, and assigns all this to *f*. Finally, script line 17 invokes the *poLCA()* function and its arguments to specify the variables (*f*), data (*weightedinput*), assumed number of latent classes (*nclass*) involved, and assign all model-related specifications and calculations to object name *m*.

A perfect measurement would be achieved if class membership was associated with all responses being concentrated in one of the possible response categories. This would lead to a response probability of one for that category and response probabilities of zero for the other categories. For class 1 and indicator y_1, for example, this would lead to a 0–0–1 pattern across the three response categories. (11.38) shows that this pattern is not achieved, but that the figures tend in this direction with 0.1014 – 0.0873 – 0.8113.

The same applies to class 1 and indicator y_2. As far as class 1 and y_3 are concerned, here too one response category clearly dominates the other two categories, although this is not quite as pronounced as with y_1 and y_2. Here the sequence 0.6888 – 0.0616 – 0.2496 would have to be related to the 1 – 0 – 0 pattern.

As far as measurement quality is concerned, a uniform distribution of responses would be the worst case, because such evenly distributed probabilities would mean that given the class membership, there is an equal chance of having answered an indicator variable with 1 or 2 or 3, in other words: somehow, arbitrary, randomly.

In addition, the pattern of response probabilities should vary *between* classes. Even if the probabilities within a class clearly deviate from the uniform distribution, this would only be of limited worth if every class had the same response pattern. Because this would mean that the classes do not differ from one another in terms of content.

However, this does not apply to the response pattern in the present example. On the contrary, the three classes differ very clearly in their most likely response category. This becomes apparent when the response patterns in (11.38) are examined one after the other for each indicator variable. For y_1, for example, we see that in class 1 most of the responses fall into category 3, in class 2 into category 1, and in class 3 into

Table 11.8: Wordings of Scale Poles and Assigned Response Codes.

Code	1	2	3
	Is the heating transition for the building sector justified ?		
y_1	"Yes, we need every possible saving in CO_2 to protect the climate."	neutral	"No, the heating transition demands far too much from citizens."
	Intergenerational justice in the financial burden of climate change		
y_2	"Climate protection justifies any taking on debts"	neutral	"This debt puts far too much of a burden on future generations."
	Climate rationality		
y_3	"Germany should not impose strict climate protection targets as long as other countries continue to put much greater strain on the earth's climate than Germany."	neutral	"Even though Germany has recently contributed only just under two percent to global CO_2 emissions, it should definitely take the lead with strict climate protection measures"

y_1 was placed in the middle part of the questionnaire, y_2 was the second question and y_3 the last question in the survey. The three survey questions were therefore asked very separately from each other.

category 2. We see a similar pattern for y_2 and a comparable pattern for y_3. As for y_3, we see that in class 1 most of the responses fall into category 1, in class 2 into category 3, and in class 3 into category 2.

We now use exactly these response patterns to draw conclusions about the meaning of the three classes. To do this, we recall which answers are represented by categories 1, 2 and 3 (Table 11.8) in order to derive a characterization of the classes from these contents as outlined in the next subsection.

11.4.5 Latent Classes

Class 1 is critical of climate protection measures. Members of this class feel that the resulting burdens on citizens and future generations are too high and believe that Germany should not impose strict climate protection targets as long as other countries continue to put much greater strain on the earth's climate than Germany. (11.39) provides information on the estimated class sizes. As to class 1, the estimated population share is 36.4 percent.

Class 2 is in favor of the heating transition in the building sector, regards the taking on of depts justified and finds that Germany should move forward with strict climate protection measures. The estimated population share is 40.6 percent.

Class 3 tends predominantly to a neutral attitude towards the heating transition in the building sector, has a neutral to critical attitude towards the debt issue, and a neutral to positive attitude towards the question of whether Germany should move

forward with strict climate protection measures. The neutral attitude is the most pronounced in each case. The estimated population share is 23 percent.

```
Estimated class population shares
 0.3642  0.4063  0.2296
```

$$(11.39)$$

```
Predicted class memberships (by modal posterior prob.)
 0.3747  0.4108  0.2144
```

Thus, 36.4 percent were opposed to too much climate protection, 40.6 percent expressed a positive attitude towards climate protection, and 23 percent expressed a
mainly neutral stance.

In addition, this section of the standard output contains information about the
predicted class memberships when these predictions are based on posterior probabilities. We will come back to this point below.

11.4.6 Model Fit

Before we interpret the outcome of an LCA as illustrated in the previous subsections,
we need to ensure that the estimated model is sufficiently consistent with the observed data. This is the question of model fit. (11.40) reprints the information available
for this purpose.

```
============================================================
Fit for 3 latent classes:
============================================================
number of observations: 443
number of estimated parameters: 20
residual degrees of freedom: 6
maximum log-likelihood: -1233.104
```

$$(11.40)$$

```
AIC(3): 2506.207
BIC(3): 2588.079
G^2(3): 6.721283 (Likelihood ratio/deviance statistic)
X^2(3): 6.354991 (Chi-square goodness of fit)
```

First, some basic information is provided. We learn that the model is estimated on the
basis of data from 443 units (respondents). We also learn that 20 parameters are estimated and that we are left with 6 degrees of freedom. The loglikelihood value is also
reported.

The residual degrees of freedom are calculated as the difference between available degrees of freedom and degrees of freedom consumed by the parameter estimation (McCutcheon 1987: 25). With 3 indicator variables, each with three values, 27 − 1 degrees of freedom are available. Of these 26 degrees of freedom,

$$
\begin{aligned}
df \quad = \quad & [(y_1 \cdot y_2 \cdot y_3) - 1] \\
- \quad & [(k-1) + k \cdot (y_1 - 1) + k \cdot (y_2 - 1) + k \cdot (y_3 - 1)]
\end{aligned}
\tag{11.41}
$$

we lose 20 for parameter estimation. This becomes evident when we replace in (11.41) y_1, y_2, y_3 and k with the respective number of categories, i. e. with 3 in each case.

$$
[(3 \cdot 3 \cdot 3) - 1] - [(3-1) + 3 \cdot (3-1) + 3 \cdot (3-1) + 3 \cdot (3-1)]
\tag{11.42}
$$

This leaves 6 degrees of freedom. Next, in this model-fit section, we obtain two information-theoretical measures. Such measures are useful for comparing models, in the present context for instance two models, one assuming 3 classes and another one assuming 2 classes. It holds the smaller the value, the better the model fit. The first measure is Akaike's information criterion (AIC)

$$
AIC = -2 \cdot LL + 2 \cdot q
\tag{11.43}
$$

and the second is Schwarz's Bayesian information criterion (BIC)[4],

$$
BIC = -2 \cdot LL + (q \cdot ln(n))
\tag{11.44}
$$

both computed for a model with 3 classes (as indicated in the brackets). In these formulae LL indicates the Loglikelihood (here, -1233.104), q the number of estimated parameters (here, 20) and n the number of units (here, 443).

Chi^2 measures of model fit are in widespread use when it comes to contingency table analysis. The model-fit section involves two standard measures, the Pearson Chi^2 goodness of fit

$$
\chi^2 = \sum_{cells} \frac{\left(f_{y_1 y_2 y_3} - \hat{f}_{y_1 y_2 y_3}\right)^2}{\hat{f}_{y_1 y_2 y_3}}
\tag{11.45}
$$

and the likelihood ratio statistic

$$
G^2 = 2 \cdot \sum_{cells} f_{y_1 y_2 y_3} \cdot ln\left(\frac{f_{y_1 y_2 y_3}}{\hat{f}_{y_1 y_2 y_3}}\right)
\tag{11.46}
$$

Both measures relate observed and expected frequencies to each other. We need such measures to be able to assess whether the observed frequencies differ systematically

---

4 Beaujean (2014: 153–166) provides a compact overview of fit measures including AIC and BIC on page 161.

from the expected ones or whether any differences can be explained by chance. The two Chi^2 values 6.35 and 6.72, each with 6 degrees of freedom, indicate a good fit, the associated p values are 0.616 and 0.652 respectively. These values relate to the null hypothesis that observed and expected frequencies differ only by chance and indicate that we cannot reject this hypothesis. For instance, assuming the null hypothesis is true, the probability of obtaining the observed frequencies is, for instance, 0.616 and thus much larger than a significance level, of say, 0.05.

Table 11.9: Script to LCA, Part 2: Design Matrix, Observed and Expected Cell Frequencies, Dissimilarity Index, and Predicted Class Memberships.

Line	R Script
1	m$predcell
2	designmatrix <- cbind(
3	m$predcell$kpo.y1,
4	m$predcell$kpo.y2,
5	m$predcell$kpo.y3)
6	obs.cell.frq <- m$predcell$observed
7	exp.cell.frq <- m$predcell$expected
8	print(DI <- sum(abs(obs.cell.frq - exp.cell.frq))/(2 * m$N))
9	# Predicted Class Memberships
10	ftable(m$y$kpo.y1, m$y$kpo.y2, m$y$kpo.y3, m$predclass)
11	table(m$predclass)
12	round(PCM <- c(prop.table(table(m$predclass))),4)

Lines explained

Line 1 extracts from object *m*, the model with all stored specifications and computations, the *predcell* data frame as displayed as (11.48). This data frame is decomposed into several components. Lines 2 to 5 create a design matrix by combining the three left columns (the row numbers not included) for subsequent use with the posterior probabilities. Lines 6 and 7 extracts from *predcell* the vectors for the observed and expected frequencies, line 8 use these vectors for computing and printing the dissimilarity index. Line 9: comment. Line 10 extracts from object *m* the *predclass* variable along with the empirical *y1*, *y2* and *y3* values from the data frame stored in *m* to build the *ftable* displayed as (11.57). Line 11 builds the frequency distribution of the predicted class memberships and line 12 the associated relative frequencies, reported as "Predicted class memberships (by modal posterior prob.)"

The validity of Chi^2-based conclusions may be limited by sample size. A sample that is too small can result in contingency tables with sparsely frequented cells. Even a respectively large data base of 443 units (respondents) result in a contingency table in which 7 of the 27 cells have an expected frequency of less than 5. This means that 25.9 percent of the 27 cells do not meet a requirement formulated for Chi^2 tests. In general, larger samples are therefore better than smaller samples. However, Chi^2 testing is not without problems even in large and very large samples, as there is a tendency for Chi^2 to indicate statistical significance hastily. This has been made particularly elaborated in the context of structural equation models, where accordingly some alternative fit measures have been developed there. Chi^2 testing is nevertheless in widespread use.

It may therefore be reasonable to consider additional fit measures in the present context too. At least as a descriptive measure, the dissimilarity index would be a good candidate for it.

$$DI = \frac{\sum_{cells}\left|f_{y_1y_2y_3} - \hat{f}_{y_1y_2y_3}\right|}{2 \cdot N} \tag{11.47}$$

In the present example we get a DI value of 0.035. This value indicates the proportion of respondents that would have to be moved in another cell of the contingency table to get a perfect fit.

```
m$predcell
   kpo.y1 kpo.y2 kpo.y3 observed expected
1       1      1      1       35   32.736
2       1      1      2        7    7.489
3       1      1      3       88   89.621
4       1      2      1        2    3.917
5       1      2      2        4    5.681
6       1      2      3       11    9.151
7       1      3      1       18   17.657
8       1      3      2        9    6.600
9       1      3      3       26   27.147
10      2      1      1        2    3.999
11      2      1      2        9    9.198
12      2      1      3       11    9.621
13      2      2      1        4    3.030
14      2      2      2       25   22.199
15      2      2      3        6    8.112
16      2      3      1       10   10.362
17      2      3      2       17   19.706
18      2      3      3       13   10.773
19      3      1      1        9    8.728
20      3      1      2        3    2.540
21      3      1      3        4    4.068
22      3      2      1        8    7.667
23      3      2      2        5    5.109
24      3      2      3        4    4.134
```

$$\tag{11.48}$$

25	3	3	1	75	74.904
26	3	3	2	10	10.477
27	3	3	3	28	28.373

11.4.7 Posterior Probabilities and Predicted Class Memberships

In addition to the estimated class populations shares, (11.39) also informs about the predicted class memberships when based on modal posterior probabilities. Posterior probabilities are calculated according to Bayes' rule

$$P(A|B) = \frac{P(B|A) \cdot P(A)}{P(B)} \tag{11.49}$$

In the present context this rule is applied to calculate the probability of class membership given a particular response configuration.

$$P(class|response\ config) = \frac{P(response\ config|class) \cdot P(class)}{P(response)} \tag{11.50}$$

Since we have 27 response combinations in this example, the prediction of class membership must be calculated for each of these 27 conditions. And since we are assuming 3 classes, three predictions must be made for each of these 27 conditions. We exemplify the calculations for one of these 27 conditions, namely the response configuration $y_1 = 1$ and $y_2 = 1$ and $y_3 = 1$. The following formula computes the posterior probabilities.

$$P_{k=1|y_1=1y_2=1y_3=1} = \frac{\left(\hat{p}_{y_1=1|1} \cdot \hat{p}_{y_2=1|1} \cdot \hat{p}_{y_3=1|1}\right) \cdot \hat{p}_{k=1}}{\sum_{k=1}^{3}\left(\hat{p}_{y_1=1|k} \cdot \hat{p}_{y_2=1|k} \cdot \hat{p}_{y_3=1|k}\right) \cdot \hat{p}_k} \tag{11.51}$$

With the relevant figures in (11.38) and (11.39)[5], (11.51) becomes

$$P_{k=1|y_1=1y_2=1y_3=1} = \frac{(0.1014 \cdot 0.0933 \cdot 0.6888) \cdot 0.3642}{(0.1014 \cdot 0.0933 \cdot 0.6888) \cdot 0.3642} = 0.0321 \tag{11.52}$$
$$+ \quad (0.9283 \cdot 0.7506 \cdot 0.2511) \cdot 0.4036$$
$$+ \quad (0.1629 \cdot 0.1756 \cdot 0.0657) \cdot 0.2296$$

---

[5] The calculation with only four decimal places introduces marginal rounding error from the 4th decimal place. This can be avoided by using 6 to 8 significant decimal places. The script line str(model), here *str(m)*, reveals how one can extract from the model computations the less-strongly rounded conditional response probabilities and estimated population shares for this purpose, namely *m$probs$kpo.y1*, *m$probs$kpo.y2*, *m$probs$kpo.y3*, and *m$P*.

$$P_{k=2|y_1=1 y_2=1 y_3=1} = \frac{(0.9283 \cdot 0.7506 \cdot 0.2511) \cdot 0.4036}{(0.1014 \cdot 0.0933 \cdot 0.6888) \cdot 0.3642} = 0.9621 \qquad (11.53)$$
$$+ \quad (0.9283 \cdot 0.7506 \cdot 0.2511) \cdot 0.4036$$
$$+ \quad (0.1629 \cdot 0.1756 \cdot 0.0657) \cdot 0.2296$$

$$P_{k=3|y_1=1 y_2=1 y_3=1} = \frac{(0.1629 \cdot 0.1756 \cdot 0.0657) \cdot 0.2296}{(0.1014 \cdot 0.0933 \cdot 0.6888) \cdot 0.3642} = 0.0058 \qquad (11.54)$$
$$+ \quad (0.9283 \cdot 0.7506 \cdot 0.2511) \cdot 0.4036$$
$$+ \quad (0.1629 \cdot 0.1756 \cdot 0.0657) \cdot 0.2296$$

The poLCA library contains the *poLCA.posterior()* function to get the posterior probabilities computed. The three probabilities computed in (11.52) to (11.54) represent the first row in this matrix of posterior probabilities. The structure of (11.55) follows the design matrix displayed as part of (11.48).

Table 11.10 reports the relevant section of the associated R script.

```
> print(postprobs <- round(pprobs,4))
          [,1]    [,2]    [,3]
  [1,]   0.0321  0.9621  0.0058
  [2,]   0.0125  0.7147  0.2727
  [3,]   0.0042  0.9882  0.0075
  [4,]   0.2308  0.6456  0.1235
  [5,]   0.0142  0.0757  0.9101
  [6,]   0.0358  0.7772  0.1870
  [7,]   0.5273  0.4493  0.0234
  [8,]   0.1260  0.2043  0.6697
  [9,]   0.1243  0.8218  0.0539
 [10,]   0.2263  0.5694  0.2043
 [11,]   0.0088  0.0421  0.9491
 [12,]   0.0341  0.6655  0.3004
 [13,]   0.2571  0.0603  0.6826
 [14,]   0.0031  0.0014  0.9955
 [15,]   0.0348  0.0634  0.9018
 [16,]   0.7740  0.0554  0.1707
 [17,]   0.0364  0.0049  0.9587
 [18,]   0.2698  0.1497  0.5805
 [19,]   0.9633  0.0178  0.0189
 [20,]   0.2958  0.0104  0.6938
 [21,]   0.7489  0.1077  0.1434
 [22,]   0.9439  0.0016  0.0544
 [23,]   0.1266  0.0004  0.8730
 [24,]   0.6344  0.0085  0.3571
```

(11.55)

```
[25,]  0.9947  0.0005  0.0048
[26,]  0.6354  0.0006  0.3639
[27,]  0.9516  0.0039  0.0445
```

In each row of the matrix, by definition the largest probability is taken to refer to the true class given the response configuration of that row. In row 1, for instance, this is class 2. If in each row the units, i. e. the respondents, are allocated accordingly to this most frequented class given the associated response configuration, this is referred to as "modal assignment". In the *poLCA* library this assignment is stored in a variable termed *predclass*, whose frequency distribution across the response configurations reveals exactly this pattern (11.57). If the absolute frequencies displayed in (11.57) are summed up column-wise, the result is the univariate distribution of predicted class memberships. We obtain this distribution and thus the "Predicted class memberships (by modal posterior prob.)" reported in (11.39) also via *table()* and *prop.table()* in (11.56)

```
> table(m$predclass)
  1   2   3
166 182  95
> round(PCM <- c(prop.table(table(m$predclass))),4)
     1      2      3
0.3747 0.4108 0.2144
```
(11.56)

Since modal assignment can represent the true class the better, the fewer units were empirically placed outside of it in a row of (11.55), an associated measure of classification quality computes exactly this expected proportion of misclassified units, below termed CQ_3. In the present example this proportion is 0.111 (11.1 percent).

```
> ftable(m$y$kpo.y1, m$y$kpo.y2, m$y$kpo.y3, m$predclass)
          1   2   3

1 1 1     0  35   0
    2     0   7   0
    3     0  88   0
  2 1     0   2   0
    2     0   0   4
    3     0  11   0
  3 1    18   0   0
    2     0   0   9
    3     0  26   0
2 1 1     0   2   0
    2     0   0   9
    3     0  11   0
```
(11.57)

```
2 1   0   0   4
  2   0   0  25
  3   0   0   6
3 1  10   0   0
  2   0   0  17
  3   0   0  13
3 1 1   9   0   0
  2   0   0   3
  3   4   0   0
  2 1   8   0   0
  2   0   0   5
  3   4   0   0
  3 1  75   0   0
  2  10   0   0
  3  28   0   0
```

11.4.8 Expected Cell and Latent-Class Frequencies

The algorithm allocates the expected cell frequencies of each response configuration to the three assumed latent classes. This can be completely expressed in *absolute* frequencies. This is shown in (11.58) for two reasons: first, to illustrate the option itself; secondly, to be able to relate to it the statement that such absolute frequencies can be converted into *relative* frequencies both horizontally (in each row, e.g., to get the posterior probabilities) and vertically (column by column), for example to evaluate classification quality. While the measure CQ_1 includes the entropy of the class probabilities calculated *for each row* of the matrix, CQ_2 is based on a comparison of the unconditional and conditional entropy, both calculated *column by column*. The absolute latent-class frequencies in (11.58), i. e. the three right columns, may also be related to the overall sample size n, i. e., quasi diagonally. We use this last-mentioned option for an illustration of how equations (11.36) and (11.37) decompose the relative frequencies in an LCA. Table 11.10 reports the segment of the R script used to build (11.58).

	exp.cell.frq	exp.frq.cl1	exp.frq.cl2	exp.frq.cl3
[1,]	32.736	1.051	31.494	0.191
[2,]	7.489	0.094	5.353	2.043
[3,]	89.621	0.381	88.564	0.676
[4,]	3.917	0.904	2.529	0.484
[5,]	5.681	0.081	0.430	5.170
[6,]	9.151	0.328	7.112	1.712
[7,]	17.657	9.310	7.933	0.414
[8,]	6.600	0.832	1.348	4.420

[9,]	27.147	3.374	22.310	1.463
[10,]	3.999	0.905	2.277	0.817
[11,]	9.198	0.081	0.387	8.730
[12,]	9.621	0.328	6.403	2.890
[13,]	3.030	0.779	0.183	2.068	(11.58)
[14,]	22.199	0.070	0.031	22.098
[15,]	8.112	0.282	0.514	7.316
[16,]	10.362	8.020	0.574	1.768
[17,]	19.706	0.717	0.097	18.892
[18,]	10.773	2.906	1.613	6.254
[19,]	8.728	8.407	0.156	0.165
[20,]	2.540	0.751	0.026	1.762
[21,]	4.068	3.047	0.438	0.583
[22,]	7.667	7.237	0.012	0.417
[23,]	5.109	0.647	0.002	4.460
[24,]	4.134	2.622	0.035	1.476
[25,]	74.904	74.508	0.039	0.357
[26,]	10.477	6.658	0.007	3.813
[27,]	28.373	27.001	0.110	1.262

The column frequencies add up to the estimated population frequencies and shares.

We use row [3,] of (11.58) to exemplify for one of the 27 configurations of $y_1 y_2 y_3$ how (11.36) and (11.37) decompose the relative frequencies. For this purpose we express each absolute frequency as share in all 443 units. Left of the equal sign in (11.36), this yields

$$\hat{p}_{y_1=1 y_2=1 y_3=3} = 89.621/443 = 0.2023 \qquad (11.59)$$

while right of the equal sign of (11.36) three frequencies are involved, one for each class

$$\hat{p}_{k_1 y_1=1 y_2=1 y_3=3} = 0.381/443 = 0.00086$$

$$\hat{p}_{k_2 y_1=1 y_2=1 y_3=3} = 88.564/443 = 0.19992 \qquad (11.60)$$

$$\hat{p}_{k_3 y_1=1 y_2=1 y_3=3} = 0.676/443 = 0.00153$$

If we take the sum over these three values we get with

$$0.00086 + 0.19992 + 0.00153 = 0.2023 \qquad (11.61)$$

the expected identity left and right the equal sign of (11.36). Finally, we can also illustrate (11.37) using this response configuration. For this purpose we form the product of class population share and the relevant combination of conditional response probabilities. Since row [3,] represents the response configuration $y_1 = 1$, $y_2 = 1$ and $y_3 = 3$, we insert the relevant figures from (11.38) for class 1, 2 and 3 in (11.62). The estimated class population shares are taken from (11.39).

$$0.3642 \cdot 0.1014 \cdot 0.0933 \cdot 0.2496 = 0.00086$$

$$0.4063 \cdot 0.9283 \cdot 0.7506 \cdot 0.7062 = 0.19992 \tag{11.62}$$

$$0.2296 \cdot 0.1629 \cdot 0.1756 \cdot 0.2324 = 0.00153$$

11.4.9 Entropy-based Classification Quality

Entropy is a very prominent measure in statistics that can be used, for instance, to determine the degree of predictability inherent in the distribution of units (e.g., respondents) over the categories of a discrete variable. The entropy is maximal when units are evenly distributed across the categories of such a variable; then predictability is lowest and the uncertainty associated with a prediction is accordingly highest. Conversely, the uncertainty of a prediction is lowest and predictability is highest, when all units are concentrated in one category of the variable. Then the entropy is zero. (11.63) shows how to compute this metric for a variable with C categories.

$$H = \sum_{cat=1}^{C} (-p_{cat} \cdot ln(p_{cat})) = -1 \cdot \sum_{cat=1}^{C} (p_{cat} \cdot ln(p_{cat})) \tag{11.63}$$

To illustrate the computation, we refer to the frequency distribution of a variable with $C = 4$ categories[6]. We used this question wording: "What can you do as an individual to protect the climate?" The four response categories are shown in (11.64) along with their associated relative frequencies (N = 449).

Very much	p_1	0.125
A lot	p_2	0.423
Not so much	p_3	0.381
Practically nothing	p_4	0.071

(11.64)

With these four relative frequencies, (11.63) becomes

$$H = -0.125 \cdot ln(0.125) - 0.423 \cdot ln(0.423) - 0.381 \cdot ln(0.381) - 0.071 \cdot ln(0.071)$$

and yields as outcome an entropy value of 1.179. This value is clearly below the value, H would attain in case of evenly distributed units. This maximum value of H is $ln(C)$, here therefore $ln(4) = 1.386$. Dividing H by this H_{max} results in the *relative entropy* with its maximum value of 1.

---

6 This variable too stems from Example Data Set 7 on Views & Insights on Climate Policy.

$$rH = \frac{\sum_{cat=1}^{C}(-p_{cat} \cdot ln(p_{cat}))}{ln(C)} \tag{11.65}$$

It is rH that represents a first core element in the assessment of classification quality via CQ_1 and it is H in the case of CQ_2. A second core element is the calculation of entropy for *conditional* frequency distributions. Both CQ_1 and CQ_2 calculate *conditional* entropy values to take a weighted sum of them over the involved conditions, with the relative size of each individual condition used as the weight. (11.66) specifies the formula for the 27 $y_1y_2y_3$ configurations and the $k = 3$ classes involved.

$$CQ_1 = 1 - \frac{\sum_{config=1}^{27}\left(\hat{f}_{y_1y_2y_3} \cdot \sum_{k=1}^{3}\left(-\hat{p}_{k|y_1y_2y_3} \cdot ln\left(\hat{p}_{k|y_1y_2y_3}\right)\right)\right)}{n \cdot ln(3)} \tag{11.66}$$

In particular, CQ_1 takes the weighted sum of the conditional entropy values *of the posterior probabilities* and subtracts this sum from 1. Here, this yields a CQ_1 value of 0.729.

A CQ_1 index value near 1 indicates an overall entropy value near 0 (high predictability, units tend to being concentrated in single classes), while a CQ_1 index value near 0 indicates an overall entropy value near 1 (posterior probabilities tend to being evenly (i. e., randomly) distributed across the three classes.

CQ_2 relates the entropy of the 27 expected cell probabilities to the entropy that results if the distribution of units across the three classes is *additionally* considered. In particular, CQ_2 relates the *unconditional* entropy of the distribution of the 27 expected cell probabilities to a corresponding *conditional* entropy by calculating the proportional reduction in prediction error.

For this purpose, the absolute frequencies in (11.58) are converted *column by column* into relative frequencies in order to calculate the entropy separately for each of these columns. Referring to the leftmost column,

$$H_{y_1y_2y_3} = \sum_{config=1}^{27}\left(-\hat{p}_{y_1y_2y_3} \cdot ln\left(\hat{p}_{y_1y_2y_3}\right)\right) \tag{11.67}$$

we obtain an entropy that can be used as a reference value. And for the remaining three columns we get three more entropy values, one for each column. We combine these three entropy values into a single value by multiplying each of them by the relative size of the class for which the entropy was computed and by forming the sum of these three weighted entropy values. The relevant R script lines are shown in Table 11.11. Now we have one unconditional entropy as reference value and one conditional entropy value that additionally considers the expected class memberships. The proportional reduction in prediction error may then be computed by combining these two values via

$$CQ_2 = \frac{H_{y_1 y_2 y_3} - H_{k y_1 y_2 y_3}}{H_{y_1 y_2 y_3}} \tag{11.68}$$

In the present example this yields a value of 0.278, i. e. a reduction by 27.8 percent.

Table 11.10: Script to LCA, Part 3: Expected Absolute Cell & Latent-Class Frequencies.

Line	R Script
1	pprobs <- poLCA::poLCA.posterior(m, y=designmatrix)
2	print(postprobs <- round(pprobs,4))
3	frq <- cbind(exp.cell.frq, pprobs)
4	exp.frq.cl1 <- c(frq [,1] * frq [,2])
5	exp.frq.cl2 <- c(frq [,1] * frq [,3])
6	exp.frq.cl3 <- c(frq [,1] * frq [,4])
7	print(exp.freqs <- round(cbind(exp.cell.frq,
8	exp.frq.cl1, exp.frq.cl2, exp.frq.cl3),3))

Lines explained
Line 1 invokes the *poLCA.posterior()* function for the posterior probabilities using the previously constructed design matrix, and assigns this matrix to object *pprobs*. Line 2 addresses this object to print a version of it rounded to 4 decimal places. This matrix is displayed as (11.55). Line 3 combines these posterior probabilities with the vector of expected cell frequencies created earlier and assigns all this to matrix *frq*. Lines 4 to 8 are used to convert the posterior probabilities to the absolute frequencies printed as (11.58).

Table 11.11: Script to LCA, Part 4: Entropy-based Measures of Classification Quality.

Line	R Script
1	H.cl <- (frq [,1] * ((-1 * frq [,2]) * log(frq [,2]) +
2	(-1 * frq [,3]) * log(frq [,3]) +
3	(-1 * frq [,4]) * log(frq [,4])))
4	print(CQ1 <- 1 - (sum(H.cl))/(m$N * log(3)))
5	exp.cell.p <- c(m$predcell$expected/m$N)
6	exp.p.cl1 <- c(exp.frq.cl1 / sum(exp.frq.cl1))
7	exp.p.cl2 <- c(exp.frq.cl2 / sum(exp.frq.cl2))
8	exp.p.cl3 <- c(exp.frq.cl3 / sum(exp.frq.cl3))
9	Hc <- -sum(exp.cell.p * log(exp.cell.p))
10	Hcl1 <- -sum(exp.p.cl1 * log(exp.p.cl1))
11	Hcl2 <- -sum(exp.p.cl2 * log(exp.p.cl2))
12	Hcl3 <- -sum(exp.p.cl3 * log(exp.p.cl3))
13	Hcl <- (Hcl1 * sum(exp.frq.cl1/m$N) +

Table 11.11 (continued)

Line	R Script
14	Hcl2 * sum(exp.frq.cl2/m$N) +
15	Hcl3 * sum(exp.frq.cl3/m$N))
16	print(CQ2 <- (Hc – Hcl)/Hc)

Lines explained

Lines 1 to 4 calculate CQ1 as explained in the context of (11.63) to (11.66). Lines 5 to 8 convert the absolute frequencies in (11.58) column by column to relative frequencies. Line 9 calculates the reference entropy and lines 10 to 12 the entropy values for the three class-related columns. Lines 13 to 15 weight these class-related entropy values with their associated relative class sizes and take the sum of these weighted entropy values. Finally, line 16 relates this latter entropy to the reference entropy from line 9, to compute the proportional reduction in prediction error.

Table 11.12: Script to the LCA, Part 5: Expected Proportion of Misclassified Units.

Line	R Script
1	pmc1 <- c(1-max(pprobs[1,]))
2	pmc2 <- c(1-max(pprobs[2,]))
3	pmc3 <- c(1-max(pprobs[3,]))
4	pmc4 <- c(1-max(pprobs[4,]))
5	pmc5 <- c(1-max(pprobs[5,]))
6	pmc6 <- c(1-max(pprobs[6,]))
7	pmc7 <- c(1-max(pprobs[7,]))
8	pmc8 <- c(1-max(pprobs[8,]))
9	pmc9 <- c(1-max(pprobs[9,]))
10	pmc10 <- c(1-max(pprobs[10,]))
11	pmc11 <- c(1-max(pprobs[11,]))
12	pmc12 <- c(1-max(pprobs[12,]))
13	pmc13 <- c(1-max(pprobs[13,]))
14	pmc14 <- c(1-max(pprobs[14,]))
15	pmc15 <- c(1-max(pprobs[15,]))
16	pmc16 <- c(1-max(pprobs[16,]))
17	pmc17 <- c(1-max(pprobs[17,]))
18	pmc18 <- c(1-max(pprobs[18,]))
19	pmc19 <- c(1-max(pprobs[19,]))
20	pmc20 <- c(1-max(pprobs[20,]))
21	pmc21 <- c(1-max(pprobs[21,]))
22	pmc22 <- c(1-max(pprobs[22,]))
23	pmc23 <- c(1-max(pprobs[23,]))
24	pmc24 <- c(1-max(pprobs[24,]))
25	pmc25 <- c(1-max(pprobs[25,]))
26	pmc26 <- c(1-max(pprobs[26,]))
27	pmc27 <- c(1-max(pprobs[27,]))

Table 11.12 (continued)

Line	R Script
28	pmc <- c(pmc1, pmc2, pmc3, pmc4,
29	pmc5, pmc6, pmc7, pmc8,
30	pmc9, pmc10, pmc11, pmc12,
31	pmc13, pmc14, pmc15, pmc16,
32	pmc17, pmc18, pmc19, pmc20,
33	pmc21, pmc22, pmc23, pmc24,
34	pmc25, pmc26, pmc27)
35	print(CQ3 <- sum(exp.cell.p * pmc))

Lines explained

Lines 1 to 27 calculates for each row of (11.55) the proportion of units outside the most-frequented cell, by definition the expected proportion of misclassified units in that row (i. e., $y_1 y_2 y_3$ configuration). Lines 28 to 34 collect these 27 values into one vector. Line 35 weights each such value with the relative size of the row for which it was computed, and takes their sum over the rows.

Chapter 12
Statistical Learning

12.1 Statistical Learning

Ghani and Schierholz (2017: 147) characterize *machine learning*[1] as "although the field originates from computer science (specifically, artificial intelligence), it has been influenced quite heavily by statistics in the past 15 years," including many concepts that "are not entirely new, but simply called something else." The way the elements of a data matrix are named is a striking example of using different technical terms for the same elements. We consider the *statistical learning* approach (James et al. 2013) to be particularly useful when the focus of the perspective is on the similarities rather than the differences between the ways data analysis is performed in the social-science and machine-learning fields. As James et al. (2013: vii, 6) wrote at the time, "inspired by the advent of *machine learning* and other disciplines, statistical learning has emerged as a new subfield in statistics, focused on supervised and unsupervised modeling and prediction." Statistical learning "blends with parallel developments in computer science and, in particular, machine learning."

The statistical learning approach shares many of its data analysis methods with social science statistics. These include the statistical methods we introduced in the previous chapters: for example, the linear and generalized linear model, as well as the metrics, methodological rules, and procedures for evaluation of model performance. These also include methods for accounting for nonlinear effects, such as polynomial regression, regression splines, and the generalized additive model. This list should be supplemented by statistical learning methods that we have not yet addressed in this textbook, namely decision trees[2] and support vector machines. We would also consider resampling methods for cross-validation and bootstrapping to be part of the common core, even if these and related ensemble methods[3] are regarded

---

1 For example, Lantz (2019) defines the field of *machine* learning, among other things, by a list of methods, including classification using nearest neighbors, Naive Bayes, decision trees and rules. He also includes these methods: regression methods for forecasting numeric data, and the black-box methods neural networks and support vector machines. He also includes association rules and clustering as well as methods for determining and improving model performance.

2 Decision trees are the subject of Section 12.4 and artificial neural networks of Section 12.5 below.

3 Kelleher et al. (2020: 158–159) define model ensembles this way: "Rather than creating a single model, they generate a set of models and then make predictions by aggregating the outputs of these models. A prediction model that is composed of a set of models is called model ensemble." [. . .] The authors point to "two standard approaches to creating ensembles: *bagging* and *boosting*" as well as "commonly used, high performing extensions" to them, namely "*random forests* in the case of bagging and *gradient boosting* in the case of boosting." The description by Ghani and Schierholz (2017: 169) is similar when they describe the intuition behind building ensembles of models as follows: "The intuition [. . .] is to build

https://doi.org/10.1515/9783110680683-012

so important in the context of statistical learning. The same applies to methods for model selection and regularization.

On the other hand, particularly high emphasis is placed on *confirmatory* proce-dures and the control of random and systematic measurement error in social science statistics, for example through confirmatory factor analysis, structural equation modeling or latent class analysis. The handling of unit and item nonresponse is also given great importance in social science data analysis.

Statistical learning methods are classified according to whether or not they serve to predict a target variable, called a *label*. If so, they are referred to as *supervised* methods.[4] It is not uncommon to refer to a supervised model as *regression* when the label is a metric scale and as *classification* when the label is a categorical variable.[5] On the other hand, *unsupervised* learning methods are used "when we do not have a target variable to predict but want to understand 'natural' clusters or patterns in the data" (Ghani and Schierholz 2017: 153). This includes clustering algorithms, principal components analysis, and association rules.

Part of the common core is also a tidy data structure. Such a structure organizes the units of analysis *row by row* and the variables *column by column*. We explained this structure of a data frame in detail in Sections 4.2 and 4.3, and present it here again in Figure 12.1 to draw attention to an important point: the machine-learning and social-science branches use different vocabularies to address the elements of such a data matrix (Ghani and Schierholz 2017: 154).

We see that a *feature* in the machine-learning vocabulary corresponds to a *predic-tor, independent*, and *explanatory variable* in the social-science branch. Accordingly, *feature engineering* is the technical term used when such variables are to be prepared, selected or created for analysis.[6] Also, the term *label* corresponds to a *response, depen-dent, target*, and *outcome variable*. And we also see that an *example*, and sometimes

several models, each somewhat different. This diversity can come from various sources such as: training models on subsets of the data; training models on subsets of the features; or a combination of these two." See also Lantz (2019: 359–373) on "Improving model performance with meta-learning". We will discuss bootstrapping in Section 12.4.5 and bagging, random forest, and boosting below in Section 12.4.6.
4 Ghani and Schierholz (2017: 161–173) introduce these supervised learning methods: k-nearest neigh-bor, support vector machines (SVM), decision trees, ensemble methods: bagging, boosting, random for-ests, stacking, neural networks and deep learning.
5 Strictly speaking, however, the conceptual contrast between regression and classification is only partially convincing due to a lack of discriminatory power. The reason: even the prediction of the probability of belonging to a category or latent class can be based on (logistic) regression. Essentially, it is only a question of whether a prediction equation is used to predict conditional means of a metric target variable (regression) or the probabilities for belonging to the categories of a – then usually – nominally scaled variable (classification).
6 See section 12.3 below.

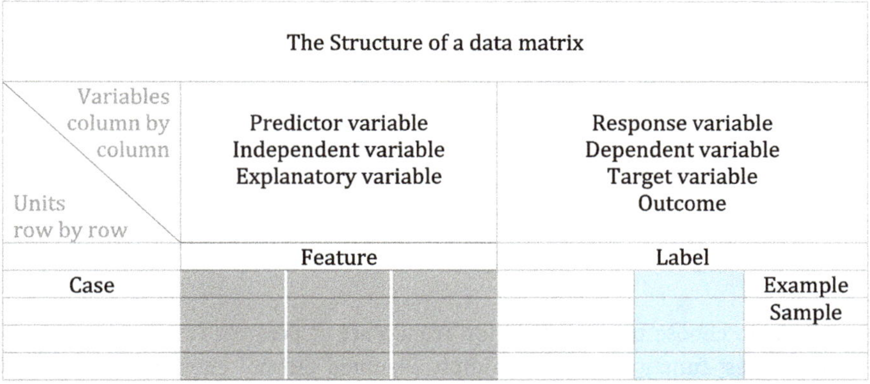

The Structure of a data matrix				
Variables column by column / Units row by row	Predictor variable Independent variable Explanatory variable		Response variable Dependent variable Target variable Outcome	
	Feature		Label	
Case				Example Sample

Figure 12.1: The Data Matrix: Different Technical Terms, with Equivalent Meaning.

even a *sample* is meant to be the same as a *case*. This means: Different technical terms are used to indicate the same thing.

12.2 Learning Functions from Data

As Ghani and Schierholz (2017: 154) outline, in the machine learning literature *learning* a model means the same "as *fitting* or *estimating* a function, or *training* or *building* a model. These terms are all synonyms and are used interchangeably in the machine learning literature." But what does it mean to say that we let a machine learn functions from data?

In machine learning, algorithms are used to recognize patterns in data sets that can be described as functions. Such a function can be defined as a mapping from input values to output values. Figure 12.2 presents two examples. Input values are denoted as x, and output values as y_1 and y_2 respectively. If we now ask which function connects y_1 to x, it quickly becomes clear that y_2 is simply x-squared, $y_1 = x^2$ (the red graph in Figure 12.3). But what connects the values of y_2 to the values of x? Here, as in general, this function is not so obvious. Then, as a rule, we use an algorithm to estimate the function that links input and output. In the illustrating example in Figure 12.2, this is the exponential function $y_2 = b_1 \cdot e^{b_1 \cdot x}$, with $b_1 = 0.5$ (the blue graph in Figure 12.3).

As Kelleher (2019: 11) describes the general task, a "machine learning algorithm is a search process designed to choose the best function, from a set of possible functions, to explain the relationships between features in a dataset." Typically, such functions are unknown and therefore have to be estimated from data. For this purpose, estimation algorithms are used, for example to obtain least-squares estimates of the unknown functional parameters.

x	Function	y_1		x	Function	y_2
1		1		1		0.82
2	?	4		2	?	1.36
3		9		3		2.24
4		16		4		3.7
5		25		5		6.09
6		36		6		10.04

Figure 12.2: Which Function Links Input and Output Values?

However, how to choose the best function from a set of possible functions? In practice, often the best functional form is simply assumed but not chosen from a set of possible alternatives. This is then usually the assumption of a *linear* relationship. If the functional form is fixed a priori in this way, only the parameters (intercept, slope) of the pertaining straight-line regression need to be estimated. In principle there is nothing wrong with this simplification, except that the functional form itself remains untested. It then simply remains unclear whether there are alternative curves that would better describe a relationship under consideration. This of course limits the scope of an analysis. However, estimating linear relationships can often be the only realistic option when a predictor variable used to estimate a target variable has only a few values. In social research, this is generally the rule rather than the exception. Even 11-point scales provide only limited space for nonlinearity to unfold. However, age and time are two variables for which *the option of* nonlinear relationships can be examined very well in empirical social research. As explained in section 10.2, a polynomial regression or a regression spline, for example, offer good options for this.

If we actually use such an option and compare with each other, for instance, the corresponding goodness of fit of a linear, polynomial or regression spline (each applied to the same data), then we can say that we not only assumed a functional form, but that we tested whether a functional form is the best out of a set of possible alternatives. In other words, a comparatively best functional form was then learned from the data.

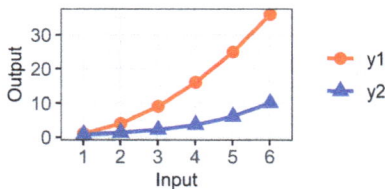

Figure 12.3: Example of an Exponential Function to Link Input and Output Values.

Let us consider an example: How much does the preference for parties on the far right of the political spectrum depend on age? To answer this question, we used Example Data

Set 8 (European Social Survey Rounds 1 to 9) to estimate the probability of right-wing vote as a function of age. The model consists of two variables, the target variable y (right-wing vote) and the predictor variable x (age). Because y is a binary variable, we use the statistical framework of Generalized Linear Models (GLMs). As detailed in chapter 8.5, a GLM consists of three parts: a systematic part that relates x to the involved linear predictor, a random part to specify the random distribution of y, and a link function.

Using the *probit* link and *binomial* distribution (in the quasibinomial specification that considers possible overdispersion), four models were fit to the data (Figure 12.4). The first model assumes a *linear* effect of age on the probability of right-wing vote (upper left, grey graph) and the second model a 3rd degree *polynomial* effect of age (upper right, light blue graph). Such a polynomial model can be further developed into a regression-spline model, as we explained in detail in Section 10.2. This is done here using third-order regression spline models that include knots at predefined points, one with two knots at the terciles (bottom left, orange graph) and another with three knots at the quartiles of the age distribution (bottom right, dark red graph).

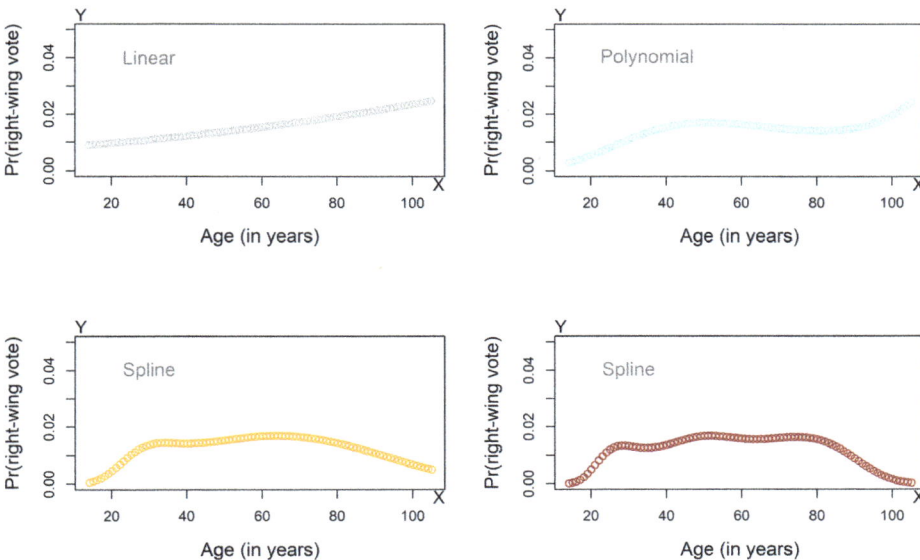

Figure 12.4: Functional Forms Assumed and Learned From Data: Illustrating Example.

Depending on the model specification, we obtain slightly different curves and would now have to check which of these curves best describes the data.[7] In a validation set

---

7 Models were fit to the units with valid values in y and x. This left us with 328,635 of 340,215 units in the data frame. The probit model assuming a linear age effect was y ~ x. This formula changed to y ~

design, this step would be part of the training phase and would possibly use a validation dataset before the resulting best model is applied to a test dataset in a subsequent step. We explained this design in Chapter 7.2, for example, in the context of Figure 7.2.

12.3 Modeling and Feature Engineering

A data science analysis typically involves a sequence of tasks. Initially, a validation approach must be defined and, along with it, the random partitioning of the entire data set must be implemented. For this purpose, resampling methods are recommended, for example in the form of cross-validation (James et al. 2013: 175–186). However, since we are working with very large to big samples here, we will use the simpler validation set design in the following two data examples. In Chapter 7.2, two basic variants of validation set design were introduced: one that randomly divides the data into two components — a training set and a test set — and another that randomly divides the data into three parts — a training set, a validation set, and a test set (Figure 7.2). Here, we will build on this former variant in the following two data examples.

It is also essential to build a model. This could be, for example, a linear model, a generalized linear model, a generalized additive model or a model that implements another statistical learning method. Once this has been decided, the expected effects must be specified. For example, these can be linear or nonlinear in some way; they can be main effects whose effects add up, or they can be interactions. There is considerable scope for practical implementation in these respects, as we have seen in chapter 6 (statistical interaction) and 10 (nonlinear relations).

In these two chapters, we have also seen how nonlinear and nonadditive effects can be estimated by extending a given set of predictors (features) with artificial terms that represent mathematical functions of them. For example, it might be meaningful to square a feature and raise it to the third power to estimate a third-order polynomial regression using an equation that includes all three predictors. Or we can include a feature in logarithmic form to estimate specific nonlinear relationships. There are other examples where we work not only with the original features, but with func-

---

poly(x,3) and y ~ bs(x, knots = c(38,58), degree = 3) to y ~ bs(x, knots = c(33,48,63), degree = 3) in the succeeding models. As to the RMSE (root mean squared error), it increases slightly from 2.24 to 2.25 to 2.26 to 2.27 in the transition from the first to the fourth model, while at the same time, McFadden's R^2 increases from 0.0043 to 0.0098 to 0.0116 to 0.0125. Thus, age explains only a marginal 0.4 to 1.25% of the variation in the probability of voting for parties on the right of the respective country's political spectrum. However, the four models ignore all other influencing factors, including systematic and random ones. They are therefore incomplete at best, but can nevertheless illustrate that even very similar model types (polynomial, spline) can lead to different curves, depending on how tuning parameters are set in them. However, since the Y-axis in each plot was limited to the relevant scale range, these differences appear somewhat more pronounced in the visual representation than in a plot that would not focus so strongly on a narrow interval.

tions of them. For example, when we conceptualize these features as manifest indicators of latent scales. Furthermore, categorical predictors may need to be recoded into a set of (0, 1) dummy terms to be included in a regression model. Or features may need to be recoded. Data science analyses often involve variable transformations related to the features of a model. And it may be necessary to decide on an appropriate selection of predictors to consider.[8] Therefore, it makes sense that Kuhn and Silge (2022) refer to this as *feature engineering.*

In addition, tasks usually need to be solved that prepare or guide data analysis. These include, for example, the use of a weighting variable to compensate for sampling bias caused by unit nonresponse. These also include measures for handling missing values in data matrices (due to item nonresponse), for example, by excluding corresponding units or by replacing missing values with plausible alternatives, such as multiple imputation. We discussed this in more detail in Chapter 2.

From previous chapters, we already know in detail how we can use *base-R* techniques to realize such tasks. Another option is the *tidymodels* metapackage (Kuhn and Silge 2022). The emphasis here is on *option*, which means that we can perform required calculations using this meta-library, or as before with base R in conjunction with any required individual libraries.[9]

We would like to illustrate this option in the two sections following the next section and first introduce the two data examples used for this illustration.

12.3.1 Example Data

As before, we would like to illustrate the discussion with data examples. In this section, we shall use two data sources: the PPSM Innovation Panel and a cumulative dataset of the European Social Survey, Rounds 1 to 9. In both cases, happiness is the target variable.

---

8 James et al. (2013: 203–228) devote considerable space to the topic of linear model selection and regularization. They present various approaches, including best subset selection, stepwise selection, and shrinkage methods, particularly ridge regression and the lasso method. Also dimension reduction methods (Principal Components Regression and Partial Least Squares). Subset selection, for example, means identifying the subset of k from p predictors considered for a model that yields the largest R^2 for the model. To do this, all $\binom{p}{k}$ models are compared with each other (using the *regsubsets()* function of *library(leaps)* (James et al. 2013: 205, 244–247). The Lasso method consists in extending the least squares algorithm by a penalty term that shrinks the coefficient estimates towards zero depending on a parameter λ. The *glmnet()* function from the library of the same name provides the relevant comparisons in terms of this parameter (James et al. 2013: 219, 255).

9 Based on our experience so far, the direct approach using base R techniques is easier and faster to implement than a meta-approach, which primarily functions as a user interface (API) for accessing required R packages even from a comprehensive programming environment. However, it is certainly advantageous that such a meta-package provides the systematic tackling of regularly occurring programming tasks from the very beginning.

We start with data from Example Data Set 1 (PPSM Innovation Panel) to predict happiness based on a set of predictors. In the following R script (Table 12.1), this target variable is denoted *q16*. The survey question on happiness consisted of a sequence of two individual questions. The first question was: "If you think about how things are going for you right now, what would you say? Are you currently rather happy or rather unhappy?" Possible answers: "rather happy," "rather unhappy," "don't know." Regardless of their answer, all respondents were then presented with the eleven-point scale used in this section: "On a scale of 1 'very unhappy' to 11 'very happy': Where on this scale would you place yourself?" Based on N = 3,918 respondents with valid values in all of the variables involved in this analysis, we encounter an almost bell-shaped albeit skewed-to-the-left frequency distribution (Figure 12.5, left graph). The first, second and third quartiles of the frequency distribution are 6, 8, and 9.

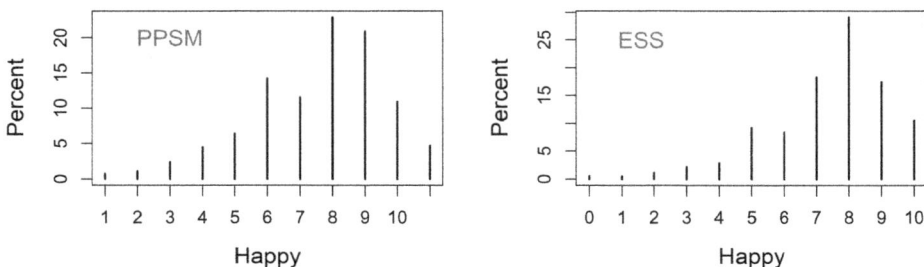

Figure 12.5: Univariate Distributions of Happiness in the two Data Examples.

As for the predictors, we include variables we had already used in Chapter 7 in the context of the cross-validation example (Section 7.4): the assessment of standard of living on an eleven-point ladder scale (*LS11*), the assessment of the extent to which it is fair to pass on wealth to children so that they have better opportunities (7-point scale from 1 = completely disagree to 7 = completely agree) (*just10*). Also gender (*male*) and age (*age*).

The initial model estimates are reported in (12.1) and the underlying R script in Table 12.1. As expected, the relationship between standard of living and happiness proves to be nonlinear. This also applies to the age effect, albeit only to a certain extent. Gender and its assumed interaction with standard of living also prove to be insignificant. When the model is reduced by these features, the reduced model predicts happiness based on standard of living and the perceived fairness of inheritance of wealth. Applying this reduced model to the test data set, both effects on happiness turn out to be substantial: Perceived fairness has a significant positive effect on happiness, and standard of living has a nonlinear effect whose five components[10] are

---

10 The five *bs()* coefficients; with *t* values, of which three are significantly above $|1.96|$, while one is a little and another one is significantly below this critical value. R^2 is 0.217 and the test dataset consists

mostly significant. The left graph in Figure 12.6 visualizes this nonlinear effect by plotting the living-standard scores against the predicted happiness values. We encounter a not atypical course, a horizontal *S*-curve. Furthermore, we observe a narrow variation in the predicted happiness values at *each* of the eleven living-standard scores (vertically), reflecting the influence of differences in the fairness assessment, which is the second predictor in the model.

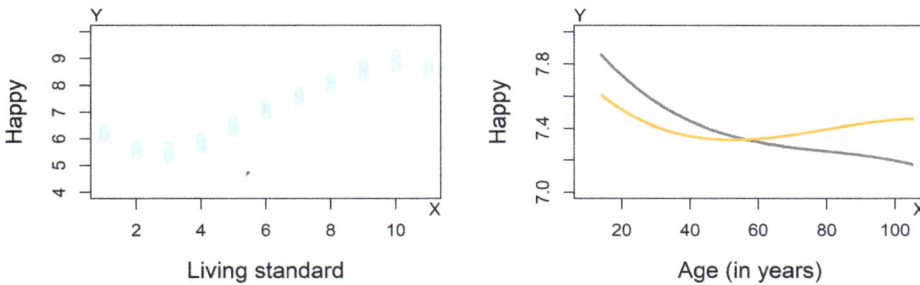

Figure 12.6: Nonlinear and Nonadditive Effects on Perceived Happiness.

The second data example uses data from Example Data Set 8. In the European Social Survey, happiness is measured as follows: "Taking all things together, how happy would you say you are?" followed by an eleven-point scale ranging from 0 = "extremely unhappy" to 10 "extremely happy". In the R script (Table 12.2 and (12.2) to (12.3)) this target variable is labeled *happy*. Based on N = 315,470 respondents with valid values in all variables included in this analysis, the right-hand diagram in Figure 12.5 also shows an almost bell-shaped, albeit left-skewed, frequency distribution. When this distribution is weighted for analysis as recommended,[11] its quartiles are 7, 8, and 9.

The predictor set consists of original variables from the ESS rounds, which have been renamed here for clarity.[12] According to the *ESS* source questionnaire,[13] the variables and scales can be described as follows: *trust* asks on an 11-point scale, "generally speaking, would you say that most people can be trusted, or that you can't be too careful in dealing with people? Please tell me on a score of 0 to 10, where 0 means you can't be too careful and 10 means that most people can be trusted." *fair* asks, "do you think that most people would try to take advantage of you if they got the chance, or

---

of 1,176 respondents (Overall N is 3,918). Based on a .7 to .3 random split, the training data consists of 2,742 respondents and the test dataset on 1,176 respondents.

11 For example, Kaminska (2023)

12 Here are the equivalents: *prej* = imdfetn, *trust* = ppltrst, *fair* = pplfair, *helpful* = pplhlp, *age* = agea, *depriv* = hincfel, *female* = cat. 2 of gndr, *eduyrs* = eduyrs. The weight variable *wt* is anweight.

13 As a possible reference, we can take the source questionnaire of an ESS Round, for example: European Social Survey (2022). *ESS Round 11 Source Questionnaire*. London: ESS ERIC Headquarters c/o City, University of London.

would they try to be fair?" (11-point scale from 0 = "Most people would try to take advantage of me", to 10 = "Most people would try to be fair"). h*elpful* asks, "Would you say that most of the time people try to be helpful or that they are mostly looking out for themselves?" (11-point scale from 0 = "People mostly look out for themselves" to 10 = "People mostly try to be helpful."). *prej* represents the second in a sequence of three questions about people from other countries coming to live in the respondent's country. This second question asks to what extent the country should allow people of a *different* race or ethnic group from most country's people to come and live here. The *ESS* uses this 4-point response scale: 1 = Allow many to come and live here, 2 = Allow some, 3 = Allow a few, 4 = Allow none. *depriv* asks, which of the following "descriptions (. . .) comes closest to how you feel about your household's income nowadays?". These descriptions are worded as follows: 1 = " Living comfortably on present income", 2 = "Coping on present income", 3 = "Finding it difficult on present income", 4 = "Finding it very difficult on present income". In addition, three sociodemographic variables are included: *age* in years, *female* (coded 1 if gndr is 2 = female, and coded 0 if gndr is 1 = male); finally *eduyrs* denotes the years of full-time education completed.

The linear mixed model applied to the test data is a random-intercept model. It is documented in Table 12.3 and is partially visualized in the right-hand graph in Figure 12.6. Here is a brief description:

Respondents who believe that people can be trusted and see them as fair and helpful are happier than respondents who believe this less. We encounter three linear effects here: the more people are seen as trustworthy, fair, and helpful, the higher the predicted happiness score. In contrast, three other linear effects have a negative sign: the effects of prejudice, income deprivation, and years of education. Accordingly, the higher a respective score, the lower the predicted happiness, and vice versa. All of these effects are main effects and are statistically significant.

The effects of age and gender are also statistically significant in the model. Age has a nonlinear effect on happiness, the shape of which can be seen in the right-hand graph of Figure 12.6. We see two graphs there, one for females (gray curve) and one for males (orange curve). The fact that the two curves cross each other is an expression of an interaction between age and gender in their effect on happiness. While *female* has a positive main effect, meaning that women are generally predicted to have slightly higher happiness values than men, we also find a negative interaction effect between age and *female*, so that the main and interaction effects together lead to the two curves in the right-hand graph of Figure 12.6.

To better understand this diagram, it should be noted that the whole spectrum of *predicted* happiness scores ranges from 4.3 to 9.6 and is thus much larger than the displayed scale range of 7 to 8. This only occurs because we inserted the respective *average* values for all predictors — except for age and female — into the prediction equation, in order to construct this graph. This is only to be able to demonstrate the curve shape for the age and gender effect; for the overall analysis, *all* occurring configurations of predictor values would, of course, be relevant.

Table 12.1: A Possible Syntax Structure in the *tidymodels* Metapackage.

Line	R Script
1	`load("jst.Rdata")`
2	`sset <- jst[complete.cases(jst$q16, jst$LS11,`
3	`               jst$just10, jst$age, jst$male),]`
4	`library(tidymodels)`
5	`sset <- as_tibble(sset)`
6	`set.seed(125)`
7	`(sset_split <- initial_split(sset, prop = 0.70))`
8	`train <- training(sset_split)`
9	`test <- testing(sset_split)`
10	`model <-`
11	`  linear_reg() %>%`
12	`  set_engine("lm")`
13	`rec <- recipe(q16 ~ LS11+just10+age+male,`
14	`              data=train) %>%`
15	`  step_interact(~LS11:male) %>%`
16	`  step_bs(LS11, degree = 3,`
17	`          options = list(knots=c(6,8))) %>%`
18	`  step_poly(age,2)`
19	`lmwflow <-`
20	`  workflow() %>%`
21	`  add_model(model)%>%`
22	`  add_recipe(rec)`
23	`fit <-`
24	`  fit(lmwflow,train)`
25	`get_model <-`
26	`  function(x) {`
27	`    extract_fit_parsnip(x) %>% tidy()`
28	`  }`
29	`get_model(fit)`
30	`fit %>% extract_fit_engine() %>% summary()`

Lines explained

The structure of this R script is explained in the text. *tidymodels* uses the % >% pipe operator, which we introduced in Section 4.12. Line 1 loads the data frame and lines 2 and 3 reduce this frame to the complete cases in the variables involved. Line 4 calls the *tidymodels* library and line 5 transforms the data frame into a *tibble*. We discussed this topic in Section 4.10. Lines 7 to 9 are used for the random split into a training and a test data set. This is followed by the model statement for calling the *lm()* function (lines 10 to 12). The feature engineering instructions bundled via *recipe()* are located in lines 13 to 18. Here we use the options to specify an interaction effect, a *b* spline and polynomial regression. In lines 19 to 22, the model and recipe instructions are integrated into a workflow object and all model parameters are estimated via lines 23 and 24. We obtain these estimates via the two *extract* instructions in lines 25 to 30.

The cumulative data set underlying this analysis is big. It contains 315,470 respondents from 22 countries with valid values in the variables involved. Via random split, 220,829 of these respondents were allocated to the training dataset and 94,641 to the test dataset.

8.0 percent is variance of *happy* between countries and 92.0 percent within countries.[14] Compared to the null model, the present model implies a proportional reduction in prediction error by $R^2 = 18.6$ percent.

12.3.2 Using the *tidymodels* Metapackage

We use the first of the two data examples presented in the last section to illustrate a possible structure and sequence of instructions in the R script. To do so, we limit ourselves to the initial step, in which we examine whether two predictors in the data may have nonlinear effects on happiness. For the predictor *standard of living*, we consider a third-order regression spline and for *age*, a second-order polynomial regression. We also examine whether standard of living and gender may interact in their effect on happiness.

The R script reported in Table 12.1 produces output (12.1). We have already briefly discussed the content of this result in the previous section 12.3.1 and would like to concentrate on the R script in this section (Table 12.1).

```
> get_model(fit)
# A tibble: 11 × 5
   term          estimate   std.error   statistic   p.value
   <chr>            <dbl>       <dbl>       <dbl>      <dbl>
 1 (Intercept)     3.26       0.341        9.55    2.72e-21
 2 just10          0.0859     0.0210       4.09    4.46e- 5
 3 male           -0.0558     0.254       -0.219   8.26e- 1
 4 LS11_x_male    -0.00672    0.0355      -0.190   8.50e- 1
 5 LS11_bs_1       1.82       0.537        3.40    6.88e- 4
 6 LS11_bs_2       2.99       0.339        8.83    1.85e-18
 7 LS11_bs_3       4.58       0.390       11.7     3.92e-31
 8 LS11_bs_4       5.59       0.402       13.9     1.55e-42
 9 LS11_bs_5       5.74       0.412       13.9     1.21e-42
10 age_poly_1     -3.08       1.80        -1.71    8.71e- 2
11 age_poly_2      0.675      1.79         0.377   7.06e- 1
```

(12.1)

---

14 If the variance decomposition also takes into account the time axis, i. e. – as a proxy variable – the *ESS* rounds 1, . . ., 9, then the variance of the target variable *happy* can be attributed to the country level (8.4%), the *ESS* round (0.6%) and residually to *within* country and round (91.0%).

The script's structure and sequence of instructions are designed to utilize the central function of the *tidymodels* library to provide a unified user interface for the various tasks that need to be accomplished in a data science analysis.

First, the random split into a training and test dataset is implemented using the *initial_split()* function. The *rsample* package is used in the background for this purpose (Kuhn and Silge 2022: 56).

Second, we include a statement in the script specifying the model to be estimated, which in this case is an ordinary linear regression via *lm()*. In the background, *tidymodels* accesses the *parsnip* package for this purpose (Kuhn and Silge 2022: 63–65).

Third, the instructions for feature engineering follow. This is done using the *recipe()* function of the *recipes* package for Preprocessing and Feature Engineering Steps for Modeling (Kuhn et al. 2025). A recipe is an object "that defines a series of steps for data processing. Unlike the formula method inside a modeling function, the recipe defines the steps via *step_*()* functions without immediately executing them; it is only a specification of what should be done" (Kuhn and Silge 2022: 91). As can be seen from the PDF documentation of the *recipes* package, a large number of *step()* functions are available for this purpose, three of which we will use here: *step_interact()*, *step_bs()*, and *step_poly()* to specify the terms for an interaction, a regression spline, and a polynomial regression.

Next, we create a workflow object. As Kuhn and Silge (2022: 75) introduce this concept, its purpose is "to encapsulate the major pieces of the modeling process [. . .] The workflow is important in two ways. First, using a workflow concept encourages good methodology since it is a single point of entry to the estimation components of a data analysis. Second, it enables the user to better organize projects." In this example, we use the *workflow()* function in particular to integrate the preceding *model* and *recipe* statements into the workflow via *add_model()* and *add_recipe()*.

Finally, the model parameters are estimated with reference to the workflow object using the *fit()* and related functions of the *parsnip* package, specifically *extract_fit_parsnip()* to produce (12.1) and *extract_fit_engine()* to get the corresponding output of the *stats::lm()* function involved.

12.3.3 Test Step

We use the second of the two data examples from Section 12.3.1 to illustrate how training and testing are bridged. For this, we'll return to the *base*-R route. The corresponding script in Table 12.2 is only intended to show how we can get a same training model via the *tidymodels* route.

```
load("ess19.Rdata")
sset <- na.omit(subset(ess19,
                    select = c( happy, trust, fair,
                                helpful, prej, depriv,
                                age, female, eduyrs,
                                essround, cntry, wt )))
set.seed(125)
tr <- sample(315470, 220829)                                          (12.2)
happy <- lm(happy ~ trust+fair+helpful+
                    prej+depriv+poly(age, 3)+female+
                    age:female+eduyrs, weights = wt,
                    data = sset, subset=tr)
(mse1 <- mean((sset$happy-predict(happy, sset))[-tr]^2))
(rmse1 <- sqrt(mse1))
```

(12.2) shows the first part of the R script, in which the dataset is loaded, missing data is handled, and the random split of 70:30 into training and test dataset is performed, before two related stages follow: the training data (*subset tr*) is used to estimate the model via *lm()* and its predicted values — for the calculation of the prediction error — are related to the observed values of the test data (*subset -tr*). We discussed this procedure in more detail in Section 7.2 and apply it here to the calculation of MSE (mean squared error) and RMSE (root mean squared error). In Section 7.2 we also discussed other important measures for evaluating the prediction error.[15]

The model estimates several linear main effects, one nonlinear effect, and one interaction, all of which appear acceptable based on the corresponding *t* values. These *t*-values are calculated by dividing the estimate of an effect by its estimated standard error. This ratio is typically used to assess the statistical significance of an effect estimate. However, the ratio of an effect estimate to its standard error can also simply be used as an indicator of the strength of an effect — a practice consistently followed, for example, by Coleman (1981). As we noted in Chapter 9, since in this practice the standard error only acts as a uniform benchmark without wanting to draw conclusions about statistical significance from the associated *t* value, this technique is suitable, for example, in big samples, because even the most minimal effects quickly reach significance in such samples simply due to the sheer sample size. And here we have indeed a big sample.

---

15 Section 7.2 in the context of Tables 7.5 and 7.7.

Table 12.2: *tidymodels* Specification for the Training Data (*ESS* Example).

Line	R Script
1	`load("ess19.Rdata")`
2	`sset <- na.omit(subset(ess19,`
3	`               select = c( happy, trust, fair,`
4	`                          helpful, prej,depriv,`
5	`                          age, female, eduyrs,`
6	`                          essround, cntry, wt )))`
7	`library(tidymodels)`
8	`sset <- as_tibble(sset)`
9	`set.seed(125)`
10	`(sset_split <- initial_split(sset, prop = 0.70))`
11	`train <- training(sset_split)`
12	`test <- testing(sset_split)`
13	`wt <- hardhat::importance_weights(train$wt)`
14	`model1 <-`
15	`  linear_reg() %>%`
16	`  set_engine("lm")`
17	`fit1 <-`
18	`  model1 %>%`
19	`    fit(happy ~ trust+fair+helpful+`
20	`        prej+depriv+poly(age, 3)+female+`
21	`        age:female+eduyrs, case_weights=wt,`
22	`        data=train)`
23	`fit1 %>% extract_fit_engine() %>% summary()`

Lines explained

Line 1 loads the data frame and lines 2 to 6 reduce this frame to the complete cases in the variables involved. Line 7 calls the tidymodels library and line 8 transforms the data frame into a tibble. Lines 9 to 12 are used for the random split into a training and a test data set. This is followed by line 13 to define *wt* as the variable that contain the individual case weights. Next comes the model statement for calling the *lm()* function (lines 14 to 16). Referring to this model statement, the *fit()* function is next specified to formulate the model to be estimated in the same way as we would essentially do for the *lm()* function. This includes the weighting variable, the dataset, and a formula that directly incorporates variable transformations required for feature engineering into the equation as inline functions (here for an interaction and a possible nonlinear effect) (lines17 to 22). Finally, we use the *extract_fit_engine()* function in line 23 to obtain the result of the model estimation as produced by *stats::lm()*.

```
rim <- lme4::lmer(happy ~
          (1 | cntry) +
          trust+fair+helpful+
          prej+depriv+poly(age, 3)+female+
          age:female+eduyrs, weights = wt,         (12.3)
          data = sset, subset=tr)
(mse2 <- mean((sset$happy-predict(rim,
          sset))[-tr]^2))
(rmse2 <- sqrt(mse2))
```

Reflecting the *t*-values, it would therefore not be necessary to simplify the model by removing terms. Furthermore, the effects appear to be clearly interpretable. Nevertheless, the model can be improved. Because we are combining data from respondents in 22 countries in the dataset, these data are hierarchically structured. As discussed in Chapter 9, it may therefore be useful to further develop the linear model into a linear mixed model by allowing the intercept to vary randomly from country to country. We did this via (12.3) and can now see how this intervention affected the MSE and RMSE. Regarding the latter, the value improved slightly from 1.69 to 1.67.

If we pursue such a testing strategy, the model is optimized (tuned) on the training set until the best model is reached – possibly sequentially in successive steps – in order to relate the model evaluation to the test set. The coefficients of this best model, as ultimately obtained in the *training* set, would then be reported, along with the prediction error that results when this best model is related to the *test* set. This is undoubtedly useful when relating the predicted values of the training model to the observed values of the test set. Furthermore, this arrangement is often unavoidable when, for small and medium sample sizes, the test set is too small to serve as a meaningful basis for a completely new estimation of the training model. But if the sample size allows, we have that option too, and we use it here. If we replace, in the *lmer()* expression of (12.3), *subset = tr* with *subset = -tr*, we get the estimates of this linear mixed model *when it is applied to the unseen test data* (Table 12.3). Not surprisingly, this approach also results in an RMSE of 1.67.

However, this measure is only of limited use for evaluating the model itself and would not even begin to fully exploit the potential of the available measures. For example, it is useful to reference the model to a null model containing only the intercept, in order to calculate the *proportional reduction in prediction error* attributable to the predictors (features) and their functional relationships to the target variable by comparing it with this reference model. For this purpose, we can use the variances of the random effects in Table 12.3, for instance by taking their respective sums across the two levels involved (*between* countries and *within* country). Using $R^2 = \left(\left(s^2_{null} - s^2_{model} \right) / s^2_{null} \right)$, this shows a reduction in the prediction error by 18.6 percent of the variance of the target variable. In addition, the reference model itself is useful for variance decomposition, as reported at the end of Section 12.3.1.

Table 12.3: Linear Mixed Model applied to the Test Data (*ESS* Example).

Line	R Output
1	Random effects:
2	Groups Name Variance Std.Dev.
3	cntry (Intercept) 0.05529 0.2351
4	Residual 2.65462 1.6293
5	Number of obs: 94641, groups: cntry, 22
6	
7	Fixed effects:
8	Estimate Std. Error t value
9	(Intercept) 8.372e+00 9.495e-02 88.170
10	trust 4.562e-02 2.961e-03 15.406
11	fair 9.364e-02 3.125e-03 29.968
12	helpful 5.494e-02 2.952e-03 18.609
13	prej -9.566e-02 6.806e-03 -14.056
14	depriv -6.260e-01 7.615e-03 -82.198
15	poly(age, 3, raw = TRUE)1 -2.678e-02 5.389e-03 -4.969
16	poly(age, 3, raw = TRUE)2 3.814e-04 1.149e-04 3.319
17	poly(age, 3, raw = TRUE)3 -1.594e-06 7.549e-07 -2.111
18	female 3.321e-01 2.961e-02 11.216
19	eduyrs -5.315e-03 1.570e-03 -3.385
20	female:age -5.898e-03 5.912e-04 -9.977

Lines explained
We introduced the linear mixed model in detail in Chapter 9. Lines 1 to 5: *Random effects* block of information. Line 3 names the group-level variable *cntry* and the variance and standard deviation of the intercept at this group level. Line 4 informs about the residual, i. e. within-group variance of the target variable *happy*. Line 5 prints the number of observations at the individual and group level. Lines 7 to 20 inform about the *Fixed effects* block. We obtain the estimates of effect, their standard errors and the effect/standard error ratio (*t* value).

12.4 Regression and Classification Trees

James et al. (2013: 314) compare trees and linear models and ask which model is better? Their answer: "If the relationship between the features and the response is well approximated by a linear model [. . .], then an approach such as linear regression will likely work well, and will outperform a method such as a regression tree that does not exploit this linear structure. If instead there is a highly non-linear and complex relationship between the features and the response [. . .], then decision trees may outperform classical approaches."

We also gained this impression when we included the last model predicting happiness (Table 12.3), particularly its predictors with linear main effects, in a tree analy-

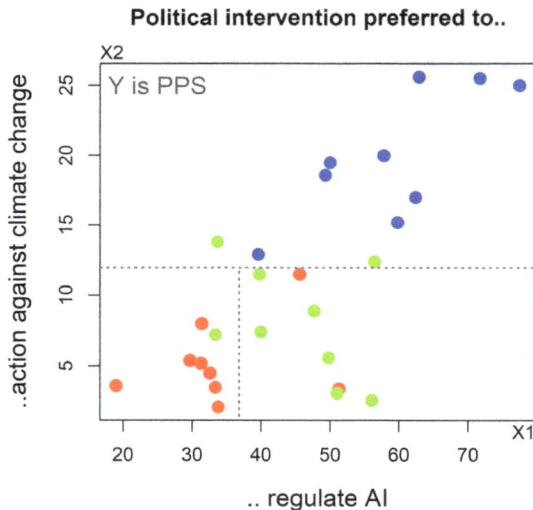

Figure 12.7: Three Regions in a Feature Space.

sis. Only two of these characteristics proved to be of at least limited[16] relevance for this type of analysis: income deprivation (*depriv*) and perceived fairness (*fair*).[17] This is not really surprising for an analysis method that is strongly focused on taking interactions into account. The fact that value *combinations* in particular play a central role in the feature space may perhaps be illustrated by the following introductory example in tree analysis.

12.4.1 Trees in the Feature Space

This analysis is based on data from Example Data Set 6 on Energy Transition in the European Green Deal. We use the same three scales that we used to visualize a scatter plot in Section 5.2.2 (Figures 5.2 and 5.3). Those two figures visualized the relationship between two population shares of a country: the percentage of those who regard action against climate change as a first priority of the European Parliament[18] and the percentage of those who think that "political intervention" is required to ensure "that artificial intelligence applications are developed ethically".[19] The third variable was

---

16 The relevance is particularly limited by the fact that the tree model narrows the spectrum of predicted happiness scores to the scale range of 5.7 to 8.1.

17 We only mention this result briefly here, without reporting the analysis in detail or visualizing it in a diagram.

18 Source: Eurobarometer 95.1

19 Source: Eurobarometer 92.3

the purchasing power standard of a country (PPS), a Eurostat[20] measure. PPS measures the price of certain goods and services relative to income in a country.

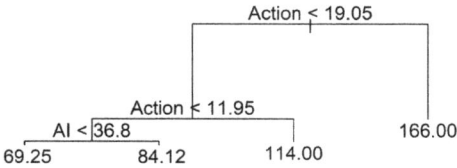

Figure 12.8: Result of the Tree Analysis of the Variables Shown in Figure 12.7.

Figure 12.7 shows the scatterplot of the three variables again, but this time with two reference lines from a tree analysis that partition the feature space into three regions. At the same time, the PPS values were colored as follows: red if a country's PPS is in the bottom third, green if it is in the middle third, and blue if it is in the top third of the EU countries. It is noticeable that the three regions generated by the reference lines almost perfectly separate the red, green and blue marked points. As James et al. (2013: 305) note, "In keeping with the *tree* analogy," such "regions [. . .] are known as *terminal nodes* or *leaves* of the tree" [. . .], to continue that the "points along the tree where the predictor space is split are referred to as *internal nodes.*" Here, we have three internal nodes as indicated by the text *Action < 19.05*, *Action < 11.95* and *AI < 36.8* (Figure 12.8). And it is the latter two internal nodes to which the two reference lines in Figure 12.7 correspond. As decision trees are typically drawn upside down, leaves are at the bottom of the tree.

In Figure 12.8, the top split assigns countries having *Action < 19.05* to the *left* branch and countries having *Action ≥ 19.05* to the *right* branch.

Following this latter branch first, leads to 166.0 which is the mean predicted response, i. e., PPS value for the countries with *Action ≥ 19.05*. On the other hand, the branch for countries with *Action < 19.05* leads to a further subdivision into countries with *Action < 11.95* and countries with *Action* values ≥ 11.95 and < 19.05. Following this latter branch, we arrive at a mean response (PPS) value of 114 for this group of countries.

On the other hand, for countries with an *Action* Value < 11.95, there is a further subdivision into countries for which the *AI* value is < 36.8 or ≥ to 36.8. These branches lead to mean PPS values of 69.25 and 84.12.

In essence, the regression tree underlying the graph in Figure 12.8 is calculated using the instructions in (12.4).[21]

---

20 Source: https://european-union.europa.eu/principles-countries-history/key-facts-and-figures/life-eu _de
21 It should be emphasized that this example only serves to illustrate how a tree analysis divides a feature space into regions with respect to a target variable. This does not imply any assumption of

```
library(tree)
(m <- tree(PPS ~ Action+AI, data=eudata,
           method = "recursive.partition" ))
summary(m)
plot(m)
text(m)
```
(12.4)

12.4.2 Example Data

In the following two sections we use data from Example Data Set 7 on Views & Insights on Climate Policy. In the following section on regression trees, the target variable is sense of responsibility. In the model this variable is termed *responsible*. Respondents were asked in the survey how much they feel personally responsible for contributing to reducing climate change. We used an eleven-point scale ranging from 0 = not at all to 10 = very much.

This is followed by a section on classification trees. To illustrate this approach, a model is presented that will have a dichotomous target variable on the question of climate-neutral (coded 1) versus secure (coded 0) energy supply. The wording of the underlying survey question was as follows: "A thought experiment: Imagine that politicians had to choose between a secure and a climate-neutral energy supply for the country, and — completely fictitiously — both could not be achieved simultaneously. What would be your recommendation: Which of these two goals should politicians then choose?" These three possible answers were offered: "For a secure energy supply", "For a climate-neutral energy supply", "I don't know, I can't say".

For the regression tree analysis example, the set of predictors (features) consists of the following five variables. For the classification tree analysis example that follows later, only two of these five predictors from this set are included, namely *too demanding* and *nimby*.

Three bipolar scales were already introduced[22] in Section 3.4.7. We use the same assigned response codes (−3, −2, −1, 0, 1, 2, 3) as described in Table 3.8. For the graphs in this Section 12.4, we have renamed the variables to indicate their meaning. *Too demanding* refers to the heating transition for the building sector in Germany, a highly contested topic at the time. The following applies here: the larger the scale value, the more a respondent tends to believe that the heating transition demands far too much

---

any "effect" of the features on the target variable. Given the contents of the three variables, such an assumption would be completely misplaced here. If one were to look for effects in these variables, the direction of the relationship would be rather the opposite: that the purchasing power of a country may influence the priority that people living there give to issues such as climate change and AI, for example, compared to issues that affect the economic security of their own living standards.

22 Also used in section 11.4.4 (Table 11.8) in trichotomized form.

from citizens. *Take lead* refers to a survey question on two opposing views on climate rationality. The following applies here: the higher the scale value, the more a respondent tends to believe that Germany should take the lead in climate protection measures, even if the country only makes a very small contribution to global CO_2 emissions. Third, the variable *unfair depts* refers to the issue of intergenerational equity in the financial burden of climate change. The higher the scale value here, the more a respondent tends to believe that such debts put far too much of a burden on future generations.

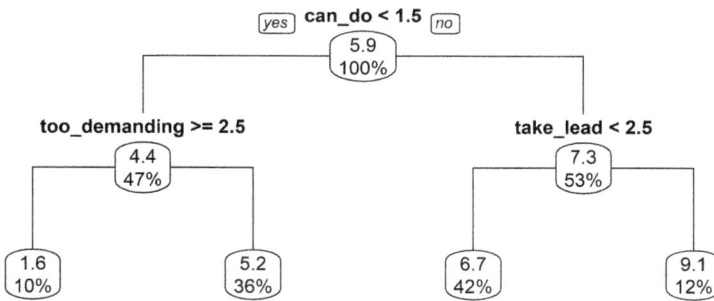

Figure 12.9: Pruned Regression Tree Example. Target: Sense of Responsibility.

Then, *can do* denotes a survey question that asks what one can do as an individual to protect the climate (0 = practically nothing, 1 = not so much, 2 = a lot, 3 = very much).

Finally, we included a survey question about wind turbines and their acceptance as long as they are not located in one's neighborhood – the well-known *nimby* (Not in my backyard) phenomenon. Regarding this phenomenon, we asked: Should climate policy respect this attitude? For the present analysis, the response codes were assigned as follows: 1 = yes, should be accepted without exception, 2 = yes, should be generally accepted (exceptions allowed), 3 = don't know, can't say, 4 = no, should not be generally accepted (exceptions allowed), 5 = no, should not be accepted without exception. The "don't know" response category actually followed the other four categories in the questionnaire and is placed in the middle of the scale only for the purposes of this analysis. The underlying auxiliary assumption is that it expresses an indifference or uncertainty that can be located between the two definitive *yes* and the two definitive *no* answers.

12.4.3 Regression Trees

Figure 12.10 shows the tree structure when the predictor set described in Section 12.4.2 is used to predict the target variable *sense of responsibility*. To calculate this analysis, we first randomly split the data set *sset* into a training and test set.

```
set.seed(125)
tr <- sample(434, 304)
traindata  <- sset[ tr, ]
testdata   <- sset[-tr, ]
```
(12.5)

It is striking that only three of the five predictors prove to be relevant. If this regression tree is pruned back slightly, the result is the image shown in Figure 12.9. Both regression trees were calculated with the *library(rpart)* for recursive partitioning and visualized with the related *library(rpart.plot)*. It is the statements in (12.6) that generate the graph in Figure 12.10 and calculate the underlying tree analysis.

```
library(rpart)
library(rpart.plot)
(sr <- rpart(responsible ~
              unfair_depts+too_demanding+
              take_lead+can_do+nimby,
              method="anova", weights = wg,
              data = traindata))
summary(sr)
rpart.plot(sr,cex=1.3,type = 1, digits=2,
            box.palette = 0, extra = "auto",
            roundint = FALSE)
```
(12.6)

Part of the calculations is a *CP* complexity measure that can be used to prune back the tree (if wanted). In the present analysis, this CP starts at 0.278 at the first node – at the very top of the decision tree – and decreases at the other five nodes below, until it finally reaches the smallest value at one of these nodes, which is 0.013 in the present tree. We can prune back the tree by fixing *CP* at a suitable value within this range. The pruned tree in Figure 12.9, for example, results if we set *cp = 0.05* using

```
psr <- prune(sr, cp=0.05)
```
(12.7)

and relate the plot instruction to the object that contains this pruned tree.

```
rpart.plot(psr,cex=1.3,type = 1, digits=2,
            box.palette = 0,
            extra = "auto",
            roundint = FALSE)
```
(12.8)

This pruned tree starts at the top node (labeled *can_do < 1.5*) with a mean predicted sense of responsibility score of 5.9 on the 0 to 10 scale. Following this topmost branch to the left brings us to the next node, at *too_demanding >= 2.5*. Following the branch to

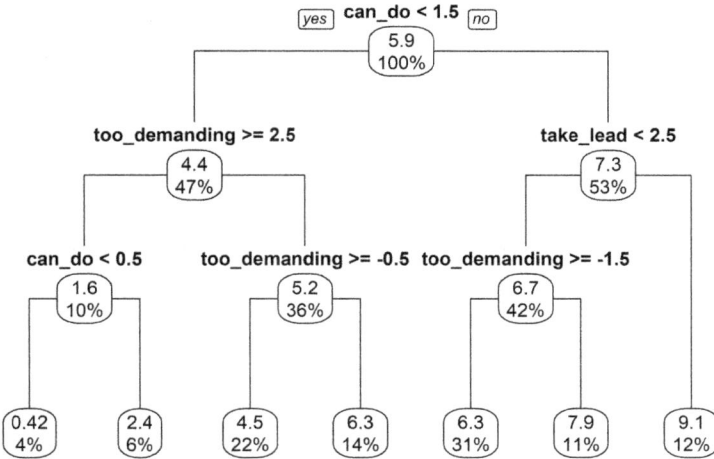

Figure 12.10: Regression Tree Example. Target: Sense of Responsibility.

the left *again at this node* leads us to a terminal node with a predicted sense of responsibility value of *1.6*. This value is expected if a respondent has a value in *can_do* less than *1.5* and in *too-demanding* a value greater than or equal to *2.5*. On the other hand, we end up with a predicted sense of responsibility value of *9.1* if respondents have a value in *can_do* that is greater than or equal to *1.5* and a value in *take_lead* that is greater than or equal to *2.5*. Following the same logic, we can also follow the other branches to finally arrive at the predicted values of the target variable within the spanned spectrum. If the decision tree is not pruned (Figure 12.10), the range of predicted values in the sense of responsibility, from 0.42 to 9.1, covers almost the entire spectrum of the 0 to 10 response scale.

Following on from (12.5) and (12.6), we can evaluate the model with respect to the test data. To do so, we use the *predict()* function and calculate, for instance, the multiple R^2 for this model, which is 0.439. In addition, the second line in (12.9) provides the test MSE (which is 4.28), while the third line calculates the training MSE (which is 3.07).

```
cor(predict(sr, sset[-tr,]), testdata$responsible)^2
mean((testdata$responsible - predict(sr, sset[-tr,]) )^2)         (12.9)
mean((traindata$responsible - predict(sr, sset[tr,]) )^2)
```

12.4.4 Classification Trees

The target variable is dichotomous and indicates the preference for a climate-neutral (coded 1) versus secure (coded 0) energy supply. As before, we first randomly split the data into a training and test set and next calculate the tree model.

```
set.seed(125)
tr <- sample(396, 277)
traindata   <- sset[ tr, ]
testdata    <- sset[-tr, ]
```

(12.10)

For this purpose, we have several libraries at our disposal, such as the *library(tree)*, the *library(rpart)*, or the *library(c50)*. We'll stick with *rpart* in conjunction with *library(rpart.plot)*. The instructions in (12.11) calculate the tree analysis and the graph displayed in Figure 12.11.

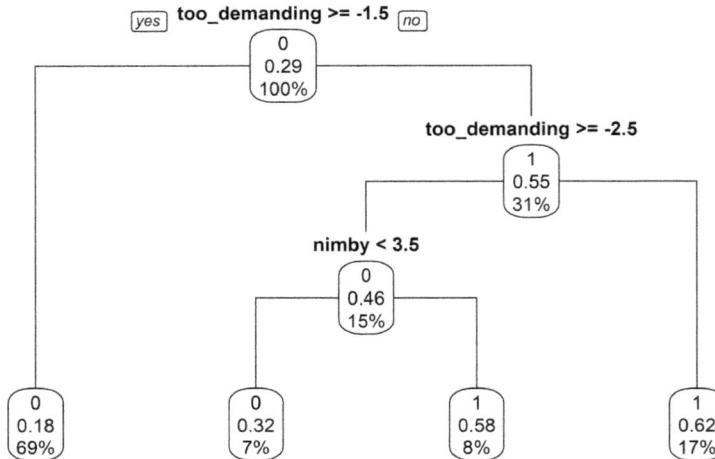

Figure 12.11: Classification Tree. Target is the Preference for Climate-Neutral (1) vs. Secure (0) Energy Supply.

Figure 12.11 presents the nodes along with three pieces of information in the boxes: the predicted class (0 or 1), the probability of being in class 1, and the probability of the node, i. e., the number of units (respondents) to which the feature configuration applies.

```
library(rpart)
library(rpart.plot)
(es <- rpart(clneutral ~
             too_demanding+nimby,
             method="class", weights = wg,
             data = traindata))
rpart.plot(es,cex=1.3,type = 1, digits=2,
           box.palette = 0,extra=106,
           roundint = FALSE)
```

(12.11)

One way to evaluate the model is to calculate a confusion matrix. This involves using the *predict()* function with respect to the test set. This also involves tabulating the predicted class memberships against the observed class memberships. To assign the *predicted* values to class 0 or class 1, an intersection point must be defined. We choose the intersection point at ≤ 0.5 versus > 0.5. The table itself is then obtained using the *table()* function of base R.

```
predicted <- predict(es, testdata)
pred <- ifelse(predicted[,2] > 0.5, 1, 0)                          (12.12)
addmargins(table(testdata$clneutral, pred))
```

In the present case, (12.12) yields the counts in (12.13) that may be used to calculate the usual measures as reported in section 11.1.

```
      pred
         0    1   Sum
0       70    9    79                                              (12.13)
1       29   11    40
Sum     99   20   119
```

12.4.5 Resampling Using the Bootstrap

As James et al. (2013: 187) note, the "*bootstrap* is a widely applicable and extremely powerful statistical tool that can be used to quantify the uncertainty associated with a given estimator or statistical learning method." For example, we can use the bootstrap to estimate the standard error of a coefficient.

Bootstrapping consists of repeatedly drawing random samples of size n from a data set of size n, with each element replaced after it has been drawn. The key term is thus sampling *with replacement* from the original data set.[23] The original dataset can itself be a random sample drawn from a population, as is common in survey research. If this random sample consists of n respondents, bootstrapping would involve repeatedly drawing random samples of this same size n from this original sample. The bootstrap approach works because each drawn element is replaced before the next draw, making it available for possible selection each time. This changes the composition of the original data set in terms of the units involved and, as a result, the numerical estimates based on the respective set of units.

---

23 James et al. (2013: 187–190, 194–197) provide a worthwhile introduction to the bootstrap in their chapter on resampling methods.

We can use the 27 units (countries) from Example Dataset 6 on the energy transition in the European Green Deal to illustrate the principle. In the dataset *eu*, the country codes are in the column (i. e., variable) *cntry*.

```
> eu$cntry
 [1] "AT" "BE" "BG" "CY" "CZ" "DE" "DK" "EE" "ES"
[10] "FI" "FR" "GR" "HR" "HU" "IE" "IT" "LT" "LU"
[19] "LV" "MT" "NL" "PL" "PT" "RO" "SE" "SI" "SK"
```

(12.14)

We first formulate a function that outputs the values contained in the original data set in this country variable (*cntry*), and then performs the resampling step by step using the *sample()* function. This is only for illustration purposes. In practice, we would rather use the *boot()* function instead, which handles the task much faster, much more simply and, above all, automatically.

```
f <- function(eu, i){
  x=eu$cntry[i]
  return(x)
  }
```

(12.15)

In the next step, we refer to the function *f* and implement – here only for 3 runs – the resampling (where *set.seed()* only serves to ensure the reproducibility of the respective result).

```
set.seed(1)
f(eu, sample(27, 27, replace=TRUE))
set.seed(2)
f(eu, sample(27, 27, replace=TRUE))
set.seed(3)
f(eu, sample(27, 27, replace=TRUE))
```

(12.16)

This gives us the following three compositions of the data set. While each country is included only once in the original dataset, it can be seen that a country can be included multiple (up to five) times in a resample, or not at all.

First resampling:

```
 [1] "SE" "CY" "DK" "AT" "BE" "PT" "FR" "HU" "LU"
[10] "SK" "LV" "AT" "NL" "NL" "FI" "PL" "HU" "FI"
[19] "DK" "ES" "IE" "NL" "CZ" "ES" "SE" "HU" "CZ"
```

(12.17)

Second resampling:

```
[1]  "NL" "IE" "DE" "DE" "EE" "LT" "LT" "GR" "ES"
[10] "LU" "FR" "AT" "BG" "PL" "IT" "LU" "LV" "PT"          (12.18)
[19] "EE" "DK" "AT" "PL" "ES" "IT" "CY" "FR" "DE"
```

Third resampling:

```
[1]  "CZ" "SI" "GR" "DK" "CY" "SI" "EE" "FR" "EE"
[10] "MT" "FI" "PT" "EE" "IT" "EE" "EE" "CZ" "BE"          (12.19)
[19] "GR" "HR" "CZ" "EE" "CZ" "ES" "ES" "RO" "PL"
```

The estimates resulting from the respective sample compositions are correspondingly different.

```
f <- function(eu, i){
  y=eu$KKS[i]
  return(mean(y))                                          (12.20)
  }
```

Just one example: If we modify function (12.15) so that the mean is calculated in the countries' purchasing power standards and then relate (12.16) to this, we obtain the following three estimates of this mean: 111.04, 111.22, and 88. The third estimate, in particular, deviates significantly from the first two. This is obviously unfortunate, but it is simply due to the special composition of this third resample (in which one country alone (*EE*) was drawn five times, for a total of only 27 units). This can result in considerable bias. To counteract this, the number of resamples should not be just three, as in this case, but considerably higher, for example, 1,000 or 5,000.

For bootstrapping, the *sample()* function wouldn't really be practical. Instead, the *boot()* function, for example, would be more suitable. This also allows increasing the number of bootstrap estimates to a large number. Based on our example, the instruction could look like this:

```
library(boot)
                                                           (12.21)
boot(eu, f, 5000)
```

For example, this would produce the following result.

```
ORDINARY NONPARAMETRIC BOOTSTRAP

Call:
boot(data = eu, statistic = f, R = 1000)                   (12.22)
```

```
Bootstrap Statistics :
    original         bias      std. error
t1* 101.5185 -0.003444444      8.017318
```

We see that the high number of bootstrap estimates results in practically negligible bias. However, there is no guarantee of this. Even then, bias may remain. However, it is often the case that the fewer bootstrap estimates are calculated, the greater the bias can be expected. In this example, reducing R to 100 resulted in a bias of −0.13, and reducing R to 10 resulted in a bias of 1.8.

12.4.6 Bagging, Random Forests, Boosting

As James et al. (2013: 316) note, decision trees suffer from *high variance*.

> This means that if we split the training data into two parts at random, and fit a decision tree to both halves, the results that we get could be quite different. In contrast, a procedure with *low variance* will yield similar results if applied repeatedly to distinct data sets; [. . .] *Bootstrap aggregation*, or *bagging*, is a general-purpose procedure for reducing the variance of a statistical learning method [. . .] which is particularly useful and frequently used in the context of decision trees (James et al. 2013: 316).

The basic idea of bagging is to reduce variance and hence increase prediction accuracy by generating many training sets, using each of them to calculate a separate prediction model, and averaging the resulting predictions. Since drawing a new sample *from the population* for each required training set would be practically impossible, we bootstrap, by taking repeated samples *from the training data set itself*, train the model on each of these bootstrapped training sets in order to average their predictions for obtaining a *bagged* prediction. "To apply bagging to regression trees, we simply construct B regression trees using B bootstrapped training sets, and average the resulting predictions. The trees are grown deep, and are not pruned. Hence each individual tree has high variance, but low bias. Averaging these B trees reduces the variance" (James et al. 2013: 317).

Random forests result when a decision tree is built in such a way that at each split only a random selection from the set of predictors of the model is considered. In the words of James et al. (2013: 319, 329):

> "*Random forests* provide an improvement over bagged trees by way of a small tweak that *decorrelates* the trees. As in bagging, we build a number of decision trees on bootstrapped training samples. But when building these decision trees, each time a split in a tree is considered, a *random sample of m predictors* is chosen as split candidates from the full set of p predictors". [. . .] That means "that bagging is simply a special case of a random forest with $m=p$".

Accordingly, we can use the *randomForest()* function from the library of the same name for the performance of both random forests and bagging. We did this for model (12.6). In a first step, $m = p$ and thus the *bagging* variant is realized by setting $mtry = 5$ in (12.23). This means that at every split *all five* predictors are considered as possible split candidates.

```
library(randomForest)
set.seed(15)
(m <- randomForest(responsible ~
                   unfair_depts+too_demanding+                    (12.23)
                   take_lead+can_do+nimby,
                    data = sset, subset=tr,
                    importance=TRUE, mtry=5))
```

Through (12.23), we obtain the output in (12.24), which first informs us about the type of random forest, namely by reference to *regression*, the number of trees or bootstrapped training sets (*500*), and the number of variables (*5*) considered as split candidates for each split. Furthermore, the output lists the result. This consists of the mean squared residual calculated for the training dataset (Training MSE), as well as the explained variance.

```
        Type of random forest: regression
              Number of trees: 500
No. of variables tried at each split: 5
                                                                   (12.24)

        Mean of squared residuals: 3.611673
                  % Var explained: 46.04
```

To obtain the test MSE, we add statement (12.25) to (12.23) and bridge training and test data using the *predict()* function. This yields an MSE of 4.45 and an R^2 of 0.425, similar to the initial, unbagged version in (12.9).[24]

```
mean((testdata$responsible - predict(m, sset[-tr,]) )^2)
                                                                   (12.25)
cor(predict(m, sset[-tr,]), testdata$responsible)^2
```

---

[24] The direct comparison is slightly limited because the random forest is calculated without the case weight. However, if (12.6) too is calculated *without* weights = *wg*, the values in (12.9) change only marginally: test R^2 is then 0.442, test MSE = 4.23 and training MSE = 3.04. Thus, in this example, bagging itself does not lead to an improved model fit, but we observe slightly better fit values for the test set if we use the option of working with *a random selection* from the set of predictors at each split. In this example, this is done by setting *mtry* in (12.23) to a number less than 5. For the possible values from 1 to 5, (12.26) informs about the results.

We move from bagging to random forest when, in the splits involved, not all predictors are included, but only a random selection of them are included as split candidates. In (12.23), we reduce the parameter *ntry* accordingly to a number smaller than the number of predictors. We do this by reducing the values successively from 5 to 1. The effect this has on MSE and R^2 is reported in (12.26). It then appears that allowing a smaller rather than a larger number of split candidates for the splits involved has a positive effect on the model's prediction accuracy. However, this may well be different in other data examples. In any case, it is not intended to draw conclusions about a more general relationship from this example.

mtry=	1	2	3	4	5	
Train *MSE*	3.24	3.34	3.48	3.56	3.61	
Train R^2	51.6	0.501	0.480	0.468	0.460	(12.26)
Test *MSE*	4.14	4.28	4.18	4.38	4.45	
Test R^2	0.467	0.452	0.442	0.432	0.425	

Both the *rpart* and *randomForest* libraries calculate the *relative importance* of predictors for a tree analysis. For example, with respect to model (12.6), the model's *summary()* returns this information: *can do* (32), *too demanding* (29), *take lead* (22), *unfair debts* (15) and *nimby* (3). In addition, the relative importance of the individual predictors will also be visible from the tree structure itself, with the comparatively stronger predictors located towards the top of the tree. Along with this, the complexity measure *CP* from the *summary()* of the tree, which we used above as a guide for pruning the tree, also reflects this importance.

Here, in the context of bagging and random forest, we also get information about the importance of the predictors – via the instruction *importance(m)* –, in fact in relation to their contribution to the criteria MSE and node purity. Depending on which criterion is used, the rankings differ slightly. In terms of the MSE criterion, *can do* is at the top, and *too demanding* is in second place. Regarding *node purity*, these two positions are reversed. Following them — equal for both criteria — are *take lead* in third place, *unfair debts* in fourth place, and *nimby* in fifth place.

Boosting is another approach to improving the predictions of a decision tree. While bagging builds a tree for each bootstrapped sample *independently from each other*, boosting works "*sequentially*: each tree is grown using information from previously grown trees. Boosting does not involve bootstrap sampling; instead each tree is fit on a modified version of the original data set" [. . .]. This is basically performed like this: "Given the current model, we fit a decision tree to the residuals from the model. That is, we fit a tree using the current residuals, rather than the outcome Y, as the response. We then add this new decision tree into the fitted function in order to update the residuals" (James et al. 2013: 321).

We did this for model (12.6) using the *gbm()* function from the library of the same name and found that the relative influence of the predictors changed significantly.

Now, *too demanding* appears to be most influential, followed by *unfair depts, nimby, take lead* and *can do*.

Lantz (2019: 131) lists a couple of strengths and weaknesses of the C5.0 decision tree algorithm for classification trees. The strengths include that the results can be interpreted without a mathematical background, that the algorithm excludes unimportant features, and that it is applicable to both small and large data sets.

Weaknesses, however, include that tree models were often biased toward splits on features with many levels, that over- or underfitting of the model is easy, and that small changes in the training data can lead to large changes to decision logic.

Similarly, James et al. (2013: 315–316) describe advantages and disadvantages of trees. Accordingly, trees are very easy to explain to people and they can be displayed graphically. On the other hand, trees generally wouldn't have the same level of predictive accuracy as some other regression and classification approaches. Furthermore, trees can be very un-robust, meaning that "a small change in the data can cause a large change in the final estimated tree" (James et al. 2013: 316). This instability is also highlighted by Ghani and Schierholz (2017: 168).

This latter insight was also conveyed to us through the analysis here.

12.5 Artificial Neural Networks

"An artificial neural network consists of a network of simple information processing units, called neurons", whose power "to model complex relationships is not the result of complex mathematical models, but rather emerges from the interactions between a large set of simple neurons" (Kelleher 2019: 67). Figure 12.12 illustrates the topological structure of a simple neural network. It consists of one input layer, one hidden layer, and one output layer. "A hidden layer is just a layer that is neither the input nor the output layer" (Kelleher 2019: 67–68). Since an artificial neural network is only called a *deep learning* network if it contains *two or more hidden* layers (Kelleher 2019: 68; Kelleher et al. 2020: 389), the network in Figure 12.12 does *not* represent *a deep* neural network. Its topological structure — with only one hidden layer — would be too simple for that. The following applies: "The *depth* of a neural network is equal to the number of hidden layers plus the output layer" (Kelleher et al. 2020: 389). This is why, in visual representations of the topological structure of a neural network, one encounters a numbering of the layers starting with 0, so that the counting of the depth of a neural network begins with the first hidden layer and ends with the output layer (Kelleher 2019: 68; Kelleher et al. 2020: 390). For the network in Figure 12.12, this count would result in a depth of 2: input layer (layer 0), hidden layer (layer 1), output layer (layer 2).

We'll stick with the data underlying a previous example in this chapter and use the respective response variable *sense of responsibility* as well as the set of predictors —*unfair debts, too demanding, take lead, can do, nimby*— to calculate a small neu-

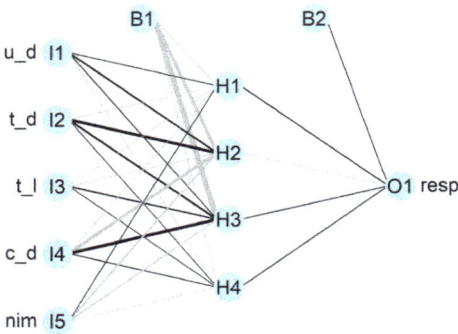

Figure 12.12: Structure of Input, Hidden and Output Layers.

ral network. Figure 12.12 shows the assumed topological structure for this example. To create this graphic, we first calculate the model using the *neuralnet* library with its function of the same name,

```
library(neuralnet)
library(NeuralNetTools)
(sr <- neuralnet(responsible ~
                 unfair_depts+too_demanding+
                 take_lead+can_do+nimby,
                 hidden = 4,
                 data = traindata,
                 act.fct = "logistic"))
```
(12.27)

and then use the *plotnet()* function from the *NeuralNetTools* library in order to produce the plot.

```
plotnet(sr, cex_val=1.5, x_names = c("u_d", "t_d", "t_l",
"c_d", "nim"),
        y_names = c("resp"))
```
(12.28)

On the left we see the input layer with its neurons *I1* to *I5*, which represent the locations in computer memory "that are used to present inputs to the network. These locations can be thought of as sensing neurons. There is no processing of information in these sensing neurons; the output of each of these neurons is simply the value of data stored at the memory location" (Kelleher 2019: 68). In this case, these are the values of the five predictors.

To the right are the circles with the "information processing neurons" in the network. "Each of these neurons takes a set of numerical values as input and maps them to a single output value. Each input to a processing neuron is either the output of a sensing neuron or the output of another processing neuron" (Kelleher 2019: 70).

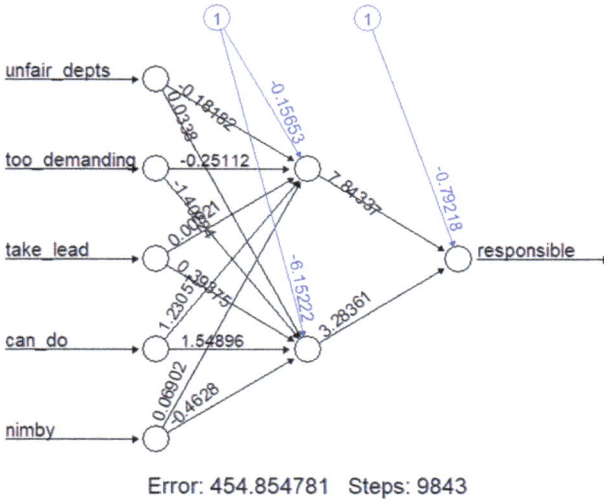

Error: 454.854781   Steps: 9843

Figure 12.13: Reduced Model, with *hidden = 2* and the *plot()* function of *neuralnet*.

Kelleher and Tierney (2018: 120–121) speak of *multiple linear regression* as a function that maps from multiple inputs to a single output, and point out that this "multi-input regression function is the basis for a range of ML algorithms, including neural networks." The authors continue that "at its core, a neuron is simply a multi-input linear-regression function", with the "only significant difference between the two" being "that in a neuron the output of the multi-input linear-regression function is passed through another function that is called the *activation function*." Common activation functions are the *logistic()*, *tanh()* and *rectifier* function, whereas *threshold* activation has been common in early neural network research (Kelleher and Tierney 2018: 121–122; Kelleher 2019: 73–75; Kelleher et al. 2020: 387). Lantz (2019: 237) also points to a smooth approximation of the rectifier known as the *softplus()* function.

Returning to Figure 12.12, we can imagine the neurons *H1* to *H4* as functions $f_1()$ to $f_4()$ of the quantities to their left, whose *predicted* scores are embedded in such an activation function (Kelleher and Tierney 2018: 126–127). Kelleher (2019: 54–56, 73, 89) illustrates this nesting using the example of a threshold function which is used to arrive at a loan decision: first, the credit solvency score is estimated, then a decision rule is applied to this prediction. In general, the output of a neuron is obtained by embedding the prediction of a multiple regression into a (nonlinear) activation function (Kelleher and Tierney 2018: 125), where the embedded equation with its weights (slopes) can also be described as a "weighted sum" plus a "bias" term. "The bias term is simply an extra value that is included in the calculation of the weighted sum" (Kelleher 2019: 88–89). The bias terms "are numeric constants that allow the value at the indicated nodes to be shifted upward or downward, much like the intercept in a linear regression" (Lantz 2019: 234).

$$\text{Output=activation function(predicted score plus bias)} \qquad (12.29)$$

Analogously, *O1* can now be considered as function $f_5()$ of the functions $f1()$ to $f4()$. Kelleher and Tierney (2018: 125–126) speak of "composing functions" in this regard, meaning "that the output of one function is used as input to another function." Here, these would be the outputs of neurons *H1* to *H4*, which are used as input for neuron *O1*, so that the function implemented by *O1* composes the functions implemented by *H1* to *H4*.

In the present model, the information flows from left to right, i. e., in the direction of the arrow as indicated by a plot such as Figure 12.13. Such a network is called a "feed-forward neural network because there are no loops in the network: all the connections points forward from the input toward the output" (Kelleher and Tierney 2018: 124–125; Kelleher et al. 2020: 389). Compared to Figure 12.12, this latter plot represents a simplified topological structure in that the hidden layer here consists of only two neurons instead of four. We show this simplified structure here only for two reasons:[25] first, to demonstrate how the topological structure of a neural network is represented when the *plot()* function of the *neuralnet* library itself is used instead of the *plotnet()* function of the *NeuralNetTools* library, but also for the second reason that this type of representation remains readable only in less complex models. If we were to choose this representation for the hidden layer with four neurons (instead of two here), the numbers for the weights on the arrows would no longer be readable due to lack of space and overwriting. However, it would still be possible to view all weights in the *$result.matrix* in tabular form. Following *library(neuralnet)* and the *neuralnet()* function in (12.27), with *hidden = 2 (instead of hidden = 4)*, the plot in Figure 12.13 was produced using:

```
plot(sr, fontsize=14)                                              (12.30)
```

One goal that is pursued when training a neural network is to find the optimal set of weights for the network. As Kelleher (2019: 70) notes, the "weight of a connection affects how a neuron processes the information it receives along the connection". The interpretability of such weights can be quite challenging if they concern a *hidden* layer in the network. If we take up a consideration by Kelleher (2019: 32–33, 76) in this regard, then it may not be possible "to put a meaningful interpretation on the output of the neuron apart from the general interpretation that it represents some sort of derived feature [. . .] that the network has found useful in generating its outputs." With such features Kelleher means features that are derived from raw features such

---

25 Reducing the assumed number of hidden-layer neurons from four to two increases the error from 383.6 to 454.9. Such a reduction would therefore be adverse.

as the BMI index, which "is a function that takes a number of attributes as input and maps them to a new value" Kelleher and Tierney (2018: 109).

Kelleher (2019: 245) is probably right in assuming that *deep* learning models are the least interpretable models. However, in less complex learning models it may be easier to assign substantive meaning to the weights along the neurons. Just as we do in social science statistics, when we interpret statistical interactions, or as it is done if functions —such as the $f_1()$ to $f_4()$ in the present case— are taken to model "the interaction between the inputs in a different way" (Kelleher 2019: 126).

With the weights that we can read either from the graph or the result matrix itself, this would then be the interpretation task in the present context. We thus transfer these weights from this matrix of model *sr* to (12.31).

	1H1	1H2	1H3	1H4	O1
Intercept	−3.60	−45.0	−79.52	−0.07	2.57
Unfair debts	0.09	13.61	1.67	−0.34	
Too demanding	−1.50	35.31	16.53	1.08	
Take lead	−0.10	−4.51	11.90	0.39	
Can do	−0.03	−44.32	37.50	3.04	
nimby	0.72	−17.69	−14.04	−0.93	
responsibility	4.29	−3.11	3.10	2.77	

$$(12.31)$$

To obtain this matrix with regard to the test data, we use the *compute()* function, to create an object *o1* with its sections on the *$neurons* and the predicted *o1* scores in *$net.result*, with the latter to be used for calculating the multiple R and R^2 (0.691 and 0.478, respectively).

```
o1 <- compute(sr, testdata)
pr <- o1$net.result
cor(pr, testdata$responsible)^2
```
$$(12.32)$$

In (12.31), except for the bottom row, we can proceed by describing each of the four columns for hidden layer 1, i. e., the neurons *1H1* to *1H4*, with their specific weighting according to the input variables to their left, in order to use the respective composition to infer the content significance of these four hidden neurons. If we do this in this way, it essentially follows the same logic as when we interpret a factor analysis or structural equation model[26] by means of the regression weights (i. e., factor load-

---

26 Hidden layer 1 then corresponds to the level of *first-order* latent factors. Just as neural networks can have more than one hidden layer and thus represent deep learning models, structural equation models can also have more than one latent level, for example, two of them: they then estimate the empirical indicators as functions of first-order factors, and these, in turn, as functions of second-order factors. We are not thinking of Curves-of-Factor models here (for a data example, see Can and Engel

ings) that link the latent quantities with their manifest indicators — here, however, without restricting these relationships to linear ones. Next, having clarified the meaning of the hidden or latent quantities in terms of their inherent compositions of weights, we can interpret the effects *of these specific configurations on the target variable O1*, using the weights in the bottom row in (12.31).

The emphasis is on the respective *configuration*, as reflected in the composition of the weights in each column. Unlike in an exploratory – or confirmatory – factor analysis, however, the key question would not be to what extent a set of indicators reflects a *content-homogeneous* latent variable. As if a set of indicators were to be used to measure a latent variable such as prejudice formation or an authoritarian attitude or trust in fellow human beings. Accordingly, the analysis criterion would not primarily be the search for high factor loadings or regression weights. Instead, we look for *patterns of* weights that appear meaningful in terms of content, even though such an approach offers no guarantee that such patterns will always allow for a meaningful interpretation. Essentially, this would be an open question in any analysis.

This is also the case in the present example with four latent or hidden variables. *1H1*, for example, is characterized by a negative and a positive weight, resulting from the indicators *too demanding* and *nimby*. This constellation would in turn have a positive effect on the *sense of responsibility*. In contrast, *1H2* is strongly characterized by a constellation in which a positive weight of *too demanding* meets a negative weight of *can do*, which subsequently has a negative influence on the *sense of responsibility*. *1H3*, on the other hand, is more strongly constituted by *can do* than by the other indicators, and also significantly weaker in *1H4*.

2015), but rather of models in which the weights connecting the two latent levels with each other are also freely estimated. For a data example on purposive and value rationality along with a description of the model architecture, we can refer to Engel et al. (2012: 263–271).

Chapter 13
Natural Language Processing

13.1 Introduction

In addition to established data collection methods such as surveys and experiments, technical progress has provided us with an enormous amount of data available on the internet. Today, a significant part of our communication takes place online, for example in the form of blog posts, message board comments and, of course: social media posts. In addition to that, we have access to all kinds of information that is not from interpersonal communication, but from other outlets sharing information with readers: news outlets inform us about what is going on in the world or in specific contexts, political parties aim to make their agendas known and archives on just about any topic are readily available to us. In addition to the availability and the enormous amount of data, another advantage is that the data was not created for research purposes. People communicate their attitudes and preferences without knowing that we, as researchers, are present.

However, in order to use these data, we need specialized knowledge about how to handle the new data formats that come with it. Survey data comes to us in the shape of datasets that rely heavily on numerical information and, in case of categorical variables, on labeled categories. Those new data sources provide us with data heavily focused on *textual information* instead. Often, the sheer amount of such data makes it impossible for researches to analyze them without computational methods. To make information stored in form of texts usable for researchers, specialized methods for data collection and data analysis are required to handle this so-called *Natural Language*. Natural Language Processing (NLP)[1] is a subfield of computer science and artificial intelligence focused on enabling computers to understand, interpret, and generate human language. The overall aim is to allow computers to process and make sense of large amounts of natural language data. While it is not a new field, the introduction of machine learning algorithms has resulted in NLP methods already being ubiquitous in our daily life. Natural Language Processing encompasses a great variety of tasks such as speech recognition, translations, text analysis and, increasingly, *Large Language Models* (LLM). In social science research, NLP allows us to extract content, meaning and sentiments from textual data. To be able to do so, knowledge of three steps is necessary: of methods of data *collection*, of data *preparation*, and of the *application of statistical models* suitable for the analysis of texts.

---

[1] Depending on discipline and context the terms Text Analytics, Text Mining, Computational Linguistics, Quantitative Text Analysis and several others are used to refer to what is called Natural Language Processing in this chapter.

https://doi.org/10.1515/9783110680683-013

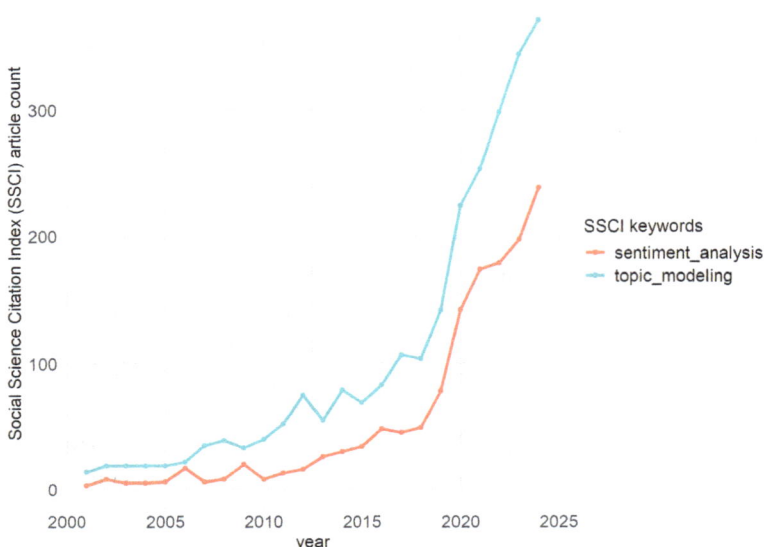

Figure 13.1: Sentiment Analysis and Topic Modeling in the Social Science Citation Index, 2000 to 2025.

With the increased availability of textual data to social scientists, the number of academic publications using, for example, topic models or sentiment analysis has also risen sharply in recent years as shown in Figure 13.1. This chapter provides insights into some beginner-friendly modeling options for both topic modeling and sentiment analysis. It also includes application examples for data collection via Application Programming Interfaces (APIs), for gaining first insights into textual data and also for data preparation, basic model estimation and interpretation.

13.2 Methods of Data Collection for Textual Data

As always, before the collection of data, sampling strategies need to be considered. In survey research, sampling often means to select a representative group of people from a well-defined population, such as all citizens eligible to vote, in order to be able to generalize our findings. This typically involves a form of random sampling and careful attention to statistical accuracy, though research based on self-selection into the sample is also common.

When planning a research project based on textual data, it is necessary to adapt the sampling strategy to the research objective. In some cases, it is possible to collect all texts relevant to answering a research question, but in many cases, this is not possible.

In research where large corpora of communication-based texts are analyzed, the population is often not clearly defined or even definable. Sampling is then often based on practical considerations consistent with the chosen scope of interest. The sample can for example consist of all posts about climate change on a specific platform, or only those written in a specific language, only those from a specific time period or a combination of all of these. Researchers might draw a sample based on convenience, such as scraping posts from the top 100 threads in a message board or consider stratification, such as selecting an equal number of articles from different news outlets. Unlike surveys, text-based research is often less concerned about sampling bias, since the goal is usually to explore patterns within the text itself rather than to make broad generalizations.

When we think about extracting text-based content from the Internet, our first thought might be simply doing the data collection by hand. Copying and pasting the texts into a file that can be imported by our data analysis software of choice is the least technical option that comes to mind. This works well for smaller research projects, but depending on the scope of the data and the structure of the website, it can be a time-consuming task. With larger amounts of data, it is necessary for us to automate the process. In order to collect data automatically, different methods can be used to systematize and automate data collection, the most common being web scraping and the use of Application Programming Interfaces (APIs).

13.2.1 Web Scraping

Web scraping is the procedure of automatically extracting data from websites using a programming environment. It involves downloading the content of a website in order to access specific parts, such as texts, images or tables. We may in fact already be familiar with the concept without identifying it as web scraping: search engines that provide us with information in response to a search query are also based on scraping and indexing the websites that are listed to us as search results.

In order to analyze the content of a website, we first need to use a function in our programming environment that downloads the HTML code so we can process it further and extract the information that is relevant to us. There are several packages for web scraping in R, the most common package being *rvest* (Wickham 2024). When pursuing a research question, the entire content of a website is rarely relevant; we are often interested in specific areas of a website. Packages like *rvest* provide functions to parse, which means to translate, the content into a more structured format, making it accessible for analysis. Websites, of course, are not designed to meet the needs of scraping-based research and can change frequently. It is therefore possible that the content of a website changes between data collection time points, requiring the parsing code to be continually adapted. For a detailed application example using the R package *rvest* see Bosse et al. (2022).

Even though web scraping is a particularly flexible way to extract publicly available data from websites, there several important considerations. Some websites prohibit scraping their content altogether in their terms of use or they may specify which content can and cannot be scraped in a file called *robots.txt*. It is important to review and to respect the websites terms of service and ensure that our activities do not overload their servers or violate legal boundaries. In some cases, websites may offer *Application Programming Interfaces* (APIs) as a more structured and ethical alternative to scraping their content. We therefore recommend to check for existing APIs as a first step when planning to access data.

13.2.2 Application Programming Interfaces (APIs)

An *Application Programming Interface* (API) is a software interface that enables different software applications to communicate with each other. Most of the time, we use APIs without even noticing. For example, a local train company's software system contains information about train punctuality that commuters rely on. On their personal devices, the public transport apps software communicates with the company's software system to display updates on train connections in real-time.

The *API protocol* consists of rules that define how requests can be sent and how data are received. APIs act as intermediaries, enabling one program to access the functionality or data of another program without the need to understand the internal programming of the provider's software system. The communication process is therefore very straightforward for us: we send a request to the API, the API checks the availability of the data and returns them to us in a structured format, in case of R for example as a list or a data frame. For research purposes, data acquisition via APIs offers several advantages. The data are typically reliable, structured, and consistent, with fast response times. APIs are authorized by their providers, significantly reducing legal risks. However, they may have access limits or usage restrictions, and users are dependent on the third-party provider for functionality. Additionally, some APIs may require a paid plan for extensive or long-term use of the service.

In order to communicate with an API, we first need access, typically through a registration on a developer platform. From our programming environment we then connect to the API and are required to authenticate ourselves with our credentials. In the context of APIs, authentication refers to the process of verifying the identity of a user or application trying to access the API. This way, the APIs operator ensures that we are authorized to receive the requested data and that all requests made are traceable. As a result, only authorized users or systems can interact with the API and access its data or services. For us, authentication typically involves supplying the R function that sends the request with credentials, such as an API key, username and password combination, or OAuth tokens, issued to us by the API operator.

Table 13.1: Common Components of APIs.

Component	Description
Developer account	Required to access API documentation and developer tools. Typically registered via the provider's developer portal or through account settings on platforms like social networks.
Oauth	A more secure and complex method where users can grant access to their data.
API key	Unique identifier used to authenticate requests in form of a string given by API provider
Client ID or secret	Credentials used in Oauth flows to identify the app, registered with the API provider
User name or handle	Identifier for a user account on a platform (e.g., social media), sometimes used as a parameter in APIs but not typically involved in authentication.

Access models, or the ways APIs can be accessed, vary widely. Many APIs require an API key or OAuth token to authenticate our requests, while others offer limited open access without requiring authentication. In some cases, especially for full-archive access or sensitive data, researchers need to apply for elevated or academic access and explicitly describe the project for which the data will be used. Depending on the platform, researchers may be able to filter content based on hashtags, language, date ranges, or user mentions; keywords or post types; video titles or upload dates; or variables such as geographic location, topic or media outlet. These filters shape the scope and focus of the collected data. Reflecting on the consequences of these decisions requires our reflection.

Access can be further regulated to ensure functionality for all users. APIs may impose rate limits, which restrict how many requests you can send in a predefined time frame. To manage this, researchers often use batching, breaking a large data collection task into smaller chunks and making requests in intervals, to stay within the allowed limits. This may involve adding pauses between requests or saving partial results across sessions. While some APIs are supported by mature libraries in Python or R that simplify authentication, filtering, and pagination, others require researchers to build more customized solutions and workarounds. Ultimately, researchers need to align their methodological considerations, technical skills, and research ethics with the specific capabilities, access models, and constraints of the APIs we choose to use.

APIs vary significantly in structure, access, and functionality, making it essential to understand their differences when planning to collect textual data (Jünger 2022). Modern APIs most commonly return data in *JSON* (JavaScript Object Notation) or *XML* (Extensible Markup Language), formats social scientists may not be very familiar with. Additionally, the structure of the data, for example how elements are organized, can vary widely. Often, the data are returned in a nested format, where multiple layers of information exist within a single object. This hierarchical organization requires researchers to apply functions that can navigate through multiple levels and extract the desired information. In many cases, R packages exist to parse the data and return more familiar data structures, such as lists and data frames. In this chapter, data collection is accomplished by using some of those beginner-friendly packages.

In the following application example, we demonstrate how to extract data using the *BlueSky API*. BlueSky is a decentralized social network platform. *Decentralized* means it is not controlled by a single central organization or company and is built on an open proto-col that allows different services and platforms to communicate with each other. BlueSky aims to reduce platform control over content while enhancing transparency, making it a particularly interesting platform for researchers. As of today, BlueSky offers an API that is one of the most open, giving *broad access* to publicly available posts, feeds, likes, and reposts (BlueSky Developer APIs 2025). The BlueSky API requires users to have an account on the app and to set up an app-specific password to access data.

Table 13.2: Requesting Data from BlueSky with the *atrrr* Package.

Line	R Script & Output
1	`library(atrrr)`
2	`auth("blueskyaccount.bsky.social")`
3	`ukpol_feed_skeets <- get_feed(`
4	`  "https://bsky.app/profile/johnlf.bsky.social/feed/UKPolitics",`
5	`  limit = 200000,`
6	`  parse = TRUE,`
7	`  verbose = TRUE)`
8	`Got 599 skeets, but there is more.. [7.7s]`
9	`names(ukpol_feed_skeets)`
10	`[1] "uri"      "cid"      "author_handle" "author_name"  "text"`
11	`[6] "author_data"   "post_data""embed_data"  "reply_count"`
12	`    "repost_count"`
13	`[11]"like_count"   "quote_count"  "indexed_at"`
14	`    "in_reply_to"  "in_reply_root"`
15	`[16] "quotes"    "tags"    "mentions"  "links"  "langs"`
16	`[21]"labels"`

Lines explained

Line 1 loads the *atrrr* package (Gruber et al. 2025) that communicates with the BlueSky API. Line 2 starts the authentication process. The personal account handle needs to be provided here instead of *blueskyaccount*. Running the *auth()* function opens a window, where the app password that can be set in the personal account settings must be provided. Lines 3 to 7 request data from a BlueSky Feed. The function *get_feed()* requires a link to the feed and an upper limit on how many skeets will be requested. If parse equals TRUE the results will be returned in a data frame instead of a nested object sent by the server. If verbose equals TRUE information on the process such as the progress bar will be visible in the console. Line 8 shows the progress bar. Lines 9 to 16 show the variable names of the returned data frame object.

As we can see in Table 13.2, when requesting data from a BlueSky feed, we not only receive the skeets, which are stored in the variable *text*, but a data frame rich in additional information. The BlueSky API, in addition to the content of the skeet itself, provides a set of metadata including author information, engagement statistics, and timing details. When using the *get_feed()* function from the *atrrr* package to extract information from feeds on BlueSky, the API returns structured information about individual posts. This includes key details such as the post URI (a unique identifier), the post CID (content ID), the text of the post, the author's handle and display name, and the timestamp indicating when the post was created. It may also include information about embedded media like links or images, as well as interaction metrics such as repost and reply counts, if available. This enables us to later apply filters to define our sample based on the metadata.

13.3 Text Quality and Challenges

Once acquired, textual data can be challenging to analyze for several reasons. Unlike numerical data or predefined categories, textual data often lacks a clear and well-defined structure. Its quality often depends on *the author* and the *context* in which it was written. We can expect texts explicitly written for publication, for example in news outlets or political party programs, to be mostly free of grammatical and typing errors. In contrast, *interpersonal* online communication often shows less concern for correctness and cohesion. Additionally, texts often include irrelevant information or *noise*, for example special characters, links to third party websites and emoticons.

Understanding the sentiment or tone behind text is another challenge for computers, as texts are naturally written with another human as the recipient in mind. Languages have been formed over a long period of time and have developed characteristics that are understandable to humans but pose challenges for computers. People often express emotions in ways that are not immediately clear through words alone, for example through sarcasm or irony, where the opposite of what is said may actually be meant. Additionally, words can have multiple meanings depending on the context, which makes it difficult to understand the intended message, even for human readers. Sometimes the meaning of a word can only be understood from context. For example, many languages include homonyms, words that share the same spelling but have different meanings. For instance, *bark* may refer to the covering of tree trunks or the sound a dog makes. Context is not as easily accessible to a machine as it is to a human reader. Text can be written in simple language or on the contrary in highly complex language with varying sentence structures. Depending on the social group, slang, idioms, abbreviations, and informal language may be present. All of this can make it more challenging to extract meaningful insights using NLP techniques.

In Natural Language Processing, supervised and unsupervised learning that represent the two main approaches to data analysis. Supervised learning involves training a model on a dataset that includes both input data (such as text) and corresponding labels that indicate the correct output. For example, in Sentiment Analysis, the *label* might indicate whether a sentence expresses a positive, negative, or neutral sentiment or conveys more complex emotions like anger or surprise. Creating these labels requires considerable effort, often involving human annotators who understand the meaning of words in context and assign the appropriate labels. This process is time-consuming and therefore costly, especially for large datasets. Unsupervised learning, on the other hand, does not rely on labeled data. These models take raw text as input and identify patterns or structures within it. For instance, an unsupervised model might analyze a collection of articles and *automatically* group them into topics or cluster similar documents based on their content. A limitation of unsupervised learning is that the results can be more difficult to interpret and evaluate, since there are no predefined *correct answers* for comparison.

In recent years, considerable progress has been made in bridging the gap between supervised and unsupervised learning. Transformer-based models are deep learning architectures that have revolutionized NLP by enabling models to understand context and relationships between words across entire texts, rather than just nearby words. These models use mechanisms called *attention layers*, which weigh the importance of each word in a sequence. Popular transformer models like BERT, GPT, and T5 are pre-trained on large amounts of text using self-supervised learning objectives and can then be fine-tuned on specific tasks using supervised learning. Their flexibility and potential in analyzing how human language works make them the foundation of most state-of-the-art NLP systems (Sajun et al. 2024). Despite this, traditional approaches, such as those demonstrated in this chapter, remain important. These models are often more computationally efficient and easier to implement for large-scale or resource-constrained environments. Moreover, they offer transparent outputs such as clear topic-word distributions or rule-based sentiment scores, which are easy to understand. Additionally, in domains with limited labeled data, these unsupervised or rule-based methods can perform robustly without requiring extensive knowledge about, or skills in, fine-tuning.

13.4 Preprocessing of Textual Data

Filtering out all the noise in a text while ideally retaining all of the meaningful content is essential for a successful analysis. To achieve this, several preprocessing steps are required to clean and standardize the data as much as possible before further analysis. Which of these steps are needed or recommended depends on the specific data analysis task or NLP model. Failing to consider and apply appropriate preprocessing has direct consequences for the results of downstream NLP tasks. For example, in the case of topic modeling, how texts are prepared influences both the parameters we consider when choosing the number of topics to estimate, and the quality of those topics (Heiberger and Galvez 2022). There are a multitude of preprocessing steps to consider, tokenization, normalization,[2] stop-word filtering, stemming and part-of-speech-tagging being the most commonly used.

Tokenization means breaking the text into smaller units, called tokens, typically individual words or sub-words. For example, a character variable containing the text *a textual data* becomes the following tokens: *analyzing, textual* and *data*. This step is necessary to enable models to recognize and compare words, for instance in the topic models described later in this chapter. An important step in preprocessing is converting all the text to lowercase. By transforming everything to lowercase, we ensure uniformity and reduce errors in subsequent processing steps and more complex modeling. Lowercasing ensures consistency by treating words like *Politics* and *politics* as the same token. In some cases, however, we might unintentionally merge words that *do not* share the same meaning. This is especially true for languages that use a lot of uppercase letters to distinguish meaning, for example in the German language where all nouns are capitalized.

Punctuation marks, such as commas, periods, and exclamation points, are also often removed from the text. Depending on the research objective, numbers may not be relevant and may add unnecessary complexity to the dataset. Of course, if the text includes numbers that are meaningful for analysis, this step should be skipped. Removing numbers helps focus on the words and their semantic meaning, which is usually more important in tasks like topic modeling or sentiment analysis. For example, the sentence *I computed 2000 cases* would be reduced to *I computed cases* removing any numerical characters. Additionally, texts from the internet often contain symbols and URLs, which should also be removed if they are not relevant for the research objective.

Words, such as *and, the* and *in* are common words that usually don't carry significant meaning in the context of text analysis. These words appear frequently in all types of documents but do not contribute much to understanding the content. By removing these so-called *stop words*, we reduce the noise in the text and improve the efficiency of algorithms, helping them focus on the more meaningful content. For instance, *I have a dog* becomes *have dog*. This can be achieved by using a predefined stop word lexicon to filter out the most common stop words, a feature readily implemented in many NLP packages. If there are topic specific stop words to be considered, a custom stop word list can be defined additionally.

Stemming reduces words to their root form, the core form of a word, that cannot be reduced any further. This process helps group different forms of the same word, such as turning *meeting* and *met* into the root form *meet*. By doing so, similar words are treated as one, which reduces the complexity of a dataset and makes analysis more efficient. A related concept is *lemmatization*, a more advanced procedure that converts words to their base or dictionary form, considering the word's meaning and

---

2 Normalization is often used as an umbrella term for multiple preprocessing steps such as lowercasing and the removal of punctuation, URLs and numbers.

context. The code example in Table 13.3 shows the preprocessing of a corpus of texts using the *quanteda* package (Benoit et al. 2025).

Table 13.3: Example of Text Preprocessing using the *quanteda* Package.

Line	R Script
1	`library(quanteda)`
2	`cleaned_data <- tokens(corpus,`
3	`remove_punct = TRUE,`
4	`remove_symbols = TRUE,`
5	`remove_numbers = TRUE,`
6	`remove_url = TRUE)`
7	`cleaned_data <- tokens_tolower(cleaned_data)`
8	`cleaned_data <- tokens_remove(cleaned_data, stopwords("en"))`
9	`cleaned_data <- tokens_wordstem(cleaned_data)`

Lines explained

Line 1 loads the *quanteda* package. Line 2 defines an object named *cleaned data* using the *tokens()* function which splits the strings in the corpus object into single words. Lines 3 to 6 specify the preprocessing steps, in this case the removal of punctuation, symbols, numbers and URLs. Lines 7 to 9 refer to transforming the tokens to lowercase characters, to the removal of stop words based on an English stop word dictionary included in the package and to stemming.

Part-of-speech (POS) tagging is a preprocessing step used to assign grammatical information to text. In the tagging process, a grammatical label, called a tag, is assigned to each word or token (Martinez 2012). For instance, in the sentence *He made a speech*, *He* will be tagged as a *pronoun*, *made* as a *verb*, and *speech* as a *noun*.

POS taggers are able to annotate text in great detail. Multiple taggers are currently available, some of which are displayed in Table 13.4, and each uses slightly different abbreviation systems for labeling text components. In addition to annotation, many POS taggers support a full text-processing pipeline, including functions such as tokenization, lemmatization, and dependency parsing.[3]

Table 13.5 shows the first rows of an output of a Part-of-Speech (POS) tagging process using the UDPipe tagger with the *udpipe* R package (Wijffels et al. 2018). In this process the texts are tokenized and lemmatized. Each row in the data frame corresponds to a token in the sentence. The *sentence* column contains the first sentence of the first text in the input data. The *start* and *end* columns represent the starting and ending positions of each token within the sentence in terms of character count. The *token_id* column provides a unique identifier for each token in the sentence, starting

---

3 Dependency parsing is an NLP technique that analyzes the grammatical structure of a sentence based on grammatical rules. For more information see Nivre (2010).

Table 13.4: POS Taggers.

Tagger[4]	R Package	Requirements
spaCy	spacyr	Python, spaCy
Stanford CoreNLP	coreNLP, cleanNLP	Java, CoreNLP (download and setup needed)
UDPipe	udpipe	None (Pretrained models can be downloaded within R)
OpenNLP	openNLP	Java, OpenNLP models
TreeTagger	koRpus	TreeTagger installation

from 1, that is assigned to the token *Days*. The column *token* displays the word extracted from the sentence before any linguistic processing, while the lemma column shows the lemmatized form of each token, which is its base or dictionary form. For example, *days* is lemmatized to *day* and *attacked* is lemmatized to *attack*.

Table 13.5: Model Output of Results of a POS Tagging Part 1.

Line		R Output					
1	sentence	start	end	token_id	token	lemma	
2	Days after the Tories...	1	4	1	Days	day	
3	Days after the Tories...	6	10	2	after	after	
4	Days after the Tories...	12	14	3	the	the	
5	Days after the Tories...	16	21	4	Tories	Tory	
6	Days after the Tories...	23	30	5	attacked	attack	

Lines explained
The output shows a part of a data frame containing the results of texts annotated using the *udpipe* POS pipeline. Line 1 shows the variable names as assigned by the Tagger. Lines 2 to 6 show the first five rows of the data frame.

Table 13.6 shows a different selection of columns from the output. The *upos* column indicates the grammatical category of each word, following the Universal Dependencies (UD) standard. In the example sentence the token *day* is tagged as a NOUN, *after* as an adposition (ADP), "the" as a determiner (DET), *Tory* as a proper noun (PROPN) and *attack* as a verb (VERB). This output helps in understanding the syntactic role of each word in the sentence and allows us to filter the dataset based on these tags to identify and retain important words for further analysis.

---

4 For the Taggers and R packages mentioned in Table 13.4, but not used in this Chapter, references are provided in the *References* section under Apache Software Foundation (2025, OpenNLP), Arnold (2025, cleanNLP), Arnold and Tilton (2025, coreNLP), Benoit et al. (2025, spacyr), Honnibal and Montani (2025, spaCy), Hornik (2025, OpenNLP), Michalke (2025, koRpus), Manning et al. (2025, Stanford CoreNLP) and Schmid (2025, TreeTagger)

Table 13.6: Model Output of Results of a POS Tagging Part 2.

Line		R Output			
1	sentence	token_id	token	lemma	upos
2	Days after the Tories...	1	Days	day	NOUN
3	Days after the Tories...	2	after	after	ADP
4	Days after the Tories...	3	the	the	DET
5	Days after the Tories...	4	Tories	Tory	PROPN
6	Days after the Tories...	5	attacked	attack	VERB

Lines explained
The output shows another part of a data frame containing the results of texts annotated using the *udpipe* POS pipeline. Line 1 shows the variable names as assigned by the Tagger. Lines 2 to 6 show the first five rows of the data frame.

13.5 Data Structures for Textual Data

Textual data, in its raw form, is unstructured. Natural language contains a vast number of unique words, phrases, and other linguistic features. It lacks a clear format or predefined structure like numbers or tables, *instead* information is stored in words and sentences. In order to perform data analysis, we need to convert the unstructured text into a structured format that can be processed by functions in general and later in the analysis by algorithms. Input data needs to be readable by there functions, but efficient computation also relies on structured formats. Specialized data structures help compare documents based on shared terms or features. These structures allow models to understand and process text data in a way that is compatible with their requirements. In the documentation of R packages, the data structure expected as input is usually specified. A corpus object in Natural Language Processing is a collection of texts designed to make working with large amounts of textual data easier. Corpora can include books, articles, posts or any other genre of written language. These objects store text in ways that allow easy access to its components, such as individual words, sentences, or phrases. They are used in tasks like text classification, keyword analysis, and language modeling. R packages like *quanteda* provide functions to create corpus objects that help researchers and developers work with text data. A *Document-Term Matrix* (DTM) is a way to organize text data in a structured form. It is similar to a table where rows represent different documents, such as articles, tweets, or book paragraphs, and columns represent words found in those documents, and the cells contain numbers showing how often a word appears in a document. This structure helps computers analyze patterns in text, such as identifying the most common words across multiple documents.

For example if we have the following three short documents:
1. "voting is important"
2. "I will go voting, voting is important"
3. "voting is finished"

their DTM will include the document number for identification purposes, and the column names are the *terms*, represented in counts. An example of a DTM for these sentences is shown in Table 13.7. A related format is the Term-Document-Matrix (TDM) where the rows represent the terms and the columns represent the documents. While *the* DTM and TDM contain the same information, some functions may require a specific format depending on the task or package used.

Table 13.7: Example of a Document Term Matrix (DTM).

document_nr	voting	is	important	I	will	go	finished
1	1	1	1	0	0	0	0
2	2	1	1	1	1	1	0
3	1	1	0	0	0	0	1

A *Document-Feature Matrix* (DFM) is a concept similar to a document term matrix but is often used in broader contexts, where *features* can refer to any type of attribute or characteristic derived from the texts, such as words, sentiments, topics, and more. Just like a data frame, a DFM is a tabular structure where data are organized in rows and columns as shown in Table 13.8 In a data frame, rows typically represent cases and columns represent variables, whereas in a DFM, rows represent text documents, and columns represent their features.

Table 13.8: Example of a Document Feature Matrix (DFM).

document_nr	words	sentences	sentiment
1	34	5	positive
2	7	1	positive
3	150	13	negative

13.6 First Insights into Textual Data

While classical summary statistics analyze values or groupings directly, text summary statistics measure features and patterns within the language itself. Summary statistics for numeric data typically involve measures of central tendency like the mean or median, as well as measures which describe the distribution and numerical variability. For categorical variables, which represent groups or labels rather than numbers, summary statistics focus on counts and proportions such as the frequency of each category, the mode and measures of diversity. Summary statistics for text data focus on structural and content-based properties rather than direct numerical operations. Common text statistics include word counts or sentence counts which give a basic understanding of the lengths and complexity of a corpus of texts. Additionally, vocabulary size, the number of unique words, and frequencies of particular terms can be calculated.

Text summaries may also involve readability scores that estimate how difficult the texts are to understand, or sentiment analysis scores that capture the emotional tone of the writing. Vocabulary size, or the number of unique words (types), provides insight into lexical diversity, often paired with the type-token ratio (TTR) to assess richness. Frequency distributions, like the most common words, highlight recurring terms or phrases, often used for topic identification. More advanced statistics can include sentiment scores or part-of-speech distributions. These summary statistics form the foundation for exploratory analysis and more complex natural language processing tasks. Table 13.9 provides summary statistics for a text corpus consisting of 798 short texts on climate change science.[5]

Table 13.9: Example of Summary Statistics using the *quanteda.textstats* Package.

Line	R Script & Output
1	library(quanteda.textstats)
2	corpus <- corpus(climatechangescience_skeets, text_field = "text")
3	text_stats <- textstat_summary(corpus)
4	
5	library(vtable)
6	sumtable(text_stats, out = "return")

Line		Variable	N	Mean	Std. Dev.	Min	Pctl. 25	Pctl. 75	Max
7		Variable	N	Mean	Std. Dev.	Min	Pctl. 25	Pctl. 75	Max
8	1	chars	798	212	85	0	149	290	301
9	2	sents	798	2.1	1.2	0	1	3	8
10	3	tokens	798	38	17	0	24	50	79
11	4	types	798	31	13	0	22	41	55
12	5	puncts	798	6	4.1	0	3	9	37
13	6	numbers	798	0.58	1.4	0	0	1	15

---

5 For more information on the dataset see chapter 13.7.2

Table 13.9 (continued)

Line										
					R Script & Output					
14	7	symbols	798	0.46	1.1	0	0		0	11
15	8	urls	798	0.82	0.83	0	0		1	5
16	9	tags	798	0.8	1.5	0	0		1	13
17	10	emojis	798	0.36	1	0	0		0	11

Lines explained

Line 1 loads the *quanteda.textstats* package which is part of the quanteda family of packages developed by Benoit et al.). It is required for running the *textstat_summary()_*function. Line 2 defines a corpus object from which the summary statistics are extracted and saved. Line 5 loads the *vtable* (Huntington-Klein 2024) package required for the *sumtable()* function. Lines 7 to 17 show the output.

The rows listed under *Variable* refer to different components of the texts. Firstly, we get information on the number of characters in each document, ranging from 0 to a maximum of 301, with a mean of 212 characters, followed by information about the number of sentences per text, ranging from 0 to 8 sentences. Since the texts from a social network such as BlueSky are expected to be rather short, the mean of 1.2 sentences seems fitting. *Tokens,* in this case, refers to the total count of words, and *types* reflect the number of unique tokens, giving a first idea of vocabulary diversity. The *puncts* row shows punctuation marks, and *numbers* sums up numeric expressions. *Symbols* captures non-alphanumeric symbols such as currency signs or special characters. The row *urls* refers to the presence of web addresses, *tags* refer to labeled metadata such as hashtags, *emojis* represents the number of emoji characters used.

To assess how easy or hard texts are to understand, readability measures offer some insight. Some texts are written in simple words and short sentences, making them very easy to read, while the usage of complicated words and long sentences makes texts harder to follow. A common and easy way to measure readability is the calculation of the Flesch Reading Ease score. The typical range of possible values is between 0 and 100, but negative and higher values are possible (Flesch 1948).

Table 13.10: Flesch Reading Ease Scores.

Score Range	Reading Difficulty
0–30	Very Difficult
30–40	Difficult
50–60	Fairly Difficult
60–70	Standard
70–80	Fairly Easy
80–90	Easy
90–100	Very Easy

The formula of the Flesch Reading Ease Score uses the average number of words per sentence and the average number of syllables per word. If a given text has short sentences and easy words, it will get a high score, meaning it is easy to read. If a text has long sentences and words consisting of a high syllable count, it will get a lower score. In the context of social sciences, political debate transcripts or academic articles tend to have lower readability scores because of their complexity, while social media posts score relatively high.

Table 13.11: Computation of the Flesch Reading Ease Score.

Line	R Script & R Output
1	library(quanteda)
2	library(quanteda.textstats)
3	corpus <- corpus(climatechangescience_skeets,
4	text_field = "text")
5	readability <- textstat_readability(corpus)
6	summary(readability)
7	document Flesch
8	Length:798 Min. :-640.18
9	Class :character 1st Qu.: 15.64
10	Mode :character Median : 34.74
11	Mean : 23.58
12	3rd Qu.: 51.83
13	Max. : 103.54
14	NA's :4

Lines explained
Line 1 and 2 load the packages to convert text data into different object types and to compute the Flesch scores. Line 3 converts the skeets into a corpus object. Lines 5 to 6 define an object containing the readability scores and request a summary. Lines 7 to 14 show the output.

In the example output displayed in Table 13.11, at least one of the documents displays a negative value, the minimum score being −640.18. This happens for example, when URLs, which usually contain a high number of syllables are still present in the corpus before the data cleaning. The range of values extends from texts with very low comprehensibility to texts that are difficult to understand. The average and median Flesch scores of the corpus point to a corpus with a readability suitable for readers with an academic or scientific background. This is consistent with what we might suspect from a social media feed dedicated to scientific dialogue.

The Type-Token Ratio (TTR) is a way to measure how rich and diverse the vocabulary in a text is (Malvern et al. 2004). It looks at how many different words, the *types*, there are compared to the total number of words, the *tokens*. If a text has a lot of repeated words, its TTR will be lower while many unique words will result in a higher TTR. A high TTR value, close to 1, suggests a text with very high lexical diversity, where most words are unique and repetition is minimal. This typically occurs in very short texts.

Table 13.12: Computation of the Type-Token Ratio.

Line	R Script & R Output
1	library(quanteda)
2	library(quanteda.textstats)
3	corpus <- corpus(climatechangescience_skeets, text_field = "text")
4	dfm <- dfm(tokens(corpus))
5	text_stats <- textstat_lexdiv(dfm)
6	summary(lexdiv)
7	document TTR
8	Length:798 Min. :0.4667
9	Class :character 1st Qu.:0.8571
10	Mode :character Median :0.9167
11	Mean :0.9073
12	3rd Qu.:0.9643
13	Max. :1.0000
14	NA's :18

Lines explained
Line 1 and 2 load the packages to convert text data into different object types and to compute the TTR. Line 3 generates a corpus object. Line 4 converts the corpus to a *Document Feature Matrix*. Lines 5 to 6 define an object containing the TTR scores and request a summary. Lines 7 to 14 show the output.

As the TTR value decreases, it indicates increasing repetition and less variety in words. Extremely low TTR values suggest heavy repetition of words and limited vocabulary in the texts. However, as Bestgen (2024) points out, the TTR is sensitive to the length of the texts. Longer texts make the repeated use of words more likely, affecting the TTR value. For the BlueSky skeets, which are *short texts*, the mean TTR suggests high lexical diversity and few repeated words.

13.7 Topic Modeling

13.7.1 Introduction

When working with large collections of texts, a common goal is to find out what their *content* is. This can be approached using qualitative or quantitative content analysis methods. Qualitative content analysis follows a manual, interpretive approach, such as coding and thematic analysis, where researchers closely read the text, identify themes or patterns, and interpret their significance. This process is more subjective and relies on the researchers' understanding of the text, often making the results rich in context but the process time-consuming and labor-intensive. In topic modeling, the key concepts include topics, documents, and words.

Topics represent *latent themes* or concepts that group together words which frequently appear in similar contexts. Documents refer to individual pieces of text, such as articles, blog posts, or reviews, within a given corpus, which is a collection of these documents. Words are the fundamental units of text that are organized into topics based on their co-occurrence patterns across the documents. In the context of quantitative analysis of texts, topic modeling is used to *automatically* extract topics from large amounts of text. It works by using statistical methods to determine which words frequently appear together in a text. It assumes that each document consists of *different topics*, and each topic is described by specific words that are *thematically related* (Blei et al. 2003). Since topic modeling methods calculate topics based on probabilities, manual review of the generated topics is still a very effective and necessary approach to determine whether the found topics are meaningful and interpretable. In this regard, interpreting the latent topics identified by a topic model is a similar process to interpreting the results of an exploratory factor analysis or a latent class model.

13.7.2 Number of Topics and Interpretability

One of the most consequential steps of topic modeling is choosing the number of topics to be estimated (Griffiths and Steyvers 2004). How many topics are appropriate depends heavily on the data, so there is no one-size-fits-all recommended number. One thing that matters is the amount of data and its complexity. For a very small corpus of texts about a very specific topic, for example open-ended survey questions as a reaction to a specific question, we can assume a comparatively low number. For larger corpora like transcripts of political debates from a comprehensive archive, hundreds of topics are a possibility.[6] Choosing the right number of topics must therefore be considered carefully. Choosing the number of topics is also about the content of the topics itself. If we choose a number of topics that is too small, the topics tend to be very broad and therefore lacking more rare but contextually important words. If the number is on the contrary too large, the topics may appear very similar to each other, making them challenging to interpret. A common approach is to test multiple values for the number of topics (e.g., 5, 10, 20, 50) and compare results based on both model fit criteria and human interpretability.

---

6 As Roberts et al. point out in the details of the *stm()* function in the *stm* package used later in this chapter "beyond rough guidelines it is application specific (. . .) Of course, your mileage may vary."

Much more than number-based model outputs, the results of topic models require human interpretation based on *semantic coherence*. In the context of topic modeling, semantic coherence refers to the degree to which the words or terms associated with a given topic are *meaningfully related* to each other. More specifically, it measures how well the terms that frequently appear together in a topic make sense when interpreted in a human-readable way, and how relevant and consistent those terms are with the central theme of the topic. For example, if a topic is labeled as *politics* we would expect words like *party, election, debate* and *vote* to appear in it together. These terms are semantically coherent because they are *conceptually related* to each other. On the other hand, if a topic is labeled *politics* and it contains terms like *party, isopod, election* and *nature*, the semantic coherence would be lower because most of these words do not have a clear or meaningful relationship with each other.

13.7.3 Common Topic Models

13.7.3.1 Latent Dirichlet Allocation (LDA)

When we review publications using *Topic Modeling*, one of the models we come across most often is the *Latent Dirichlet Allocation* (LDA) topic model introduced by Blei et al. in 2003. The LDA model assumes that each document in a corpus is a mixture of multiple topics, and each topic is a distribution of multiple words. The LDA algorithm tries to find the most probable topic distributions that could explain the observed words in each document. One of its advantages is that it operates as an unsupervised learning method, so it does not require labeled data to identify the underlying topics in the documents. LDA utilizes a Bayesian net, incorporating prior beliefs about the data and producing easily interpretable results.

Despite this, LDA has some disadvantages that may lead us to consider other topic modeling methods instead. When it comes to the attributes of the data, the LDA model has data requirements that not every corpus meets equally. LDA works less well when the data are sparse, i. e., when a corpus contains many documents that contain little information. Additionally, the LDA model treats words as if their order in the underlying document were irrelevant, as a *Bag of Words* (BOW) model. In this framework, only the frequency with which a word occurs in a document matters. We, as researchers that are familiar with how human languages, work know from firsthand experience that grammar, word order, sentence structure, and of course context are essential to understand the meaning of texts. For this reason, the results of a LDA model can seem less coherent when it comes to the interpretation of the topics. On top of that, the model assumes that the found topics are equally likely across all documents, which can lead to issues when topics vary significantly in their prevalence across different document sets.

Additionally, the LDA model assumes the topics to be uncorrelated. While this assumption may hold in some cases, we can oftentimes form an argument about our expected topics being correlated quite easily. News articles, for example, tend to cover content that is related because of geographical proximity, events happening in the same political environment, or report repeatedly about the same topic. The *Correlated Topic Model* (CTM) introduced by Blei and Lafferty in 2007 is an improvement on the LDA model in that regard. Like LDA, CTM assumes that each document is made up of a mixture of topics, however unlike in LDA, CTM allows topics to be correlated. To make this possible the Dirichlet distribution used in LDA is replaced with a logistic normal distribution, which includes a covariance structure. This change makes CTM more realistic in capturing how topics actually co-occur in real-world text. Blei/Lafferty (2007) showed that CTM outperforms LDA in practice. *The Structural Topic Model* (STM) introduced by Roberts et al. covered in a later section in this chapter builds directly on the CTM framework. Often, textual data comes with additional information, called metadata, that cannot be used in the LDA framework, but can be incorporated in a Structural Topic Model.

13.7.3.2 Biterm Topic Model (BTM)

The length of texts on the internet varies greatly, depending on the purpose for which they were written. Longer sections of text can for example be found in book reviews, news articles, and blog posts. Although these types of texts are relevant in research, many texts we are interested in are, on the contrary, quite short. Especially when we want to explore the opinions and attitudes of private individuals, we are dependent on texts that are written in everyday life as a reaction to other web content. Examples of such texts are social media posts on short message apps like X or BlueSky, open ended answers in surveys, or customer reviews. For these types of short texts traditional topic models like Latent Dirichlet Allocation are less suited. The *Biterm Topic Model* (Watanabe 2021) is especially useful to identify topics in such collections of very short texts. Unlike LDA and similar models that focus on document-level word distributions, a Biterm Topic Model captures word co-occurrence patterns directly by modeling unordered word pairs called biterms. A *biterm* is a pair of words that co-occur within a local context, typically within the same short text. The general idea is that co-occurring

words in short texts carry stronger topical signals than individual word frequencies. The BTM is a generative probabilistic model that uses the Gibbs sampling algorithm. In its generative process, a topic is first drawn from a corpus-level topic distribution. Then, two words are independently sampled from the word distribution associated with the topic, forming a biterm. This allows it to generalize better to short texts (Yan et al. 2013).

For the application example of the BTM model, we analyze a sample of 200000 short texts published in the BlueSky feed *ukpolitics*.[7] The goal of the analysis is to identify the most important topics and trends in British politics as seen by users of

---

7 The data collection process for this application example is demonstrated in Table 13.2

the BlueSky feed. Before running the model, we need to preprocess the data. Because the BTM models word co-occurrence patterns, it is important that the words included in the text corpus are actually meaningful. This can be achieved by performing Part-of-Speech Tagging on the data before running the model.

Table 13.13: Part of Speech Tagging Process.

Line	R Script
1	`library(udpipe)`
2	`lang_model <- udpipe_load_model("english-ewt-ud-2.5-191206.udpipe")`
3	`processed_skeets <- udpipe(ukpol_skeets$text,`
4	`                    object = lang_model,`
5	`                    parralel.cores = 16,`
6	`                    trace = TRUE)`
7	`custom_stopwords <- c("UK", "MP")`
8	`cleaned_processed_skeets <- processed_skeets %>%`
9	`            filter(upos %in% c("NOUN", "VERB", "ADJ", "PROPN")) %>%`
10	`            filter(!lemma %in% custom_stopwords)`

Lines explained
Line 1 loads the "udpipe" package to provide a language model for the Part of Speech Tagging. Line 2 imports the pretrained linguistic model to process texts written in English language. Lines 3 to 6 apply the model to the texts. The *udpipe()* function performs tokenization, tagging and lemmatization. Line 7 defines custom stop words. Lines 8 to 10 filter the dataset for nouns, verbs, adjectives, proper nouns and remove the predefined custom stop words.

In the process, we also specify additional stop words. These are not included in the pre-implemented stop words list, but are specific to the topic of the texts. *UK* and *MP* refer to the abbreviations for the United Kingdom and Member of Parliament which can be expected to occur in many skeets and may confound the topics. After the data preparation, a Biterm Topic Model consisting of 5 topics is estimated.

Table 13.14: Estimation of a Biterm Topic Model using the BTM Package.

Line	R Script & R Output
1	`library(BTM)`
2	`set.seed(212)`
3	`btm_model <- BTM(cleaned_processed_skeets,`
4	`            k = 5,`
5	`            trace = TRUE,`
6	`            detailed = TRUE)`
7	
8	`2025-07-12 17:38:07 Start Gibbs sampling iteration 1/100`

Table 13.14 (continued)

Line	R Script & R Output
9	. . .
10	2025-07-12 17:45:25 Start Gibbs sampling iteration 100/100
11	btm_model
12	Biterm Topic Model
13	trained with 100 Gibbs iterations, alpha: 10, beta: 0.01
14	topics: 5
15	size of the token vocabulary: 19567
16	topic distribution theta: 0.175 0.384 0.144 0.109 0.188

Lines explained

Line 1 loads the *BTM* package to estimate the model. Line 2 sets the seed. Lines 3 to 6 run the function for the BTM model for a five-topic solution. *Trace* and *detailed* are set to TRUE to print out the Gibbs sampling iterations and to return model information to the console. Lines 11 to 16 request and show information about the model.

In the model output in Table 13.14 we are given the topic distribution, theta. *Theta* represents the probability that a randomly selected biterm in the corpus is generated from topic k. Theta values add up to a value of 1 and can be interpreted as proportions.

Based on the theta values of our model, topic 2 has the highest proportion by far. This means that topic 2 is more dominant in the overall corpus. Figure 13.2 shows a bar plot of the topic distribution.

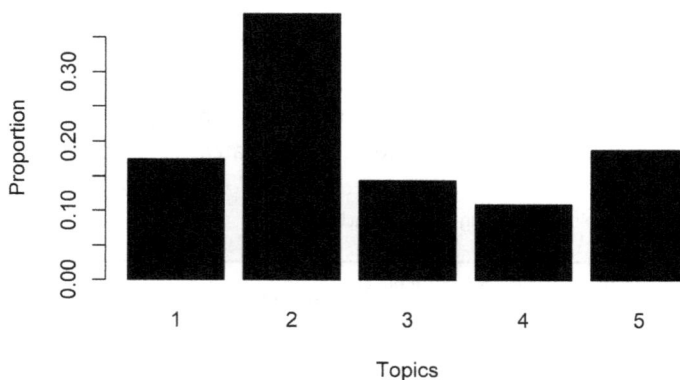

Figure 13.2: Topic Proportions for the Biterm Topic Model.

As the name of the model suggests, *biterms* play a central role in the model estimation. When we look at the output of the *terms()* function in Table 13.15, we can see a section of the generated biterms and their associated topic assignments. Each row is a biterm occurring in the corpus that was assigned to the same topic. The output also informs us that the number of biterms is 22,543,941. As it is often the case, the output is not understandable without either context knowledge or additional research into unfamiliar terms. In this case FBPE might refer to the *Follow Back Pro EU* hashtag under which users of a platform could find like-minded users to follow.

Table 13.15: Biterms from the Biterm Topic Model.

Line		R Script & R Output		
1	biterms <- terms(btm_model, type = "biterms", top_n = 5)			
2	biterms			
3	$n			
4	[1] 22543941			
5	$biterms			
6		term1	term2	topic
7	1	FBPE	lot	2
8	2	FBPE	shaking	2
9	3	FBPE	heads	2
10	4	FBPE	Starmer	2
11	5	FBPE	get	2
12	6	FBPE	feeling	2
13	7	cheated	FBPE	2
14	8	lot	shaking	5
15	9	heads	lot	2
16	10	lot	Starmer	4

Lines explained
Lines 1 to 2 call the *terms()* function the BTM package includes to extract all biterms for a topic number of k = 5 and sends information to the console. Lines 3 to 16 show the output.

Additionally, we can use the same function to show *token probabilities* in relation to the topics, as seen in Table 13.16. The function returns a list of data frames, one for each topic, where each data frame contains columns *token* and *probability* ordered from high to low. These token probabilities help us with identifying the most representative words for each topic, aiding in the interpretation and labeling of the topics.

The analysis shows that while we get information about the contents of the skeets, *human knowledge* is needed to make sense of them. In this case without information on how the political landscape in the United Kingdom is structured, we could only guess that some of the tokens are proper names of meaningful political figures. It is up to us as researchers to interpret the information given by the model and to research contexts that are unknown to us so far. In the example, those proper names are meaningful in all of the topics which makes sense considering the data source. On short message social networks as BlueSky, sharing news into a feed is a common way to use the app. We can expect central political decision makers to be connected to all political topics that are widely discussed on the feed. The same reasoning applies to the political parties

Table 13.16: Token Probabilities for the Biterm Topic Model.

Line	R Script & R Output
1	`topicprobs <- terms(btm_model, type = "tokens", top_n = 5)`
2	`topicprobs`
3	`[[1]]` `[[2]]`
4	`        token probability         token probability`
5	`1 government 0.016976838   1 Starmer 0.020600799`
6	`2    Starmer 0.010460406   2 Farage 0.019999994`
7	`3         AI 0.008245050   3 Labour 0.019013118`
8	`4 Government 0.007681136   4 Reform 0.015311667`
9	`5        new 0.006565475   5 Tories 0.012344912`
10	`6     people 0.004155093   6 people 0.009297315`
11	`7     Labour 0.003716508   7  right 0.008182095`
12	`[[3]]` `[[4]]`
13	`        token probability         token probability`
14	`1    Starmer 0.008654583   1   Starmer 0.014027572`
15	`2     Labour 0.008059488   2    Reeves 0.009942841`
16	`3      House 0.007307230   3       tax 0.009044660`
17	`4 government 0.006589915   4      Keir 0.008608587`
18	`5     Farage 0.005799174   5    Rachel 0.007981325`
19	`6      Tories 0.004616220  6    Farage 0.007228162`
20	`7       Bill 0.004568963   7 Minister 0.005434851`
21	`[[5]]`
22	`        token probability`
23	`1    Starmer 0.026844626`
24	`2   Badenoch 0.021024538`
25	`3     Labour 0.012621375`
26	`4       Keir 0.012089263`
27	`5       Kemi 0.011549014`
28	`6       PMQs 0.007998774`
29	`7     leader 0.006598090`

Lines explained
Line 1 calls the *terms()* function the BTM package includes to extract the token probabilities for a topic number of K = 5. Lines 3 to 29 request and show the output.

mentioned. In the differences between the topics often lies the most meaningful information, we can see that *reforms*, *taxes*, *people* and *AI* are mentioned in the topics. For further analysis, we might consider filtering the tagged skeets and removing the proper nouns to get topics more focused on content than on political personas.

13.7.3.3 Structural Topic Model (STM)

The Structural Topic Model (STM) is an advanced topic modeling technique that extends traditional approaches mentioned in earlier subchapters by incorporating metadata. Similar to control variables in a regression model, the STM can take additional information into account when estimating the topics. Compared to traditional approaches that estimate topics based on the textual information only, STM can be used to uncover not only the latent themes but also how these themes vary systematically with attributes such as author characteristics, geographic contexts or the time a text was published. Metadata can influence the model in two main ways: it can affect topic *prevalence* (how much each topic contributes to a document) and/or topic *content* (how word distributions within a topic change based on metadata). This is particularly useful in social sciences, where researchers may want to examine how discourses play out across voters of different party affiliations, demographic groups, or time periods. Additionally, STM can estimate correlations between topics.

The estimation process in Structural Topic Model uses Variational Expectation-Maximization (EM) to perform approximate Bayesian inference.[8] The estimation works by iteratively uncovering patterns in texts. The model starts with random guesses about which topics are in each document and which words belong to which topics. E-step, it estimates topic proportions and word-topic assignments using a simpler approximation method called variational inference. In the M-step, it updates how metadata influences topic prevalence and/or topic content. This process repeats until the model stabilizes, resulting in a set of topics, their associated words, and insights into how these topics vary with metadata. The STM framework is implemented in the *stm* package in R, providing functions for estimation, evaluation, model selection, visualization and hypothesis testing (Roberts et al. 2019).

For the following application example, the data used are based on articles published by the US newspaper *The New York Times*. The services the New York Times offers consists of multiple API endpoints, each serving a different purpose and returning different data. The Article Search API, which we used for this application example enables users to search for articles based on keywords, dates, or filters, while the Top Stories API delivers the latest news across different categories. The Most Popular API provides access to the most read, shared, or commented articles. To access the New York Times' API, the registration of a developers account is necessary to be able to complete authentication when using R to extract data from the service.[9] In the application example, the R package *nytimes* (Coene 2025) is used to communicate with the API to collect information on news articles from the Article Search API (The New York Times Developer Network 2025). For the application example we are interested in articles the API returns when using the query "education". While we do not get articles in full length, we do get titles, abstracts and the first paragraph of every article returned. Since the first paragraphs of news articles are generally used to in-

---

8 For further explanation of the model estimation see Roberts et al. (2019).
9 For signing up for an API key and documentation on the APIs the New York Times offers see https://developer.nytimes.com/ (The New York Times Developer Network 2025).

troduce to the articles topic they will be analyzed in this example. The API returns data for the search query in form of a "Large list" object.

Table 13.17: Requesting and Inspecting Data from the New York Times Article API.

Line	R Script & R Output
1	`library(nytimes)`
2	`library(quanteda)`
3	`library(tidyverse)`
4	
5	`nytimes_key("YourAPIkey")`
6	`education_articles <- ny_search("education",`
7	`since = Sys.Date() - 90, pages = 100)`
8	`education_articles <- tibble(education) %>%`
9	`unnest_wider(education, names_sep = NULL)`
10	`education_articles <- select(education_articles,`
11	`lead_paragraph,`
12	`type_of_material)`
13	`fct_count(education_articles$type_of_material,`
14	`sort = T,`
15	`prop = T)`
16	`# A tibble: 13 × 3`
17	`f                              n          p`
18	`<fct>                        <int>      <dbl>`
19	`1 News                       576      0.632`
20	`2 Op-Ed                      111      0.122`
21	`3 Interactive Feature         61      0.0669`
22	`4 Obituary (Obit)             58      0.0636`
23	`5 briefing                    43      0.0471`
24	`6 Letter                      21      0.0230`
25	`7 Review                      12      0.0132`
26	`8 Editorial                   10      0.0110`
27	`9 Video                        7      0.00768`
28	`10 NA                          6      0.00658`
29	`11 News Analysis               5      0.00548`
30	`12 Correction                  1      0.00110`
31	`13 NYT Cooking                 1      0.00110`

Lines explained

Lines 1 to 3 load the required packages. Line 5 runs the function to authenticate to the New York Times Article API. *YourAPIkey* has to be replaced with the personal key. Lines 6 to 7 run the article search function using the query *education* to access article information. It is specified via the since argument that articles from the systems current date minus 90 days will be requested. This function returns a nested list. Lines 8 to 9 convert the list to a tibble. Lines 10 to 12 select variables from the tibble object. Lines 13 to 15 request a table sorted by frequencies with a column of proportions added. Lines 16 to 31 show the output.

Since a strength of the Structural Topic Model is the possibility to include metadata, and the NYTimes API returns metadata variables in addition to the textual data, we include the variable *type_of_material* in the model and assume it influences topic prevalence in the lead paragraphs. The variable contains information about what kind of article the first paragraphs come from. The frequency table included in Table 13.17 tells us that the most common article genre in the data are news articles, making up 63.3% of the texts, but other materials such as Op-Eds, interactive features, obituaries, and briefings are also common. The *NAs* shows, that not all articles returned by the API have a type of material assigned, so a proportion of metadata is missing for the texts.

Table 13.18: Text Preprocessing using the *quanteda* Package.

Line	R Script
1	library(quanteda)
2	education_articles <- education_articles[education_articles$lead_pa
3	ragraph !="",]
4	education_articles <- na.omit(education_articles)
5	corpus <- corpus(education_articles, text_field = "lead_paragraph",
6	meta = "type_of_material")
7	cleaned_data <- tokens(corpus,
8	remove_punct = T,
9	remove_symbols = T,
10	remove_numbers = T,
11	remove_url = T)
12	cleaned_data <- tokens_tolower(cleaned_data)
13	cleaned_data <- tokens_remove(cleaned_data, stopwords("en"))
14	cleaned_data <- tokens_wordstem(cleaned_data)

Lines explained
Line 1 loads the *quanteda* package. Lines 2 to 3 remove rows with empty cells in the *lead_paragraph* variable from the data. Line 4 removes NA rows. Lines 5 to 6 create a corpus document specifying *lead_paragraph* as the text field and *type_of_material* as metadata. Lines 7 to 14 pre-process the data as explained in section 13.4

To prepare the data for analysis, rows that cannot be used in the model are removed. Rows that either have no metadata present or contain empty cells in the text variable can prevent the model from running successfully. Afterwards, the texts are prepared for analysis as described previously. After tokenizing, punctuation, symbols, numbers and URLs are removed. The tokens are converted to lowercase, and stop words are filtered out before applying stemming.

After preprocessing a number of topics to be estimated must be chosen. The diagnostic values across varying values of K displayed in Table 13.19 offer insights into the fit of the estimated models. Contradictions between the metrics are a common occurrence and part of the model selection process is to consider which number of topics provides the best fit given those conflicting results.

Table 13.19: Model Fit Measures for Structural Topic Models.

Line	R Script & R Output

Line			R Script & R Output			
1	dfm <- dfm(cleaned_data)					
2	prepped_articles <- convert(dfm, to = "stm")					
3	docs <- prepped_articles$documents					
4	vocab <- prepped_articles$vocab					
5	meta <- prepped_articles$meta					
6	set.seed(133)					
7	k <- searchK(docs, vocab, K= seq(2, 10, by = 1),					
8	prevalence = ~type_of_material,					
9	data = meta)					
10	plot(k)					
11	k					
12	$results					
13	K	exclus	semcoh	heldout	residual	bound	lbound
14	1 2	6.971593	-103.8625	-7.741806	9.010067	-154799.3	-154798.6
15	2 3	7.845256	-114.2866	-7.769401	6.946862	-152939.8	-152938
16	3 4	8.342191	-123.1027	-7.701014	6.115303	-150176.8	-150173.6
17	4 5	8.560005	-124.1668	-7.944474	4.816948	-148252.8	-148248
18	5 6	8.756279	-129.8768	-8.025858	4.338544	-147394.7	-147388.1
19	6 7	8.951741	-139.5685	-8.031802	3.812076	-145670.4	-145661.9
20	7 8	9.087698	-137.2016	-7.980207	3.402737	-144329.8	-144319.2
21	8 9	9.174514	-137.199	-8.14792	3.081764	-143428.3	-143415.5
22	9 10	9.27366	-141.4537	-8.103419	2.852155	-142565.5	-142550.4

Lines explained

Lines 1 to 2 create a document feature matrix of the *cleaned_data* object in Table 13.18 and covert it to an STM object. Lines 3 to 5 extract and store the *documents*, the *vocab* and the *metadata*. Line 6 sets the seed. Lines 7 to 9 run multiple STMs. The sequence specifies that topics from 2 (the minimum) to 10 are estimated. Line 10 plots diagnostic values as seen in Figure 13.4. Lines 12 to 22 show the model fit measures.

The *exclusivity* (exclus) metric measures how exclusive the top words in each topic are, with higher values indicating that topics have a more unique composition of words. In this case exclusivity increases with K, from 6.97 at K = 2 to 9.27 at K = 10. However, very high exclusivity can come at the cost of *semantic coherence* (semcoh), which measures how coherent or interpretable the topics are based on word co-occurrence. Semantic coherence, introduced from a human perspective previously in this chapter, is a way to ascertain the relationships between the words of a found topic. The concept of semantic coherence in a structural topic model context is similar. The core idea is that in models which are semantically coherent the words which are most probable in a topic should co-occur within the same document. (Mimno et al. 2011).

Solutions with higher values of semcoh are preferred. As K increases, semantic coherence becomes more negative, starting at −103.86 and dropping to −141.45 by K = 10. This suggests that the interpretability of topics declines with more topics, highlighting a

Diagnostic Values by Number of Topics

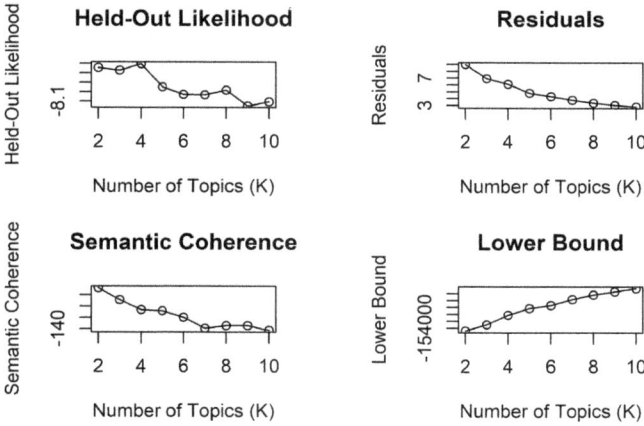

Figure 13.3: Diagnostic Values for Models with 2 to 10 Topics.

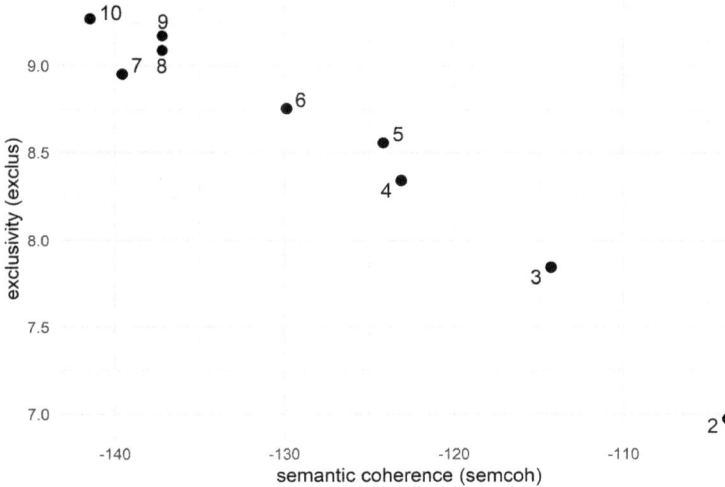

Figure 13.4: Exclusivity and Semantic Coherence for Models with 2 to 10 Topics.

common trade-off between exclusivity and coherence that is shown in Figure 13.4, where the values for exclusivity and semantic coherence are plotted jointly.

Exclusivity and semantic coherence can be used in conjunction with other metrics, such as the held-out likelihood and residual variance to get a more comprehensive picture of the model fit. In the case of the residual variance or *residuals* in the output, lower values are indicative for a better fit. The held-out likelihood *heldout* is a measure to evaluate a model's ability to make accurate predictions on heldout data that it hasn't "seen" before using cross validation to measure predictive performance. In the example in Table 13.19 the heldout remains relatively flat or worsens slightly across different K values, ranging from −7.74 to −8.1. K = 4 has the best (least negative) heldout value at −7.7, suggesting that K = 4 offers the best generalization. Meanwhile, the residual variance in the document-topic matrix decreases with more topics, from 9.01 at K = 2 to 2.85 at K = 10, indicating a better model fit as more topics are included, although this trend is expected and not always meaningful by itself. The *bound* and *lbound* metrics, which represent bounds on the log-likelihood, become less negative with increasing K, suggesting better log-likelihood approximation as more parameters are introduced. However, this improvement may lead to overfitting as the number of topics increases.

Given these trends, K = 4 or K = 5 strike the best balance between exclusivity, coherence, and predictive performance. These values provide a good mix of exclusivity and coherence while avoiding the overfitting risks and diminishing returns seen with higher values of K.[10] Based on those results a Structural Topic Model with K = 5 topics is estimated for the application example.

Table 13.20: Estimation of the Structural Topic Model.

Line	R Script
1	`library(stm)`
2	`stm_model <- stm(documents = prepped_articles$documents,`
3	`vocab = prepped_articles$vocab,`
4	`data = prepped_articles$meta,`
5	`prevalence = ~type_of_material,`
6	`K = 5,`
7	`seed = 133,`
8	`init.type = "Spectral",`
9	`verbose = T)`
10	`plot(stm_model)`

Lines explained
Line 1 loads the stm package to estimate the model. Lines 2 to 9 specify the model. Line 1 in the function specifies the documents to be used. Lines 3 and 4 specify the data to be used. Line 5 specifies the metadata to be used as a covariate. Line 6 refers to the chosen number of topics. Line 7 sets a seed. Line 8 specifies the initialization type to be used, Spectral being the default option. For more detailed information on different initialization types see Roberts et. al. (2016). Line 10 plots the expected topic proportions as seen in Figure 13.5.

---

10 In this chapter, values of K ranging from 2 to 10 were chosen for the purpose of showing a comprehensible and clear output. Given the variety of topics that can be assumed to occur in the news articles returned with the rather general keyword *education*, an even higher number of K than 10 to be a better fit is likely and to be considered.

Figure 13.5 shows the expected topic proportions. The expected topic proportion is the average proportion of each topic across all documents in the corpus. Topic 2, centered on words like *presid*, *trump*, and *feder* is the most prevalent across the documents, indicating a strong focus on political content.

Top Topics

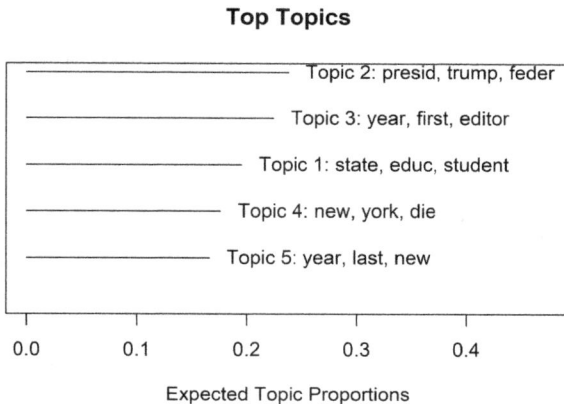

Expected Topic Proportions

Figure 13.5: Expected Topic Proportions for the Structural Topic Model.

Because, as mentioned before in section 13.7.3.1, the STM model builds on the *Correlated Topic Model*, a key advantage is the possibility to find out if the found topics are correlated with each other. Using the *topicCorr()* function, we can plot possible correlations between the topics. If the topics are correlated, the plot shows dotted lines between the topics. In this case none of the topic correlations are high enough to show in the plot.

Table 13.21: Plotting the Topic Correlations.

Line	R Script
1	`mod.out.corr <- topicCorr(stm_model)`
2	`plot(mod.out.corr)`

Lines explained
Line 1 runs the *topicCorr()* function on the stm model object. Line 2 plots the correlations between topics as seen in Figure 13.6

Using the *labelTopics()* function implemented in the *stm* package, we get insights into the words that the topics consist of. The function offers different perspectives on the 5 estimated topics based on different metrics.

Topic 3

Topic 5

Topic 2

Topic 1

Topic 4

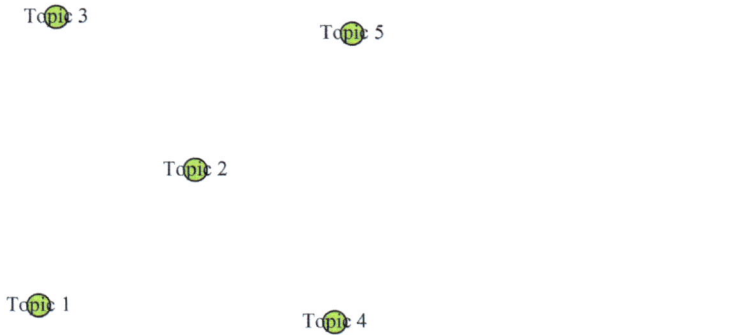

Figure 13.6: Correlations between the Topics of the Model.

Table 13.22: Insights into the Topics of the Structural Topic Model.

Line	R Script
1	labelTopics(stm_model)
2	Topic 1 Top Words:
3	Highest Prob: state, educ, student, univers, said, school, public
4	FREX: equiti, inclus, loan, episod, discrimin, antisemit, district
5	Lift: compli, isra, jone, prosecutor, reli, religi, 11-year-old
6	Score: episod, loan, equiti, inclus, israel', antisemit, protest
7	
8	Topic 2 Top Words
9	Highest Prob: presid, trump, feder, administr, trump, order, govern
10	FREX: trump, order, donald, elon, musk, j, president-elect
11	Lift: demand, here', price, wildfir, zelenski, 90-minut, abolish
12	Score: trump, trump', presid, elon, musk, feder, donald
13	
14	Topic 3 Top Words:
15	Highest Prob: year, first, editor, peopl, can, time, like
16	FREX: editor, act, jr, articl, charact, mcmahon, linda
17	Lift: badg, commerci, committe, feet, korean, tibetan, you'r
18	Score: editor, jr, charact, film, art, doctor, quechua
19	
20	Topic 4 Top Words:
21	Highest Prob: new, york, die, citi, home, mayor, school
22	FREX: mayor, adam, eric, gov, clear, hill, york'
23	Lift: #metoo, 110th, 11th, 12th, 17-year-old, 1930s, 40s
24	Score: eric, adam, mayor, clear, chocol, die, ballet
25	
26	Topic 5 Top Words:
27	Highest Prob: year, last, new, one, get, show, citi

Table 13.22 (continued)

Line	R Script
28	FREX: we'll, app, might, transcript, audio, appl, nyt
29	Lift: ezra, iheartradio, klein, must, western, advantag, affair
30	Score: audio, appl, nyt, spotifi, wherev, app, ezra

Lines explained

Line 1 runs the *labelTopics()* function for the stm object. Lines 2 to 30 show the generated output.

Highest Prob lists the most frequent words within the documents assigned to a specific topic. Those words may also appear frequently in other topics. The most frequent words in Topic 2 which accounts for the highest proportion in the documents, *presid, trump, feder, administr, order* and *govern,* suggest a general focus on the Trump administration. *FREX, Lift* and *Score* refer to different metrics used to determine the most distinct words of a given topic.[11] FREX is a mixture of the words frequent and exclusive and the metric displays words that are both frequent and exclusively associated with a given topic. Identifying words combining these two traits is especially informative as frequent words are often functional words necessary to discuss any topic; while looking at exclusive words only could bring up words that are just rare words in general. The words listed under this metric, trump, *order, donald, elon, musk, j* and *president-elect* point to persons associated with the Trump administration in the articles. The *Lift* metric shows words that are unusually common in this topic compared to others, even if they aren't frequent overall. Hence *Lift* will show words that appear almost exclusively in a given topic. Lift is calculated as the ratio of the probability of the word in the topic to the probability of the word in the corpus. The more frequent the word is in the corpus, the lower will be its Lift. The presence of *demand, here', price, wildfir,* zelenski, *90-minut* and *abolish* suggest contextual events linked with political or governmental actions e.g., international relations, climate policy, or economic issues that tie back to the Trump administration. Lastly, Score identifies words that best capture what distinguishes this topic based on statistical association. The score value largely suggests words that are also listed under *Highest Prob.*

Based on this information, Topic 2 appears to center on the Trump administration and related events. Given the output, the other topics center around religious conflicts in the educational system (1), films and media (3), education related events in New York City (4) and media and apps (5). However, the information about the topics is prone to individual interpretation and should be approached as a starting point and validating the interpretation with domain knowledge may strengthen it.

---

[11] For more information on the calculations of the metrics see the package documentation of labelTopics() function in the stm package (Roberts et al.) and the further readings listed there.

13.8 Sentiment Analysis

13.8.1 Introduction

Sentiment Analysis, also known as *opinion mining*, is an NLP technique used to determine the emotional tone behind a text, the *sentiment*. It helps identify whether the sentiment expressed in the text is positive, negative, neutral or absent. For example, words like *friendly* or *nice* typically indicate a positive sentiment, while words like *hate* or *violent* suggest a negative sentiment. In addition to basic polarities such as positive and negative, the functions of some sentiment analysis packages can also detect specific emotions like joy, anger, or sadness. For insightful sentiment analysis, it is necessary that emotional tones are indeed present in the acquired data. The method is therefore suitable for research topics where emotional responses in written communication can be reasonably expected. Sentiment Analysis is commonly applied to social media posts, product reviews, customer feedback, and other types of textual data to examine public opinion, customer satisfaction, or general sentiment about a specific subject. Multiple established approaches exist to extract sentiments from texts including rule-based methods relying on lexicons, machine learning models and deep learning models (Loynes and Elliot 2022).

13.8.2 Lexicon-based Sentiment Analysis

When using lexicon-based approaches, we have to provide the model with a lexicon in which the sentiments for the words in our documents are already classified. Identifying the sentiment a word carries is a relatively easy task for humans, who participated in the creation of the lexicons, assigning labels. Lecicons require frequent updates as words not present in them are ignored in the analysis. Several established sentiment lexicons, including AFINN from Finn Årup Nielsen, bing from Bing Liu and collaborators, and NRC from Saif Mohammad and Peter Turney, are publicly available. These lexicons are based on unigrams, or single words, and contain many English words assigned scores for positive or negative sentiment, as well as emotions like joy, anger, and sadness. The NRC lexicon categorizes words in a binary manner into categories such as positive, negative, anger, anticipation, disgust, fear, joy, sadness, surprise, and trust (Mohammad and Turney 2013). The bing lexicon also categorizes words in a binary fashion into positive and negative categories (Hu and Liu 2004).

The AFINN lexicon assigns scores to words ranging from −5 to 5, with negative scores indicating negative sentiment and positive scores indicating positive sentiment (Nielsen 2011). Analyzing textual data written in different languages require lexicons of the respective language.

In the application example we want to find out how climate change is discussed on the BlueSky feed #climatechangescience. As the name of the feed suggests it is a feed for users who are interested in conversing about climate change in a scientific

Table 13.23: Sentiment Lexicons.

Lexicon	Author/s	Sentiment	Coding	Languages
AFINN	Finn Årup Nielsen	neg/pos	−5 to 5	English, Danish
bing	Liu et al.	neg/pos	neg/pos	English
nrc	Mohammad/ Turney	neg/pos, emotions	neg/pos, anger, anticipation, disgust, fear, joy, sadness, surprise, and trust	English, translated into many languages

way. As demonstrated in Table 13.24, the texts are collected using the *BlueSky API* and the *atrrr* package.

Table 13.24: Collection of skeets on Climate Change Science from BlueSky.

Line	R Script & R Output
1	`library(atrrr)`
2	`auth("blueskyaccount.bsky.social")`
3	
4	`ukpol_feed_skeets <- get_feed(`
5	`  "https://bsky.app/profile/kesma.bsky.social/feed/aaamxvffjaodq",`
6	`  limit = 200000,`
7	`  parse = TRUE,`
8	`  verbose = TRUE)`
9	
10	`Got 629 skeets, but there is more.. [11.7s]`
11	
12	`names(climatechangescience_skeets)`
13	`[1] "uri"   "cid"   "author_handle"  "author_name"   "text"`
14	`[6] "author_data"   "post_data" "embed_data"   "reply_count"`
15	`    "repost_count"`
16	`[11] "like_count"   "quote_count"   "indexed_at"`
17	`    "in_reply_to"   "in_reply_root"`
18	`[16] "quotes"   "tags"   "mentions"   "links"   "langs"`
19	`[21] "labels"`

Lines explained

Line 1 loads the *atrrr* package that communicates with the BlueSky API. Line 2 starts the authentication process. The personal account handle needs to be provided instead of *blueskyaccount*. Line 2 is running auth() to opensa window, where one is asked to provide the previously set *app password*. Lines 4 to 9 request data from a BlueSky Feed. The *get_feed()* function requires a link to the feed, an upper limit on how many skeets will be requested. If parse equals TRUE the results will be returned in a data frame instead of the nested object sent by the server. If verbose equals TRUE information on the process such as the progress bar will be visible in the console. Line 10 shows the progress bar. Lines 12 to 19 show the variable names of the returned data frame object.

Climate change may evoke strong emotions due to its profound implications for the planet and future generations. Many scientists in climate change-related disciplines potentially feel a personal connection to the environment, making discussions about climate change resonate deeply with their values and beliefs. The topic often intersects with political, economic, and social issues, which can polarize opinions and create heated debates. The urgency of the climate crisis can inspire advocacy, prompting individuals to express their concerns. Since this is a feed presumably followed by scientists, we also expect positive sentiments when new studies are published and discussed.

Table 13.25: Preprocessing of skeets on Climate Change Science from BlueSky.

Line	R Script & R Output
1	library(quanteda)
2	corpus <- corpus(climatechangescience_skeets, text_field = "text")
3	tokens_clean <- tokens(corpus,
4	remove_punct = T,
5	remove_symbols = T,
6	remove_numbers = T,
7	remove_url = T)
8	cleaned_data <- tokens_tolower(tokens_clean)
9	cleaned_data <- tokens_remove(tokens_clean, stopwords("en"))
10	climatechangescience_skeets$clean_text <- sapply(cleaned_data,
11	paste, collapse = "")

Lines explained
Line 1 loads the *quanteda* package Line 2 creates a corpus object from the dataset climatechangescience_skeets, specifying "text" as the column containing the text data. Lines 3 to 7 tokenize the text and remove punctuation, symbols, numbers, and URLs. Line 8 converts all tokens to lowercase. Line 19 removes stop words from the tokenized data. Lines 10 to 11 add the cleaned tokens to the original data frame as a new column named *clean_text*.

After the data preprocessing, as shown in Table 13.25, we use the *syuzhet* package (Jockers 2015) to extract the sentiments from the skeets. The package provides functions to use multiple lexicons, including the ones listed in Table 13.23, to extract sentiments from the skeets. For our skeets we use the *get_nrc_sentiment()* function to extract emotions and valence from the texts to get more nuanced insights than just the positive and negative sentiments. Afterwards, we summarize the results with the *sumtable()* function.

We see in Table 13.26 that not all texts include a sentiment. This may be because a user is just sharing a news article or a link, or simply because of the absence of sentiments. Text 3 is the first skeet in the dataset to include a word that is classified as being connected to the feeling of anticipation, and a word that conveys trust and to carry a positive sentiment. Text 6, in comparison, offers a variety of emotions as well

Table 13.26: Sentiment Analysis.

Line	R Script & R Output
1	`library(syuzhet)`
2	`s_nrc <- get_nrc_sentiment(climatechangescience_skeets$clean_text)`
3	`head(s_nrc)`

	anger	anticipation	disgust	fear	joy	sadness	surprise	trust	neg	pos
4										
5	1	0	0	0	0	0	0	0	0	0
6	2	0	0	0	0	0	0	0	1	0	0
7	3	0	1	0	0	0	0	0	1	0	1
8	4	1	0	0	0	1	1	1	0	0	2
9	5	1	1	1	2	1	0	1	1	1	1
10	6	3	2	1	3	1	3	1	0	6	1

Line	R Script & R Output
11	`library(vtable)`
12	`sumtable(s_nrc, out = "return")`

	Variable	N	Mean	Std. Dev.	Min	Pctl. 25	Pctl. 75	Max
13								
14	1	anger	798	0.41	0.71	0	0	1	4
15	2	anticipation	798	0.65	0.9	0	0	1	5
16	3	disgust	798	0.25	0.52	0	0	0	3
17	4	fear	798	0.61	0.9	0	0	1	5
18	5	joy	798	0.43	0.7	0	0	1	4
19	6	sadness	798	0.37	0.65	0	0	1	4
20	7	surprise	798	0.33	0.6	0	0	1	3
21	8	trust	798	0.9	1.1	0	0	1	7
22	9	negative	798	0.92	1.2	0	0	1	7
23	10	positive	798	1.6	1.5	0	0	3	8

Lines explained
Line 1 loads the *syuzhet* package. Line 2 extracts sentiments from the cleaned texts. Lines 3 to 10 request and show the results from the first 6 texts. Line 11 loads the *vtable* package. Lines 12 to 23 request and show summary statistics.

as negative sentiments and a positive one. On average, the skeets contain 0.92 negative and 1.6 positive words. Of the more nuanced emotional dimensions, trust, anticipation and fear are most common on average, while words connected to disgust are the least common. As expected, when analyzing short texts, the texts' maximum values for sentiments are low in comparison to the numbers longer texts may contain. Overall, the skeets extracted from the Climate Change Science feed on BlueSky display a variety of emotions, despite being short texts and published in a feed closely connected to science.

References

Adler, Joseph. 2010. *R in a Nutshell*. Sebastopol: O'Reilly

Agresti, Alan. 1990. *Categorical Data Analysis*. New York: Wiley

Agresti, Alan & Barbara Finlay. 2009 [1979]. *Statistical Methods for the Social Sciences*. Fourth Edition. Upper Saddle River: Pearson Prentice Hall

Aldrich, John H. & Forrest D. Nelson. 1984. *Linear Probability, Logit, and Probit Models*. Newbury Park: Sage

Alipourfard, Nazanin, Keith Burghardt & Kristina Lerman. 2022. Disaggregation via Gaussian regression for robust analysis of heterogeneous data. In Uwe Engel, Anabel Quan-Haase, Sunny Xun Liu & Lars Lyberg (Eds.), *Handbook of Computational Social Science, Volume 2: Data Science, Statistical Modelling, and Machine Learning Methods*, 269-288. London/New York: Routledge. https://doi.org/10.4324/9781003025245

Allison, Paul. 2015. *Imputation by Predictive Mean Matching: Promise & Peril*. https://statisticalhorizons.com/predictive-mean-matching (last access: Feb 14, 2025)

Apache Software Foundation. 2025. *Welcome to Apache OpenNLP*. https://opennlp.apache.org/ (last access: Jul 20, 2025)

Arnold, Taylor. 2025. *cleanNLP: Clean 'NLP' Text Annotation*. https://CRAN.R-project.org/package=cleanNLP

Arnold, Taylor & Lauren Tilton. 2025. *coreNLP: R Interface to Stanford CoreNLP*. https://CRAN.R-project.org/package=coreNLP

Attewell, Paul & David B. Monaghan. 2015. *Data Mining for the Social Sciences*. An Introduction. Oakland: University of California Press

Bache, Stefan Milton, Hadley Wickham & Lionel Henry. 2025. *Package 'magrittr'*. https://CRAN.R-project.org/package=magrittr

Bates, Douglas, Martin Mächler, Benjamin M. Bolker & Steven C. Walker. 2015. *Fitting Linear Mixed-Effects Models Using lme4*. https://cran.r-project.org/web/packages/lme4/vignettes/lmer.pdf

Bates, Douglas, Martin Maechler, Ben Bolker & Steven Walker. 2025. *Package 'lme4'*. https://CRAN.R-project.org/package=lme4

Bates, Douglas, William Venables. 2025. *Package 'splines'*. https://CRAN.R-project.org/package=splines

Beaujean, A. Alexander. 2014. *Latent Variable Modeling Using R*. New York: Routledge

Beck, Marcus W. 2025. *Package 'NeuralNetTools'*. https://CRAN.R-project.org/package=NeuralNetTools

Beetz, Michael, Uwe Engel, Nina Hoyer, Lorenz Kähler, Hagen Langer, Holger Schultheis & Sirko Straube. 2023. Trustworthiness and Well-Being: The Ethical, Legal, and Social Challenge of Robotic Assistance. In Uwe Engel (Ed.). *Robots in Care and Everyday Life. Future, Ethics, Social Acceptance*, 1–26. Cham: Springer. https://doi.org/10.1007/978-3-031-11447-2

Benoit, Kenneth, Akitaka Matsuo & Johannes Gruber. 2025. *spacyr: R Wrapper for spaCy NLP Library*. https://CRAN.R-project.org/package=spacyr

Benoit, Kenneth, Kohei Watanabe, Haiyan Wang, Paul Nulty, Adam Obeng, Stefan Müller, Akitaka Matsuo & William Lowe. 2025. *Package 'quanteda'*. https://CRAN.R-project.org/package=quanteda

Benoit, Kenneth, Kohei Watanabe, Haiyan Wang, Jiong Wei Lua & Jouni Kuha. 2025. *Package 'quanteda.textstats'*. https://CRAN.R-project.org/package=quanteda.textstats

Berry, William D. & Stanley Feldman. 1985. *Multiple Regression in Practice*. Newbury Park: Sage

Bestgen, Yves. 2024. Measuring lexical diversity in texts: The twofold length problem. *Language Learning*, 74(3), 638-671. https://doi.org/10.1111/lang.12630

Bethlehem, Jelke. 2009. *Applied Survey Methods. A Statistical Perspective*. Hoboken: Wiley

Bethlehem, Jelke, Fannie Cobben & Barry Schouten. 2011. *Handbook of Nonresponse in Household Surveys*. Hoboken: Wiley

Bethlehem, Jelke & Silvia Biffignandi. 2012. *Handbook of Web Surveys*. Hoboken: Wiley

Blalock, Hubert M. 1981. *Social Statistics*. Revised 2nd Edition. Auckland: McGraw-Hill

https://doi.org/10.1515/9783110680683-014

Blei, David, Andrew Ng, & Michael. I. Jordan. 2003. Latent Dirichlet Allocation. *Journal of Machine Learning Research*, 3, 993–1022

Blei, David., & John. D. Lafferty. 2007. A correlated topic model of science. *Annals of Applied Statistics*, 1(1), 17–35. https://doi.org/10.1214/07-AOAS114

BlueSky Developer APIs. 2025. https://docs.bsky.app/ (last access: Jul 20, 2025)

Bollen, Kenneth A. 1989. *Structural Equations with Latent Variables*. New York: Wiley.

Bosse, Stefan, Lena Dahlhaus & Uwe Engel. 2022. Web data mining. Collecting textual data from web pages using R. In Uwe Engel, Anabel Quan-Haase, Sunny Xun Liu & Lars Lyberg (Eds.), *Handbook of Computational Social Science, Volume 2: Data Science, Statistical Modelling, and Machine Learning Methods*, 46-70. London/New York: Routledge. https://doi.org/10.4324/9781003025245

Breiman, Leo, Adele Cutler, Andy Liaw, Matthew Wiener. 2025. *Package 'randomForest'*. https://CRAN.R-project.org/package=randomForest

Browne, Michael. W. & Robert Cudeck. 1993. Alternative Ways of Assessing Model Fit. In Kenneth A. Bollen & J. Scott Long (Eds.). *Testing Structural Equation Models*, 136–162. Newbury Park: Sage

Burmeister, Laura, & Uwe Engel. 2015. Collecting MTMM Data on Satisfaction with Life. In Uwe Engel (Ed.). *Survey Measurements. Techniques, Data Quality and Sources of Error*, 97 –111. Frankfurt/New York: Campus

Buttrey, Samuel E. & Lyn R. Whitaker. 2018. *A Data Scientist's Guide to Acquiring, Cleaning, and Managing Data in R*. Chichester: Wiley

Byrne, Barbara M. 2012. *Structural Equation Modeling With Mplus. Basic Concepts, Applications, and Programming*. New York: Routledge.

Can, Suat & Uwe Engel. 2015. Nonresponse, Measurement Error, and Estimates of Change – Lessons from the German PPSM Panel. In Uwe Engel (Ed.). *Survey Measurements. Techniques, Data Quality and Sources of Error*, 160 –191. Frankfurt/New York: Campus

Canty, Angelo & Brian Ripley. 2025. *Package 'boot'*. https://CRAN.R-project.org/package=boot

Chatterjee, Samprit & Bertram Price. 1977. *Regression Analysis by Example*. New York: Wiley

Cioffi-Revilla, Claudio. 2017 [2014]. *Introduction to Computational Social Science. Principles and Applications*, 2nd edition. Cham: Springer

Coene, John. 2025. *Package 'nytimes'*. https://github.com/news-r/nytimes

Coleman, James S. 1964. *Introduction to Mathematical Sociology*. New York: The Free Press of Glencoe

Coleman, James S., Ernest Q. Campbell, Carol J. Hobson, James McPartland, Alexander M. Mood, Frederic D. Weinfeld & Robert L. York. 1966. *Equality of Educational Opportunity*. Washington, D. C.: US Government Printing Office

Coleman, James. S. 1971 [1968]. The Mathematical Study of Change. In Hubert M. Blalock & Ann B. Blalock (Eds.), *Methodology in Social Research*, 428–478. International Student Edition. London: McGraw-Hill

Coleman, James S. 1981. *Longitudinal Data Analysis*. New York: Basic Books.

Coleman, James S. 1990. *Foundations of Social Theory*. Cambridge/London: Belknap Press of Harvard University Press

D' Alberto, Riccardo & Meri Raggi. 2024. Integrating rather than collecting: statistical matching in the data flood era. *Statistical Papers 65*, 2135-2163. https://doi.org/10.1007/s00362-023-01468-3

Daniel, Cuthbert & Fred S. Wood. 1999. *Fitting Equations to Data. Computer Analysis of Multifactor Data*. 2nd Edition. New York: Wiley

Daly, F., D. J. Hand, M. C. Jones, A. D. Lunn & K. J. McConway. 1995. *Elements of Statistics*. Harlow: Addison-Wesley

De Queiroz, Gabriela, Colin Fay, Emil Hvitfeldt, Os Keyes, Kanishka Misra, Tim Mastny, Jeff Erickson, David Robinson & Julia Silge. 2025. *Package 'tidytext'*. https://CRAN.R-project.org/package=tidytext

De Vaus, David A. 2001. *Research Design in Social Research*. London: Sage

Diekmann, Andreas. 2007. *Empirische Sozialforschung* [Empirical Social Research]. Reinbek: Rowohlt

Draper, Norman. R. & Harry Smith. 1981 [1966]. *Applied Regression Analysis*, 2nd Edition. New York: Wiley

Elliot, Michael R. & Richard Valliant. 2017. Inference for Nonprobability Samples. *Statistical Science* 32 (2), 249-264, https://doi.org/10.1214/16-STS598

Enamorado, Ted. 2022. A primer on probabilistic record linkage. In Uwe Engel, Anabel Quan-Haase, Sunny Xun Liu & Lars Lyberg (Eds.), *Handbook of Computational Social Science, Volume 2: Data Science, Statistical Modelling, and Machine Learning Methods*, 95-107. London/New York: Routledge. https://doi.org/10.4324/9781003025245

Enders, Craig K. 2010. *Applied Missing Data Analysis*. New York: Guilford Press.

Engel, Uwe. 1991. Schätzung kurz- und längerfristiger Effekte, wenn die Meßperiode nicht der Wirkungsweise des Kausalfaktors entspricht [Estimation of short- and longer-term effects when the measurement period does not correspond to the mode of action of the causal factor]. In J.J.G. Schmeets, M. E. P. Odekerken & F. J. R. van de Pol (Eds.). *Developments and applications in structural equation modelling. Proceedings of the twelfth meeting of the 'Working group structural equation modelling' (AG 'Strukturgleichungsmodelle') at the Netherlands Central Bureau of Statistics in Heerlen, 4 and 5 April 1991*, 19-41. Amsterdam: Sociometric Research Foundation

Engel, Uwe & Wolfgang Meyer. 1996. Structural Analysis in the Study of Social Change. In Uwe Engel & Jost Reinecke (Eds.), *Analysis of Change. Advanced Techniques in Panel Data Analysis*, 221–252. Berlin/New York: De Gruyter.

Engel, Uwe, Alexander Gattig & Julia Simonson. 2007. Longitudinal Multilevel Modelling: A Comparison of Growth Curve Models and Structural Equation Modelling using Panel Data from Germany. In Kees van Montfort, Johan Oud & Albert Satorra (Eds.). *Longitudinal Models in the Behavioral and Related Sciences*, 295–314. Mahwah/London: Lawrence Erlbaum Associates.

Engel, Uwe, Simone Bartsch, Christiane Schnabel & Helen Vehre. 2012. *Wissenschaftliche Umfragen. Methoden und Fehlerquellen* [Scientific Surveys. Methods and Sources of Error]. Frankfurt/New York: Campus

Engel, Uwe. 2013. *Access Panel and Mixed-Mode Internet Survey. PPSM Panel Report*. University of Bremen. https://www.viewsandinsights.com/fileadmin/bilder/referenzen/ppsm-panel-report.pdf

Engel, Uwe. 2015. Response Behavior in an Adaptive Survey Design for the Setting-Up Stage of a Probability-Based Access Panel in Germany. In Uwe Engel, Ben Jann, Peter Lynn, Annette Scherpenzeel & Patrick Sturgis (Eds.), *Improving Survey Methods. Lessons from Recent Research*, 207–222. New York/London: Routledge.

Engel, Uwe & Britta Köster. 2015. Response Effects and Cognitive Involvement in Answering Survey Questions. In Uwe Engel, Ben Jann, Peter Lynn, Annette Scherpenzeel & Patrick Sturgis (Eds.), *Improving Survey Methods. Lessons from Recent Research*, 35–50. New York/London: Routledge.

Engel, Uwe & Britta Köster. 2015a. Framing Effects. In Uwe Engel (Ed.). *Survey Measurements. Techniques, Data Quality and Sources of Error*, 58 –75. Frankfurt/New York: Campus

Engel, Uwe & Suat Can. 2017. Studiendesign [Study Design]. In Uwe Engel (Ed.), *Bremen und seine Ausstellungen. Wie die Bevölkerung Bremens ihre Stadt, ihr Interesse an der Wissenschaft und die Ausstellungsangebote in Bremen und Bremerhaven sieht* [Bremen and its exhibitions. How the people of Bremen see their city, their interest in science and the exhibitions on offer in Bremen and Bremerhaven], 37-40. Booklet. University of Bremen

Engel, Uwe. 2020. Interest in Science: Response Order Effects in an Adaptive Survey Design. In Mays, Anja, André Dingelstedt, Verena Hambauer, Stephan Schlosser, Florian Berens, Jürgen Leibold, Jan Karem Höhne (Eds.). *Grundlagen – Methoden – Anwendungen in den Sozialwissenschaften* [Fundamentals – Methods – Applications in the Social Sciences], 247 –261. Wiesbaden: Springer VS. https://doi.org/10.1007/978-3-658-15629-9_13

Engel, Uwe. 2022. Causal and predictive modeling in computational social science. In Uwe Engel, Anabel Quan-Haase, Sunny Xun Liu & Lars Lyberg (Eds.), *Handbook of Computational Social Science, Volume 1: Theory, Case Studies and Ethics*, 131-149. London/New York: Routledge. https://doi.org/10.4324/9781003024583-10

Engel, Uwe. 2022a. *Zukunftsperspektive Energiewende. Umfrage in Bremen und Bremerhaven zur Rohstoffabhängigkeit der Energiewende und Empfehlungen der Enquetekommission „Klimaschutzstrategie für das Land Bremen" zu den Bereichen Mobilität und Wärmeversorgung* [Future perspective energy transition. Survey in Bremen and Bremerhaven on the dependence on raw materials and recommendations of the Enquete commission "Climate Protection Strategy for the State of Bremen"]. Bremen https://www.viewsandinsights.com/fileadmin/bilder/referenzen/zukunftsperspektive_energie wende.pdf

Engel, Uwe. 2022b. *Energiewende im europäischen Green Deal. Einsichten in die Akzeptanz von Klimaschutzmaßnahmen, die wir aus Auswertungen des Eurobarometer, des European Social Survey und der amtlichen EU-Statistik gewinnen können* [Energy transition in the European Green Deal. Insights into the acceptance of climate protection measures that we can gain from the Eurobarometer, the European Social Survey and the official EU statistics]. Bremen. https://www.viewsandinsights.com/fil eadmin/bilder/referenzen/energiewende-in-europa.pdf

Engel, Uwe. 2022c. Online appendix to Causal and predictive modeling in computational social science. In Uwe Engel, Anabel Quan-Haase, Sunny Xun Liu & Lars Lyberg (Eds.), *Handbook of Computational Social Science, Volume 1: Theory, Case Studies and Ethics*, 131-149. London/New York: Routledge. https://www.viewsandinsights.com/forschung

Engel, Uwe & Lena Dahlhaus. 2022. Data quality and privacy concerns in digital trace data. Insights from a Delphi study on machine learning and robots in human life. In Uwe Engel, Anabel Quan-Haase, Sunny Xun Liu & Lars Lyberg (Eds.), *Handbook of Computational Social Science, Volume 1: Theory, Case Studies and Ethics*, 343-362. London/New York: Routledge. https://doi.org/10.4324/9781003024583-23

Engel, Uwe, Anabel Quan-Haase, Sunny Xun Liu & Lars Lyberg (Eds.). 2022a. *Handbook of Computational Social Science, Volume 1: Theory, Case Studies and Ethics*, 343-362. London/New York: Routledge. https://doi.org/10.4324/9781003024583

Engel, Uwe, Anabel Quan-Haase, Sunny Xun Liu & Lars Lyberg (Eds.). 2022b. *Handbook of Computational Social Science, Volume 2: Data Science, Statistical Modelling, and Machine Learning Methods*, 95-107. London/New York: Routledge. https://doi.org/10.4324/9781003025245

Engel, Uwe. 2023. *Ansichten & Einsichten zur Klimapolitik. Repräsentative Umfrage für den Zwei-Städte-Staat Bremen* [Views & Insights on Climate Policy. Representative Survey for the Two-City State of Bremen]. Bremen. https://www.viewsandinsights.com/fileadmin/bilder/referenzen/umfrage-zur-klimapolitik2023.pdf

European Social Survey Cumulative File, ESS 1–8. 2018. Data file edition 1.0. NSD – Norwegian Centre for Research Data, Norway – Data Archive and distributor of ESS data for ESS ERIC. doi:10.21338/NSD-ESS-CUMULATIVE

European Social Survey Round 9 Data. 2018. Data file edition 2.0. NSD – Norwegian Centre for Research Data, Norway – Data Archive and distributor of ESS data for ESS ERIC. doi:10.21338/NSD-ESS9-2018

European Social Survey. 2020. *ESS Round 10 Source Questionnaire*. London: ESS ERIC Headquarters c/o City, University of London

European Social Survey European Research Infrastructure (ESS ERIC). 2023. ESS10 Self-completion – integrated file, edition 3.1 [Data set]. Sikt – Norwegian Agency for Shared Services in Education and Research. https://doi.org/10.21338/ess10sce03_1

European Social Survey European Research Infrastructure (ESS ERIC). 2022. ESS10 Data Documentation. Sikt – Norwegian Agency for Shared Services in Education and Research. https://doi.org/10.21338/NSD-ESS10-2020

European Social Survey. 2022. *ESS Round 11 Source Questionnaire*. London: ESS ERIC Headquarters c/o City, University of London.

European Social Survey European Research Infrastructure (ESS ERIC). 2023. ESS11– integrated file, edition 2.0. [Data set]. Sikt – Norwegian Agency for Shared Services in Education and Research. https://doi.org/10.21338/ess11e02_0

Evans, Merran, Nicholas Hastings & Brian Peacock. 2000. *Statistical Distributions*. 3rd Edition. New York: Wiley

Flesch, Rudolph. 1948. A New Readability Yardstick. *Journal of Applied Psychology*, 32(3), 221.

Forthofer, Ron N. & Robert G. Lehnen. 1981. *Public Program Analysis. A New Categorical Data Approach*. Belmont: Lifetime Learning Publications

Fox, John. 2009. *A Mathematical Primer For Social Statistics*. Los Angeles: Sage

Fox, John. 1991. *Regression Diagnostics*. Newbury Park: Sage

Fox, John, Sanford Weisberg & Brad Price. *Package 'car'*. https://CRAN.R-project.org/package=car

Freese, Jeremy, & David Peterson. 2017. Replication in Social Science. *Annual Review of Sociology* 43, 147–165.

Frick, Hannah, Fanny Chow, Max Kuhn, Michael Mahoney, Julia Silge & Hadley Wickham. 2025. *Package 'rsample'*. https://CRAN.R-project.org/package=rsample

Friedman, Jerome, Trevor Hastie, Rob Tibshirani, Balasubramanian Narasimhan, Kenneth Tay, Noah Simon, James Yang. 2025. *Package 'glmnet'*. https://CRAN.R-project.org/package=glmnet

Fritsch, Stefan, Frauke Guenther & Marvin N. Wright. 2025. *Package 'neuralnet'*. https://CRAN.R-project.org/package=neuralnet

Fuller, Wayne A. 2009. *Sampling Statistics*. Hoboken: Wiley

Galtung, Johan. 1969 [1967]. *Theory and Methods of Social Research*, Revised Edition. Oslo: Universitetsforlaget

Ghani, Rayid & Malte Schierholz. 2017. Machine Learning. In Ian Foster, Rayid Ghani, Ron S. Jarmin, Frauke Kreuter, & Julia Lane (Eds.), *Big Data and Social Science. A Practical Guide to Methods and Tools*. 147–186. Boca Raton: CRC Press.

Goodman, Leo A. 1955. Generalizing the problem of prediction. In Paul F. Lazarsfeld & Morris Rosenberg (Eds.), *The Language of Social Research*, 277–283. New York: The Free Press.

Griffiths, Thomas L., & Mark Steyvers. 2004. Finding scientific topics. *Proceedings of the National Academy of Sciences*, 101(suppl_1), 5228-5235

Groves, Robert M., Don A. Dillman, John L. Eltinge & Roderick J. A. Little. 2002. *Survey Nonresponse*. New York: Wiley

Groves, Robert M. 2011. Three eras of survey research. *Public Opinion Quarterly*, 75(5), 861-871

Gruber, Johannes B., Benjamin Guinaudeau & Fabio Votta. 2025. *Package 'atrrr'*. https://CRAN.R-project.org/package=atrrr

Guo, Shenyang & Mark W. Fraser. 2010. *Propensity Score Analysis. Statistical Methods and Applications*. Thousand Oaks: Sage

Hagle, Timothy M. 1995. *Basic Math For Social Scientists. Concepts*. Thousand Oaks: Sage

Hammill, Dillon. 2025. *Package 'DataEditR'*. https://CRAN.R-project.org/package=DataEditR

Hastie, Trevor, Robert Tibshirani & Jerome Friedman. 2009. *The Elements of Statistical Learning. Data Mining, Inference, and Prediction*. 2nd Edition. New York: Springer

Hastie, Trevor. 2025. *Package 'gam'*. https://CRAN.R-project.org/package=gam

Hatzinger, Reinhold, Kurt Hornik, Herbert Nagel, Marco J. Maier. 2014. *R — Einführung durch angewandte Statistik* [R — Introduction through applied statistics]. 2nd Edition. Hallbergmoos: Pearson

Heeringa, Steven G., Brady T. West & Patricia A. Berglund. 2010. *Applied Survey Data Analysis*. Boca Raton: Chapman & Hall/CRC Press

Heiberger, Raphael. H. & Sebastian M.N. Galvez. 2022. Text mining and topic modeling. In Uwe Engel, Anabel Quan-Haase, Sunny Xun Liu & Lars Lyberg (Eds.), *Handbook of Computational Social Science, Volume 2: Data Science, Statistical Modelling, and Machine Learning Methods*, 352-365. London/New York: Routledge

Hilbe, Joseph M. 2009. *Logistic Regression Models*. Boca Raton: Chapman & Hall/CRC

Hofman, Jake M., Amit Sharma & Duncan J. Watts. 2017. Prediction and explanation in social systems. *Science*, 355 (6324), 486–488. https://doi.org/10.1126/science.aal3856

Honnibal, Matthew & Ines Montani. 2025. *spaCy – Industrial-strength NLP*. https://spacy.io/ (last access: Jul 20, 2025)

Hornik, Kurt. 2025. *openNLP: Interface to Apache OpenNLP Tools*. https://CRAN.R-project.org/package= openNLP

Hox, Joop J. 2010. *Multilevel Analysis. Techniques and Applications*. 2nd Edition. New York: Routledge

Hox, Joop J. 2017. Computational social science methodology, anyone? *Methodology*, 13, 3–12. https://doi. org/10.1027/1614-2241/a000127

Hu, Minquing, & Bing Liu. 2004. Mining and summarizing customer reviews. *Proceedings of the Tenth ACM SIGKDD International Conference on Knowledge Discovery and Data Mining*, 168–177. https://doi.org/10. 1145/1014052.1014073

Huntington-Klein, Nick. 2024. *Package 'vtable'*. https://CRAN.R-project.org/package=vtable

Jaccard, James. 2001. *Interaction Effects in Logistic Regression*. Thousand Oaks: Sage

James, Gareth, Daniela Witten, Trevor Hastie, & Robert Tibshirani. 2013. *An Introduction to Statistical Learning. With Applications in R*. New York: Springer

Jann, Ben. 2002. *Einführung in die Statistik* [Introduction to Statistics]. München: Oldenbourg

Jockers, Matthew. 2015. *Package 'syuzhet'*. https://CRAN.R-project.org/package=syuzhet

Johnson, Norman L., Samual Kotz & N. Balakrishnan. 1994. *Continuous Univariate Distributions. Volume 1*. 2nd Edition. New York: Wiley

Jünger, Jakob. 2022. A brief history of APIs: Limitations and opportunities for online research. In Uwe Engel, Anabel Quan-Haase, Sunny Xun Liu & Lars Lyberg (Eds.), *Handbook of Computational Social Science, Volume 2: Data Science, Statistical Modelling, and Machine Learning Methods*, 17 –32. London/ New York: Routledge. https://doi.org/10.4324/9781003025245-3

Kaminska, Olena. 2023. *Guide to Using Weights and Sample Design Indicators with ESS Data*. V1.2. European Social Survey. https://doi.org/10.21338/NSD-ESS10-2020

Kelleher, John D., Brendan Tierney. 2018. *Data Science*. Cambridge/London: MIT Press.

Kelleher, John D. 2019. *Deep Learning*. Cambridge/London: MIT Press

Kelleher, John D., Brian Mac Namee & Aoife D'Arcy. 2020. *Fundamentals of Machine Learning for Predictive Data Analytics*. 2nd Edition. Cambridge/London: MIT Press

Kessler, Ronald C., & David F. Greenberg. 1981. *Linear Panel Analysis. Models of Quantitative Change*. New York: Academic Press

Keusch, Florian & Frauke Kreuter. 2022. Digital trace data. Modes of data collection, applications, and errors at a glance. In Uwe Engel, Anabel Quan-Haase, Sunny Xun Liu & Lars Lyberg (Eds.), *Handbook of Computational Social Science, Volume 1: Theory, Case Studies and Ethics*, 100-118. London/New York: Routledge. https://doi.org/10.4324/9781003024583-8

King, Gary, Robert O. Keohane & Sidney Verba. 1994. *Designing Social Inquiry. Scientific Inference in Qualitative Research*. Princeton: Princeton University Press

Kish, Leslie. 1965. *Survey Sampling*. New York: Wiley

Kmenta, Jan. 1986. *Elements of Econometrics*. 2nd Edition. New York: Macmillan Publ. Co.

Kreuter, Frauke (Ed.). 2013. *Improving Surveys with Paradata. Analytic Uses of Process Information*. Hoboken: Wiley

Kühnel, Steffen-M. & Dagmar Krebs. 2006. *Statistik für die Sozialwissenschaften* [Statistics for the Social Sciences]. 3rd Edition. Hamburg: Rowohlt

Kuhn, Max, & Kjell Johnson. 2013. *Applied Predictive Modeling*. New York: Springer

Kuhn, Max & Julia Silge. 2022. *Tidy Modeling with R. A Framework for Modeling in the Tidyverse*. Beijing: O'Reilly

Kuhn, Max & Ross Quinlan. 2025a. *Package 'C50'*. https://CRAN.R-project.org/package=C50

Kuhn, Max & Davis Vaughan. 2025b. *Package 'parsnip'*. https://CRAN.R-project.org/package=parsnip

Wickham, Hadley, Davis Vaughan & Maximilian Girlich. 2025. *Package 'tidyr'*. https://CRAN.R-project.org/package=tidyr

Kuhn, Max, Hadley Wickham & Emil Hvitfeldt. 2025. *Package 'recipes'*. https://CRAN.R-project.org/package=recipes

Kuhn, Max & Hadley Wickham. 2025. *Package 'tidymodels'*. https://CRAN.R-project.org/package=tidymodels

Lantz, Brett. 2019. *Machine Learning with R*. 3rd Edition. Birmingham: Packt>

Lazarsfeld, Paul F. 1955. Interpretation of statistical relations as a research operation. In Paul F. Lazarsfeld & Morris Rosenberg (Eds.), *The Language of Social Research*, 115–125. New York: Free Press

Lazarsfeld, Paul F., Bernard Berelson & Hazel Gaudet. 1955. The process of opinion and attitude formation. In Paul F. Lazarsfeld & Morris Rosenberg (Eds.), *The Language of Social Research*, 231–242. New York: Free Press

Lazarsfeld, Paul F. & Herbert Menzel. 1969 [1961]. On the relation between individual and collective properties. In Amitai Etzioni (Ed.), *A Sociological Reader on Complex Organizations*, 499–516. London: Holt, Rinehart and Winston

Lazer, David M. J., Alex Pentland, Duncan J. Watts, Sinan Aral, Susan Athey, Noshir Contractor, Deen Freelon, Sandra Gonzalez-Bailon, Gary King, Helen Margetts, Alondro Nelson, Matthew J. Salganik, Markus Strohmaier, Alessandro Vespignani & Claudia Wagner. 2020. Computational social science: Obstacles and opportunities. Data sharing, research ethics, and incentives must improve. *Science* 369 (6507), 1060-1062. https://doi.org/10.1126/science.aaz8170

Levy, Paul S. & Stanley Lemeshow. 1999. *Sampling of Populations. Methods and Applications*. Third Edition. New York: Wiley

Linzer, Drew & Jeffrey Lewis. 2025. *Package 'poLCA'*. https://CRAN.R-project.org/package=poLCA

Little, Roderick J. A. & Donald B. Rubin. 2002. *Statistical Analysis With Missing Data*. 2nd Edition. Hoboken: Wiley

Long, J. Scott. 1997. *Regression Models for Categorical and Limited Dependent Variables*. Thousand Oaks: Sage

Long, J. Scott & Jeremy Freese. 2006. *Regression Models for Categorical Dependent Variables Using Stata*. 2nd Edition. College Station: Stata Press

Loynes, Niklas M., & Mark Elliot. 2022. Understanding political sentiment: Using Twitter to map the US 2016 Democratic primaries. In Uwe Engel, Anabel Quan-Haase, Sunny Xun Liu & Lars Lyberg (Eds.), *Handbook of Computational Social Science, Volume 1*, 256-286. London/New York: Routledge, https://doi.org/10.4324/9781003024583

Lumley, Thomas. 2010. *Complex Surveys. A Guide to Analysis Using R*. Hoboken: Wiley

Lumley, Thomas, Peter Gao & Ben Schneider. 2024. *Package 'survey'*. http://r-survey.r-forge.r-project.org/survey/

Lumley, Thomas. 2025. *Package 'leaps'*. https://CRAN.R-project.org/package=leaps

Lumley, Thomas, Peter Gao & Ben Schneider. 2025. *Package 'survey'*. https://CRAN.R-project.org/package=survey

Lyberg, Lars & Steven G. Heeringa. 2022. A changing survey landscape. In Uwe Engel, Anabel Quan-Haase, Sunny Xun Liu & Lars Lyberg (Eds.), *Handbook of Computational Social Science, Volume 1: Theory, Case Studies and Ethics*, 83-99. London/New York: Routledge. https://doi.org/10.4324/9781003024583-7

Lynn, Peter. 2003. PEDAKSI: Methodology for collecting data about survey non-respondents. *Quality & Quantity* 37, 239-261

Malvern, David, Brian Richards, Ngoni Chipere & Pilar Durán. 2004. *Lexical Diversity and Language Development*. Palgrave Macmillan UK.

Manning, Christopher D., Mihai Surdeanu, John Bauer, Jenny Finkel, Steven Bethard & David McClosky. 2025. *Stanford CoreNLP*. https://stanfordnlp.github.io/CoreNLP/.

Martinez, Angel R. 2012. Part-of-speech tagging. *Wiley Interdisciplinary Reviews: Computational Statistics*, 4(1), 107-113. https://doi.org/10.1002/wics.195

Matloff, Norman. 2011. *The Art of R Programming. A Tour of Statistical Software Design*. San Francisco: No Starch Press

McCullagh, P. & John A. Nelder. 1989 [1981]. *Generalized Linear Models*. 2nd Edition. London: Chapman & Hall

McCutcheon, Allan L. 1987. *Latent Class Analysis*. Newbury Park: Sage

Michalke Meik, Earl Brown, Alberto Mirisola, Alexandre Brulet & Laura Hauser, 2025. *koRpus: Text Analysis and Readability*. https://cran.r-project.org/package=koRpus

Milborrow, Stephen. 2025. *Package 'rpart.plot'*. https://CRAN.R-project.org/package=rpart.plot

Mimno, David, Hanna Wallach, Edmund Talley, Miriam Leenders & Andrew McCallum. 2011. "Optimizing semantic coherence in topic models." In *Proceedings of the Conference on Empirical Methods in Natural Language Processing*, 262-272. Association for Computational Linguistics. Chicago

Mohammad, Saif M., & Peter D. Turney. 2013. Crowdsourcing a word-emotion association lexicon. *Computational Intelligence*, 29(3), 436–465 https://doi.org/10.1111/j.1467-8640.2012.00460.x

Morgan, Stephen L., & Christopher Winship. 2007. *Counterfactuals and Causal Inference. Methods and Principles for Social Research*. Cambridge: Cambridge University Press.

Müller, Kirill & Hadley Wickham. 2025. *Package 'tibble'*. https://CRAN.R-project.org/package=tibble

Murrell, Paul. 2011. *R Graphics*. 2nd Edition. Boca Raton: CRC Press

Nelder, John A. & Robert W. M. Wedderburn. 1972. Generalized linear models. *Journal of the Royal Statistical Society* A 135, 370-384

Nielsen, Finn Å. 2011. A new ANEW: Evaluation of a word list for sentiment analysis in microblogs. arXiv preprint arXiv:1103.2903 https://arxiv.org/abs/1103.2903

Nivre, Joakim. 2010. Dependency parsing. *Language and Linguistics Compass* 4.3, 138-152.

Parsonage, Hugh. 2025. *Package 'hutils'*. https://CRAN.R-project.org/package=hutils

Pearl, Judea, Madelyn Glymour & Nicholas P. Jewell. 2016. *Causal Inference in Statistics*. Chichester: Wiley

Pinheiro, José, Douglas Bates & R Core Team. 2025. *Package 'nlme'*. https://CRAN.R-project.org/package=nlme

Plewis, Ian. 1985. *Analysing Change. Measurement and Explanation Using Longitudinal Data*. Chichester: Wiley

Quan-Haase, Anabel, & Luke Sloan. 2017. Introduction to the Handbook of Social Media Research Methods: Goals, Challenges and Innovations. In Luke Sloan and Anabel Quan-Haase (Eds.). *The Sage Handbook of Social Media Research Methods*. Kindle edition, Pos. 606–859. Los Angeles: SAGE

R Core Team. 2025. *R: A language and environment for statistical computing*. R Foundation for Statistical Computing, Vienna, Austria. URL: https://www.R-project.org/

Reinecke, Jost. 2014. *Strukturgleichungsmodelle in den Sozialwissenschaften* [Structural Equation Models in the Social Sciences]. 2nd Edition. Berlin/Boston: De Gruyter/Oldenbourg

Revelle, William. 2025. *Package 'psych'*. https://CRAN.R-project.org/package=psych

Ridgeway, Greg & GBM Developers. 2025. *Package 'gbm'*. https://CRAN.R-project.org/package=gbm

Ripley, Brian. 2025. *Package 'tree'*. https://CRAN.R-project.org/package=tree

Roberts, Margaret E., Brandon M. Stewart & Dustin Tingley. 2016. Navigating the Local Modes of Big Data: The Case of Topic Models. In *Data Analytics in Social Science, Government, and Industry*. New York: Cambridge University Press.

Roberts, Margaret E., Brandon M. Stewart & Dustin Tingley. 2019. stm: R package for structural topic models. *Journal of Statistical Software*, 91(2), 1–40. https://doi.org/10.18637/jss.v091.i02

Roberts, Margaret E., Brandon M. Stewart & Dustin Tingley. 2025. *Package 'stm'*. https://CRAN.R-project.org/package=stm

Robinson, David & Julia Silge. 2025. *Package 'tidytext'*. https://CRAN.R-project.org/package=tidytext

Rosenberg, Morris. 1968. *The Logic of Survey Analysis*. New York/London: Basic Books.

Rosseel, Yves, Terrence D. Jorgensen & Luc De Wilde. 2025. *Package 'lavaan'*. https://CRAN.R-project.org/package=lavaan

Rubin, Donald B. 1976. Inference and missing data. *Biometrika* 63, 581-592

Rubin, Donald B. 1987. *Multiple Imputation for Nonresponse in Surveys*. New York: Wiley

Särndal, Carl-Erik, Bengt Swensson & Jan Wretman. 1992. *Model Assisted Survey Sampling*. New York: Springer

Särndal, Carl-Erik & Sixten Lundström. 2005. *Estimation in Surveys with Nonresponse*. Chichester: Wiley

Sajun, Ali Reza, Imran Zualkernan & Donthi Sankalpa. 2024. A historical survey of advances in transformer architectures. *Applied Sciences*, 14(10), 4316 https://doi.org/10.3390/app14104316

Salganik, Matthew J. 2018. *Bit by Bit. Social Research in the Digital Age*. Princeton: Princeton University Press.

Schafer, Joseph L. 1997. *Analysis of Incomplete Multivariate Data*. Boca Raton: Chapman & Hall/CRC

Schmid, Helmut. 2025. *TreeTagger – A Language Independent Part-of-Speech Tagger*. http://www.cis.uni-muenchen.de/~schmid/tools/TreeTagger/

Schnell, Rainer. 2015a. Linking Surveys and Administrative Data. In Uwe Engel, Ben Jann, Peter Lynn, Annette Scherpenzeel & Patrick Sturgis (Eds.), *Improving Survey Methods. Lessons from Recent Research*, 273–287. New York/London: Routledge

Schnell, Rainer. 2015b. Enhancing Surveys with Objective Measurements and Observer Ratings. In Uwe Engel, Ben Jann, Peter Lynn, Annette Scherpenzeel & Patrick Sturgis (Eds.), *Improving Survey Methods. Lessons from Recent Research*, 288–302. New York/London: Routledge

Schnell, Rainer, Paul B. Hill & Elke Esser. 2018. *Methoden der empirischen Sozialforschung* [Methods of empirical social research]. 11th Edition. Berlin/Boston: De Gruyter Oldenbourg

Shadish, William R., Thomas D. Cook & Donald T. Campbell. 2002. *Experimental and Quasi-Experimental Designs for Generalized Causal Inference*. Boston/New York: Houghton Mifflin Co.

Silge, Julia & David Robinson. 2017. *Text Mining with R. A Tidy Approach*. Beijing: O'Reilly

Som, Ranjan K. 1996. *Practical Sampling Techniques*. Second Edition. New York: Marcel Dekker, Inc.

Stinchcombe, Arthur L. 1987 [1968]. *Constructing Social Theories*. Chicago: The University of Chicago Press.

The New York Times. 2025. *The New York Times Developer Network* https://developer.nytimes.com/apis (last access: Jul 20, 2025)

Therneau, Terry & Beth Atkinson. 2025. *Package 'rpart'*. https://CRAN.R-project.org/package=rpart

Tourangeau, Roger, Lance J. Rips & Kenneth Rasinski. 2000. *The Psychology of Survey Response*. Cambridge: Cambridge University Press

Tourangeau, Roger, Brad Edwards, Timothy P. Johnson, Kirk M. Wolter & Nancy Bates (Eds.). 2014. *Hard-to-Survey Populations*. Cambridge: Cambridge University Press

Valliant, Richard, Jill A. Dever & Frauke Kreuter. 2013. *Practical Tools for Designing and Weighting Survey Samples*. New York: Springer

Van Buuren, Stef & Karin Groothuis-Oudshoorn. 2011. mice: Multivariate Imputation by Chained Equations in R. *Journal of Statistical Software 45(3)*, 1-67. https://doi.org/10.18637/jss.v045.i03

Van Buuren, Stef. 2018. *Flexible Imputation of Missing Data*. 2nd Edition. Boca Raton: CRC Press

Van Buuren, Stef & Karin Groothuis-Oudshoorn. 2024. *Package 'mice'*. https://CRAN.R-project.org/package=mice

Voelkel, Jan G. and Jeremy Freese. 2022. Open computational social science. In Uwe Engel, Anabel Quan-Haase, Sunny Xun Liu & Lars Lyberg (Eds.), *Handbook of Computational Social Science, Volume 1: Theory, Case Studies and Ethics*, 119-130. London/New York: Routledge. https://doi.org/10.4324/9781003024583

Warnes, Gregory R., Ben Bolker, Thomas Lumley, Randall C. Johnson, Nitin Jain, Mark Schwartz, Jim Rogers. 2025. *Package 'gmodels'*. https://CRAN.R-project.org/package=gmodels

Warshaw, Christopher. 2016. The Application of Big Data in Surveys to the study of Elections, Public Opinion, and Representation. In R. Michael Alvarez (Ed.), *Computational Social Science. Discovery and Prediction*, 27–50. Cambridge: University Press

Watanabe, Kohei. 2021. Latent topic modeling with btm: An R package for the biterm topic model. *R Journal*, 13(2), 300–323. https://doi.org/10.32614/RJ-2021-111

Webb, Eugene J., Donald T. Campbell, Richard D. Schwartz, & Lee Sechrest. 2000. *Unobtrusive Measures* (1st Edition, 1966). Sage Classics 2. Thousand Oaks: Sage

Weisberg, Herbert F. 2005. *The Total Survey Error Approach. A Guide to the New Science of Survey Research.* Chicago/London: University of Chicago Press

Wickham, Hadley. 2016. *ggplot2*. 2nd Edition. New York: Springer

Wickham Hadley. 2024. *rvest: Easily Harvest (Scrape) Web Pages*, https://github.com/tidyverse/rvest

Wickham, Hadley & Garrett Grolemund. 2017. *R for Data Science. Import, Tidy, Transform, Visualize, and Model Data.* Sebastopol: O'Reilly

Wickham, Hadley, Romain Francois, Lionel Henry, Kirill Müller & Davis Vaughan. 2023. *Package 'dplyr'.* https://CRAN.R-project.org/package=dplyr

Wickham, Hadley, Winston Chang, Lionel Henry, Thomas Lin Pedersen, Kohske Takahashi, Claus Wilke, Kara Woo, Hiroaki Yutani, Dewey Dunnington & Teun van den Brand. 2025a. *Package 'ggplot2'.* https://CRAN.R-project.org/package=ggplot2

Wickham, Hadley, Evan Miller & Danny Smith. 2025b. *Package 'haven'.* https://CRAN.R-project.org/package=haven

Wickham, Hadley & Jennifer Bryan. 2025c. *Package 'readxl'.* https://CRAN.R-project.org/package=readxl

Wickham, Hadley. 2025d. *Package 'tidyverse'.* https://CRAN.R-project.org/package=tidyverse

Wickham, Hadley, Davis Vaughan & Maximilian Girlich. 2025. *Package 'tidyr'.* https://CRAN.R-project.org/package=tidyr

Wijffels, Jan, Milan Straka & Jana Straková. 2018. *Package 'udpipe'.* https://CRAN.R-project.org/package=udpipe

Wijffels, Jan. 2025. *Package 'BTM'.* https://CRAN.R-project.org/package=BTM

Wood, Simon N. 2017. *Generalized Additive Models. An Introduction with R.* 2nd Edition. Boca Raton: CRC Press

Yan, Xiaohui, Jiafeng Guo, Yanyan Lan & XueqiCheng, X. 2013. A biterm topic model for short texts. In *Proceedings of the 22nd international conference on World Wide Web*, 1445-1456

Yarkoni, Tal & Jacob Westfall. 2017. Choosing Prediction Over Explanation in Psychology: Lessons From Machine Learning. *Perspectives on Psychological Science* 12 (6), 1–23. https://doi.org/10.1177/1745691617693393

Yee, Thomas W. 2015. *Vector Generalized Linear and Additive Models. With an Implementation in R.* New York: Springer

R Libraries Used

Throughout this textbook, we have relied on R and its programming capabilities[1]. The R libraries we used for data analysis or referenced in the text are listed here. These *libraries*, or *packages* as they are also called, are either part of the core of R or were contributed by the larger R community.

From the *System Library*, we primarily used the *base*, *graphics*, and *stats* packages. These packages are automatically available when you load R. Access to the respective documentation is possible within R via the functions *library(help="base")* or *library(help="graphics")* or *library(help="stats")*. We'd like to begin by acknowledging the authors of this core R resources and refer you to the official page,[2] which introduces the *R Core Team* along with other key contributors:

https://www.r-project.org/contributors.html

In addition, there is a list of *Contributed Packages*, whose description or documentation files contain, among other things, a link to a reference manual and information about the program authors. These files are accessible via

https://cran.r-project.org/web/packages/

As of July 2025, the CRAN repository claims to contain approximately 22,500 available packages. Such files can be downloaded in RStudio via *Tools > Install Packages*.

In the following list, we cite the name, title, and authors[3] of the packages used in this textbook, along with the canonical form of the link to the respective documentation page. Each reference manual is also cited in the References.

Package	Title & Authors
atrrr	Wrapper for the 'AT' Protocol Behind 'Bluesky'
	Johannes B. Gruber, Benjamin Guinaudeau, Fabio Votta
	https://CRAN.R-project.org/package=atrrr
base	The R Base Package (Part of System Library)
	R Core Team & Contributors Worldwide
	Access to information on the package via library(help="base")

---

1 About R: At https://www.r-project.org/about.html, the *R Project* starts its introduction with this sentence: "R is a language and environment for statistical computing and graphics."

2 When we cite reference pages in the context of R, as here, we assume they are trustworthy, but we *disclaim any liability* for them. This also applies to the packages used, etc. In general, it must also be pointed out that following a link or downloading information from the Internet can always pose a risk.

3 The documentation or description files cited in this overview show that some packages have a large number of contributors. These files distinguish between the roles of authors ('aut'), contributors ('ctb') and copyright holders ('cph'). Here as well as in the References of this textbook, we cite the names explicitly named as *authors* in the documentation files. In addition, this overview also cites the cph. For an overview of the *complete* list, *please refer to the respective documentation file cited in this overview*. The different roles in the author field of the description files is explained in a CRAN Repository Policy file at its page 2. (https://cran.r-project.org/web/packages/policies.pdf).

https://doi.org/10.1515/9783110680683-015

(continued)

Package	Title & Authors
boot	Bootstrap Functions (Originally by Angelo Canty for S)
	Angelo Canty, Brian Ripley
	https://CRAN.R-project.org/package=boot
BTM	Biterm Topic Models for Short Text
	Jan Wijffels, BNOSAC, Xiaohui Yan
	https://CRAN.R-project.org/package=BTM
car	Companion to Applied Regression
	John Fox, Sanford Weisberg, Brad Price
	https://CRAN.R-project.org/package=car
C50	C5.0 Decision Trees and Rule-Based Models
	Max Kuhn, Ross Quinlan, RuleQuest Research, Rulequest Research Pty Ltd
	https://CRAN.R-project.org/package=C50
DataEditR	An Interactive Editor for Viewing, Entering, Filtering & Editing Data
	Dillon Hammill
	https://CRAN.R-project.org/package=DataEditR
dplyr	A Grammar of Data Manipulation
	Hadley Wickham, Romain Francois, Lionel Henry, Kirill Müller, Davis Vaughan, Posit Software
	https://CRAN.R-project.org/package=dplyr
gam	Generalized Additive Models
	Trevor Hastie
	https://CRAN.R-project.org/package=gam
gbm	Generalized Boosted Regression Models
	Greg Ridgeway, GBM Developers
	https://CRAN.R-project.org/package=gbm
ggplot2	Create Elegant Data Visualisations Using the Grammar of Graphics
	Hadley Wickham, Winston Chang, Lionel Henry, Thomas Lin Pedersen, Kohske Takahashi, Claus Wilke, Kara Woo, Hiroaki Yutani, Dewey Dunnington, Teun van den Brand, Posit, PBC
	https://CRAN.R-project.org/package=ggplot2

(continued)

Package	Title & Authors
glmnet	Lasso and Elastic-Net Regularized Generalized Linear Models
	Jerome Friedman, Trevor Hastie, Rob Tibshirani, Balasubramanian Narasimhan, Kenneth Tay, Noah Simon, James Yang
	https://CRAN.R-project.org/package=glmnet
gmodels	Various R Programming Tools for Model Fitting
	Gregory R. Warnes, Ben Bolker, Thomas Lumley, Randall C. Johnson, Nitin Jain, Mark Schwartz, Jim Rogers
	https://CRAN.R-project.org/package=gmodels
graphics	The R Graphics Package (Part of System Library)
	R Core Team & Contributors Worldwide
	Access to information on the package via library(help="graphics")
haven	Import and Export 'SPSS', 'Stata' and 'SAS' Files
	Hadley Wickham, Evan Miller, Danny Smith, Posit Software, PBC
	https://CRAN.R-project.org/package=haven
hutils	Miscellaneous R Functions and Aliases
	Hugh Parsonage
	https://CRAN.R-project.org/package=hutils
lavaan	Latent Variable Analysis
	Yves Rosseel, Terrence D. Jorgensen, Luc De Wilde
	https://CRAN.R-project.org/package=lavaan
leaps	Regression Subset Selection
	Thomas Lumley
	https://CRAN.R-project.org/package=leaps
lme4	Linear Mixed-Effects Models using 'Eigen' and S4
	Douglas Bates, Martin Maechler, Ben Bolker, Steven Walker, Pavel N. Krivitsky
	https://CRAN.R-project.org/package=lme4
magrittr	A Forward-Pipe Operator for R
	Stefan Milton Bache, Hadley Wickham, Lionel Henry, RStudio
	https://CRAN.R-project.org/package=magrittr

(continued)

Package	Title & Authors
mice	Multivariate Imputation by Chained Equations
	Stef van Buuren, Karin Groothuis-Oudshoorn
	https://CRAN.R-project.org/package=mice
neuralnet	Training of Neural Networks
	Stefan Fritsch, Frauke Guenther, Marvin N. Wright
	https://CRAN.R-project.org/package=neuralnet
NeuralNetTools	Visualization and Analysis Tools for Neural Networks
	Marcus W. Beck
	https://CRAN.R-project.org/package=NeuralNetTools
nlme	Linear and Nonlinear Mixed Effects Models
	José Pinheiro, Douglas Bates, R Core Team
	https://CRAN.R-project.org/package=nlme
nytimes	R wrapper to New York Times APIs
	John Coene
	https://github.com/news-r/nytimes
Parsnip	A Common API to Modeling and Analysis Functions
	Max Kuhn, Davis Vaughan, Posit Software, PBC
	https://CRAN.R-project.org/package=parsnip
poLCA	Polytomous Variable Latent Class Analysis
	Drew Linzer, Jeffrey Lewis
	https://CRAN.R-project.org/package=poLCA
psych	Procedures for Psychological, Psychometric, and Personality Research
	William Revelle
	https://CRAN.R-project.org/package=psych
quanteda	Quantitative Analysis of Textual Data
	Kenneth Benoit, Kohei Watanabe, Haiyan Wang, Paul Nulty, Adam Obeng, Stefan Müller, Akitaka Matsuo, William Lowe
	https://CRAN.R-project.org/package=quanteda

(continued)

Package	Title & Authors
quanteda. textstats	Textual Statistics for the Quantitative Analysis of Textual Data
	Kenneth Benoit, Kohei Watanabe, Haiyan Wang, Jiong Wei Lua, Jouni Kuha
	https://CRAN.R-project.org/package=quanteda.textstats
randomForest	Breiman and Cutlers Random Forests for Classification and Regression
	Leo Breiman, Adele Cutler, Andy Liaw, Matthew Wiener
	https://CRAN.R-project.org/package=randomForest
readxl	Read Excel Files
	Hadley Wickham, Jennifer Bryan, Posit, PBC, Marcin Kalicinski, Komarov Valery, Christophe Leitienne, Bob Colbert, David Hoerl, Evan Miller
	https://CRAN.R-project.org/package=readxl
recipes	Preprocessing and Feature Engineering Steps for Modeling
	Max Kuhn, Hadley Wickham, Emil Hvitfeldt, Posit Software, PBC
	https://CRAN.R-project.org/package=recipes
rpart	Recursive Partitioning and Regression Trees
	Terry Therneau, Beth Atkinson
	https://CRAN.R-project.org/package=rpart
rpart.plot	Plot 'rpart' Models: An Enhanced Version of 'plot.rpart'
	Stephen Milborrow
	https://CRAN.R-project.org/package=rpart.plot
rsample	General Resampling Infrastructure
	Hannah Frick, Fanny Chow, Max Kuhn, Michael Mahoney, Julia Silge, Hadley Wickham, Posit Software, PBC
	https://CRAN.R-project.org/package=rsample
splines	Regression Spline Functions and Classes
	Douglas Bates, William Venables
	https://cran.r-project.org/package=splines
stats	The R Stats Package (Part of System Library)
	R Core Team & Contributors Worldwide
	Access to information on the package via library(help="stats")

(continued)

Package	Title & Authors
stm	Estimation of the Structural Topic Model
	Margaret Roberts, Brandon Stewart, Dustin Tingley
	https://CRAN.R-project.org/package=stm
survey	Analysis of Complex Survey Samples
	Thomas Lumley, Peter Gao, Ben Schneider
	https://CRAN.R-project.org/package=survey
syuzhet	Extracts Sentiment and Sentiment-Derived Plot Arcs from Text
	Matthew Jockers
	https://CRAN.R-project.org/package=syuzhet
tibble	Simple Data Frames
	Kirill Müller, Hadley Wickham, RStudio
	https://CRAN.R-project.org/package=tibble
tidymodels	Easily Install and Load the 'Tidymodels' Packages
	Max Kuhn, Hadley Wickham, Posit Software, PBC
	https://CRAN.R-project.org/package=tidymodels
tidyr	Tidy Messy Data
	Hadley Wickham, Davis Vaughan, Maximilian Girlich, Posit Software, PBC
	https://CRAN.R-project.org/package=tidyr
tidytext	Text Mining using 'dplyr', 'ggplot2', and Other Tidy Tools
	David Robinson, Julia Silge
	https://CRAN.R-project.org/package=tidytext
tidyverse	Easily Install and Load the 'Tidyverse'
	Hadley Wickham, Rstudio
	https://CRAN.R-project.org/package=tidyverse
tree	Classification and Regression Trees
	Brian Ripley
	https://CRAN.R-project.org/package=tree

(continued)

Package	Title & Authors
udpipe	Tokenization, Parts of Speech Tagging, Lemmatization and Dependency Parsing with the 'UDPipe' 'NLP' Toolkit
	Jan Wijffels, BNOSAC, Institute of Formal and Applied Linguistics, Faculty of Mathematics and Physics, Charles University in Prague, Milan Straka, Jana Straková
	https://CRAN.R-project.org/package=udpipe
vtable	Variable Table for Variable Documentation
	Nick Huntington-Klein
	https://CRAN.R-project.org/package=vtable

List of Figures

https://doi.org/10.1515/9783110680683-016

List of Tables

https://doi.org/10.1515/9783110680683-017

About the Authors

Uwe Engel is a Professor at the University of Bremen (Germany), where he held a chair in sociology from 2000 until his retirement in October 2020. In 2007, he founded the Social Science Methods Centre of Bremen University and has directed this institution until his retirement. His previous academic positions were the universities in Hannover, Bielefeld, Duisburg, Chemnitz and Potsdam. From 2008 to 2013, Uwe coordinated the Priority Programme 1292 "Survey Methodology" of the German Research Foundation (DFG). His research focuses on survey methodology, social science statistics, and field research (experiments, surveys). Uwe is a founding member of the European Association of Methodology (EAM) and the Bremen International Graduate School of Social Sciences (BIGSSS). He earned a doctorate in sociology at the University of Hannover in 1986. http://orcid.org/0000-0001-8420-9677

Lena Dahlhaus is a lecturer at the Institute of Social Sciences (IFSOL) at the Carl von Ossietzky University of Oldenburg, where she teaches statistics, social research methods and urban sociology to students of sociology and political science. Previously, Lena has worked at the Social Science Methods Centre and the Working Group Statistics and Social Research at the University of Bremen, where she was involved in research projects about the role of artificial intelligence in society. Following a bachelor's degree in sociology, she received a master's degree in social research with distinction from the University of Bremen in 2020. Her research interests include survey methodology, natural language processing, research ethics, and integrating traditional and new forms of data. https://orcid.org/0000-0003-4244-5545

https://doi.org/10.1515/9783110680683-018

Subject Index

https://doi.org/10.1515/9783110680683-019

www.ingramcontent.com/pod-product-compliance
Lightning Source LLC
Chambersburg PA
CBHW061750260326
41914CB00006B/1056